A LEVEL COMPUTER SCIENCE FOR AQA UNIT 2

KEVIN R BOND

Educational Computing Services Ltd

Structure of the book

The structure of this book follows closely the structure of AQA's A Level Computer Science specification for first teaching from September 2015. The content of the book has been constructed with the aim of promoting good teaching and learning, so where relevant practical activities have been suggested and questions posed for the student to answer. The book includes stimulus material to promote discussion and deeper thinking about the subject. Additional material to support teaching and learning will be available from the publisher's website.

About the author

Dr Kevin R Bond is an experienced author. Kevin has 24 years of examining experience. He also has many more years of experience teaching AS and A Level Computing and Computer Science. Before becoming a computer science teacher, he worked in industry as a senior development engineer and systems analyst designing both hardware and software systems.

Published in 2016 by

Educational Computing Services Ltd

42 Mellstock Road

Aylesbury

Bucks

HP21 7NU

United Kingdom

Tel: 01296 433004

e-mail: mail@educational-computing.co.uk

Every effort has been made to trace copyright holders and to obtain their permission for the use of copyrighted material. We apologise if any have been overlooked. The author and publisher will gladly receive information enabling them to rectify any reference or credit in future editions.

First published in 2016

ISBN 978-0-9927536-2-7

Approval message from AQA - Print

This textbook has been approved by AQA for use with our qualification. This means that we have checked that it broadly covers the specification and we are satisfied with the overall quality. Full details of our approval process can be found on our website.

We approve textbooks because we know how important it is for teachers and students to have the right resources to support their teaching and learning. However, the publisher is ultimately responsible for the editorial control and quality of this book.

Please note that when teaching the A-level (7517) course, you must refer to AQA's specification as your definitive source of information. While this book has been written to match the specification, it cannot provide complete coverage of every aspect of the course.

A wide range of other useful resources can be found on the relevant subject pages of our website: aqa.org.uk

Acknowledgements

The author and publisher are grateful to the following for permission to reproduce images, clipart and other copyright material in this book under licence or otherwise:

Chapter 5.1.1

Figure 1.1.1 "Late Babylonian clay tablet: table of numerals representing

lunar longitudes", image ID 00851897001, British Museum

Pages 1, 2: Clip art www.123rf.com: green apple: 123rf / 14199537; red apple: 123rf / 1419906;

banana: 123rf / 39056131; orange: 123rf / 38547844; purse: 123rf / 27347756

Chapter 5.1.2

Page 4: Thermometer - "Thermometre froid a plat" Fotolia / 11368653 © Albachiara

Page 5: Cake - 123rf / 33382329 (www.123rf.com)

Chapter 5.1.4

Page 12: Greek character - 123rf / 32698394 (www.123rf.com)

Chapter 5.1.5

Page 14: Road going off into the desert - www.canstockphoto.com / csp9388362

Chapter 5.1.7

Page 20: Dreaming sheep - Shutterstock / 110338271; Page 20: Ruler - Shutterstock / 198850166

Chapter 5.2.1

Figure 2.1.1 Microsoft® Windows® 7 Calculator screenshot used with permission from Microsoft

Microsoft and Windows are either registered trademarks or trademarks of

Microsoft Corporation in the United States and/or other countries

Figure 2.1.4 Microsoft® Windows® 7 Device Manager version

6.1.7600.16385 screenshot used with permission from Microsoft

Chapter 5.3.1

Page 34: Penguins - Shutterstock / 114208987; Page 34: Peacock - 123rf / 36970936 (www.123rf.com)

Page 34: Highway code signs used in question 2, and page 35 are based on Highway Code signs,

© Crown copyright 2007, and are reproduced under Open Government Licence v3.0.

Page 35: Tree rings - Shutterstock / 97674011; Figure 3.1.4 red apples - 123rf / 1419906 (www.123rf.com)

Page 36: Pound coin showing head - 123rf / 20150613_ml (www.123rf.com)

Page 36: Pound coin showing tail - 123rf / 35831780 (www.123rf.com)

Chapter 5.3.2

Figure 3.2.2 Microsoft® Windows 7 command line window screenshot used with permission from Microsoft

Figure 3.2.3 Apple® MacBookPro® and OS X® are trademarks of Apple Inc., registered in the U.S. and other countries

Chapter 5.4.3

CPU - Shutterstock / 222009121

Chapter 5.5

Figure 5.5.1 Shutterstock / 157001045; Figure 5.5.2 Shutterstock / 1226401

Figure 5.5.3 Shutterstock / 185237537; Figure 5.5.5 123rf / 31206024 (www.123rf.com)

Figure 5.5.6 123rf / 32168839 (www.123rf.com)

Chapter 5.6.2

Figure 5.6.2.2 Adapted from www.engineeringtoolbox.com/air-altitude-pressure-d462.html

with kind permission of the editor

Chapter 5.6.10

Figure 6.10.14 "A one-time pad" - reproduced with kind permission of Paul Reuvers, Crypto Museum

(www.cryptomuseum.com)

Figure 6.10.16 (a) "Image generated from random numbers generated by the PHP rand() function on Microsoft Windows."
idea for this courtesy of Bo Allen, http://boallen.com/ who kindly provided permission
to use his PHP script to generate this image.

Figure 6.10.16 (b) image generated from random numbers obtained from atmospheric
noise, reproduced with permission of RANDOM.ORG

Figure 6.10.17 "Gilbert Vernam" - image in public domain

Figure 6.10.19(a) "Plaintext image to be encrypted using a one-time pad." - Mathematician & computer scientist
Claude Shannon, Getty Image library, image 5337874

Chapter 7.4.1

Figure 7.4.1.3 CCD SONY ICX493AQA 10.14 Mpixels APS-C 1.8" (23.98 x 16.41mm) sensor side
CC A-Share Alike 4.0 Int. license, Andrzej w k 2.

Page 347: Subtractive colour model image - Public domain SharkD

Figure 7.4.1.5 Schematic of the operation of a laser printer

Reproduced with permission from Computer Desktop Encyclopedia, www.computerlanguage.com

Chapter 7.4.2

Figure 7.4.2.5 SSD drive image reproduced with kind permission of StorageReview.com from
http://www.storagereview.com/samsung_ssd_840_pro_review

Chapter 8.1

Page 331: "Information Technology alone has this capacity to both automate and reflect information (informate)" - Professor
Shoshana Zuboff, Charles Edward Wilson Professor of Business Administration at the Harvard Business School.

Page 344: Memories for life: Page 99 "The Spy in the Coffee Machine" © Kieron O'Hara and Nigel
Shadbolt 2008, reproduced with permission of the publishers Oneworld Publications.

Page 333: Case study: "From Forbes.com, 16/02/2012 © 2012 Forbes LLC. All rights reserved. Used by
permission and protected by the Copyright Laws of the United States. The printing, copying, redistribution,
or retransmission of this Content without express written permission is prohibited." http://www.forbes.com/
sites/kashmirhill/2012/02/16/how-target-figured-out-a-teen-girl-was-pregnant-before-her-father-did/

Chapter 11.1

Figure 11.1.2 Schematic of several servers connected via a network switch
Shutterstock / 53738941 (server), Shutterstock / 133413857 (switch)
Figure 11.1.3 Racks of commodity servers at one of Google's data centres
(image Google/Connie Zhou) reproduced with permission of Google.

Chapter 12.1

Figure 12.1.1 screenshot of WinGhci, a simple GUI to run GHCI (the Glasgow Haskell Interpreter) on Windows - written by Pepi
Gallardo (http://www.lcc.uma.es/~pepeg/). Haskell - https://www.haskell.org/
- is a purely functional programming language developed by an open source community.

Figure 12.1.2 another screenshot of WinGhci.

The author would like to thank

- Richard Dobson for helpful comments on drafts of Chapters 5.6.1, 5.6.2, 5.6.3, 5.6.7, 5.6.8, and Chapter 6.3

- Marjory Joan and Edwin Sidney Bond for their unstinting and devoted support over
the years and for laying the foundations that made this book possible

- Sue Poh-Cheng Bond for her patience and constant support during the making of this book

Contents

10.5 Client server databases 533

11.1 Big Data 543

12.1 Functional programming paradigm 561

12.2 Writing functional programs 581

12.3 Lists in functional programming languages 592

Index 597

13.1 Aspects of software development - See Unit 1

Glossary - www.educational-computing.co.uk/CS/Unit2/Glossary.pdf

Exam practice questions -

www.educational-computing.co.uk/CS/Unit2/ExamPracticeQuestions.pdf

Exam practice solutions -

www.educational-computing.co.uk/CS/Unit2/ExamPracticeSolutions.pdf

How to use this book

The structure and content of this book maps to sections 4.5 to 4.12 of AQA's A-level Computer Science specification (7517). For example, the chapter number of the first chapter is 5.1.1 and its title is Number systems: Natural numbers. This chapter maps to section 4.5.1.1 of AQA's A-level Computer Science specification (7517). The chapters in the book do not use the leading 4 as this designates Subject content – A-level in the specification.

Flipped classroom

This textbook has been written with the flipped classroom approach very much in mind. This approach reverses the conventional classroom lesson and homework model of teaching. Instead, chapters in this textbook should be used to prepare for a lesson so that classroom-time can be devoted to exercises, projects, and discussions.

The features in this book include:

Learning objectives

Learning objectives linked to the requirements of the specification are specified at the beginning of each chapter.

Key concept	Concepts that you will need to understand and to be able to define or explain are highlighted in blue and emboldened, e.g. Integers. The same concepts appear in the glossary for ease of reference.
Key principle	Principles that you will need to understand and to be able to define or explain are highlighted in blue and emboldened, e.g. Abstraction. The same principles appear in the glossary for ease of reference.

Key fact   Key point   Key term

Facts, points and terms that are useful to know because they aid in understanding concepts and principles are highlighted in blue and emboldened, e.g. Whole number: Whole number is another name for an integer number.

Information   Background

References information that has the potential to assist and contribute to a student's learning, e.g. Read Unit 1 section 4.2.2 for more background on sets and set comprehension. Background knowledge that could also contribute to a student's learning.

Did you know?   Extension Material

"Did you know?" - interesting facts to enliven learning. "Extension Material" - content that lies beyond the specification.

Task	Activity to deepen understanding and reinforce learning.
Programming tasks	Practical activity involving the use of a programming language to deepen understanding and reinforce learning of concepts and principles.
Questions	Short questions that probe and develop your understanding of concepts and principles as well as creating opportunities to apply and reinforce your knowledge and skills.

Web links for this book

The URLs of all websites referenced in this book are recorded at

www.educational-computing.co.uk/aqacs/alevelcs.html

Educational Computing Services is not responsible for third party content online, there may be some changes to this content that are outside our control. If you find that a Web link doesn't work please email webadmin@educational-computing.co.uk with the details and we will endeavour to fix the problem or to provide an alternative.

Introduction

If you are reading this book then you will already have chosen to be a part of an exciting future, for Computer Science is at the heart of an information processing revolution. This revolution applies not just to seeking patterns of meaning in data accumulated on an unprecedented scale by the huge growth in connected computing devices but also the realisation that all forms of life are controlled by genetic codes. Genetic codes are instructions in a procedural information sense that together with the environment that they inhabit control and guide the development of organisms.

Computer scientists concern themselves with
- representations of information in patterns of symbols, known as data or data representations,
- the most appropriate representation for this data
- the procedures in the form of instructions that can transform this data into new forms of information.

The procedures themselves are also a form of information of an instructional kind.

The key process in Computer Science is **abstraction** which means building models which represent aspects of behaviour in the real-world which are of interest. For example, if we wanted to build an automated recommendation system for an online book store, we might choose to record the types of book and number of each type purchased as well as details that identify the respective customer.

Computer Science is not alone in building abstractions, mathematics and the natural sciences also build abstractions but their models only serve to describe and explain whereas Computer Science must, in addition, perform actions on and with the data that has been modelled if it is to solve problems. These actions are described by **algorithms** or step-by-step instructions which form what is called the **automation** stage of problem solving. Whilst it is true that automation of tasks existed before Computer Science, their nature involved concrete, real-world objects, e.g. the Jacquard loom, not informational abstractions such as an online book recommendation system.

So far it has not been necessary to mention digital computers. Digital computers are just the current means by which algorithms can be implemented to execute on data. Both algorithms and the models on which they act need to be **implemented**: algorithms in the form of code or instructions that a digital computer can understand, i.e. a computer program; models in data structures in a programming language. Unit 1 was largely about the fundamentals of programming, data structures, algorithms and their efficiency, i.e. algorithms to run quickly while taking up the minimal amount of resources (e.g. memory, hard disk, electricity), and the limits of computation.

Unit 2 covers the fundamentals of computing devices, how data is represented and communicated between devices, the logic gate circuits that enable computing devices to perform operations and to store information. It covers the fundamentals of computer organisation and architecture, the structure and role of the processor, the language of the machine, binary (machine code) and how it is used to program the hardware directly. The fundamentals of networking are covered which leads onto data models for storing structured and unstructured data that can be accessed from networked machines. The simpler case of structured data is covered first using the relational database model. The limitations of this model are exposed for data that lacks structure and which is too big to fit into a single server. Such data is known as "Big Data". Machine learning techniques are needed to discern patterns in this data and to extract useful information. Big Data also requires a different programming paradigm, functional programming, one that facilitates distributed programming.

It is right that having journeyed through Unit 1 and Unit 2 that a student should have an opportunity to discuss using hypotheticals and case studies what kind of philosophy of information is appropriate for any advanced information society. This is explored in Unit 2 in the section Consequences of uses of computing where guiding principles of behaviour are explored.

Task

1 Try your hand at counting: https://www.youtube.com /watch?v=vJG698U2Mvo video.

Key principle

Abstraction:

An abstraction is a representation that is arrived at by ignoring or removing unnecessary detail.

Key concept

Number:
Quantity of things.
Numeral:
The representation of a number is called a numeral.
Numerals are written symbols for numbers.

Task

2 Investigate the Babylonian numeral system.
What symbols did the Babylonian numeral system use?
Evaluate the following:

(Use http://en.wikipedia.org/ wiki/Babylonian_numerals)

5.1.1 Natural numbers

What does it mean to count?

We learn to count from an early age. We notice that in the real world objects can be grouped together in collections, for example three apples. In doing so, we use abstraction in ignoring the differences between the individual apples in the collection – for example, one of them is green, the other two are red.

The concept of number

By considering collections of items we can get an understanding of the concept

of number. For example, a collection of three oranges, a collection of three bananas. If we choose to ignore the differences between these collections and concentrate on their similarity, then we can form a relatively abstract concept of the number three. The same process could lead to the concept of the number 4, 5 and so on.

Numerals – representation of number

Representations of the concept of number have been carved in stone, and scratched on clay tablets since early times. The representation of a number is called a numeral. The early Roman numerals were originally pictorial. For example, three strokes carved in stone, III, represented the number three.

Figure 1.1.1 Late Babylonian clay tablet: table of numerals representing lunar longitudes

The Arabic (decimal) representations are less pictorial, but again there is some choice in the numerals to represent a number. For example, both 3 and 03 (and indeed 003 and so on) are all recognised as valid numerals, representing the same number.

0 0 3

Numeral systems

V   A numeral system (or system of numeration) is

VI   a writing system for expressing numbers, using

VII   symbols in a consistent manner.

Questions

1 For the following numbers represented by Roman numerals, change the symbols from Roman numeral representation to the equivalent Arabic numeral representation:

(a) VII   (b) LXXVII   (c) MCMXCVI

Digits of numerals

In a basic digital system, a numeral is a sequence of digits, which may be of arbitrary length. The most commonly used system of numerals is the Hindu–Arabic numeral system, based on Hindu numerals. It uses ten symbols called digits (0, 1, 2, 3, 4, 5, 6, 7, 8, and 9) to represent any number, no matter how large or how small. This system is referred to as the decimal or denary system.

Key concept

Natural number:
Natural numbers are the counting numbers, either
$\{1, 2, 3, ... \}$, or $\{0, 1, 2, 3, ... \}$.

The symbol $\mathbb{N}_1$ is used to denote the set $\{1, 2, 3, ... \}$, and the symbol $\mathbb{N}_0$ is used to denote the set $\{0, 1, 2, 3, ... \}$.

Where it is clear which set applies, the symbol $\mathbb{N}$ is used.

What is a counting number?

We use the counting numbers $\{1, 2, 3, 4, ... \}$ to keep track of things such as how much money we have in our pocket. The braces $\{\}$ indicate a set (a collection of objects). The objects in the set are written inside the braces. "…" indicates that there are infinitely more objects. Informally, the counting numbers are all the numbers you can get to by counting, starting at 1.

What is a natural number?

Counting numbers are known as natural numbers.

$\mathbb{N}$

Thus natural numbers can mean either "Counting Numbers" $\{1, 2, 3, ... \}$, or the "Counting Numbers" and zero, $\{0, 1, 2, 3, ... \}$. Sometimes the special symbol $\mathbb{N}$ or $\mathbb{N}_1$ is used to denote $\{1, 2, 3, ... \}$ and the special symbol $\mathbb{N}_0$ is used to denote $\{0, 1, 2, 3, ... \}$.

Did you know?

What is the sum of the first 100 natural numbers?

The mathematician Karl Friedrich Gauss when in elementary school in the eighteenth century amazed his teacher by finding, in a few minutes, the sum of the natural numbers from 1 to 100. Gauss wrote the sum down twice as shown below, once in ascending order, the second time in descending order, directly beneath the first.

$$1 + 2 + 3 + 4 + 5 + \ldots + 96 + 97 + 98 + 99 + 100$$
$$100 + 99 + 98 + 97 + 96 + \ldots + 5 + 4 + 3 + 2 + 1$$

Each vertical pair adds up to 101.

In total, there are 100 vertical pairs.

This makes the sum of all the natural numbers across the two rows $= 100 \times 101 = 10100$.

The sum for one of the rows is one-half of this, i.e. **5050**.

The alternative to Gauss' method involves laboriously performing **99** addition steps, adding **1** to **2** then **3** to the resulting sum and so on. This long-winded and laborious calculation is an example of a **brute-force** approach.

Questions

2 Find the sum of the following range of natural numbers using Gauss's method

       (i) **1 to 50**   (ii) **1 to 200**

3 Write a formula, in terms of n, to calculate the sum of all the natural numbers from 1 to n.

Programming tasks

1 Write a program to find the sum of the natural numbers from 1 to n. Your program should use the brute-force approach. Test your program with the following values of n

       (i) **100**   (ii) **1000 000**

2 Write a program to find the sum of the natural numbers from 1 to n. Your program should use the formula approach. Test your program with the following values of n.

       (i) **100**   (ii) **1000 000**

Investigation

1 Compare the execution times of programming tasks 1 and 2 for the two test values. What do you observe?

In this chapter you have covered:

- What it means to count
- The concept of number
- Numerals – representation of number
- Numeral systems
- Digits of numerals
- What is a counting number?
- What is a natural number?

5 Fundamentals of data representation

5.1 Number systems

Key concept

Integer numbers:

Integer numbers are the natural numbers, $\mathbb{N}$, plus the negative numbers formed by subtracting one natural number from another.

The special symbol $\mathbb{Z}$ is used to denote the set of integers

$\mathbb{Z} = \{ \ldots, -5, -4, -3, -2, -1, 0, 1, 2, 3, 4, 5, \ldots \}$

Information

Read Unit 1 section 4.2.2 for more background on sets and set comprehension:

$\{m - n: m \in \mathbb{N} \text{ and } n \in \mathbb{N}\}$ means to generate the members of the set $\mathbb{Z}$ by subtracting n from m where $m \in \mathbb{N}$ means m is a member of the set $\mathbb{N}$ and $n \in \mathbb{N}$ means n is a member of the set $\mathbb{N}$.

Programming Task

1 What are the maximum and minimum integers for the programming language that you use?

If your programming language has several integer data types, find these values for all the supported integer data types.

■ 5.1.2 Integer numbers

Is the set of natural numbers, $\mathbb{N}$, enough?

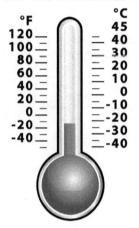

Are the natural numbers sufficient for all simple arithmetic? What about 3 – 5? The answer is clearly not a counting number so negative numbers have to be added to the set of natural numbers to create the integers.

Integers are like the set of natural numbers, $\mathbb{N}$, but they also include negative numbers. For example, when the temperature is 10 degrees below zero, it is -10 degrees.

So, integers can be negative {-1, -2, -3, -4, -5, ... }, positive {1, 2, 3, 4, 5, ... }, or zero {0}.

The special symbol $\mathbb{Z}$ is used to denote the set of integers

$$\mathbb{Z} = \{ \ldots, -5, -4, -3, -2, -1, 0, 1, 2, 3, 4, 5, \ldots \}$$

There are infinitely many elements in this set.

Questions

1 Are the following numbers (Hindu-Arabic numerals representing numbers) integers?

(a) -10   (b) 5⅓   (c) 3.5?

2 Is the result of evaluating the following expression an integer?

(367 × 42) / 7

Whole numbers

What are whole numbers?

We will consider whole numbers to be numbers without a fractional part although other definitions of whole numbers exist which take a different interpretation. A fractional part is a fraction. A fraction is any number greater than 0 and less than 1. For example, a slice of cake is a part of the whole, say $^1/_{10}$ and clearly not the whole. On the other hand, we may have 3 whole cakes or 3 whole degrees of temperature below zero, i.e. -3.

Whole numbers can be positive, negative or zero according to this interpretation. Whole number is another name for integer.

In this chapter you have covered:

- Integer numbers which are numbers which belong to the set
$$\{ ..., -5, -4, -3, -2, -1, 0, 1, 2, 3, 4, 5, ... \}$$
- Whole number is another name for integer

5 Fundamentals of data representation

5.1 Number systems

Learning objectives:

- *Rational numbers*

- *The set $\mathbb{Q}$ of rational numbers*

Key concept

Rational number:
A rational number, x, is one that can be expressed in the form $x = {}^m/_n$ where m and n are integers, excluding zero for n.

5.1.3 Rational numbers

Is the set of integers, $\mathbb{Z}$, enough for all arithmetic operations?

$$\frac{10}{7}$$ If we carry out an arithmetic operation of division such as 3 ÷ 5 the result is not a natural number or an integer. Therefore, we need to extend our number system to include the rational numbers, e.g. ½, ⅓, ¼, ⅜, ⅛, ${}^{10}/_7$ and so on. $$\frac{1}{4}$$

The definition of a rational number is as follows

"For x to be a rational number it must be expressible in the form

$$x = {}^m/_n$$

where m and n are integers, excluding zero for n."

By this definition, ${}^2/_1$, ${}^{11}/_1$, ${}^3/_2$, ${}^4/_1$, ${}^5/_3$, $-{}^3/_2$, ${}^{24}/_{11}$, ${}^9/_7$, $-{}^1/_2$, are rational numbers as are ${}^8/_4$, ${}^6/_3$, ${}^{24}/_3$. $$\frac{11}{1}$$

Key point

Simplest form:
A rational number in its simplest or lowest form is one that cannot be reduced any further because the only common factor of m and n, the numerator and denominator respectively, is 1.

For x to be a unique rational number then we need to insist that m and n have no common factor except 1. ${}^8/_4$, is not a unique rational number because 8 and 4 have the common factors 2 and 1. ${}^8/_4$, can be reduced to ${}^2/_1$ which is a unique rational number because the only common factor is 1. A rational number in its simplest form is one that cannot be reduced any further because the only common factor of m and n, the numerator and denominator respectively, is 1. Such rational numbers are called simple fractions.

Information

The word "rational" comes from the word "ratio" because a rational number can always be written as the ratio, or quotient, of two integers.

Formally, $\mathbb{Q}$ is the set of rational numbers.

There are infinitely many elements in this set.

Questions

1. Determine whether each of the following statements is true or false:

   (a) -13 ∈ $\mathbb{N}$ (b) ${}^{36}/_{77}$ ∈ $\mathbb{Q}$ (c) -11 ∈ $\mathbb{Q}$?

Key term

Set of rational numbers, $\mathbb{Q}$:
Formally, the symbol $\mathbb{Q}$ is used to mean the set of rational numbers.

Information

Read Unit 1 section 4.2.2 for more background on sets and set comprehension:

$$\mathbb{Q} = \{^m/_n : m \in Z \text{ and } n \in \mathbb{N}_1\}$$

Programming Task

1 A program that computes the quotient q and the remainder r when dividing an integer x by an integer y must satisfy the following two conditions as follows:

1) $x \geq 0$ and $y > 0$

2) $x = y * q + r$ and $0 \leq r < y$

Pseudo-code for the algorithm to compute q and r when dividing an integer x by an integer y:

```
r ← x
q ← 0
While r >= y
    r ← r - y
    q ← q + 1
```

Write a program for this algorithm. Does your program meet the two conditions? If your programming language supports assertions, then use assertions to check that the two conditions are met. If not use appropriate tests.

Is the set of rational numbers $\mathbb{Q}$ countable?

Just for the moment, consider the set of positive rational numbers

$$\{^1/_1, \, ^2/_1, \, ^1/_2, \, ^1/_3, \, ^3/_1, \, ^4/_1, \, ^3/_2, \, ^2/_3, \, ^1/_4, \, ^1/_5, \, ^5/_1, \, \ldots\}$$

arrived at by following the arrows in Table 1.3.1.

This set is represented by the symbol $\mathbb{Q}^+$.

Key point

Simplest form:
The entries in Table 1.3.1 that have common factors greater than 1 are greyed out because they can be reduced to their simplest form which is already in the table e.g. $^2/_8$ becomes $^1/_4$.

	1	2	3	4	5	6	7	8	...
1	1/1	1/2	1/3	1/4	1/5	1/6	1/7	1/8	
2	2/1	2/2	2/3	2/4	2/5	2/6	2/7	2/8	
3	3/1	3/2	3/3	3/4	3/5	3/6	3/7	3/8	
4	4/1	4/2	4/3	4/4	4/5	4/6	4/7	4/8	
5	5/1	5/2	5/3	5/4	5/5	5/6	5/7	5/8	
6	6/1	6/2	6/3	6/4	6/5	6/6	6/7	6/8	
7	7/1	7/2	7/3	7/4	7/5	7/6	7/7	7/8	
8	8/1	8/2	8/3	8/4	8/5	8/6	8/7	8/8	
...									

Table 1.3.1

If you think about it all possible positive rational numbers will be generated, e.g. $^{147}/_{91457}$ will be in the table at the intersection of row 147 and column 91457 and will get added in turn. Therefore, it is possible to order the rational numbers of the set $\mathbb{Q}'$ and to show a one-to-one correspondence with the natural numbers as indicated in *Table 1.3.2*.

1	2	3	4	5	6	7	8	9	10	11	...
1/1	2/1	1/2	1/3	3/1	4/1	3/2	2/3	1/4	1/5	5/1	...

Table 1.3.2

To generate $\mathbb{Q}$, we can place zero /1 before 1/1 and insert the negative of each positive rational number other than zero immediately after the positive rational number as shown in *Table 1.3.3*.

1	2	3	4	5	6	7	8	9	...
0/1	1/1	-1/1	2/1	-2/1	1/2	-1/2	1/3	-1/3	...

Table 1.3.3

Table 1.3.3 shows that it is possible to order the rational numbers $\mathbb{Q}$ and to place them in a one-to-one correspondence with the natural numbers. Therefore, the set of rational numbers $\mathbb{Q}$ is countable. It is also infinite because the set of natural numbers is infinite.

In addition, all integers are in $\mathbb{Q}$ because every integer n can be expressed as n/1.

Representing rational numbers as terminating decimals

Long division is used to convert a rational number into decimal form.

Examples: (a) $189/9 = 189 \div 9 = 21$ (b) $13/20 = 13 \div 20 = 0.65$

| 9 goes into **189** |
| 21 times remainder 0 |

| 20 goes into 13 |
| 0 times remainder 13 |
| . 20 goes into 130 |
| 6 times remainder 10 |
| 20 goes into 100 |
| 5 times remainder 0 |

If the final remainder is 0, e.g. 189/9, the quotient is a whole number, e.g. 21, or a finite or terminating decimal, i.e. a decimal with a finite number of digits after the decimal point, e.g. 0.65.

The rational numbers in lowest form whose only prime factors in their denominator are 2 or 5 or both, convert to terminating decimals.

Key point

$\mathbb{Q}$ is countable:
It is possible to order the rational numbers, $\mathbb{Q}$, and to show a one-to-one correspondence with the natural numbers. Therefore, $\mathbb{Q}$ is countable.

Key point

The rational numbers in lowest form whose only prime factors in their denominator are 2 or 5 or both, convert to **terminating decimals**.

Examples: (a) $^1/_2 = ^1/_2 \times ^5/_5 = ^5/_{10} = 0.5$

(b) $^1/_4 = ^1/_2 \times ^1/_2 \times ^5/_5 \times ^5/_5 = ^{25}/_{100} = 0.25$

Key point

All **recurring decimals** are **infinite decimals**. This occurs when the denominator involves the prime factors from the set {3, 7, 11, 13, 17, 19, …}.

Questions

2 Without performing a decimal conversion, determine whether the following rational numbers will convert to a terminating decimal

(a) $^5/_{125}$ (b) $^{16}/_{1024}$ (c) $^2/_3$

Representing rational numbers as recurring decimals

Sometimes when converting a rational number by long division, the division never stops as there is always a remainder. Such rational numbers convert to a recurring decimal.

All recurring decimals are infinite decimals.

This occurs when the denominator involves the prime factors from the set

{3, 7, 11, 13, 17, 19, …}

Examples: (a) $^{19}/_{12} = 19 \div 12 = 1.58333...$ (b) $^1/_3 = 1 \div 3 = 0.333...$

Remainder	70	10
	100	10
	40	10
	40	1
	40	…
	4	
	…	

The repeating pattern may consist of just one digit or of any finite number of digits. The number of digits in the repeating pattern is called the period. The repeating pattern is indicated by placing a period mark or a bar over each digit in the repeating pattern, e.g.

(a) $^1/_3 = 0.333... = 0.\overset{\bullet}{3}$

(b) $^8/_{11} = 0.727272... = 0.\overline{72}$

Questions

3 Convert the following rational numbers to decimal:
(a) $^{16}/_3$ (b) $^{10}/_7$ (c) $^{13}/_{11}$

4 What is the repeating pattern for each decimal in Q3?

Rational numbers are terminating or recurring decimals

A rational number is either a terminating or recurring decimal. Every terminating or recurring decimal can be converted to $^a/_b$ where $a \in \mathbb{Z}$ and $b \in \mathbb{N}_1$.

Key point

A **rational number** is either a terminating decimal or a recurring decimal.

Questions

5 Convert the following decimals to their rational number equivalent:
(a) 5.25 (b) $0.9\overline{0}$

In this chapter you have covered:

■ The set of integers $\mathbb{Z}$ is not enough for all arithmetic operations

■ A rational number, x, is one that can be expressed in the form x = m/n where m and n are integers, excluding zero for n.

■ The set of rational numbers $\mathbb{Q}$ is countable

■ The rational numbers in lowest form whose only prime factors in their denominator are 2 or 5 or both, convert to **terminating decimals**.

■ Rational numbers are terminating or recurring decimals

■ Recurring decimals are infinite decimals

5 Fundamentals of data representation

5.1 Number systems

Learning objectives:

- *Irrational numbers*
- *Decimal expansion of an irrational number*

5.1.4 Irrational numbers

Are rational numbers sufficient to model all numbers?

The answer is no. The following boxed yellow section explains why but this is for information only.

Figure 1.4.1 shows a rectangle with sides of length a, and b. We use multiplication to work out the area of the rectangle as follows

$$\text{Area} = ab$$

where ab means a times b. To measure the length of the sides we use a ruler marked with the rational numbers as shown in *Figure 1.4.2*. The integers were marked first. Next the multiples of $^1/_2$ were added followed by the multiples of $^1/_3$ and so on. It would seem that this process would leave little room for any further points on the line.

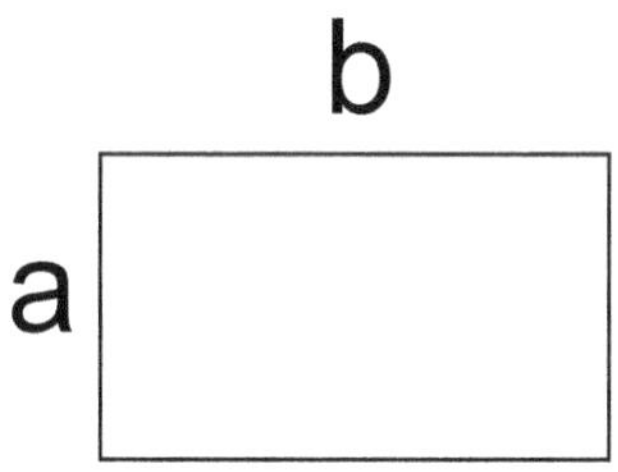

Figure 1.4.1 Rectangle of sides a and b

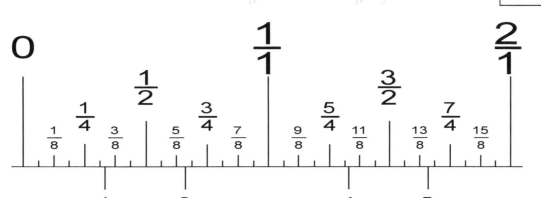

Figure 1.4.2 Ruler of the rational numbers

Information

Pythagoras' theorem states that the square on the hypotenuse of a right-angled triangle is the sum of the squares on the other two sides.

However, this intuition is not consistent with Pythagoras' theorem which requires that the length *h* of the hypotenuse in the right-angled triangle in *Figure 1.4.3* should satisfy

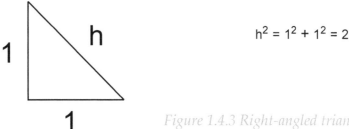

$$h^2 = 1^2 + 1^2 = 2$$

Figure 1.4.3 Right-angled triangle sides 1, 1, h

If it is true that every length in Euclidean geometry can be measured by a rational number, then it must be true that there is a positive rational number such that x = h, $x^2 = 2$, and $x = \sqrt{2}$. That makes $\sqrt{2}$ a rational number but we will discover that it can't be.

If x is rational then it can be expressed as the ratio of two integers, m and n with common factor 1 only and n <> 0.

$$x = {}^m/_n$$

It follows that $\quad x^2 = {}^{m^2}/_{n^2} \quad$ because $x = \sqrt{2}$

Therefore, $\quad m^2 = 2n^2$

And so m^2 is even. This implies that m is even.

We may therefore write   m = 2k   (Multiplying k, any natural number, by 2 ensures evenness).

Substituting 2k for m in $m^2 = 2n^2$

we get $\quad (2k)^2 = 2n^2$

Or $\quad 4k^2 = 2n^2$

$\quad 2k^2 = n^2$

Rearranging $\quad n^2 = 2k^2$

Thus n is even.

For both m and n to be even they must be divisible by 2 but by definition ${}^m/_n$ is a rational number divisible by 1 only.

Therefore, $\sqrt{2}$ cannot be defined as a rational number and therefore it is not a member of the set of rational numbers.

What is the set of irrational numbers?

Conclusion, we need more than the set of rational numbers. We require in addition, a new set which contains those numbers that like $\sqrt{2}$ are not rational numbers. We call this new set the set of irrational numbers. $\sqrt{2}$ is therefore an irrational number.

Irrational numbers are numbers that can be written as decimals but not as simple fractions. Irrational numbers have decimal expansions that neither terminate nor are periodic with some repeating sequence. For example, the decimal expansion of $\sqrt{2}$ to 50 decimal places is

1.41421356237309504880168872420969807856967187537694

To see more decimal places go to

http://apod.nasa.gov/htmltest/gifcity/sqrt2.1mil

Square roots and irrational numbers?

If a number could be the area of a square with a side that is a whole number, then the number is called a "perfect square", e.g. 4. However, if the area of a square is not a perfect square, then the side of the square is an irrational number, i.e. the square root of the area. For example, if the area is 3 cm² then 1.73205..... is an irrational number.

Key point

Irrational number:
Irrational numbers are numbers that can be written as decimals but not as simple fractions.

Irrational numbers have decimal expansions that neither terminate nor are periodic with some repeating sequence.

Questions

1. Which of the following numbers are irrational?

(a) $\sqrt{8}/2$ (b) $\sqrt{8}$ (c) $\sqrt{300}$
(d) $\sqrt{361}$ (e) $3.777... = 3.\overline{7}$
(f) $0.12112111211112...$ (g) $325/7$

In this chapter you have covered:

■ The set of rational numbers $\mathbb{Q}$ is not enough to model all numbers

■ An irrational number is a number that can be written as a decimal but not as a simple fraction.

■ Irrational numbers have decimal expansions that neither terminate nor are periodic with some repeating sequence

> ### Key concept
>
> **Real number:**
> A real number is either a rational number or an irrational number.
> Real numbers are represented by decimals using an infinite decimal expansion.

> ### Key point
>
> The real number system of rational numbers and irrational numbers forms a continuum.

> ### Key point
>
> **Real number line:**
> The real number line is a useful way of modelling the set of real numbers.

> ### Key concept
>
> **Set of real numbers:**
> The set of real numbers, $\mathbb{R}$, is formed from the union of the set of rational numbers and the set of irrational numbers.

■ 5.1.5 Real numbers

Real number system forms a continuum

We need more than the set of rational numbers to model numbers because marking a straight line with the rational numbers will still leave points of the line unmarked. These 'holes' are filled by irrational numbers. When both rational and irrational numbers are marked on the line, they fill it completely  and stretch unbroken in both directions to form the real number system. The real number system of rational numbers and irrational numbers forms a continuum.

What is the real number line?

The real number line is a useful way of modelling the set of real numbers. It is an infinite line on which points are taken to represent the real numbers by their distance from a fixed point labelled O and called the origin. Every point of this line represents a real number. Some real numbers are shown on this line in *Figure 1.5.1*.

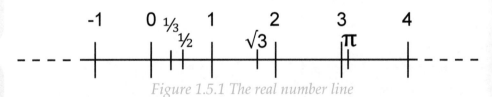

Figure 1.5.1 The real number line

Ideally, one would like to show and label every point on the number line, but no matter how dense one makes the points there are always points in between.

What is the set of real numbers?

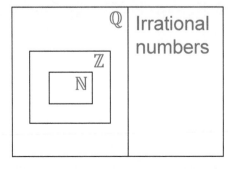

The set interpretation of real numbers is an alternative to thinking of real numbers as points on an infinitely long line. The special symbol $\mathbb{R}$ is used to denote the set of real numbers. It is a set formed from the union of the set of rational numbers and the set of irrational numbers – *Figure 1.5.2*.

Figure 1.5.2 The composition of the set of real numbers, $\mathbb{R}$

Questions

1   Determine whether each of the following statements is true or false:

(a) $^{16}/_3 \in \mathbb{R}$ (b) $3.142 \in \mathbb{R}$

(c) $^1/_4 \in \mathbb{Q}$ and $^1/_4 \in \mathbb{R}$ (d) $\pi \in \mathbb{R}$ (e) $\sqrt{2} \in \mathbb{Q}$

(f) $\sqrt{361} \in \mathbb{N}$ and $\sqrt{361} \in \mathbb{R}$ (g) $-3 \in \mathbb{R}$

What is a real number?

Real numbers describe real-world quantities such as distances, amounts of things, temperature, and so on. They are represented by decimals using an infinite decimal expansion and which define a real number.

Using this definition a real number is an expression of the form

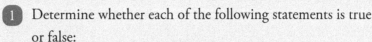
$$\pm a_1a_2a_3...a_k \cdot b_1b_2b_3...$$

For example, $-4328.5000000...$ where ... indicates infinitely many zeroes.

$\pm$ represents a choice between plus and minus.

Each of the digits a_1, a_2, a_3, ..., a_k is an integer between 0 and 9 inclusive except a_1 when there is more than one digit in which case a_1 is restricted to being between 1 and 9, since it is the leading digit, e.g. $13 \cdot 56...$.

The infinitely many b digits are integers between 0 and 9 inclusive.

Questions

2   A line of exact length 1 is repeatedly shortened an infinite number of times by cutting exactly $^9/_{10}$ths from the line each time. Each bit removed is added to the end of its immediate predecessor to make a new and separate line. How much in total is removed after

(a) one cut   (b) two cuts   (c) four cuts

(d) a very large but finite number of cuts

(e) infinitely many cuts

Investigation

Find out why 0.9999... and 1.0000... represent the same real number.

Programming Task

1 The ratio of the circumference of a circle to its diameter, π can be calculated using the formula below. The more terms in the sequence the more accurate the calculated value for π will be.

$$\pi = 3 + \frac{4}{2\cdot3\cdot4} - \frac{4}{4\cdot5\cdot6} + \frac{4}{6\cdot7\cdot8} - \frac{4}{8\cdot9\cdot10} + \cdots$$

… means that there are more terms modelled on what is given already, e.g. the next two terms in the sequence are

$$\frac{4}{10\cdot11\cdot12} - \frac{4}{12\cdot13\cdot14}$$

Write a program that uses this formula to calculate π for a given number of terms, n. Test your program with the following values of n

(a) 2   (b) 3   (c) 5   (d) 7

If we evaluate

$$1 + \frac{1}{1!} + \frac{1}{2!} + \frac{1}{3!} + \frac{1}{4!} + \cdots + \frac{1}{r!} + \cdots$$

the result tends towards the value 2.718… which is given the symbol e.

We can arrive at a value for e by evaluating the formula

$$e = \sum_{0}^{n} \frac{(2n+2)}{(2n+1)!}$$

Using a value for n of 6 we can evaluate e to 9 decimal places of accuracy.
Write a program that uses this formula to calculate e for the following values of n.

(a) 1   (b) 3   (c) 6   (d) 8

In this chapter you have covered:

■ Real number system forms a continuum

■ A real number is either a rational number or an irrational number

■ Real numbers are represented by decimals using an infinite decimal expansion

■ Every real number has a unique decimal expansion unless it is a rational number of the form $^m/_{10^n}$

Information

$\sum_{1}^{n=6} n$ is shorthand for

$1 + 2 + 3 + 4 + 5 + 6$.

$\sum$ means summate or sum.

! means factorial,
e.g. $3! = 3\times2\times1$.

This special number e was known in the early 17th century, and probably was discovered around this date in connection with the growth of money with time when invested.

Did you know?

There are some irrational numbers that can be contemplated in their entirety. For example,

0.2200022200000 222222000000022…

defines an irrational number in which each string of 0's and 2's increases in length each time by two of each. Thus we have a rule for constructing the decimal expansion of this irrational number. The rule can be expressed as an algorithm to generate successive digits. Real numbers whose expansions can be generated by algorithms are called **computable numbers.** They are the real numbers that can be computed to within any desired precision by a finite, terminating algorithm. However, there are also many real numbers that are not computable in this sense.

- The set of real numbers, ℝ, is formed from the union of the set of rational numbers and the set of irrational numbers
- The set ℝ is an uncountable set
- Real numbers describe real-world quantities such as distances, amounts of things, temperature, and so on.

5 Fundamentals of data representation

5.1 Number systems

Key concept

Ordinal or ordinal number:
Ordinals or ordinal numbers are used to label the positions of objects in a list, ordered set or sequence of objects.

■ 5.1.6 Ordinal numbers

What is an ordinal number?

The natural numbers are used for counting or quantifying something, i.e. how much of something we have, but we have another type of number which we use when we need to talk about where something comes in relation to something else, e.g. first or second and so on. This number type is called ordinal number or just ordinal.

Ordinal numbers are therefore used when we need to position something. Ordinal numbers are used to label the positions of objects in a list, ordered set or sequence of objects. The objects must be ordered so that there is a first element, a second element and so on. We use the natural numbers to describe the position of an element in a sequence as follows

$$1^{st}, \ 2^{nd}, \ 3^{rd}, \ 4^{th}, \ 5^{th}, \ \text{etc.}$$

In English, this is

first, second, third, fourth, fifth, etc.

We could also have started at 0 and labelled the first element as the zeroth element in which case we use the natural numbers including zero as follows

$$0^{th}, \ 1^{st}, \ 2^{nd}, \ 3^{rd}, \ 4^{th}, \ 5^{th}, \ \text{etc.}$$

Information

An array index is a way of labelling a cell of an array. The term subscript is also used to mean the same thing.

Questions

1. An index is used in programming to specify the position of an element in an ordered collection, e.g. an array. An index may start from 0 or 1 depending on programming language used or programmer preference.
   (a) If you were told that i was the 100th element of an array:
       (i) How many elements would you consider come before this element?
       (ii) What would be the index for this 100th element if the indexing starts at 0?
       (iii) What would be the index for this 100th element if the indexing starts at 1?
   (b) If you were told that there are 100 elements in an array:
       (i) What would be the index of the last element if the indexing starts at 0?

(ii) What would be the index of the last element if the indexing starts at 1?

2 An element's ordinal (index) equals the number of elements preceding it in the sequence, e.g. an array or a string.
Should the index start with 0 or 1 to make this statement true?

3 The length of a range is the difference of its endpoints, e.g. 0 <= i < 5 has 5 elements, as does 5 <= i < 10.
Give the length of these two ranges if in each case '<' is replaced by '<='. Comment on your answer.

Discussion

4 Some programming languages only allow array indexing to begin from zero whilst other languages are more flexible and allow the programmer to choose whether to start indexing from 0, 1 or any integer, e.g. -2.
Discuss the advantages and disadvantages of each.

Programming Task

1 Write a program that accepts a letter of the alphabet typed at the keyboard, uppercase or lowercase, and outputs its numeric position in the alphabet followed by either "st", "nd", "rd" or "th" as appropriate.

In this chapter you have covered:

■   Ordinals or ordinal numbers which are used to label the positions of objects in a list, ordered set or sequence of objects.

5 Fundamentals of data representation

5.1 Number systems

Learning objectives:

- *Be familiar with the use of*
- *natural numbers for counting*
- *real numbers for measurement*

Key point

The process of counting is known as enumeration. To enumerate is to count. Enumeration is counting with natural numbers.

Information

url for Cantor's diagonal argument:
Su, Francis E., et al. "Cantor Diagonalization."
Math Fun Facts.
https://www.math.hmc.edu/funfacts/ffiles/30001.4.shtml

5.1.7 Counting and measurement

Enumeration

When we count things we start at **1** for the first item, **2** for the second and so on. Anything that can be counted out is said to be enumerable. The process of

counting is known as enumeration and we use the natural numbers for counting.

Can we count the integers? If we can they can be said to be enumerable. We can in actual fact. Similarly, we can enumerate, i.e. count, the positive rational numbers greater than **0** using a for loop as follows

```
for i ← 1 to infinity
    for j ← 1 to i
        display i/j
```

By a similar for-loop argument we could enumerate all rational numbers and thereby count them. We conclude that the set of rational numbers is also countable.

We are not so lucky when it comes to the irrational numbers. The irrational numbers cannot be enumerated (for a formal proof see Cantor's diagonal argument).

Using real numbers for measurement

When we make a physical measurement, we use a measuring instrument. For example, for measuring the lengths of pieces of wood we could use a ruler such as the one shown in *Figure 1.7.1*. This ruler is marked off in whole centimetres and tenths of centimetres. A tenth of a centimetre in the decimal numeral system is the fraction $^1/_{10}$.

Figure 1.7.1 Ruler marked in centimetres and tenths of a centimetre

Clearly, using this ruler, we would not be able to measure the length of a piece of wood to hundredths of a centimetre, but instead are limited to measuring to tenths of a centimetre. We conclude that when dealing with fractions, we shall have to approximate some by using a suitably close fraction that does have a representation on the ruler, e.g. $^1/_9$ would be approximated by $^1/_{10}$ with an error of $^1/_9 - ^1/_{10} = ^1/_{90}$. The more divisions that we have on the ruler, the better our approximation can be, but the need for approximation cannot be removed. Between one tenth and two tenths, for example, there are infinitely many fractions. We are limited therefore to using a rational number approximation to a real number.

Questions

1   Calculate the decimal expansion of $^1/_9$.

2   If the decimal expansion of $^1/_9$ is restricted to each of the following number of decimal places, what fraction results in each case
    (a) 2   (b) 3   (c) 6?

3   What is the difference between $^1/_9$ and each of the fractions that result from answering (a), (b), (c) in Q2?

Programming task

Write a program that outputs the result of performing the following calculations:
(a) $^1/_3$
(b) $^1/_7$
(c) $^1/_5$
(d) $^1/_{10}$
Comment on the results.

Rational number approximation to a real number

Any real number can be approximated to any desired degree of accuracy by rational numbers with finite decimal representations, i.e. terminating decimals. If the real number is x and assuming

$$x \geq 0$$

Then for every integer $n \geq 1$ there is a finite decimal

$$r_n = + a_1 a_2 a_3 \ldots a_k \cdot b_1 b_2 b_3 \ldots b_n$$

such that

$$r_n \leq x < r_n + \frac{1}{10^n}$$

For example, assuming $x = 368.78456789123\ldots\ldots\ldots$

then for $n = 2$, $r_2 = 368.78$ and $r_2 + \frac{1}{100} = 368.79$

That is, x, lies somewhere between 368.78 and 368.79.

> ## Questions
>
> For each real number x where $x \geq 0$ write down
>
> $$r_n \text{ and } r_n + \frac{1}{10^n}$$
>
> where $r_n = + a_1 a_2 a_3 \ldots a_k \cdot b_1 b_2 b_3 \ldots b_n$ and $n \geq 1$
>
> (a) $x = 0.3245995632\ldots\ldots$ and $n = 4$
> (b) $x = 85.994467285\ldots\ldots$ and $n = 3$

Rounding off

We usually apply the process of rounding off to real numbers when using a rational number approximation. The rules for rounding off to n decimal places are:

- If the value of the $(n + 1)^{\text{th}}$ digit is less than five (0, 1, 2, 3, or 4), we leave the nth digit alone.

- If the value of the $(n + 1)^{\text{th}}$ digit is greater than or equal to five (5, 6, 7, 8, or 9), we increase the value of the nth digit by one.

For example, if the real number is $368.78456789123\ldots\ldots$

then rounding off to 2 decimal places, it becomes 368.78.

Whilst if the real number is $368.78546789123\ldots\ldots$

then rounding off to 2 decimal places, it becomes 368.79.

Questions

 Round off the following real numbers to the specified number of decimal places

(a) x = 0.3245995632......... to 4 decimal places

(b) x = 85.994467285......... to 3 decimal places

(c) x = 5.884467285......... to 3 decimal places

In this chapter you have covered:

- To count is to enumerate.

- Enumeration is counting with natural numbers.

- When making measurements we are limited to using a rational number approximation to a real number.

- All fractional representations run the risk of being imprecise.

- Any real number can be approximated to any desired degree of accuracy by rational numbers having finite decimal representations.

- We usually apply the process of rounding off to real numbers when using a rational number approximation.

Fundamentals of data representation

5.2 Number bases

Learning objectives:

- *Number base*

- *Decimal (base 10)*

- *Binary (base 2)*

- *Hexadecimal (base 16)*

- *Converting between decimal, binary and hexadecimal*

- *Hexadecimal as a shorthand for binary and why*

Background

The abacus is a calculating tool based on moving beads in a counting frame to positions that represent the size of a number. It was invented long before the adoption of the written modern numeral system and is still in use today.

Information

Base 10 system is an example of a positional number system. This type of system was first used by the Babylonians over 4000 years ago in Mesopotamia, modern day Iraq. Positional number systems are good for doing arithmetic with.

■ 5.2.1 Number base

Meaning of number base

The number base system specifies how many digits are used in constructing a numeral (representation of a number) and by how much to multiply each digit.

For example, in the decimal system the numeral 734 is interpreted as meaning

$$7 \times 100 + 3 \times 10 + 4 \times 1$$

Decimal (base 10)

The number base of the decimal system is ten because it has ten digits 0, 1, 2, 3, 4, 5, 6, 7, 8, 9 and the digit multiplier is a power of ten, 10^n where n is

$$\cdots -3, -2, -1, 0, 1, 2, 3, \cdots$$

The number represented by the numeral 734 in base 10 is constructed using the place values indicated in *Table 2.1.1* as follows

$$7 \times 100 + 3 \times 10 + 4 \times 1$$

	10^2	10^1	10^0	
...	100	10	1	...
	7	3	4	

Table 2.1.1 Place values for the decimal system

Table 2.1.2 shows how the place values can be extended to include fractions, thousands and ten thousands.

	10^4	10^3	10^2	10^1	10^0	10^{-1}	10^{-2}	
...	10000	1000	100	10	1	$^1/_{10}$	$^1/_{100}$	...
	2	7	7	3	4	3	5	

Table 2.1.2 Some more place values for the decimal system

The number represented by the numeral 27734·35 in base 10 is constructed using the place values shown in *Table 2.1.2* as follows

$$2 \times 10000 + 7 \times 1000 + 7 \times 100 + 3 \times 10 + 4 \times 1 + 3 \times {}^1/_{10} + 5 \times {}^1/_{100}$$

To indicate the base we use a suffix attached to the numeral, e.g. 34_{10}.

Binary (base 2)

The number base of the binary system is two because it has two digits 0, 1 and the digit multiplier is a power of two, 2^n where n is $\cdots -3, -2, -1, 0, 1, 2, 3, \cdots$

Decimal:
The number base of the decimal system is ten because it has ten digits 0, 1, 2, 3, 4, 5, 6, 7, 8, 9 and the digit multiplier is a power of ten, 10^n where n is $\cdots, -3, -2, -1, 0, 1, 2, 3, \cdots$

Key point

To indicate the base we use a suffix attached to the numeral, e.g. 34_{10}.

Key concept

Binary:
The number base of the binary system is two because it has two digits 0, 1 and the digit multiplier is a power of two, 2^n where n is $\cdots, -3, -2, -1, 0, 1, 2, 3, \cdots$

	2^4	2^3	2^2	2^1	2^0	2^{-1}	2^{-2}	
$\cdots$	16	8	4	2	1	$1/2$	$1/4$	$\cdots$
	1	0	1	1	1	1	1	

Table 2.1.3 Place values for the binary system

The number in decimal represented by the binary numeral $10111 \cdot 11$

is constructed using the place values in *Table 2.1.3* as follows

$$1 \times 16 + 0 \times 8 + 1 \times 4 + 1 \times 2 + 1 \times 1 + 1 \times {}^1/_2 + 1 \times {}^1/_4$$

To indicate the base we use a subscript attached to the numeral, e.g. $10111 \cdot 11_2$.

Now the "There are 10 types of people in the world those that understand binary and those that don't" quote might make more sense because

$$10_{Binary} = 2_{Decimal}$$

Questions

1 Write out each of the following in the form

$$\text{digit} \times \text{multiplier} + \text{digit} \times \text{multiplier} + \ldots$$

(a) 1010_2 (b) $1111 \cdot 11_2$ (c) $10 \cdot 0101_2$

2 Convert the following numbers expressed in binary to their decimal equivalent:

(a) 1010_2 (b) 1111_2 (c) 10010111_2 (d) 11111111_2

3 Convert the following numbers expressed in binary to their decimal equivalent:

(a) $10 \cdot 10_2$ (b) $0 \cdot 1111_2$ (c) $100 \cdot 10111_2$ (d) $1 \cdot 1111111_2$

Hexadecimal (base 16)

The number base of the hexadecimal system is sixteen because it has sixteen digits 0, 1, 2, 3, 4, 5, 6, 7, 8, 9, A, B, C, D, E, F and the digit multiplier is a power of sixteen, 16^n where n is $\cdots, -3, -2, -1, 0, 1, 2, 3, \cdots$

The number in decimal represented by the hexadecimal numeral D4

is constructed using the place values in *Table 2.1.4* as follows

$$13 \times 16 + 4 \times 1$$

where D has been replaced by 13.

16^1	16^0
16	1
D	4

Table 2.1.4 Place values for the hexadecimal system

The hexadecimal digits A, B, C, D, E and F are in decimal 10, 11, 12, 13, 14 and 15 respectively.

The number in decimal represented by the hexadecimal numeral 38AD4•95 is constructed using the place values in *Table 2.1.5* as follows

$3 \times 65536 + 8 \times 4096 + 10 \times 256 + 13 \times 16 + 4 \times 1 + 9 \times 1/16 + 5 \times 1/256$

To indicate the base we use a subscript attached to the numeral, e.g. 38AD4•95$_{16}$.

16^4	16^3	16^2	16^1	16^0	16^{-1}	16^{-2}
65536	4096	256	16	1	$^1/_{16}$	$^1/_{256}$
3	8	A	D	4	9	5

Table 2.1.5 Some more place values for the hexadecimal system

Questions

4   Write out each of the following in the form

$$\text{digit} \times \text{multiplier} + \text{digit} \times \text{multiplier} + \cdots$$

(a) 1023$_{16}$ (b) 1F$_{16}$ (c) F•13$_{16}$

5   Convert the following numbers expressed in hexadecimal to their decimal equivalent:

(a) 1023$_{16}$ (b) 1F$_{16}$ (c) FFFF$_{16}$ (d) DEAD$_{16}$

Converting from decimal to binary

Method 1

Take the decimal number to be converted and find between which two column place values it lies, e.g. 35$_{10}$ lies between columns with place values 32 and 64, respectively. Place 1 in the column with the lower of the two place values and 0 in the higher of the two as shown in *Table 2.1.6*. With the given example, take the place value 32 away from the decimal number, leaving 3$_{10}$. Place 0 in all the columns with place values greater than 3$_{10}$. It is then trivial to see that we need one 2 and one 1 to match 3$_{10}$.

...	2^6	2^5	2^4	2^3	2^2	2^1	2^0	...
...	64	32	16	8	4	2	1	...
	0	1	0	0	0	1	1	

Table 2.1.6 Some place values for the binary system

Questions

6 Convert the following numbers expressed in decimal to their binary equivalent using Method 1.

(a) 33_{10} (b) 24_{10} (c) 58_{10} (d) 127_{10}

Key method

Example:
Decimal to decimal by successive division, picks out the individual digits
e.g. $n = 462_{10}$

n	$n/10$	r
462	46	2
46	4	6
4	0	4

Where r is the remainder.
The remainder supplies the individual digits, one at a time, e.g. 2.

Method 2 - the method of successive division

Take the decimal number and repeatedly divide by 2 writing down the remainder each time as shown in Table 2.1.7, stopping when zero is reached.

The binary equivalent of 35_{10} is read from the remainder column beginning at the last row and working up the table.

Quotient	New number	Remainder
35/2	17	1
17/2	8	1
8/2	4	0
4/2	2	0
2/2	1	0
1/2	0	1

Table 2.1.7 Successive division by 2 method

Questions

7 Convert the following numbers expressed in decimal to their binary equivalent using Method 2. Show the intermediate results in a table with structure similar to Table 2.1.7.

(a) 33_{10} (b) 24_{10} (c) 58_{10} (d) 127_{10}

Why does the method of successive division work?

We note that if a decimal number, n, is even then there is some integer, k for which

$$n = 2k \qquad \text{i.e.} \qquad n = 2k + 0$$

e.g. n = 62, k = 31,

$$\therefore 62 = 2 \times 31 + 0$$

We call 0 the remainder. In this example, 2 goes into 62, 31 times exactly.

On the other hand, if a decimal number, n, is odd then there is some integer, k for which

$$n = 2k + 1$$

e.g. n = 63, k = 31

$$\therefore 63 = 2 \times 31 + 1$$

We call 1 the remainder. In this example, 2 does not divide 63 exactly.

The first 1 or 0 remainder is the least significant bit of the decimal number's binary equivalent and the final remainder 1 or 0 remainder, the most significant bit of the binary equivalent.

Successive division algorithm decimal to binary

For decimal number, n.

```
Make k the value of n
If k is equal to 0 write down the answer 0
While k is not equal to 0
  Make the new value of k the old value
        divided by 2 using integer division
  If this is the first pass write down remainder
  Else write down remainder to the left
        of the previous remainder
```

Programming task

1 Code this successive division algorithm in a programming language with which you are familiar. Test your program by converting the following decimal numbers

(a) 0_{10} (b) 24_{10} (c) 59_{10} (d) 127_{10} (e) 33_{10}

Converting from decimal to hexadecimal

We can use the method of successive division similar to the one used for decimal to binary conversions, this time dividing by 16. *Table 2.1.8* shows a worked example for $n = 319_{10}$. The last column is read from the last row upwards giving $13F_{16}$.

Quotient	New number	Remainder
319/16	19	15 (F)
19/16	1	3
1/16	0	1

Table 2.1.8 Successive division by 16 method

Questions

8 Convert the following numbers expressed in decimal to their hexadecimal equivalent using the algorithm above. Show the intermediate results in a table with structure similar to Table 2.1.8.

(a) 47_{10} (b) 302_{10} (c) 65517_{10} (d) 285562_{10}

Successive division algorithm decimal to hexadecimal

For decimal number, n.

```
Make k the value of n
If k is equal to 0 write down the answer 0
While k is not equal to 0
  Make the new value of k the old value
          divided by 16 using integer division
    If this is the first pass write down remainder
                    using hexadecimal digit
    Else write down remainder to the left
          of the previous remainder
                    using hexadecimal digit
```

Programming task

2 Code this successive division algorithm in a programming language with which you are familiar. Test your program by converting the following decimal numbers

(a) 0_{10} (b) 47_{10} (c) 302_{10} (d) 65517_{10} (e) 285562_{10}

Use of Microsoft Windows programmer calculator

It is possible to use Microsoft Windows' calculator to perform number conversions by selecting the programmer view mode, entering a value in the chosen base and then by changing to one of the other available bases.

You could use this calculator to check your answers to questions about number bases.

Figure 2.1.1 Screenshot of Microsoft® Windows® calculator in decimal mode

Converting from hexadecimal to binary

This can be done in a straightforward way as follows:

```
Write down the number in hexadecimal
Replace each hexadecimal digit
by its binary equivalent
using 4 binary digits
```

$$B47A_{16} = 1011010001111010_2$$

1011 0100 0111 1010

The method relies on the fact that the hexadecimal digits 0 to F map to 0 to 15 in decimal and this decimal range can be coded by just four binary digits. When a number represented in four binary digits is multiplied by 16_{10}, it becomes a number represented by eight binary digits with zeroes in the least significant four bit positions, twelve binary digits when multiplied by 16_{10} again and so on.

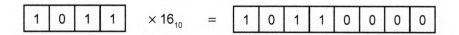

Questions

9 Convert the following numbers expressed in hexadecimal to their binary equivalent using the method described above.

(a) 47_{16} (b) $3A2_{16}$ (c) $6FE7_{16}$ (d) $BEEF_{16}$

Converting from binary to hexadecimal

This can be done in a straightforward way as follows:

```
Write down the number in binary
Add leading 0s to the left-hand side of
        the bit pattern so that the number of bits
                is a multiple of 4 (if necessary)
Replace each block of four binary digits
                        by their hexadecimal equivalent
```

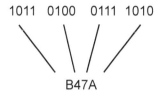

$$1011010001111010_2 = B47A_{16}$$

Questions

 Convert the following numbers expressed in binary to their hexadecimal equivalent using the method described above.

(a) 1111_2 (b) 10101101_2 (c) 101100_2

(d) 110011100011_2

Hexadecimal as shorthand for binary

Long strings of 1s and 0s are difficult for a human to read so programmers often switch to the hexadecimal equivalent because it is much easier to read. If the strings of 1s and 0s represent executable code then debugging this code is much easier if the code is displayed in hexadecimal form. Its meaning is easier to determine than its binary form.

Similarly, writing numbers in hexadecimal form is less error prone than writing the same numbers in binary especially if the binary form consists of long strings of 1s and 0s. For example, it would be cumbersome and error prone to specify the colour for text on a page of HTML in 24 binary digits, better to use the

0000011000010000	0000000000000101	0000000001000001
0000011000010000	0000000000000110	0000000001110011
0000011000010000	0000000000000111	0000000001101101
0000011000010000	0000000000001000	0000000001010100
0000011000010000	0000000000001001	0000000001110101
0000011000010000	0000000000001010	0000000001110100
0000011000010000	0000000000001011	0000000001101111
0000011000100000	0000000000000000	0000000001110010
0000011011000000	0000000000000000	0000000000001100
0000001100000000	0000000000000000	0000000000000000
0000000000000000	0000000000000000	0000000000000000
0000000000000000	0000000000000000	0000000000000000
0000000000000000	0000000000000000	0000000000000000
0000000000000000	0000000000000000	0000000000000000
0000000000000000	0000000000000000	0000000000000000
0000000000000000	0000000000000000	0000000000000000

Figure 2.1.2 Machine code displayed in binary

shorthand form of hexadecimal, e.g. #1F040A. Here the # symbol is used to indicate that the numeral is in hexadecimal.

The contents of memory or registers of a computer system can be displayed for debugging purposes. It is usual for the software that does this to display these contents in hexadecimal because it is much easier for a human to read the numbers in this form as well as taking up less space on the display screen. Software is needed because the numbers are actually stored in the memory locations and the registers in base 2 form.

Memory addresses are more conveniently expressed in hexadecimal than binary. For example, the memory limit of Windows 7 is 4 GiB. This requires the use of 32 binary digits to express the address of a particular memory word or location but in hexadecimal it requires only 8 hexadecimal digits. Incidently, it would require 10 decimal digits. However, hexadecimal is more suitable when working with digital hardware than decimal because hexadecimal uses 4x fewer digits than binary ($^{32}/_4$) but decimal uses 3.2x fewer ($^{32}/_{10}$), an awkward factor to work with.

0610	0005	0041
0610	0006	0073
0610	0007	006D
0610	0008	0054
0610	0009	007C
0610	000A	0074
0610	000B	006F
0620	0000	0072
06C0	0000	000C
0300	0000	0000
0000	0000	0000
0000	0000	0000
0000	0000	0000

Figure 2.1.3 The same machine code expressed in hexadecimal

Key point

Long strings of 1s and 0s are difficult for a human to read so programmers often switch to the hexadecimal equivalent because it is

- much easier to read
- more compact, 4x fewer digits
- less error prone
- easier to debug code expressed in hexadecimal
- suitable for working with digital hardware because an integral factor relationship with binary unlike decimal.

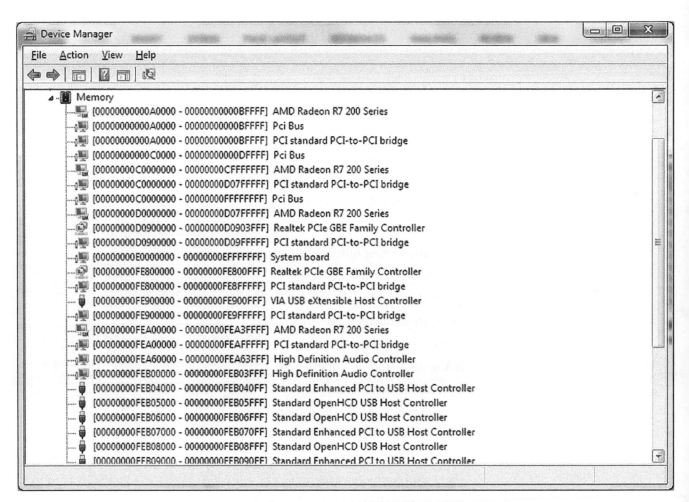

Figure 2.1.4 Microsoft® Windows® Device manager showing the allocation of memory

Task

1   Explore memory with the memory viewer of a debugger in the programming language environment that you use, e.g. memory window in Visual Studio 2013, Xcode on Apple Mac, or use a command line tool such as cat /proc/<processid>/maps in Linux, e.g. using Raspberry Pi.

In this chapter you have covered:

- The meaning of number base
- The decimal number base
- The binary number base
- Converting from decimal to binary
- The method of successive division
- Converting from decimal to hexadecimal
- Converting from hexadecimal to binary
- Converting from binary to hexadecimal
- Hexadecimal as a shorthand for binary.

5 Fundamentals of data representation

5.3 Units of information

Learning objectives:

- *The bit is the fundamental unit of information*
- *A byte is a group of 8 bits*
- *Know that 2^n different values can be represented with n bits*

Background

Sounds can have symbolic meaning i.e. are symbols for something.

Gestures or movement can have symbolic meaning i.e. are symbols for something.

Key point

Symbols communicate information.

A symbol is an information carrier.

Key principle

A representation is a pattern of symbols that conveys information, e.g. a pattern of 1s and 0s.

Background

The words *sign* and *symbol* are equivalent.

5.3.1 Bits and bytes

Information

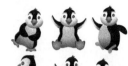

The number of penguins can be represented by many symbols,

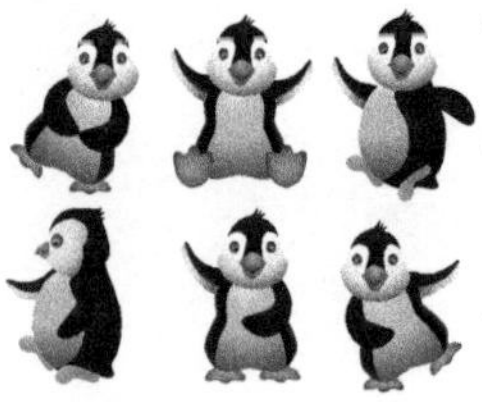

e.g. 6 VI six 0110 |||||| 3 + 3 六

We use symbols all the time when we communicate. Animals also use symbols to communicate. Special sounds or movements are used by animals to attract a partner and other sounds and movements are used to warn of danger. *Figure 3.1.1* shows a peacock with its tail fully extended. This display of tail feathers is a form of communication.

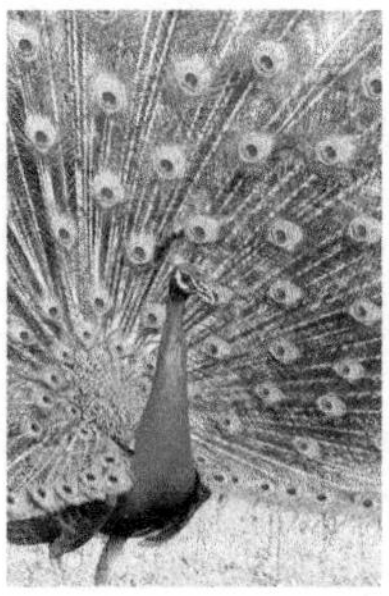

Figure 3.1.1 Peacock display

Special sounds are made by humans too when we speak but our use of such symbols is considerably more advanced than that of animals.

Humans also use symbols when writing words and sentences on paper and on electronic devices; when drawing pictures on paper and painting paintings. We also use gestures and write music using musical notation and so on.

The use of the symbols is not decorative instead their use is to communicate something. That something is **information**.
In other words, the symbol is an **information carrier**.

Questions

1. State the information conveyed by the following symbols:

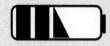

♩ ♪ ☺ He Ar

2. The word sign is sometimes used in place of the word symbol. Figure 3.1.2 shows road signs. State the information conveyed by these signs.

(a) (b) (c)

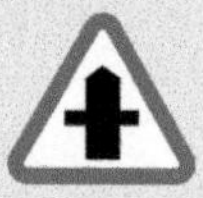

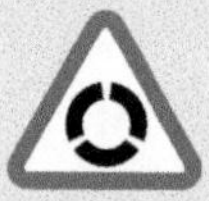

Figure 3.1.2 Road signs

Information and data

Information is made of data put together according to the rules (*syntax*) that govern the way the chosen symbols are used. Syntax determines the form, construction, composition, or structuring of something. The data must also have meaning or be meaningful. This means that data must comply with the meanings (*semantics*) of the chosen symbol system, code, or language in question. It is not restricted to language but could, for example, be pictorial. The data-based definition of information is thus summarised as

Information = data + meaning

Types of information

The road signs shown in Q2(a), (b) and (c) are informational of a factual kind, e.g. Q2(a) has the meaning, the road ahead narrows, that is a fact. On the other hand, information of the instructional kind is supplied by, for example, the GIVE WAY sign. The sign has a meaning but that meaning is an instruction.

Both factual and instructional data belong to a category of information called semantic content. Semantic content is associated with an intelligent producer/consumer pair. Figure 3.1.3 shows the datum *True* being sent from a producer to a consumer. This datum has the status of information at the producer end and at the consumer end where the information = *it is raining*. If the datum *False* was sent instead, then this would be interpreted at the producer and the consumer ends as the information = *it is not raining*.

The datum *True* in transit is an uninterpreted symbol, i.e. its meaning is not yet processed. It is the responsibility of the consumer to interpret this datum and extract its meaning.

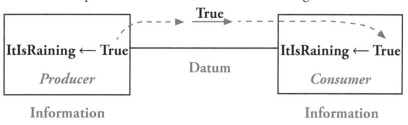

Figure 3.1.3 Semantic content information = data + meaning

Environmental information on the other hand is information that is defined relative to an observer who relies on it instead of having direct access to the original data, e.g. the concentric rings visible in the wood of a cut tree trunk provide information on the age of the tree and the growing conditions at the time a ring was laid down. Note, environmental doesn't mean it has to be natural, e.g. the low battery indicator in Q1 is environmental information because it reflects the state of the battery but it is not the battery.

Bits

We have seen how to represent the
natural numbers in the decimal

Figure 3.1.4 A collection of apples

and the binary numeral systems.

In the binary system, we use just two symbols, the binary digits 0 and 1
to represent a natural number, for example, the number of apples shown
in *Figure 3.1.4* in binary is 101_2. Rather than use the term binary digit
we can abbreviate it to bit. So we need three bits to count five apples.

This digital data 101_2 encodes the information that we have five apples. If
we remove one apple, our digital data must change to 100_2 to convey the
new information that we have four apples. Note that digital data always
changes in discrete steps. The minimum step in our apples' example is one.
Removing more apples, say three, leaves just one apple and to convey this
information we must change our digital data to 1_2. Removing the last apple
leaves none and our digital data becomes 0_2 to convey this information.

In a similar manner, the datum True and the datum False in
Figure 3.1.3 could be encoded as 1 and 0, respectively.

Coin tossing

Now rather than counting objects and recording their number, let's suppose
that we wish to convey the outcome of a coin tossing experiment. For the
experiment, assume our coin will land either head up (h) or tail up (t) with
equal probability when tossed and we will call a single toss of the coin, a trial.

Now before we toss the coin, we cannot say that the outcome is (h) or the
outcome is (t). We are in a state of *data deficit* and therefore, in possession
of no information about the outcome. However,
as soon as the coin is tossed we have an outcome,
(h) or a (t) which we can represent as 1 or 0. We
now have data, a single bit of data which conveys
information, the result of the trial. We say that
to represent the outcome we require one bit
of information or one bit of information per
symbol where a symbol is either (h) or (t).

Outcome	2-bit encoding
(tt)	00
(th)	01
(ht)	10
(hh)	11

Table 3.1.1

Now let's conduct a coin tossing experiment
using two unbiased coins. We have four possible outcomes, encoded as the
symbols (hh), (tt), (ht) and (th). Before conducting the experiment, the
data deficit is four units, the four symbols, because we have no information
about which outcome will actually occur. However, when we have an
outcome, say the symbol (ht), we remove a greater data deficit than we
do for the single coin experiment because each symbol in the two coin
experiment provides more information by excluding more alternatives.

We need two bits to encode the possible two-coin experiment outcomes as shown in *Table 3.1.1*, or **two bits of information per symbol**.

Questions

3 Complete a copy of Table 3.1.2 by replacing the blanks in the Alphabet column and entering the missing information in the Bits of information per symbol column.

No of coins	Alphabet	Bits of information per symbol
1	2 equiprobable symbols (h), (t)	1
2	4 equiprobable symbols (hh), (ht), (th), (tt)	2
3	8 equiprobable symbols (hhh), (___), (___), (___) (thh), (___), (___), (ttt)	
4	16 equiprobable symbols (hhhh), (____), (____), (____) (hthh), (____), (____), (____) (thhh), (____), (____), (____) (tthh), (____), (____), (tttt)	

Table 3.1.2

Key principle

Unit of information:
The bit is the fundamental unit of information.

The bit is the fundamental unit of information

Imagine a machine that can answer only "**42**" to any question. There is no data deficit because the answer to any question can be predicted with absolute certainty, it is always the symbol "**42**". Therefore, the machine produces an amount of information which is zero.

The smallest amount of information occurs when we have two equally likely choices which we know requires one bit. We therefore use the **bit as the fundamental unit of information**.

Key concept

Byte:
The name used for a group of 8 bits is *byte*.

A byte is a group of 8 bits

It is convenient to group together bits and refer to the group by name. The name used for a group of 8 bits is byte.

Task

1 Investigate whether or not the programming language that you use has a byte data type. If it doesn't how could one be created for use in programs that you might write?

How different arrangements of n bits are there?

Figure 3.1.5 shows all possible arrangements for 1, 2, 3, 4 bits. Notice that the number of arrangements doubles each time we add another bit. Starting at one bit, the number of arrangements is 2 or 2^1. To double the number of arrangements to 4 or 2^2 we just add another bit making 2 bits. To double again from 4 to 8 or 2^3 we add another bit making 3 bits. Doubling again we obtain 16 or 2^4 different arrangements and we now have used 4 bits.

This suggests the relationship between number of bits and number of different arrangements is as follows

2 ways	4 ways	8 ways	16 ways
0	0 0	0 0 0	0 0 0 0
1	0 1	0 0 1	0 0 0 1
	1 0	0 1 0	0 0 1 0
	1 1	0 1 1	0 0 1 1
		1 0 0	0 1 0 0
		1 0 1	0 1 0 1
		1 1 0	0 1 1 0
		1 1 1	0 1 1 1
			1 0 0 0
			1 0 0 1
			1 0 1 0
			1 0 1 1
			1 1 0 0
			1 1 0 1
			1 1 1 0
			1 1 1 1

Figure 3.1.5 No of different arrangements of n bits where n = 1, 2, 3, 4

Number of different arrangements of n bits = 2^n

If each arrangement represents a value, e.g. a natural number, then we can also say that

Number of different values that can be represented in n bits = 2^n

No of bits	Decimal integers	No of integers	Binary integers
1	0, 1	2	0, 1
2	0, 1, 2, 3	4	00, 01, 10, 11
3	0, 1, 2, 3, 4, 5, 6, 7	8	000, 001, 010, 011, 100, 101, 110, 111

Table 3.1.3 Number of different values for a given number of bits

Questions

4 How many different arrangements are possible if the number of bits is
   (a) 5   (b) 8   (c) 16   (d) 24   (e) 32?
   Express your answers as both powers of 2 and fully evaluated.

5 How many different values are possible for the following number of bytes
   (a) 1   (b) 2   (c) 8?
   Express your answers as powers of 2.

Questions

 6   Write all possible bit patterns for **4** bits and their corresponding decimal natural number values in table format.

In this chapter you have covered:

- Symbols are used to communicate information
- The data-based definition of information:

    Information = data + meaning

- Data is how information is represented
- Information can be factual or instructional
- A bit is a single binary digit, 0 or 1
- The bit is the fundamental unit of information
- Byte: The name used for a group of 8 bits is byte.
- Number of different values that can be represented in n bits = 2^n

■ 5.3.2 Units

Quantities of bytes

Storage device manufacturers measure capacity using the decimal system (base 10), so 1 gigabyte (GB) is calculated as exactly 1,000,000,000 bytes or 1 billion bytes.

Figure 3.2.1 shows the reporting of the capacity of a Western Digital hard disk.

On the other hand, the memory capacity of RAM installed in machines and quoted in GB is usually reported by the OS using the binary system (base 2) of measurement. In binary, 1 GB means 1,073,741,824 bytes, 2 GB is therefore 2147483648 bytes as shown in *Figure 3.2.2*. The RAM capacity GB is therefore a different unit from the disk storage GB.

Figure 3.2.1 Image of a part of the exterior of a hard disk showing storage capacity of 160.0 GB quoted to 4 significant figures

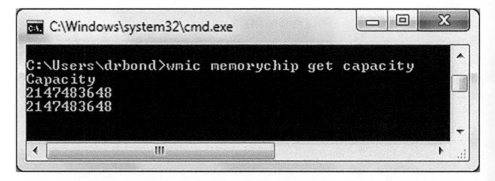

Figure 3.2.2 Command line Microsoft® Windows® 7 showing capacity in bytes of RAM chips – 2 in total each 2GB

This rather confusing situation has been resolved by the gradual adoption of the International Electrotechnical Commission (IEC) standard for binary prefixes, which specify the use of gigabyte (GB) to strictly denote 1000000000 bytes and gibibyte (GiB) to denote 1073741824 bytes. This standard is now part of the International System of Quantities.

Background

The *bi* in prefix *gibi* refers to binary.

Figure 3.2.3 shows the use of Gi and Ki for reporting disk storage capacity using the command *df –h* in terminal mode on an Apple® MacBook Pro® running operating system OS X® 10.8.5. The About This Mac window is also shown.

```
[Kevin-Bonds-MacBook-Pro:~ drbond$ df -h
Filesystem                              Size
/dev/disk0s2                           232Gi
devfs                                  184Ki
map -hosts                               0Bi
map auto_home                            0Bi
```

Figure 3.2.3 shows the use of the units Gi and Ki

Task

1 Using the command line of your computer, investigate the capacity of the

(a) hard disk drive attached to your computer

(wmic diskdrive get size on Microsoft Windows,

wmic diskdrive get /? for more options)

(b) RAM installed in your computer

(hostinfo | grep memory on Apple Mac computers,

wmic memorychip get capacity on Microsoft Windows)

Information

The following command to obtain disk capacity is available at the command line in Windows:

wmic logicaldisk get size, freespace, caption

Powers of 2

Table 3.2.1 shows some numbers in decimal numerals expressed as powers of 2 and their equivalent binary numeral. In 2 raised to the power of 10, 10 is known as the exponent. The exponents 10, 20, 30, 40 specify the number of zeroes in the binary numeral.

Decimal numeral	Power of 2	Binary numeral
1024	2^{10}	10000000000
1048576	2^{20}	100000000000000000000
1073741824	2^{30}	1000000000000000000000000000000
109951162776	2^{40}	10000000000000000000 00000000000000000000

Questions

1 Express the following binary numerals in the form 2^n.

(a) 1000_2 (b) 1000000_2 (c) 1000000000000000_2

2 Express the following decimal numerals in the form 2^n.

(a) 1024   (b) 512   (c) 2048   (d) 4096   (e) 2097152

To avoid writing out long strings of zeroes, the names, symbols and corresponding powers of 2 are used as shown in *Table 3.2.2*.

Name	Symbol	Power of 2
kibi	Ki	2^{10}
mebi	Mi	2^{20}
gibi	Gi	2^{30}
tebi	Ti	2^{40}

Table 3.2.2 Unit name, symbol and corresponding power of 2

If the binary numeral refers to a quantity of bytes then we can express the quantity using the units of **Ki, Mi, Gi** and **Ti** as shown in *Table 3.2.3*.

B refers to byte.

Decimal numeral	Power of 2	Using units	Using symbol form of unit for quantities of bytes	Using named unit for quantities of bytes
1024	2^{10}	1Ki	1KiB	1 kibibyte
1048576	2^{20}	1Mi	1MiB	1 mebibyte
1073741824	2^{30}	1Gi	1GiB	1 gibibyte
109951162776	2^{40}	1Ti	1TiB	1 tebibyte

Table 3.2.3 Quantities of bytes expressed in units

Questions

3 Convert the following to bytes
(a) 1MiB   (b) 1.5KiB   (c) 1.75GiB

4 Convert the following quantities in bytes to KiB
(a) 1024   (b) 512   (c) 2048   (d) 4096

5 Convert the following quantities in bytes to MiB
(a) 1048576   (b) 6291456   (c) 4718592   (d) 9437184

Powers of 10

Figure 3.2.4 shows the decimal numeral corresponding to a given power of 10. The power is known as the exponent. The exponent specifies the number of zeroes in the decimal numeral.

To avoid writing out long strings of zeroes, the names, symbols and corresponding powers of 10 are used as shown in *Table* 3.2.4.

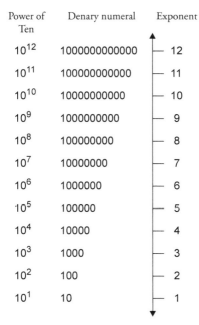

Power of Ten	Denary numeral	Exponent
10^{12}	1000000000000	12
10^{11}	100000000000	11
10^{10}	10000000000	10
10^9	1000000000	9
10^8	100000000	8
10^7	10000000	7
10^6	1000000	6
10^5	100000	5
10^4	10000	4
10^3	1000	3
10^2	100	2
10^1	10	1

Figure 3.2.4 Powers of 10

Name	Symbol	Power of 10
kilo	k	10^3
mega	M	10^6
giga	G	10^9
tera	T	10^{12}

Table 3.2.4 Unit name, symbol and corresponding power of 10

Table 3.2.5 shows how to express a decimal numeral which is a power of 10 in units of k, M, G and T.

If the decimal numeral refers to a quantity of bytes then we can express the quantity using the units of k, M, G and T.

Decimal numeral	Power of 10	Using units	Using symbol form of unit for quantities of bytes	Using named unit for quantities of bytes
1000	10^3	1k	1kB	1 kilobyte
10000	10^4	10k	10kB	10 kilobytes
100000	10^5	100k	100kB	100 kilobytes
1000000	10^6	1M	1MB	1 megabyte
10000000	10^7	10M	10MB	10 megabytes
100000000	10^8	100M	100MB	100 megabytes
1000000000	10^9	1G	1GB	1 gigabyte
10000000000	10^{10}	10G	10GB	10 gigabytes
100000000000	10^{11}	100G	100GB	100 gigabytes
1000000000000	10^{12}	1T	1TB	1 terabyte

Table 3.2.5 Quantities of bytes expressed in units k, M, G and T

Questions

6   Express the following decimal numerals in the form 10^n
   (a) 1000   (b) 1000000   (c) 10000000

7   Convert the following quantities in bytes to kB
   (a) 1000   (b) 10000

8   Convert the following quantities in bytes to MB
   (a) 500000   (b) 2000000   (c) 30000000

Data transfer units

Data transfer rates are normally expressed in bits per second using the units k, M, G, T, e.g. 1Mb/s, where the meaning of 1Mb/s is 1 megabit per second or 1000000 bits per second. A lowercase b is used to indicate bits.

Questions

9 Convert the following data transfer rates to bits per second
   (a) 1Mb/s   (b) 100kb/s   (c) 1Gb/s

In this chapter you have covered:

■ *How quantities of bytes are named*

■ *The use of the prefixes kibi, mebi, gibi, tebi*

■ *The use of the prefixes kilo, mega, giga, tera*

5.4 Binary number system

5.4.1 Unsigned binary

Non-negative values

In this coding scheme, the numbers that can be coded are limited to nonnegative values. For example, the numbers expressible in four bits for unsigned binary are as shown in *Figure 4.1.1*. This figure also shows the decimal equivalent values.

Key fact

Unsigned binary:
In unsigned binary numbers are limited to non-negative values.

Decimal value	Unsigned binary value	Decimal value	Unsigned binary value
0	0000	8	1000
1	0001	9	1001
2	0010	10	1010
3	0011	11	1011
4	0100	12	1100
5	0101	13	1101
6	0110	14	1110
7	0111	15	1111

Figure 4.1.1 Table of unsigned binary codes in four bits and their decimal equivalent values.

When coding numbers in unsigned binary, the weights of each binary position in decimal are as shown in *Figure 4.1.2*. Notice that the next significant digit weighting in decimal is obtained from the previous one by multiplying by 2.

Figure 4.1.2 shows that the number with decimal representation 12 has an unsigned binary representation of **00001100** in 8 bits.

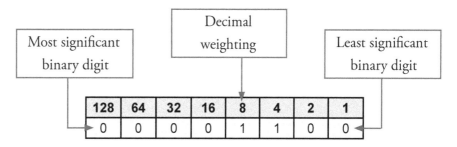

Figure 4.1.2 Decimal weighting of binary digits in unsigned binary coding.

Questions

1 Convert the following decimal values to unsigned binary using 8 bits:

(a) 5   (b) 129   (c) 253

2 Convert the following unsigned binary numbers to decimal:

(a) 10100001   (b) 01111010   (c) 11111111

Minimum and maximum values

The range of numbers that can be coded in unsigned binary depends upon the number of bits that are allocated to represent the number. Obviously, with just one bit only two numbers can be coded, zero and one, giving a range of

$$\text{minimum} = 0_2$$

$$\text{maximum} = 1_2$$

With two bits, four numbers can be coded in unsigned binary as follows:

00, 01, 10, 11, giving a range with

$$\text{minimum} = 00_2$$

$$\text{maximum} = 11_2$$

The minimum number is always zero but the maximum varies with the number of bits used to represent the number. *Figure 4.1.3* shows the maximum binary numeral for 1, 2, 3, 4, 5, 6, 7 and 8 bits and the weighting in decimal for each bit position.

> **Key fact**
>
> **Range of numbers in unsigned binary in n bits:**
> Min value = 0
> Max value $= 2^n - 1$

128	64	32	16	8	4	2	1
1	1	1	1	1	1	1	1
	1	1	1	1	1	1	1
		1	1	1	1	1	1
			1	1	1	1	1
				1	1	1	1
					1	1	1
						1	1
							1

Figure 4.1.3 Maximum binary numeral for a given number of bits

Figure 4.1.4 shows the maximum number expressed as a decimal numeral for 1, 2, 3, 4, 5, 6, 7, 8 and n bits.

No of bits	Maximum number in decimal	In unsigned binary	In compact decimal form
1	1	1	$2^1 - 1$
2	3	11	$2^2 - 1$
3	7	111	$2^3 - 1$
4	15	1111	$2^4 - 1$
5	31	11111	$2^5 - 1$
6	63	111111	$2^6 - 1$
7	127	1111111	$2^7 - 1$
8	255	11111111	$2^8 - 1$
n		1111...1111	$2^n - 1$

Figure 4.1.4 Maximum number for a given number of bits

Generalising, the minimum and maximum values expressible in unsigned binary for a given number of bits n is in decimal as follows

$$\text{Minimum value} = 0$$
$$\text{Maximum value} = 2^n - 1$$

Questions

3   What is the largest number that can be represented in unsigned binary for the following number of bits? Express your answer in binary and decimal.

(a) 6 bits   (b) 10 bits   (c) 16 bits

In this chapter you have covered:

- Unsigned binary
- Range of unsigned binary
  Min value = 0
  Max value = $2^n - 1$ for n bits

47

5.4 Binary number system

Learning objectives

- *Adding two unsigned binary integers*
- *Multiplying two unsigned binary integers*

5.4.2 Unsigned binary arithmetic

Adding two unsigned binary integers

The rules for adding numbers expressed in the binary numeral system are basically the same as for any other system. We add the contents of each column in turn, starting from the right with the least significant digit column and moving progressively leftward. Any carry from a column must be added to the sum of the digits in the next column as shown in *Figure 4.2.1* which shows the sum $01101100_2 + 00101010_2$ of two 8-bit unsigned binary integers.

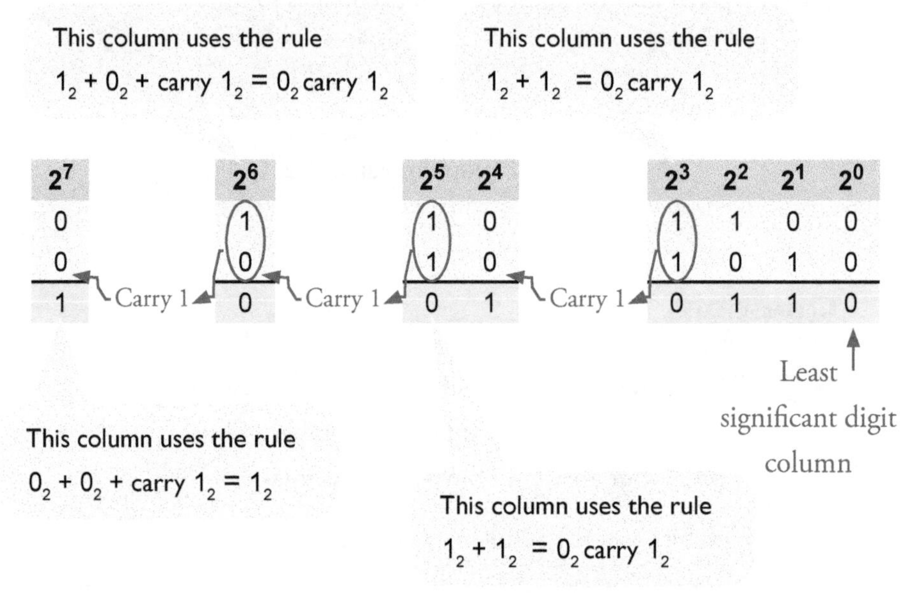

Figure 4.2.1 Addition of two 8-bit unsigned binary integers

The basic rules are as follows

$0_2 + 0_2 = 0_2$

$0_2 + 1_2 = 1_2$

$1_2 + 0_2 = 1_2$

$1_2 + 1_2 = 0_2$, carry 1_2 to the next column since there is no symbol for 2.

The last rule states that $1_2 + 1_2 = 10_2$.

Key principle

Addition of two unsigned binary integers:
Apply the following rules to each digit column

$0_2 + 0_2 = 0_2$
$0_2 + 1_2 = 1_2$
$1_2 + 0_2 = 1_2$
$1_2 + 1_2 = 0_2$ carry 1_2
$0_2 + 0_2 +$ carry $1_2 = 1_2$
$0_2 + 1_2 +$ carry $1_2 = 0_2$ carry 1_2
$1_2 + 0_2 +$ carry $1_2 = 0_2$ carry 1_2
$1_2 + 1_2 +$ carry $1_2 = 1_2$ carry 1_2

If we have a carry from the previous column then the carry must be added to the sum of the two digits of the current column. So we have the additional rules

$$0_2 + 0_2 + \text{carry } 1_2 = 1_2$$

$$0_2 + 1_2 + \text{carry } 1_2 = 0_2 \text{ carry } 1_2$$

$$1_2 + 0_2 + \text{carry } 1_2 = 0_2 \text{ carry } 1_2$$

$$1_2 + 1_2 + \text{carry } 1_2 = 1_2 \text{ carry } 1_2$$

Normally addition of two binary numerals representing unsigned binary integers is set out in the manner of the example below

```
  01101011
+ 00011011
----------
  10000110
```

Questions

1 Complete the following additions of two 4-bit unsigned binary integers:

(a) `  0 1 1 0`
     `+ 0 0 0 1`
     `---------`

(b) `  0 1 0 1`
     `+ 0 1 0 1`
     `---------`

2 Complete the following additions of two 8-bit unsigned binary integers:

(a) `  0 1 1 0 1 0 1 1`
     `+ 0 0 0 1 1 0 1 1`
     `-----------------`

(b) `  1 1 0 1 0 1 0 1`
     `+ 0 1 0 1 1 1 0 1`
     `-----------------`

Multiplication of two unsigned binary integers

Multiplication in binary is performed in a similar manner to a decimal long multiplication problem. For example, the decimal long multiplication problem $456_{10} \times 43_{10}$ would be done as follows

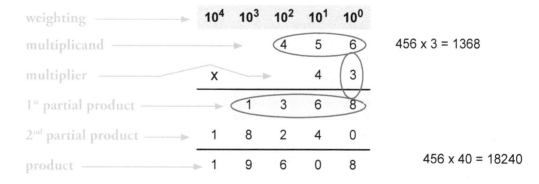

	weighting	10^4	10^3	10^2	10^1	10^0	
multiplicand				4	5	6	456 × 3 = 1368
multiplier		X			4	3	
1st partial product			1	3	6	8	
2nd partial product		1	8	2	4	0	
product		1	9	6	0	8	456 × 40 = 18240

The multiplicand 456_{10} is multiplied by each digit of the multiplier 43_{10} separately and then the partial products are added giving appropriate weighting to the implied power of 10 of each digit of the multiplier.

If we wanted the result of $101_2 \times 11_2$ where each numeral represents an unsigned binary integer then the binary long multiplication would be done as follows

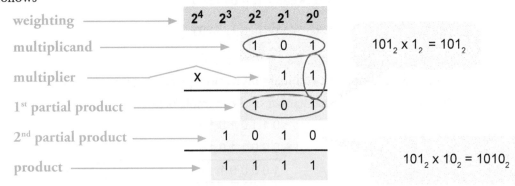

	2^4	2^3	2^2	2^1	2^0	
weighting						
multiplicand			1	0	1	$101_2 \times 1_2 = 101_2$
multiplier		x		1	1	
1st partial product			1	0	1	
2nd partial product		1	0	1	0	
product		1	1	1	1	$101_2 \times 10_2 = 1010_2$

Notice that because each digit of the multiplier 11_2 in the above example is a 1, the multiplicand 101_2 is just copied and then shifted either zero or one places to the left to produce the corresponding partial product, 101_2 or 1010_2. The number of shifts to perform is the same as the exponent of the weighting, i.e. 0 or 1.

Extending this to a multiplication of larger numbers we see that binary multiplication consists of copying and shifting the multiplicand, e.g. $11011101_2 \times 1011_2 = 100101111111_2$ as shown in *Figure 4.2.2*.

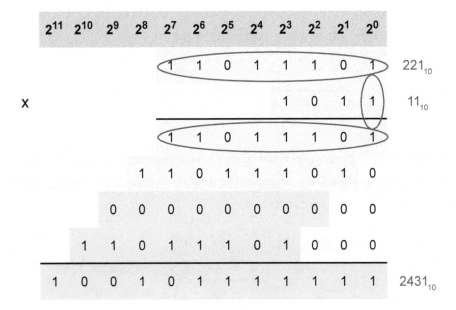

Figure 4.2.2 Long multiplication of 11011101_2 by 1011_2

Key principle

Multiplication of two unsigned binary integers:

For each 1 in the multiplier, copy the multiplicand and place below the last partial product but shifted left by a number of columns equal to the exponent of the weight for this 1.

For each 0 in the multiplier, change every digit in a copy of the multiplicand to 0 and place the copy as before.

Sum the partial products to obtain the product.

$1_2 + 1_2 + \text{carry } 1_2 = 1_2 \text{ carry } 1_2$

Questions

 3   Use the long multiplication method for the multiplication of two unsigned binary integers to evaluate the following. Check your answer is correct by converting the multiplicand and multiplier to decimal, multiplying out and then comparing with your unsigned binary answer.

(a) 101_2 x 10_2 (b) 101_2 x 11_2 (c) 1001_2 x 10_2

(d) 1001_2 x 11_2 (e) 1001_2 x 101_2

(f) 1001011_2 x 1101_2 (g) 1011100_2 x 1010_2

(h) 10111101_2 x 11101_2

In this chapter you have covered:

- Adding two unsigned binary integers
- Multiplying two unsigned binary integers

5.4 Binary number system

5.4.3 Signed binary using two's complement

Representing negative integers

Numbers smaller than zero are called negative numbers. Most humans but not all, accountants are the exception, place the symbol, '-', before a natural number greater than zero, e.g. 2, to indicate a negative integer, e.g. -2.

-2 -1 0 1 2 3 4

The term, negative or minus sign, is used for '-'. The '+' symbol used to indicate a positive integer, is called the positive or plus sign. If there is no sign before the number, it is assumed to be positive. Integers can be positive or negative or zero.

Computations are carried out in digital computers using binary to represent numbers because the binary system is ideally suited to the electronic circuits in digital computers. These circuits operate using two different levels of voltage which map easily to the two symbols, 0 and 1, of the binary system. However, there is no third level of voltage to map to the symbol '-'. Therefore, we have to rely on the two symbols, 0 and 1 to indicate both the magnitude (size) and the sign of a number.

There are several choices of representation for positive and negative integers in binary one of which is two's complement.

In *Table 4.3.1*, the column headed `Bin` contains 3-bit binary integer numerals and the column headed `Dec` contains the corresponding decimal numerals for these integers. If you study *Table 4.3.1* carefully, you will observe that `Dec` is a negative integer only when the most significant digit of `Bin` is 1 and `Dec` is a positive integer or zero only when the most significant digit of `Bin` is 0. This representation in binary of integers is known as two's complement.

Bin	Dec
0 0 0	0
0 0 1	1
0 1 0	2
0 1 1	3
1 0 0	-4
1 0 1	-3
1 1 0	-2
1 1 1	-1

Table 4.3.1 Two's complement representation of negative and positive integers

Key fact

For integers represented in two's complement binary:

- 1 in the most significant bit position indicates a negative integer and a 0, a positive integer
- The most negative integer occurs with 1 in the most significant bit position and all 0s in the other positions
- For -1, every bit is 1
- For the most positive integer every bit is 1 except the most significant bit which is 0.

Bin	Dec
0000	0
0001	1
0010	2
0011	3
0100	4
0101	5
0110	6
0111	7
1000	-8
1001	-7
1010	-6
1011	-5
1100	-4
1101	-3
1110	-2
1111	-1

Table 4.3.2 Two's complement representation of negative and positive integers

Key fact

Two's complement sign bit:
The most significant bit is the sign bit.
Its weighting is always negative.

Table 4.3.2 shows Bin using 4 bits to represent integers in binary. Again, negative numbers are represented in binary with the most significant digit 1 and positive numbers with the most significant digit 0.

Whatever the number of bits:

- 1 in the most significant bit position indicates a negative integer and a 0, a positive integer
- The most negative integer occurs with 1 in the most significant bit position and all 0s in the other positions
- For -1, every bit is 1
- For the most positive value every bit is 1 except the most significant bit which is 0.

The sign bit in two's complement is always the most significant digit.

To achieve the range -8_{10} to $+7_{10}$ the weighting for each bit must be as shown in *Table 4.3.3*. Notice that the most significant digit, the sign bit, also has magnitude or size, i.e. a weighting of -8_{10}.

Table 4.3.4 shows how the weighting of each bit position varies for integers in two's complement binary for a given number of bits, e.g. for 5 bits the most significant bit has a weighting of -16 in decimal. The most significant digit is always the sign bit and its weighting is always negative.

The bit positions are labelled starting with the least significant digit which is given bit position 0.

The most significant bit has weighting, -2^{n-1} where n is the number of bits,

e.g. $n = 8$, $-2^{8-1} = -2^7 = -128_{10}$.

-8	4	2	1
0	0	0	0
0	0	0	1
0	0	1	0
0	0	1	1
0	1	0	0
0	1	0	1
0	1	1	0
0	1	1	1
1	0	0	0
1	0	0	1
1	0	1	0
1	0	1	1
1	1	0	0
1	1	0	1
1	1	1	0
1	1	1	1

Table 4.3.3 4-bit two's complement representation of integers

No of bits	Weighting							
8	-128	64	32	16	8	4	2	1
7		-64	32	16	8	4	2	1
6			-32	16	8	4	2	1
5				-16	8	4	2	1
4					-8	4	2	1
3						-4	2	1
2							-2	1
	7	6	5	4	3	2	1	0

Bit position

Table 4.3.4 Two's complement representation of integers showing weighting of bit positions for different numbers of bits

Questions

1. What is the weighting in decimal of the most significant bit if the following number of bits are used to represent integers in two's complement binary
   (a) 3 (b) 5 (c) 8 (d) 10 (e) 16?

2. Express your answers to Q1 in 2^x format.

3. What is the binary numeral for the most negative integer in two's complement binary when the number of bits for the numeral is as follows
   (a) 3 b) 5 (c) 8 (d) 10 (e) 16?

4. What is the binary numeral for the most positive integer in two's complement binary when the number of bits for the numeral is as follows
   (a) 3 (b) 5 (c) 8 (d) 10 (e) 16?

Converting an integer from decimal to two's complement binary

We have two cases to consider, negative integers and non-negative integers.

Non-negative integers

Treat the integer as unsigned and convert using one of the available methods for converting unsigned decimal numerals such as Repeated Division By Two.

Write down the result in binary and place one or more zeroes in front of the binary numeral up to the specified number of bits. For example, convert $+13_{10}$ to two's complement binary using 5 bits as follows

$$+13_{10} \rightarrow 1101_2 \rightarrow 01101_2$$

The most significant bit will always be 0 for non-negative integers.

Negative integers

Treat the integer as unsigned and convert using one of the available methods for converting unsigned decimal numerals such as Repeated Division By Two.

Write down the result in binary and place one or more zeroes in front of the binary numeral up to the specified number of bits.

Now there are two possible methods for the next stage.

Method 1

- Flip the bits

- Then add 1.

Key principle

To convert from decimal to 2's complement binary:

Non-negative

- Treat the integer as unsigned
- Convert to unsigned binary
- Pad out with leading zeroes up to the specified number of bits

Negative

Method 1

- As for non-negative
- Flip the bits
- Add 1

Method 2

- As for non-negative
- Starting from the right, leave all the digits alone up to and including the first 1
- Flip all the other digits

For example, if the specified number of bits is **5** proceed as follows

$$-13_{10} \xrightarrow{\text{Change to unsigned decimal}} 13_{10} \xrightarrow{\text{Convert}} 1101_2 \xrightarrow{\text{Insert 0}} 01101_2 \xrightarrow{\text{Flip bits}} 10010_2 \xrightarrow{\text{Add 1}} 10011_2$$

Check: $10011_2 = -16_{10} + 2_{10} + 1_{10} = -13_{10}$

Method 2

- Starting from the right, leave all the digits alone up to and including the first **1**

- Then flip all the other digits.

For example,

$$-13_{10} \xrightarrow{\text{Change to unsigned decimal}} 13_{10} \xrightarrow{\text{Convert}} 1101_2 \xrightarrow{\text{Insert 0}} 01101_2 \xrightarrow{\text{Leave 1st bit alone}} 0110\,|\,1_2 \xrightarrow{\text{Flip all other bits}} 10011_2$$

Questions

5 Convert the following integers expressed in decimal to 5-bit two's complement binary.

(a) +12   (b) -12   (c) +7   (d) -7   (e) -1

6 Convert the following integers expressed in decimal to 8-bit two's complement binary.

(a) +12   (b) -12   (c) -7   (d) +32   (e) -32   (f) -128

(g) -1   (h) -63   (i) -76

Converting an integer from two's complement binary to decimal

- Set out the decimal weighting for each binary digit remembering that the most significant digit's weighting is negative.

- Sum the products of each bit value and the corresponding decimal weighting.

Key principle

Two's complement to decimal: Sum the products of each bit value and the corresponding decimal weighting.

For example, for 11110001_2 proceed as follows

-128_{10}	64_{10}	32_{10}	16_{10}	8_{10}	4_{10}	2_{10}	1_{10}
1	1	1	1	0	0	0	1

$1 \times -128 + 1 \times 64 + 1 \times 32 + 1 \times 16 + 0 \times 8 + 0 \times 4 + 0 \times 2 + 1 \times 1 = -15_{10}$

Questions

7 Convert the following integers expressed in two's complement binary to decimal.

(a) 01011100   (b) 10100100   (c) 1000000   (d) 11111111
(e) 10000000   (f) 01111111

Subtraction in two's complement

Given two integers in two's complement binary, it is possible to subtract one, B, from the other, A, by two's complementing B and then adding the result to A.

$$A - B \rightarrow A + (-B)$$

For example, $0101_2 - 0011_2$ would be evaluated as follows

$$0101_2 - 0011_2 \rightarrow 0101_2 + (-0011_2) \rightarrow 0101_2 + 1101_2 \rightarrow (1)0010_2$$

The addition carried out is just binary addition but this can generate a carry (1) which is ignored because we restrict the answer to the same number of bits as we started with, i.e. 4.

$$\text{Check: } 0101_2 - 0011_2 = 5_{10} - 3_{10} = +2_{10} = 0010_2$$

Another example, $0101_2 - 1111_2$ would be evaluated as follows

$$0101_2 - 1111_2 \rightarrow 0101_2 + (-1111_2) \rightarrow 0101_2 + 0001_2 \rightarrow 0110_2$$

$$\text{Check: } 0101_2 - 1111_2 = 5_{10} - (-1_{10}) = +6_{10} = 0110_2$$

Key principle

Subtraction:
Perform addition with 2's complement of B

$$A - B \rightarrow A + (-B)$$

Questions

8 Evaluate the following 4-bit two's complement binary integer expressions using steps that involve only binary.

(a) 0111 - 0100   (b) 0100 - 1110   (c) 1101 - 1110
(d) 1111 - 1100   (e) 1100 - 0011

Computer hardware engineers like to use two's complement binary for arithmetic because they only need to design addition circuits and circuits that flip bits (complement), no subtraction circuitry is required. The addition and complementing circuits are easy to design.

Computer engineers also like to use two's complement binary because there is only one binary numeral for zero. Other representations have two binary numerals for zero. Comparisons of two numerals is often done by subtracting one from the other and checking to see if the answer is zero or not. Zero means that the two numerals represent the same number.

Key fact

Range:

For 2's complement the range of a given number of bits, n is

$$-2^{n-1} \text{ to } 2^{n-1} - 1$$

Range for a given number of bits

The range of integers that can be coded in two's complement binary depends upon the number of bits that are allocated to represent the integer.

For example, in 8 bits, the most negative integer that can be represented in two's complement binary is 10000000_2 whose bits are associated with the following decimal weightings:

-2^7	2^6	2^5	2^4	2^3	2^2	2^1	2^0
-128_{10}	64_{10}	32_{10}	16_{10}	8_{10}	4_{10}	2_{10}	1_{10}
1	0	0	0	0	0	0	0

and the most positive integer is 01111111_2 whose bits are associated with the following decimal weightings:

-2^7	2^6	2^5	2^4	2^3	2^2	2^1	2^0
-128_{10}	64_{10}	32_{10}	16_{10}	8_{10}	4_{10}	2_{10}	1_{10}
0	1	1	1	1	1	1	1

Thus, the range in decimal is

$$-2^7 \text{ to } (2^6 + 2^5 + 2^4 + 2^3 + 2^2 + 2^1 + 2^0)$$

but $(2^6 + 2^5 + 2^4 + 2^3 + 2^2 + 2^1 + 2^0) = 127_{10} = 128_{10} - 1 = 2^7 - 1$

Therefore,

$$\text{the range for 8 bits is } -2^7 \text{ to } 2^7 - 1$$

In general,

$$\text{for n bits the range is } -2^{n-1} \text{ to } 2^{n-1} - 1$$

Questions

9 What is the range in decimal of integers represented in two's complement binary using

(a) 4 bits   (b) 6 bits   (c) 10 bits

(d) 16 bits?

Express your answers first in 2^x format before evaluating.

In this chapter you have covered:

■ Two's complement representation of negative and positive integers

■ Converting between signed binary and decimal and vice versa

■ Subtraction using two's complement

■ Range of two's complement representation for a given number of bits

5.4 Binary number system

Learning objectives

- *Representing numbers with a fractional part in*
  - *Fixed point form*
  - *Floating point form*
- *Decimal to binary fixed point*
- *Binary to decimal fixed point*
- *Decimal to binary floating point*
- *Binary to decimal floating point*

5.4.4 Numbers with a fractional part

Fixed point form

Calculations often produce results that are not whole numbers, e.g. 5¼, so there is a need to represent values that have a fractional part in the language of the digital computer, i.e. binary. The decimal system gives a clue to how to do this in binary

```
100   10    1      1/10  1/100
-------------------------------
  1    3    6   •    7     5
```

The number 136 • 75 represents 1 hundred, 3 tens, 6 units, 7 tenths and 5 hundredths.

Figure 5.4.4.1 shows how unsigned numbers with a fractional part can be represented in binary using 8 bits. The weighting of each bit has been selected to allow three bits for the fractional part but we could have chosen a different number of bits for the fractional part, if we had wanted to. Notice that the weighting decreases by a factor of 2 between adjacent columns as shown.

	÷2	÷2	÷2	÷2	÷2	÷2	÷2	
Weighting	16	8	4	2	1	½	¼	⅛
	16	8	4	2	1	0.5	0.25	0.125
	1	0	1	1	0	1	1	1

Figure 5.4.4.1 Interpreting a bit pattern when it represents an unsigned number with a fractional part

$$10110 \cdot 111_2 = 16 + 4 + 2 + \tfrac{1}{2} + \tfrac{1}{4} + \tfrac{1}{8} = 22\tfrac{7}{8} = 22.875_{10}$$

This coding is known as **fixed point coding** because the binary point is fixed in position, in this example between the third and fourth bits from the right.

Questions

1. Given 8 bits with the binary point fixed in position between the third and fourth bits from the right as in Figure 5.4.4.1, what is the decimal representation for each of the following unsigned binary numbers?

   (a) 00011•100 (b) 00101•110 (c) 10000•101
   (d) 11111•111

Questions

2 Given 8 bits with the binary point fixed in position between the fourth and fifth bits from the right what is the decimal representation for each of the following unsigned binary numbers?

(a) 0001•0001   (b) 0010•0011   (c) 1111•0100   (d) 1010•0111

3 Given 12 bits with the binary point fixed in position between the sixth and seventh bits from the right what is the decimal representation for each of the following unsigned binary numbers?

(a) 100000•000001   (b) 111000•000010
(c) 001111•000011   (d) 110001•000111

Fixed point form of signed numbers

We use two's complement representation to represent signed numbers with a fractional part in binary as shown in the example in *Figure 5.4.4.2.*

-16	8	4	2	1	½	¼	⅛
1	0	1	1	0	1	1	1

Figure 5.4.4.2 Interpreting a bit pattern when it represents a signed number with a fractional part

$$10110 \cdot 111_2 = -16 + 4 + 2 + ½ + ¼ + ⅛ = -9⅛ = -9.125_{10}$$

Questions

4 Given 8 bits with the binary point fixed in position between the third and fourth bits from the right as in Figure 5.4.4.2, what is the decimal representation for each of the following signed binary numbers?

(a) 11100•100   (b) 11010•010   (c) 10111•011
(d) 11100•001

Floating point form

In decimal, large and small numbers are often represented using scientific notation which is of the form

$$A \times 10^B$$

where A is any real number greater than -10 and less than +10 and B is any integer, e.g. A = 1.356, B = 1.

For example,

$6 \cdot 58723 \times 10^4 = 65872 \cdot 3$ where A = $6 \cdot 58723$ and B = 4, the number of decimal places to shift the point right

$6 \cdot 5 \ 8 \ 7 \ 2 \ 3 = 65872 \cdot 3$

$-8 \cdot 0000 \times 10^3 = -8000 \cdot 0$ where A = $-8 \cdot 0000$ and B = 3

$6 \cdot 0 \times 10^{-4} = 0 \cdot 0006$ where A = $6 \cdot 0$ and B = -4, the number of decimal places to shift the point right, i.e. shift right -4 places which translates to a shift left of 4 places.

A similar notation is used when two's complement binary is used to represent signed numbers that range from small to large

$$M \times Base^E$$

where M is called the *mantissa* or significand, E the *exponent* and the number base *Base* equals 2 in decimal.

The mantissa is any real number greater than or equal to -1_{10} and less than $+1_{10}$. The exponent expresses the number of binary places to shift the point right or left.

For example,

$M = 0 \cdot 1000000_2$ and $E = 0010_2 = 2_{10}$

$0 \cdot 1 \ 0 \ 0 \ 0 \ 0 \ 0 \ 0_2 \quad = 10 \cdot 000000_2$

and another example,

$M = 0 \cdot 1000000_2$ and $E = 1110_2 = -2_{10}$

$0 \ 0 \ 0 \cdot 1 \ 0 \ 0 \ 0 \ 0 \ 0 \ 0_2 \quad = 0 \cdot 001000000_2$

Shifting the point by one binary place to the right is equivalent to multiplying by 2 and shifting the point by one binary place to the left is equivalent to dividing by 2. This *floating or shifting of the point* gives *floating point representation* its name.

Information

IEEE floating point standard:

IEEE floating point standard is another representation of real numbers commonly used in computer design.

S is one bit representing the sign of the number

E is an 8-bit biased integer representing the exponent

F is an unsigned integer

The true value represented is

$$(-1)^S \times f \times 2^e$$

S = sign bit

$(-1)^S \to (-1)^0 = +1$

and $(-1)^1 = -1$

where

e = E − bias

$f = F/2^n + 1$

For single precision numbers n=23, bias=127.

Representation of two's complement floating point binary

Figure 5.4.4.3 shows how, given 8 bits, the representation can be divided into a mantissa field, 4 bits, and an exponent field, 4 bits, and their corresponding weighting.

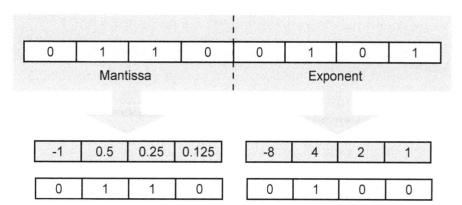

Figure 5.4.4.3 shows mantissa and exponent fields of a floating point number, 0•110 x Base^0101 where Base equals 2 in decimal

The most significant bit of the mantissa is the sign bit. Its weighting is always -1. Therefore, the binary point is situated between the most significant bit and the next most significant bit of the mantissa.

Likewise, the most significant bit of the exponent is a sign bit. The exponent is always integral, i.e. a whole number, either negative or positive or zero.

Example 1: To evaluate $0•110 \times Base^{0101}$ in decimal, where Base equals 2 in decimal, first calculate exponent in decimal

$$Exponent = 0101_2 = 4 + 1 = +5_{10}$$

Then move the binary point of the mantissa **+5$_{10}$ places to the right** and then convert the mantissa to decimal (plus sign means move binary point right)

$$0•110_2 \to 011000•0_2 = +24_{10}$$

Example 2: To evaluate $0•110 \times Base^{1000}$ where Base equals 2 in decimal.

Exponent = $1000_2 = -8_{10}$ (minus sign means move binary point left)

Move binary point of the mantissa **8$_{10}$ places to the left** and convert mantissa to decimal

$$0•110_2 \to 0•0000000011_2 = {}^1/_{512} + {}^1/_{1024} = + 0.0029296875_{10}$$

Questions

5 Given 8 bits to represent a signed number in two's complement floating point form, with 4 bits for the mantissa and 4 bits for the exponent as shown in Figure 5.4.4.3, write down separately, for each of (a) to (f), the binary forms of the mantissa and the exponent then the decimal expansion

(a) 01000100   (b) 10100100   (c) 01001111   (d) 01110011   (e) 10000000   (f) 11111100

Converting from decimal to fixed point binary

Unsigned decimal to unsigned fixed point binary

To convert an unsigned decimal number, W . F, e.g. 5.75_{10} where W = 5 and

F = 0.75, to fixed point binary proceed as follows

1. Consider the whole number part, W, and the fractional part, F separately.

2. Convert the whole number part, W, from decimal to binary using, for example, the repeated division by two algorithm.

3. Convert the fractional part, F, from decimal to binary in a given number of bits using the following algorithm.

Repeated multiplication by two algorithm:

```
n ← 0

OrigF ← Fractional part F

Repeat

  R ← F x 2

  Write down the digit to the left of the

  decimal point of R, call it D

  n ← n + 1

  F ← R - D

Until F = 0 Or F = OrigF

      Or n = AllocatedFractionalNoOfBits
```

Table 5.4.4.1 shows how the fractional part 0.75_{10} is converted to 0.11_2 by this algorithm. The algorithm terminates for 0.75_{10} on the condition F = 0. It will always terminate on F = 0 when the denominator of the fractional part involves the prime factor 2 only, if a sufficient number of bits are allocated to the fractional part.

Fractional part, F	R	Digit D
0.75	0.75 x 2 = 1.5	1
0.5	0.5 x 2 = 1.0	1
0		

Most significant bit

Table 5.4.4.1 Conversion of fractional part, 0.75_{10} to 0.11_2

Table 5.4.4.2 shows an example where the algorithm terminates on the condition F = OrigF. Under these circumstances, the fractional decimal part converts to a repeating binary part, e.g. 0.8_{10} is converted to $0 \cdot \overline{1100}_2$.

Key principle

Decimal to binary fixed point:

1. Consider the whole number part, W, and the fractional part, F separately.

2. Convert the whole number part, W, from decimal to binary using the repeated division by two algorithm.

3. Convert the fractional part, F, from decimal to binary in a given number of bits using the repeated multiplication by two algorithm.

Fractional part, F	R	Digit D
0.8	0.8 x 2 = 1.6	1
0.6	0.6 x 2 = 1.2	1
0.2	0.2 x 2 = 0.4	0
0.4	0.4 x 2 = 0.8	0
0.8	(Previous 4 steps now repeat)	

Most significant bit

Table 5.4.4.2 shows an example of a conversion which results in a repeating binary pattern.

Table 5.4.4.2 shows an example of a conversion which results in a repeating binary pattern.

Table 5.4.4.3 shows an example of a conversion which results in a repeating binary pattern for which $F \neq 0$ and $F \neq OrigF$ so condition

`n = AllocatedFractionalNoOfBits` is necessary to terminate loop.

Fractional part, F	R	Digit D
0.1	0.1 x 2 = 0.2	0
0.6	0.2 x 2 = 0.4	0
0.2	0.4 x 2 = 0.8	0
0.4	0.8 x 2 = 1.6	1
0.6	0.6 x 2 = 1.2	1
0.2	0.2 x 2 = 0.4	0
0.4	0.8 x 2 = 1.6	1
0.6	0.6 x 2 = 1.2	1
0.2	(Previous 3 steps now repeat)	

Most significant bit

Table 5.4.4.3 Repeating binary pattern for which $F \neq 0$ and $F \neq OrigF$.

Repeating bit patterns occur whenever the denominator of the fractional part involves prime factors other than 2, e.g. $0.8 = {}^8/_{10} = {}^4/_5$ so the denominator has a prime factor (5) other than 2.

Questions

6 Convert the following decimal numbers to fixed point binary using the *repeated multiplication by two algorithm*.

(a) 0.375   (b) 0.4   (c) 0.7   (d) 0.703125

(e) 0.1

Questions

7 Convert the following decimal numbers to fixed point binary using the repeated division by two algorithm for the whole number part and the *repeated multiplication by two algorithm* for the fractional part.

(a) 101.875   (b) 333.55

Programming tasks

1 Write a program that implements the repeated multiplication by two algorithm. Test your program for cases (a) to (e) in Question 6.

Signed decimal to signed two's complement fixed point binary

To convert a signed non-zero decimal number to two's complement fixed point binary:

- Ignoring the sign, convert decimal number to two's complement fixed point binary in given number of bits

- If the sign was negative

  Use one of the following two methods

  Either

  Method 1: Flip all bits then add 1 to the least significant bit

  Or

  Method 2: Starting from the right, leave all the digits alone up to and including the first 1 then flip all the other digits.

For example, -3.75_{10} becomes in 8-bit fixed point binary 11100.010_2 if three bits are allocated to the fractional part.

Using method 1:

$$3.75_{10} \rightarrow 00011.110_2 \rightarrow 11100.001_2$$

$$\rightarrow 11100.001_2 + 1_2 \rightarrow 11100.010_2$$

Key principle

Signed decimal to signed 2's complement binary:

Method 1: Flip all bits then add 1 to the least significant bit

Method 2: Starting from the right, leave all the digits alone up to and including the first 1 then flip all the other digits.

Questions

8 Convert the following decimal numbers to 8-bit fixed point binary in which three bits are allocated for the fractional part.

(a) -1.25   (b) -7.5   (c) -1   (d) -15.875

Key principle

Decimal to binary floating point form:

```
Convert decimal to two's
complement fixed point
binary using just as many
bits as required
While point is not between
most significant and next
most significant bit
  Shift point left
    (divide by 2)
  Increment exponent
```

Converting from decimal to binary floating point form

The following algorithm is used to convert decimal numbers to binary floating point form when both mantissa and exponent use two's complement and the binary point is positioned between the most significant and next most significant bit of the mantissa.

```
Convert decimal number to two's complement fixed point
binary using just as many bits as required

While point is not between most significant and next most
significant bit

    Shift point left (divide by 2)

    Increment exponent
```

For example, 3.75_{10} is in two's complement 8-bit floating point binary with 3 bits for the exponent and 5 bits for the mantissa

$$0.1111_2 \quad 010_2$$

as shown in Table 5.4.4.4, which starts from the fixed point form 011.1100_2.

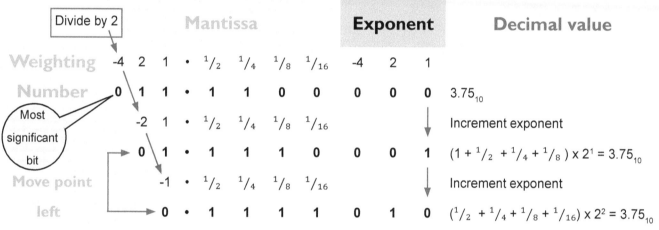

Divide by 2	Mantissa							Exponent			Decimal value
Weighting	-4	2	1 •	$^1/_2$	$^1/_4$	$^1/_8$	$^1/_{16}$	-4	2	1	
Number	0	1	1 •	1	1	0	0	0	0	0	3.75_{10}
		-2	1 •	$^1/_2$	$^1/_4$	$^1/_8$	$^1/_{16}$				Increment exponent
	0	1	1 •	1	1	1	0	0	0	1	$(1 + ^1/_2 + ^1/_4 + ^1/_8) \times 2^1 = 3.75_{10}$
Move point		-1 •		$^1/_2$	$^1/_4$	$^1/_8$	$^1/_{16}$				Increment exponent
left	0 •		1	1	1	1	0	1	0		$(^1/_2 + ^1/_4 + ^1/_8 + ^1/_{16}) \times 2^2 = 3.75_{10}$

Table 5.4.4.4 Stages of conversion of +3.75$_{10}$ to 8-bit floating point form

Table 5.4.4.5 shows the algorithm applied to -3.75_{10} to produce $1.0001_2\ 010_2$ (mantissa exponent) in 8-bit floating point form with 3 bits for the exponent. The tables starts with the fixed point form 100.0100_2.

	Mantissa							Exponent			Decimal value
Weighting	-4	2	1 •	$^1/_2$	$^1/_4$	$^1/_8$	$^1/_{16}$	-4	2	1	
Number	1	0	0 •	0	1	0	0	0	0	0	$(-4 + ^1/_4) = -3.75_{10}$
		-2	1 •	$^1/_2$	$^1/_4$	$^1/_8$	$^1/_{16}$				Increment exponent
	1	0 •		0	0	1	0	0	0	1	$(-2 + ^1/_8) \times 2^1 = -3.75_{10}$
Move point		-1 •		$^1/_2$	$^1/_4$	$^1/_8$	$^1/_{16}$				Increment exponent
left	1 •		0	0	0	1	0	1	0		$(-1 + ^1/_{16}) \times 2^2 = -3.75_{10}$

Table 5.4.4.5 Stages of conversion of -3.75$_{10}$ to 8-bit floating point form

Questions

9 Convert the following decimal numbers to floating point binary storing the mantissa in 5 bits in two's complement form and the exponent in 3 bits, also in two's complement form. The binary point should be between the most significant bit and the next most significant bit of the mantissa.

(a) 1.25   (b) -5.5   (c) 7.5   (d) +1   (e) -1

(f) 7.25 (remember mantissa is stored in 5 bits not 6)

Converting from binary floating point to decimal

Floating point representation in any number base takes the form

$$M \times Base^E$$

where M is the mantissa, E is the exponent and Base is the number base, for example, it is **2** in decimal for binary floating point numbers.

Method 1:

If we know the values of the mantissa and exponent we can use the formula above to convert from binary floating point to decimal as follows

1. Convert M to decimal → M_d

2. Convert E to decimal → E_d

3. Calculate $M_d \times 2^{E_d}$

For example,

$$M = 0 \cdot 110_2 \quad \text{(two's complement)}$$

$$E = 0101_2 \quad \text{(two's complement)}$$

$M_d = + (\,^1/_2 + \,^1/_4) = \,^3/_4 = 0.75_{10}$

-1	½	¼	⅛
0	1	1	0

$E_d = 0101_2 = +5_{10}$

-8	4	2	1
0	1	0	1

$M_d \times 2^{E_d} = \,^3/_4 \times 2^5 = \,^3/_4 \times 32 = 24_{10}$

Therefore,

Mantissa	Exponent		
0·110	0101	→	24_{10}

Key principle

Binary floating point to decimal:

$M \times Base^E$

1. Convert M to decimal → M_d
2. Convert E to decimal → E_d
3. Calculate $M_d \times 2^{E_d}$

Alternatively, convert the exponent to decimal and move binary point of mantissa **right** if exponent positive, **left** otherwise.

Questions

10 Using method 1 convert the following floating point binary numbers which store the mantissa in **4** bits in two's complement form and the exponent in **4** bits, two's complement form, into decimal. The binary point is between the most significant bit and the next most significant bit of the mantissa.

(a) 0•101 0111   (b) 1•000 0110 (c) 0•100 1000

(d) 0•111 1011   (e) 1•001 1111

Method 2:

Alternatively, convert the exponent to decimal and move the binary point of the mantissa **right** if exponent positive, **left** otherwise.

For example,

$$M = 0\text{•}110_2 \qquad \text{(two's complement)}$$

$$E = 0101_2 \qquad \text{(two's complement)}$$

$$E_d = 0101_2 = +5_{10}$$

Shift binary point 5_{10} places to the **right**, but first add trailing zeroes

$$0\text{•}110_2 \rightarrow 0\text{•}110000_2$$

$$\rightarrow 011000\text{•}0_2$$

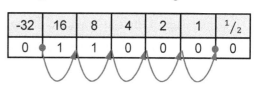

The result of the conversion to decimal is 24_{10}

Another example but this time with a negative exponent,

$$M = 0\text{•}110_2 \qquad E = 1101_2$$

$$E_d = 1101_2 = -3_{10}$$

Shift binary point 3 places to the **left**, but first add leading zeroes

$$0\text{•}110_2 \rightarrow 0000\text{•}110_2$$

$$\rightarrow 0\text{•}000110_2$$

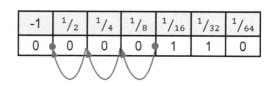

The result of the conversion to decimal is $^3/_{32} = 0.09375_{10}$

Example with a negative mantissa and a negative exponent,

$$M = 1 \cdot 010_2 \qquad E = 1100_2$$

$$E_d = 1100_2 = -4_{10}$$

Shift binary point 4 places to the **left**, but first add leading 1s,

(note: $1 \cdot 010_2$ is equivalent to $11111 \cdot 010_2$, to check just convert each to decimal remembering that the most significant bit is negative in each case).

$$1 \cdot 010_2 \rightarrow 11111 \cdot 010_2$$

$$\rightarrow 1 \cdot 1111010_2$$

-1	$^1/_2$	$^1/_4$	$^1/_8$	$^1/_{16}$	$^1/_{32}$	$^1/_{64}$	$^1/_{128}$
1	1	1	1	1	0	1	0

The result of the conversion to decimal is $- \, ^3/_{64} = -0.046875_{10}$

Example with negative mantissa and positive exponent,

$$M = 1 \cdot 010_2 \qquad E = 0100_2$$

$$E_d = 0100_2 = 4_{10}$$

Shift binary point 4 places to the **right**, but first add trailing zeroes

$$1 \cdot 010_2 \rightarrow 1 \cdot 01000_2$$

$$\rightarrow 10100 \cdot 0_2$$

-16	8	4	2	1	$^1/_2$
1	0	1	0	0	0

The result of the conversion to decimal is $- \, 12_{10}$

Questions

11 Using method 2, convert the following floating point binary numbers which store the mantissa in 4 bits in two's complement form and the exponent in 4 bits, two's complement form, into decimal. The binary point is between the most significant bit and the next most significant bit of the mantissa.

(a) $0 \cdot 101 \quad 0111$ (b) $1 \cdot 000 \quad 0110$ (c) $0 \cdot 100 \quad 1000$

(d) $0 \cdot 111 \quad 1011$ (e) $1 \cdot 001 \ 1111$

In this chapter you have covered:

■ Representing numbers with a fractional part in

  • Fixed point form

  • Floating point form

■ Decimal to binary fixed point

■ Binary to decimal fixed point

■ Decimal to binary floating point

■ Binary to decimal floating point

5.4 Binary number system

Learning objectives

■ *For both fixed point and floating point representation of real numbers, know and explain why when the decimal form is converted to binary the result may be inaccurate.*

■ 5.4.5 Rounding errors

The units of the decimal and binary numeral systems

Remember that a numeral system is a writing system for expressing numbers. In the decimal numeral system, we work with the decimal digits and use these to express a number as multiples of units such as 1000, 100, 10, 1, $^1/_{10}$, $^1/_{100}$, etc. For example,

$$(6 \times 10) + (0 \times 1) + (7 \times ^1/_{10}) + (1 \times ^1/_{100}) = 60.71$$

Questions

1. Write down the following decimal numerals as sums of the decimal units 1000, 100, 10, ..., shown above

   (a) 302.034   (b) 5120.2007   (c) 0.4567

In binary, we are restricted to the numerals 0 and 1.

Also, when we convert from decimal to binary, we need to break the decimal numeral into powers of 2 such as 32, 16, 8, 4, 2, 1, $^1/_2$, $^1/_4$, $^1/_8$, $^1/_{16}$.

For example, 5.25_{10} is broken into

$$(1 \times 4) + (0 \times 2) + (1 \times 1) + (0 \times ^1/_2) + (1 \times ^1/_4) = 101.01_2$$

Questions

2. Write down the following binary numerals as sums of the decimal units 32, 16, 8, 4, ..., shown above
   (a) 1100.11   (b) 101.0101   (c) 11.1011

3. Write down the binary numerals from Q2 in the decimal form $^x/_{2^n}$, e.g. $101.01_2 = ^{21}/_{2^2}$ (because $^{21}/_4 = 5.25$)

   (a) 1100.11   (b) 101.0101   (c) 11.1011

Representation problem

We don't have a representational problem in binary with the whole number part of a decimal providing we have enough bits but we do have a representational problem with the fractional part. We break a decimal into $x/2^n$ when we convert it exactly to its binary equivalent, e.g.

$$5.25_{10} = (1 \times 4) + (0 \times 2) + (1 \times 1) + (0 \times \tfrac{1}{2}) + (1 \times \tfrac{1}{4})$$

$$= (1 \times \tfrac{16}{4}) + (0 \times \tfrac{8}{4}) + (1 \times \tfrac{4}{4}) + (0 \times \tfrac{2}{4}) + (1 \times \tfrac{1}{4}) = \tfrac{21}{4} = \tfrac{21}{2^2}$$

Notice in binary the only possible prime factor for the denominator is 2. However, the denominator of a decimal such as $0.8 = \frac{(2 \times 2)}{5}$ doesn't consist of multiples of 2. There are in fact many decimals that cannot be broken down into the form $x/2^n$.

Questions

4 Write down the factors of the following fixed point decimal numbers in $Factors/Factors$ format, for some you may want to use a factoring calculator

(a) 0.1   (b) 0.7   (c) 5.7   (d) 8.75   (e) 67.03125

5 For each of the fixed point decimal numbers in Q4, state whether it can be represented in the form $x/2^n$.

6 Using a decimal to binary converter, write down the fixed point binary equivalent of the decimal numerals in Q4. Comment on your answers.

Fixed point decimal	Fixed point binary
0.1	0.00011
0.2	0. 0011
0.25	0.01
0.3	0.01001
0.4	0.0110
0.5	0.1
0.6	0.1001
0.7	0.10110
0.75	0.11
0.8	0.1100
0.9	0.11100
1.0	1.0

Table 5.4.5.1 shows the fixed point binary equivalent of some unsigned fixed point decimals.

Notice that some binary equivalents contain a repeating sequence of 1s and 0s indicated with a line.

Table 5.4.5.2 shows the same decimals expressed in rational form x/y with the numerator and denominator factored. It also shows the closest binary fixed point numeral in 8 bits with binary point between the most significant digit and the next.

Table 5.4.5.1 Fixed point decimals and their fixed point binary equivalent

Unsigned Fixed point decimal	x/y	Closest $x/2^n$ form for $0 \le n \le 7$	Closest 8-bit fixed point binary form	Closest 8-bit binary numeral in decimal form
0.1	$\dfrac{1}{(2 \times 5)}$	$\dfrac{13}{2^7}$	0.0001101	0.1015625
0.2	$\dfrac{1}{5}$	$\dfrac{13}{2^6}$	0.0011010	0.203125
0.25	$\dfrac{1}{(2 \times 2)}$	$\dfrac{1}{2^2}$	0.0100000	0.25
0.3	$\dfrac{3}{(2 \times 5)}$	$\dfrac{19}{2^6}$	0.0100110	0.296875
0.4	$\dfrac{2}{5}$	$\dfrac{51}{2^7}$	0.0110011	0.3984375
0.5	$\dfrac{1}{2}$	$\dfrac{1}{2^1}$	0.1000000	0.5
0.6	$\dfrac{3}{5}$	$\dfrac{77}{2^7}$	0.1001101	0.6015625
0.7	$\dfrac{7}{(2 \times 5)}$	$\dfrac{45}{2^6}$	0.1011010	0.703125
0.75	$\dfrac{3}{(2 \times 2)}$	$\dfrac{3}{2^2}$	0.1100000	0.75
0.8	$\dfrac{(2 \times 2)}{5}$	$\dfrac{51}{2^6}$	0.1100110	0.796875
0.9	$\dfrac{9}{(2 \times 5)}$	$\dfrac{115}{2^7}$	0.1110011	0.8984375
1.0	$\dfrac{2}{2}$	$\dfrac{1}{2^0}$	1.0000000	1.0

Table 5.4.5.2 Decimals expressed in rational form x/y

Missing rational numbers

Figure 5.4.5.1 shows the weighting for the 8-bit unsigned fixed point binary that was used for *Table 5.4.5.2*.

$\frac{1}{1}$	$\frac{1}{2}$	$\frac{1}{4}$	$\frac{1}{8}$	$\frac{1}{16}$	$\frac{1}{32}$	$\frac{1}{64}$	$\frac{1}{128}$
0	0	0	0	0	0	0	0

Figure 5.4.5.1 Weighting for 8-bit fixed point binary

If we construct all the possible fixed point binary numerals from these weightings we end up with a finite subset of rational numbers, S, as follows

$$S = \left\{ \frac{255}{128}, \frac{254}{128}, \frac{253}{128}, \dots, \frac{239}{128}, \dots, \frac{47}{128}, \frac{46}{128}, \dots, \frac{128}{128}, \dots, \frac{31}{128}, \frac{30}{128}, \dots, \frac{8}{128}, \frac{7}{128}, \dots, \frac{2}{128}, \frac{1}{128}, \frac{0}{128} \right\}$$

Rational numbers are missing from this subset, S.

Take any two consecutive members of the set, e.g. $\frac{255}{128} = \frac{510}{256}$ and $\frac{254}{128} = \frac{508}{256}$. Notice that, for this example, $\frac{509}{256}$ is missing from the set S. Lots more rational numbers can be found that are missing from the set S.

This leads to inaccuracies when we represent a given fixed point decimal in fixed point binary using the specified number of bits, e.g. we cannot represent $^{509}/_{256}$ for example using 8-bit fixed point binary.

Questions

7   For each of the following values of x, write down the nearest 8-bit fixed point binary numeral to $^{x}/_{128}$ using Figure 5.4.5.1 weighting

(a) 0   (b) 1   (c) 2   (d) 3   (e) 5   (f) 254

8   For each of the following values of x, write down the nearest 8-bit fixed point binary numeral to $^{x}/_{256}$ using Figure 5.4.5.1 weighting.

(a) 510   (b) 508   (c) 509

9   For each part of Q8 write down the decimal expansion of $^{x}/_{256}$ (e.g. 1.99…) and the decimal equivalent of your answers to Q8. Comment on your results.

Rounding error

Table 5.4.5.3 shows for each given unsigned fixed point decimal, the difference or error between it and the closest decimal that can be represented in 8-bit unsigned binary fixed point form. We call this error the rounding error.

Fixed point decimal	Closest 8-bit binary in decimal	Difference or Error
0.1	0.1015625	0.0015625
0.2	0.203125	0.003125
0.25	0.25	0
0.3	0.296875	0.003125
0.4	0.3984375	0.0015625
0.5	0.5	0
0.6	0.6015625	0.0015625
0.7	0.703125	0.003125
0.75	0.75	0
0.8	0.796875	0.003125
0.9	0.8984375	0.0015625
1.0	1.0	0

Table 5.4.5.3 Fixed point decimals and the error difference

Truncation or rounding down

Unsigned fixed point decimal 0.1_{10} converts to fixed point binary $0.0\overline{0011}$, 0.3_{10} to $0.0\overline{1001}$ and so on as shown in *Table 5.4.5.4*.

When these fixed point binary numerals with recurring bit patterns are limited to a given numbers of bits, e.g. 9, we can just drop the bits in bit positions greater than this given number. This is known as truncation or rounding down. For example, 0.1_{10} truncated to 9 bits becomes 0.00011001_2 just by dropping $\overline{10011}$ from the 10th bit position onwards.

Rounding off

Alternatively, we can choose to round off. This means

- Add 1 to the last retained digit if the following digit is 1 otherwise leave unaltered.

For example, if we round off $0.0\overline{0011}$ to 8 bits then we need to look at the binary expansion as far as the 9th bit which is 0.00011001.

The 9th bit is 1 so we drop the 9th bit but add 1 to the 8th bit so arriving at 0.0001101_2, the rounded off result in 8 bits.

On the other hand, if we round off $0.0\overline{1001}$ to 8 bits then we don't add 1 because the binary expansion to 9 bits is 0.01001100_2 and the 9th bit is 0. Therefore, $0.0\overline{1001}$ rounded off to 8 bits is 0.0100110_2.

Rounding off is usually used where the representation is inexact, because less error can result compared with rounding down.

Fixed point decimal	Fixed point binary	Fixed point binary truncated after 9-bits	Closest binary form in 8 bits
0.1	$0.0\overline{0011}$	0.00011001	0.0001101
0.2	$0.\overline{0011}$	0.00110011	0.0011010
0.25	0.01	0.01000000	0.0100000
0.3	$0.0\overline{1001}$	0.01001100	0.0100110
0.4	$0.\overline{0110}$	0.01100110	0.0110011
0.5	0.1	0.10000000	0.1000000
0.6	$0.\overline{1001}$	0.100110011	0.1001101
0.7	$0.1\overline{0110}$	0.10110011	0.1011010
0.75	0.11	0.11000000	0.1100000
0.8	$0.\overline{1100}$	0.11001100	0.1100110
0.9	$0.1\overline{1100}$	0.11100110	0.1110011
1.0	1.0	1.00000000	1.0000000

Table 5.4.5.4 Fixed point decimals and their equivalents

Rounding errors in signed fixed point

Everything that has been stated for unsigned fixed point binary is also true of signed fixed point binary.

Rounding errors in floating point

Everything that has been stated for fixed point binary is also true of the mantissa of floating point representation because the mantissa takes on fixed point form.

In this chapter you have covered:

- Why both fixed point and floating point representation of decimal numbers may be inaccurate. For both fixed point and floating point representation of real numbers, there are in fact many decimals that cannot be broken down into the form $^x/_{2}n$. This leads to inaccuracies when we represent a given fixed point decimal in fixed point binary using a specified number of bits or in the mantissa of a floating point binary.

5.4 Binary number system

■ 5.4.6 Absolute and relative errors

Approximating a number

In the previous chapter we learned that when storing a number in a computer, if the number contains more digits than can be accommodated, an approximation to the number is stored (obtained by either rounding off or truncating). When using truncated results, the machine representation is constructed by simply discarding significant digits that cannot be stored; when rounding off it approximates a quantity with the closest machine representation possible.

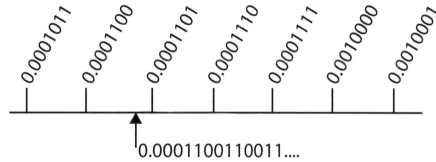

Figure 5.4.6.1 Binary number line showing 8-bit unsigned fixed point binary

For example, if only 8 bits are available as shown in *Figure 5.4.6.1* then 0.1_{10} which in unsigned fixed point binary is $0.0\overline{0011}$ will be represented by 0.0001100_2 if truncated and 0.0001101_2 if rounded off because it lies between these two values as shown.

Absolute error

The difference between the actual number and the nearest representable value is known as the absolute error. For example, 0.1_{10} is stored as 0.0001101_2 in 8-bit unsigned fixed point binary form which is 0.1015625_{10}. Therefore,

$$\text{Absolute error} = 0.1015625_{10} - 0.1_{10} = 0.0015625_{10}$$

Absolute means that the sign is ignored e.g. differences of 0.0015625 and -0.0015625 are the same absolute error.

Key principle

Absolute error:
The difference between the actual number and the nearest representable value.

Questions

1 Calculate the absolute error when the following fixed point decimal numbers are stored in 8-bit unsigned fixed point binary as shown in Figure 5.4.6.1. Round off if a number cannot be represented exactly.

(a) 0.2_{10} (b) 0.6_{10}

Key principle

Relative error:
The absolute error divided by the actual number.

Relative error

The relative error is defined as the absolute error divided by the actual number. For example, the absolute error when 0.1_{10} is stored as 0.0001101_2 in 8-bit unsigned fixed point binary form is 0.0015625_{10}. Therefore,

$$\text{Relative error} = \frac{0.0015625_{10}}{0.1_{10}}$$

$$= 0.015625$$

This is 1.5625% when represented as a percentage.

Questions

2. Calculate the percentage relative error when the following fixed point decimal numbers are stored in 8-bit unsigned fixed point binary as shown in Figure 5.4.6.1. Round off if a number cannot be represented exactly.

   (a) 0.2_{10} (b) 0.6_{10}

Comparing absolute and relative errors

Absolute error calculations are not as useful as relative error calculations. For example, Table 5.4.6.1 shows how the relative error can vary for a given absolute error if the magnitude of the actual value varies from small to large.

Absolute error in decimal	Actual value in decimal	Relative error %
1.0	1000000.0	0.0001
1.0	10.0	10
1.0	1.0	100
16	128	12.5
$1/2048$	$1/256$	12.5

Table 5.4.6.1 Variation of relative error for a given absolute error

Questions

3. The percentage relative error is 1% for the following decimal numbers. Calculate the absolute error.

   (a) 1.00   (b) 1.00×10^{38} (c) 1.00×10^{-39}

In this chapter you have covered:

- How to calculate for stored and processed numerical data
  - absolute error: the difference between the actual number and the nearest representable value.
  - relative error: the absolute error divided by the actual number.
- Comparing absolute and relative errors for large and small magnitude numbers, and numbers close to one - see Table 5.4.6.1.

5.4 Binary number system

5.4.7 Range and precision

Using fixed point representation

In the previous chapter, we learned that it becomes necessary to approximate a number sometimes if a representation of it is to be stored in a digital computer. A digital computer is not designed to allocate an infinite number of bits instead it must allocate a fixed number of bits because computer memory is finite.

In a simplified example of fixed point, we allocate 8 bits and use these as shown in Figure 5.4.7.1.

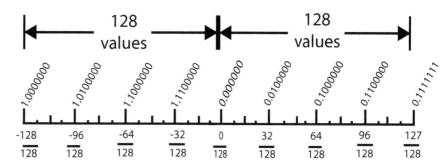

Figure 5.4.7.1 Number line for 8-bit signed two's complement fixed point binary.

For 8 bits there are 2^8 or 256 different arrangements of the bits or bit patterns. The example uses these to code numbers in fixed point signed two's complement binary arranged in decimal from $^{-128}/_{128}$ to $^{+127}/_{128}$ or binary 1.0000000 to 0.1111111 with the most significant bit as the sign bit, and weighted $^{-128}/_{128}$ as shown in Figure 5.4.7.2 .

$^{-128}/_{128}$	$^{64}/_{128}$	$^{32}/_{128}$	$^{16}/_{128}$	$^{8}/_{128}$	$^{4}/_{128}$	$^{2}/_{128}$	$^{1}/_{128}$
0	0	0	0	0	0	0	0

Figure 5.4.7.2 Weightings in the example for 8-bit signed two's complement fixed point binary

The (128 + 128) or 256 different representations referenced in Figure 5.4.7.1 are distributed evenly across the range. Any number that needs to be stored is coded by assigning to it the nearest representation, e.g. 0.2_{10} will be stored as the bit pattern 0.0011010_2 or in decimal, $^{26}/_{128}$, an approximation to 0.2_{10}.

The smallest difference of any two 8-bit patterns in the example coding is $^1/_{128}$ or $^1/_2{}^{8-1}$ in decimal. In general, for n bits, the smallest difference for fixed point binary with the given weighting is $^1/_2{}^{n-1}$.

If we think of the number line shown in *Figure 5.4.7.1* as a ruler then the precision with which we can record measurements with this ruler is to the nearest $^1/_{128}$.

Thus, for any positive or negative number inside the range that can be represented, the maximum absolute error in a measurement in this coding scheme will be $^1/_{256}$ (one half of $^1/_{128}$ because we round off). The maximum percentage relative error will be $^1/_{256}/_{127/_{128}}$ x 100 = 0.39% and the largest $^1/_{256}/_{1/_{128}}$ x 100 = 50%.

> ## Questions
>
> 1 With the binary point placed between the sign bit and the next bit what is the smallest positive number that can be represented in two's complement fixed point binary for the following number of bits ?
>
> (a) 4 (b) 16 (c) 24 (d) 32 (e) 64

Using floating point representation

The range of numbers that can be stored in 8-bit signed two's complement fixed point form as shown above, $^{-128}/_{128}$ to $^{+127}/_{128}$, is very limited. If we divide these 8 bits into a 4-bit signed fraction, f, and a 4-bit signed multiplier , 2^e, then we can represent numbers differently in 8-bits as follows

$$f \times 2^e$$

We are still restricted with 8 bits to choosing from 2^8 or 256 different bit patterns but we achieve a much greater range of representable numbers than with fixed point coding. If we use the weightings shown in *Figure 5.4.7.3* then the range of representable numbers is

$$^{-8}/_8 \times 2^7 \quad \text{to} \quad ^{+7}/_8 \times 2^7 \text{ (i.e. -128 to 127)}$$

or

$$^{-128}/_{128} \times 2^7 \quad \text{to} \quad ^{+112}/_{128} \times 2^7$$

This range is larger than the 8-bit fixed point coding by a factor 2^7.

Mantissa				Exponent			
$^{-8}/_8$	$^4/_8$	$^2/_8$	$^1/_8$	-8	4	2	1
0	0	0	0	0	0	0	0

Figure 5.4.7.3 Weightings for 8-bit floating point, two's complement 4-bit mantissa and 4-bit exponent

Figure 5.4.7.4 shows the range of expressible negative and positive numbers for a normalised 4-bit mantissa and a 4-bit exponent weighted as described above in *Figure 5.4.7.3*. The negative value closest to zero is $1011\ 1000_2$ in 4-bit mantissa 4-bit exponent form or -0.625×2^{-8} in decimal. The mantissa has been normalised for maximum precision as will be explained in *Chapter 5.4.8*. The positive value closest to zero is 0.100 1000 in 4-bit mantisa 4-bit exponent form or +0.5 x 2^{-8} in decimal. The mantissa has been normalised for maximum precision.

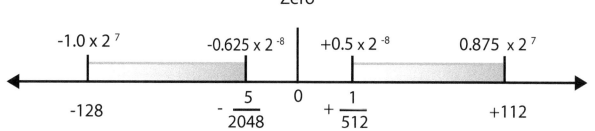

Essentially, the mantissa f is restricted to the following ranges to ensure maximum precision

$$½ ≤ f < 1 \text{ and } -1 ≤ f < -½$$

or in two's complement binary

$$0.100_2 ≤ f ≤ 0.111_2 \text{ and } 1.000_2 ≤ f < 1.100_2$$

or

$$0.100_2 ≤ f ≤ 0.111_2 \text{ and } 1.000_2 ≤ f ≤ 1.011_2$$

0.111_2 is the nearest positive mantissa to 1_2 or 1_{10}.

The nearest two's complement binary representation less than 1.100_2 is

$$1.100_2 - 0.001_2 = 1.011_2 = -0.625_{10}.$$

We consider zero as a special case. For zero, f is 0 and exponent e is also 0. This means that for our 8-bit example we will use only **128** bit patterns excluding zero, but **129** bit patterns if zero is included. For zero to be excluded then the bit before the binary point must always be different from the bit after this point.

The 129 different representations are distributed unevenly across the range as illustrated in a section of the number line in *Figure 5.4.7.5*.

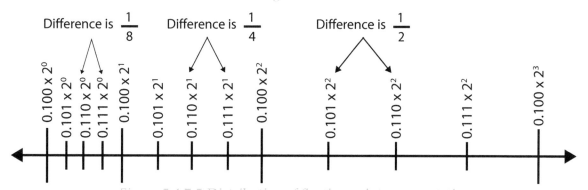

Thus for largest positive numbers, the difference between the representations is as much as $⅛ × 2^7$ or 16, so a somewhat large absolute error of half of this because we round off when approximating. The approximate percentage relative error is $^8/_{2^7} \times 100 = ^8/_{128} \times 100 = 6.25\%$ for the largest positive number.

For the smallest positive numbers, the difference between the representations is as little as $^1/_8 \times 2^{-8}$ or $^1/_{2048}$, a small absolute error of half this. The approximate percentage relative error is $^1/4096 /_{2^{-8}} \times 100 = 6.25\%$ for the smallest positive number. The relative error is similar across the whole range.

Questions

2   Evaluate the following where the mantissa is in two's complement form
    (a) $0.111_2 \times 2^2$ (b) $0.101_2 \times 2^6$ (c) $1.011_2 \times 2^2$ (d) $0.101_2 \times 2^{-6}$

3   Explain why the gaps between adjacent numbers expressed in floating point form are not constant.

Comparing fixed point and floating point ranges

Floating point representation can store numbers chosen from a much greater range, larger and smaller, positive and negative, than fixed point, for a given number of bits n for each.

Representation	Range
The fixed point range in decimal for n bits where n = 32, and using two's complement representation with 8 of the 32 bits allocated to the fractional part is approximately	$+8.4 \times 10^6$ to $+3.9 \times 10^{-3}$, 0, -3.9×10^{-3} to -8.4×10^6
The floating point range in decimal, for the same number of bits 32, for an 8-bit two's complement exponent and 24-bit normalised mantissa, is approximately	$+1.7 \times 10^{38}$ to $+1.5 \times 10^{-39}$, 0, -1.5×10^{-39} to -1.7×10^{38}

Table 5.4.7.1 Comparison of ranges of fixed point and floating point representations where the number of bits is 32 in each case

Questions

4   What are the most positive and most negative numbers that can be represented using the following fixed point two's complement representations? Give your answers in decimal.

    (a) 4 bits of which 2 bits are allocated to the fractional part
    (b) 8 bits of which 4 bits are allocated to the fractional part
    (c) 10 bits of which 5 bits are allocated to the fractional part

5   What are the most positive and most negative numbers that can be represented using the following floating point two's complement representations? Give your answers in decimal.

    (a) 16 bits of which 8 bits are allocated to mantissa and 8 bits to the exponent
    (b) 32 bits of which 16 bits are allocated to mantissa and 16 bits to the exponent
    (c) 64 bits of which 32 bits are allocated to mantissa and 32 bits to the exponent

Precision and significant figures or digits

To compare the precision of fixed point with floating point we need first of all to understand what is meant by precision. To understand precision we need first to understand what is meant by significant figures or digits.

Significant figures or digits

Rulers, tape measures and other measuring devices enable length measurements to be made. Here are some measurements and their units

| 11.1 cm | 120 cm | 12.23 km | 12.2 km |

The first 11.1 cm is also 111 mm. This indicates that this measurement has been made to the nearest millimetre. The second, 120 cm is ambiguous. It is not clear whether the measurement is exactly 120 cm or the measurer was just measuring to the nearest 10 cm.

The third, 12.23 km in metres is 12230 m. The measurement was performed to the nearest 10 m, i.e. the real value lies somewhere between 12225 and 12235. The last measurement 12.2 km in metres is 12200 m, a measurement performed to the nearest 100 m, i.e. the real value lies somewhere between 12150 and 12250.

The latter two measurements, 12.23 km and 12.2 km, clearly show a different degree of precision, one is a measurement to the nearest 10 m and the other to the nearest 100 m. We call the digits which provide information about the precision of a measurement, significant digits or significant figures and the more significant digits used the greater the precision of the measurement.

Table 5.4.7.2 shows the number of significant digits for some measurements.

Measurement	Precision	Explanation
11.1 cm	111 3 significant figures	11.1 cm is 111 mm measurement has been made to the nearest millimetre
12.23 km	1223 4 significant figures	12230 m measurement has been made to the nearest 10 metres
12.2 km	122 3 significant figures	12200 m measurement has been made to the nearest 100 metres
120. cm	120 3 significant figures	Decimal point indicates measurement made to nearest centimetre, the 0 is not just a placeholder
0.03000 km	3000 4 significant figures	By changing the units to centimetres it becomes 3000 cm which suggests measurement to nearest centimetre and therefore the three zeroes after 3 are significant, the zeroes before are not
9.0 cm	90 2 significant figures	Measurement made to nearest millimetre (90 millimetres) therefore the zero is significant
2.001 m	2001 4 significant figures	2.001 m is 2001 mm Measurement made to nearest millimetre

Table 5.4.7.2 Number of significant digits for various measurements

Key concept

Significant digits/figures:
Digits which provide information about the precision of a measurement, are called significant digits or significant figures.

Rules of significant figures or digits

1. Any non-zero digits and zeroes between non-zero digits are significant, e.g. in 2.001m the two zeros are significant

2. Leading zeroes, i.e. zeroes that come before the non-zero digits are not significant, e.g. in 0.03000 km the first two zeros are not significant

3. Trailing zeroes after the last non-zero digit are significant if a decimal point occurs anywhere in the number, e.g. 0.03000 km, the last three zeros are significant

4. If there is no decimal point anywhere in the number then its precision is ambiguous.

Questions

6 State the number of significant figures for each of the following measurements made in the decimal system

(a) 12.23 (b) 130.04 (c) 0.03 (d) 0.00450 (e) 34 (f) 0254.

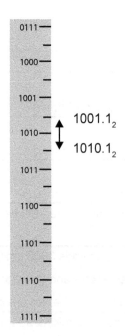

Figure 5.4.7.6 Section of a binary ruler

Significant digits in floating point representation

The number of significant digits for the measurement 1010_2 is ambiguous, it is not clear whether the measurement was exactly 1010_2, i.e. 1010.0_2 or the measurement was made to the nearest unit, i.e. the actual value was between 1001.1_2 and 1010.1_2.

If the measurement was between 1001.1_2 and 1010.1_2, the ambiguity in 1010_2 could be removed if we expressed the measurement in the form showing that we have just 3 significant digits of precision

$$1.01_2 \times 2^3$$

Multiplying by 2^3 is equivalent to shifting the binary point **three** places to the right as follows

$$1.01 \xrightarrow{\times 2} 10.1 \xrightarrow{\times 2} 101. \xrightarrow{\times 2} 1010$$

The number of significant digits is unambiguous, it is 3, i.e. 101. This representation is known as scientific form. Floating point representation resembles scientific form in structure but differs slightly on detail. The significant digits are contained in the mantissa. The exponent records how many places to shift the binary point, left or right to obtain the fixed point form of the number.

Questions

7 State the number of significant figures, if you can, for each of the following measurements made in fixed point binary. If you cannot, explain why.

(a) 10.1_2 (b) 0.111_2 (c) 0.011_2 (d) 0.101_2 (e) 0.1100100_2 (f) 1010_2

Precision

The more significant digits recorded for a measurement the greater its precision. Precision is indicated by the number of significant digits.

Comparison of the advantages and disadvantages of fixed point and floating point

Precision versus range

We focus on the mantissa of the floating point representation when comparing the precision of floating point with fixed point as the size of the mantissa in bits determines the number of significant digits that can be stored.

If fixed point representation has the same number of bits as the mantissa in a floating point representation then both forms will (assuming the floating point representation is normalised – see *Chapter 5.4.8*) have the same precision.

However, if the total number of bits is the same for each then the number of bits in the floating point's mantissa will be less and so will possess fewer significant digits than fixed point. Therefore, a number stored in floating point form will be stored with less precision than it will in fixed point form if the same total number of bits are used for each form.

However, floating point, for a given number of bits, can store numbers chosen from a greater range than fixed point, but only at the expense of precision.

For example, *Figure 5.4.7.7* shows a floating point number representation in 32 bits using a 24-bit mantissa and an 8-bit exponent.

The mantissa has storage space for 23 significant digits + 1 sign bit.

However, the same 32 bits could store 31 significant digits + 1 sign bit in fixed point form.

Mantissa						Exponent				
Sign bit −1						Sign bit −128				
1	0	⋯	1	0		0	1	⋯	1	0

Figure 5.4.7.7 32-bit floating point number, two's complement 24-bit mantissa and 8-bit exponent

Questions

8 How many significant digits can two's complement floating point store if the representation is as follows

(a) 16 bits in total of which 6 bits are allocated to the exponent?

(b) 32 bits in total of which 6 bits are allocated to the exponent?

(c) 64 bits in total of which 8 bits are allocated to the exponent?

Key concept

Precision:
The number of significant digits used to represent the number. The more significant digits used the greater the precision.

Key fact

Precision of floating point vs fixed point:
For a given number of bits, fixed point representation can store more significant digits than floating point.

Therefore, a number stored in floating point form will be stored with less precision than fixed point representation which uses the same total number of bits.

Key fact

Range of floating point vs fixed point:
For a given number of bits, floating point represents a much greater range of numbers than fixed point.

Questions

9   How many significant digits can two's complement fixed point store in the following number of bits

(a) 16 bits?

(b) 24 bits?

(c) 64 bits?

Speed of calculation

In general, calculations take longer with numbers stored in a digital computer in floating point form than they do with numbers stored in fixed point form because floating point inevitably involves floating or shifting the decimal or binary point of operands whereas fixed point doesn't.

If the central processing unit (CPU) does not have circuitry to perform floating point operations directly then the steps of the operations have to be written in software and accessed by the CPU. Fetching and executing code to perform calculations is considerably slower than doing these calculations directly in hardware designed just for this task.

Although modern general purpose computers contain CPUs that have access to hardware floating point units, even with a hardware floating point unit floating point calculations still take longer than fixed point calculations.

In this chapter you have covered:

- The advantages and disadvantages of fixed point and floating point forms in terms of
  - Range: For a given number of bits, floating point represents a much greater range of numbers than fixed point.
  - Precision: For a given number of bits, fixed point representation can store more significant digits than floating point. Therefore, a number stored in floating point form will be stored with less precision than fixed point representation which uses the same total number of bits.
  - Speed of calculation: In general, calculations take longer with numbers stored in floating point form than they do with numbers stored in fixed point form.

5.4 Binary number system

5.4.8 Normalisation of floating point form

Uniqueness of representation

The decimal number, 323.142 can be represented in floating point form in many different ways, some of which are as follows

$$32314.2 \times 10^{-2}$$

$$323.142 \times 10^{0}$$

$$0.323142 \times 10^{3}$$

$$0.00323142 \times 10^{5}$$

> #### Questions
>
> 1. Write down the floating point form of 323.142 for which the power of ten multiplier is
>
> (a) 10^{7} (b) 10^{9} (c) 10^{-5}

Having more than one representation is not a good idea. For example, adding 323.142 to itself using two different floating point representations is not straight forward. Try this for yourself

$$32314.2 \times 10^{-2}$$

$$+ \ 0.323142 \times 10^{3}$$

Neither is comparing two numbers straightforward if they use different floating pointing representations, e.g. 323.142×10^{0} and 0.00323142×10^{5}.

It makes good sense therefore to allow just one floating point representation of a number to ensure the uniqueness of the representation and to reduce the effort required to perform arithmetic operations.

Normalisation in decimal

Computer memory is finite and therefore it is necessary to allocate a fixed number of bits to each representation of a number. Just for the moment, imagine that the computer is able to store the decimal digits, sign and decimal point as shown in *Figure 5.4.8.1* with the position of the mantissa's decimal point **fixed** to ensure uniqueness of representation. This memory is shown to store up to six significant decimal digits in the mantissa.

Mantissa							Exponent	
+	3	•	2	3	1	4	2	+	2

Figure 5.4.8.1 Mantissa exponent store for decimal digits, sign and decimal point in fixed position as shown to ensure uniqueness of representation

Now imagine that after a floating point number calculation the result obtained is

$$+\ 0.00516838 \times 10^6$$

We now face a problem. Although the mantissa of the answer has six significant digits, and our fixed point memory arrangement can accommodate six significant digits, if we do not adjust the exponent of the result we will lose precision as shown in *Figure 5.4.8.2* where rounding off has been applied

Mantissa							Exponent	
+	0	•	0	0	5	1	7	+	6

Figure 5.4.8.2 Loss of precision

On the other hand, we can preserve precision by adjusting the exponent as follows

Mantissa							Exponent	
+	5	•	1	6	8	3	8	+	3

Figure 5.4.8.3 Regaining maximum precision

This form of the result is said to be normalised

The goal for normalising floating point representations of numbers is to maximise precision by maximising the number of significant digits in the representation.

Questions

2 Using the form of representation shown below, in which six significant digits are allowed in the mantissa and one in the exponent, normalise the following floating point decimal numbers

Mantissa							Exponent	
sign	d	•	d	d	d	d	d	sign	d

(a) 0.0000456789×10^7 (b) 0.0000456789×10^4

(c) $0.00456789 \times 10^{-5}$ (d) $0.00004567895 \times 10^6$

Normalising an un-normalised floating point binary representation

Numbers expressed in floating point form are normalised to maximise the precision with which the number is expressed, i.e. to maximise the number of significant digits present in the representation.

Normalisation also provides a unique representation for a number.

0.1875_{10} is 0.0011_2 in binary fixed point form. In un-normalised floating point form, this is

$$0.0011_2 \quad 0000_2$$

where the mantissa is 0.0011_2 and the exponent is 0000_2.

What if only 4 bits instead of 5 bits were available for the mantissa? Do we just round off to 0.010_2? No, we normalise the 5 bits first and then round off, if we have to.

Figure 5.4.8.4 shows in stages how this is done, for a 4-bit mantissa and a 4-bit exponent for the result, by shifting the bits of the mantissa left whilst decrementing the exponent. Shifting/incrementing stops when the bit before the binary point is different from the bit after the point. The mantissa bit shown in red is unavailable to use for the result. The normalised representation is

$$0.11_2 \quad 1110_2$$

	Mantissa					Exponent				Decimal value
Weighting	-1	$^1/_2$	$^1/_4$	$^1/_8$	$^1/_{16}$	-8	-4	2	1	
	0 •	0	0	1	1	0	0	0	0	$^3/_{16} \times 2^0 = 0.1875_{10}$
	0 •	0	1	1		1	1	1	1	$^3/_8 \times 2^{-1} = 0.1875_{10}$
	0 •	1	1			1	1	1	0	$^3/_4 \times 2^{-2} = 0.1875_{10}$

Figure 5.4.8.4 Normalising a positive number expressed in un-normalised floating point binary form

The normalisation process essentially identifies where the significant digits of the representation begin and then adjusts the mantissa so that digit positions are not wasted by being taken up by non-significant digits, For example, in the two's complement floating point representation 0.0011_2 0000_2 , the mantissa is 0.0011_2 and has significant digits that begin at the first 1_2 after the point, i.e. 11_2. The 0_2 before the binary point is the sign bit so needs to be retained. The 00_2 between the point and 11_2 is not significant. So moving the point two places to the right results in a mantissa of 0.11_2. To compensate we need to take 2 away from the exponent, $0000_2 \rightarrow 1110_2$.

Normalisation algorithm

We start by expressing the decimal number in floating point form with the leftmost bit position of the mantissa weighted -1_{10}. For example, 10.75_{10} in two's complement fixed point binary is shown in Table 5.4.8.1.

	Decimal No	Fixed point 2's complement binary	Floating point 2's complement binary	Normalised floating point form?
(a)	10.75_{10}	1010.11_2	$0.10111_2\ 0011_2$	Yes
(b)	0.234375_{10}	0.0000011_2	$0.0000011_2\ 0000_2$	No
(c)	0.234375_{10}	0.0000011_2	$0.11_2\ 1011_2$	Yes

Table 5.4.8.1 Normalised floating point form?

Normalisation algorithm for positive mantissa

Algorithm:

```
While bit before point = bit after point
   Do
      Remove bit after point
        then shift all remaining mantissa bits left one place and
           insert a zero in least significant bit position
      Decrement exponent
   EndWhile
```

For example, the algorithm applied to (b) in Table 5.4.8.1 produces $0.11_2\ 1011_2$ when truncated to a 3-bit mantissa, which is (c) in the table.

Questions

3 Using the form of representation shown below for your answer in which six bits are assigned to the mantissa and four to the exponent, normalise the following un-normalised floating point binary numbers whose mantissa and exponent are shown below in (a) to (c)

Mantissa						Exponent			
-1	$^1/_2$	$^1/_4$	$^1/_8$	$^1/_{16}$	$^1/_{32}$	-8	4	2	1
d • d	d	d	d	d	d	d	d	d	d

(a) $0.000011101_2\ 0011_2$ (b) $0.0010101_2\ 1100_2$

(c) $0.00000011101_2\ 0111_2$

Normalisation algorithm for negative mantissa

Express decimal number in floating point form with the leftmost bit position of the mantissa weighted -1_{10}.

Algorithm:

```
While bit before point = bit after point
   Do
      Remove bit after point
         then shift all remaining mantissa bits left one place and
            insert a zero in least significant bit position
      Decrement exponent
   EndWhile
```

Figure 5.4.8.5 shows this algorithm applied to $1.1101_2\ 0000_2$. Four bits are allocated to the mantissa and four to the exponent for the result. The fifth mantissa bit shown in red is not available to use in the result. For each iteration of the algorithm a 1 in the $^1/_2$ column is removed and then the lesser significant bits are shifted left one bit position and a zero inserted in the least significant bit position. The normalised form shows that we have avoided rounding off and thereby a loss of precision.

Weighting	Mantissa					Exponent				Decimal value
	-1	$^1/_2$	$^1/_4$	$^1/_8$	$^1/_{16}$	-8	-4	2	1	
	1 •	1	1	0	1	0	0	0	0	$-^3/_{16} \times 2^0 = -0.1875_{10}$
	1 •	1	0	1	0	1	1	1	1	$-^3/_8 \times 2^{-1} = -0.1875_{10}$
	1 •	0	1	0	0	1	1	1	0	$-^3/_4 \times 2^{-2} = -0.1875_{10}$

Figure 5.4.8.5 Normalising a negative number expressed in un-normalised floating point binary form

Also note that the algorithm for normalizing a negative mantissa is exactly the same as for normalizing a positive mantissa.

The normalisation process for a negative mantissa essentially identifies where the significant digits of the representation begin and then adjusts the mantissa so that digit positions are not wasted by being taken up by non-significant digits. For example, in the two's complement floating point representation $1.1101_2\ 0000_2$, the mantissa is 1.1101_2 and has significant digits that begin at the first 0_2 after the point, i.e. 01_2 (this is the opposite of the case when the mantissa is positive). The 1_2 before the binary point is the sign bit so needs to be retained. The 11_2 between the point and 01_2 is not significant. So moving the point two places to the right results in a mantissa of 1.01_2. To compensate we need to take 2 away from the exponent, $0000_2 \rightarrow 1110_2$. Notice that when the mantissa is negative we look for the occurrence of the first 0_2 after the binary point as this is where the significant digits begin.

By a similar argument, if the mantissa had been 111.1101_2 , the first two 1's are insignificant, they are equivalent to leading zeroes in a positive mantissa, e.g. 000.1010_2, and therefore can be dropped producing 1.1101_2 which then needs to undergo normalisation.

Questions

4 Write down the result of eliminating unnecessary digits, if possible, from the following two's complement representations

(a) 1111.01_2 (b) 1101.011_2 (c) 00011.01_2

(d) 101.01_2 (e) 101.0100_2

5 Using the form of representation shown below for your answer in which six bits are assigned to the mantissa and four to the exponent, normalise the following un-normalised floating point binary numbers whose mantissa and exponent are shown below in (a) to (c)

Mantissa						Exponent			
-1	$1/2$	$1/4$	$1/8$	$1/16$	$1/32$	-8	4	2	1
d	d	d	d	d	d	d	d	d	d

(a) 1.111101110_2 0011_2 (b) 1.1101011_2 1100_2

(c) 1.11111100010_2 0111_2

In this chapter you have covered:

- Why floating point numbers are normalised:
  - To maximise precision by maximising the number of significant digits that are represented in mantissa. This is achieved by ensuring that bit to the immediate right of point is a significant digit, 1 for positive mantissas, 0 for negative mantissas
  - Ensures that the representation is unique.
- Normalising un-normalised floating point numbers with positive and negative mantissas: see algorithms

5.4 Binary number system

Key principle

Underflow:

Underflow occurs when a number is too small in magnitude to be represented.

■ 5.4.9 Underflow and overflow

Underflow

Underflow occurs when a number is too small in magnitude to be represented.

Fixed point underflow

If the smallest fraction that can be represented is in decimal, let's say, ¼, for the given number of bits and fixed point representation (see Table 5.4.9.1), then multiplying together ½ and ¼ results in something smaller than ¼, i.e. ⅛. For the given fixed point representation shown in Table 5.4.9.1, e.g. 8 bits with 2 bits after the binary point, ⅛ is too small to be represented. We say underflow has occurred. The number is too small in magnitude to be represented.

32	16	8	4	2	1	½	¼
0	0	0	0	0	0 •	0	1

Table 5.4.9.1 8-bit fixed point representation with 2 bits allocated to the fractional part

Floating point underflow

When we normalise a two's complement floating point binary representation of a number we ensure that the mantissa lies in the decimal ranges as shown in Table 5.4.9.2.

Positive mantissa	+½ ≤ mantissa < +1
Negative mantissa	-1 ≤ mantissa < -½

Table 5.4.9.2 Ranges of positive and negative mantissa

Therefore, the least positive and the least negative decimal numbers that can be represented in two's complement normalised binary floating point form are as shown in Table 5.4.9.3 where n is the number of bits assigned to the exponent.

Magnitude	n = no of exponent bits	Example n = 3
Least positive number	$\frac{1}{2} \times 2^{-2^{(n-1)}}$	$\frac{1}{2} \times 2^{-2^{(n-1)}}$ $= 0.5 \times 2^{-2^{(3-1)}}$ $= 0.5 \times 2^{-2^2} = 0.5 \times 2^{-4}$
Least negative number	less negative than $-\frac{1}{2} \times 2^{-2^{(n-1)}}$	$< -\frac{1}{2} \times 2^{-2^{(n-1)}}$ $= -0.5 \times 2^{-2^{(3-1)}}$ $< -0.5 \times 2^{-2^2} = -0.5 \times 2^{-4}$

Table 5.4.9.3 Least positive and negative numbers

This means that there is a range of numbers either side of zero for which a floating representation does not exist as shown in Figure 5.4.9.1. Zero can be treated as a special case by assigning it with its own un-normalised representation, e.g. an all zeroes mantissa and exponent or we have to use the least positive or least negative number representations for zero. For the specifics of how it is done in current computer systems look up the IEEE standard.

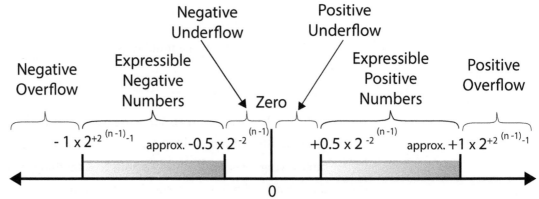

Figure 5.4.9.1 Number range for floating point two's complement binary where n is the number of exponent bits

If a calculation produces a final result that lies in this range then it cannot be represented and underflow has said to have occurred. Intermediate results of the calculation may encroach into this range but after normalisation the final result is restricted to the range of representable numbers for the specified number of storage bits.

Simplified example

Figure 5.4.9.2 shows the least positive and the least negative normalised floating point binary representations in 7 bits for a 4-bit mantissa and a 3-bit exponent, 0100_2 100_2 and 1011_2 100_2, respectively, or in decimal $+\frac{1}{2} \times 2^{-4}$ and $-\frac{5}{8} \times 2^{-4}$.

	Mantissa				Exponent		
	-1	½	¼	⅛	-4	2	1
Least positive normalised	0	1	0	0	1	0	0
Least negative normalised	1	0	1	1	1	0	0

Figure 5.4.9.2 7-bit two's complement floating point binary least positive and least negative number normalised representations

If we represent in two's complement floating point form, the fraction $\frac{1}{64}$ which is in fixed point two's complement representation 0.00000100_2, we obtain 0.100_2 1011_2 or in decimal $\frac{1}{2} \times 2^{-5}$. This requires a 4-bit exponent. Therefore, $\frac{1}{64}$ cannot be represented in the 4-bit mantissa, 3-bit exponent form shown in Figure 5.4.9.2. This is an example of underflow.

Circumstances when underflow can occur

Underflow can occur when dividing a small number by a very large number or when subtracting two numbers of the same sign which are close in magnitude.

Questions

1 Using the form of representation shown below in which six bits are assigned to the mantissa and four to the exponent, state whether underflow occurs when attempting to represent the following numbers expressed in fixed point two's complement binary.

Mantissa							Exponent			
-1	$^1/_2$	$^1/_4$	$^1/_8$	$^1/_{16}$	$^1/_{32}$		-8	4	2	1
d	d	d	d	d	d		d	d	d	d

   (a) 0.000000000111011_2 (b) 0.000000001_2

   (c) 1.1111111101111_2 (d) 1.11111111101111_2

2 The least positive number that can be represented in a particular computer system is 2^{-129}. The following expression is to be evaluated by this computer system

$$2^{10} \times {^{2^{-2}}/_{2^{129}}}$$

In which order should the evaluation be arranged and why?

Overflow

Overflow occurs when a number is too large in magnitude to be represented.

Integer overflow

Overflow can occur when representing integers. For example, when 8 bits are allocated to store an integer in two's complement form, as shown in Figure 5.4.9.3, the most positive number that can be represented is 01111111_2 in binary. If 1 is added to this then the representation becomes 10000000_2, a change of sign. Overflow has occurred.

Similarly, if 1 is subtracted from the most negative number that can be represented in binary, 10000000_2, the representation becomes 01111111_2, a change of sign. Again overflow has occurred. Subtracting 1_2 is equivalent to adding -1_2.

-128	64	32	16	8	4	2	1
0	1	1	1	1	1	1	1

Figure 5.4.9.3 Most positive number that can be represented in 8-bit two's complement binary

It should be clear that overflow can occur when adding two positive integers or two negative integers because in each case there is the potential to produce an even larger positive or negative integer that cannot be represented.

On the other hand overflow can never occur if adding two numbers of opposite sign.

Key principle

Overflow:
Overflow occurs when a number is too large in magnitude to be represented.

Key fact

Overflow can never occur if adding two numbers of opposite sign only when adding numbers of the same sign.

Key point

When adding numbers of the same sign, overflow can be detected by observing a change of sign.

Questions

3 State whether performing the following arithmetic with integers represented in 8-bit two's complement form will result in overflow.

(a) $11110011_2 + 00001101_2$ (b) $10000011_2 - 00000100_2$

(c) $10001111_2 + 11110000_2$ (d) $1000000_2 + 01111111_2$

Floating point overflow

The most positive and negative decimal numbers that can be represented using two's complement binary floating point form are as shown in *Table 5.4.9.4* where n is the number of bits assigned to the exponent.

Magnitude	n = no of exponent bits	Example n = 3
Most positive number	less than $+1 \times 2^{(2^{(n-1)} - 1)}$	$< +1 \times 2^{(2^{(3-1)} - 1)}$ $= +1 \times 2^{(2^2 - 1)}$ $= +2^{4-1} = +2^3 = 8$
Most negative number	more negative than $-1 \times 2^{(2^{(n-1)} - 1)}$	$-1 \times 2^{(2^{(3-1)} - 1)}$ $= -1 \times 2^{(2^2 - 1)}$ $= -2^{4-1} = -2^3 = -8$

Table 5.4.9.4 Two's complement binary floating point representation of most positive and negative decimal numbers

Key fact

Circumstances when overflow can occur:
Overflow can occur when adding two very large numbers of the same sign or in multiplication involving large numbers or when dividing a number by a very small number.

If a calculation produces a final answer which is more positive than the most positive number then positive overflow has occurred.

Conversely, if a calculation produces a final answer which is more negative than the most negative number that can be represented then negative overflow has occurred.

Circumstances when overflow can occur

Overflow can occur when adding two very large numbers of the same sign or in multiplication involving large numbers or when dividing a number by a very small number.

Questions

4 Using the form of representation shown below in which six bits are assigned to the mantissa and four to the exponent, state whether overflow occurs when attempting to represent the following numbers expressed in signed fixed point binary.

Mantissa						Exponent			
-1	$^1/_2$	$^1/_4$	$^1/_8$	$^1/_{16}$	$^1/_{32}$	-8	4	2	1
d	d	d	d	d	d	d	d	d	d

(a) $+10000000.0_2$ (b) $+1111100.0_2$ (c) -10000000.0_2 (d) -100000000.0_2

Questions

5 The most negative number that can be represented in a particular computer system is -2^{127}.
The following expression is to be evaluated by this computer system

$$-2^{127} \times 2^{20} / 2^{30}$$

In which order should the evaluation be arranged and why?

6 Discuss whether it is preferable to use the right hand side of the identity shown below, or the left, when writing a program to evaluate $x^2 - y^2$. State the circumstances for your choice(s).
Both x and y represent real numbers.

$$x^2 - y^2 = (x + y)(x - y)$$

In this chapter you have covered:

- Underflow - underflow occurs when a number is **too small in magnitude to be represented**.
- Overflow - overflow occurs when a number is **too large in magnitude to be represented**.
- The circumstances in which they occur
  - Underflow can occur when dividing a small number by a very large number or when subtracting two numbers of the same sign and close in magnitude.
  - Overflow can occur when adding two very large numbers of the same sign or in multiplication involving large numbers or when dividing a number by a very small number.
  - Overflow can never occur if adding two numbers of opposite sign only when adding numbers of the same sign.
  - When adding numbers of the same sign, overflow can be detected by observing a change of sign.

Key concept

Machine to machine communication of human readable text:

Digital computers and their components send and receive binary codes that are mapped in terminal devices such as keyboards and visual display units to symbols which humans use to communicate, i.e. letters of an alphabet. Two such coding schemes that do this are ASCII and Unicode.

5.5 Information coding systems

ASCII

Figure 5.5.1 shows the states of traffic lights, *amber, green, red & amber, red.* Each state encodes a message using light codes, e.g. green means GO, red means STOP.

Figure 5.5.1 Traffic lights and their states

Traffic lights are able to use light codes successfully to convey information of an instructional form to road users because the communication is between machine, the traffic lights, and humans in control of another kind of machine, e.g. a motor car. Humans can interpret the light codes from the traffic lights and decide whether to proceed through the junction controlled by the lights or not.

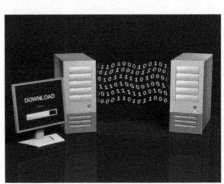

Figure 5.5.2 Two computing machines communicating in binary

In computing, we often want to send data between one computer or part of one computer and another, e.g. between the central processing unit (CPU) and a flat screen display, that map to symbols which humans use for communication, i.e. letters of an alphabet. Light codes are not used because the language of digital computers is binary not coloured lights, instead binary codes in electrical form are used. Human readable text and their binary-coded equivalent are mapped to each other in terminal devices such as keyboards and their controllers, and visual display units and their controllers. Two coding schemes that map between human readable symbols and binary codes that represent them are ASCII and Unicode.

In ASCII, the symbols corresponding to the letters of the alphabet (upper case and lower case), punctuation marks, special symbols and the decimal digits 0 to 9 are assigned different 7-bit binary codes according to a look up table, *Table 5.5.1* which shows 96 of the possible 128 codes (2^7). For example, the ASCII code for the letter A is 1000001 in binary and 65 in decimal.

All 128 codes are called character codes because they encode what is collectively known as characters. However, only 95 codes are actually used for symbols, the other 33 are control codes, codes 0 to 31 and the code 127 which is reserved for an instruction *delete a character code.*

ASCII was invented in the 1960s so that information could be exchanged over telephone wires between data processing equipment. ASCII stands for American Standard Code for Information Interchange. Messages were prepared on paper tape, similar to that shown in Figure 5.5.3, by punching holes in the tape (a hole = 1, an absence of a hole = 0) and then the tape was read by a sending machine connected to a telephone line. At the other end of the line was another machine that would interpret the received ASCII codes and then print the corresponding message in symbol form on paper for a human to read.

Figure 5.5.3 5-bit Punched paper tape large black dot = a hole = 1, absence of a hole = 0

Table 5.5.2 shows a lookup table for ASCII control codes, 0 to 31. The codes with a blank character field are codes used for controlling communication over a telephone line. Line feed and carriage return are used to break a long string of characters into separate lines. When characters are organised on a line-by-line basis we call this text, e.g. the text that you are reading on this page.

Text files therefore consist of one long string of ASCII character codes with the line breaks marked by a combination of ASCII code 10 (line feed) and ASCII code 13 (carriage return). These control codes reposition a VDU's cursor at the beginning of the next line when displaying a text file on a VDU.

Code in decimal	Character	Code in decimal	Character	Code in decimal	Character	Code in decimal	Character
32	Space	56	8	80	P	104	h
33	!	57	9	81	Q	105	i
34	"	58	:	82	R	106	j
35	#	59	;	83	S	107	k
36	$	60	<	84	T	108	l
37	%	61	=	85	U	109	m
38	&	62	>	86	V	110	n
39	'	63	?	87	W	111	o
40	(	64	@	88	X	112	p
41	)	65	A	89	Y	113	q
42	*	66	B	90	Z	114	r
43	+	67	C	91	[	115	s
44	,	68	D	92	\	116	t
45	-	69	E	93	]	117	u
46	.	70	F	94	^	118	v
47	/	71	G	95	_	119	w
48	0	72	H	96	`	120	x
49	1	73	I	97	a	121	y
50	2	74	J	98	b	122	z
51	3	75	K	99	c	123	{
52	4	76	L	100	d	124		
53	5	77	M	101	e	125	}
54	6	78	N	102	f	126	~
55	7	79	O	103	g	127	DEL

Table 5.5.1 ASCII code lookup table

Code in decimal	Character	Code in decimal	Character
0	Null	16	
1		17	
2		18	
3		19	
4		20	
5		21	
6		22	
7	Bell	23	
8	Backspace	24	
9	Horizontal tabulation	25	
10	Line feed	26	
11	Veetical tabulation	27	Escape
12	Form feed	28	
13	Carriage return	29	
14		30	
15		31	

Table 5.5.2 ASCII code lookup table for some control codes

Questions

1. What is the ASCII character code for
   (a) the letter H (b) the decimal digit 3 (c) the symbol ?

2. What is the symbol or character corresponding to the following ASCII character codes
   (a) 97 (b) 37 (c) 48?

3. Encode the message "Hello" in ASCII.

4. Why is ASCII code 127 the control code for the instruction delete a character code (HINT: a clue is in the holes punched in 5-bit paper tape - see *Figure 5.5.3*)?

5. Encode the text
   > "Hello
   > World!"
   in ASCII.

6. Convert the following string of ASCII character codes to its equivalent text form
   72 101 108 108 111 10 13 87 111 114 108 100 33

Key concept

ASCII or American Standard Code for Information Interchange:
In ASCII, the symbols corresponding to the letters of the alphabet (upper case and lower case), punctuation marks, special symbols and the decimal digits 0 to 9 are assigned different 7-bit binary codes according to a look up table.

Information

Extended ASCII:
This is the 8-bit version of ASCII consisting of 2^8 or 256 character codes or code points. The code points beyond 127 use the eighth bit. These map to symbols that are not covered in 7-bit ASCII, e.g. £ sign.
A code point or code position is any of the numerical values that make up the code space.

Information

Scan codes:
When a key on a keyboard is pressed a scan code is generated. Scan codes are binary codes as well. The scan code that is generated is converted into an ASCII code that corresponds to the current setting for the keyboard's keys. The mapping between scan codes and ASCII codes can be changed. For example, the mapping for a key marked in one currency symbol can be changed so that when pressed it maps to the ASCII code for another currency symbol, e.g. $ to £ (extended ASCII code 163_{10}). This was the only way to overcome ASCII's limited character set until the adoption of Unicode.

Unicode

ASCII provides only 128 numeric values, and 33 of those are reserved for special functions - the control codes and delete. Many of the control codes are no longer needed because they have their origin in the days of the teletype, punched cards and paper tape. ASCII does not cater for many Western European languages which have accented letters, and special symbols such as £, as it was designed for the North American market and it certainly doesn't cater for Asian languages which are logogram-based (symbols represent concepts), not alphabetic. The 95 ASCII codes for characters found in text are wholly inadequate for a universal standard for information interchange.

Unicode was designed to provide a single character set that covers the languages of the world. Unicode UTF-16 uses either one or two 16-bit code units for its character codes. A single 16-bit unit supports 2^{16} or 65536 different codes. Unicode UTF-32 uses 32-bit code units each representing a single character code. Unicode includes all the ASCII codes in addition to codes for characters in foreign languages (e.g. complete sets of Chinese characters), and many mathematical and other symbols.

UTF-8 encodes each of the 1,112,064 valid code points in the Unicode code space using one to four bytes. The first 128 characters of Unicode, which correspond one-to-one with ASCII, are encoded using a single byte with the same binary value as ASCII.

Character form of a decimal digit

Table 5.5.3 has been constructed by copying the code points for the decimal digits 0 to 9 from Table 5.5.1.

Humans work with numerals consisting of decimal digits, e.g. 261, when they do a calculation or record a number. If a decimal numeral sent from one computer or computer component to another is used by a human at the receiving end for a calculation, the decimal digits of the numeral must first be mapped to their ASCII code equivalents before sending, and mapped back on receipt from ASCII code to decimal digit form.

Code in decimal	Symbol
48	0
49	1
50	2
51	3
52	4
53	5
54	6
55	7
56	8
57	9

Table 5.5.3 ASCII codes for the decimal digit symbols 0 to 9

For example, if 261 is typed at the keyboard, the sequence of ASCII codes 50, 54, 49 is generated and sent. A visual display unit (VDU) receiving these ASCII codes knows that it should display 261 on its screen - see Figure 5.5.4.

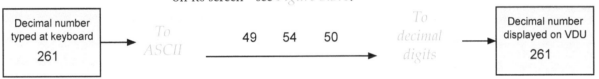

Figure 5.5.4 From decimal numeral to ASCII codes and back to decimal numeral

The ASCII codes 50, 54, 49 are called the character code form of the decimal digits 261 e.g. 50 is the character code form of the decimal digit 2. To convert this character code form 50 into the number 2 we need to subtract 48. The character code form of the decimal number 2 in 7-bits is 0110010 whereas its pure binary representation is 000 0010 in 7-bits.

Symbolically, the character code form 50, 54, 49 can be written as '2' '6' '1'. The single apostrophes around each digit are used to differentiate the character form from the decimal digit form.

Questions

7 What needs to be done to convert the following ASCII codes to their equivalent decimal digit
   (a) 53   (b) 48   (c) 57?

8 What is the ASCII character code form of the following decimal digits and combination of decimal digits
   (a) 6   (b) 34   (c) 908   (d) 444?

9 Why is it difficult to do arithmetic with the character form of a decimal numeral?

10 What would need to be done with the character form of a decimal numeral in order to do arithmetic in the conventional way?

11 What is the ASCII character code form of the following characters and character strings
   (a) '6'   (b) '54'?

Error checking and correction

Every time information is transmitted it may get corrupted by electrical interference or faulty hardware, and result in errors in the information received. Faulty hardware may also cause errors to suddenly appear in information stored in a storage device.

Figure 5.5.5 Error detected in data bits

The solution to this problem is to use redundancy to add reliability to information in transit or in storage. The data (data is how information is represented) is extended by including additional data used for error checking and correction.

Majority voting

Majority voting is an error correction method that duplicates or copies each bit in the message an odd number of times before sending these copies. For example, if the message consists of three bits, 101, then the thrice duplicated message would consist of nine bits as follows 111 000 111. The size of the message is thus increased but without increasing the amount of information. The message therefore contains additional redundancy (it may already be redundant, e.g. message = " It is hot. It is hot."). However, this additional redundancy can be used for error correction.

Let's first see how error detection can be achieved by just duplicating the message bits twice. If the data 1011 have to be transmitted then the bits 11 00 11 11 are sent instead. If the receiver receives a pair of bits with non-identical bits then it knows an error has occurred but it won't know if, for example, 01 was originally 00 or 11. Duplication twice has allowed error detection but not correction.

To allow for error correction, we need to copy the message bits an odd number of times. For example, 1011 becomes 111 000 111 111.

On receipt of this redundant bit pattern, the receiver compares the three bits of each triplet. If for each triplet all three bits are identical then the receiver assumes that they are correct (it is possible but very unlikely that 111 gets corrupted to 000). If only two bits in a triplet are the same and the third is different, the receiver assumes that the two bits the same are correct and the third bit is in error. This is what is meant by majority voting. The message bits need to be duplicated an odd number of times, n, for majority voting to make a decision.

For the above example, if transmission errors change 111 000 111 111 to 110 010 101 111, majority voting applies error correction producing 111 000 111 111 and the recovered message 1011.

Majority voting does not guarantee absolute reliability. Careful consideration of this example will tell you that majority voting can get it wrong, but the probability of this happening can be minimised if it isn't already low enough by choosing a bigger value for *n*.

Parity bits

If error detection rather than error correction is sufficient then the parity bit method can be used. The parity bit is computed from a group of *n* data bits and then added to the group, making it *n* + 1 bits long. For example, a 7-bit ASCII code becomes 8 bits long after a parity bit is added. The parity bit is computed by counting the number of ones in the *n* bit data group, and then setting the parity bit to make the count for the *n* + 1 group (parity + data) either even or odd. The former is called even parity and the latter odd parity.

For example, the count of 1s for the 7-bit ASCII code 0101101 is 4.

Figure 5.5.6 7-bit ASCII character code

With even parity this becomes the 8-bit code 00101101 with the parity bit set to 0 to make the count of 1s across the 8 bits an even number. With odd parity this becomes the 8-bit code 10101101 with the parity bit set to 1 to make the count of 1s across the 8 bits an odd number. Now suppose that even parity is used and 00101101 is sent. If the pattern 01101101 is received then an error has occurred because the count of 1s is now odd.

The parity bit can be computed by applying the exclusive-OR (XOR) to the *n* data bits because an XOR operation performs modulo-2 addition. Thus a series of XOR operations can perform the counting.

Suppose the data is the 7-bit ASCII code, 0101101, and the XOR operation is denoted by $\oplus$ then

$$0 \oplus 1 \oplus 0 \oplus 1 \oplus 1 \oplus 0 \oplus 1 = 1 \oplus 1 \oplus 1 \oplus 1 = 0 \oplus 0 = 0$$

The XOR-computed parity bit for the 1011010 is 0 for even parity. Inverting the computed XOR-computed result gives 1 for odd parity. The result for parity + data is thus as follows

EVEN parity: 00101101   ODD parity: 10101101

Now suppose that the byte 00101101 (most significant bit(MSB) a parity bit) is read from disk and even parity is used. To check that this byte has been read reliably, the parity bit for its 7 data bits is computed (by hardware or software) using XOR (0) and compared with the MSB using XOR again (0 $\oplus$ 0 = 0). The transmission or disk read is judged reliable if the regenerated parity bit agrees with the received parity bit. This judgement is not always correct as two bits or an even number of bits may be corrupted during transmission. However, use of a single parity bit is usually sufficient except when circumstances dictate that full error-detection capability is required.

Checksums

Parity checking is good for checking asynchronous serial transmission of data over short distances but not very good for synchronous serial transmission over long distances. For the latter, checking must be applied to a block of data. The data is treated as a sequence of fixed size numbers, e.g. each one byte in size. These numbers are added together to form a total which is then truncated to the same size as the number size, e.g. one byte, often by hashing. This truncated total is known as the checksum. The checksum is appended to the end of the block and for this reason is also referred to as a block check character. When the data arrives at the receiver, the checksum is regenerated and compared with the transmitted checksum. In this way the received data can be checked for errors that have arisen in transmission.

Two common checksum methods are LRC and CRC. LRC is an acronym for Longitudinal Redundancy Check or Longitudinal Redundancy Character. CRC is an acronym for Cyclic Redundancy Check or Cyclic Redundancy Character.

Parity bit							
1	1	0	0	1	0	1	0
0	0	1	0	1	1	0	1
1	1	1	0	1	0	0	0
1	0	1	1	1	1	1	0
0	0	1	1	[1]	1	1	1
1	1	0	0	0	1	0	1
1	1	0	1	1	1	1	0
Checksum 1	0	0	1	0	1	0	1

Figure 5.5.7 Longitudinal Redundancy Check using a checksum formed by computing the parity bit for each column (vertical parity)

LRC uses a block check character made up of a parity bit for each column as shown in *Figure 5.5.7*. By using horizontal parity bits as well, it is possible to correct some errors. If the indicated bit □ is flipped to become a 0 then both the vertical parity and the horizontal parity checking will indicate an error has occurred. The horizontal parity bit will indicate the row and the vertical parity the column. Thus the data bit in error can be located and corrected.

Questions

15 What is a checksum?

16 The checksum for the block of data opposite uses even vertical parity. Horizontally the most significant bit is an even parity bit. There is a single bit error in this block. Can you identify which bit is in error?

```
1 1 0 0 1 0 1 0
0 0 1 0 1 1 0 1
1 1 1 0 1 0 0 0
1 0 1 0 1 1 1 0
0 0 1 1 1 1 1 1
1 1 0 0 0 1 0 1
1 1 0 1 1 1 1 0
1 0 0 1 0 1 0 1
```

Key concept

Check digit:
A check digit is a decimal digit added to a number (either at the end or the beginning) to validate the number, e.g. a valid book ISBN.
The main task of a check digit is to detect a single corrupted digit and a transposition of two adjacent digits.

Check digits

Check digits and parity bits are special cases of checksums. The maths used for parity bits works for binary numbers but not decimal numbers. Thus different methods must be used for making decimal number data such as credit card numbers and book ISBNs reliable.

A check digit is a decimal digit added to a number (either at the end or the beginning) to validate the number, e.g. a valid book ISBN.

For example, the check digit in ISBN 978-0-9927536-2-7 shown in *Figure 5.5.8*, is the rightmost 7 digit. This 7 is computed by an algorithm applied to the information digits of the number, i.e. 978-0-9927536-2. On entering this ISBN into a computer, the check-digit generating algorithm is applied to the information digits of the ISBN as before, and the re-computed check digit compared with the check digit that was entered (see later for a more efficient way of doing this). In this way it is possible to check that the book ISBN has been read correctly.

Figure 5.5.8 ISBN-13 book code 978-0-9927536-2-7 showing check digit 7

The three most common errors made by humans when keying numbers into a computer, or reading and saying them, are omitting or adding a digit, transposing adjacent digits and changing a single digit.

For example, transposing the digits 2 and 7 in 978-0-9927536-2-7 or changing the triplet 992 to 922. The omission or addition of a digit is easily detected without a check digit. Therefore, the main task of a check digit is to detect a single corrupted digit and a transposition of two adjacent digits. Other types of error are rare.

Check digits normally use modular arithmetic. The mathematical function $a \bmod b$ returns the remainder of the integer division a / b, an integer in the range 0 to b - 1. Given a number N that consists of decimal digits $d_1 d_2 d_3 ...$, the simplest way to compute a check digit C for N is to solve the equation

$$(C + d_1 + d_2 + d_3 + ...) \bmod p = 0$$

choosing an appropriate value for p. Note that for the lefthand side of this equation to be 0

$$(C + d_1 + d_2 + d_3 + \cdots) \text{ must be a multiple of } p$$

Therefore, this equation can be solved by first computing the sum S as follows

$$S = (d_1 + d_2 + d_3 + \cdots) \bmod p$$

and then using the fact that if C is restricted to the range 0 to p - 1,

$$C + S = p$$

Rearranging, $\quad\quad\quad C = p - S$

Example

Suppose N is a three-digit number and each digit is in the range 0 to 4, inclusive, then a good choice for p is 5.

If N = 342, $\quad\quad\quad S = (3 + 4 + 2) \bmod 5 = 4$

then $\quad\quad\quad\quad\quad\quad C = 5 - 4 = 1$

The check digit 1 is appended to the number N and the 4-digit number 3421 is given over the telephone, stored in a computer or transmitted over a communication line. At the receiving end, the 4-digit number is checked. If no digits have been corrupted, the calculation (3 + 4 + 2 + 1) mod 5 will yield 0 (remember $(C + d_1 + d_2 + d_3 + \cdots) \bmod p = 0$). However, if the received 4-digit number has been corrupted in a single digit, e.g. it became 3221, then the calculation (3 + 2 + 2 + 1) mod 5 yields 3 when it should be 0. Detection of single-digit errors are possible with this simple check digit mechanism.

However, it is not possible to detect any transposition of digits.

Therefore, the check digit is calculated by applying weights to each digit as follows

$$(C + w_1 \cdot d_1 + w_2 \cdot d_2 + w_3 \cdot d_3 + \cdots) \bmod p = 0$$

or $\quad\quad\quad S = (w_1 \cdot d_1 + w_2 \cdot d_2 + w_3 \cdot d_3 + \cdots) \bmod p$

and $\quad\quad\quad C = p - S$

Example

Suppose N is a three-digit number and each digit is in the range 0 to 4, inclusive, then a good choice for p is 5. The weights chosen are 2, 3, and 4 because they are relatively prime to 5, i.e. 5 does not divide any of them evenly.

If N = 342, $\quad\quad\quad S = (2 \cdot 3 + 3 \cdot 4 + 4 \cdot 2) \bmod 5 = 1$

then $\quad\quad\quad\quad\quad\quad C = 5 - 1 = 4$

The check digit 4 is appended to the number N and the 4-digit number 3424 is read over the telephone, stored in a computer or transmitted over a communication line. At the receiving end, the 4-digit number is checked. If no digits have been corrupted, the calculation (2·3 + 3·4 + 4·2 + 4) mod 5 will yield 0. However, if two adjacent digits of the 4-digit number have been swapped because of an error, e.g. it became 3244, then the calculation (2·3 + 3·2 + 4·4 + 4) mod 5 yields 2 when it should be 0, thereby detecting an error.

ISBN

ISBN-13 has a total of 13 digits and includes a check digit. It conforms to EAN-13, the European Article Numbering barcode system. The commonly used ISBN-10 book codes have been turned into ISBN-13 by prepending 978. ISBN-13 book codes can use an EAN-13 barcode and therefore be barcode scanned. For example, ISBN-13 book code 978-0-9927536-2-7 has 978 followed by language/country code 0, publisher code 9927536, book number 2, and check digit 7.

To calculate the check digit:

Add up all the even numbered positions and multiply the sum by 3.

Sum the odd numbered positions.

Total the two sums.

Add a number that rounds up this total to the nearest multiple of ten.

This number is the check digit.

Algebraically

$S = (1·9 + 3·7 + 1·8 + 3·0 + 1·9 + 3·9 + 1·2 + 3·7 + 1·5 + 3·3 + 1·6 + 3·2)$ mod $10 = 3$

$C = p - S$

$C = 10 - 3 = 7$

The check digit C is therefore 7.

Questions

17 What is a check digit?

18 What are the **three** most common errors made by humans when keying numbers into a computer, or reading and saying them?

19 Using an example, describe how a check digit is calculated so that it can be used to detect two of these commonest errors?

In this chapter you have covered:

- The following coding systems for coding character data
    - ASCII
    - Unicode
- Why Unicode was introduced
- The difference between the character code representation of a decimal digit and its pure binary representation
- The meaning of and uses of
    - parity bits
    - majority voting
    - checksums
    - check digits

■ 5.6.1(1) Bit patterns, images, sound and other data

Binary, the language of the machine

The language of digital computers is binary. Whether the communication is instructions, e.g. calculate the square of 9, or data, e.g. speech, the communication must be transformed into discrete signals of a binary nature for the hardware of the computer to be able to process them.

Instructions or data at this level are seen logically as sequences of bit patterns or bits, e.g. 01101010 10001111 11000010 ...., although physically they are patterns of electrical voltage (or electric charge) in the memory of a computer, for example zero volts and five volts.

A bit pattern is just a unit of bits (binary digits) such as a byte. 01101010 is an 8-bit bit pattern. For convenience, bit patterns are usually shown in hexadecimal or decimal form to make viewing easier for humans - *Figure 5.6.1.1*.

0000011000010000	0000000000000101	0000000001000001	0610	0005	0041
0000011000010000	0000000000000110	0000000001110011	0610	0006	0073
0000011000010000	0000000000000111	0000000001101101	0610	0007	006D
0000011000010000	0000000000001000	0000000001010100	0610	0008	0054
0000011000010000	0000000000001001	0000000001110101	0610	0009	0075
0000011000010000	0000000000001010	0000000001110100	0610	000A	0074

Figure 5.6.1.1 Binary bit patterns and their equivalent hexadecimal

We can view a sequence of bit patterns representing instructions or data as just a sequence of numbers. Each bit pattern can be treated as a binary value with an equivalent hexadecimal or decimal value, e.g. 01101010_2 is $6A_{16}$ or 106_{10} if treated as an unsigned integer.

When data or instructions are organised as files and stored on a computer's backing store, e.g. magnetic disk, a stream of bits is sent to the backing store device. Similarly, when a file is opened for reading and its contents transferred to the CPU or main memory of a computer, the contents are transferred as a stream of bits. To interpret a bit stream of bit patterns as a digitised image/ digitised sound/text instructions, for example, requires that the sequence of bit patterns is organised into an appropriate structure for viewing/playing/ displaying/executing. Applying the wrong structuring can have unintended consequences, e.g. interpreting data as code and vice versa.

Questions

1. Explain why instructions, e.g. calculate square of 9, and data, e.g. speech, must be transformed before the hardware of a digital computer is able to process these instructions or data.

2. What is a bit pattern?

Graphics

One way of structuring bit patterns is the Joint Photographic Experts Group (JPEG) method for images produced by digital photography.

A JPEG file stores a digitised image as a sequence of bit patterns obtained, for example, from a digital camera that captures a scene photographically by sampling the brightness (or intensity) of the colour components of the scene before digitising the result in numbers to produce a JPEG formatted digital image representation of the scene – see Figure 5.6.1.2.

0	255	255	255	255	255	255
255	255	255	255	255	255	255
255	255	255	255	255	255	255
255	255	255	255	255	20	0
255	255	255	255	255	255	255
255	255	255	255	255	255	255
255	255	255	255	255	255	255
255	255	255	21	0	255	255

Figure 5.6.1.2 Image data taken from a section of the JPEG formatted file, Redang.jpg and displayed in decimal for ease of viewing.

When this JPEG file's contents are accessed and processed correctly the digitised recording of the original scene can be displayed as shown in Figure 5.6.1.3. The sequence of bit patterns serves to convey both the digitised image itself plus information (metadata) about the image such as its dimensions, in this case 600 x 800.

Figure 5.6.1.3 600 × 800 digital image stored in file Redang.jpg

Questions

3. Outline a method by which an image of a scene can be captured in digital form so that it can be displayed on an image display device.

Information

MatLab:
http://uk.mathworks.com/products/matlab

GNU Octave:
http://mxeoctave.osuv.de/

Redang.jpg:
www.educational-computing.co.uk/CS/Images/Redang.jpg

Information

Octave:
You will need to add the command disp(info); to output the value of the info.

A relatively easy way to explore digital images is to use either Matlab from MathWorks or GNU Octave, an open source system. The same scripts and commands execute in either. For example, the following script

```
Z = imread('Redang.jpg');
info=imfinfo('Redang.jpg');
image(Z);
```

executes in either Matlab or GNU Octave and extracts and displays image and format information data from `Redang.jpg`.

Figure 5.6.1.4 shows the extracted format information and *Figure 5.6.1.5* the image displayed by the command

`image (Z).`

The digital image is actually made of three separate monochrome digital images, one red, one green and one blue that are combined by the command `image(Z)` to produce the 600 × 800 image shown in *Figure 5.6.1.5* with labelled x and y axes.

When the digital camera snapped the scene it sampled the scene through three filters: a red filter, recording each red sample's intensity value in 8 bits, a green filter recording each green sample's intensity value in 8 bits and a blue filter recording each blue sample's intensity value in 8 bits.

The red, green and blue samples are combined to produce an RGB image of 600 × 800 samples in all. For each sample, a total of 8 + 8 + 8 = 24 bits is used as indicated by the `BitDepth` field.

A quick calculation indicates by comparison with the format information `FileSize` that the whole collection of digital samples has undergone compression. The JPEG format uses compression throwing away image information that the viewer would not notice.

To process the bit patterns from the file `Redang.jpg` appropriately, i.e. according to the JPEG standard, the bit patterns must be structured as follows using two-dimensional arrays of the following dimensions:

- The 600 × 800 red samples into a 600 × 800 array

- The 600 × 800 green samples into a 600 × 800 array

- The 600 × 800 blue samples into a 600 × 800 array

It is the metadata on image dimensions 600 × 800 extracted from this file that is used to determine the dimensions 600 × 800 of the arrays.

Therefore when all three two-dimensional arrays are stacked together we obtain a 600 × 800 × 3 three-dimensional array as shown in *Figure 5.6.1.6*.

The script command:

`Z = imread('Redang.jpg');`

reads the contents of `Redang.jpg`, decompresses it and performs the processing just described, storing the image samples' intensity values in a three-dimensional array Z with dimensions 600 × 800 × 3.

```
Filename: 'C:\Images\Redang.jpg'
FileModDate: '11-Jul-2003 12:12:16'
FileSize: 58014
Format: 'jpg'
FormatVersion: ''
Width: 800
Height: 600
BitDepth: 24
ColorType: 'truecolor'
FormatSignature: ''
NumberOfSamples: 3
CodingMethod: 'Huffman'
CodingProcess: 'Progressive'
Comment: {}
```

Figure 5.6.1.4 Produced in MatLab's command window by >>info

Figure 5.6.1.5 The output of the script command image(Z). Z contains the image data.

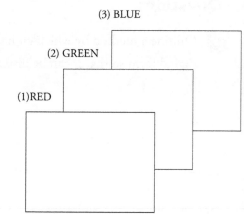

Figure 5.6.1.6 Three-dimensional array Z with dimensions 600 × 800 × 3.

Using MatLab's Pixel region Image Tool as shown in Figure 5.6.1.7, the Red (R), Green (G) and Blue (B) sample values of any region of the displayed image can be retrieved.

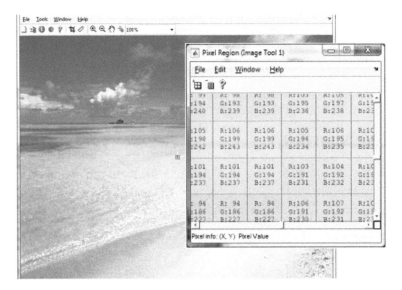

Figure 5.6.1.7 Pixel Region Image Tool showing Red (R), Green (G) and Blue (B) values in a region of the image.

Questions

4   A digital image file stores bit patterns representing intensity values of samples of the scene captured by the imaging device. What other information about the image is also stored in the image file and why?

In this chapter you have covered:

■   How bit patterns may represent graphics

Information

MatLab:
http://uk.mathworks.com/products/matlab

GNU Octave:
http://mxeoctave.osuv.de/

Redang.jpg:
www.educational-computing.co.uk/CS/Images/Redang.jpg

■ 5.6.1(2) Bit patterns, images, sound and other data

Manipulating digital images

Having digitised an image, it is now just a sequence of numbers (bit patterns) to which arithmetic operations may be applied to produce new numbers and new forms of the digital image. For example, the following MatLab/GNU Octave script will double every value in the Red array, $C(:, :, 1)$ obtained after reading the JPEG image file Redang.jpg with the command

```
W = imread('Redang.jpg');
```

and storing a copy of W in C with the command

```
C = W;
```

```
% Introduces a comment in the script
close all; % Closes all figures
clear all; % Deletes all stored variables in workspace
clc; % Removes all lines in the command window
W = imread('Redang.jpg'); % Populate 3-D array W
figure(1); % Draw contents of W as figure 1 appropriately rendered as an image
image(W); % Renders the digital image for values in W
C = W; % makes a copy of W and assigns it to C
% Every value in the 600 x 800 Red array (1) of C is now doubled and written
back into the corresponding cell of this array. This will enhance the redness
of the image
% :, :, means the entire 600 x 800 array
C(:,:,1) = 2*C(:,:,1);
figure(2); % Draw the result as Figure 2
image(C); % Render C as a digital image
% Write C to a new JPEG file RedangChanged.jpg.

imwrite(C, 'RedangChanged.jpg');
```

The outcome is shown in *Figure 5.6.1.8(b)* alongside the original image, *Figure 5.6.1.8(a)*.

Figure 5.6.1.8(a) Array W rendered.

Figure 5.6.1.8(b) Array C rendered showing the effect of doubling every red value in W

Questions

  Explain how each of the red and the green components of an RGB image can be reduced by 50% in MatLab or GNU Octave.

Information

PlaneGrey.jpg:
www.educational-computing.
co.uk/CS/Images/PlaneGrey.jpg

Information

Octave:
 You will need to add the command disp(info); to output the value of the info.

The greyscale digitised image shown in *Figure 5.6.1.9(a)* occupies a single 480 × 640 two-dimensional array, C, when loaded by the MatLab/GNU Octave script

```
clear all;
C = imread('PlaneGrey.jpg');
figure(1);
image(C);
C(:,:) = 255 - C(:,:);
figure(2);
imshow(C);
imwrite(C, 'PlaneGreyNegative.jpg');
```

If the intensity values in array C are subtracted from 255 then an intensity value of 255 becomes an intensity value of 0, and an intensity value of 0 becomes an intensity value of 255, and so on.

Thus we get the negative of this image when we update C as follows

```
C(:,:) = 255 - C(:,:);
```

Figure *5.6.1.9(b)* shows the result.

Figure 5.6.1.9(a) 480 × 640 greyscale image   *Figure 5.6.1.9(b) 480 x 640 negative greyscale image*

Programming tasks

1 Whenever the red, green and blue components of an image sample have the same value, the colour displayed is a shade of grey. This means that a digitised image of sampled red, green and blue colours has the potential for **256** shades of grey if each colour is encoded with **8** bits (0..255). We can use the intensity of the overall colour, i.e. red + green + blue, to assign a shade or level of grey. The intensity of a colour called the luminance is calculated as follows

$$\frac{\text{red + green + blue}}{3}$$

Write a program or script in MatLab or GNU Octave that uses this formula to set the colour of each pixel of an RGB image to a shade of grey to produce an equivalent greyscale image.

2 If you succeeded in turning an RGB image into a greyscale image you may have noticed that the result is not as expected. This is because the formula method used in Programming task **1** did not take into account the way that the human eye perceives luminance, e.g. the eye is less sensitive to blue light than red. We need to adjust for this by weighting as follows

$$\frac{0.299 \times \text{red} + 0.587 \times \text{green} + 0.114 \times \text{blue}}{3}$$

Change your program or script to take account of this new formula.

3 Write a program or MatLab/GNU Octave script to rotate an image through 180 degrees, i.e. turn the image upside down.

A digital image can be created without using a camera. We can instead create a digital coloured image by creating a three-dimensional array of numbers, D, as shown in *Figure 5.6.1.10*. D is populated with values, **0** and **255** or in binary **00000000** and **11111111**, representing the intensity of red, green and blue with **255** being the strongest and **0** the weakest.

The MatLab/GNU Octave script to generate this array, to render it as an image and write the data to a file Squares.jpg is as follows

```
close all; % Closes all figures
clear all; % Deletes all stored variables in workspace
D(:,:,1) = [0 255 0 255; 255 0 255 0; 0 255 0 255];
D(:,:,2) = [0 255 0 255; 255 0 255 0; 0 255 0 255];
D(:,:,3) = [0 255 0 255; 255 0 255 0; 0 255 0 255];
figure(4);
image(D);
imwrite(D, 'Squares.jpg');
```

[0 255 0 255; 255 0 255 0; 0 255 0 255] is the way that MatLab/GNU Octave creates a two-dimensional array, each sequence of numbers is a row vector with rows separated by ' ; ' so putting the row vectors together we get, in this instance,

0	255	0	255
255	0	255	0
0	255	0	255

As we have three primary colours, three of these 2-D arrays are required, one for each colour, Red, Green, Blue.

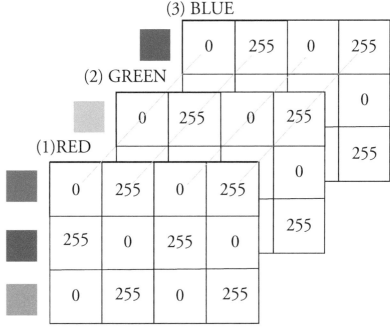

Figure 5.6.1.10 Three-dimensional array, D, containing cells values, 0 or 255.

The outcome when the command image(D) is executed is a 3 x 4 grid of black and white squares on the screen. The black square is produced by the triplet 0, 0, 0 taken from the arrays for (1) RED, (2) GREEN, (3) BLUE. The white square is produced by the triplet 255, 255, 255 taken from the arrays for (1) RED, (2) GREEN, (3) BLUE.

The command:

```
imwrite(D, 'Squares.jpg')
```

scans array D, as it does so writing its values to a bit stream for file Squares.jpg using the format required by JPEG.

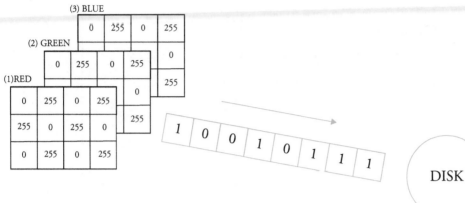

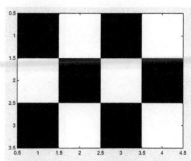

Figure 5.6.1.11 Outcome of executing image(D), an image of 3 by 4 squares.

Figure 5.6.1.12 Writing array D to disk

Reading file contents byte by byte

Files of any type, e.g. JPEG, BMP, XLS, TXT, can be opened as a file of byte and their contents read as bit patterns of unit size one byte. For example, given access to a bitmapped file Fruit1.bmp the following Python 3.4 script will open, read and display both a running count and each byte of this file in decimal.

Programming tasks

4. Write a script for execution in MatLab or GNU Octave that creates a file Squares.bmp for a black and white chequer board image with dimensions 4 × 4 with white as the colour of the top left square.

Information

Spyder python:

https://store.continuum.io/

cshop/anaconda/

Spyder is part of the Anaconda system that gives access to scientific routines including support for arrays and digital signal processing in Python.

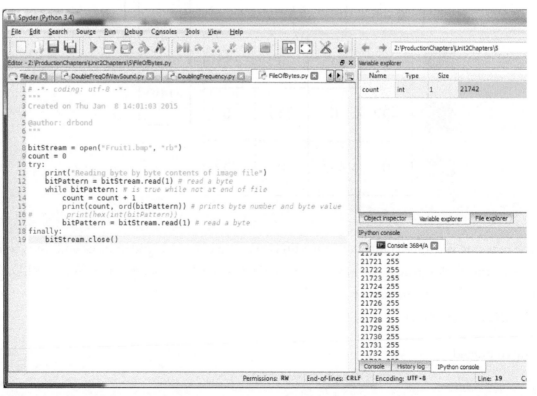

Figure 5.6.1.13 Python 3.4 script to read byte by byte contents of a bitmap file Fruit1.bmp

The size of this file is calculated as follows.

The total number of bytes necessary to store one row of pixels is

$$\texttt{RowSize} = \frac{\texttt{BitsPerPixel} \times \texttt{ImageWidth}}{8}$$

where `ImageWidth` is expressed in pixels. A pixel is a picture element and is the smallest area of the picture that is sampled and digitised.

The total number of bytes to store an array of pixels, `ArraySize`, is

$$\texttt{RowSize} \times \texttt{ImageHeight}$$

where `ImageHeight` is measured in pixels.

Image Fruit1.bmp when displayed has dimensions 126 × 161, i.e. 126 rows each of 161 pixels. This bitmap stores 8 bits per pixel.

Therefore, $\qquad \texttt{RowSize} = (8 \times 161) / 8 = 161$
and

$$\texttt{ArraySize} = 161 \times 126 = 20286 \text{ bytes}$$

The metadata occupies 1078 bytes

Therefore, total size in bytes of `Fruit1.bmp` = 20286 + 1078 = 21364

This calculation is close to the result obtained from running the Python 3.4 script in *Figure 5.6.1.13* above. The discrepancy is caused by the fact that RAM stores bytes in groups of four so our calculation for the `RowSize` is an underestimate. It should be 164 bytes. This gives 164 × 126 bytes for total file size, i.e. 20664 + 1078 = 21742 bytes. This agrees exactly with the output of the Python 3.4 script.

Programming tasks

5 Write a program that opens a BMP image file as a file of byte. The program should copy the first 1078 bytes of the file into a new file, then write the 8-bit ASCII codes for "HELLO WORLD" to the new file after this. It should skip copying the next 11 bytes of the original file (which are effectively replaced by "HELLO WORLD") and then copy the rest of the data in the original file into the new BMP file. Note where the message starts. View the new BMP file in an image viewer. Can you detect where the original image has been altered?

Now write a program to extract the message that has been stored in the image file. The program should use the same message starting position as was used in the program that stored the message.

Tasks

1 Investigate steganography and digital watermarking.

In this chapter you have covered:

■ *How bit patterns may represent graphics*

Information

Audacity:
http://audacity.sourceforge.net/

JES:
http://coweb.cc.gatech.edu/mediaComp-teach

Information

The beginning of a WAVE file comprises a "header" storing information about the sound data :

- number of channels
- number of sample frames
- word size (16bit, 24bit, etc)
- sample type (int, float)
- sample rate

■ 5.6.1(3) Bit patterns, images, sound and other data

Sound

A WAV file, Me2.wav, is just a sequence of bit patterns or numbers recording the sampled and digitised waveform of a sound.

File Me2.wav was sampled, and recorded in digitised form, using a microphone connected to a computer running Audacity, the free, open source, cross-platform software for recording and editing sounds.

This WAV file was then read from disk as a bit stream of bit patterns using JES, free, cross-platform software for interacting with graphics and sound files. The sequence of bit patterns read from the disk was stored in sound, a one-dimensional array. JES' Sound Tool is able to render the bit patterns stored in array sound as an on screen waveform of amplitude against sample number as shown in *Figure 5.6.1.14*. Each sample value can be shown on screen using this tool. The samples are stored in as 16-bit twos' complement integers (−32768 to 32767). JES displays the sample values in decimal.

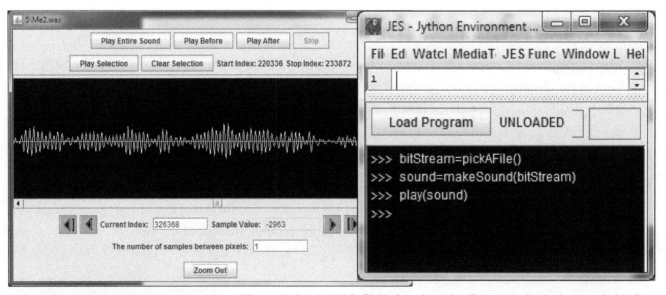

Figure 5.6.1.14 JES GUI showing the Command window and the Sound Tool window and sample 326368 whose value is -2963.

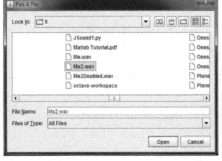

The command makeSound(bitStream) reads the bit patterns from bit stream bitStream which itself is connected to WAV file Me2.wav. It extracts the sampling rate, the number of bits per sample and the type of recording (mono or stereo) all of which are stored in this file. With this information, makeSound(bitStream) constructs either a one-dimensional

Information

For sound file I/O by far the best add-in module for Python is "pysoundfile".

http://pysoundfile.readthedocs.org/en/0.8.1/

array (mono) or a two-dimensional array (stereo) and then stores the bit stream bit patterns in the constructed array.

Figure 5.6.1.15 shows `Me2.wav` opened by a Python 3.4 script running in Spyder. It extracts the sampling rate and assigns this to variable `samplingRate` and the sound data which it assigns to variable `soundData`. Before printing both, samples per second (**44100**) and array `soundData` [**9 -2 12** …, **-50, -48 -47**].

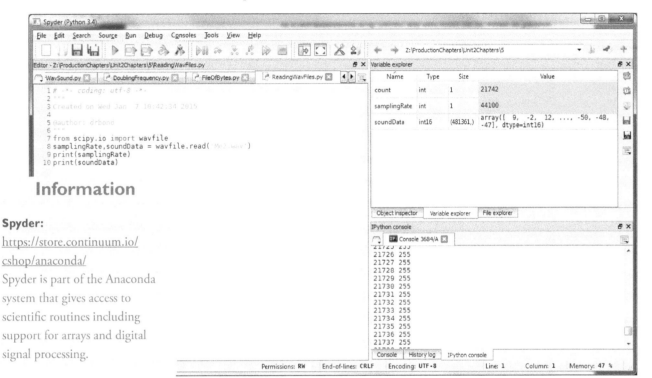

Figure 5.6.1.15 WAV file Me2.wav opened in Spyder by a Python 3.4 script.

Information

Spyder:

https://store.continuum.io/cshop/anaconda/

Spyder is part of the Anaconda system that gives access to scientific routines including support for arrays and digital signal processing.

Programming tasks

6 Using JES, Spyder Python 3.4 or another programming/scripting system that supports exploration of digitally recorded sound, write a program/script/commands to open WAV files, read the stored sampled sound values and display these. Try also to extract the sampling rate and bits per sample.

Information

MatLab
http://uk.mathworks.com/products/matlab

GNU Octave
http://mxeoctave.osuv.de/

Creating digital sound files

The MatLab/GNU Octave script shown in *Figure 5.6.1.16* creates a sequence of numbers or bit patterns, allocating 16 bits to each bit pattern, to represent the digital equivalent of a continuous tone of a frequency/pitch 1000 Hz sampled every $\frac{1^{th}}{20000}$ of a second. The bit patterns or numbers are stored in WAV format in file `Tone.Wav` together with the sampling rate and the bits per sample.

`Tone.wav` can be played using Windows Media Player or any other suitable media player.

```
SampleRate = 2e4; % 20000 samples per second
t = 0:1/2e4:1-(1/2e4); % time step 1/2e4 from 0 to 1 - 1/2e4
x = 1/2^cos(2*pi*1000*t); % cosine value at time t
% write the signal x to Tone.wav file using 16 bits per sample
wavwrite(x, SampleRate,16, 'Tone.wav');
```

Figure 5.6.1.16 Generating mathematically a sequence of numbers that represent a time sequence of samples of a continuous tone of frequency 1000 Hz sampled at a rate of 20000 samples per second or one every 1/20000th of a second. The sequence is written together with the sampling frequency and the bits per sample, to file Tone.wav.

Programming tasks

 Using MatLab or GNU Octave, mathematically generate separate WAV files of the following tones (use trigonometric function cosine and then repeat using trigonometric function sine)

(a) 500 Hz (b) 2000 Hz (c) 4000 Hz (d) 8000 Hz

Use sampling rate 20000 samples per second, bits per sample 16 and collect 20000 samples (0 to 1 − 1/20000 in time steps of 1/20000 second).

Play your generated tones in a media player.

Manipulating digital recordings of sounds

Just as it is possible to manipulate digital images because they are represented by bit patterns/numbers so it is possible to manipulate digital recordings of sounds because they too can be accessed as a sequence of bit patterns/numbers. A simple way of demonstrating this is to create a WAV file using a script similar to that shown in *Figure 5.6.1.16*.

The sampled points of the wave are indicated in *Figure 5.6.1.17* with ☆ and ★. The height (amplitude) of the wave is normalised (adjusted to a desired value) in the figure for convenience, 1 corresponds to +32767 and -1 to -32768.

The chosen frequency for this explanation is deliberately low in order that the numbers are manageable.

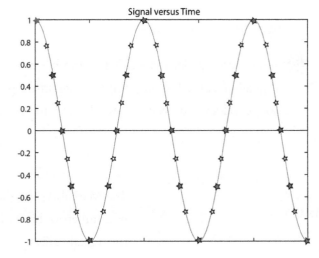

Figure 5.6.1.17 Cosine wave marked with sample points ★ and ☆

Using normalised values we have a sequence of samples

1.0, 0.9239, 0.707, 0.3826, 0.0, -0.3826, -0.707, -0.9239, -1.0, -0.9239, -0.707, -0.3826, 0.0, 0.3826, 0.707, 0.9239, etc

The values in this sequence are separated in time by $\frac{1^{th}}{20000}$ of a second because the sampling rate used was 20000 samples per second. The "sampling interval" or "sampling period" for this sample rate is $\frac{1^{th}}{20000}$.

If we read this sequence from the beginning and write the sequence to a new WAV file, `ToneFreqDoubled.wav`, omitting every other value, then the sequence in the new file is

1.0, 0.707, 0.0, -0.707, -1.0, -0.707, 0.0, 0.707, 1, etc

These are the samples indicated by ★ in *Figure 5.6.1.17*.

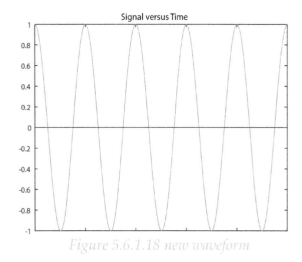

Figure 5.6.1.18 new waveform

If we record the sampling frequency as 20000 samples per second in this new file, then when it is read back, a sample will be separated in time from the next sample by $\frac{1^{th}}{20000}$ of a second. If the sequence of numbers is plotted on the same time scale as *Figure 5.6.1.17* then we get the waveform shown in *Figure 5.6.1.18*. This has 5 complete waves to the 2.5 waves in *Figure 5.6.1.17*, i.e. the frequency of the wave has been doubled. A script to double frequencies of digitally recorded sounds in WAV files is shown in *Figure 5.6.1.19*. We appear to have brought about a doubling of frequency of the sound by halving the sampling rate. We have to be careful when sampling a waveform to sample at a sufficiently high rate to avoid creating frequencies which don't exist in the waveform, i.e. spurious frequencies. If we get spurious frequencies we have produced a situation called aliasing.

```
#Spyder (Python 3.4) script
import numpy as np
import scipy.io.wavfile
samplingRate, soundSamples = scipy.io.wavfile.read('Tone.wav')
soundSamplesNew = []
for i in range(len(soundSamples)):
    if (i % 2) == 0:
        soundSamplesNew.append(soundSamples [i])
#Convert from soundSamplesNew list to array
soundSamplesNew = np.asarray(soundSamplesNew)
scipy.io.wavfile.write('ToneFreqDoubled.wav', samplingRate, soundSamplesNew)
```

Figure 5.6.1.19 Spyder Python 3.4 script to double frequencies of digitally recorded sounds in a WAV file.

Play `Tone.wav` and `ToneFreqDoubled.wav` in a media player such as Windows Media Player and note the difference in frequency.

Questions

6 Writing every other sample is one way of doubling frequencies of digitally recorded sound. Can you think of another way that this could be done without having to omit sampled values and which could alter frequencies by factors other than 2?

Programming tasks

8 Using JES, Spyder Python 3.4 or another programming/scripting system that supports exploration of digitally recorded sound, write a program/script/commands to double frequencies of digitally recorded sounds in WAV files.

Test your results in a media player.

Sound and text files

The numbers representing samples of digitised sound may be read from a WAV file, converted to their string equivalent and then written to a text file, one sample per line (text files are strings of characters organised on a line-by-line basis). The text file may now be opened in a spreadsheet and the numbers displayed on a chart as shown in *Figure 5.6.1.20*.

A Python script that creates the text file equivalent of a sound file, Tone.wav, is shown in *Figure 5.6.1.21*.

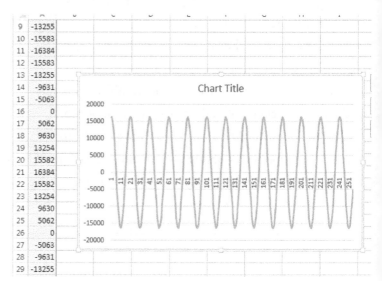

Figure 5.6.1.20 Excel spreadsheet that displays and charts Tone.txt

```
#Spyder (Python 3.4) script
import scipy.io.wavfile
samplingRate, soundSamples = scipy.io.wavfile.read('Tone.wav')
bitStream = open('Tone.txt', "wt") # open file in write text mode
for i in range(len(soundSamples)):
    # str converts number to string representation, \n add end of line
    bitStream.write(str(soundSamples[i]) + "\n")
bitStream.close()
```

Figure 5.6.1.21 Spyder Python 3.4 script to transfer sound samples to a text file

Likewise, it is possible to convert a text file into a sound file. Using Tone.txt for convenience, the Spyder Python 3.4 script shown in *Figure 5.6.1.22* creates a WAV file, TextToSound.wav, of digitised sound samples. It sets the sampling rate to 20000 samples per second but this can be changed easily to change the frequency of the tone represented by this file and it sets the number of bits per sample to be 16.

```
#Spyder (Python 3.4) script
import numpy as np
import scipy.io.wavfile
bitStream = open('Tone.txt', "rt")
contents = bitStream.readlines()
bitStream.close()
fileIndex = 0
soundData = []
samplingRate = 20000
while (fileIndex < len(contents)):
  sample = int(contents[fileIndex].replace("\n", ""))
  soundData.append(sample)
  fileIndex = fileIndex + 1
soundData = np.asarray(soundData, dtype='int16')
scipy.io.wavfile.write('TextToSound.wav', samplingRate, soundData)
```

Figure 5.6.1.22 Spyder Python 3.4 script to create a sound file from a text file

The Matlab command `audioinfo` can be used as shown in *Figure 5.6.1.23* to obtain the metadata stored in file `TextToSound.wav`.

Information

audioinfo:
The audioinfo command is not yet implemented in Octave

Principle

Text, digitised sound and images:
Text, digitised sound and images are all just bits or bit patterns under the hood. As such they can be mapped between each other by transforming the way that the bit patterns are arranged and interpreted.

```
>> info = audioinfo('TextToSound.wav')
info = Filename: 'TextToSound.wav'
        CompressionMethod: 'Uncompressed'
        NumChannels: 1
        SampleRate: 20000
        TotalSamples: 20000
        Duration: 1
        Title: []
        Comment: []
        Artist: []
        BitsPerSample: 16
```

Figure 5.6.1.23 MatLab command line >>info = audioinfo('TextToSound.wav')

Programming tasks

9 Using JES, Spyder Python 3.4 or another programming/scripting system that supports exploration of digitally recorded sound and text files, write a program/script/commands to convert WAV files to text files and vice versa.

Test your results in a media player.

Questions

7 It has been demonstrated that it is possible to transform sound and image files to text files and back again. Give **three** reasons why this is useful.

In this chapter you have covered:

■ *How bit patterns may represent sound*

Learning objectives:

■ Understand the difference between analogue and digital

• data

• signals

5.6.2 Analogue and digital

What is data?

Recording your body weight over time, say six months, would generate a set of values of a quantitative and discrete nature. Discrete because the values are not recorded continuously but sampled at intervals of time. The recorded values are known individually by the term datum and collectively as data. The data is quantitative in nature because it is obtained by measurements performed by some measuring instrument calibrated by reference to some continuous scale of values.

Data may also be qualitative and discrete. For example, recording name and eye colour of every individual in a class of students, e.g. "John Smith, blue", "Carol Jennings, green", produces a set of values or value-pairs of a qualitative nature. The recorded values or value-pairs are also known collectively as data and a single value or value-pair as a datum. The data is qualitative because it is descriptive in nature and constitutes a characteristic, e.g. eye colour or a property, e.g. a person has a name rather than a measurement.

Key concept

Analogue data:
Data that varies in a continuous manner or is recorded in a continuous form and that is similar to its original structure.

What is analogue data?

Air temperature and air pressure vary in a continuous manner. For example, if you were to climb a mountain you would find that as you rose in height the air pressure would lessen in a continuous manner as the total amount of air pressing down on you from above became less – see Figure 5.6.2.1.

The relationship between air pressure and height above sea level is shown in Figure 5.6.2.2. This variation in pressure could have been observed with a Torricellian barometer carried up the mountain. The height of the column of mercury, the data, would have been observed to vary in a continuous manner. Data that varies in a continuous manner is known as analogue data. The barometer is a source of analogue data.

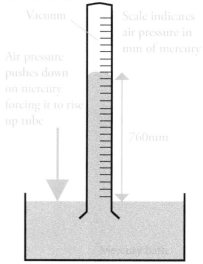

Figure 5.6.2.1 Toricelli barometer

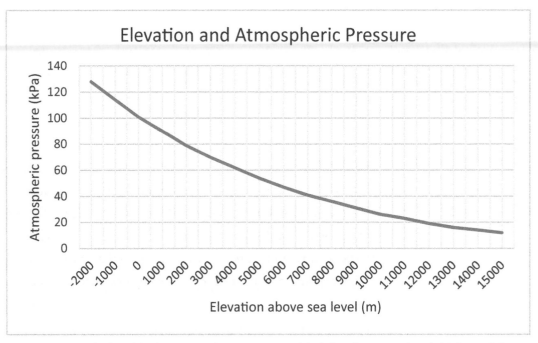

Figure 5.6.2.2 Relationship between air pressure and height above sea level (Adapted from www.engineeringtoolbox.com/air-altitude-pressure-d462.html with kind permission of the editor)

Key concept

Discrete data:
Information represented by separate values is discrete. We say that these values are discrete data.

Information that is recorded in a continuous form and that is similar to its source's original structure is also analogue data. The phonograph invented in 1877 by Thomas Edison, known today as a record player, recorded speech directly onto wax cylinders by making physical deviations of a groove, impressed into the wax, a replica of the variation in air pressure caused by the speech.

The pattern of variation recorded on the wax cylinder is an example of analogue data because it varies in a continuous fashion and is similar in form to that which caused it, the variation in air pressure caused by the spoken word. The modern equivalent of the wax cylinder is the vinyl LP.

What is discrete data?

Information represented by separate values (quantities), e.g. words in a list, is "discrete". Here are three sets of discrete quantities:

- 1, 2, 3, 4 (set 1)
- 0, 1, 0, 1, 1, 0 (set 2)
- A, B, C, D (set 3)

When analogue data are sampled and their values recorded, in the appropriate units, they become discrete data. The decimal number 45 is discrete because it belongs to a set of discrete numbers,

Hour	Temperature	Hour	Temperature
1	8	7	13
2	7	8	14
3	6	9	16
4	8	10	16
5	10	11	17
6	10	12	16

Table 5.6.2.1 Discrete temperature data (sampled from analogue data)

the set of all positive integers. *Table 5.6.2.1* shows discrete data in the form of temperature readings taken at hourly intervals.

What is digital data?

To store data digitally in a computer, it has first to be represented in discrete form, and then converted (encoded) to digital (binary) values.

Figure 5.6.2.3 shows discrete data being encoded in binary by a process which represents each discrete datum by a specific binary value, e.g. 4.70_{10} and 4.93_{10} are both represented by 100_2. This digitising process introduces errors called quantisation errors, e.g. 4.70_{10} is represented by 100_2 which is 4_{10}.

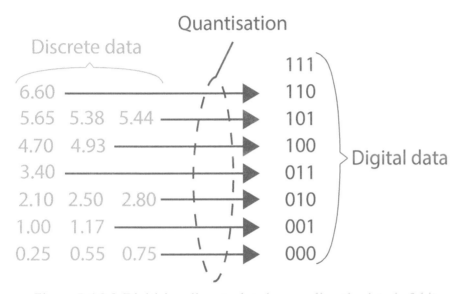

Figure 5.6.2.3 Digitising discrete data by encoding the data in 3 bits

What is a signal?

Many countries around the world have used beacons, i.e. bonfires, strategically sited, to warn of or signal danger. Some animals use sound for a similar purpose. Internally, the human body uses both electrical and chemical means to convey signals some of which are in response to danger, e.g. to cause an adrenaline response to a threatening situation.

Signals are used for all sorts of purposes. Essentially a signal is that which conveys a message or information from one place to another. As such, signals are subject to the laws of Physics, in particular Einstein's special theory of relativity that states that signals or the information that they carry cannot travel faster as a group than the speed of light which is 3×10^8 metres per second in a vacuum.

The information carried by a signal is in the form of energy that can activate a detector or sensor in a receiver of the signal. For example, the light from a warning beacon is conveyed as photons or light particles, each of which carries a certain amount of electromagnetic energy, enough to stimulate cells in the retina of the eyes of the receiver. This stimulation of the retina results in an electrical signal to the receiver's brain which responds accordingly.

What are analogue signals?

In order to process analogue data it must be sensed and then converted into an equivalent electrical form. The electrical equivalent for this purpose is called an analogue electrical signal or just analogue signal. In telecommunications and computer engineering, an analogue signal is an electrical or electromagnetic signal that varies in a continuous manner. The conversion process takes place in a device known as a transducer. A transducer is designed to convert energy from one form to another. A microphone is an example of a transducer. It converts continuously varying sound pressure waves into an equivalent continuously varying electrical signal. Another example of a transducer is a loudspeaker. A loudspeaker converts electrical energy into sound energy.

Figure 5.6.2.4 shows an electrical circuit for converting sound energy into electrical energy. *Figure 5.6.2.5* shows the variation in pressure produced by the speaker whistling a pure tone. *Figure 5.6.2.6* shows the equivalent analogue signal.

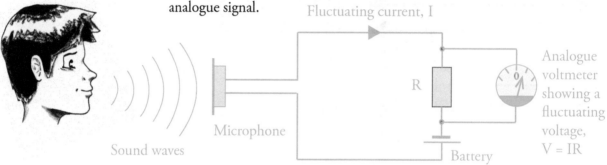

Figure 5.6.2.4 Electrical circuit for converting sound energy into electrical energy

Information

Speech:

When a person speaks, they emit a continuous stream of sound, essentially - the final syllable of one word prefixes the starting syllable of the next. However, the words spoken are nevertheless semantically discrete, and can be written down accordingly. The "raw" data is arguably the (continuous) sound. The information it carries is discrete – the words and their meaning.

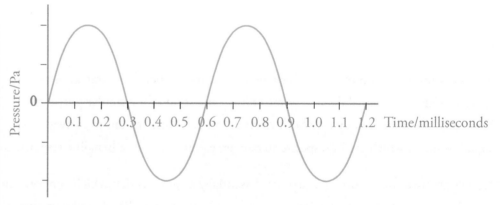

Figure 5.6.2.5 Variation in pressure produced by speaker whistling a pure tone

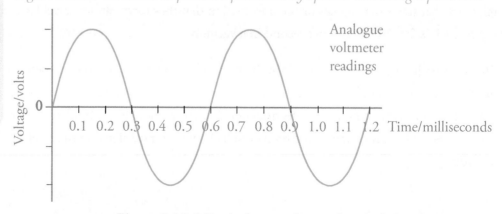

Figure 5.6.2.6 Equivalent analogue electrical signal

What are digital signals?

In contrast to analogue signals, a digital signal is a signal that represents a sequence of discrete values. It may be considered to be a sequence of codes represented by a physical quantity such as an alternating current or voltage, the signal strength of a radio signal, the light intensity of an optical signal, etc.

Figure 5.6.2.7 shows a digital signal with 7 distinguishable voltage levels. In this example, the voltage levels available to the signal were -7.5, -5 , -2.5, 0, 2.5, 5, 7.5.

Each voltage level encodes a binary datum (single item of binary data) as shown in Table 5.6.2.2. The most significant binary digit is a sign bit with 0 representing + and 1 representing −. Unfortunately this leads to two binary patterns representing zero.

Key concept

Digital signal:
A digital signal is a signal that represents a sequence of discrete values. It may be considered to be a sequence of codes represented by a physical quantity such as an alternating current or voltage or the signal strength of a radio signal or the light intensity of an optical signal.

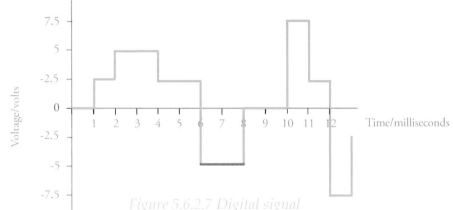

Figure 5.6.2.7 Digital signal

Voltage level	Binary
+7.5	011
+5	010
+2.5	001
0	000
0	100
−2.5	101
−5	110
−7.5	111

Table 5.6.2.2 Using digital signals to encode binary data

It is possible to use just two distinguishable levels of voltage, 0 volts and 5 volts as shown in Figure 5.6.2.8. The digital signal is then a binary digital signal. The ⎍ shape in Figure 5.6.2.8 is called a voltage pulse.

Each voltage represents a binary datum, binary datum 1 by +5 volts and binary datum 0 by 0 volts as shown in Table 5.6.2.3.

Voltage level	Binary
5	1
0	0

Table 5.6.2.3 Using binary digital signals to encode binary data

The stream of voltage pulses shown in Figure 5.6.2.8 encodes the binary data 0110101010 (the least significant digit is the first pulse to be produced).

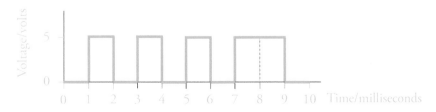

Figure 5.6.2.8 Using binary digital signals to encode binary data

Questions

1 What is analogue data?

2 What is digital data? Give an example.

3 What is a signal?

4 Differentiate between analogue and digital signals.

In this chapter you have covered:

■ The difference between

- analogue data: data that varies in a continuous manner or is recorded in a continuous form and that is similar to its original structure

and

- digital data: discrete data which has been encoded in digital form, i.e. binary, using some algorithm

■ The difference between

- analogue signals: in telecommunications and computer engineering, an analogue signal is an electrical or electromagnetic signal that varies in a continuous manner

and

- digital signals: a digital signal is an electrical signal which conveys information represented by digital data, i.e. it is a signal that represents a sequence of discrete values. It may be considered to be a sequence of codes represented by a physical quantity such as an alternating current or voltage or the signal strength of a radio signal or the light intensity of an optical signal. The digital signal can also change voltage level or amplitude in an abrupt manner or in abrupt steps.

Key principle

Analogue to digital converter (ADC):
Converts an analogue signal into an equivalent digital signal.

Key principle

Pulse Amplitude Modulation(PAM):
Pulse Amplitude Modulation is a process of measurement of the amplitude (height) of an analogue signal at fixed and regular intervals of time determined by the sampling frequency. The process outputs a series of pulses whose amplitudes correspond to these measurements and whose duration in time is the time elapsed between one sampling and the next (the sampling interval).

5.6.3 Analogue/digital conversion

Analogue to digital converter (ADC)

Using a transducer to generate an analogue signal

Sound waves travel through air causing vibrations in your ear that you perceive as sound. Sound waves are classified as analogue data because they vary continuously in shape and size. Sound waves may be converted into an equivalent analogue electrical current or voltage using a microphone which is an example of a transducer, a device for converting energy from one form to another. The variation in frequency (pitch) and amplitude (loudness) of the sound is converted to an equivalent electrical form in the microphone to produce an analogue signal.

Converting to digital form

An analogue signal representing a sound may be recorded by converting it with an analogue to digital converter (ADC) into a digital signal suitable for transmitting and storing in a digital computer system. Figure 5.6.3.1 shows an analogue signal plotted on a voltage-time graph.

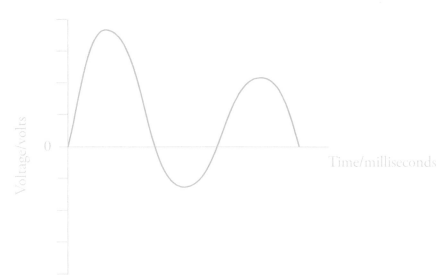

Figure 5.6.3.1 Analogue signal plotted on a voltage-time graph

The analogue to digital conversion process consists of several stages:

1. The analogue signal is sampled at fixed and regular intervals of time using sample and hold circuitry – see Figure 5.6.3.2 - to produce an equivalent digital signal as shown in Figure 5.6.3.3.
   This form of digital signal is known as a Pulse Amplitude Modulation (PAM) signal.

2. The size or amplitude of each sample is measured and coded in binary in a given number of bits, e.g. 4 bits, as shown in *Figure 5.6.3.4*.

3. The binary form of the measurements is represented by electric pulses suitable for transmission over a bus system, serial or parallel, connected to the ADC. This form of the digital signal is known as a **Pulse Code Modulation (PCM) signal**.

Key principle

Pulse Code Modulation (PCM):
Pulse Code Modulation is a process for coding sampled analogue signals by recording the amplitude of each sample in a binary electrical equivalent.

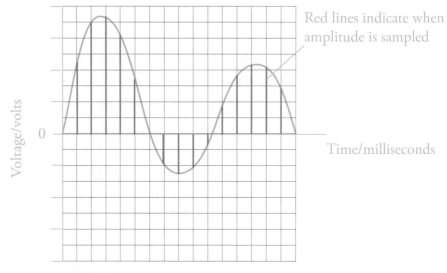

Figure 5.6.3.2 Analogue signal sampled at fixed and regular intervals of time

Figure 5.6.3.2 shows this analogue signal sampled at fixed and regular time intervals. A **sample is a single measurement of amplitude**. The number of measurements of amplitude per second is known as the **sampling rate**. Sampling rate is expressed as **number of samples per second**, e.g. 1000 samples per second. Sampling rate is also called **sampling frequency**. Sampling frequency is expressed in Hz, e.g. 1000 Hz is the equivalent of 1000 samples per second, and 1 KHz, which is the equivalent of 1000 samples per second.

Figure 5.6.3.3 shows the digital signal produced from the sampled analogue signal by a circuit that holds the current sampled value steady until the next sampled value is obtained.

Questions

1 What is a sample?

2 What is the sampling rate for the following sampling frequencies
(a) 20000 Hz (b) 40 kHz
(c) 44.1 kHz?

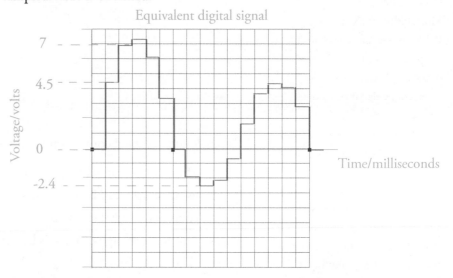

Figure 5.6.3.3 Digital signal produced from the sampled analogue signal.

A 4-bit ADC is helpful in explaining how the measurements of voltage are converted to binary but not very useful in practice; commercially available ADCs use a higher number of bits, e.g. 8, 10, 12, 16.

If we are dealing with a bipolar signal, i.e. one where the voltage may be positive or negative then the ADC must be set to work across a voltage range that includes both positive and negative values. For the conversion shown in Figure 5.6.3.4 the range is set from −8.5 to +7.5 volts i.e. 16 volts.

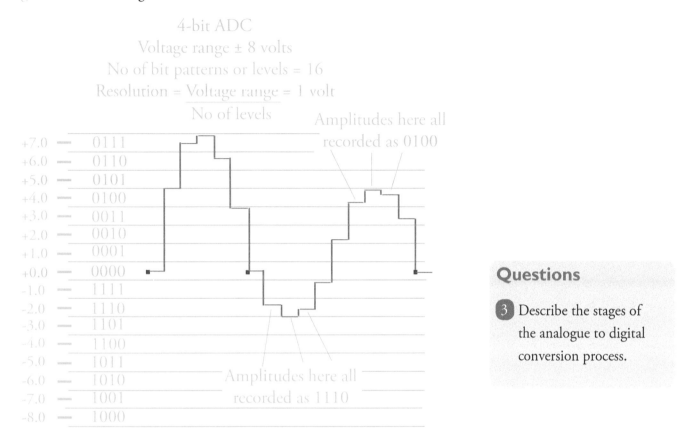

Figure 5.6.3.4 Levels for a 4-bit ADC and voltage range -8.5 to + 7.5 volts coded in 4-bit two's complement binary

Questions

3 Describe the stages of the analogue to digital conversion process.

Encoding samples using 4 bits gives 16 different bit patterns from 0000 to 1111. To cover both positive and negative values of voltage, these bit patterns are interpreted as representing two's complement binary, so voltages in the range −0.5 to +0.5 are coded as 0000, −0.5 to -1.5 volts are coded as 1111, +6.5 to +7.5 volts as 0111 and −7.5 volts to −8.5 volts as 1000. Table 5.6.3.1 shows the correspondence between voltage and binary code.

Sample value in volts	Binary Two's Complement	Voltage equivalent of code	Sample value in volts	Binary Two's complement	Voltage equivalent of code
-0.5 to +0.5	0000	0	-0.5 to -1.5	1111	-1.0
+0.5 to +1.5	0001	+1.0	-1.5 to -2.5	1110	-2.0
+1.5 to +2.5	0010	+2.0	-2.5 to -3.5	1101	-3.0
+2.5 to +3.5	0011	+3.0	-3.5 to -4.5	1100	-4.0
+3.5 to +4.5	0100	+4.0	-4.5 to -5.5	1011	-5.0
+4.5 to +5.5	0101	+5.0	-5.5 to -6.5	1010	-6.0
+5.5 to +6.5	0110	+6.0	-6.5 to -7.5	1001	-7.0
+6.5 to +7.5	0111	+7.0	-7.5 to -8.5	1000	-8.0

Table 5.6.3.1 4-bit ADC set to range -8.5 to +7.5 volts

We can imagine that the ruler shown in *Figure 5.6.3.5* has been used to measure the amplitude of the digital signal shown in *Figure 5.6.3.4*, rounding up or down to a value from the set {−8.0, −7.0, …, +6.0, +7.0}. For example, 3.6 volts would be rounded up to 4.0 volts and coded as 0100, as would 3.5 volts. But 3.4 volts would be rounded down to 3.0 volts and coded as 0011.

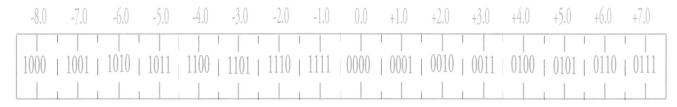

Figure 5.6.3.5 Ruler for a 4-bit ADC

The ADC stores the binary code, e.g. 0110, for the current measurement of amplitude in an internal register before transfer to the processor of the computer to which the ADC is connected. ADCs may be connected by serial (SIP or I2C) or parallel interface depending on its design. *Figure 5.6.3.6* shows the pulse code form of one 4 bit sample. Binary code 1 is a 5 volts high pulse and binary code 0 is a 0 volts high pulse.

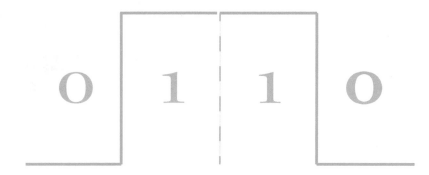

Figure 5.6.3.6 Pulse Code Modulation (PCM) form of one four bit sample.

Questions

4   Draw a ruler for a 3-bit ADC to measure an analogue signal that varies from −9.0 to +7.0 volts over a range of 16 volts. The ruler uses two's complement representation (HINT: see Figure 5.6.3.5).

5   What binary code would be used for a voltage of
(a) +2.0 volts   (b) +2.9 volts   (c) −2.9 volts   (d) +5.0 volts?

6   Draw a ruler for a 3-bit ADC to measure an analogue signal that varies within the range 0.0 to 8.0 volts. The ruler uses unsigned binary representation (HINT: see Figure 5.6.3.5).

Resolution

The purpose of an ADC is to output a PCM digital signal that represents measurements of the amplitude of an analogue signal at fixed and regular intervals of time. The accuracy of the measurements are determined by the number of bits that the ADC uses for its measurements, the more bits the greater the accuracy. Stating the resolution of the ADC is one way of expressing this accuracy.

Resolution of an ADC is measured in terms of the number of bits per sample. The number of bits per sample is referred to as the bit depth of the ADC or word length.

Resolution for a given analogue signal is defined in terms of the range of voltage measured and the number of levels or bit patterns available as follows

$$\text{Resolution} = \frac{\text{Voltage range}}{\text{No of levels}}$$

where No of levels = $2^{\text{No of bits}}$

Table 5.6.3.2 shows resolution for a voltage range 0 to +8 volts and various number of bits

No of bits available to ADC	No of levels $2^{\text{No of bits}}$	Resolution in volts
4	16	0.5
8	256	0.03125
12	4096	0.001953125
16	65536	0.0001220703125

Table 5.6.3.2 Resolution for a voltage range of 0 to +8 volts

Quantisation

The measurement process can be visualised using a ruler to measure the amplitude of an analogue signal to the nearest binary code or corresponding voltage. Imagine that the range of voltage for the analogue signal is from 0 to 4 volts and the number of bits available to represent the measurement is 2 then the ruler would be marked as shown in Figure 5.6.3.7 with 0.5 volts corresponding to 00, 1.5 volts to 01 and so on.

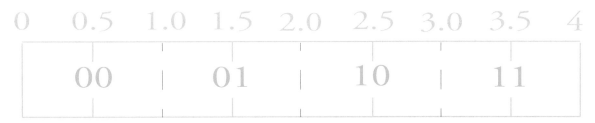

Figure 5.6.3.7 Ruler for measuring voltages in range 0 to 4 volts in 2 bits.

A voltage measurement that lies between 0 and 1 volts would be therefore be coded as 00, a voltage measurement between 1 and 2 volts as 01, and so on. The resolution is $\frac{4 \text{ volts}}{4} = 1$ volt .

However, given, for example, 01 as the coded measurement, we can only say that the analogue signal's amplitude at the time of measurement was in the range 1 to 2 volts or 1.5 ± 0.5 volts.

If the actual amplitude was 1.7 volts then the measurement would be rounded down to 1.5 volts and coded as 01.

If the actual amplitude was 1.2 volts then the measurement would be rounded up to 1.5 volts and coded as 01.

Therefore, the ADC can introduce errors when it converts an analogue signal to a PCM signal.

The error in measurement introduced by an ADC because of rounding down or up is known as quantisation error. The process of rounding up or down is called quantisation. It results in a distorted recording of the true shape of the original analogue signal. This is known as quantisation distortion.

The maximum possible error because of rounding down or up is, in this example, ± 0.5 volts. This is known as the maximum quantisation error.

Key concept

Quantisation error:
The error in measurement introduced by an ADC because of rounding down or up when measuring the amplitude of an analogue signal.

The effects of quantisation errors produced by an ADC are most apparent when the number of bits is small. The greater the number of bits the smaller the effects of quantisation error. Unfortunately, more bits means the quantity of digital data is greater and therefore file sizes that store this data are greater too. Quantity of data is calculated as follows

Quantity of data = No of bits per sample × Sample rate × Length in time of analogue signal

Music CDs are PCM recordings of analogue signals sampled at 44,100 samples per second using ADCs with a resolution of 16 bits. So three minutes of mono sound would occupy 15.876 MB of storage according to *Table 5.6.3.3*. If two channels are used then three minutes of stereo sound would occupy 31.752 MB of storage.

No of bits per sample	Sample rate (samples per second)	Length in time of analogue signal (seconds)	Quantity of data (megabytes)
8	40000	60	2.4
16	40000	60	4.8
16	44100	180	15.876

Table 5.6.3.3 Quantity of data for various no of bits per sample and sample rates

Questions

7 (a) Draw a ruler for a 4-bit ADC to measure an analogue signal that varies in the voltage range 0 to 4 volts.

(b) What is the resolution of this ADC?

(c) What is the resolution in volts for the measurements of this analogue signal?

(d) What is the maximum quantisation error?

8 An ADC with a resolution of 10 bits is used to digitize an analogue signal of duration 180 seconds using a sampling rate of 40000 samples per second. How many bytes will the ADC's PCM produce?

9 A CD-ROM has a capacity of 737 MB (1MB = 1000000 bytes). How many 3 minute two-channel stereo music recordings can be stored on this CD-ROM if the recordings were made in PCM from an ADC with a resolution of 16 bits using a sampling rate of 44,100 samples per second per channel?

Digital to analogue converter (DAC)

To turn a PCM signal back into an analogue signal requires the use of a digital to analogue converter (DAC). The DAC produces an analogue signal which is an approximation of the original analogue signal as illustrated in *Figure 5.6.3.9*. The PCM signal is first turned into a PAM signal - *Figure 5.6.3.8*. The staircase effect is a result of the approximation at the PCM quantisation stage of the analogue to digital conversion of the original analogue signal. The deviation from the original is known as quantisation noise. The DAC applies smoothing to the PAM signal before it is output as shown in *Figure 5.6.3.9*.

Key principle

Digital to analogue converter: Converts a digital signal into an analogue signal approximately equivalent to the original analogue signal from which the digital signal is derived.

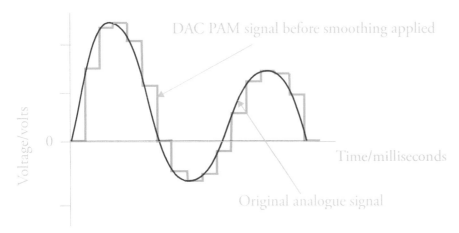

Figure 5.6.3.8 DAC reconstructed analogue signal and the original analogue signal

Key concept

Quantisation noise:
The deviation in the DAC – produced analogue signal from the original analogue signal.

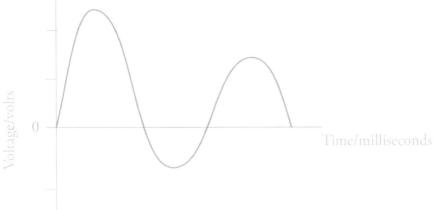

Figure 5.6.3.9 Output of DAC after smoothing applied

Questions

10 What is the purpose of a digital to analogue converter?

ADCs and analogue sensors

What is a sensor?

A sensor is a device that measures something of interest using a variety of mechanisms. A sensor is usually integrated with a transducer which converts the output of the sensing into a signal as shown in Figure 5.6.3.10. This conversion process is known as transduction. Sensors play a key role in connecting the physical world (temperature, light level, pressure, moisture, concentration levels of gases such as CO_2) with the digital world.

Key concept

Sensor:
A sensor is a device that measures something of interest in the physical world and using a transducer converts what is sensed into an equivalent electrical signal.

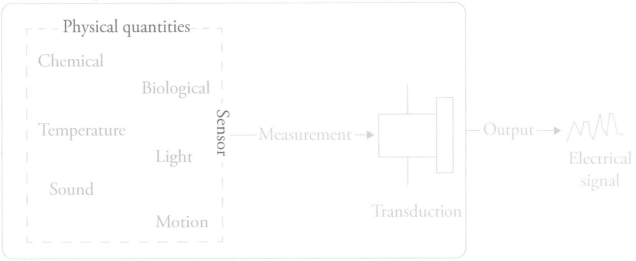

Figure 5.6.3.10 The sensing process

Analogue sensors

The output signal from the majority of sensors is analogue so the signal must first be converted into a digital signal before it can be passed to a digital computer system for recording and further processing.

To convert the analogue signal from an analogue sensor, the signal is fed to an analogue to digital converter (ADC). The output of the ADC is a PCM signal (digital) suitable for transmission to a digital computer system.

Transmitting the PCM signal to a digital computer system is usual done through a serial interface such as a UART or I2C or SPI (see *Chapter 9.1.1*).

The analogue signal may also need to undergo some conditioning before being applied to the ADC.

This signal conditioning takes the form of filtering

- to remove unwanted frequency components
- signal conversion to ensure its voltage range is correct for the ADC
- signal isolation for safety reasons in healthcare applications where there may be direct contact between a patient's body and the sensor.

The need to perform sense-transduce-signal condition-signal convert-output PCM onto a serial bus with analogue sensors has led to the development of integrated circuits called MEMS that do all this.

Information

MEMS

MEMS stands for microelectromechanical systems. They consist of mechanical microstructures, microsensors, microactuators, and microelectronics, all integrated onto the same silicon chip. *Figure 5.6.3.11* shows a schematic for a MEMS integrated circuit digital gyroscope and an actual MEMS 3-axis gyroscope that can be connected to a Raspberry Pi.

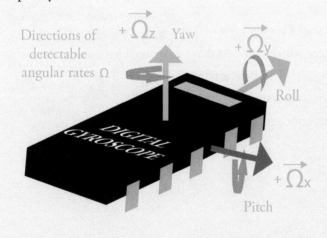

Figure 5.6.3.11 MEMS 3-axis gyroscope

MEMS are known as smart sensors because they incorporate into a single integrated package or chip,

- sensing + transduction with an analogue signal conditioning interface circuit
- an integrated analogue-to-digital converter (ADC)
- a microcontroller and an I/O bus to provide serial output to other computer systems.

Figure 5.6.3.12 shows a simplified block diagram of a smart sensor on a chip.

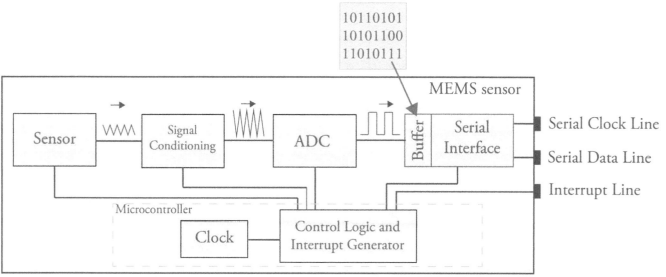

Figure 6.5.3.12 Single integrated circuit smart sensor

MEMS applications

MEMS can be found in smartphones, tablets, game console controllers, digital cameras and camcorders as well as healthcare devices such as pacemakers. Two of the most important and widely used forms are accelerometers and gyroscopes.

Smartphones often have embedded within them a range of analogue smart sensors such as accelerometers, gyroscopes, magnetometers, pressure sensors, optical sensors, silicon microphones, etc.

Sensor platforms

Sensor platforms are a subset of smart sensors. Like smart sensors they feature a microcontroller, a wired/wireless interface, and memory. However, sensor platforms are designed for non-specific platforms, i.e. not just dedicated to generating a PCM signal from an analogue sensor such as a gyroscope. Sensor platforms can provide their services to a range of sensors that may be optionally connected to them by direct wiring, Wi-Fi or Bluetooth. Examples are the Arduino, smartphones, and the electric imp.

Converting digital audio signals to analogue using a DAC

Much of today's music is available in digital format (digital audio) as are radio broadcasts and sound tracks accompanying video. The digital format is not suitable for direct replay through loudspeakers, it would sound like a morse code transmission, so the digital signal from a digital recording or a digital broadcast must be converted by a DAC into an analogue signal that approximates closely the original audio. The loudspeakers convert the electrical energy in the DAC-produced analogue signal into sound energy. If the quantisation noise is low then the quality of the sound produced in the loudspeakers will be high, reproducing faithfully the original analogue sound from which the digital form was created. Figure 6.5.3.13 shows a schematic for a typical sound card.

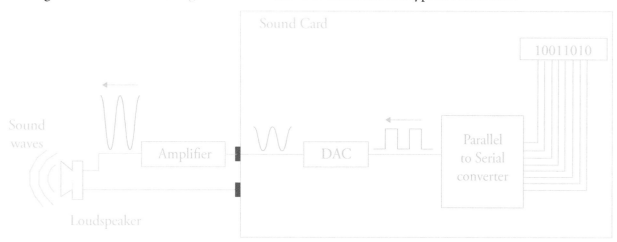

Figure 6.5.3.13 Use of a DAC in a sound card

Questions

11 What is the most common use for a Digital to Analogue Converter (DAC)?

12 What is a sensor? Why is an Analogue to Digital Converter (ADC) often required before the signal from a sensor can be processed by a digital computer?

13 Name **three** analogue sensors found in smartphones.

14 Name **four** components of a single integrated circuit smart sensor.

15 Why is a Digital to Analogue Converter (DAC) needed in order to play digitally recorded sound?

16 With the aid of diagrams, describe the process of converting a PCM signal into its equivalent analogue signal.

17 An audio signal from a microphone was converted into a PCM signal using an 8-bit ADC and replayed through a loudspeaker via a sound card employing an 8-bit DAC. A listener complained that the quality of the reproduced sound was inferior to a PCM signal generated from the same audio signal using a 16-bit ADC and replayed through the same loudspeaker via a sound card employing a 16-bit DAC. Explain why the quality of the reproduced sound could have been perceived as different for the two systems.

In this chapter you have covered:

- The principles of operation of:
  - An analogue to digital converter (ADC)
    - Sample analogue signal
    - Measure amplitude of sample
    - Encode amplitude in binary to produce PCM signal
  - A digital to analogue converter (DAC)
    - Convert PCM signal into a PAM signal
    - Smooth PAM signal to produce analogue signal
- ADCs are used with analogue sensors
  - Analogue sensors produce analogue signals which must be converted into digital form to be stored and processed by a digital computer. The conversion is performed by an ADC.
- The most common use for a DAC is to convert a digital audio signal into an analogue signal
  - Digital audio signals are not suitable for direct replay through loudspeakers. This form of signal would sound through a loudspeaker like morse code. Therefore, a DAC is required to convert the digital audio signal into an analogue signal that approximates closely the original audio. The output of the DAC when played through a loudspeaker should then resemble the sound of the original audio signal.

5.6.4 Bitmapped graphics

Image sensing and acquisition

If an object is illuminated by a source of light it will reflect that light to varying degrees, reflecting some colours more than others. If the reflected light is captured in, say, a digital camera then the energy in the light is converted by light-sensitive sensors (photosensors) into an analogue electrical voltage as shown in Figure 5.6.4.1.

This analogue electrical voltage must then be digitised to produce digital output.

In a digital camera, many such photosensors are arranged as shown in Figure 5.6.4.1. The whole array is just called a sensor.

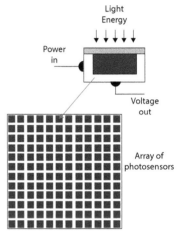

Figure 5.6.4.1 Sensor and its array of photosensors

Sampling and quantisation

When, for example, a digital camera takes a picture of an object such as shown in Figure 5.6.4.2, light from the object is projected through the imaging system onto an array of light sensitive sensors (photosensors).

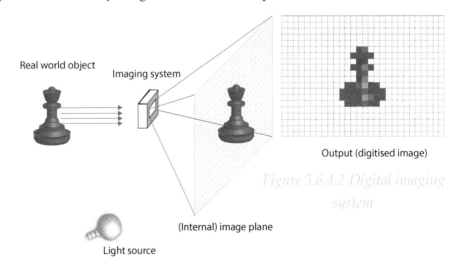

Figure 5.6.4.2 Digital imaging system

The intensity of the image is sampled in the photosensor array at specific X- and Y-coordinate positions. Each photosensor produces a voltage proportional to the intensity of the light falling on it. Making intensity measurements at specific X- and Y- coordinates positions is called sampling. Digitising the analogue voltages representing intensity of light is called quantisation.

Did you know?

Digital single-lens reflex cameras:

These use an aspect ratio of 3:2. Aspect ratio is the ratio of the width of the image to its height. The Canon EOS 600D (released February 2011) uses an APS-C CMOS sensor consisting of a sensor array of dimensions 5184 x 3456.

Tasks

1 Digital cameras currently use either a CCD or a CMOS light sensor array. How does each work and why are two types used?

2 Find out the dimensions of the array of photosensors for a digital camera that you have access to (it will be specified in pixels).

Key concept

Pixel:

A pixel is the smallest addressable region or element of a digital image. Each pixel is a sample of the original image.

Key concept

Pixel:

A pixel is also the smallest controllable element of a digital image represented on the screen i.e. the smallest element or region of a digital image that can be changed or edited when editing bitmapped images using software such as iPhoto, Photoshop, Windows Paint, and other "paint" style packages.

Key fact

Pixel-based graphics:

Pixel-based graphics are made up of small individual pieces of the whole, and each can be changed via editing.

Its strength is in creating complex patterns and displaying photographs with many colour changes.

Its weakness is in changing size. Pixel images can be reduced in size, but lose quality when they are increased in size.

Pixel

Figure 5.6.4.3 shows the result of sampling the image in *Figure 5.6.4.2* at discrete coordinate positions ranging in the X-direction from 0 to 27 and the Y-direction from 0 to 19, and digitising the analogue voltage representing the intensity of the light of the primary colours Red(R), Green(G) and Blue(B) in this light, e.g. at X = 18, Y = 12.

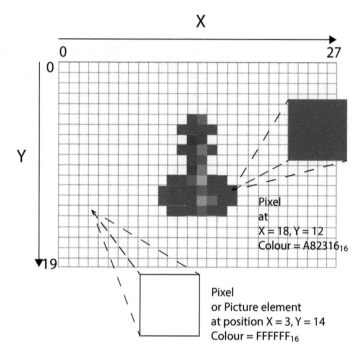

Figure 5.6.4.3 Result of sampling the image plane and digitising the intensity of light of the primary colours for each sample.

Each coordinate position in this discrete coordinate space is known as a pixel or picture element. It is the smallest addressable region of the image plane that can be sampled and the intensity of light falling on it quantised.

At the position (18, 12),

- the red component has an 8-bit value representing its intensity of $A8_{16}$ or 168_{10} (measured on a scale that ranges from 0 to 255)
- the green component has an intensity of 23_{16} or 35_{10}
- the blue component has an intensity of 16_{16} or 22_{10}

At position X = 3 and Y = 14, the corresponding red, green and blue intensities are each represented by FF_{16} or 255_{10}, the maximum value.

Figure 5.6.4.4 shows a smiley face drawn in pixel mode using Photoshop. The pixels for the eyes, nose and mouth were drawn individually by selecting the relevant pixel and changing its colour.

Figure 5.6.4.4 Smiley face drawn in Photoshop in pixel mode at 50 x 50 pixels

Questions

1. What is a pixel?

2. Explain sampling and quantisation in the context of a taking a picture with a digital camera.

3. How many pixels make up a digitised image if the image plane is sampled over the following X and Y coordinates:

   (a) X from 0 to 719, Y from 0 to 479?
   (b) X from 0 to 1919, Y from 0 to 1279?
   (c) X from 0 to 5183, Y from 0 to 3455?

4. Express the result for 3(c) in megapixels by dividing your answer by 1,000,000.

Bitmapped image or bitmap

If we wish to store a digitised image, such as the one shown in *Figure 5.6.4.2* then each quantised sample must be stored, i.e. pixel by pixel, by recording the bit pattern representing the digitised intensity of each pixel.

Figure 5.6.4.5 shows a section of memory from locations **308** to **335** and the corresponding row of pixels that it maps to. Note that the white pixels are stored as **FFFFFF** and the red pixels as **A82316**, **CA1719**, **F29476**.

We say that the digitised image is mapped to bits in memory.

The stored bits in memory are a digital representation of the image or just a bitmap. We say that the image has been bitmapped.

A bitmapped image is a pixel-based digital image.

Key concept

Bitmapped image or bitmap:
A bitmapped image is a pixel-based digital image.
The digitised image is mapped to bits in memory representing the intensity and colour of light of each pixel.

MEMORY

MAPPED TO

DIGITISED
SAMPLES

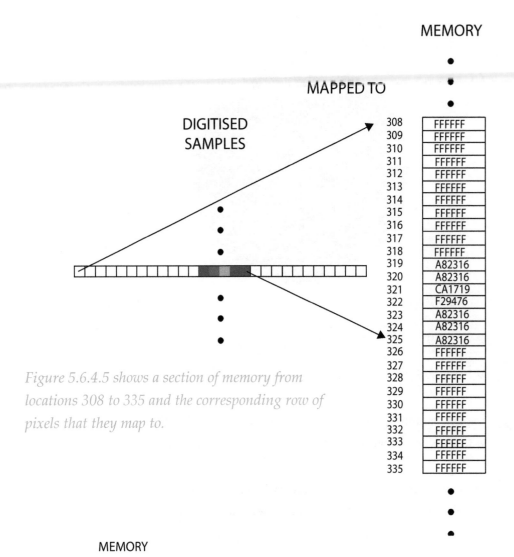

308	FFFFFF
309	FFFFFF
310	FFFFFF
311	FFFFFF
312	FFFFFF
313	FFFFFF
314	FFFFFF
315	FFFFFF
316	FFFFFF
317	FFFFFF
318	FFFFFF
319	A82316
320	A82316
321	CA1719
322	F29476
323	A82316
324	A82316
325	A82316
326	FFFFFF
327	FFFFFF
328	FFFFFF
329	FFFFFF
330	FFFFFF
331	FFFFFF
332	FFFFFF
333	FFFFFF
334	FFFFFF
335	FFFFFF

Figure 5.6.4.5 shows a section of memory from locations 308 to 335 and the corresponding row of pixels that they map to.

MEMORY

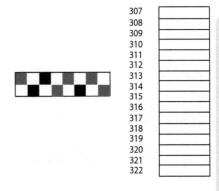

307
308
309
310
311
312
313
314
315
316
317
318
319
320
321
322

Figure 5.6.4.6

Questions

5 *Figure 5.6.4.6* shows an image of a section of a chequered board and a section of memory for storing the bitmap for this image. The pixel size is defined as the size of a single square. Each memory cell, e.g. cell **311**, can store one byte. A bitmap is to be created in the memory that will record the colour of each pixel as any one of **256** different colours. White will be coded as **255**, black as **0** and the red used in the image as **125**.

(a) Show how this image could be stored as a bitmap. Use the given memory cells in your explanation.

(b) With each memory cell still representing one pixel the memory is changed so that each cell can store 3 bytes. How many different colours can be coded in one memory cell? Express your answer as a power of 2.

Bitmap size in pixels

The output of the sampling and quantisation processes is a sequence of digital values, one per sample, corresponding to each discrete coordinate position or pixel. Image size is usually expressed as number of pixels in the X-direction by number of pixels in the Y-direction, e.g. 28 × 20 in the example in *Figure 5.6.4.3*.

Tasks

3 What is the image size in pixels produced by the digital camera in a typical smartphone? Use number of columns (X) × number of rows (Y) notation.

Key concept

Bitmap size in pixels:
Bitmap size = w x h
where
w = width of image in pixels
h = width of image in pixels

Colour depth or bit depth

Colour depth, also known as bit depth, is expressed as the number of bits used to indicate the colour of a single pixel, e.g. 8 bits, in a digitised image.

When the voltage representing intensity of light is quantised, it is represented by an integer number chosen from some range beginning at zero, e.g. 0 to 255 in decimal.

Key concept

Colour depth or bit depth:
Colour depth, also known as bit depth, is expressed as the number of bits used to indicate the colour of a single pixel, e.g. 8 bits, in a digitised image.

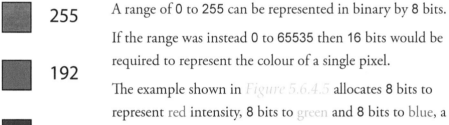

255   A range of 0 to 255 can be represented in binary by 8 bits.

If the range was instead 0 to 65535 then 16 bits would be required to represent the colour of a single pixel.

192

The example shown in *Figure 5.6.4.5* allocates 8 bits to represent red intensity, 8 bits to green and 8 bits to blue, a total of 24 bits. *Figure 5.6.4.7* shows the intensity of red, coded in 8 bits, for some selected values.

128

64   Each possible combination of quantised red, green and blue intensities represents a different resultant colour.

0   The number of different bit patterns that 24 bits can represent is

$$2^{24} = 16777216$$

Figure 5.6.4.7

Therefore, the number of different intensities of colour that can be recorded using 24 bits for each is 16777216.

Questions

6 How many different intensities of colours can be represented for an individual pixel if the number of bits used for each quantised sample is

(a) 12   (b) 15   (c) 18?

Express your answer as a power of 2.

Information

Did you know?
The Hubble telescope used a CCD detector array size of 4096 x 4096 and a field of view of 160 x 160 arcsecs. This gave a pixel size of 160/4096 or 0.04 arcsec, i.e. a pixel for every 1/90000 degrees of view.

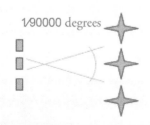

1/90000 degrees

This is approximately the angle subtended by a penny viewed at 52 km, meaning it could be distinguished from another penny immediately next to it.

Resolution

A popular convention is to describe the resolution of a bitmapped image as the number of pixel columns (width) by the number of pixel rows (height), for example, 3264 × 2448.

Image resolution = width of image in pixels × height of image in pixels

For a given dimension of image, say 1.5 inches by 1 inch, the more samples that are taken across the image the smaller the pixels and the greater the recorded detail.

To resolve the detail in a barcode, for example, it must be possible to pick out both white and black bands in the image. If the photosensors are too big then this detail will be missed.

However, the pixel dimensions of a bitmapped image, such as 5184 × 3456 pixels, doesn't give the image a physical size. The bitmapped image's dimensions in pixels state only how many pixels there are, not how big each is.

Two objects that cannot be resolved by sensor as two objects — Voltage out — Sensor — Imaging system — Power in

Figure 5.6.4.8 Sensor too large to resolve two objects

Display and print resolution

The size of each pixel is set by specifying how many pixels should be fitted into an inch when the bitmapped image is displayed or printed.

This is expressed as pixels per inch or ppi.

The choice of ppi for a clear, sharp image depends on the viewing distance.

At the viewing distance, it should not be possible to see individual pixels.

For example, a 4" × 6" standard photographic print, printed at 300 ppi and viewed at about 11 inches appears fine, whereas a billboard-sized photograph also appears fine because its viewing distance is so much greater, even though it is only printed at about 15 ppi.

Figure 5.6.4.9 shows a bitmapped image originally prepared for printing at (a) 10 ppi, (b) 50 ppi and (c) 300 ppi.

The image in (a) of 40 × 30 pixels still reveals its pixels at normal viewing distance. We say that the image is pixelated because the individual pixels are visible. Image (b) is 200 × 150 pixels and shows much less pixelation but the sharpest image is (c) which has dimensions 1200 × 900 pixels.

(a)

(b)

(c)

Figure 5.6.4.9 bitmapped image printed at (a) 10 ppi, (b) 50 ppi and (c) 300 ppi

Physical dimensions of printed images

It should be clear that for practical purposes, the clarity of the image displayed or printed is decided by its spatial resolution, not the number of pixels in an image.

In effect, when a digital image is displayed or printed, resolution refers to the number of independent pixel values per unit length, e.g. pixels per inch or ppi. This is also known as pixel density.

This is an alternative meaning of digital image resolution or bitmap resolution.

Bitmap resolution is measured in number of pixels per inch (ppi).

This definition determines the size of the pixel of the display unit when displaying digital images or the number of image pixels that will fit inside each inch of paper when printed.

Specifying a resolution gives a size to the pixels of the printed image.

Scanned and digital camera images

For images produced by scanning or by a digital camera, the clarity and resolution of a captured image is determined by the size of the photosensors (one photosensor = one pixel).

Resolution of computer displays

A bitmapped digital image produced by a digital camera is composed of digitised or quantised samples that a computer screen displays as pixels because the screen of a computer display is divided into pixels.

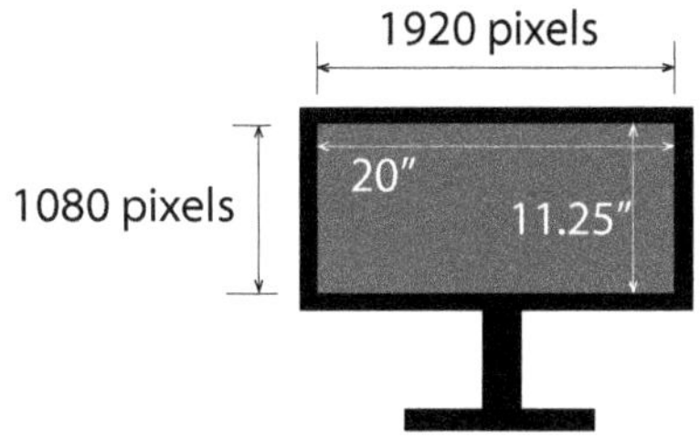

The pixels are the addressable units of the screen that are individually illuminated to create an image or text on the screen. Pixels per inch (ppi) or pixels per centimetre (ppcm) is a measure of pixel density and therefore screen or display resolution. It is defined as the number of pixels in the horizontal direction per unit measurement, e.g. inch, or the number in the vertical direction per unit measurement which is the same thing for square pixels. The ppi of a computer display is therefore related to the size of the display in inches and the total number of pixels in the horizontal or vertical directions.

For the display in Figure 5.6.4.11,

$$\text{Resolution} = 1920 \text{ pixels}/20 \text{ inches}$$
$$= 1080 \text{ pixels}/11.25 \text{ inches}$$
$$= 96 \text{ ppi}$$

PPI is a display resolution not an image resolution.

Figure 5.6.4.11 LCD monitor with screen dimensions 20 inches by 11.25 inches, filled with 1920 x 1080 pixels.

Information

Spatial resolution:

Spatial resolution is the capability of the sensor to observe or measure the smallest object clearly and distinctly, distinguishing it from other objects that surround it.

Figure 5.6.4.10 is composed of two objects which are straight lines separated from each other by a small amount of white space. At the distance at which you are viewing this page, most people will be able to see these as two separate objects, i.e. lines. The sensor in this case is your eye.

However, if you gradually increase the distance between your eye and the page, you will reach a distance at which the two lines are seen as just one thicker line. You are no longer able to resolve the two lines spatially (i.e. in space). Thus spatial resolution depends upon object separation and viewing distance, ignoring any deficiencies of the sensor itself.

Figure 5.6.4.10

Did you know?

Retina displays:

Retina displays use **326** ppi
When introducing the iPhone **4**, Steve Jobs said that the number of pixels needed for a Retina Display is about **326** ppi for a device held **10** to **12** inches from the eye. At a distance of **12** inches, the average eye will not be able to resolve the individual pixels of the screen and therefore the display will be acceptable for viewing.

Image resolution is measured in samples per inch or loosely in horizontal pixels × vertical pixels. Display screens used by desktop computers typically have a resolution of 96 ppi or lower.

For the LCD monitor in *Figure 5.6.4.11*, 96 ppi is the maximum pixel density. Display devices usually allow the display settings to be changed, e.g. for the given display, choosing 1280 pixels by 720 pixels changes the pixel density or resolution to

$$1280 \text{ pixels/20 inches} \text{ or } 720/11.25 = 64 \text{ ppi}$$

for the same screen real estate of 20 × 11.25 inches.

Figure 5.6.4.12 shows the same section of a digitised image at different screen resolutions or ppi. The dimensions of the image in pixels is unchanged but the image's size in the display goes from small to large as the resolution of the screen is reduced. The displayed pixels become larger as the screen resolution is lowered.

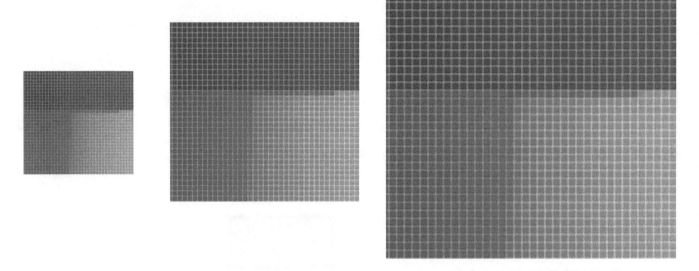

Figure 5.6.4.12 The same section of a digitised image at different screen resolutions, with the pixel density of the screen or ppi decreasing from left to right.

Questions

7 Calculate the screen resolution in number of pixels per inch for the following
   (a) Apple MacBook Pro Retina 13.3"
       screen size in pixels = 2560 × 1600 screen dimensions = 11.3 × 7.04 inches
   (b) Microsoft Surface Pro 3 12" screen size in pixels = 2160 x 1440 screen dimensions = 10.0 × 6.67 inches
   (c) Dell Ultrasharp U2414M 24 inch monitor
       screen size in pixels = 1920 × 1200 screen dimensions = 20.43 × 12.77 inches
   (d) Google Nexus 6
       screen size in pixels = 2560 × 1440 screen dimensions = 5.19 × 2.92 inches

8 Large screens can get away with lower pixel densities because viewing distance is important with regards to resolution. Use your answers for question 7 to justify this statement.

Camera resolution

The iPhone 5s' iSight camera uses a chip with light sensors of width and height 1.5×10^{-6} metre in size, giving dimensions for each pixel of 1.5×10^{-6} metres (1.5μm where μm is a micrometre) . This camera uses an aspect ratio of 4:3 and therefore is 3264 pixels across by 2448 pixels down (3264 × 2448) or 7990272 pixels in total. Expressed to 2 decimal places this is 7.99 megapixels or to none, 8 megapixels.

Apple actually increased pixel size in the iPhone 5s to 1.5μm (from 1.4 μm in iPhone 5) and kept the pixel count the same by using a 15% larger sensor. The slightly larger sensor size and therefore pixel size improved low light sensitivity and reduced the ratio of image signal to noise emanating from within the sensor in low light conditions. This actually improved the quality of the image.

Sony Xperia 's primary camera uses a chip of width and height 4128 × 3096 pixels. The total quoted number of pixels is 13.1 megapixels. This is actually greater than the number which contribute to the final image because some pixels are unused or are shielded from the light because they are around the edges of the sensor.

Questions

 Why is it useful for smartphone cameras to have 4 megapixels or greater?

Printing a bitmapped image on paper

Paper is an analogue material so it differs from a typical computer screen which is digital, i.e. divided up into pixels. The coordinate system for drawing by hand on paper is a continuous one whereas that for a digital screen is a discrete one. However, when a digital image is printed on paper, it is pixels which are printed, i.e. discrete units. There is a difference, however, for the printer controls the size of the printed image pixel, all that the digitised image supplies by way of control is the number of pixels horizontally and the number of pixels vertically.

For example, a 100 × 100 pixel image that is printed in a 1 inch square has a resolution of 100 pixels per inch (ppi). To produce good quality printed photographs, the printer must be capable of printing 300 pixels per inch, at 100% size, and the paper printed on must be coated paper stock.

A printer creates an image on paper by laying down a series of dots of ink or toner. Its resolution is therefore measured in number of dots per inch (DPI).

An ink-jet printer prints by moving a printhead across and down the paper. It has a basic movement of 1200 steps across and 1200 steps down, typically. Each pixel of the

A pixel made up of 16 blue dots

Key fact

Printer resolution and Dots per inch (DPI):
Dots per inch is a measure of the resolution of a printer. It properly refers to the dots of ink or toner used by an imagesetter, laser printer, or other printing devices to print text and graphics. In general, the more dots, the better and sharper the image. DPI is printer resolution.

image is created by a series of tiny dots and every pixel output is made up of different coloured inks (usually 4 colours, CMYK - Cyan, Magenta, Yellow, and Key which is black - though professional printing uses more) deposited by the print head on the paper.

If the printer can print 1200 dots of ink per inch (1200 dpi) and a bitmapped image is sent to the printer for printing at 300 pixels per inch, then each printed pixel will be consist of 16 smaller ink dots.

Questions

10 An image of size **640 × 480** pixels is to be printed at **300** pixels per inch. What will be the size of the printed image in inches to one decimal place?

11 The size of a photographic print printed at **300 ppi** is **4.2 × 3.2** inches. What was the size in pixels of the digital image that was printed?

Stretch & challenge question

12 A bimapped image is produced by scanning a 35mm film slide (**0.94** inches by **1.42** inches) with a scanner designed for this purpose. A print of size **9.4 × 14.2** inches is to be made of the bitmapped image on a printer that prints at **300** pixels per inch, i.e. photographic quality.

    (a) How many pixels are printed in a 9.4 inch wide row?

    (b) If the scanning resolution is n samples per inch, how many samples, in terms of n, would be taken in a scan of one row across the film slide (**0.94** inches)?

    (c) What must the minimum value of the scanning resolution be in samples per inch to produce a print of acceptable quality?

    (d) Using your answer to part (c), what is the size of the bitmap in pixels produced by the scanner? Express your answer in the form of number of pixel columns (width) by the number of pixel rows (height). Both numbers are integers.

Key concept

Metadata:

The header part of the bitmap file contains information about the bitmap data part of the file, such as number of bits per pixel. This is metadata because it is data about data, i.e. the data in the bitmap part of the file.

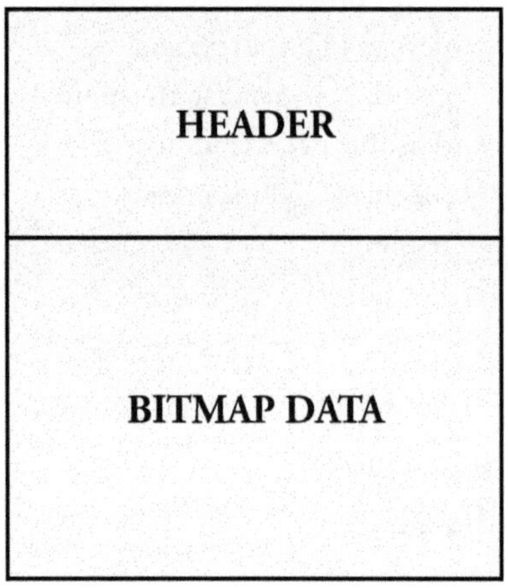

Figure 5.6.4.13 Structure of a Windows bitmap file

Metadata

Microsoft's Paint program that comes with the Windows operating system enables bitmaps to be created and saved. Bitmap files saved in Windows Paint with file extension ".bmp" have a file structure which conforms to the Windows bitmap format shown in *Figure 5.6.4.13*. The header contains information about the bitmap data part of the file, such as

- number of bits per pixel
- horizontal width of bitmap in pixels
- whether it is compressed or not, etc.

This is called metadata because it is data about data.

The actual detailed structure and content of the header is shown in *Figure 5.6.4.14* for an uncompressed, RGB, 24 bits per pixel, 4 × 2 pixel bitmap produced with Microsoft Paint and shown in *Figure 5.6.4.15*.

Figure 5.6.4.16 shows the data part of the bitmap file for *Figure 5.6.4.13*. Bytes **54, 55** and **56** correspond to the first pixel in the bottom row of the image. The colour of each pixel is controlled by three bytes, the first in the triplet controls red, the second green, and the third blue. Thus this first pixel of the bottom row is green because its colour is controlled by the triplet **0, 255, 0**. The second pixel in the bottom row is black because it is controlled by the triplet, **0, 0, 0**.

Figure 5.6.4.16, byte **10** states that the bitmap data begins at byte **54**. Byte **34** states that the length of the bitmap data is **24** bytes, which indeed it is as *Figure 5.6.4.15* shows. Microsoft chose to store the bytes in little-endian fashion. In little-endian, the least significant byte is stored in the smallest address. For example, "Where the data starts" is four bytes long and has value **0, 0, 0, 54** which in decimal is just **54**.

Questions

13 Using *Figure 5.6.4.16* as a reference, list **nine** items of metadata found in the header of a bitmap file.

Figure 5.6.4.15 Image produced when 24-bit bitmap rendered on screen

77	0	Top row fourth pixel
76	0	BLACK
75	0	0, 0, 0
74	0	Top row third pixel
73	0	BLUE
72	255	0, 0, 255
71	255	Top row second pixel
70	0	RED
69	0	255,0 ,0
68	0	Top row leftmost pixel
67	0	BLACK
66	0	0, 0, 0
65	0	Bottom row fourth pixel
64	0	BLUE
63	255	0, 0, 255
62	255	Bottom row third pixel
61	0	RED
60	0	255, 0, 0
59	0	Bottom row second
58	0	pixel BLACK
57	0	0, 0, 0
56	0	Bottom row leftmost
55	255	pixel GREEN
54	0	0, 255, 0

Figure 5.6.4.14 Bytes 54 to 77 of bitmap file represent bitmap data for 4 x 2 pixels image, 24-bit Windows bitmap.

Information

Reading and writing bytes:
The source code of programs to read and write a file of bytes can be downloaded from www. educational-computing.co.uk.

0	identifier	The file type	66	'B'
1	identifier	must be 'BM'.	77	'M'
2	file size	The size, in bytes, of the bitmap file.	78	
3	file size		0	
4	file size		0	
5	file size		0	
6	reserved	Reserved; must be zero.	0	
7	reserved		0	
8	reserved		0	
9	reserved		0	
10	bitmap data offset	The offset, in bytes, from the	54	
11	bitmap data offset	beginning of the	0	
12	bitmap data offset	BITMAPFILEHEADER	0	
13	bitmap data offset	structure to the bitmap bits.	0	
14	bitmap header size		40	
15	bitmap header size		0	
16	bitmap header size		0	
17	bitmap header size		0	
18	Horizontal width of bitmap in pixels		4	
19	Horizontal width of bitmap in pixels		0	
20	Horizontal width of bitmap in pixels		0	
21	Horizontal width of bitmap in pixels		0	
22	Vertical width of bitmap in pixels	If Height is positive, the	2	
23	Vertical width of bitmap in pixels	bitmap is a bottom-up DIB.	0	
24	Vertical width of bitmap in pixels	DIB = Device Independent	0	
25	Vertical width of bitmap in pixels	Bitmap.	0	
26	Number of planes in the bitmap	The number of planes for the target	1	
27	Number of planes in the bitmap	device.This value must be set to 1.	0	
28	Bits per pixel		24	
29	Bits per pixel		0	
30	Compression	The type of compression for a	0	
31	Compression	compressed bottom-up bitmap	0	
32	Compression	RGB uncompressed= 0x0000	0	
33	Compression	JPEG = 0x0004, PNG = 0x0005	0	
34	Bitmap data size	Size in bytes	24	
35	Bitmap data size		0	
36	Bitmap data size		0	
37	Bitmap data size		0	
38	Horizontal resolution in pixel/metre of the target device	An application can use this value to select a bitmap from	0	
39	Horizontal resolution in pixel/metre	a resource group that best	0	
40	Horizontal resolution in pixel/metre	matches the characteristics	0	
41	Horizontal resolution in pixel/metre	of the current device.	0	
42	Vertical resolution in pixel/metre of the target device		0	
43	Vertical resolution in pixel/metre		0	
44	Vertical resolution in pixel/metre		0	
45	Vertical resolution in pixel/metre		0	
46	Number of colours used	If zero, the bitmap uses the maximum	0	
47	Number of colours used	number of colours corresponding to the	0	
48	Number of colours used	value of the bits per pixel.	0	
49	Number of colours used		0	
50	Number of important colours used	If zero, all colours are important.	0	
51	Number of important colours used		0	
52	Number of important colours used		0	
53	Number of important colours used		0	

Bitmap, BM

4 bytes,
0, 0, 0, 78

Where the data starts
0, 0, 0, 54

4 bytes,
0, 0, 0, 40

4 bytes,
0, 0, 0, 4

4 bytes,
0, 0, 0, 2

2 bytes,
0, 24

4 bytes,
0, 0, 0, 24

Figure 5.6.4.16 Header part of bitmap file. It contains metadata.

Programming Tasks

1. Using Microsoft Paint (or equivalent), create and save a **4 × 2** pixels **24**-bit uncompressed Windows bitmap similar to Figure 5.6.4.15. Use the pencil tool to change the colour of individual pixels. You will need to zoom in to make the pixels large enough to manipulate.

2. Write a program that opens and reads the contents of this file, byte by byte, displaying each byte as a decimal integer on the console. Number these bytes starting from **0** so that the console output displays number followed by byte value read from file. Check that your output shows similar values to those shown in *Figures 5.6.4.14* and *5.6.4.16*.

3. Using Paint, change the colours of the pixels in the bitmap, noting the RGB values and re-run your program. Check that the output from your program now reflects the new RGB values of the colours.

4. Using Paint, create and save an 8 x 2 pixels **24**-bit uncompressed Windows bitmap, with differently coloured pixels.

5. Re-run you program and note the relevant changes in the header (metadata) and the data part of the bitmap displayed on the console. Do the displayed changes agree with what you expect?

6. Edit your program so that it also writes each byte that it reads from the opened bitmap file to a new file. Save your edited program under a new name. The new bitmap file produced by running the new program should be given a suitable name and the extension ".bmp". At the moment it should be just a copy of the original.

7. Edit your new program so that it alters the three bytes of a chosen pixel before writing these to the new bitmap file. Now open the changed bitmap file in Paint and check that your program has changed the colour of a pixel.

8. How could a short sequence of 8-bit ASCII character codes be placed in a bitmap file? Choose a much larger image bitmap file than you have been working with, e.g. **640 x 480** pixels, and use your program suitably modified to replace pixel bytes in this bitmap with a sequence of 8-bit ASCII codes. Check the result by displaying the new image bitmap file in an image viewer, e.g. Paint. Can you detect the ASCII codes?

9. Write a program that reads an altered image bitmap file and recovers the sequence of 8-bit ASCII codes. Display these as characters on the console.

Calculating storage requirements for bitmapped images

Ignoring the storage space taken up by metadata, the storage requirements of the data part of a bitmapped image is calculated as follows

Key fact

Storage requirements for bitmapped images):

Storage requirements = width in pixels × height in pixels × colour depth

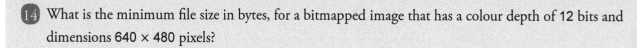

$$\textit{Storage requirements = width in pixels} \times \textit{height in pixels} \times \textit{colour depth}$$

This is sometimes referred to as being the minimum file size for a bitmapped image.

For example, a bitmapped image has dimensions 5184 × 3456 pixels and uses 24-bit colour. What is the size of the data part of the bitmap in bits? In bytes? What is it in megabytes (1000000 bytes), to 1 decimal place?

Size in bits = 5184 × 3456 × 24 = 429981696

Size in bytes = (5184 × 3456 × 24)/8 = 53747712

Size in megabytes = (5184 × 3456 × 24)/(8 x 1000000) = 53.7

Questions

14 What is the minimum file size in bytes, for a bitmapped image that has a colour depth of 12 bits and dimensions 640 × 480 pixels?

In this chapter you have covered:

- *How bitmaps are represented*
- *For bitmaps the meaning of*
  - *resolution*
  - *colour depth*
  - *size in pixels*
- *How to calculate storage requirements for bitmapped images*
- *Bitmap image files may also contain metadata*
- *Typical metadata*

5.6.5 Vector graphics

How does a vector graphic represent images?

A vector graphic image is created in a similar way to the way we draw with coloured pencils by hand, i.e. by drawing lines from point to point in different colours, drawing and shading closed shapes such as rectangles in different colours, etc.

A vector graphic such as the one shown in Figure 5.6.5.1 is just a collection of objects of various types, (e.g. circle, line, arc) together with their properties (e.g. radius of circle).

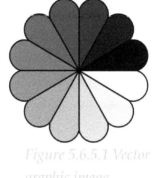

Figure 5.6.5.1 Vector graphic image

Key principle

Vector graphic:

A vector graphic can be represented as a list of objects or a list of drawing commands that reference geometric objects

A vector graphic can be represented as a list of objects or a list of drawing commands that reference geometric objects such as

- points in space,
- straight lines or curves connecting these points
- shapes formed from closed paths (such as rectangles, circles, ellipses, triangles, other polygons, and non-regular shapes created from straight and curved lines).
- Other commands apply fill operations to shapes or set the thickness of lines.

All of these points, lines, curves and shapes make up what is seen as the image.

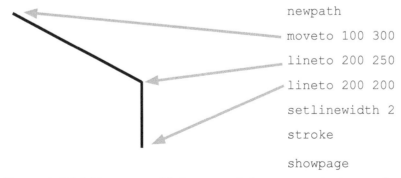

```
newpath
moveto 100 300
lineto 200 250
lineto 200 200
setlinewidth 2
stroke
showpage
```

Figure 5.6.5.2 Vector graphic image and the commands that produced it

Figure 5.6.5.2 shows a vector graphic image of two black lines and the SCRIPT commands that produced it.

A command in this vector graphic scripting language consists of operands (parameters) and an operator written *operator operand1 operand2*.

For example,

- `moveto 100 300`, moves a "phantom" pen to the point whose coordinates are 100, 300.

- The command `lineto 200 250` creates the path for a straight line from the position of the current point to the new current point at 200,250.

- The command `setlinewidth 2` sets the pen to draw lines with a thickness of **2** units which means 2/72 inch if the unit is 1/72 inch (72 ppi).

- The command stroke causes the pen to move along the defined path inking it in.

- The final command in the script, showpage displays the page on the screen.

The parameters supplied to the commands, e.g. **200** and **250** in command `lineto 200,250` are just numbers. Therefore, to apply a change, such as resize or reshape, to a part of a vector graphic image we simply do arithmetic on these numbers and then draw the vector graphic again.

This means we can resize a vector shape as many times as we like, making it any size we need, without any loss of image quality.

This is why vector graphic images retain crisp, sharp edges to graphic elements/shapes no matter by how much we enlarge them, and, unlike pixel-based graphics, vector graphic images are resolution-independent.

This means that when printing, the resolution of the printed image is determined by the highest resolution that the printer can print at.

Figure 5.6.5.3 shows the original vector graphic and a separate scaled by **2** version.

In *Figure 5.6.5.3*, the `scale 2 2` command is applied to all the operand numbers in the other commands, e.g. `moveto 100 300` becomes `moveto 200 600`, `setlinewidth 2` becomes `setlinewidth 4`.

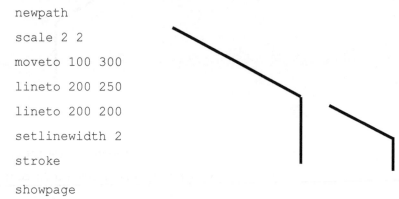

```
newpath

scale 2 2

moveto 100 300

lineto 200 250

lineto 200 200

setlinewidth 2

stroke

showpage
```

Figure 5.6.5.3 Vector graphic image from Figure 5.6.5.2, its scaled counterpart, and the commands that produced the scaled version.

Questions

1　How does a vector graphic represent images?

2　Why are vector graphic images resolution-independent?

Display devices are mainly digital so to display a vector graphic image, it must be rasterised, i.e. turned into pixels. There are some display devices that can display the vector graphic image without needing to rasterise at all. These essentially are Cathode Ray Tube-based (CRT) displays with a single colour continuous phosphor coating applied to the screen. These are ideal for being controlled by commands in a vector graphic script. Some radar displays, monitors used in medicine and laser shows are operated directly in this way as are X-Y plotters which are a kind of printer that uses vector data.

Questions

3　Explain why a vector graphic image is still displayed without any loss of image quality on a digital display when it is scaled.

Tasks

These activities are designed to familiarise you with a vector graphic format.
Download and install Ghostscript 9.15 or later for Windows and GSview 5.0 or later.

1　Create the following file in a text editor, e.g. Microsoft Wordpad, and save with extension .ps

```
newpath
0 1 0 setrgbcolor
256 500 100 0 360 arc fill
newpath
1 0 0 setrgbcolor
100 500 50 0 360 arc fill
showpage
```

Open this file in GSview.
(a) What do you see?
(b) Change the fill colour of the first object to blue.
(c) Change the dimension of the second object from 100 to 50
(d) Change the arc from 0 360 to 0 180.

Information

Postscript interpreter and viewer Ghostscript:
Download from
http://www.ghostscript.com/download/gsdnld.html and instal then download and install GSview 5.0 or later: Download from
http://pages.cs.wisc.edu/~ghost/gsview/get50.htm

Download postscript language tutorial and cookbook, PSBlueBook.pdf from
http://partners.adobe.com/public/developer/ps/sdk/sample/index_psbooks.html

Tasks

2   The code folder of the cookbook, PSBlueBook.pdf contains several postscript vector graphic files. Explore the following in GSview and Wordpad. You are not required to understand the commands only to observe that the vector graphic files contain lists of commands that reference objects and that the contents can be viewed in a text editor

(a) Prog_01.ps

(b) Prog_02.ps

(c) Prog_03.ps

3   GSView can convert postscript files to bitmapped files and pdfs. Convert Prog_02.ps to a bmp16m 72ppi bitmapped image file, Prog_02.bmp. Compare the file size of Prog_02.ps with its bitmapped equivalent. What do you observe?

4   Convert Prog_02.ps to a pdfwrite 72ppi file, Prog_02.pdf. Launch Acrobat reader and open Prog_02.pdf. What do you observe? Is the pdf format vector graphic or bitmapped?

Using vector graphic primitives to create a simple vector graphic

Scalable Vector Graphics (SVG) is an XML-based vector image format for two-dimensional graphics.

The specification of SVG is an open standard developed by the World Wide Web Consortium (W3C) since 1999.

SVG images can be created and edited with any text editor because the images are defined in XML text files.

Figure 5.6.5.4 shows an SVG image rendered in a browser window. All modern web browsers have some degree of support for rendering SVG images.

The XML-text of this SVG image shown below was produced with a text editor and saved as BasicRecSVG.svg.

```
<svg xmlns="http://www.w3.org/2000/svg" xmlns:xlink="http://www.w3.org/1999/xlink" >
   <rect x="10px" y="10px" width="150px"
       height="150px" fill="rgb(0,255,0)"
       stroke-width="1" stroke="rgb(0,0,0)" />
</svg>
```

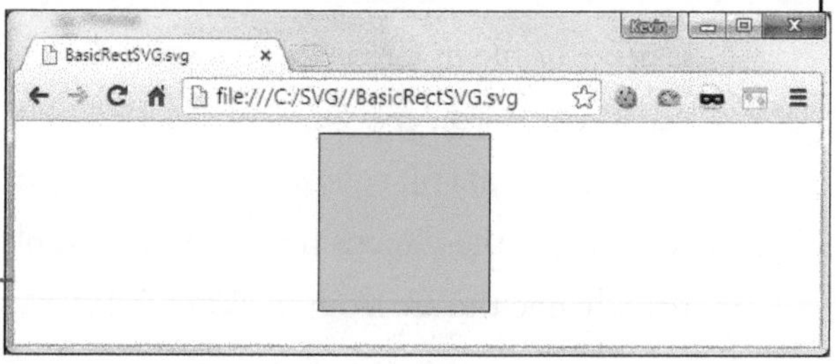

Figure 5.6.5.4 Scalable Vector Graphics image produced from XML and rendered in a browser

The root element of all SVG images is the `<svg>` element. Here is how it looks:

```
<svg xmlns="http://www.w3.org/2000/svg" xmlns:xlink="http://www.w3.org/1999/xlink" >
```

Namespaces are defined in the `<svg... />` part to avoid the names in the rest of this file clashing with similar names elsewhere:

```
xmlns="http://www.w3.org/2000/svg" xmlns:xlink=http://www.w3.org/1999/xlink
```

The vector graphic part `<rect.../>` element specifies a rectangle of width 150 pixels, height 150 pixels, 10 pixels in from the left side of the browser window and 10 pixels from the top.

In the SVG coordinate system the point x = 0, y = 0 is the upper left corner.

The rectangle has a black outline

```
stroke="rgb(0, 0, 0)" of width 1px (stroke-width="1")
```

and is filled in the green colour defined in the rgb triplet,

```
rgb(0, 255, 0)
```

Nesting SVG elements, as shown in *Figure 5.6.5.5*, enables shapes to be drawn relative to the position (x, y) of its enclosing svg element.

```
<svg xmlns="http://www.w3.org/2000/svg" xmlns:xlink="http://www.w3.org/1999/xlink" >
  <svg x="10">
    <rect x="10px" y="10px" width="150px" height="150px" fill="rgb(0,255,0)"
          stroke-width="1" stroke="rgb(0,0,0)" />
  </svg>
  <svg x="300">
    <rect x="10px" y="10px" width="150px" height="150px" fill="rgb(255,0,0)"
          stroke-width="1" stroke="rgb(0,0,0)" />
  </svg>
</svg>
```

Figure 5.6.5.5 Scalable Vector Graphic script

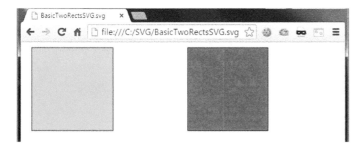

Figure 5.6.5.6 Scalable Vector Graphic image produced using nested svg elements and rendered in a browser.

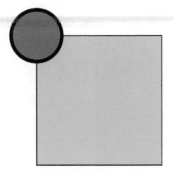

So the position of the first rectangle will be measured from $x = 10, y = 10$ and therefore be drawn starting from $x = 10+10, y = 10$.

The position of the second rectangle will be measured from $x = 300, y = 10$ and therefore be drawn starting from $x = 300 + 10, y = 10$.

The result is shown in *Figure 5.6.5.6*.

Figure 5.6.5.7 shows another SVG image produced from XML and rendered in a browser. The XML defines two shapes, a green rectangle and a red circle. The XML-text of this SVG image was also produced with a text editor and is shown in *Figure 5.6.5.8*.

Figure 5.6.5.7 SVG image

```
<svg xmlns="http://www.w3.org/2000/svg"  xmlns:xlink="http://www.w3.org/1999/xlink" >
  <rect x="50" y="150"  width="150" height="150" fill="rgb(0,255,0)" stroke-width="1"
        stroke="rgb(0,0,0)" />
  <circle cx="50" cy="150" r="30" fill="red" stroke-width="4" stroke="black" />
</svg>
```

Figure 5.6.5.8 SVG image file contents

Tasks

5　Using a text editor such as Wordpad, create a copy of the vector graphic script shown in Figure 5.6.5.5 and save as TwoRects.svg. Experiment with changing the properties of each rectangle and observe the outcome by opening TwoRects.svg in a web browser.

6　Repeat activity Task 5 for the vector graphic script shown in Figure 5.6.5.8. Save as RectAndCircle.svg.

7　Using a text editor such as Wordpad, create a copy of the vector graphic script shown below, save it as Text.svg.

```
<svg
  xmlns="http://www.w3.org/2000/svg"
  xmlns:xlink="http://www.w3.org/1999/xlink">
<text x="10" y="30"  fill="red"
   font-family=" 'Lucida Grande',sans serif"
   font-size="32" transform="rotate(90 20,30)">
   I love SVG!
  </text>
</svg>
```

(a)　　Display Text.svg in a web browser.

(b)　　Experiment with changing the properties of the text and observe the outcome by opening Text.svg in a web browser.

Tasks

8 Inkscape is an open-source vector graphics editor similar to Adobe Illustrator, Corel Draw, Freehand, or Xara X but it differs from these because it uses Scalable Vector Graphics (SVG), an open XML-based W3C standard, as the native format. Download and install.

Information

Inkscape:
Download and install https://inkscape.org/en/download/

Examples of typical properties of objects

The properties of a vector graphic object specify its dimensions, its position in coordinate space and its appearance, e.g.

Rectangle

- Dimensions: width, height

- Position: bottom left or top left corner x, y coordinates

- Appearance: filled with colour green, rgb(0,255,0), outline stroked in black, stroke width 1 px

Circle

- Dimensions: radius

- Position: centre x, y coordinates

- Appearance: filled with colour green, rgb(0,255,0), outline stroked in black, stroke width 1 px

Questions

4 List **three** types of object that could be found in a vector graphic image file.

5 List **four** properties associated with one of the objects in your answer to Q4 that could be found in a vector graphic image file.

In this chapter you have covered:

- How vector graphics represents images using lists of objects

- Examples of typical properties of objects:
  - dimensions - width, height, radius, line thickness; position in coordinate space - x, y coordinates;
  - appearance - filled and fill colour, outline stroke colour

- Using vector graphic primitives to create a simple vector graphic

5.6 Representing images, sound and other data

■ 5.6.6 Vector graphics versus bitmapped graphics

Figure 5.6.6.1 shows a vector graphic image of a black circle on a white background and a bitmap image of the same circle, at their original size and each magnified seven times. The vector graphic image was produced from the following script and rendered in GSview, a graphical interface for displaying interpreted PostScript:

```
newpath
300 500 10 0 360 arc fill
```

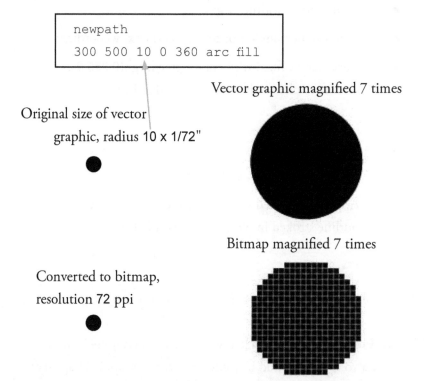

Original size of vector graphic, radius 10 x 1/72"

Vector graphic magnified 7 times

Bitmap magnified 7 times

Converted to bitmap, resolution 72 ppi

Figure 5.6.6.1 Vector graphic image and its equivalent bitmap image, original size and magnified 7 times

GSview was also used to produce the **24 bit, 72 ppi** bitmap image from its vector graphic equivalent.

Bitmap, or raster images as they are sometimes called, use a rather primitive form of representation consisting of no more than a lattice of small rectangular areas called pixels. In a bitmap file, the only information that is stored about a pixel is its colour. Therefore, for the bitmap image of a black circle on a white background displayed in *Figure 5.6.6.1*, there is no stored black circle as such in the bitmap file. All that the computer knows about the image from the bitmap file is that some of its pixels are black and some are white. When the bitmap image is rendered on screen it appears as a black circle to the viewer because that is how the viewer perceives the black and white pixels, but the larger the pixels, in the displayed image, the harder this task for the viewer.

As the computer does not see the bitmap image representation as a circle object with properties, such as position, radius, stroke (outline) colour, it cannot move the circle or transform it by, for example, changing its radius. All it can do is to change the colour of pixels, e.g. all white pixels to red or all black pixels to green, say.

Even using a pixel editing package, moving the black circle is difficult to do precisely, especially if the edge of the circle is antialiased so that some pixels on the edge have intermediate values between black and white as in *Figure 5.6.6.2*.

> ### Questions
>
> **1** For a bitmapped graphic, explain why it is difficult to move objects from one position in the image to another.

Figure 5.6.6.2 Enlarged antialiased bitmap

However, storing the black circle on a white background image as a vector graphic avoids using pixels altogether. Instead, the actual definition of the circle is stored as a circle object with its properties specified. Its properties are its (x, y) centre position in the coordinate system of the image, its radius, its stroke (or outline) colour, stroke thickness and its fill colour.

The immediate advantage is that the circle object can be treated separately from the rest of the image and its properties adjusted to move or transform it.

Indeed, if the vector graphic image contains many circles, each can be selected separately and individually manipulated. Also, with such an image, a computer can automatically, say, delete all circles or scale all black circles to three times their size or paint all green objects red. There is no pixel selection taking place only object selection.

> ### Questions
>
> **2** For a vector graphic, explain why it is relatively easy to move objects from one position in the image to another and to manipulate objects in other ways

As an example of the way that a vector graphic allows easy selection of image objects, *Figure 5.6.6.3* shows the contents of the part of an SVG file produced in Inkscape by drawing a red circle. If there was another circle in the image then another <circle ..../> block of text would be stored in the file.

Information

Inkscape:

Download and install

https://inkscape.org/en/download/

Some of the properties of the circle object referenced in *Figure 5.6.6.3* are

    radius of circle, r : 117.14286

    centre of circle x coordinate, cx : 382.85715

    centre of circle y coordinate, cy : 495.21939

    fill colour : #ff0000 (red)

    colour of stroke : #000000 (black)

    stroke-width : 0px

```
<circle
  r="117.14286"
  cy="495.21939"
  cx="382.85715"
  id="path3338"
  style="fill:#ff0000;
  fill-rule:evenodd;stroke:#000000;
  stroke-width:0px;
  stroke-linecap:butt;
  stroke-linejoin:miter;stroke-opacity:1" />
```

Figure 5.6.6.3 Part of SVG file produced in Inkscape by drawing a red circle

Advantages of the vector graphics approach

Vector images are scalable

Since vector shapes are essentially represented by their geometric properties, each time a change is made to the shape, either by resizing or reshaping it In some way, it is these properties that are changed. The vector graphic image is simply redrawn on the screen using the new definition. This means that a vector graphic shape can be scaled in size any number of times without any loss of image quality. Vector graphic drawn shapes retain their crisp, sharp edges no matter how large they are made. Vector graphic images are resolution-independent. This is in contrast to bitmapped (raster) images which are not.

A big disadvantage of bitmapped images or shapes is that they don't scale very well, at least not when making them larger than their original size. Enlarge a bitmapped image or shape too much and it will lose its sharpness. Enlarge it even more and the pixels that make up the image or shape can become visible, resulting in a blocky or pixelated appearance.

Vector images tend to produce smaller file sizes than bitmapped image files

The original vector graphic image file for the black circle on a white background consisted of 44 bytes. Its bitmapped equivalent was 1400 bytes. Thus, a vector image usually takes up less storage space than a bitmapped image.

Bitmapped (raster) images always have a fixed size in pixels, e.g. 300 x 240 pixels. In an uncompressed bitmap, doubling the dimensions, e.g. from 300 x 240 to 600 x 480 pixels, quadruples the size of its file because extra pixels need to be stored. This is not the case for vector graphic image files because the number of vector shape definitions remains the same no matter by what factor the image is scaled. All that changes are the property values for each shape; the file size, or computer memory requirements, remain the same.

Vector images are easy to create, read and edit

Vector graphic image files are (generally) plain text files and as such they can easily be generated by hand or as the output of user written programs. As text files, they are human-readable as well as generally free format, that is, the text can be split across lines and indented to highlight its logical structure. A vector graphic image file can be directly edited in a text editor. This is not the case with bitmap images.

Vector image has no resolution

Unlike bitmaps, vector graphic images are resolution-independent. Vector graphic images always print at the highest possible resolution of the printer that they are sent to. They also display without loss of image quality at different screen resolutions, keeping their dimensions the same, more or less.

On the other hand, when bitmapped images are printed, how they look always depends very heavily on their resolution. Even though the bitmapped image may look good on the computer screen, printing requires much higher resolution than computer screens display at. If the bitmapped image doesn't have enough pixels to print at the size required, its printed equivalent will be of poor quality.

Vector objects are reusable

It is very easy to pick an object from one vector graphic image, transform it or restyle it without any loss of quality, and then to insert it into another vector graphic.

Disadvantages of the vector graphic approach compared with the bitmapped approach

Vector graphic images are constructed from a limited number of object types, e.g. circles, rectangles, lines. There are many images that are difficult or even impossible to reproduce exactly in vector form. For example, images that require complex textures, such as human skin or hair. These images are typically present in digital photographs. For these, tasks such as colour corrections and retouching are best done in a bitmap or raster image editor such as GIMP or Photoshop. Similarly, for any image where the texture of the coloured surface is important, vector graphics' flat colours and colour gradients are insufficient whereas the bitmap approach can emulate painting in oils, pastels and watercolours when done in a specialised raster tool such as ArtRage or Corel Painter.

Key fact

Disadvantages of the vector graphics approach compared with the bitmapped approach:

There are many images that are difficult or even impossible to reproduce exactly in vector form:

- Images that require complex textures such as human skin
- Where the texture of the coloured surface is important such as when emulating painting in oils, pastels and watercolours.

Questions

 State **two** disadvantages that vector graphics has compared with bitmapped graphics.

Appropriate uses of vector graphics

Vector graphics are appropriate to use when the task is a drawing one. For example, when producing charts, diagrams, cartoons, maps, illustrations, typography of all kinds, leaflets, posters, web graphics, etcetera, because these can all be constructed from shape and text objects.

Appropriate uses of bitmapped graphics

Bitmapped graphics are best suited to capturing a record of the real world such as in photographic images or where the task is a painting one because they can represent texture in a realistic way.

Key fact

Appropriate uses of vector graphics:

Vector graphics are appropriate to use when the task is a drawing one, e.g. maps.

Appropriate uses of bitmapped graphics:

Bitmapped graphics are best suited to capturing a record of the real world such as in photographic images because they can represent texture in a realistic way.

Questions

 For what type of use is vector graphics appropriate and why?

 For what type of use is bitmapped graphics appropriate and why?

In this chapter you have covered:

- Comparing the vector graphics approach with bitmapped graphics approach
- The advantages and disadvantages of each approach
- Appropriate uses of each approach

Learning objectives:

- *Describe the digital representation of sound in terms of:*
  - *sample resolution*
  - *sampling rate and Nyquist theorem.*
- *Calculate sound sample sizes in bytes*

5.6.7 Digital representation of sound

Classification of waveforms

Periodic and aperiodic

It is useful when working with sounds to graph their waveforms (amplitude of air pressure, or voltage from a microphone, as a function of time). *Figure 5.6.7.1(a)* shows the waveform of the sound "Laa" spoken into a microphone. *Figure 5.6.7.1(b)* shows the waveform of white noise, the sort of sound heard from an analogue radio not tuned to any radio station.

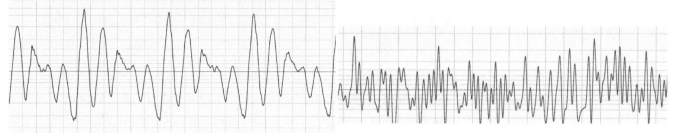

Figure 5.6.7.1(a) "Laa" sound recording

Figure 5.6.7.1(b) White noise sound recording

Key concept

Frequency of a sound:
The pitch of a sound is what humans perceive as frequency. Frrequency is measured as the number of cycles per second of a repeating pattern in a periodic waveform or vibration or oscillation. Its unit is the Hz which is one cycle per second.

Sounds are caused by vibrations or oscillations of a column of air in a woodwind instrument or in a stretched string such as a violin or guitar string when bowed or plucked.

The waveform in *Figure 5.6.7.1(a)* consists of a repeating pattern called a periodic oscillation, with maybe a few minor deviations. This is characteristic of sounds that have pitch. Pitch is what humans perceive as frequency and recognise by its position in a range of audible frequencies that range from low to high. The pitch of a sound is varied when you sing or whistle a song melody. Musicians use a notation for indicating the pitch of a sound to be played.

The waveform in *Figure 5.6.7.1(b)* does not repeat in time (aperiodic) because it is essentially random in nature.

Waveforms are broadly divided into two classes:

1. periodic (repeat in time)
2. aperiodic (don't repeat in time)

The first class is subdivided into simple (sinusoidal) and complex (non-sinusoidal) waveforms. It turns out that these complex (non-sinusoidal) waveforms are composed of sinusoidal waveforms of different frequencies and amplitudes added together. This means that complex waveforms can be synthesised by selecting the right sinusoids to add together.

The second class is subdivided into impulsive (occur once) and noise (continuous but random) waveforms.

Sinusoids

If we imagine the red dot inside the circle in Figure 5.6.7.2 is a cyclist cycling round the circle at constant speed of, say, one complete loop of the circle per minute then we are imagining a periodic system because it has a repeating pattern. If we were to lie down in the plane of the circle, i.e. view the circle sidewise-on, then looking along the time axis across the page we would see the vertical distance of the cyclist from this axis vary in time as shown in red. Mathematically, this waveform is called a sine waveform or sine wave.

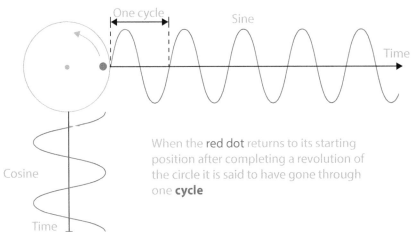

When the **red dot** returns to its starting position after completing a revolution of the circle it is said to have gone through one **cycle**

Figure 5.6.7.2 Generating sinusoids - sine and cosine waveforms

If we look along the time axis going down the page we see the vertical distance of the cyclist from this new axis also vary in time as shown in red. Mathematically, this waveform is called a cosine waveform or cosine wave. Both sine and cosine waveforms are called sinusoids. A sinusoid is characterised by three quantities:

1. Peak amplitude or just amplitude which is the maximum vertical distance of the waveform from the time axis. In circle terms this is the radius of the circular path that the cyclist follows.

2. Frequency which in circle terms is the number of cycles of the circle per second, e.g. 60 loops of the circle per second. In pitch or frequency terms it is expressed in Hz, e.g. 60 Hz.

3. Phase which in circle terms is where the red dot starts. Conventionally, this is measured in angle from the time axis, e.g. for the sine waveform time axis, angle = 0 degrees; for the cosine waveform time axis this is 90 degrees.

Task

To see a demonstration of generating a sinusoid from circular motion visit http://treeblurb.com/dev_math/sin_canv00.html

Task

Download and install SFS/ESynth from https://www.phon.ucl.ac.uk/resource/sfs/esynth.php Experiment with generating sinusoids using ESythn.

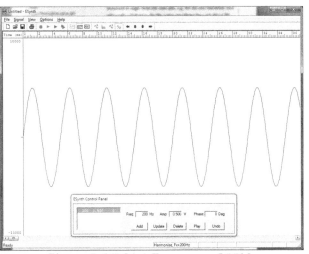

Figure 5.6.7.3(a) Frequency 200Hz, amplitude 0.5, phase 0 degrees

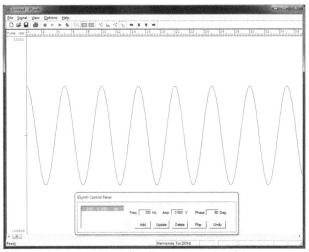

Figure 5.6.7.3(b) Frequency 200Hz, amplitude 0.5, phase 90 degrees

Figure 5.6.7.3 shows waveforms generated by ESynth with frequency 200 Hz, amplitude 0.5 and phases 0 and 90 degrees.

Sampling a waveform

Sampling rate and bit depth (sample resolution)

We have learned that the term periodic refers to any waveform that can be described in terms of going round in a circle.

Figure 5.6.7.4 shows one cycle of a sine wave generated along the time axis by recording the vertical distance of the clock hand from this axis in time. The clock hand rotates anticlockwise and the recording starts when this hand is pointing along the time axis (phase = 0 degrees).

To create a sine-wave generator (oscillator) in a digital computer all that is needed is to store, at successive intervals of time, the vertical distance of the clock hand from the time axis. This is called sampling.

The positions marked in red on the clock face indicate the moments in time when the vertical distance is sampled.

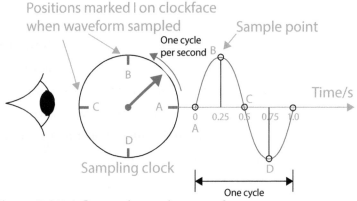

Let's suppose that the clock hand rotates at **1** revolution per second, i.e. 1Hz, then in one revolution **4** samples are taken at A, B, C and D, measured and recorded, i.e. a sampling rate of **4** samples per second (4 Hz).

Each measurement made by the digital computer is stored in binary. This is the process of quantisation. The number of binary digits used for each measurement is called the bit depth. Bit depth is one way of specifying sample resolution.

Figure 5.6.7.5 shows the first stage in the process of generating a sine wave digitally with Adobe® Audition CC 2015. At this stage, the sampling rate is set at **44100** Hz and the bit depth at **16** bits.

Figure 5.6.7.4 Generating a sine wave by the circle method and sampling it 4 times per cycle

<div class="key-concept">

Key concept

Sampling rate:
Sampling rate or sampling frequency is the number of samples taken per second.

Bit depth:
Bit depth or sampling resolution is the number of bits allocated to each sample.

</div>

Figure 5.6.7.5 Setting sampling rate and bit depth

Figure 5.6.7.6 shows sampling occurring at a rate of **8** samples per cycle. If the clockhand rotates at **1** revolution per second then the sampling rate is **8** samples per second, i.e. one sample every ⅛ second.

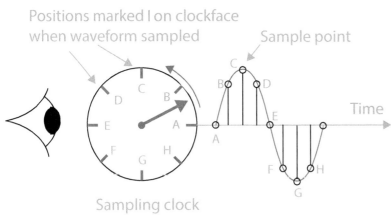

Positions marked I on clockface when waveform sampled

Sample point

Time

Sampling clock

Figure 5.6.7.6 Generating a sine wave by the circle method and sampling it 8 times per cycle

To convey an important point about sampling frequency Figure 5.6.7.7 and Figure 5.6.7.8 have been simplified by omitting any filtering which would normally be applied during the reconstruction process.

Figure 5.6.7.7 One cycle of reconstructed wave, sampling rate 4 samples per second

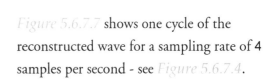

Sample point

Time

Figure 5.6.7.7 shows one cycle of the reconstructed wave for a sampling rate of **4** samples per second - see Figure 5.6.7.4.

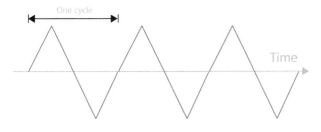

One cycle

Time

Figure 5.6.7.8 Three cycles of reconstructed wave

Figure 5.6.7.8 shows several cycles of the reconstructed wave for a sampling rate of **4** samples per second. It is still periodic with a frequency of 1 Hz, the same frequency as the original sine wave. However, its shape is no longer a sine wave. The waveform is now triangular in shape. We need to sample at a higher rate to get a better approximation to a sine wave - see Figure 5.6.7.6.

Key concept

Jean Baptiste Joseph Fourier (1768-1830), introduced the concept by which a signal can be synthesised by adding up its constituent frequencies.

He introduced the concept of frequency for elementary signals that belong to a set of sinusoidal signals (sines and cosines) with various periods of repetition.

However, if this triangular waveform was played through a sound card and loudspeakers it would still have a pitch of 1 Hz (we would need to work with higher frequencies to make a sound that the ear would perceive in a tone-like way, e.g. 200 Hz) but it would sound different from a sine wave of the same frequency. We say that its timbre is different. Higher frequencies have been added which are whole number multiples of the frequency with which the waveform repeats. These are called harmonics. The repetition frequency of the waveform is called the fundamental frequency.

The triangular waveform is thus made up of a fundamental frequency plus harmonics of the fundamental frequency. Figure 5.6.7.9 shows that adding two harmonics, $3f$ and $5f$ to the fundamental frequency f in just the right amounts and phase produces a triangle-like waveform.

Figure 5.6.7.10 shows a screenshot of a triangle-like waveform being synthesised in ESynth using a fundamental of 200 Hz and harmonics of 600 Hz and 1000 Hz. Joseph Fourier was the first person to realise that complex periodic waveforms could be synthesised in this way.

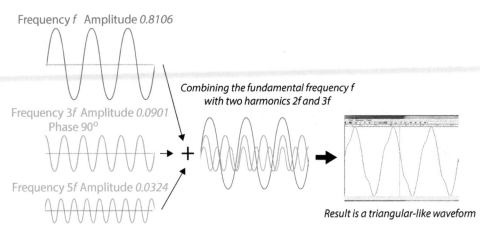

Frequency *f* Amplitude *0.8106*

Frequency *3f* Amplitude *0.0901* Phase *90°*

Frequency *5f* Amplitude *0.0324*

Combining the fundamental frequency *f* with two harmonics *2f* and *3f*

Result is a triangular-like waveform

Figure 5.6.7.9 Fundamental + two harmonics = triangle-like waveform

It led to the concept of bandwidth. To preserve the shape of this signal any communication system through which it passes must pass not only the fundamental frequency but also its harmonics, 600 Hz and 1000 Hz, i.e. frequencies located in the band 0 to 1000 Hz.

Lower limit on sampling rate - Nyquist's theorem
We have seen that to achieve a better approximation to the original signal we need to sample at a higher rate but is there a lower limit? The answer is yes. Figure 5.6.7.11 shows a **2.5 Hz**

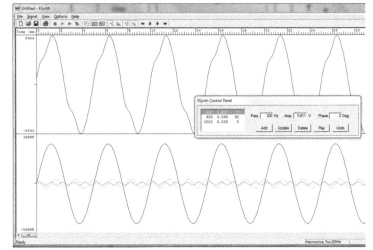

Figure 5.6.7.10 ESynth screenshot

sine waveform sampled at **4 samples per second (4 Hz)**. The sampling points in the sampling cycle are A, B, C, D.

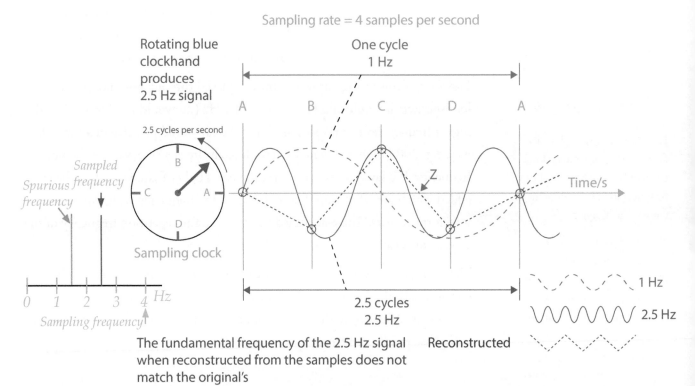

The fundamental frequency of the 2.5 Hz signal when reconstructed from the samples does not match the original's

Figure 5.6.7.11 Sampling a waveform at a sampling frequency which is less than twice the waveform's frequency results in an alias (spurious) frequency replacing the sampled waveform's frequency

168

Key principle

Nyquist's theorem:
When sampling a (complex) periodic waveform, we must sample at twice the highest frequency present in the waveform, at least, if all the frequencies present in the (complex) periodic waveform are to be preserved.

Task

Sampling a rotating image at too low a frequency can result in the rotating image appearing to rotate at a lower frequency than it actually is.
Try observing rotating ceiling fan blades whilst blinking your eyes. The fan blades may appear to rotate at a lower frequency than they really are. We call the false frequency of rotation a spurious frequency. It is a consequence of Nyquist's theorem.

However, the waveform constructed from these samples has a repeating pattern frequency which is not **2.5 Hz**. Its frequency is approximately **1.25 Hz**. This is an artifact called a spurious or alias frequency, i.e. one that does not really exist. This known as aliasing. However, the waveform that could be constructed from samples of the **1 Hz** sine waveform (red dotted curve) does have a repeating pattern frequency of 1 Hz.

It turns out that when sampling a (complex) periodic waveform, we must sample at twice the highest frequency present in the waveform, at least, if all the frequencies present in the (complex) periodic waveform are to be preserved. This is known as Nyquist's theorem. Figure 5.6.7.12 illustrates this with a sinusoid (cosine waveform) of frequency 1 Hz. The sampling rate is twice this at 2 samples per second but it is still possible to construct a waveform with fundamental frequency, 1 Hz, the same frequency as the original.

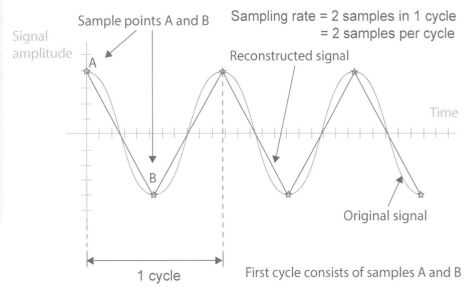

Figure 5.6.7.12 Applying Nyquist's theorem, sampling rate is at least twice highest frequency in waveform

Questions

1. Explain the terms (a) sampling rate (b) bit depth or sample resolution.

2. An analogue waveform made up of the following sinusoids with frequencies 1 kHz, 5 kHz, and 10 kHz is sampled and the samples digitised. When the digitised result is processed, it is discovered that it is made up of sinusoids with frequencies, 1 kHz, 5 kHz and 7.5 kHz but not 10 kHz. Suggest the most likely reason why this has happened and suggest one possible solution.

3. Why are music CDs recorded at a sampling rate of **44100** samples per second?

4. State Nyquist's theorem.

Nyquist's theorem and recording sound

Music CDs are recorded at a sampling rate of **44100** samples per second for a good reason. The human ear is capable of hearing sound over a frequency range of **20 Hz to 20 kHz** with its greatest sensitivity to frequencies between **2000** and **5000** Hz. Thus the sampling rate at which music is recorded for music CD production is greater than the minimum sampling frequency according to Nyquist's theorem. A note from a violin pitched at **2000** Hz still must be sampled at **44100** samples per second because what makes the note sound like a violin note are the harmonic frequencies that are also present. This is called the quality of the note or timbre that distinguishes it from other

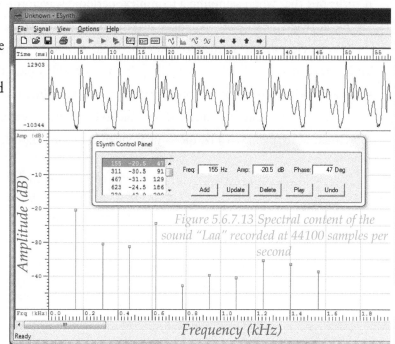

Figure 5.6.7.13 Spectral content of the sound "Laa" recorded at 44100 samples per second

sounds of the same pitch and volume, e.g. a violin note from a trumpet note. The fundamental plus harmonics of a sound are called the spectral content. *Figure 5.6.7.13* shows the spectral content of a recording of the sound "Laa". A Discrete Fourier Transform(DFT) has been applied to the recorded waveform to reveal a fundamental at **155** Hz and 22 harmonics, some of which are not displayed because their amplitude is too small. The highest harmonic frequency is **3895** Hz. Fourier analysis is the process of finding which sine waves need to be added together to make a particular waveform shape. The DFT works with digital samples. If the sound "Laa" had been sampled at, say **4000** samples per second, which is not at least twice the frequency of the highest frequency and ten other harmonics, the recording would have been distorted by including frequencies not in the original - see *Figure 5.6.7.11*.

Calculate sound sample sizes in bytes - See *Chapter 5.6.3*.

In this chapter you have covered:

■ The digital representation of sound in terms of:
- sample resolution or bit depth which is the number of bits allocated to each sample.
- sampling rate or sampling frequency is the number of samples taken per second.
- Nyquist theorem -when sampling a (complex) periodic waveform, we must sample at twice the highest frequency present in the waveform, at least, if all the frequencies present in the (complex) periodic waveform are to be preserved. If we don't then spurious(false) frequencies appear called alias frequencies and their corresponding original frequencies do not.

Key principle

MIDI: MIDI stands for Musical Instrument Digital Interface. It is a hardware and software specification for the exchange of information (musical notes, expression control, etc) between different musical instruments or other devices such as sequencers, computers, lighting controllers, etc.

Korg Wavestation synthesiser emulator running on Windows 7

USB cable

5.6.8 Musical Instrument Digital Interface(MIDI)

What is MIDI?

MIDI stands for Musical Instrument Digital Interface. It is a hardware/ software protocol adopted in the 1980s to enable electronic instruments to communicate with each other using the same set of agreed-upon codes and numbers. For example, a Korg keyboard (MIDI controller) can instruct suitable software running on a computer (MIDI instrument) to play a note by sending the software a "Note On" message. *Figure 5.6.8.1* shows a Korg MIDI 61-key keyboard connected via USB (using a USB-MIDI driver) to a computer running an emulator for a Korg synthesiser called Wavestation.

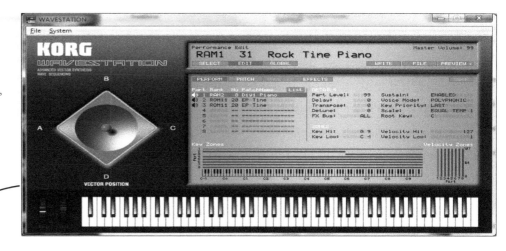

Figure 5.6.8.1 Korg 61-key keyboard connected to Korg's Wavestation synthesiser emulator

Information

Introduction to computer music:

http://www.indiana.edu/~emusic/etext/toc.shtml

Pressing a key on the Korg keyboard sends a message to the computer program to play the note corresponding to this key. A note number is assigned to each key on a MIDI keyboard. For the keyboard in *Figure 5.6.8.1*, note numbering starts at **36** and runs consecutively up to **95** as shown in *Figure 5.6.8.2*.

MIDI note number **60** has been assigned to middle C on this keyboard. Note, number **60** corresponds to frequency **261.63** Hz but the MIDI specification allows this mapping to be changed.

Table 5.6.8.1 shows the usual correspondence between MIDI note number and frequency for this and some other MIDI note numbers. The name given to each note is also shown. Note that musical pitch (note frequency) is not embedded in any way in MIDI Note messages, thereby allowing mapping from note number to pitch to be changed. Nor is note name tied to a specific frequency (tuning a musical instrument adjusts frequency).

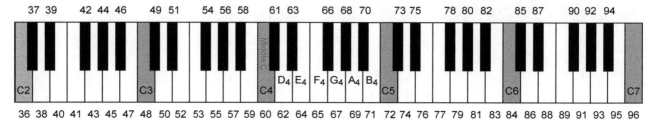

Figure 5.6.8.2 Some notes from an octave (white and grey keys only), their MIDI note number and one possible assignment of frequencies

MIDI note no	60	62	64	65	67	69	71	72
Frequency Hz	261.63	293.67	329.63	349.23	392.00	440	493.88	523.25
Note name	C4	D4	E4	F4	G4	A4	B4	C5

Table 5.6.8.1 MIDI note no, its usual corresponding frequency in Hz and its usual note name

MIDI itself does not make sound. It is just a series of messages to turn notes on and off, etc. These messages are interpreted by a MIDI instrument to produce sound. A MIDI instrument can be a piece of hardware (a synthesizer) or a software tool (Wavestation emulator, MuLab, Logic Pro).

The most common tool used to generate MIDI messages is an electronic keyboard. These messages may be routed to a digital synthesiser inside the keyboard or they may be patched (wired) to some other MIDI instrument such as a computer running synthesiser software. Almost all MIDI devices are equipped to receive MIDI messages on one or more of 16 selectable MIDI Channel numbers, labelled 1 to 16 (supports "multi-timbral" performance).

MIDI messages

The most common MIDI messages are Voice Channel messages. Voice Channel messages convey information about whether to turn a note on or off on a particular channel, what instrument sound to change to, and so on.

Voice Channel MIDI messages consist of two or three bytes as shown in *Figure 5.6.8.3* (Status byte followed by one or two Data bytes). For the serial hardware interface, each byte is surrounded by a start bit and a stop bit, making each packet 10 bits long. Within a MIDI software system data is 8-bit bytes. The first byte, called the Status byte, takes on values ranging from 0x80 to 0xFF in hexadecimal or 128 to 255 in decimal - most significant bit (MSB) is '1'. The Data bytes, take on values in the range 0x00 to 0x7F or 0 to 127 - most significant bit of each byte is a '0'.

The transmission bit rate of the hardware interface in the MIDI standard is 31,250 bits per second. Therefore, one start bit, eight data bits, and one stop bit result in a maximum transmission rate of 3125 bytes per second.

MIDI uses the fact that the Status byte is in a different range from the Data bytes. If MSB = 1, the byte is a "Status" byte. If MSB = 0, the byte is a "Data" byte. The first four bits of a Status byte are the code for the command, and the last four bits the channel to which the command applies (e.g. 0000_2 is Channel 1, 1111_2 is Channel 16).

Information

Octave:

The range from C4 to C5 is an octave. The grey keys indicate the musical interval of an octave (12 semitones) between notes. An octave has the property that the ratio of the frequencies at the ends of the range is 2:1. In equal temperament, an octave is defined to be 12 equal semitones in the modern scale. Each semitone therefore has a ratio of $2^{1/12}$ (approximately 1.059). Note A4 is assigned frequency 440 Hz. Therefore, the frequency of the nth semitone above or below A4 is

$$2^{n/12} \times 440 \text{ Hz.}$$

For example, when a key is pressed, the keyboard creates a "Note On" (Status byte = 0x91, 145_{10}, 10010001_2) message for Channel 2 consisting of three bytes, e.g. **145 45 100**. The first four bits of the Status byte (1001_2) tell MIDI that the message is a Note On command, while the last four bits tell MIDI what MIDI channel the message is for (0001_2= MIDI Channel 2).

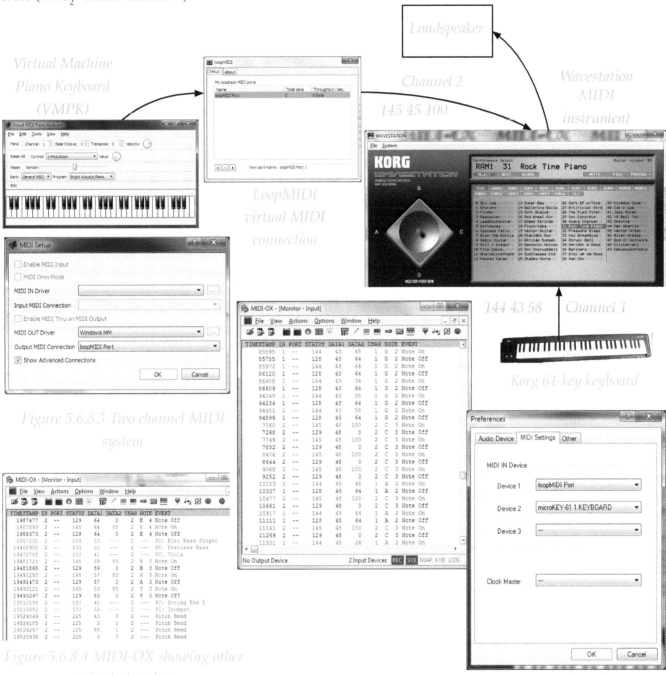

Virtual Machine Piano Keyboard (VMPK)

LoopMIDI virtual MIDI connection

Loudspeaker

Channel 2

145 45 100

Wavestation MIDI instrument

Figure 5.6.8.3 Two channel MIDI system

144 43 58

Channel 1

Korg 61-key keyboard

Figure 5.6.8.4 MIDI-OX showing other status byte values

The second byte, the nore number **60**, selects the frequency used by the receiving instrument, in this example middle C (261.63 Hz). The third byte, **85**, specifies how fast the key was pressed (velocity).

Velocity is a number that is used mainly to describe the volume (gain) of a MIDI note (higher velocity = greater volume or loudness) because it refers to how hard a key was pressed. The harder a key is pressed the greater will be the volume or loudness but the mapping is performed by the receiving instrument.

Information

MIDI-OX:

http://www.midiox.com/

Information

VMPK:

Information on VMPK can be viewed at http://vmpk.sourceforge.net/.

It can be downloaded from http://vmpk.sourceforge.net/#Download

To generate messages that use different velocities requires a MIDI keyboard. Computer keyboards are not velocity sensitive. Using a computer's keys to play notes into a software synthesiser will generate note messages that all have the same velocity.

When a key is released the keyboard creates another MIDI message, a "Note Off" message, e.g. 129 60 85. The first byte, 129, is the Status byte - the first four bits of the Status byte (1000_2) correspond to "Note Off", the second four bits (0001_2) to the channel, i.e. Channel 2 (0000 is Channel 1). The second byte is the key, 60 (middle C) in this example, and the third byte is the velocity which indicates how quickly the key was released. The MIDI instrument can use the velocity value of 85 to know how quickly it should dampen the note.

Figure 5.6.8.3 shows an on screen piano keyboard (VMPK) connected via a virtual MIDI connection (LoopMIDI) to a running copy of the Wavestation emulator. A Korg 61-key keyboard is connected via USB to the computer and Wavestation emulator. The output from Wavestation goes to a loudspeaker. The input channels 1 & 2 are monitored by a piece of software called MIDI-OX.

In *Figure 5.6.8.3* MIDI-OX shows that the "Note On" and "Note Off" Status bytes for Channel 1 have codes 144 and 128, respectively, whilst for Channel 2, these are 145 and 129, respectively. Wavestation uses the Channel values to route the messages on each Channel to different voices.

Messages can also have other purposes, e.g. to change the instrument sound. *Figure 5.6.8.4* shows messages that do this, e.g. 193 41 which is a two-byte code to change the MIDI instrument for Channel 2 (code 193 - 1100 0001_2, 1100_2 is the change code and 0001_2 is the Channel) to a viola (code 41). Such messages are control messages.

Pitch Bend (control to vary pitch) is another type of control message that a MIDI controller can send, e.g. 225 43 0 (*Figure 5.6.8.4*), causes pitch bend in a Channel 2 note. For Channel 1 the same control message would use a leading byte with value 224 (1110 0000_2). There are many more ways to control the playing of a note and each has a corresponding control code.

The playing of multiple notes "together" events in MIDI are sent as a string of serial commands so, for example, a 2-note chord will be transmitted as two separate messages, *Status(Note On, Ch 1) key1-velocity Status(Note On, Ch 1) key2-velocity* unless the synthesiser supports Running Status. In this case, a single Status byte's action is allowed to persist for an unlimited number of Data byte pairs which follow.

MIDI messages

A MIDI message is the means by which an event in one system, e.g. key pressed on a keyboard, is communicated or transported to another to produce an event in the receiving system, e.g. a synthesiser plays a note.

Keyboard-event → MIDI message → synthesiser event.

For example, the "Note On" message sent by a MIDI controller to a MIDI instrument causes an event to take place, i.e. the synthesiser plays the note

```
While True
  Do
    Wait for message
    Process message
```

Figure 5.6.8.5 Event handler

specified in the message by note number. The Virtual MIDI Piano Keyboard shown in *Figure 5.6.8.3* is a MIDI events generator and receiver. Event-driven systems rely upon a piece of software called an *event handler* which consists of a non-terminating loop that "sleeps" when there are no messages to process, i.e. is suspended - *Figure 5.6.8.5* - and springs into action when there is (in Chuck the loop takes the form of a "polling loop").

Extension material

Chuck is an open-source and freely available programming language for real-time sound synthesis and music creation. *Figure 5.6.8.6* shows an event handler written in Chuck.

```
MidiIn midiIn; //create an event object
0 => int port; // select MIDI port 0
if( !midiIn.open(port) ) // if MIDI port 0 not open exit
    {
        <<< "Error: MIDI port did not open on port: ", port >>>;
        me.exit();
    }
MidiMsg msg; // makes object to hold next MIDI message
Wurley piano => dac; // select Wurley piano to play with MIDI controller
while( true ) // loop forever
{
    midiIn => now; // wait on MIDI event, shred suspended but time advances
    while( midiIn.recv(msg) )
    {
        if (msg.data1 == 144) //check that status byte = 144 which is Note On Channel 1
        {
            Std.mtof(msg.data2) => piano.freq; //convert MIDI no to corresp. frequency
            msg.data3/127.0 => piano.gain; //set piano gain (data3 in range 0 to 127)
            1 => piano.noteOn; //trigger note on
        }
        else //status byte not equal to 144 so switch note off
        {
            1 => piano.noteOff; //trigger note off
        }
```
Figure 5.6.8.6 Event handler written in Chuck programming language
```
    }
}
```

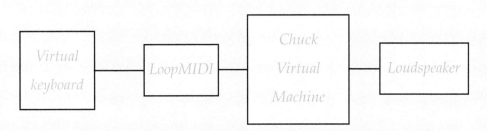

Figure 5.6.8.7 Playing music via an executing Chuck event handling program

Figure 5.6.8.7 shows the use of VMPK virtual piano connected via LoopMIDI to the running Chuck event handler shown in *Figure 5.6.8.6*. The output of the Chuck program is sent to a loudspeaker connected to the computer.

Advantages of using MIDI files for representing music

MIDI consists of a series of event messages that instruct a MIDI controlled instrument how to play music. These messages can be stored in a file before being read from the file and transmitted serially byte by byte to a MIDI-controlled instrument.

This has four main advantages over audio data produced from analogue sounds by sampling thousands of times per second and recording the digitised samples (sounds) in, for example, a .wav file.

- compact compared to sampled audio data. With MIDI, an entire song can be stored within a few hundred MIDI messages saving on memory whilst the equivalent sampled audio data would occupy many more bytes, possibly millions

- easy to modify/manipulate notes, e.g. change pitch, duration, and other parameters without having to record the sounds again which would be the case with sampled audio data recordings

- easy to change instruments - MIDI only describes which notes to play, these notes can be sent to any instrument to change the overall sound of the composition whilst with sampled audio data the sampling and recording process would have to be repeated

- it offers a simple means to compose and notate algorithmically which sampled audio does not. MIDI data is mostly a glorified note list, and such lists can easily be generated by code, and translated as needed into MIDI, whether for live output or via a MIDI file.

Questions

1. What is MIDI?

2. "MIDI itself does not make sound". Explain this statement.

3. The following MIDI message consisting of three bytes is generated when a key is pressed on a MIDI keyboard: 144 60 64
Explain the purpose of each of three bytes.

4. Note On is one example of a MIDI message. Give **three** other examples, each must be a different type.

5. Explain the statements "A MIDI keyboard is an events generator" and "MIDI messages are associated with events". What is the fundamental structure of event-handling software such as that found running in a MIDI instrument?

6. State **three** main advantages of MIDI file representation of music over audio data file representation, e.g. .wav file

In this chapter you have covered:

- The purpose of MIDI - to instruct via messages a MIDI controlled instrument how to make sound, e.g. Note On, Note Off, pitch, duration of note, loudness

- The use of event messages in MIDI - MIDI controller sends messages to a MIDI controlled instrument to turn notes on and off, etc. These are events that a MIDI controlled instrument responds to. It waits in a loop for messages and then acts on these received messages accordingly

- The advantages of using MIDI files for representing music - compact, easy to modify/manipulate and change instruments compared with sampled audio data stored in, e.g., .wav files

Key principle

Compression:

Data can be compressed because its original representation is not the shortest possible. The original data has redundancies and compressing the data reduces or eliminates these redundancies.

Non-random data is non-random because it has structure in the form of regular patterns. It is this structure that is the cause of redundancy in the data. Random data has no structure and therefore has no redundancy. Therefore, random data cannot be compressed.

■ 5.6.9 Data compression

Why are images, sound files and other files compressed?

There are two main reasons why files are compressed:

- To reduce the amount of storage space required to store the data

- To reduce the time taken to transmit the data because fewer bytes need to be transmitted.

Essentially, the purpose of data compression is to squeeze the data into a smaller number of bytes than the data would occupy if uncompressed.

For example, text may be compressed by replacing each common character/letter combination with a single byte-coded integer number from *Table 5.6.9.1*.

Integer Code	Character Combination
1	'TH'
2	'BL'
3	'CK'
4	'AT'
5	'ON'

Table 5.6.9.1 Codes for common character combinations

Uncompressed text = 'THE BLACK CAT SAT ON A MAT'

Compressed text = '1E 2A3 C4 S4 5 A M4.'

If each character in the uncompressed text is coded in one byte (including spaces and full stop) then this text requires 27 bytes of storage. For the compressed text the storage requirement is just 20 bytes, a saving of seven bytes. This represents a 26% saving, approximately.

Not every file can be compressed significantly, in fact most files cannot.

Beyond A level

Suppose that we arbitrarily but quite reasonably decide that significantly means at least 50% or greater, i.e. an n-bit file should be compressed to one of length $n/2$ or less. There are 2^n of these n-bit files. The number of $n/2$ bit compressed files will be $2^{n/2}$, the number of $n/2 - 1$ bit compressed files will be $2^{n/2 - 1}$, ..., the number of 2-bit files will be $2^2 = 4$, the number of 1-bit files will be 2.

Total number of compressed files, $S = 2 + 4 + ... + 2^{n/2} = 2^{1 + n/2} - 2 \approx 2^{1 + n/2}$

For n = 800 bits (100 bytes), the total number of different files is 2^{800} and the number of files that can be compressed by at least 50% or more is 2^{51}.

The fraction of compressed files is thus $2^{51}/2^{800} = 2^{-749} \approx 3 \times 10^{-226}$. This is an extremely small number. Further analysis shows that no compression method can compress all files or even a significant percentage of them.

The redundancies in data depend on the type of data (text, images, audio, etc) which is why different compression methods have been developed. Each works best with a particular data type.

Questions

1. What does it mean to compress data?

2. Why is it possible to compress data that has structure without losing information?

3. Give two reasons why files are compressed.

4. Can random data be compressed?

5. Why is it necessary to have different compression methods?

Key principle

Lossless and lossy compression:
Data is how information is represented.
It is possible using compression to alter the representation without losing information - this is called **lossless compression**.
It is also possible using compression to alter the representation and lose information - this is called **lossy compression**.

Key concept

Lossless compression and redundancy:
In general, information can be compressed if it is redundant. Lossless compression is possible when information is redundant.

Key concept

Lossy compression and irrelevancy:
Even when no redundancy exists it is still possible to compress by removing irrelevant information, e.g. removing image features to which the eye is not sensitive.

What are the differences between lossless and lossy compression?

Lossless compression

In lossless compression, the compression algorithm does not remove information from the original uncompressed data only redundancies. This allows the original uncompressed data to be restored by reversing the process. Lossless compression is used for text because it must be compressed without any loss of information. Imagine uncompressing an essay that you wrote for an assignment and finding that it looked nothing like the original that you spent hours constructing.

Lossy compression

In lossy compression, the compression algorithm may remove information which is irrelevant from the original uncompressed data. For example, in audio data, harmonics to which the human ear is not sensitive may be removed because they are not important to the listener. However, this means that the original uncompressed data cannot be fully restored when the reverse process is carried out. This does not matter for most images, video and audio data because these can tolerate much loss of data when compressed and later decompressed. Some exceptions are text files, executable files, and medical X-ray images where artefacts introduced into lossy compressed images could matter.

Advantages and disadvantages of lossless and lossy compression

Better compression ratios can be achieved with lossy compression than with lossless compression. Compression ratio is the size of the compressed file as a fraction of the uncompressed file, e.g. 50% expressed as a percentage.

This means that data compressed with a lossy compression method will occupy less storage space than with a lossless compression method. The time taken to transmit the data will also be less, e.g loading a file from disk.

However, a disadvantage with lossy compression is that the lost data are not retrievable. The compressed data will have very limited potential for adjustments or changes and every time the compressed data is uncompressed, edited, compressed again and saved, more data is lost.

With lossless compression the original uncompressed data is always recoverable.

Online high-quality image retailers often display their images in low quality form, i.e. they use a lossy, compressed version of high compression ratio, so potential customers can view what is on offer before purchasing. This protects against theft of data as it prevents customers from accessing and downloading a higher-quality version. It is the ability of lossy compression methods to allow the compression ratio to be varied from low to high that supports this way of marketing images. Alternative, an uncompressed or lossless version can be made available to customers on receipt of payment.

Questions

6 What is meant by lossless compression?

7 What is meant by lossy compression?

8 State **one** advantage that lossy compression has over lossless compression.

9 State **one** advantage that lossless compression has over lossy compression.

10 For each of lossless and lossy compression, give **one** example where it is used and why.

Principles of lossless compression
Run length encoding (RLE)

In run length encoding a run of contiguous bytes all with the same value can be condensed into two bytes, one byte that stores the count or run length and a second byte that stores the value in the run. These two bytes are called an RLE packet. Figure 5.6.9.1 shows run length encoding applied to a run of six contiguous bytes each of value 128.

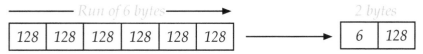

Figure 5.6.9.1 Run length encoding compression of 6 bytes into 2 bytes

RLE can be used to compress greyscale images. Each run of pixels of the same intensity (gray level) is encoded as a pair (run length pixel value). It doesn't make sense to encode a run of one and so the raw value is used. The following example shows how RLE could be applied to a greyscale bitmap that encodes the gray level of each pixel in 8 bits and that starts with the sequence

Information

Contiguous:

Means next to each other or together in sequence.

15, 15, 15, 15, 15, 15, 15, 15, 46, 81, 123, 58, 98, 98, 98, 98, 7, 7, 7, 8, ...

The compressed sequence of bytes is

8, 15, 46, 81, 123, 58, 4, 98, 3, 7, 8, ...

where the red values indicate counts. The problem is to distinguish a byte containing a greyscale value (such as 15) from one containing a count (such as 8). There are several possible solutions.

In one solution, the 256 different greyscale values are reduced to 255 so that the 256th can be used as a flag to precede every byte containing a count. Suppose this flag value is 255 then the sequence above becomes

255, 8, 15, 46, 81, 123, 58, 255, 4, 98, 255, 3, 7, 8

RLE works well with images that contain large areas of the same colour e.g. black and white images which are mostly white, such as the page of a book. This is due to the large amount of contiguous bytes that are all the same colour.

However, an image with many colours and relatively few runs of the same colour such as a photograph containing a high degree of colour variation will not lend itself to compression using RLE so well.

The direction of scan can also affect the compression ratio. For example, an image that has lots of vertical lines will not compress well if it is scanned horizontally for same-pixel runs but will if scanned vertically. A good RLE image compressor should be able to scan a bitmap by rows, columns, or in a zig-zag pattern and be able to choose the scan output that produces the best compression ratio.

Questions

11 Explain the principles of run length encoding lossless compression.

12 The following numbers, restricted to the range 0..254, represent the intensities of a contiguous block of pixels in a greyscale bitmap

15, 112, 112, 112, 98, 76, 76, 15, 46, 46, 46, 46, 46, 19, 101, 6, ...

Using run length encoding, compress this block of pixels using 255 as the flag that prefixes an RLE packet.

13 Run length encoding works well, i.e. achieves a good compression ratio, with some images but not others. Why?

14 Why is run length coding normally not a good choice for text compression?

Dictionary-based methods

We compress naturally in everyday life when, for example, referring to months of the year by number, e.g. September by the number 9. Dictionary-based methods compress by using this technique. The dictionary is a kind of look-up table, e.g. entry 9 is September. Dictionary-based compression methods vary in how the dictionary is constructed and represented but they all use the principle of replacing substrings in a text, e.g. 'th' in 'the' with a codeword, e.g. 1, that identifies that substring in a dictionary or codebook - see *Table 5.6.9.1*. The substring is called a phrase. Codewords for the dictionary are chosen so that they need less space than the phrase that they replace, thus achieving compression. The process of compression is called encoding. The reverse process is called decoding. The compressor is an encoder and the decompressor is a decoder.

If we have to use a dictionary containing a large number of entries then the overhead of storing or transmitting the dictionary is significant, and choosing which substrings to place in the dictionary to maximise compression is also difficult. The solution is to use an adaptive dictionary scheme based on methods developed by Jacob Ziv and Abraham Lempel in the 1970s.

Key concept

Token:

A unit of data written on the compressed file. A token consists of two or more fields. In LZ78, the token consists of two fields, the first is a pointer to an entry in the dictionary and the second is the code of a symbol, e.g. "A".

A token is sometimes written surrounded by chevrons < and > e.g. <2, A>

In the 1978, Ziv and Lempel described a dictionary-based algorithm (LZ78) that encodes a phrase (substring) of n characters from the input in a codeword that points back to an earlier phrase in the input which it matches in all but the last character, e.g. the B in BA matches B at position 2 in the example shown in Figure 5.6.9.2 so is encoded as the two-field token 2, A. The first field of the token is the pointer 2 and the second the code of the symbol, e.g. ASCII A.

The dictionary starts empty with the empty string at position 0 (not shown in Figure 5.6.9.2). As substrings or phrases are read and encoded, phrases are added to the dictionary at positions 1, 2, and so on. For the given input string, ABAABABAA, the first phrase consisting of the single character A is added at position 1, the next, B, at position 2.

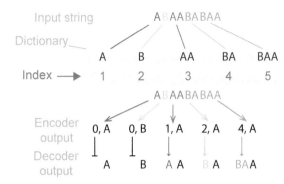

0 means no dictionary entry, i.e. nothing for a substitution

Figure 5.6.9.2 Lev-Zimpel 1978 (LZ78) compression simple example

This happens because when the first substring, A, is read from the input, no dictionary entry with the one-character string A is found, so A is added at the next available position in the dictionary which is 1, and the token 0, A is output. This token indicates the string *empty string* followed by A.

The next symbol read from the input is the character B but there is no entry yet in the dictionary for this phrase, and so B is added at position 2.

The third character read from the input, is A. This is matched with the A at position 1 in the dictionary. The goal of dictionary encoding is to find the longest dictionary substring that matches the input so the next symbol is read. This is another A. The dictionary is now searched for an entry containing the two-symbol string AA.

None is found, so the string AA is added to the next available position in the dictionary which is 3, and the token 1, A is output. This is the "compressed" version of the substring AA. We actually need to build up phrases in the dictionary with at least three characters before we can replace a phrase with something shorter. Figure 5.6.9.3 shows that this happens at entry 5 in the dictionary.

An efficient way of representing the dictionary is a tree-like structure called a trie as shown in Figure 5.6.9.3 which grows as more characters of the input are processed. All strings that start with the empty string (dictionary index 0) are added as children of the root which is labelled 0.

In the example, all strings that begin with A are located in the subtree with node labelled 1 (index 1 in the dictionary).

All strings that begin with B are located in the subtree with root labelled 2.

All strings that begin with AA are located in subtree with root labelled 3 and so on.

The example in Figure 5.6.9.2 is too trivial to achieve a reduction in the number of bytes (assuming each character is represented in one byte). We need a much longer input string to achieve compression.

The dictionary shown in Figure 5.6.9.2 and Figure 5.6.9.3 is constructed as the input string is parsed (processed). This dictionary is empty when the first

Information

Trie:

A tree data structure in which the string of characters represented by node n is the sequence of characters along the path from the root to n. Given a string, the trie consists of nodes for exactly those substrings that are prefixes of some other substring.

The word 'trie' comes from the middle of the word 'retrieval'.

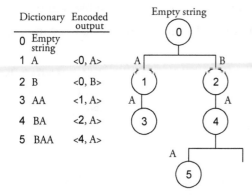

Dictionary		Encoded output
0	Empty string	
1	A	<0, A>
2	B	<0, B>
3	AA	<1, A>
4	BA	<2, A>
5	BAA	<4, A>

Figure 5.6.9.3 Data structure for LZ78 coding - numbers in nodes refer to dictionary index

character, A, of the input string is read. The characters about to be encoded are used to traverse the tree until the path is blocked, either because there is no onward path for the current character or because a leaf is reached.

The node at which the block occurs gives the index/phrase number to be used in the output, e.g. 1 in <1, A>.

A new node, e.g. 3, is added and joined by a new branch to the node at which the block occurred.

The new branch is labelled with the last character of current string, e.g. A.

For example, suppose we append BAB to the input string to form the new input ABAABABABAA**BAB**. We need to add a new node 6 to *Figure 5.6.9.3* and connect it to node 4. The path from node 4 to node 6 is labelled BAB.

The encoder output is now the string of tokens

0, A 0, B 1, A 2, A 4, A 4, B

If we extend the input with BABB to form input ABAABABAABAB**BABB** the encoder output is now the string of tokens

0, A 0, B 1, A 2, A 4, A 4, B 6, B

The compressed form (ignoring commas which have been included to aid readability) occupies less space than the uncompressed form, 14 bytes compared with 16 bytes.

On decoding, the decoder reconstructs the tree data structure so it can decode the token string - *Figure 5.6.9.4*.

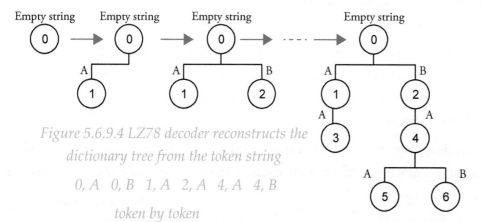

Figure 5.6.9.4 LZ78 decoder reconstructs the dictionary tree from the token string

0, A 0, B 1, A 2, A 4, A 4, B

token by token

Our examples have used an alphabet of two symbols A and B but what if the alphabet of symbols was A, B, C, D, E?

The tree data structure dictionary would then consist of a root for the empty string and then all strings that start with the empty string (strings for which the token pointer is zero) are added to the tree as children of the root. *Figure 5.6.9.5* shows the dictionary tree for the input string ABAAEACBDCBBDE.

Figure 5.6.9.5 LZ78 coding dictionary tree constructed for ABAAEACBDCBBDE

Dictionary		Encoded output
0	Empty string	
1	A	<0, A>
2	B	<0, B>
3	AA	<1, A>
4	E	<0, E>
5	C	<0, C>
6	BD	<2, D>
7	CB	<5, B>
8	BDE	<6, E>

Using the token structure <pointer, symbol> the output of the encoder for this input string is,

<0, A> <0, B> <1, A> <0, E> <0, A> <0, C> <2, D> <5, B> <6, E>

Questions

15 Explain the principles of dictionary-based lossless compression.

16 This tree data structure was created when encoding a string using a dictionary-based lossless compression technique.

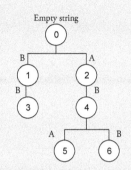

(a) What is the dictionary?

(b) What was the input if the encoded output was

<0, B>, <0, A>, <1, B>, <2, B>, <0, B>, <1, B> <4, A> <4, B>

17 The output from a dictionary-based encoder is

<0, B> <1, B> <0, A> <1, B> <3, A> <1, D> <1, A> <2, B>

Draw the dictionary tree for this output and then decode the output.

In this chapter you have covered:

■ Why images and sound files are often compressed and that other files, such as text files, can also be compressed

- to reduce the amount of storage space required to store the data

- to reduce the time taken to transmit the data

■ The differences between lossless and lossy compression and the advantages and disadvantages of each

- In lossless compression,

  ◆ the compression algorithm does not remove information from the original uncompressed data only **redundancies**

  ◆ the original uncompressed data is always recoverable.

- In lossy compression,

  ◆ the compression algorithm may remove information which is **irrelevant** from the original uncompressed data

  ◆ the original uncompressed data cannot be fully restored when the reverse process is carried out but compression ratios are higher than for lossless compression.

  ◆ limited potential for adjustments or changes and every time the compressed data is uncompressed, edited, compressed again and saved, more data is lost

■ The principles behind the techniques for lossless compression:

- run length encoding (RLE)

- dictionary-based methods

5.6.10 Encryption

What is cryptography?

Cryptography has typically concerned itself with methods of protecting information by transforming the contents of messages and documents into representations called "secret codes" that make the message and document contents incomprehensible except to those granted the means to reverse the process. A cryptosystem, or cipher, is a system or method for achieving this.

Figure 6.10.1 illustrates this with two pieces of similar-looking text, one an encrypted message and the other gobbledegook. The text on the left hand side is a message rendered incomprehensible by a process called encryption, i.e. turned into text that resembles random gibberish, whilst the text on the right hand side is random gibberish. The reverse of the encryption process is known as decryption. Decryption restores the message to a form that is comprehensible.

Encrypting a message is one way to keep the message's contents secret from others who are not authorised to view its contents. The encrypted messages look just like random gibberish as illustrated in *Figure 6.10.1*.

VWXGHQWV VKRXOG EH IDPLOLDU ZLWK WKH WHUPV FLSKHU SODLQWHAW DQG FLSKHUWHAW FDHVDU DQG YHUQDP FLSKHUV DUH DW RSSRVLWH HAWUHPHV RQH RIIHUV SHUIHFW VHFUHFB WKH RWKHU GRHVQW

LUBD YEAQJFF TEW PBDNJKFD FDSFD ND JQHD JBDCJBC EQBVAX VSS MCVN VAJGOTH HGVCCB HSXGWEFR GVCBC BCB BC W APQV VXVBBSCX YREGEVD NHEPHJVBBSP NDJ BGBWRSE SFDHJ GDHJBD MJOVQZXGT VBSH HBSV

Figure 6.10.1 A secret message and random gibberish

A cryptographer is someone who uses and studies secret codes (encrypted messages). On the other hand, someone who analyses other peoples' secret codes in order to discover the secret message is a cryptanalyst. Cryptanalysts are also known as code breakers. The most famous of code breakers is Alan Turing who during the Second World War was a key member of the team which broke the German's Enigma machine coded messages daily during World War 2, revealing important information that aided the war effort.

Key concept

Encryption:
Encryption is the process of obtaining ciphertext from plaintext.

Key concept

Decryption:
Decryption is the process of obtaining plaintext from ciphertext.

Key concept

Cipher:
The processes of encryption and decryption are called the cryptosystem or cipher.

Key point

Encoding and decoding are processes that are applied using coding systems that are publicly available and open, e.g. ASCII, whereas encrypting and decrypting are processes in a cipher system which is by definition closed to all but the participants using it to exchange secret or private messages or information.

Key concept

Caesar cipher:
The Caesar cipher is a shift cipher which shifts plaintext letters by an amount called the key to produce ciphertext.

What is encryption?

Encryption is the process of obtaining ciphertext from plaintext. Before it is encrypted, the understandable (English) text is normally referred to as plaintext and after encryption it is referred to as ciphertext. The left hand side of Figure 6.10.1 is an example of ciphertext.

The encryption process requires two inputs: the plaintext and the key.

The decryption process also requires two inputs, the ciphertext and the key, in order to produce as output the plaintext equivalent of the ciphertext.

The processes of encryption and decryption are called the cryptosystem or cipher. Thus a cryptosystem is a set of rules for converting between plaintext and ciphertext.

Codes versus ciphers

Common parlance and the media apply the term *code* to the practice and science of transforming messages in order to protect a secret when in fact the correct term is cipher.

Morse code and ASCII are examples of codes.

Morse code is a system which was designed to allow communication across a telegraph link by translating English into electrical pulse codes in a process called encoding and electrical pulse codes into English in a process called decoding. Unlike a cipher system, codes are intentionally understandable and publicly available so cannot be used to protect a secret.

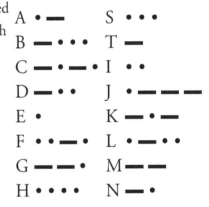

Figure 6.10.2 Sample of Morse code

Figure 6.10.2 shows a sample of Morse code. A short pulse is called a dot (•) and a long pulse a dash (—).

Caesar cipher

The ciphertext (secret message) shown in Figure 6.10.1 was produced using a cipher called the Caesar cipher, so named because it is believed that it was first used by Julius Caesar two thousand years ago. A writer at the time, Suetonius, wrote that Julius Caesar's cryptosystem replaced the plaintext letter **A** by the letter **D**, **B** by **E** and so on. The last three letters of the alphabet were replaced, respectively, by the first three letters of the alphabet. The Caesar cipher is a type of cipher called a shift cipher because the plaintext letters are shifted to produce the ciphertext.

The easiest way of visualising this is to use something called a cipher wheel or disk to convert plaintext to ciphertext. The wheel consists of an inner wheel of letters + numbers and an outer wheel of letters as shown in Figure 6.10.3.

The outer wheel in *Figure 6.10.3* is set to map the plaintext letter to its equivalent ciphertext letter, e.g. letter **A** maps to letter **D** for the current setting. The encryption key is the number on the inner wheel corresponding to the letter **A** on the outer wheel. For the current wheel setting it is the number **3**. The dot under the letter **A** in the outer wheel is to remind the user that the encryption key is the corresponding number on the inner wheel.

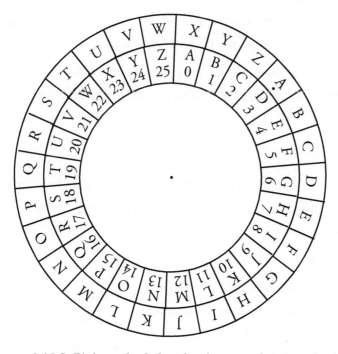

Figure 6.10.3 Cipher wheel showing inner and outer wheels

You can make your own cipher wheel by downloading copies of the inner and outer wheels from www.educational-computing.co.uk/cipherwheels and cutting out and pinning these shapes with a brad fastener or you can try an online version at https://www.khanacademy.org/computing/computer-science/cryptography/ciphers/a/ciphers-vs-codes.

How to encrypt with the cipher wheel

First write down the plaintext form of the message to be encrypted across the page, as shown below. Set the cipher wheel for the given key, let's say **3**. For each letter of the message find the corresponding letter on the outer cipher wheel then read off the corresponding letter from the inner wheel. Write this below the plaintext letter as shown below.

Decrypting with the cipher wheel

To decrypt ciphertext, first write it down as shown below. Set the cipher wheel to the key used to encrypt the plaintext. For each letter of the ciphertext, find the corresponding letter on the inner cipher wheel then read off the corresponding letter from the outer wheel. Write this below the ciphertext letter as shown below. When finished you have the decrypted message.

```
F R P S X W H U   V F L H Q F H   L V   F R R O
↓ ↓ ↓ ↓ ↓ ↓ ↓ ↓   ↓ ↓ ↓ ↓ ↓ ↓ ↓   ↓ ↓   ↓ ↓ ↓ ↓
C O M P U T E R   S C I ENC E   I S   C O O L
```

Questions

1 Convert the following plaintext message using the Caesar cipher and a key of **7**:

THE SUN HAS GOT ITS HAT ON

2 Decrypt the following ciphertext which was produced using Caeser's cipher and a key of **5**:

MNU MNU MTTWFD

3 Decrypt the ciphertext shown in the left hand side of Figure 6.10.1 which was produced by Caesar cipher using a key of **3**.

Online exercises for encryption and decryption using the Caesar cipher are available at

https://www.khanacademy.org/computing/computer-science/cryptography/ciphers/e/

Mathematical description

To describe the Caesar cipher mathematically, we represent each letter of the alphabet by an integer between **0** and **25**:

0 for A, 1 for B, …, 25 for Z as shown in *Figure 6.10.4*.

```
A  B  C  D  E  F  G  H  I  J  K  L  M  N  O  P  Q  R  S  T  U  V  W  X  Y  Z
0  1  2  3  4  5  6  7  8 9 10 11 12  13 14 15 16 17 18 19  20 21 22 23 24 25
```

Figure 6.10.4 alphabet and integer equivalent representation

To encrypt the plaintext COMPUTER SCIENCE IS COOL with key 8, first convert the plaintext letters to their integer equivalent using *Figure 6.10.4*. Next add the key **8** to each integer. If the resulting integer is **26** or greater then subtract 26 to convert 26 to 0, 27 to 1, 28 to 2, and so on, otherwise leave alone. Finally, convert each resulting integer to its equivalent letter using *Figure 6.10.4* again. The steps of the process are shown in *Figure 6.10.5*.

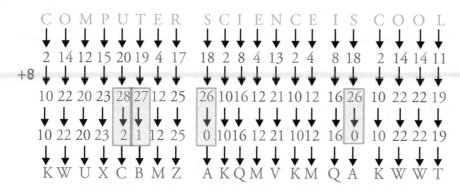

Figure 6.10.5 Encrypting with key 8

To decrypt the ciphertext KWUXCBMZ AHQMVKM QA KWWT with key 8, first convert the plaintext letters to their integer equivalent using *Figure 6.10.4*. Next subtract the key 8 from each integer. If the resulting integer is less than 0 then add 26 to convert −1 to 25, −2 to 24, −3 to 23, and so on. Finally convert each integer to its equivalent letter using *Figure 6.10.4* again. The steps of the process are shown in *Figure 6.10.6*.

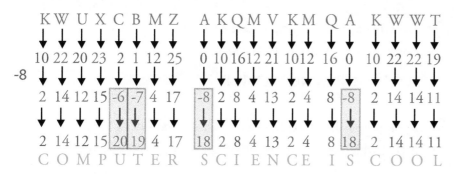

Figure 6.10.6 Decrypting with key 8

The number circle

The number circle shown in *Figure 6.10.7* is useful for visualising addition and subtraction performed in the Caesar cipher.

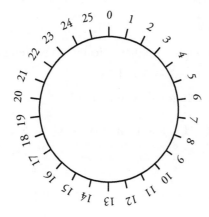

Figure 6.10.7 Number circle

If we add **6** to **22** then we move to position **2** on the number wheel. If we subtract **6** from **2** then we end up at position **22** on the number wheel as shown in *Figure 6.10.8*.

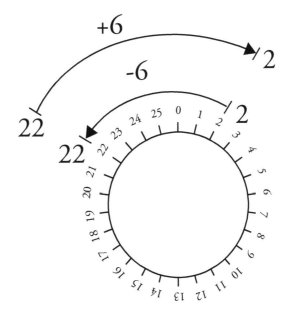

Figure 6.10.8 Number circle

Modular arithmetic

Addition using this number circle is called modulo 26 addition. Likewise subtraction using this number circle is called modulo 26 subtraction. In the world of modulo 26, there are exactly 26 numbers, {0, 1, 2, …, 23, 24, 25}. These are indicated on the number circle as 0 through 25. The number 26 is called the modulus. This particular arithmetic is called modular arithmetic.

Key concept

Modular arithmetic:
Addition using the number circle is called modulo n addition where n is the modulus. Likewise subtraction using the number circle is called modulo n subtraction.

Questions

4 Evaluate the following using modulo 26 addition:

(a) 13 + 13 (b) 20 + 16 (c) 19 + 26 (d) 10 + 26

5 Evaluate the following using modulo 26 subtraction:

(a) 6 – 12 (b) 11 – 20 (c) 13 – 26 (d) 18 – 26

6 (a) How many numbers are there in the world of modulo 12 arithmetic?

(b) What are the numbers in modulo 12 arithmetic?

It is conventional to indicate modulo arithmetic as follows

$$13 + 13 = 0 \ (\mathrm{mod}\ 26)$$

Where (mod 26) indicates that modulo 26 arithmetic has been used.

Modular arithmetic in daily life

People use modular arithmetic in their daily lives often without realising that they are doing so. For example, consider the clock face shown in *Figure 6.10.9*, ignore the fact that 12 has been replaced by 0. Suppose it is eight o'clock, and you want to know what time it will be in 7 hours. You would use modulo 12 arithmetic: 8 + 7 is 3 (mod 12).

Figure 6.10.9 Unconventional 12 hour clock

In the case of days of the week represented by numbers as shown in *Table 6.10.1* it is useful to use modulo 7 arithmetic.

Day	Number
Sunday	0
Monday	1
Tuesday	2
Wednesday	3
Thursday	4
Friday	5
Saturday	6

Table 6.10.1 Numbered days of the week

Suppose today is Wednesday.

What will the day of the week be in 6 days?

To answer this we add 6 to 3, the latter being the number for Wednesday, obtaining 9. But 9 modulo 7 is 2 (mod 7) which is Tuesday.

What day of the week will it be in 490 days?

To solve this, imagine travelling around the number circle for modulo 7. How many times does one travel around in 490 days, i.e. how many times does 7 go into 490? The answer is 70 times. This means we would arrive on a Wednesday, i.e. 3 + 490 = 3 (mod 7).

Congruence

This last example illustrates that adding 7 has the same effect as adding 14, as adding 21 or adding 0 or subtracting 7 and so on. We call this congruence (remember congruent triangles from maths lessons, it is a similar idea).

Questions

7 Suppose today is Tuesday.

(a) What day of the week will it be in 492 days?

(b) What day of the week was it 210 days ago?

8 In dealing with compass bearings, the modulus to use is 360.
Whole number bearings are chosen from the set

{0, 1, 2, ..., 358, 359}.

Suppose that you are headed due East, your bearing is 90 degrees.
You turn right 130 degrees onto a bearing 220 degrees. You then turn right 150 degrees, what is your new bearing?

9 Suppose that you are headed due East, your bearing is 90 degrees.
You turn left 130 degrees, what is your new bearing?

Key concept

Congruence:

Two integers are said to be congruent with respect to a given modulus if they differ by a multiple of that modulus. For example, if the modulus is 12 then 2, 14, 26, 38 are congruent.

Two integers are said to be congruent with respect to a given modulus if they differ by a multiple of that modulus. For example, if the modulus is 12 then 2, 14, 26, 36 are congruent. *Figure 6.10.10* shows some more congruence for modulus *12*.

A statement that two expressions are congruent is called a congruence.

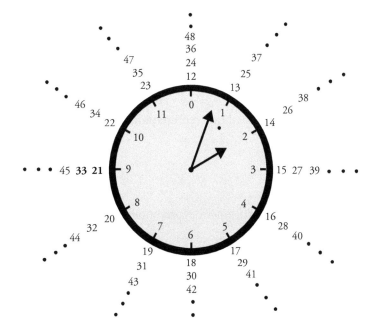

Figure 6.10.10 Unconventional 12 hour clock showing congruence

Congruence modulo 12

Two integers are congruent modulo 12 if they differ by a multiple of 12.

For example 5 is congruent to 17 (which is 5 + 12) and to
29 (which is 5 + 2 • 12).

5 is also congruent to −7 (which is 5 + (−1) • 12).

The mathematical notation for writing a congruence is similar to the mathematical notation for writing an equation but where the equality symbol has two horizontal bars ("="), the congruence symbol has three ("≡").

For example, we write the congruence

$$5 \equiv 17 \ (\text{mod } 12)$$

to state that 5 is congruent (modulo 12) to 17.

The notation requires that the modulus is specified in brackets together with the word "mod" short for "modulo".

Here are more modulo 12 examples. To verify that the numbers are indeed congruent check that the difference between them is a multiple of 12:

$$6 \equiv 42 \ (\text{mod } 12)$$

$$-13 \equiv 11 \ (\text{mod } 12)$$

$$-13 \equiv -1 \ (\text{mod } 12)$$

$$-21 \equiv 3 \ (\text{mod } 12)$$

$$12 \equiv 0 \ (\text{mod } 12)$$

$$7 + 5 \equiv 12 \ (\text{mod } 12)$$

Representative theorem

Every integer is congruent modulo m to exactly one of the integers

$$0, 1, 2, 3, \ldots, m-1.$$

For example, modulo 7: every integer is congruent to exactly one of the integers 0, 1, 2, 3, 4, 5, 6.

The 0, 1, 2, 3, ..., m − 1 are called the representatives.

Questions

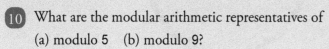 10 What are the modular arithmetic representatives of
    (a) modulo 5   (b) modulo 9?

Key principle

Quotient and remainder theorem:

For every integer b and every positive integer m, there is exactly one integer q and exactly one integer r among 0, 1, 2, 3, …, m − 1 such that

$$b = q \bullet m + r$$

r is the remainder when b is divided by m.
q is the quotient.

The equation b = q • m + r shows that b and r differ by a multiple of m, which shows that b is **congruent** to r (mod m).

Quotient and remainder theorem

For every integer b and every positive integer m, there is exactly one integer q and exactly one integer r among 0, 1, 2, 3, …, m − 1 such that

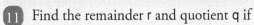

$$b = q \bullet m + r$$

Example:

> Let b = 23 and let m = 7.
>
> Then the above equation is satisfied by q = 3 and r = 2
>
> (That is, 23 = 3 • 7 + 2)

As this example suggests, r is the remainder when b is divided by m.

q is the quotient.

The remainder r is thus the value of (b mod m)'s representative.

The equation b = q • m + r shows that b and r differ by a multiple of m, which shows that b is **congruent** to r (mod m).

Questions

11 Find the remainder r and quotient q if
(a) b = 37 m = 12 (b) b = 38 m = 24   (c) b = 76 m = 60
(d) b = 576 m = 365

Representatives and negative integers

What is the remainder for −15 mod 7?

To answer this we must remember that the result must be a mod 7 representative, i.e. one of 0, 1, 2, 3, 4, 5, 6.

> −15 divided by 7 is −2 with −1 left over.

The representative that is congruent to −1 is 6
(difference between 6 and −1 is 7).

Therefore −15 mod 7 = 6.

Questions

12 Find the remainder r and quotient q if
(a) b = −37 m = 12 (b) b = −38 m = 24   (c) b = −76 m = 60
(d) b = −576 m = 365

Programming Tasks

1 Write a program to encrypt a line of uppercase text using the Caesar cipher. Represent each character by a number between 0 and 26 (A ↦ 0, B ↦ 1, …, Z ↦ 25, space ↦ 26).

Use only these characters. Allow a user to choose a key within the range 0…26.

Encrypt each character of the text using the equation

ciphertext_character = (plaintext_character + key) mod 27

2 Write a program to decrypt a line of text encrypted using the Caesar cipher. Assume that each character was represented by a number between 0 and 26 (A ↦ 0, B ↦ 1, …, Z ↦ 25, space ↦ 26) and only these characters were used when producing the line of encrypted text. The user should enter a key in range 0…26.

Decrypt each character of the text using the equation

ciphertext_character = (plaintext_character − key) mod 27

Questions

13 What is it unnecessary to use a key range wider than 0..26 for the Caesar cipher in this case?

Breaking the Caesar cipher
Brute force approach

The Caesar cipher is easily broken by an attacker thus revealing the plaintext and the key used to produce the ciphertext. A brute-force search is sufficient. Assuming that the plaintext consisted of the 26 uppercase letters of the alphabet. A brute force search on the ciphertext consists of just trying all the possible keys except 0 on the ciphertext until the plaintext is discovered. It is assumed that key 0 would not have been used when encrypting the plaintext because it doesn't alter the plaintext.

For example, take a five letter name, choose a key between 1 and 25 and then, with this key, use the Caesar cipher to encrypt the name. If we choose ALICE for the name and 3 for the key then the ciphertext is DOLFH. *Table 6.10.2* shows the outcome of the brute force search from which it can be deduced that the key was 3 and the plaintext was ALICE.

Key	Plaintext	Key	Plaintext	Key	Plaintext
1	CNKEG	10	TEBVX	19	KVSMO
2	BMJDF	11	SDAUW	20	JURLN
3	ALICE	12	RCZTV	21	ITQKM
4	ZKHBD	13	QBYSU	22	HSPJL
5	YJGAC	14	PAXRT	23	GROIK
6	XIFZB	15	OZWQS	24	FQNHJ
7	WHEYA	16	NYVPR	25	EPMGI
8	VGDXZ	17	MXUOQ		
9	UFCWY	18	LWTNP		

Table 6.10.2 Brute force attack on ciphertext DOLFH

Task

1   Choose a four letter name and a key. Use the key and the Caesar cipher to encrypt the name. Now give the ciphertext to another student and ask them to use a brute force attack to discover the name and the key used.

Letter frequency attack

The Caesar cipher is also susceptible to letter frequency analysis. If an attacker knows that the plaintext was written in English then because the Caesar cipher applies the same shift to each plaintext letter, the frequencies of occurrence of the letters in the ciphertext match those in the plaintext shifted by the key. When the plaintext is sufficiently long or a series of ciphertexts are intercepted, a good guess is that the ciphertext(s) matches the relative frequency of letters common to a large number of English texts when shifted by the key.

Frequency analysis of a large number of English texts has revealed that each letter of the alphabet occurs with unequal likelihood as shown in *Figure 6.10.11*. The letter E occurs most frequently, 12.7% of the time on average, and so is roughly twice as likely on average to occur in a piece of text as the letter S which has relative frequency of approximately 6.3%.

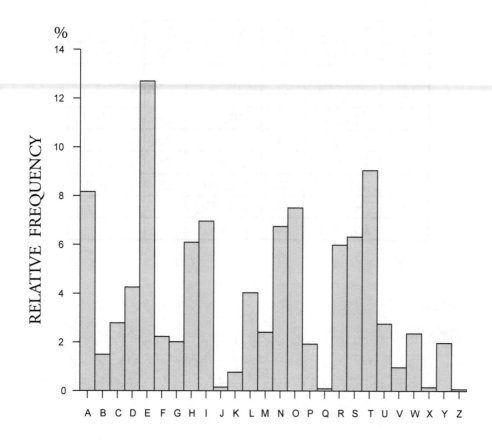

Figure 6.10.11 Relative frequency analysis for English

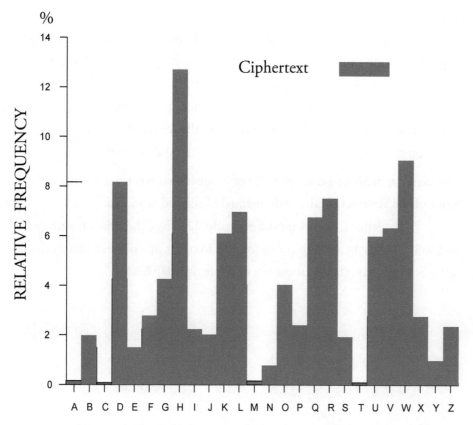

Figure 6.10.12 Ciphertext relative frequency analysis

Figure 6.10.12 shows what the relative frequency distribution would be if the Caesar cipher was applied with key **3** to plaintext with relative letter frequency distribution as shown in *Figure 6.10.11*. It is relatively easy to see that an E has been shifted to become an H, therefore the key must be **3**. The ciphertext is said to leak information about the plaintext.

> ### Task
>
> Try the Caesar frequency analysis exercise at
> https://www.khanacademy.org/computing/computer-science/cryptography/ciphers/e/

Programming Task

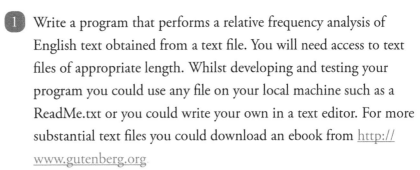 Write a program that performs a relative frequency analysis of English text obtained from a text file. You will need access to text files of appropriate length. Whilst developing and testing your program you could use any file on your local machine such as a ReadMe.txt or you could write your own in a text editor. For more substantial text files you could download an ebook from http://www.gutenberg.org

The NLTK toolkit from www.nltk.org written for Python is a very powerful text processing resource that could be used for this and other work.

Caesar cipher weaknesses

Key point

Caesar cipher weaknesses:
1.   The number of possible keys is too small
2.   The same shift is applied to each character making it easy to use relative letter frequency analysis.
3.   The same shift is likely to be used for each message.

Summarising, the Caesar cipher has three major weaknesses:

1.   The number of possible keys is too small

2.   The same shift is applied to each character making it easy to use relative letter frequency analysis.

3.   The same shift is likely to be used for each message.

The solution:

4.   Make the number of possible keys so large that it becomes infeasible to employ a brute force approach of trying all possible keys

5.   Arrange for the occurrence of each letter/character in the ciphertext to be equally likely by applying a random shift to each.

One-time pad

One way of making the number of possible keys large is to choose a new key value for each letter/character of the plaintext message and a new set of key values for each new message. If key values are chosen randomly then the second bullet point above can also be satisfied.

For example, if the plaintext message is

CLOCK TOWER USUAL TIME TONIGHT J

then 32 key values are needed because there are 32 characters – 27 letters and 5 spaces in this message. We randomly choose a different combination of 32 key values for each new 32 character long message from the set of all possible permutations of 32 key values. Each key value can be one of 26 possible letters or a space. This is done 32 times therefore there are 27^{32} different key patterns to choose from at random.

Applying a random shift to each letter/character in the plaintext ensures that each ciphertext character is equally likely.

For our example, first convert each plaintext character to numeric form. The 26 letters of the alphabet are coded as 0...25, respectively and the space character as 26.

If we use p_i to refer to the numeric code for the ith character of the plaintext, and c_i for the numeric code of the corresponding letter in the ciphertext, then to obtain c_i from p_i and key k_i we use

$$c_i = (p_i + k_i) \bmod 27$$

To obtain the ciphertext character we convert c_i into its equivalent character.

Let's suppose the 32 key values, k_i where i is in {1...32}, chosen at random from the range {0...26} are

22 23 8 8 3 13 14 15 24 22 5 9 8 18 25 16 10 7 21 1 2 4 23
1 12 11 4 14 4 23 15 6

Call this sequence of keys the cipher key K. (To obtain these 32 keys you could use all the hearts and diamonds from a pack of cards and a joker because this gives 27 cards. Shuffle the pack then take the top card, write down its corresponding number: the joker is 0, hearts are 1...13, diamonds are 14...26 with Ace 1 or 14, Jack 11 or 24, etc, Put the card back and shuffle the pack again, repeat the process until you have 32 randomly chosen numbers.)

Background

The use of a truly random key, as long as the plaintext, is an essential part of the one-time pad algorithm. The one-time pad algorithm itself is mathematically secure. Thus the codebreaker cannot retrieve the plaintext by examining the ciphertext. The best that the codebreaker can do is to try to retrieve the key. If the random values for the one-time key are not truly random but generated by a deterministic mechanism or algorithm then there is a possibility of predicting the key. Thus, selecting a good random number generator is the most important part of the system. To see one way of manually generating a truly random key using ten-sided dice visit http://users.telenet.be/d. rijmenants/en/onetimepad.htm

Questions

 Why is it unnecessary for this cipher to choose numbers greater than 26?

The plaintext codes p_i where i is in {1...32} are

2 11 **14** 2 **10** 26 **19** 14 **22** 4 **17** 26 **20** 18 **20 0 11** 26 **19** 8 **12** 4 **26** 19 **14** 13 **8** 6 **7** 19 **26** 9

The ciphertext codes [$c_i = (p_i + k_i) \bmod 27$ where i is in {1...32}]

are

24 22 **22** 10 **1** 12 **6** 2 **19** 26 **15** 7 **1** 9 **18** 16 **21** 6 **13** 9 **14** 8 **22** 20 **26** 24 **12** 20 **11 15 14** 15

The ciphertext is

YGWKLMGCT FGBJSQVGNJOIWU YMULPOP

The tendency of applying random shifts is to flatten the distribution. Analysis reveals that applying random shifts to a large number of plaintext messages leads to the following two powerful properties possessed by ciphertexts

1. The shifts do not fall into a repetitive pattern, e.g. E → H every time is avoided

2. The ciphertext distribution is flattened and has a uniform frequency distribution

Achieving a uniform frequency distribution as in *Figure 6.10.13* will mean that there is no frequency differential and therefore no leak of information about the plaintext message that an attacker or eavesdropper could exploit to guess the plaintext.

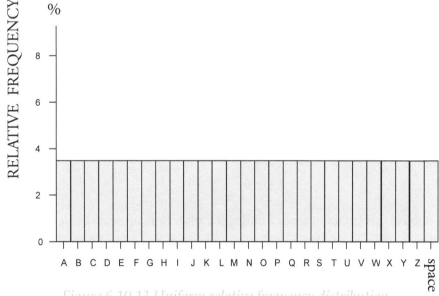

Figure 6.10.13 Uniform relative frequency distribution

Task

3   Watch the Khan Academy polyalphabetic video and try the tool to
see how a non-uniform plaintext distribution can be flattened as
described in this section.

https://www.khanacademy.org/computing/computer-science/
cryptography/crypt/v/polyalphabetic-cipher

Questions

15   Suppose Alice and Bob communicate messages to each other which
have been encrypted using the Caesar cipher and a previously
agreed secret key. Now suppose that Eve intercepts the ciphertext
and that she happens to know or suspect that Alice starts all
her messages to Bob with the characters "DEAR BOB". The
corresponding ciphertext is GHDUCERE. Alice and Bob make
no secret of the fact that they use the Caesar cipher believing that
keeping the key secret is sufficient to maintain the security of their
messages. The encryption equation that Alice and Bob use is

ciphertext_character = (plaintext_character + key) mod 27

Explain how Eve using the plaintext and ciphertext could recover
the secret key used by Alice and Bob.

16   Alice and Bob decide to use a new key for each character, generated
randomly, and apply the stream of random keys using the Caesar
cipher to future messages. Explain why this could offer greater
security over the scheme described in Q15 even though Eve
continues to intercept the ciphertext and Alice continues to start
messages with "DEAR BOB".

To subject this cipher to closer scrutiny we ask how many ways can a particular
plaintext message consisting of only uppercase letters of the alphabet be
encrypted by a shift cipher which chooses key values randomly? Well consider
that for the first character, there are 26 different possible key values, for the
second character, 26 different possible values again and so on. If plaintext
messages of length 32 characters are encrypted then a key will consist of 32 key
values. The total number of keys of length 32 is therefore

$$26 \times 26 \times 26 \times .... \times 26 \times 26 = 26^{32} \approx 2 \times 10^{45}$$

Key principle

One-time pad:
Plain text of a message is 'mixed' with random text taken from a one-time pad resulting in cipher text which is truly random. The same one-time pad is used to 'unmix' the random text from the cipher text, which results in the original plain text.

One only has to guarantee that the one-time pad is safe, that it comprises truly random numbers, that there are only two copies of it, and that both copies are destroyed immediately after use to prevent it being used again (the one-time property), for it to be used to send a message safely without the risk of being deciphered by an attacker or eavesdropper.

Background

The "red phone" used in the 1980s for secure communication between the USA and the USSR was based on a one-time pad. The random key sequences or pads were delivered by courier.

The total number of possible ciphertexts corresponding to any particular 32 character plaintext message is thus 2×10^{45} one for each possible key consisting of 32 key values.

If each of these possible ciphertexts is written on a separate piece of paper then the entire stack would be

$$2 \times 10^{45} \times 5 \times 10^{-5} \text{ metres high} = 1 \times 10^{40} \text{ metres}$$

taking the thickness of a piece of paper to be 5×10^{-5} metres.

By comparison the Milky Way galaxy is estimated to be 9.5×10^{20} metres across. If the key values were generated randomly then each ciphertext will be equally likely.

The decryption cipher is

$$p_i = (c_i - k_i) \bmod 27$$

Likewise a particular ciphertext could have come from any one of 2×10^{45} possible plaintext messages. The chance of an attacker guessing which one correctly is therefore vanishingly small. It is impossible therefore for an attacker or eavesdropper to break this encryption scheme because the ciphertext yields no possible information about the plaintext (except its length).

This is the strongest possible method of encryption. It is known as the one-time pad because when first used the key was written on a sheet of paper or pad and used only once.

Summarising, the one-time pad method is based on the principle that the plain text of a message is 'mixed' with truly random text taken from a one-time pad. Because the resulting cipher text is still truly random it can safely be sent without the risk of being deciphered by an attacker or eavesdropper.

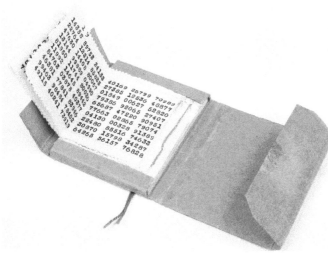

At the receiving end, the same one-time pad is used to 'unmix' the random text from the cipher text, which results in the original plain text. One only has to guarantee that the one-time pad is safe, that it comprises truly random numbers, that there are only two copies of it, and that both copies are destroyed immediately after use to prevent it being used again (the one-time property) on another plaintext message.

Figure 6.10.14 A one-time pad reproduced with kind permission of Paul Reuvers, Crypto Museum (www.cryptomuseum.com)

Task

4   Watch the Khan Academy one-time pad video
https://www.khanacademy.org/computing/computer-science/cryptography/crypt/v/one-time-pad

5   The Venona project was a counter-intelligence program initiated by the United States Army Signal Intelligence Service (a forerunner of the National Security Agency) that lasted from 1943 to 1980. The program attempted to decrypt messages sent by Soviet Union intelligence agencies, including its foreign intelligence service and military intelligence services. The project produced some of the most important breakthroughs for western counter-intelligence in this period, including the discovery of the Cambridge spy ring and the exposure of Soviet espionage targeting the Manhattan Project. The NSA declassified the program in 1995. It can be read about in a NSA document at

https://www.nsa.gov/about/_files/cryptologic_heritage/publications/coldwar/venona_story.pdf

Background

Hardware random number generators have been built into some processor systems or made possible in some operating system. E.g. Raspberry Pi includes a hardware-based random number generator that can generate cryptographic quality random numbers.
In Unix-like operating systems /dev/random is a special file that serves as a blocking pseudorandom number generator:

   .dev>more –f random

Randomness

Randomness means lack of pattern or predictability of events. Randomness abounds in the physical world and in man-made devices such as electrical circuits as fluctuations of an unpredictable nature which we call noise. Electrical storms, the microwave background left over from the Big Bang and other events induce random currents of electricity in aerials connected to radio receivers and televisions that cause the hissing noise that we hear in their loudspeakers. This atmospheric noise can be captured, sampled and digitised to provide a source of truly random bits. Such a service is provided by https://www.random.org.

Another source is https://www.fourmilab.ch/hotbits/secure_generate.html which uses the unpredictable nature of radioactive decay to generate truly random bits.

A random number is one that is drawn from a set of possible values, each of which is equally probable, i.e., a uniform distribution, e.g. the throw of a six-sided die. When discussing a sequence of random numbers, each number drawn must be statistically independent of the others, i.e. knowledge of an arbitrarily long sequence of numbers is of no use whatsoever in predicting the next number to be generated. Each possible arbitrarily long sequence is thus equally likely.

Key principle

Randomness:
Randomness means lack of pattern or predictability of events.

Background

RandomX package for Java has an option to get random bits from hotbits.
http://www.fourmilab.ch/hotbits/source/randomX/randomX.html

Pseudorandom

Pseudorandomness is an important concept in cryptography.

Informally pseudorandom means:

cannot be distinguished from uniform i.e. random.

The cryptographic definition of pseudorandom however is

a distribution is pseudorandom if it passes all efficient statistical tests.

This definition has been arrived at by considering the need to resist an attack from an adversary who is trying to obtain information from ciphertexts about the corresponding plaintext messages.

Generating large numbers of truly random numbers is extremely difficult so people have turned to the computer and algorithms programmed into the computer to generate pseudorandom numbers from an initial seed. These pseudorandom numbers are generated deterministically and can only approximate a truly random distribution because numbers calculated by a computer through a deterministic process, cannot, by definition, be random. Given knowledge of the algorithm used to create the numbers and the seed, it is possible to predict all the numbers returned by subsequent calls to the algorithm, whereas with genuinely random numbers, knowledge of one number or an arbitrarily long sequence of numbers is of no use whatsoever in predicting the next number to be generated. Therefore, computer-generated "random" numbers are more properly referred to as pseudorandom numbers, and pseudorandom sequences of such numbers. Pseudorandom generated sequences eventually repeat with the periodicity determined by the seed and the algorithm used. Pseudorandom generated sequences are also reproducible, i.e. for a given algorithm, starting from the same seed generates the same sequence.

Pseudorandom number generators (PRNGs)

A pseudorandom number generator is an efficient, deterministic algorithm that expands a short, uniform seed into a longer, pseudorandom output in polynomial time. It is useful whenever

1. It would be difficult to communicate a long sequence of numbers needed in a symmetric key cipher instead the seed is communicated

2. A large number of random numbers are required and access to truly random numbers is restricted to a much smaller number

The seed may be chosen from the small number of truly random numbers that are available but doesn't have to be.

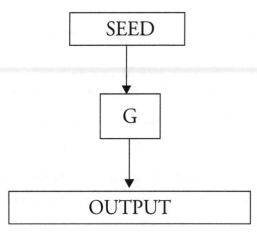

Figure 6.10.15 A pseudorandom number generator, G, producing a longer stream of "random" bits from a shorter length seed of true random bits

Care must be taken when relying on pseudorandom number generators for cryptographic purposes because they are deterministic. However, a class of improved random number generators, termed cryptographically secure pseudorandom number generators (CSPRNG) exist that rely on truly random seeds external to the software.

<div class="background">

Background

Security experts have long suspected the National Security Agency (NSA) has been introducing weaknesses into CSPRNG standard 800-90 that they can exploit in ciphers that use this standard; this being confirmed for the first time by one of the top secret documents leaked to the Guardian by Edward Snowden.

</div>

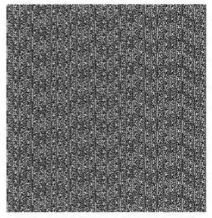

Figure 6.10.16 (a) Image generated from random numbers generated by the PHP rand() function on Microsoft Windows.

Figure 6.10.16 (b) reproduced with permission of RANDOM.ORG – image generated from random numbers obtained from atmospheric noise.

The image in *Figure 6.10.16(a)* (reproduced using a PHP script with kind permission of Bo Allen, http://boallen.com) exhibits patterns because the pseudorandom number generator, the programming language PHP's rand() function, is deterministic with a relatively short periodicity whereas the bitmap in *Figure 6.10.16(b)* does not because it relies on truly random numbers.

Task

6 Download the test program at http://www.fourmilab.ch/random/ Use it to test sequences of bytes/bits for their randomness. Run this program on data generated by a high-quality pseudorandom sequence generator. You should find it generates data that are indistinguishable from a sequence of bytes chosen at random. Indistinguishable, but not genuinely random.

7 Watch the video on pseudorandom number generators at https://www.khanacademy.org/computing/computer-science/cryptography/crypt/v/random-vs-pseudorandom-number-generators

Background

The Vernam cipher was exploited in the design of a high security teleprinter cipher machine that the Lorenz company made for the German Army High Command to enable them to communicate by radio in complete secrecy during WW2.

These transmissions were broken by Bill Tutte. The process of decrypting Lorentz machine ciphertexts was later automated using a refinement suggested by Max Newman and some clever engineering by Tommy Flowers who designed and built Colussus, the world's first stored program computer to decrypt Lorentz encrypted messages. Colussus reduced the time taken from weeks to hours. Colussus came online just in time to decrypt messages which gave vital information to Eisenhower and Montgomery prior to D-Day - http://www.codesandciphers.org.uk/lorenz/colossus.htm

The Vernam cipher

The Vernam Cipher is named after Gilbert Sandford Vernam (1890-1960) who, in 1917, invented the stream cipher and later co-invented the one-time pad (OTP). His patent US1310719 was filed in 1918 and is, according to the National Security Agency (NSA), perhaps one of the most important in the history of cryptography.

At the time of the invention, Vernam was working at AT & T Bell Labs in the USA. Messages were then sent by telegraph, a system that used pulses of electrical current to encode characters according to the Baudot code. The characters were entered into and read from the system using a teleprinter.

Figure 6.10.17
Gilbert Vernam

Vernam proposed a teleprinter cipher in which a previously prepared key, kept on paper tape, was combined character by character with the plaintext message to produce the ciphertext. To decrypt the ciphertext, the same key would be again combined character by character, producing the plaintext.

Working with Joseph Mauborgne, at that time a captain in the US Army Signal Corps, they proposed that the paper tape key should contain random information (the key stream). The incorporation of this proposal into Vernam's machine implemented an automatic form of the one-time pad.

Task

8 Watch AT & T Labs' video of the Vernam cipher http://techchannel.att.com/play-video.cfm/2009/10/12/From-the-Labs:-Encryption1

9 Read about the details of the Vernam cipher machine by visiting the website http://www.cryptomuseum.com/crypto/vernam.htm

The Vernam cipher relies on the bit-wise eXclusive-OR (XOR) Boolean function. This is symbolised by $\oplus$ and is represented by the following truth table, *Table 6.10.3*, where 1 represents true and 0 represents false

INPUT		OUTPUT
A	**B**	**A $\oplus$ B**
0	0	0
0	1	1
1	1	1
1	0	0

Table 6.10.3 Exclusive-Or truth table

A very useful property of the exclusive-or operation is that it is possible to recover an input given the output and the other input. For example, if the inputs A and B are 0 and 1 respectively, then A $\oplus$ B = 1. If we exclusive-or this output 1 with, say, input B which was 1, 1 $\oplus$ 1 = 0, we recover input A which was 0. It works for all inputs.

Therefore the same key stream can be used both to encrypt plaintext to ciphertext and to decrypt ciphertext to yield the original plaintext:

$$\text{Plaintext} \oplus \text{Key} = \text{Ciphertext}$$

and:

$$\text{Ciphertext} \oplus \text{Key} = \text{Plaintext}$$

If the key stream is truly random, and used only once, this is effectively a one-time pad.

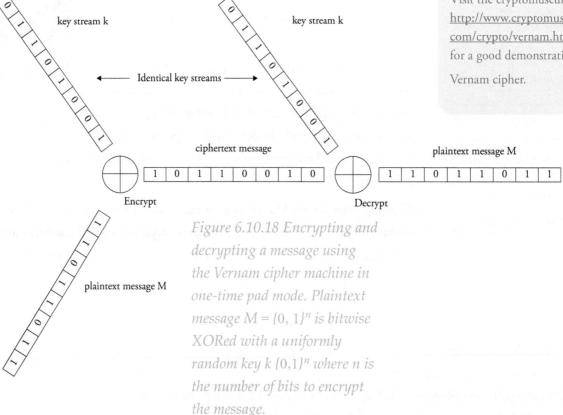

Figure 6.10.18 Encrypting and decrypting a message using the Vernam cipher machine in one-time pad mode. Plaintext message M = {0, 1}^{n} is bitwise XORed with a uniformly random key k {0,1}^{n} where n is the number of bits to encrypt the message.

Background

RC4 is an example of a Vernam cipher. It has been and still is used in popular protocols such as Transport Layer Security (TLS) (to protect Internet traffic) and WEP (to secure wireless networks) although it is now considered insecure.

Substituting pseudorandom data generated by a cryptographically secure pseudorandom number generator is a common and effective construction for a stream cipher.

RC4 has been a very widely used software stream cipher. RC4 is an example of a Vernam cipher. It has been and still is used in popular protocols such as Transport Layer Security (TLS) (to protect Internet traffic) and WEP (to secure wireless networks) although it is now considered insecure.

WEP relies on a short secret key that is shared between a mobile station (e.g. a laptop with a wireless Ethernet card) and an access point (i.e. a base station).

The short secret key is expanded into an infinite pseudorandom key stream which is XORed with the message packets before they are transmitted.

Programming task

3. RC4 is a stream cipher used in WEP. The infinite pseudorandom key stream for RC4 is generated from a secret key using the following two algorithms. Code these in your preferred language and run the test below on secret key = AQACS and plaintext = Computer Science

Key-scheduling algorithm

```
for i from 0 to 255
   S[i] := i
endfor
j := 0
for i from 0 to 255
   j := (j + S[i] + key[i mod keylength]) mod 256
   swap values of S[i] and S[j]
endfor
```

PseudoRandom Number Generator

```
i := 0
j := 0
while PseudoRandom Numbers required:
   i := (i + 1) mod 256
   j := (j + S[i]) mod 256
   swap values of S[i] and S[j]
   PSRNumber := S[(S[i] + S[j]) mod 256]
   output PSRNumber
endwhile
```

Test

The keys and plaintext are ASCII, the keystream and ciphertext are expressed below in hexadecimal but stored as bytes.

Key: AQACS

Keystream: F163D4497F1C801DCB4E3C...

Plaintext: Computer Science

Ciphertext: B20CB9390A68E56FEB1D5FC4720A7BD7

Task

 Attacks on RC4 have shown that it is possible to distinguish its output from a random sequence. Why does this make RC4 insecure? Use a search engine to research an RC4 attack.

RC4 is still installed on some operating systems. For example, running the *openssl ciphers* command on an Apple Mac running Mac OS X 10.8 reveals that the SSL(Secure Sockets Layer) cipher RC4 (128 bit) is being used for encryption on this machine because it has not been deselected:

```
$ openssl ciphers -tls1 -v RC4-SHA

RC4-SHA SSLv3 Kx=RSA Au=RSA Enc=RC4(128) Mac=SHA1
```

Perfect secrecy

Claude Shannon, at Bell Labs, proved that the one-time pad is unbreakable, and that it is the only cryptosystem that achieves perfect secrecy. He published his proof in a research paper in 1949. In it he defined a mathematical model of what it means for a cryptosystem to be secure. Essentially, any unbreakable system must have the same characteristics as the one-time pad:

The key

1. must be truly random

2. must be as long as the plaintext message

3. must never be reused in whole or part

4. and must be kept secret.

Points 1 and 2 mean that the number of possible keys must be at least as large as the number of possible messages of a given length.

*Claude Shannon
(Getty Image library)*

Task

 Watch the video on Perfect Secrecy from Khan Academy -
www.khanacademy.org/computing/computer-science/cryptography/crypt/v/perfect-secrecy

Perfect secrecy means an eavesdropper would not, by gaining knowledge of the ciphertext but not of the key, be able to improve their guess of the plaintext even if given unlimited computing power.

Key point

Unconditional or Perfect Security (Perfect secrecy)
Regardless of any prior information the attacker has about the plaintext, the ciphertext leaks no additional information about the plaintext in a ciphertext-only attack.

Such cryptosystems are considered cryptoanalytically unbreakable and information-theoretically secure meaning they will not be vulnerable to future developments in computer power such as quantum computing.

The one-time pad is an example of an information-theoretically secure cryptosystem. These systems have been used for the most sensitive governmental communications, such as diplomatic cables and high-level military communications.

What if the plaintext was a sequence of bits that represented an image? If we apply a bitwise exclusive-or to this image using a sequence of randomly generated bits for the key, we get an image that contains no information about the original image because each ciphertext bit is just as likely to be a 0 as a 1 - Figure 6.10.19(a) and Figure 6.10.19 (b).

The original image can only be recovered by using the same key, i.e. the exact sequence of randomly generated bits that produced the ciphertext.

Applying the "wrong" key will result in recovering a different image.

Information

Figure 6.10.19(a) Claude Elwood Shannon was an American mathematician, electronic engineer, and cryptographer famous for having founded information theory with a landmark paper that he published in 1948.

Shannon was also the first person to show how the logical algebra of 19th-century mathematician George Boole could be implemented using electronic circuits of relays and switches in which open or closed switches could represent. "true" and "false" and "0" and "1". Furthermore he showed how the use of electronic logic gates could be used to make decisions and to carry out arithmetic.

Figure 6.10.19(a) Plaintext image to be encrypted using a one-time pad.
(Getty Image Library)

Figure 6.10.19(b) One-time pad ciphertext image of (a).

Task

 Try the reversible XOR demonstration at https://www.khanacademy.org/computer-programming/reversible-xor-demo/5580322717564928

How XOR and a random key achieves perfect secrecy

Let's suppose that Alice needs to send a private message to Bob and therefore encrypts the message with a secret key known only to her and Bob. Furthermore before encrypting the message, the letters of the plaintext message are replaced by their equivalent ASCII values expressed in binary. We would then have the problem of encrypting 0s and 1s. For the sake of argument, let's just focus on one bit of the message, call it p, and encrypt this obtaining a one-bit ciphertext, c.

Next, Alice chooses the key, k, at random and uniformly (with no bias) from the set of symbols {☺, ☺, ☹}. These symbols have equal likelihood, $\frac{1}{3}$, of being chosen by Alice, i.e. $\frac{1}{3}$ of the time Alice chooses ☺, $\frac{1}{3}$ of the time ☺ and $\frac{1}{3}$ of the time ☹. The chosen secret key is known only to Alice and Bob.

When Alice needs to send the message she uses the chosen key to encrypt her plaintext message bit p obtaining ciphertext, c according to the following table, *Table 6.10.4*.

p	k	c
0	☺	0
0	☺	1
0	☹	1
1	☺	1
1	☺	0
1	☹	0

Table 6.10.4 Look up table for encrypting p into c using key k

Let's suppose that Alice has chosen ☺ for k. The values in *Table 6.10.4* have been carefully chosen so that no two rows have the same k-value and c-value, so on receipt of c, Bob will be able to decrypt c.

Unfortunately, this encryption scheme leaks information to Eve, an eavesdropper who wishes to learn something about the plaintext so that she can read what Bob is able to read.

Here is the method that Eve uses:

Suppose plaintext message bit $p = 1$,

Then if the key was ☺, the ciphertext $c = 1$

But if it was ☺ or ☹ then $c = 0$

However, one of ☺ or ☹ are twice as likely as ☺ to have been chosen

Therefore, for $p = 1$, $c = 0$ is twice as likely as $c = 1$.

Suppose, plaintext message bit $p = 0$,

Then if the key was ☺, the ciphertext $c = 0$

But if it was ☺ or ☹ then c = 1

However, one of ☺ or ☹ are twice as likely as ☺ to have been chosen

Therefore, for p = 0, c = 1 is twice as likely as c = 0.

Although having knowledge of c doesn't allow Eve to determine the value of p with certainty, it does allow her to revise her estimate of the chance that p = 0 or p = 1, as follows:

If before seeing c, Eve believed that p = 0 and p = 1 were equally likely, then if she sees that c = 1 she can infer that p = 0 is twice as likely as p = 1. On the other hand, if she sees c = 0 then she can infer that p = 1 is twice as likely as p = 0 - *Table 6.10.5*.

The solution is to remove ☹ as a possible value for k. Encryption then takes place using the values in *Table 6.10.6*.

Alice randomly chooses the key, k, from the set of symbols {☺, ☺}. These symbols have equal likelihood, ½, of being chosen, i.e. ½ of the time Alice will choose ☺, ½ of the time ☺. The chosen secret key is known only to Alice and Bob.

Why does this new cryptosystem thwart Eve's attempt to learn something about the plaintext by examining the ciphertext?

Suppose p = 0,

Then if the key was ☺, c = 0

But if it was ☺ then c = 1

Since ☺ is equally likely as ☺ to have been chosen

c = 1 is as equally likely to occur as c = 0.

Suppose, p = 1,

Then if the key was ☺, c = 1

But if it was ☺ then c = 0

Since ☺ is equally likely as ☺ to have been chosen

c = 0 is as equally likely to occur as c = 1.

If before seeing c Eve believed that p = 0 and p = 1 were equally likely, then seeing c = 1 or seeing c = 0 cannot alter that belief because c = 1 and c = 0 are equally likely whichever value of key k is chosen.

For this encryption scheme, the probability distribution of the output does not depend upon whether 0 or 1 is being encrypted, so knowing the output gives Eve no information about which is being encrypted. We say that the scheme achieves perfect secrecy or perfect security.

Value of c seen by Eve	Probability p = 1	Probability p = 0
not seen	½	½
0	⅔	⅓
1	⅓	⅔

Table 6.10.5 How probability changes when Eve gets sight of value of c

p	k	c
0	☺	0
0	☺	1
1	☺	1
1	☺	0

Table 6.10.6 Look up table for encrypting p into c using key k

Key principle

Perfect security:
When the probability distribution of the output, the ciphertext, for the encryption system does not depend upon whether 0 or 1 is being encrypted we say that the scheme achieves perfect secrecy or perfect security because the output will leak no information about the input, the plaintext.

Encrypting long messages

If we replace ☺ with 0 and ☹ with 1, the encryption *Table 6.10.6* becomes the modulo 2 addition table for GF(2), *Table 6.10.7*.

p	k	c
0	0	0
0	1	1
1	0	1
1	1	0

Table 6.10.7 Look up table for encrypting p into c using key k

The exclusive-or operator $\oplus$ can be used to implement this table and encrypt plaintext p using key k to produce ciphertext c as follows

$$c = k \oplus p$$

Similarly, the exclusive-or operator can be used to decrypt ciphertext c using key k to produce plaintext p as follows

$$p = k \oplus c$$

Key point

VERY IMPORTANTLY by using XOR and choosing the key randomly, the XOR operator has a **50%** chance of outputting a **0** or a **1**.

To encrypt a long message, we first represent it as a string of n bits. Next, Alice and Bob should agree an equally long sequence of key bits, $k_1, \ldots, k_n$ chosen randomly. Now once Alice has produced the plaintext $p_1, \ldots, p_n$, she obtains the ciphertext $c_1, \ldots, c_n$, one bit at a time as follows:

$$c_1 = k_1 \oplus p_1$$
$$c_2 = k_2 \oplus p_2$$
$$\bullet$$
$$\bullet$$
$$\bullet$$
$$c_n = k_n \oplus p_n$$

The previous section argued that each bit c_i of ciphertext tells Eve nothing about the corresponding bit p_i of plaintext and nothing about any of the other bits of plaintext. From this we can draw the conclusion that the cryptosystem has **perfect secrecy** or **security**.

Questions

 A 3-symbol message, AQA is encrypted as follows. Each symbol is represented by a number between 0 and 26 (A ↦ 0, B ↦ 1, ..., Z ↦ 25, space ↦ 26). Each number is represented by a five-bit binary sequence (0 ↦ 00000, 1 ↦ 00001, ..., 26 ↦ 11010). Finally, the resulting sequence of 15 bits is encrypted using the key consisting of 15 randomly chosen bits 110000000101110 (obtained from random.org) and modulo 2 addition.

Compute the ciphertext.

Computational security
Limitations of the one-time pad

The success of the one-time pad is that it achieves perfect secrecy. However the following limitations have prevented more widespread use:

- The key is as long as the message

- Only secure if each key is used to encrypt a single message (i.e. key not used more than once)

This means that the parties wishing to communicate in secret, e.g. Washington, DC and Moscow, Russia via the "red phone" must share keys of total length equal to the total length of all messages that they might ever send.

If the same key k is used twice, e.g

$$c_1 = k \oplus m_1$$

$$c_2 = k \oplus m_2$$

the attacker can compute

$$c_1 \oplus c_2 = (k \oplus m_1) \oplus (k \oplus m_2) = m_1 \oplus m_2$$

This leaks information about m_1 and m_2 because it reveals where these differ: the characteristics of the ASCII coding scheme can be exploited to identify some letters and frequency analysis can be brought to bear as well.

Information

The "red phone" used in the 1980s for secure communication between the USA and the USSR was based on a one-time pad. The random key sequences or pads were delivered by courier.

Questions

 Study the ASCII code table and note that letters all begin with 01 and the space character begins with 00. Also note that XOR of two letters gives 00... and XOR of a letter and a space gives 01... It is easy to identify XOR of letter and space. If the identified XORed letters and spaces are XORed with space's ASCII code, the plaintext letter is recovered. The following two ciphertexts were intercepted. It is suspected that the same random key has been used to produce these. Assuming 8-bit ASCII, can you recover any letters of the plaintext messages?

c_1 = 010100001010110011001000111101111101000011101110
c_2 = 010000011010010011011101100100111101110011110011

(The key that was used so that you can check your answer:
000100011111110110001001110110111001001110111101)

Computational secrecy

In practice it is more convenient to allow the leak of information with a tiny probability to eavesdroppers with bounded computational resources, i.e. not unlimited. This means relaxing perfect secrecy by

- Allowing security to fail with tiny probability
- Only considering "efficient" attackers

To set this in perspective we need to consider what is meant by a tiny probability and "efficient" attackers.

Let's say we allow security to fail with probability 2^{-60} or 1 in 10^{18} times.

This is of the order of probability that a person will be struck by lightning in the next year.

Now consider a brute-force search of the key space.

Assuming for argument's sake that one key can be tested per clock cycle of the CPU (2014 commodity PC CPU):

- Desktop computer $\approx 2^{57}$ keys per year
- Supercomputer $\approx 2^{80}$ keys per year
- Supercomputer since Big Bang $\approx 2^{112}$ keys

The meaning of "efficient" attackers is attackers who can try 2^{112} keys.

Well, if we choose a key space of 2^{128}, i.e. keys of length 128 bits then we should meet the requirement for secrecy.

This kind of secrecy is called computational secrecy. It relies on allowing

1. security to fail but with a probability negligible in n where n is a measure of the challenge of breaking the system, e.g. factoring a given integer n
2. restricting attention to attackers running in time polynomial in n

The notion of computational secrecy leads to the classification of an encryption method as being computational secure if it safe to assume that no known attack can break it in a practical amount of time.

However, this is very different from a proof of security. Thus in theory, every cryptographic algorithm except for the Vernam cipher (one-time pad) can be broken, given enough ciphertext and time.

Key principle

Computational secrecy:
Computational secrecy relies on allowing

1. security to fail but with a probability negligible in *n* where *n* is a measure of the challenge of breaking the system, e.g. factoring a given integer *n*
2. restricting attention to attackers running in time polynomial in *n*

Key principle

Computational security:
An encryption method is computational secure if it safe to assume that no known attack can break it in a practical amount of time.

Information

IBM Quantum computer:
IBM makes quantum computer available to members of the public, 4th May 2016 - www-03.ibm.com/press/us/en/pressrelease/49661.wss
See www.research.ibm.com/quantum/

Task

13 Research why quantum computing might be a threat to ciphers that rely on computational security and not information-theoretical security.

Task

14 Look at the Kryptos transcript available from
www.elonka.com/kryptos/. Can you decrypt the four ciphertexts?
Don't worry if you can't –
see www.wired.com/2013/07/nsa-cracked-kryptos-before-cia

In this chapter you have covered:

- What is meant by encryption and its definition

- Caesar cipher and applied it to encrypt a plaintext message and to decrypt
  a ciphertext

- The limitations of the Caesar cipher

- Vernam cipher or one-time pad and applied it to encrypt a plaintext
  message and to decrypt a ciphertext

- Why Vernam cipher is considered as a cipher with perfect security

- Comparison of Vernam cipher with ciphers that depend on
  computational security

6 Fundamentals of computer systems

6.1 Hardware and software

Key concept

Hardware:
The hardware of a computer is the physical components, electronic and electrical, that it is assembled from. It is the platform on which software executes.

6.1.1 Relationship between hardware and software

What is hardware?

The hardware of a computer is the physical components, electronic and electrical, that it is assembled from. It is the platform on which software executes.

What is software?

Software consists of sequences of instructions called programs which can be understood and executed by the hardware in its digital electronic circuits or a virtual machine equivalent.

Questions

1. What is meant by hardware?

2. What is meant by software?

6.1.2 Classification of software

Computer software may be classified as follows:

1. The system programs (or system software), which control the operation of the computer itself, e.g. the operating system

2. The application programs (or application software), which solve problems for their users, e.g. constructing a letter using word processing software for printing and sending to someone.

What is system software?

A computer system uses a layer or layers of software to enable users to operate the computer without having to be familiar with its internal workings. This layer or layers is called systems software and includes the operating system and other forms of systems software.

What is application software?

Applications software is an application program or programs designed to support user-oriented tasks which would need to be carried out even if computers did not exist. For example, communicating in written form, placing orders for goods, looking up information.

Key concept

Software:
Consists of sequences of instructions called programs which can be understood and executed by the hardware in its digital electronic circuits or a virtual machine equivalent.

Key concept

System software:
A layer or layers of software which enables users to operate the computer without having to be familiar with its internal workings.

Key concept

Application software:
Application software is an application program or programs designed to support user-oriented tasks which would need to be carried out even if computers did not exist.

Key concept

Different types of software:
1. General purpose
2. Special purpose
3. Bespoke

Questions

 Describe the classification of computer software.

The need for and attributes of different types of software

Application software cannot execute unless it has been first translated into the language of the computer, machine code. or a form that is executable by a computer.

It needs to be loaded into main memory and it needs to obtain input from input devices such as keyboards and to write output to output devices such as printers and it may need to communicate with other computers.

Application software may need to store information permanently and to subsequently access stored information. The stored information should be backed up so, if necessary, it may be restored from a back-up copy. These services are provided by the operating system and utility software without which it would not be possible to run application software.

Application software may be classified as

- **General purpose application software**: software that is appropriate for many application areas is described as general-purpose application software. For example, word processing can be applied in writing-up project work, in personal correspondence, writing memos, writing a book, creating standard business letters. The software is relatively cheap because its development costs are spread among all the purchasers of the software, which in the case of popular application software will be a large number. It is likely to be very reliable because it has been produced by an experienced team of programmers and tested on a large customer base.

- **Special purpose applications software**: special purpose application software is used for a particular application. For example, a dentist might use application software written specifically to record and process dental treatments, a task that every dentist needs to do. A business might use an accounting package for its accounts of sales. It is likely to be very reliable because it has been produced by an experienced team of programmers and tested on a large but specialised customer base.

- **Bespoke software**: when no general purpose or special purpose software exists that could do the job, software must be written from scratch to solve the specific problem or to support the required task. This software is called bespoke (tailor-made) software. For example, a teacher interested in finding out how frequently his students logged on to the college's computer network and for how long, wrote a program using the programming language C to handle this task because no application program existed which could do this job.

6.1.3 System software

Systems software can be classified as follows:

- **Operating system software:** an operating system is a program or suite of programs which controls the entire operation of a computer

- **Utility programs:** a utility program is a systems program designed to perform a common place task, for example, formatting and partitioning a disk or checking a disk for viruses. Some utility programs are supplied with the operating system, others can be installed at a later time.

- **Library programs:** a program library is a collection of compiled routines that other programs can link to and use. Linking may be done at compile-time when building an executable or at run-time. Run-time library programs are loaded on demand and shared by different software applications. Loaded run-time libraries remain resident in memory until the last executing application is closed. In the Microsoft Windows operating system, the run-time libraries are called dynamic linked libraries or dlls.

- **Compilers, assemblers, interpreters:** these are computer language translators.

  - Compiler: a compiler translates a high-level language program into a computer's machine code or some other low-level language. Machine code is a language that the hardware of a computer can understand and execute. It consists of executable binary codes.

  - Assembler: an assembler translates a program written in assembly language into machine code. Assembly language is a symbolic form of machine code. The symbolic form consists of mnemonics such as ADD and SUB that denote the machine operation to be performed. An assembler simply substitutes the corresponding executable binary code for the mnemonics.

  - Interpreter: translates and executes a high-level language or intermediate-code program one statement at a time. It provides a way of executing programs not in the machine code of the computer.

Key concept

System software classification:
1. Operating systems
2. Utility programs
3. Library programs
4. Translators
   1. Compilers
   2. Assemblers
   3. Interpreters.

Information

Intermediate code:
This is a language which lies between a high-level language (HLL) and machine code. It is closer to machine code than an HLL. It supports operations for a fictitious machine. Compilers consist of several stages, one of which is intermediate-code generation. It is a much simpler task to write an interpreter for a new machine designed with a different instruction set than it is to write a compiler. Any program in intermediate-code form, including a compiler, can be "executed" by interpreting its intermediate-code form with the interpreter written for the new machine.
Examples of intermediate-code are p-code and bytecode.

Questions

6   What are the functions of each of the following software:

(a) operating systems   (b) utility programs   (c) libraries   (d) translators?

7   Name **three** different types of utility program.

6.1.4 Role of an operating system

The most fundamental of all the system programs is the operating system.

An operating system has two major roles:

- Hide the complexities of the hardware from the user so that the user is presented with a machine which is much easier to use.

- Manage the hardware resources to give an orderly and controlled allocation of the processors, memories and input/output (I/O) devices among the various programs competing for them, and manage data storage.

Key concept

Role of an operating system:
1. To hide the complexities of the hardware from the user.
2. Manage the hardware resources.

Questions

8   What is the role of the operating system?

In this chapter you have covered:

- The relationship between hardware and software and be able to define the terms:
  - hardware
  - software
- What is meant by:
  - system software
  - application software
- The need for, and attributes of, different types of software
- The need for, and functions of the following software:
  - operating systems (OSs)
  - utility programs
  - libraries
  - translators (compiler, assembler, interpreter)
- The role of the operating system

6.2 Classification of programming languages

Learning objectives:

■ *Show awareness of the development of types of programming languages and their classification into low- and high-level languages*

■ *Know that the low-level languages are considered to be:*

  • *machine code*

  • *assembly language*

■ *Know that high-level languages include imperative high-level language*

■ *Describe machine-code language and assembly language*

■ *Understand the advantages and disadvantages of machine-code and assembly language programming compared with high-level language programming*

■ *Explain the term 'imperative high-level language' and its relationship to low-level languages.*

Information

EDSAC film:

http://www.tnmoc.org/special-projects/edsac/edsac-history

Maurice Wilkes' 1976 commentary on the 1951 film about how EDSAC was used in practice.

6.2.1 Classification of programming languages

Low-level programming languages

Low-level programming languages are classified as

  • machine code

  • assembly language.

EDSAC and machine code

On May 6th, 1949, EDSAC ran its first program which printed a table of squares for integers in the range 0 to 99. The programme (sic) took two minutes to run. The program of order codes had been punched on paper tape as 5-bit binary codes (see *Figure 5.3.3* in *Chapter 5.5*). The order codes represented arithmetic and logical orders, shifts, jumps, data transfer orders, input and output orders and stop orders. The word "order" was literally an order for EDSAC to do something. These order codes were the first programming language, a low-level language known as machine code that was interpreted directly by the hardware of EDSAC. Two examples of these order codes are shown in *Table 6.2.1.1* where each 5-bit order code is expressed as a single letter. The single letter order codes were typed on a machine that punched the corresponding 5-bit code directly onto paper tape (see Information panel opposite for the 1951 film on how EDSAC was used in practice). Addresses were also expressed in decimal and then translated into binary.

Order code	Address	Description
A	n	Add the content of location n to the accumulator.
S	n	Subtract the content of location n from the accumulator.

Table 6.2.1.1 Examples of EDSAC order codes

Figure 6.2.1.1 shows a snippet of an EDSAC order code program. Each character represents a 5-bit code

```
T123SE84SPSPSP10000SP1000SP100SP10SP1S

QS#SA40S!S&S@SO43SO33SPSA46S

T65ST129SA35ST34SE61ST48SA47ST65SA33SA40S
```

Figure 6.2.1.1 EDSAC order code

Key concept

Machine code:
Machine code is a language consisting of bit patterns/binary codes that a machine can interpret, i.e. executable binary codes.

Key concept

Machine code instruction:
A machine code instruction is an operation which a machine is capable of carrying out.

Key concept

Low-level programming language:
The direct relationship with the hardware gives machine code instructions their low-level classification.

What is machine code?

Machine code is a language consisting of bit patterns/binary codes that a machine can interpret, i.e. execute. For this reason, machine code is referred to as executable binary codes. For example, the EDSAC order code program instruction

0010100000010101

means "transfer the content of the accumulator to storage location 21."

A machine code instruction is an operation which a machine is capable of carrying out. This direct relationship with the hardware gives machine code instructions their low-level classification. Therefore, higher-level operations for which there is no direct machine counterpart have to be broken down into a sequence of machine code instructions.

What is a machine code program?

A machine code language program is a program consisting of executable binary codes.

Questions

1 What is machine code?

2 What is a machine code instruction?

3 Why is machine code classified as a low-level programming language?

Assembly language

Writing programs directly in machine code is challenging. The EDSAC programmers wrote their programs using letters for the operation to be performed and addresses in decimal using the digit characters '0'..'9'.

The hardware on which they typed these letters and digit characters was wired to punch paper tape with the 5-bit equivalent of each.

We would call the form of the program shown in Figure 6.2.1.1 which uses letters, an assembly language program. In assembly language, a (symbolic) name is assigned to each operation/instruction code. The operation/instruction code name is called a mnemonic or memory jogger. The operation code mnemonic should describe in some way what the instruction does, e.g. LDR means LoaD a Register, ADD means add - see Table 6.2.1.2. The address field &1234 is expressed in hexadecimal (& is used to indicate this).

Assembly language	Description
LDR R_d, &1234	LDR means LoaD a Register with content of a memory location or word, R_d is the symbolic name for the register, &1234 is the memory location's address expressed in hexadecimal.
ADD R_d, R_n, R_m	ADD means add content of registers R_n and R_m, store result in register R_d.
STR R_d, &4321	STR means STore the content of the specified Register in a memory location or word.

Table 6.2.1.2 Some assembly language instructions

There is a ONE-to-ONE mapping between an assembly language instruction and its equivalent machine code language instruction.

For example,

LDR R_d, &1234 might be assembled to 000000 0001 01001000110100

The one-to-one mapping makes translating instruction mnemonics into the binary of machine code a simple task that can be assigned to a computer. The translator is called an assembler.

Questions

4 What is assembly language code?

5 What is the mapping between assembly language instructions and machine code?

6 What language translator is required to translate assembly language into machine code?

High-level languages

As the 1951 EDSAC film showed, a problem had to be recast by hand into a form that could use the machine code language of EDSAC. Wouldn't it be much better if the problem could be expressed in a programming language much closer to the problem space, leaving the task of translating to machine code to the computer? This thought led to the development in the 1950s of high-level languages, some of which are still used. For example, Fortran (1957) was designed for numerical applications and is still used by mathematicians, scientists and engineers, today.

High-level languages are closer to English than they are to the machine. This means that the mapping from a high-level language statement to machine code will be a one-to-many mapping because each high-level language statement will need to be broken down into several machine code operations. For example, the assignment statement

$$x \leftarrow y + z$$

when translated could become in the assembly language form of machine code

LDR R_0, &1234

LDR R_1, &1235

ADD R_2, R_0, R_1

STR R_2, &1236

Questions

7 What is meant by the term *high-level programming language*?

8 What is the mapping between high-level language statements and machine code?

Key concept

Assembly language:
Assembly language is the symbolic form of machine code. Each operation/instruction code of machine code is assigned a symbolic name or mnemonic describing what the instruction does, e.g. ADD.
There is a ONE-to-ONE mapping between an assembly language instruction and its equivalent machine code language instruction.

Information

GNU Fortran:
GNU Fortran is the primary open source version of the Fortran compiler widely used both in and out of academia. It is one of the Fortran compilers available for the Raspberry Pi.

Key concept

High-level programming language:
High-level programming languages are problem-oriented and therefore closer to English than they are to the machine. This means that the mapping from a high-level language statement to machine code will be a one-to-many mapping because each high-level language statement will need to be broken down into several machine code operations.

Information

High-level language classification:
Imperative:
- Procedural
- Object-oriented

Declarative:
- Logic
- Functional

Imperative high-level languages (HLL)

The word "imperative" is derived from the Latin word imperare meaning "to command". High-level languages that are classified as imperative do just that. They consist of a sequence of commands for actions such as *assign*, *add*, *write*, *read* which a programmer has written to solve some problem or accomplish some task. Table 6.2.1.3 shows a snippet of program code for an imperative high-level language. Procedural and Object-Oriented Programming languages are classified as imperative high-level languages, e.g. Pascal, Delphi, Basic, C, C++, Java, C#, Python and Javascript.

Imperative program	Description
y := 6;	assign 6 to y
z := 7;	assign 7 to z
x := y + z;	add z to y and store result in x

Table 6.2.1.3 Imperative high-level program

Another important feature of imperative languages is that their commands change a program's state, e.g. Table 6.2.1.3 shows that the variable *y* has its state changed by the action of the assign command from whatever value it was before to 6.

Questions

 Explain the term *imperative high-level language*.

Advantages of programming in machine code and assembly language compared with HLL programming

High-level language programs are converted into machine code by a translator called a compiler. Most compilers attempt to optimise the machine code which is produced. The compiler scans the machine code to see if it contains any unnecessary code which it then attempts to remove or adapt. Fewer machine code instructions means the code will take up less memory (smaller footprint) as well as running more quickly when executed. However, the process is not perfect, for example, where floating-point operations are concerned. In embedded computer systems, where speed of execution is paramount or memory is at a premium, the compiled code can be examined by hand and sections that are not already optimised replaced by hand-coded assembly language code, which is then assembled into machine code.

For short sections of code which need to run quickly or take up little space, it may be better to code directly in assembly language. Some high-level programming languages allow assembly language code to be embedded (inline) in the HLL program to take advantage of the time and space efficiency of assembly language coding.

Assembly language and machine code programming allow direct access to registers and low-level operating system routines which is not generally possible with most high-level language programming languages.

Questions

10 State **three** advantages of programming in assembly language compared with programming in a high-level language.

Disadvantages of programming in machine code and assembly language compared with HLL programming

Code written in assembly language or machine code is less readable than code written in a high-level language and therefore more difficult to understand and maintain, debug and write without making errors. Code written in assembly language or machine code uses the instruction set of a particular processor (processor family). It is therefore machine dependent and will only execute on processors that use this instruction set. High-level languages are machine independent. An HLL program is expressed in an English-like language which is turned into machine code by a compiler. As long as a compiler exists for a particular instruction set, the HLL program may be ported to and its compiled version run on a computer with a different instruction set processor from the one it was written on. HLL programs are easier to understand and therefore maintain than assembly language programs because they are written using statements that are close to English. They are less error-prone when writing for the same reason.

Questions

11 State **three** disadvantages of programming in assembly language compared with programming in a high-level language.

In this chapter you have covered:

 Classification of programming languages into low- and high-level languages

 Low-level languages classified as:

- machine code
- assembly language

 Imperative high-level language is a type of high-level language

 Machine-code language and assembly language

 The advantages and disadvantages of machine-code and assembly language programming compared with high-level language programming

 The meaning of the term 'imperative high-level language' and its relationship to low-level languages.

Key fact

Adv. of programming in machine code and assembly language:

Hand-coded assembly language when assembled can

- achieve a smaller memory footprint in machine code than compiled high-level language code
- achieve better code optimisation than compiled high-level language code and therefore code that will run faster
- directly access registers and low-level operating system routines which is not possible with most high-level programming languages.

Key fact

Disadv. of programming in machine code and assembly language:

Code written in assembly language or machine code is less readable than code written in a high-level language and so more difficult to

- understand and maintain
- debug
- write without making errors

Code written in assembly language or machine code is machine dependent making it difficult to port to a different instruction set processor compared with code written using high-level languages which do port readily because they are not machine-oriented.

6.3 Types of program translator

Key principle

Assembler:

An assembler translates assembly language into machine code.
One assembly language statement maps to one machine code statement.

■ 6.3.1 Types of program translator

Types of program translator

There are three types of program translator:

 • Assembler

 • Compiler

 • Interpreter

Role of an assembler

Programs written in assembly language have to be translated into machine code before they can be executed. This is done with an assembler.

Machine code is a language that the machine can execute, i.e. it is executable binary code (binary patterns for which machine operations are defined).

Assembly language is the mnemonic form of these executable binary codes. Thus there is a one-to-one correspondence between an assembly language statement and its machine code equivalent: one assembly language statement maps to one machine code statement. This is in contrast to a high level language statement which typically maps to several machine code statements.

Role of a compiler

A compiler is a program that reads a program (the source code) written in a high level programming language (the source language) and translates it into an equivalent program (the object code) in another language - the target language. As an important part of this translation process, the compiler reports the presence of errors in the source code program.

A compiler translates (compiles) a high level programming language source code program into a separate and independently executable object code target language program. The target language program or object code produced by the process could be

 • Machine code of an actual machine (in which case the compiler is called a native language compiler)

 • Intermediate code which can, if necessary, be interpreted by an interpreter, e.g. Java bytecode is an intermediate language produced by a Java compiler

 • Executable code for execution by a virtual machine.

A compiler translates one high level language statement into several machine code or target language statements.

Key principle

Compiler:

A compiler translates a high level programming language source code program into a separate and independently executable object code target language program. Object code is typically machine code.

A compiler translates one high level language statement into several machine code or target language statements.

Key principle

Interpreter:

An interpreter is a program that executes a high level programming language program, statement by statement, by recognising the statement type of a statement and then calling a pre-written procedure/function for the statement type, to execute the statement.

Key principle

Interpreter vs compiler:
An interpreter both "translates" and executes whereas a compiler only translates.

Key principle

Interpreter vs compiler:
A compiler produces a separate independently executable form of the source code program whereas an interpreter does not.

A compiler only translates a high level language program (the whole of the program), it does not execute it.

The process that the compiler engages in is called compiling,

A compiler consists of several stages:

- Lexical analysis – splits the source into user-defined "words", e.g. variable identifiers and language-defined "words", e.g. While
- Syntax analysis – checks that statements are grammatically correct
- Semantic analysis – e.g. type checking, "A" + 3.142 is incorrect as you can't add a real to a string
- Intermediate code generation
- Code optimising
- Code generation

Role of an interpreter

An interpreter is a program that executes a high level programming language program, statement by statement, by recognising the statement type of a statement, e.g. $X = X + 1$, and then calling a pre-written procedure/function for the statement type, to execute the statement. Therefore, an interpreter does not, unlike a compiler, produce an independently executable target language equivalent of the source language program. The application of interpreter to a source code program is called interpreting.

The differences between compilation and interpretation

The major differences between the compilation and interpretation are:

- An interpreter both "translates" and executes whereas a compiler only translates.
- A compiler produces a separate independently executable form of the source code program whereas an interpreter does not.
- A compiler is not needed when target form of source program is executed whereas in the case of the interpreter, execution requires the source code form of the program together with the interpreter, i.e. the interpreter needs to be available on the machine where the program is being run.
- If an interpreter is used then only the source code form of program is needed to execute the program whereas, if a compiler is used then the object code form of program is needed in order to execute the program.
- Interpreters are usually easier to write than compilers.
- With the compiler approach, if an error is discovered while the program is executing the source form of program must be located. An editor and the source form of the program must be loaded. The error must be pin-pointed which is not always easy and then corrected.

The compiler must be loaded and a compilation carried out. The new target form of program must then be loaded and executed. With an interpreter, the execution is halted at the point where the error occurs. The interpreter gives precise details of location of error. The error is corrected with an editor which may be co-located with interpreter. If it isn't, an editor will have to be loaded. However, no time-consuming compilation is involved and execution can resume immediately.

Situations in which assemblers, compilers and interpreters would be appropriate

Assemblers

For time-critical sections of code where execution speed is important, e.g. interrupt service routines, assembly language still has a role to play because in the hands of a skilled programmer, assembly language code can be written that is highly optimised for speed. As an assembler simply translates one assembly language statement into one machine code statement, that optimisation is preserved. Compilers can optimise code but the binaries produced cannot be guaranteed to be fully optimised for the given hardware. In the pecking order of speed, interpreters come after compilers.

Assembly language is still used where direct access to hardware is required e.g. processor registers or I/O controller registers. This is the case when writing device drivers, e.g. a screen driver. In this instance an assembler would be required to translate the assembly language program into machine code.

Compilers and interpreters

It is considerably more productive to write programs in high-level languages than in assembly language. There are relatively few programmers who are skilled in writing assembly language programs compared with the number of programmers skilled in writing in one or more high-level programming languages.

Compiled code which has been compiled into machine code of the computer will execute a lot faster than its interpreted source code equivalent (i.e. interpreter + the source code equivalent of the compiled code).

The immediate feedback and ease of locating errors in source code give interpreters an advantage over compilers when developing programs. This advantage is particularly beneficial for novice programmers or when programs are being prototyped and the write, compile, debug, edit cycle can be too time consuming.

Compiling has an advantage over interpreting because it produces a separate executable which means that the source code program does not have to be distributed. There are plenty of situations where this is desirable such as when producing commercial software or where there is a requirement is to protect the algorithm or coding technique used.

Key principle

Interpreter vs compiler: Where speed of execution and/ or direct access to hardware is required, use assembly language and an assembler.

Key principle

Interpreter vs compiler: Compiled code which has been compiled into machine code of the computer will execute a lot faster than its interpreted source code equivalent (i.e. interpreter + the source code equivalent of the compiled code).

Key principle

Interpreter vs compiler: Where rapid debugging and immediate feedback on errors is required including pinpointing the location of both syntax and runtime errors, use an interpreter.

Key principle

Interpreter vs compiler: Where a separate executable that can execute independently of its source code equivalent is required, use a compiler.

Key concept

Bytecode:
Bytecode is an intermediate language between machine code and high-level language source code.
It is produced by a compiler which has been designed to translate source code into object code for execution on a virtual machine based on a stack machine

Bytecode

Bytecode is an intermediate language between machine code and high-level language source code. Bytecode is produced by a compiler which has been designed to translate source code into object code for execution on a virtual machine based on a type of machine architecture called a stack machine. You will learn about an alternative type of machine architecture called a register machine in *Chapter 7.3.1*.

Compilers for stack machines are simpler and quicker to build than compilers for other machine architectures. For example, for a simple stack machine architecture, the compiled code for the statement $x \leftarrow x * y + z$ would take, minus the comments, the form:

```
push x        /transfer a copy of local variable x to top of stack

push y        /transfer a copy of local variable y to top of stack

multiply      /multiply the top two items on the stack,replace with result

push z        /transfer a copy of local variable z to top of stack

add           /add the top two items on the stack,replace with result

pop x         /remove top item from stack and store in local variable
```

The stack operations `push` and `pop` are covered in Chapter 2.3.1 of the Unit 1 textbook and evaluating expressions using a stack covered in Chapter 3.3.1 of the same textbook. A compiler for this simple stack machine would output byte-long numeric codes, called opcodes, for the operations push, pop, multiply and add. These opcodes are known as bytecodes because they are one byte long and they form the instruction set of the stack machine.

The bytecode stream issued by the compiler for this example might be as follows `1a 1b 68 1c 60 3b`. This bytestream example uses bytecodes for the Java Virtual Machine which is a stack-based machine that is able to interpret Java bytecodes. *Table 6.3.1.1* shows the corresponding interpretation of these bytecodes.

Bytecode	Operation
1a	push first local variable onto stack
1b	push second local variable onto stack
68	pop top two items on stack, multiply them together, push result on stack
1c	push third local variable onto stack
60	pop top two items on stack, add them together, push result on stack
3b	pop top item on stack, store in first local variable

Table 6.3.1.1 Java bytecodes and their interpretation

To execute bytecode on a virtual machine requires that it be interpreted by the underlying real machine, i.e. the bytecode is executed in software running on the underlying real machine. This software is called an interpreter.

Writing a software interpreter to interpret bytecode is an easier task than writing an interpreter to interpret high-level language source code. All that a bytecode interpeter has to do is parse (identify) and directly execute the bytecodes, one at a time. This also makes the bytecode interpreter very portable, i.e. very easy to move onto a new machine with a different instruction set, and very compact.

Interpreting bytecode programs is also much faster than interpreting their high-level language source code program equivalents because the interpreter written to interpret bytecode has to perform much less work and is therefore simpler.

Bytecode targets a virtual machine not a real machine and so can run on any machine or operating system for which a bytecode interpreter has been written.

This means that the same object code can run on different platforms by simply creating an interpreter for the platform. A compiler that outputs bytecode thus produces object code that is portable.

However, bytecode may be further compiled into machine code for better performance. Some systems, called dynamic translators, or "just-in-time" (JIT) compilers, translate bytecode into machine language as necessary at runtime.

Questions

1. Explain the role of each of the following:
   (a) assembler
   (b) compiler
   (c) interpreter

2. State **three** differences between compilation and interpretation.

3. (a) Give two reasons why programs are still written in assembly language
   (b) What is the relationship between
      (i) assembly language statement and machine code
      (ii) high level programming language statement and machine code?

4. Given a choice, under what circumstances would it be preferable to use:
   (a) a compiler;
   (b) an interpreter?

Stretch & Challenge question

5 A particular computer has two compilers for a high level language HLL. The compilers are called HLL1 and HLL2. HLL1 compiles a program written in HLL into the machine code of this computer, whereas HLL2 compiles an HLL program into intermediate code, which can then be executed by an interpreter running on this computer, if one exists.

On purchase, compiler HLL2 was supplied in intermediate code form without an interpreter, the same intermediate code that is produced by HLL2, and HLL1 in source code program form.

(a) With only a means to write assembly language programs and to run an assembler on the computer at this stage, explain carefully what could be done to enable HLL2 to compile HLL programs for this computer.

(b) Explain carefully how HLL1 can now be executed.

(c) Explain carefully how the machine code form of HLL1 can now be produced on this computer.

In this chapter you have covered:

- The role of each of the following:
  - assembler
  - compiler
  - interpreter
- The differences between compilation and interpretation
- Situations in which each would be appropriate.
- Why an intermediate language such as bytecode is produced as the final output by some compilers and how it is subsequently used.
- The difference between source code and object (executable) code

6.4 Logic gates

■ 6.4.1 Logic gates

Boolean variables

In 1847 George Boole, an English mathematician, introduced a shorthand notation for a system of logic originally set forth by Aristotle. Aristotle's system dealt with statements considered either true or false. Here are two examples:

It is sunny today.

Today is Tuesday.

Quite clearly these two statements are either True or False. If today is Wednesday then the statement "Today is Tuesday" is False. *Table 6.4.1.1* shows the possible outcomes of examining the truth of each statement.

Statement	Outcome	
It is sunny today	False	True
Today is Tuesday	False	True

Table 6.4.1.1 Possible outcomes for truth of statements

Just as we might use an integer variable G to record the number of goats in a farmer's field so we can use variable X as shorthand for "It is sunny today", and Y for "Today is Tuesday". The values that G can be assigned are the natural or counting numbers. For X and Y, we have only two possible values, True or False, to assign. We call X and Y Boolean variables, after George Boole who introduced this form of algebra called Boolean algebra. *Table 6.4.1.2* shows the Boolean variable equivalent of *Table 6.4.1.1* for "It is sunny today" expressed as Boolean variable X. Boolean algebra deals with Boolean values that are typically labelled True/False (or 1/0, Yes/No, On/Off).

X (It is sunny today)	Meaning
False	It is not sunny today
True	It is sunny today

Table 6.4.1.2 Boolean variable representation of truth statements

Boolean algebra had very little practical use until digital electronics and digital computers were developed. As digital computers rely for their operation on using the binary number system, Boolean algebra can be applied usefully in the design of the electronic circuits of a digital computer. Using Boolean values 1 and 0 instead of True and False, True in *Table 6.4.1.2* becomes 1 and False becomes 0 as shown in *Table 6.4.1.3*. X = 1 now means that "It is true that it is sunny today" and X = 0 means "It is not true that it is sunny today".

X	Meaning
0	It is not sunny today
1	It is sunny today

Table 6.4.1.3 Boolean variable representation of truth statements using 0 in place of False and 1 in place of True

It is then a small step to use Boolean variables to represent the state of components such as switches and indicator lamps as follows:

- a switch can be either closed (1) or open (0) and

- an indicator lamp can be either on (1) or off (0).

Y	Meaning
0	Switch is not closed
1	Switch is closed

Table 6.4.1.4 Boolean variable representation for state of a switch Y

Z	Meaning
0	Lamp is not on
1	Lamp is on

Table 6.4.1.5 Boolean variable representation for state of an indicator lamp Z

Logical OR operation

Things become interesting when switches and lamps are combined together in circuits. *Figure 6.4.1.1* shows a simple circuit consisting of two switches wired in parallel, one indicator lamp and one battery.

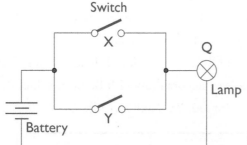

X	Y	Q
Open	Open	Off
Open	Closed	On
Closed	Open	On
Closed	Closed	On

X	Y	Q
0	0	0
0	1	1
1	0	1
1	1	1

Figure 6.4.1.1 OR logical operation: switch arrangement, switch state combinations and corresponding lamp state

The lamp is on if switch X is closed OR if switch Y is closed OR if both are closed, otherwise the lamp is off. The state of the switches can be expressed in the two Boolean variables, X and Y, as open or closed or using 0 for open and 1 for closed. The state of the lamp can also be expressed in a Boolean variable, Q, because the state has two possible values, off or on, which can be coded as 0 and 1, respectively.

Just as we can write the number equation for the total number of goats G, a farmer possesses,

$$G = X + Y$$

where X is the number in the first goat pen and Y is the number in the second, so we can write for the lamp circuit the Boolean equation

$$Q = X + Y$$

The operator "+" denotes the logical OR operation that behaves according to the tables in *Figure 6.4.1.1*, e.g. if X = 1 and Y = 1 then Q = 1, i.e. the lamp is on.

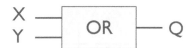

Logical OR Truth Table

If the logical operator "+" is represented by a rectangle labelled OR (*Figure 6.4.1.2*) then Boolean variables X and Y become its inputs and Q becomes its output. The inputs X and Y are transformed by the logical OR operation into Q.

In fact, the logical OR operation defines a Boolean function OR because it operates on binary inputs and returns a single binary output (*Figure 6.4.1.4*).

Figure 6.4.1.2 is called a block diagram. A single block in a block diagram is sometimes called a black box even though it is not coloured black.

The black box approach is a convenient way of representing the logical OR operation with the details of how it is implemented abstracted away. We now define the logical OR operation by its truth table (*Figure 6.4.1.3*) not by the particular details of its implementation which could be, for example, electronic, magnetic, optical, biological, hydraulic, or pneumatic.

X	Y	Q
0	0	0
0	1	1
1	0	1
1	1	1

Figure 6.4.1.3 Logical OR truth table

Logical OR		
Inputs: X, Y		
Output: Q		
Function: OR = X + Y		

Figure 6.4.1.4 Logical OR function

Logical AND operation

Figure 6.4.1.5 shows a simple circuit consisting of two switches wired in series, one indicator lamp and one battery.

X	Y	Q
Open	Open	Off
Open	Closed	Off
Closed	Open	Off
Closed	Closed	On

X	Y	Q
0	0	0
0	1	0
1	0	0
1	1	1

Figure 6.4.1.5 AND logical operation: switch arrangement, switch state combinations and corresponding lamp state

In this case, the lamp is only on if both switch X is closed AND switch Y is closed, otherwise the lamp is off. Again, the state of the switches can be expressed in the two Boolean variables, X and Y, as open or closed or using 0 for open and 1 for closed. The state of the lamp can also be expressed in a Boolean variable, Q, because the state has two possible values, off or on, which can be coded as 0 and 1 respectively.

We can write for the lamp circuit the Boolean equation

$$Q = X \cdot Y$$

Key point

Boolean function:
A Boolean function is a function that operates on binary inputs and returns a single binary output.

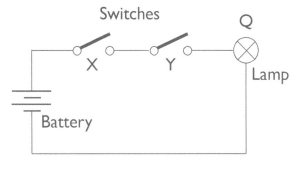

Switches

Lamp

Battery

X	Y	Q
0	0	0
0	1	0
1	0	0
1	1	1

Figure 6.4.1.6 AND truth table

Figure 6.4.1.7 Logical AND operation: block diagram

Figure 6.4.1.8 Logical NOT operation: block diagram

The operator "." denotes the logical AND operation that acts according to the truth table in Figure 6.4.1.6, e.g. if X = 1 and Y = 1 then Q = 1, i.e. the lamp is on.

Figure 6.4.1.7 shows the block diagram representation of the logical AND operation with inputs X and Y transformed into output Q.

Questions

1 Draw the arrangement of switches that produce output Q where $Q = X.Y + X.Z$

Logical NOT operation

It is the convention to use Boolean value 1 for the active state, e.g. lamp on, Q = 1, and the Boolean value 0 for the inactive state, e.g. lamp off, Q = 0. Another way of expressing lamp off is NOT lamp on. This insight leads to

NOT lamp on = lamp off

Or, NOT 1 = 0

And, NOT lamp off = lamp on

Or, NOT 0 = 1

X	Q
0	1
1	0

Figure 6.4.1.9 NOT truth table

The NOT black box in Figure 6.4.1.8 transforms input X into output Q using the logical NOT operation which inverts its input, $0 \rightarrow 1$, $1 \rightarrow 0$.

$$Q = NOT\ X$$
$$Q = \overline{X}$$

The line or bar placed over X is shorthand for NOT or the invert operation.

Logical NAND operation

If the output of the AND operation is inverted (Figure 6.4.1.10) then we have the NAND logical operation. Its Boolean equation is

$$Q = \overline{X . Y}$$

X	Y	Q
0	0	1
0	1	1
1	0	1
1	1	0

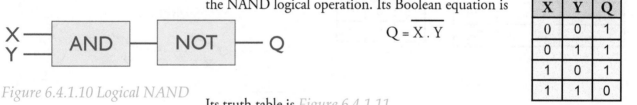

Figure 6.4.1.10 Logical NAND operation: constructed from an AND and a NOT, block diagram

Its truth table is Figure 6.4.1.11.

Figure 6.4.1.11 NAND truth table

Logical NOR operation

If the output of the OR operation is inverted (Figure 6.4.1.12) then we have the NOR logical operation. Its Boolean equation is

$$Q = \overline{X + Y}$$

X	Y	Q
0	0	1
0	1	0
1	0	0
1	1	0

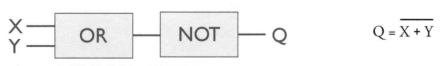

Figure 6.4.1.12 Logical NOR operation: constructed from an OR and a NOT, block diagram

Its truth table is Figure 6.4.1.13.

Figure 6.4.1.13 NOR truth table

Logical XOR operation

The truth table for the eXclusive-OR (XOR) operation (*Figure 6.4.1.14*) shows Q to be 1 if X is 1 and Y is 0 (Y not 1) or if X is 0 (X not 1) and Y is 1. Its Boolean equation is thus

$$Q = X . \overline{Y} + \overline{X} . Y$$

X	Y	Q
0	0	0
0	1	1
1	0	1
1	1	0

Figure 6.4.1.14 XOR truth table

It has its own symbol ⊕ so the Boolean equation is written as follows

$$Q = X \oplus Y$$

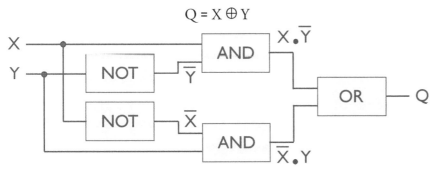

Figure 6.4.1.15 XOR logical operation: block diagram constructed from NOTs, ANDs and an OR

Key point

Logic gate:
A logic gate is a physical device that implements a Boolean function.

Questions

2 Q is only 1 if both X and Y are 1 and Z is 0 or if both Y and Z are 1 and X is 0 or if X, Y and Z are 1. Complete the truth table.

3 Draw the block diagram using AND and OR operations that produces output Q where $Q = X . Y + X . Z$

4 Draw the block diagram for logical operations that produce output Q where $Q = \overline{X . Y} + \overline{X . Z}$

X	Y	Z	Q
0	0	0	
0	0	1	
0	1	0	
0	1	1	
1	0	0	
1	0	1	
1	1	0	
1	1	1	

Logic gates

The logical operations above are implemented in electronic circuits as logic gates. The circuit symbols for these logic gates are shown in *Table 6.4.1.6*.

Drawing and interpreting logic gate circuit diagrams

Logic gates may be connected together to perform a variety of logical operations. The output of one gate is used as the input to other gates.

For example, in *Figure 6.4.1.16*, Boolean variable, E, is the output of an AND gate and the input to an OR gate.

The full circuit uses Boolean variables, A, B, C, D, E, F, Q as follows

E = A . B

F = C . D

Q = E + F

therefore   Q = A . B + C . D

Logic gate symbol	Logical operation
	OR
	NOR
	AND
	NAND
	XOR
	NOT

Table 6.4.1.6 Logic gate symbols (ANSI/IEEE standard 91-1984)

Questions

5   What is the output of this logic gate circuit
when its input is   (a) 0   (b) 1?

6   What is the output of this logic gate circuit when its
input is   (a) 0   (b) 1?

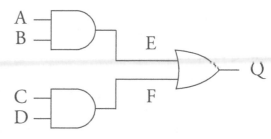

Figure 6.4.1.16 Three gates
connected to perform a logical
operation

Questions

7   What is the output, Q, of this logic gate circuit when its
inputs A and B are   (a) both 0   (b) both 1
(c) different from each other?

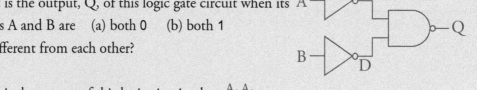

8   What is the output of this logic circuit when
(a) $A_0 = B_0$ and $A_1 = B_1$?
(b) $A_0 \neq B_0$ and $A_1 \neq B_1$?
(c) $A_0 \neq B_0$ and $A_1 = B_1$?
(d) $A_0 = B_0$ and $A_1 \neq B_1$?

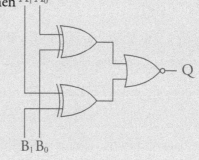

9   What is the purpose of the logic circuit in Q8?

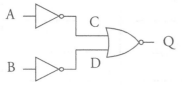

Figure 6.4.1.17 Three gates
connected to perform a logical
operation

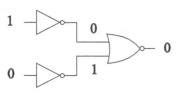

Figure 6.4.1.18 Tracing
Boolean values through the
three gates

Truth table equivalent of a logic gate circuit

A truth table can be used to analyse the behaviour of a logic gate circuit when
inputs are applied to it. For the logic gate circuit shown in Figure 6.4.1.17,
there are two inputs, A and B, and one output Q. The first two columns in
Table 6.4.1.7 contain all possible combinations of values for inputs A and B.
Column C contains the values NOT A and column D the values NOT B. Q's
column contains the values for C NORed with D, e.g. 1 NOR 1 → 0.

Figure 6.4.1.18 traces Boolean values through
the three gates, for A = 1 and B = 0.

Information

Logic simulator:
A freeware logic simulator is
available from
http://www.cburch.com/logisim/

A	B	C	D	Q
0	0	1	1	0
0	1	1	0	0
1	0	0	1	0
1	1	0	0	1

Table 6.4.1.7 Truth table
for logic circuit shown in
Figure 6.4.1.17

Questions

10 Complete the truth table for this logic gate circuit using Boolean variables A, B, C, D and Q.

A	B	C	D	Q
0	0			
0	1			
1	0			
1	1			

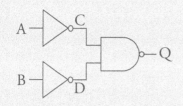

11 Draw the truth table for this logic gate circuit using Boolean variables A, B and Q.

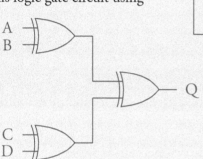

12 Draw the truth table for this logic gate circuit using Boolean variables A, B, C, D and Q. (Note: the table will have 16 rows for the values of the Boolean variables).

Questions

13 Complete the truth table for this logic circuit.

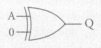

A	0	Q
0	0	
1	0	

14 Complete the truth table for this logic circuit.

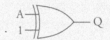

A	1	Q
0	1	
1	1	

15 Complete the truth table for this logic gate circuit.

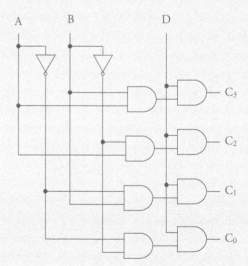

A	B	D	C_3	C_2	C_1	C_0
0	0	1				
0	1	1				
1	0	1				
1	1	1				
0	0	0				
0	1	0				
1	0	0				
1	1	0				

See Figure 6.4.1.32 for an example of how this circuit could be used.

Boolean expression equivalent of a logic gate circuit

The logic gate circuit in *Figure 6.4.1.19* may be expressed using Boolean variables, A, B, C, D and Q and the logical operators, NOT and NOR

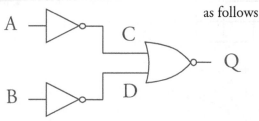

Figure 6.4.1.19 Three gates connected to perform a logical operation

as follows

$$C = NOT\ A = \overline{A}$$

$$D = NOT\ B = \overline{B}$$

$$Q = \overline{C + D}$$

therefore

$$Q = \overline{\overline{A} + \overline{B}}$$

$\overline{\overline{A} + \overline{B}}$ is the Boolean expression equivalent of the logic gate circuit shown in *Figure 6.4.1.19*. If we examine *Figure 6.4.1.6* carefully we see that the output from this logic gate circuit for inputs A and B is that of the truth table for an AND logic gate. Therefore, another equivalent Boolean expression is A . B.

Thus for the two Boolean expressions

$$A\ .\ B \text{ is equivalent to } \overline{\overline{A} + \overline{B}}$$

This means that we could replace the logic circuit in *Figure 6.4.1.19* by an AND gate with inputs A and B.

Logic gate circuit equivalent of a given Boolean expression

Consider the following Boolean expression

$$\overline{\overline{A}\ .\ \overline{B}}$$

To convert this into an equivalent logic gate circuit we must take each term in the expression, starting with the innermost, and apply each operation in turn. The innermost terms are

$$A \text{ and } B$$

applying the NOT operation to each

$$\overline{A} \text{ and } \overline{B}$$

turning these into equivalent logic gates

$$A \ \rightarrow\!\!\!\!\bigtriangledown\!\!\!\!\circ\ \overline{A} \qquad\qquad B \ \rightarrow\!\!\!\!\bigtriangledown\!\!\!\!\circ\ \overline{B}$$

applying the next operation AND

$$\overline{A}\ .\ \overline{B}$$

turning this Boolean expression into its equivalent logic gate circuit

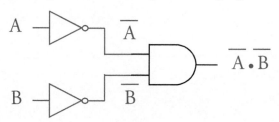

Finally applying the NOT operation to

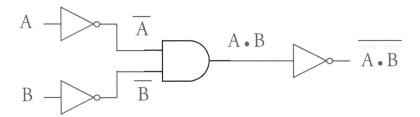

The number of gates can be reduced to three by replacing the AND-NOT combination by its logic gate equivalent NAND. The logic gate circuit becomes

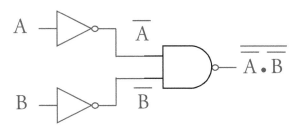

For more complicated Boolean expressions the same approach is used to arrive at the equivalent logic gate circuit, e.g.

$$\overline{\overline{A}.\overline{B}} + \overline{\overline{A}.B}$$

$\overline{\overline{A}.\overline{B}}$ is converted to its equivalent logic gate circuit W

$\overline{\overline{A}.B}$ is converted to its equivalent logic gate circuit Z

the output of these two circuits, W and Z is then ORed together, W + Z

If the order of evaluation needs to be controlled, brackets are used as the following example demonstrates

$$(\overline{A}+\overline{B}).(\overline{A}+B)$$

$(\overline{A}+\overline{B})$ is converted to its equivalent logic gate circuit W

$(\overline{A}+B)$ is converted to its equivalent logic gate circuit Z

the output of these two circuits, W and Z is then ANDed together, W . Z

Questions

16 Write an equivalent Boolean expression in terms of A, B, C and D for this logic gate circuit.

17 Write an equivalent Boolean expression in terms of A, B for this logic gate circuit.

Half-adder

To make a system to add together two binary digits A and B to produce a Sum and a Carry digit requires the following understanding of binary arithmetic

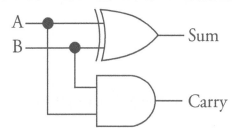

Figure 6.4.1.20 Half-adder constructed from an exclusive-OR and an AND logic gate

A	+	B	=	Sum	and	Carry
0	+	0	=	0	and	0
0	+	1	=	1	and	0
1	+	0	=	1	and	0
1	+	1	=	0	and	1

Table 6.4.1.8 Binary addition with Sum and Carry

You will notice that the A, B and Sum columns mirror the truth table for the exclusive-OR logical operation which means that A + B = Sum can be implemented with an XOR logic gate (Figure 6.4.1.20). The A, B and Carry columns mirror the truth table for the AND logical operation and so Carry can be generated with an AND logic gate.

Figure 6.4.1.21 shows the block diagram for a half-adder and Table 6.4.1.9 shows its truth table. This is the first step towards adding binary numbers which is to be able to add two bits. The result of the operation A + B is a two-bit number (Figure 6.4.1.22). If we label the least significant bit of the addition Sum, and the most significant bit Carry, then we can treat the half-adder as two functions as shown in Table 6.4.1.10.

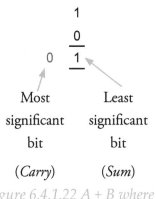

Figure 6.4.1.22 A + B where A = 1 and B = 0

Figure 6.4.1.21 Half-adder block diagram

Inputs		Outputs	
A	B	Carry	Sum
0	0	0	0
0	1	0	1
1	0	0	1
1	1	1	0

Table 6.4.1.9 Truth table for half-adder

Half-adder	
Inputs:	A, B
Outputs:	Sum, Carry
Function:	Sum = Least significant bit of A + B
	Carry = Most significant bit of A + B

Table 6.4.1.10 Half-adder as two Boolean functions, Sum and Carry

Questions

18 Trace the operation of the half-adder logic gate circuit shown in Figure 6.4.1.20 for inputs A = 1 and B = 1.

Full-adder

A pair of binary numbers, A and B, can be added digit by digit from right to left, by the simple rules of arithmetic. First, the two right-most digits, also called the least significant bits (LSB) of the two binary numbers, are added.

Next, the resulting carry bit (which is either 0 or 1) is added to the sum of the next pair of bits up the significance ladder. The process is continued until the two most significant bits (MSB) are added. If the last bit-wise addition generates a carry of 1, overflow has occurred, otherwise, the addition completes successfully. Figure 6.4.1.23 shows two different cases, one with overflow and one without.

Computer hardware for binary addition of two n-bit numbers can be built from logic gates designed to calculate the sum of three bits (pair of bits plus carry bit). The transfer of the resulting carry bit forward to the addition of the next significant pair of bits can be easily accomplished by appropriate wiring of logic gates. The logic gate circuit that does this is called a full-adder.

Figure 6.4.1.24 shows the block diagram for a full-adder, designed to add three bits, a pair of bits A, B, and a carry bit C. In a similar way to the half-adder case, the full-adder produces two outputs: the least significant bit of the addition, and the carry bit.

You should note that the Sum column of the first half of the full-adder truth table (Figure 6.4.1.24) is the same as that for the half-adder Sum function (Table 6.4.1.9).

You should also note that the Sum column of the second half of the truth table (Figure 6.4.1.24) is the same as that for the half-adder Sum function plus another half-adder Sum function with one input set to 1 (Figure 6.4.1.25) – see Q14.

In fact, the first half of the truth table (Figure 6.4.1.24) is the same as that for the half-adder Sum function plus another half-adder Sum function with one input set to 0 (Figure 6.4.1.25).

Setting this input to 0 simply causes the other input to be unchanged (see Q13)

0	0	0	1	Carry	1	1	1	1
	0	1	0	1	A		0	1	1	1
+	1	0	0	1	B	+	1	0	1	1
0	1	1	1	0	A + B	1	0	0	1	0

| no overflow | overflow |

Figure 6.4.1.23 Adding two binary numbers with carry, one case with overflow and one without

Inputs			Outputs	
A	B	C	Carry	Sum
0	0	0	0	0
0	1	0	0	1
1	0	0	0	1
1	1	0	1	0
0	0	1	0	1
0	1	1	1	0
1	0	1	1	0
1	1	1	1	1

Full-adder

Inputs:	A, B, C
Outputs:	Sum, Carry
Function:	Sum = Least significant bit of A + B + C
	Carry = Most significant bit of A + B + C

Figure 6.4.1.24 Full-adder block diagram and its truth table

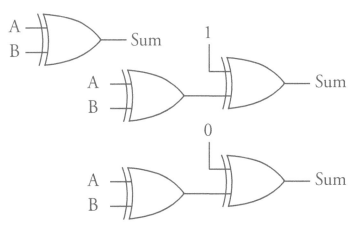

Figure 6.4.1.25 XORs of two half-adders implement the Boolean function Sum = A + B + C

241

Figure 6.4.1.26 shows the conditions for generating Carry = 1.

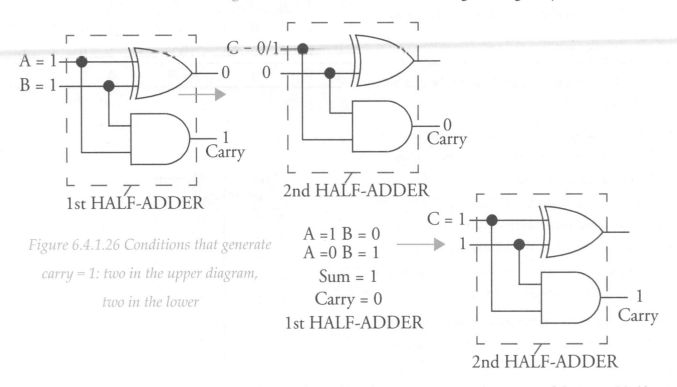

Figure 6.4.1.26 Conditions that generate

carry = 1: two in the upper diagram,

two in the lower

Note that the first half-adder carry output is the inverse of the second half-adder output: 1/0 and 0/1 respectively. Therefore if the two carry outs, one from the first half-adder and one from the second are made the first and second inputs of an OR-gate then its output will be the final carry. Figure 6.4.1.27 shows the final circuit. C becomes the CARRY IN from the previous digit column. A and B are the current digit column's bits to be added and CARRY OUT is the final carry from the current column.

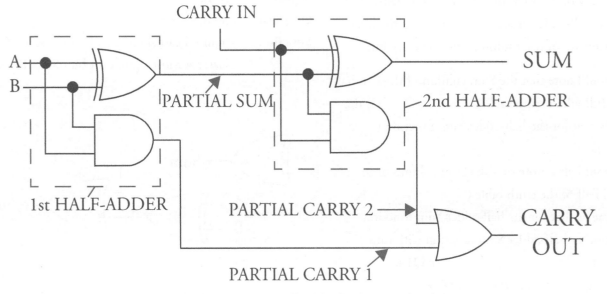

Figure 6.4.1.27 Full-adder logic gate circuit

Questions

19 Trace the operation of the full-adder logic gate circuit shown in Figure 6.4.1.27 for inputs A = 1 and B = 1 and CARRY IN = 1.

The logic gates and logic gate circuits that we have considered so far are known as combinational logic circuits. Combinational logic circuits compute functions that depend solely on combinations of input values. Combinational logic circuits are used in the construction of the Arithmetic and Logic Unit (ALU) which lies at the heart of the central processing unit (CPU) – see Chapter 7.3.1.

Edge-triggered D-type flip-flop

Although combinational logic circuits provide many important processing functions, they cannot maintain state. In addition to computing values such as 5 + 6, computers must also be able to store and recall values, i.e. they must be equipped with memory elements that preserve data over time. These memory elements are built from sequential logic gate circuits called flip-flops. Flip-flops are the elementary building blocks of all memory devices used in typical modern computers.

A flip-flop sequential logic circuit is one in which data is captured and "committed to memory" at a specific moment in time. Time in a computer is provided by a master clock that delivers a continuous train of alternating binary signals. The master clock is an oscillator that alternates between two phases labelled 0 and 1, or low and high with the transition between the two phases called an edge (Figure 6.4.1.28).

Figure 6.4.1.28 Clock signal of alternating binary signals

A clock signal applied to a flip-flop triggers the flip-flop, on an edge of the clock signal, into updating its "memory". It is this characteristic that gives the flip-flop its name. The flip-flop is designed to be triggered by either a rising edge (low to high) or a falling edge (high to low).

A data or D-type flip-flop is one that consists of a single-bit data input, a single-bit data output and a single clock input as shown in Figure 6.4.1.29. The description "edge-triggered" in edge-triggered D-type flip-flops is redundant because all flip-flops are edge-triggered. If it wasn't edge-triggered but was level-triggered it would be a latch.

Table 6.4.1.11 describes the behaviour of an edge-triggered D-type flip-flop for the case when triggering takes place on a rising edge.

The symbol ↑ means a rising edge clock signal. "Not rising" means the clock signal is not producing a rising edge currently, either because it is at another

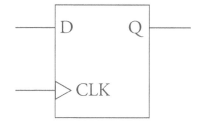

Figure 6.4.1.29 Edge-triggered D-type flip-flop triggered by a rising edge

D	Clock	Q
0	↑	0
1	↑	1
0 or 1	not rising	Q is unchanged

Table 6.4.1.11 States of an edge-triggered D-type flip-flop triggered by a rising edge

part of its low-high cycle or it is disabled. The state of the device changes on the rising edge of the clock signal only.

D	Clock	Q
0	↓	0
1	↓	1
0 or 1	not falling	Q is unchanged

Table 6.4.1.12 States of an edge-triggered D-type flip-flop triggered by a falling edge

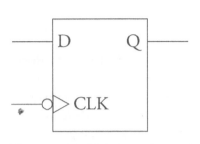

Figure 6.4.1.30 Edge-triggered D-type flip-flop triggered by a falling edge

Table 6.4.1.12 describes the behaviour of an edge-triggered D-type flip-flop for the case when triggering takes place on a falling edge. *Figure 6.4.1.30* shows the circuit symbol for an edge-triggered D-type flip-flop triggered by a falling edge (○).

Figure 6.4.1.31 shows a typical circuit for using a D-type flip-flop to "memorise" a datum. While the datum bit is being set up on the D input, the clock signal is prevented from reaching the clock input, CLK, of the D-type flip-flop by setting the Enable Clock Signal to the AND gate to 0.

The output of the AND gate is then guaranteed to be zero. Next, the Enable Clock Signal is set to 1, enabling the AND gate to pass the clock signal through to the CLK input of D-type flip-flop. On the rising edge of the clock signal, the output Q assumes the same value as applied to input D. The Enable Clock Signal is then set to 0, disabling the AND gate from passing the clock signal to input CLK.

The input to D may now be changed without affecting output Q. The D-type flip-flop remembers the value applied to input D at the time the clock signal last reached CLK.

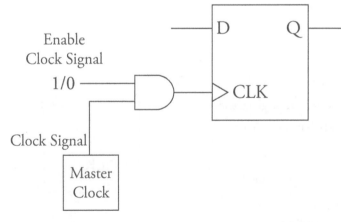

Figure 6.4.1.31 Edge-triggered D-type flip-flop connected via an AND gate to master clock

Questions

20 The output Q of an edge-triggered D-type flip-flop is currently 0. Explain how this output could be updated to Q = 1 using the circuit shown in *Figure 6.4.1.31*. Pay particular attention to the order of events.

Stretch and challenge extension

Questions

21 *Figure 6.4.1.32* shows a **4 x 2 memory**.

(a) Which row is selected when $A_0 = 0$ and $A_1 = 0$?

(b) What is the value of each Q for the selected row when $D_0 = 1$ and $D_1 = 0$ and the Write signal has been applied?

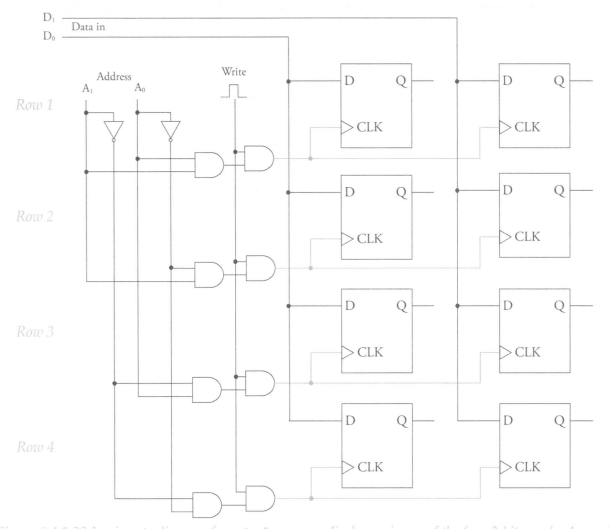

Figure 6.4.1.32 Logic gate diagram for a 4 x 2 memory. Each row is one of the four 2-bit words. A row is selected by setting the value of $A_0 A_1$. Data is sent along the Data in wires $D_0 D_1$ and written to the selected D-type flip-flops by the Write signal.

In this chapter you have covered:

■ Constructing truth tables for the following logic gates:

- NOT

- AND

- OR

- XOR

- NAND

- NOR
- ■ Drawing and interpreting logic gate circuit diagrams involving one or more of the above graphs
- ■ Completing a truth table for a given logic gate circuit
- ■ Writing a Boolean expression for a given logic gate circuit
- ■ Drawing an equivalent logic gate circuit for a given Boolean expression
- ■ Recognising and tracing the logic of the circuits of a half-adder and a full-adder
- ■ The use of the edge-triggered D-type flip-flop as a memory unit

■ 6.5.1 Using Boolean algebra

Boolean algebra

In Boolean algebra as in the algebra you have studied in Maths, variables are combined into expressions with Boolean operators that obey certain laws (rules).

Boolean variables

The variables that we have used so far are known as Boolean variables because they are two-state variables whose states have the values 0 and 1. These are not the 0 and 1 of arithmetic but represent True and False.

Boolean operators

We need only consider **three** operators because all other operators can be expressed in terms of these. They are the

+   operator denoting Boolean addition

•   operator denoting Boolean multiplication

−   operator denoting Boolean inversion

Boolean functions

We have encountered the Boolean AND function, the Boolean OR function and the Boolean NOT function in *Chapter 6.4.1* where they were implemented by logic gates with inputs, A and B, for AND and OR, and A for NOT. A and B are Boolean variables.

A	B	A • B
0	0	0
0	1	0
0	1	0
1	1	1

Table 6.5.1.1 Truth table for AND function

A	B	A + B
0	0	0
0	1	1
0	1	1
1	1	1

Table 6.5.1.2 Truth table for OR function

A	B	A • B	A + B	A • B + (A + B)
0	0	0	0	0
0	1	0	1	1
1	0	0	1	1
1	1	1	1	1

Table 6.5.1.3 Truth table for the two pairs of switches in parallel shown in Figure 6.5.1.1

These Boolean functions and Boolean expressions containing Boolean operators are equivalent as shown below

$$AND(A, B) = A \cdot B \qquad OR(A, B) = A + B \qquad \text{and} \qquad NOT(A) = \overline{A}$$

This means that Boolean algebra can be used to design logic gate circuits.

Combining Boolean functions

We also learned in *Chapter 6.4.1* that we can combine Boolean functions. The functions AND and OR may be combined in exactly the same way that we can, for example, combine pairs of switches that can perform these functions.

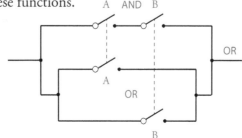

Figure 6.5.1.1 Pairs of switches connected in parallel

Table 6.5.1.3 shows the truth table for the combination of switches in *Figure 6.5.1.1.* The two switches labelled A are ganged together as shown by a dotted line, as are the two switches labelled B. This means that when the first switch A is open so is the second switch A and when the first switch A is closed so is the second A. Likewise for the two switches B.

Note that the A + B column of *Table 6.5.1.3* is exactly the same as the A • B + (A + B) column. Therefore, we can say that A • B + (A + B) is equivalent to A + B.

We draw the conclusion that the Boolean expression A • B + (A + B) can be simplified to A + B.

In general, many Boolean expressions may be simplified to Boolean expressions containing fewer terms. This is important if we are using Boolean algebra to design logic gate circuits because fewer terms means fewer gates.

Simplifying Boolean expressions

Boolean identities

In mathematics, an identity is a statement true for all possible values of its variable or variables. For example, the algebraic identity of A x 1 = A tells us that anything (A) multiplied by 1 equals the original "anything," no matter what value that "anything" (A) may be. Like ordinary algebra, Boolean algebra has its own unique identities based on the states 0 and 1 of Boolean variables as shown in *Figure 6.5.1.2.*

> ### Did you know?
>
> **Simplifying Boolean expressions:**
> Inspecting truth tables is a useful way of identifying simplifications.

$A + 0 = A$

A	0	A + 0
0	0	0
1	0	1

$A + 1 = 1$

A	1	A + 1
0	1	1
1	1	1

$A + A = A$

A	A	A + A
0	0	0
1	1	1

$A + \overline{A} = 1$

A	$\overline{A}$	A + $\overline{A}$
0	1	0
1	0	1

$0 • A = 0$

0	A	0 • A
0	0	0
0	0	0

$1 • A = A$

1	A	1 • A
1	0	0
1	1	1

$A • A = A$

A	A	A • A
0	0	0
1	1	1

$A • \overline{A} = 0$

A	$\overline{A}$	A • $\overline{A}$
0	1	0
1	0	0

$\overline{\overline{A}} = A$

A	$\overline{A}$	$\overline{\overline{A}}$
0	1	0
1	0	1

Figure 6.5.1.2 Boolean identities and their truth tables

Laws of Boolean algebra

Commutative law

Does it matter in which order inputs A and B are presented to an OR-gate or an AND-gate? The answer is no. Similarly, placing A to the left of the + operator or to the right doesn't matter, we still get the same answer. The same applies to the • operator. That is what is meant by saying that the + operator and the • operator are commutative.

$$A + B = B + A$$

≡ means identical to

$$A • B = B • A$$

Associative law

Does it matter whether the operator is applied to B and C first or to A and B first? The answer is no as long as it is the same operator. That is what is meant by saying that the + operator and the • operator obey the associative law.

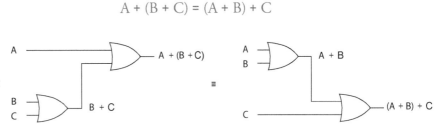

$$A + (B + C) = (A + B) + C$$

Take care because the associative law does not say that A + (B • C) has to be the same as (A + B) • C where the term in brackets is evaluated first. It is not. When written as A + B • C B • C is evaluated first because • has a higher precedence than +.

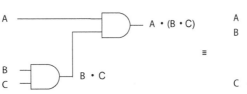
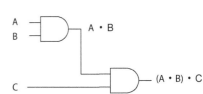

$$A • (B • C) = (A • B) • C$$

Distributive law

This law applies where a term or terms have been bracketed as follows

    A *operator1* (B *operator2* C) = A *operator1* B *operator2* A *operator1* C

where *operator1* may be • and *operator2* + or *operator1* may be + and *operator2* • as shown in Table 6.5.1.4.

Note the use of brackets to define the order of evaluation. A • B + C is not the same as A • (B + C) because • has a higher order of precedence than + and is therefore evaluated before + unless brackets are used.

operator1	operator2
•	+
+	•

Table 6.5.1.4 Operators for distributive law

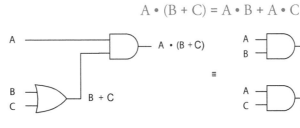
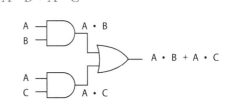

$$A • (B + C) = A • B + A • C$$

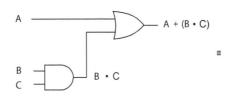
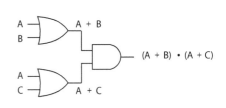

$$A + (B • C) = (A + B) • (A + C)$$

However, A + (B • C) = A + B • C because the brackets are redundant since • has higher precedence than +. Similarly, (A + B) • C is not the same as A + B • C because B • C is evaluated first in A + B • C whereas A + B is evaluated first in (A + B) • C and (A + B) • C = A • C + B • C.

Examples

Simplify A • A + B • 1

A • A + B • 1 = A + B • 1   using   A • A = A

A + B • 1 = A + B   using   B • 1 = B

The Boolean identities used in the examples and their truth tables are shown below

A • A = A

A	A	A • A
0	0	0
1	1	1

Simplify A • (B + 1)

A • (B + 1) = A • 1   using   B + 1 = 1

A • 1 = A   using   A • 1 = A

1 • A = A

1	A	1 • A
1	0	0
1	1	1

Simplify B • A + B

B • A + B = B • (A + 1)   using the distributive law

B • (A + 1) = B • 1   using A + 1 = 1

B • 1 = B   using B • 1 = B

A + 1 = 1

A	1	A + 1
0	1	1
1	1	1

Simplify A • ($\overline{A}$ + B)

A • ($\overline{A}$ + B) = A • $\overline{A}$ + A • B using the distributive law

A • $\overline{A}$ + A • B = 0 + A • B   using A • $\overline{A}$ = 0

0 + A • B = A • B   using 0 + X = X

A • $\overline{A}$ = 0

A	$\overline{A}$	A • $\overline{A}$
0	1	0
1	0	0

A + 0 = A

A	0	A + 0
0	0	0
1	0	1

Show that ($\overline{A}$ + $\overline{B}$) • (A + B) = $\overline{A}$ • B + $\overline{B}$ • A

($\overline{A}$ + $\overline{B}$) • (A + B) = $\overline{A}$ • A + $\overline{A}$ • B + $\overline{B}$ • A + $\overline{B}$ • B   using distribution law

$\overline{A}$ • A + $\overline{A}$ • B + $\overline{B}$ • A + $\overline{B}$ • B = 0 + $\overline{A}$ • B + $\overline{B}$ • A + 0   using $\overline{A}$ • A = 0 and $\overline{B}$ • B = 0

0 + $\overline{A}$ • B + $\overline{B}$ • A + 0 = $\overline{A}$ • B + $\overline{B}$ • A   using 0 + X = X and X + 0 = X

Questions

Using Boolean algebra show that

1 ($\overline{A}$ + B) • (A + $\overline{B}$) = $\overline{A}$ • $\overline{B}$ + B • A

2 A($\overline{A}$ + B)($\overline{B}$ + C) = ABC

3 Use a truth table for each question above to verify that the identities are true.

Information

Writing A • B as AB:
We can omit the • operator and write the Boolean variables one after another, e.g. A • B as AB.

Key principle

Redundancy theorem:
In a sum of products Boolean expression, e.g. A + A • B, a product such as A • B that contains all the factors of another product, A • 1, is redundant.

Distributive law for Boolean variables X, Y, Z:
$X + (Y • Z) = (X + Y) • (X + Z)$

Information

Product:
A • B is known as a product Boolean expression.

Sum:
A + B is known as a sum Boolean expression.

Sum of products:
A • B + B • C is known as a sum of products Boolean expression.

Product of sums:
(A + B) • (B + C) is known as a product of sums Boolean expression.

Show that $A + A • B = A$

$A + A • B = A • (1 + B)$ A is common factor

$A • (1 + B) = A • 1$ using (1 + B) = 1

$A • 1 = A$ using A • 1 = A

Show that $B + A • \overline{B} = A + B$

$B + A • \overline{B} = (B + A) • (B + \overline{B})$ using distributive law

$(B + A) • (B + \overline{B}) = (B + A) • 1$ using $B + \overline{B} = 1$

$(B + A) • 1 = B + A$ using X • 1 = X

$B + A = A + B$ using commutative law

Simplify $A + A • \overline{B}$

We could use the distributive law immediately but it is useful to be aware of other techniques:

$A + A • \overline{B} = A • 1 + A • \overline{B}$ using A • 1 = A

$A • 1 + A • \overline{B} = A • (1 + \overline{B})$ using distributive law

$A • (1 + \overline{B}) = A$ using $1 + \overline{B} = 1$

Questions

Using Boolean algebra show that

4 $\overline{A} + \overline{A} • B = \overline{A}$

5 $A + \overline{A} • B = A + B$

6 $A + \overline{A} • B + \overline{B} • C = A + B + C$

7 $A + \overline{A} • C + B + D • (\overline{B} • \overline{C} + A • \overline{C}) = A + B + C + D$

(HINT: Use the result proved in question 5)

Using Boolean algebra simplify the following

8 $A\overline{B}C + A\overline{B}\,\overline{C}$

9 $A • (\overline{A} + B) + A • \overline{B}$

10 $(\overline{A} • \overline{B} + \overline{A} • B) • A • B + A • \overline{B}$

11 Show that $(\overline{A} + B) • (A + \overline{B}) = \overline{A} • \overline{B} + B • A$

De Morgan's laws

De Morgan's laws expressed in a form that is useful for designing logic circuits are as follows

$$A + B = (\overline{\overline{A} \cdot \overline{B}})$$

$$A \cdot B = (\overline{\overline{A} + \overline{B}})$$

Table 6.5.1.4 demonstrates the equivalence of $A + B$ and $(\overline{\overline{A} \cdot \overline{B}})$.

Table 6.5.1.5 demonstrates the equivalence of $A \cdot B$ and $(\overline{\overline{A} + \overline{B}})$.

$$A + B = (\overline{\overline{A} \cdot \overline{B}})$$

A	B	A+B	$\overline{A}$	$\overline{B}$	$(\overline{A} \cdot \overline{B})$	$\overline{(\overline{A} \cdot \overline{B})}$
0	0	0	1	1	1	0
0	1	1	1	0	0	1
1	0	1	0	1	0	1
1	1	1	0	0	0	1

Table 6.5.1.4 Truth table for $A + B$ *and* $(\overline{\overline{A} \cdot \overline{B}})$

$$A \cdot B = (\overline{\overline{A} + \overline{B}})$$

A	B	A·B	$\overline{A}$	$\overline{B}$	$(\overline{A} + \overline{B})$	$\overline{(\overline{A} + \overline{B})}$
0	0	0	1	1	1	0
0	1	0	1	0	1	0
1	0	0	0	1	1	0
1	1	1	0	0	0	1

Table 6.5.1.5 Truth table for $A \cdot B$ *and* $(\overline{\overline{A} + \overline{B}})$

Examples

Show using Boolean algebra and De Morgan's laws that $\overline{A \cdot B} = \overline{A} + \overline{B}$

$$\overline{A \cdot B} = \overline{\overline{\overline{A} + \overline{B}}} \qquad \text{Using De Morgan's law} \quad X \cdot Y = \overline{(\overline{X} + \overline{Y})}$$

$$\overline{\overline{\overline{A} + \overline{B}}} = \overline{A} + \overline{B} \qquad \text{Using the Boolean identity} \quad \overline{\overline{X}} = X$$

Show using Boolean algebra and De Morgan's laws that $\overline{A + \overline{B}} = \overline{A} \cdot B$

$$\overline{A + \overline{B}} = \overline{\overline{\overline{A} \cdot B}} \qquad \text{Using De Morgan's law} \quad X + Y = \overline{(\overline{X} \cdot \overline{Y})}$$

$$\overline{\overline{\overline{A} \cdot B}} = \overline{A} \cdot B \qquad \text{Using the Boolean identity} \quad \overline{\overline{X}} = X$$

Information

Propositional logic form of De Morgan's laws:

1. $\neg(A \vee B) = (\neg A \wedge \neg B)$

2. $\neg(A \wedge B) = (\neg A \vee \neg B)$

where $\vee$ means OR, $\wedge$ means AND, $\neg$ means NOT.

Using + and • in place of $\vee$ and $\wedge$ respectively, and $^-$ in place of $\neg$, De Morgan's laws become

1. $\overline{(A + B)} = (\overline{A} \cdot \overline{B})$

2. $\overline{(A \cdot B)} = (\overline{A} + \overline{B})$

Key point

Cancelling NOTs:
Care should be exercised when cancelling NOTs. The following examples illustrate when you may cancel and when you may not:

$\overline{\overline{(A + B)}} = (A + B)$ cancellation possible

$\overline{\overline{(\overline{A} + \overline{B})}} = (A + B)$ cancellation possible

$\overline{\overline{(\overline{A} \cdot \overline{B})}} = \overline{(\overline{A} \cdot \overline{B})}$ cancellation not possible

$\overline{\overline{(\overline{A} \cdot \overline{B})}} = \overline{A} \cdot \overline{B}$ cancellation possible

Show using Boolean algebra and De Morgan's laws that $A \cdot \overline{B} + \overline{A} \cdot B = (A + B) \cdot (\overline{A} + \overline{B})$

$A \cdot \overline{B} + \overline{A} \cdot B = \overline{(\overline{A} + B)} + \overline{(A + \overline{B})}$ Using De Morgan's law $X \cdot Y = \overline{(\overline{X} + \overline{Y})}$

$\quad\quad\quad = \overline{\overline{(\overline{A} + B)} \cdot \overline{(A + \overline{B})}}$ Using De Morgan's law $X + Y = \overline{(\overline{X} \cdot \overline{Y})}$ and $\overline{\overline{X}} = X$

$\quad\quad\quad = \overline{\overline{A} \cdot A + \overline{A} \cdot \overline{B} + B \cdot A + B \cdot \overline{B}}$ Multiplying out the bracketed terms

$\quad\quad\quad = \overline{0 + \overline{A} \cdot \overline{B} + B \cdot A + 0}$ Using the Boolean identities $\overline{A} \cdot A = 0$ and $B \cdot \overline{B} = 0$

$\quad\quad\quad = \overline{\overline{A} \cdot \overline{B} + B \cdot A}$ Using the Boolean identity $0 + X = X$

$\quad\quad\quad = \overline{\overline{(\overline{A} \cdot \overline{B})} \cdot \overline{(B \cdot A)}}$ Using De Morgan's law $X + Y = \overline{(\overline{X} \cdot \overline{Y})}$ and $\overline{\overline{X}} = X$

$\quad\quad\quad = (A + B) \cdot (\overline{B} + \overline{A})$ Using De Morgan's law $X \cdot Y = \overline{(\overline{X} + \overline{Y})}$ and $\overline{\overline{X}} = X$

Show using Boolean algebra and De Morgan's laws that $\overline{(\overline{A} + B)} + \overline{(A + \overline{B})} = \overline{(A \cdot B)} \cdot \overline{(\overline{A} \cdot \overline{B})}$

Let $\overline{(\overline{A} + B)} + \overline{(A + \overline{B})} = \overline{X} + \overline{Y}$ Where X = $(\overline{A} + B)$ and Y = $(A + \overline{B})$

$\quad\quad \overline{X} + \overline{Y} = \overline{X \cdot Y}$ Using De Morgan's law $\overline{C} + \overline{D} = \overline{(C \cdot D)}$

$\quad\quad \overline{(X \cdot Y)} = \overline{(\overline{A} + B) \cdot (A + \overline{B})}$ Substituting for X and Y

$\overline{(\overline{A} + B) \cdot (A + \overline{B})} = \overline{\overline{A} \cdot A + \overline{A} \cdot \overline{B} + B \cdot A + B \cdot \overline{B}}$ Multiplying out the bracketed terms

$\quad\quad\quad = \overline{0 + \overline{A} \cdot \overline{B} + B \cdot A + 0}$ Using $\overline{A} \cdot A = 0$ and $B \cdot \overline{B} = 0$

$\quad\quad\quad = \overline{\overline{A} \cdot \overline{B} + B \cdot A}$ Using $0 + X = X$ and $X + 0 = X$

$\quad\quad\quad = \overline{(\overline{A} \cdot \overline{B})} \cdot \overline{(B \cdot A)}$ Using De Morgan's law $C \cdot D = \overline{(\overline{C} + \overline{D})}$

$\quad\quad\quad = \overline{(B \cdot A)} \cdot \overline{(\overline{A} \cdot \overline{B})}$ By commutative law

$\quad\quad\quad = \overline{(A \cdot B)} \cdot \overline{(\overline{A} \cdot \overline{B})}$ By commutative law

---

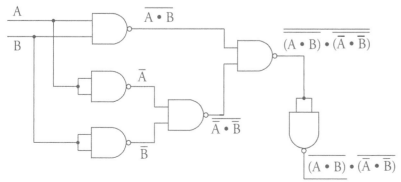

The original Boolean expression has been transformed into one that can be implemented just with NAND gates as shown in *Figure 6.5.1.3*.

Figure 6.5.1.3 NAND gate implementation

Questions

Using Boolean algebra and De Morgan's laws show for questions 12 to 15 that

12 $\overline{\overline{A \cdot \overline{B}} + \overline{A \cdot B}} = (A + B) + (\overline{A} + \overline{B})$

13 $\overline{(\overline{A} + B) + (A + \overline{B})} = \overline{A} \cdot \overline{B} + B \cdot A$

14 $\overline{\overline{A \cdot B} + A} = 1$

15 $\overline{\overline{A \cdot \overline{B}} \cdot \overline{\overline{A} \cdot B}} = \overline{B}$

16 Simplify the following:

(a) $\overline{\overline{A + \overline{B}} + (A \cdot \overline{B})}$

(b) $\overline{A} \cdot \overline{(A + \overline{B})}$

(c) $\overline{A} \cdot B \cdot C + \overline{A} \cdot B$

(d) $\overline{\overline{A} + \overline{(A \cdot B)}}$

(e) $\overline{(A \cdot B)} + \overline{(A \cdot \overline{B})}$

17 An electronic control circuit is used to switch off an industrial process when certain parameters, indicated by two-state electronic signals W, X, Y and Z, reach critical values. The process must be stopped if either W and X or W, Y and Z become critical at the same time. Write a Boolean expression for these parameters that when evaluated will output 1 to switch off the process and 0 otherwise.

18 The Boolean expression for EXCLUSIVE-OR is $A \cdot \overline{B} + \overline{A} \cdot B$.

(a) Convert this expression into a form that could be implemented with NAND logic gates each with two inputs.

Draw the NAND logic gate circuit for this expression.

(b) Convert this expression into a form that could be implemented with NOR gates each with two inputs.

Draw the NOR logic gate circuit for this expression.

19 For a process to proceed the following Boolean expression must be true $W \cdot (X + Y \cdot Z)$.

(a) Convert this expression into a form that could be implemented with NAND logic gates each with two inputs.

Draw the NAND logic gate circuit for this expression.

(b) Convert this expression into a form that could be implemented with NOR gates each with two inputs.

Draw the NOR logic gate circuit for this expression.

20 Given that

(1) Alice never gossips

(2) Bob gossips if anyone else is present

(3) Dick gossips under all conditions even when alone

(4) Soria gossips if and only if Alice is present

Determine the conditions when there is no gossip in the room.

Questions

21 A security light outside a house is controlled by two switches, which can be turned on or off from inside the house, and a light level sensor. The switches are named A and B. The light level sensor is named C. The security light is labelled L.

If the light level is low (i.e. it is night time) the output of the sensor is on otherwise it is off.

- If both switches A and B are off then the light L is always off.
- If switch A is on the light L is always on.
- If switch B is on and switch A is off then:
    o the light L turns on if the light level is low
    o the light L turns off if the light level is not low.

Write a Boolean expression to represent the logic of the security light system.

22 A second sensor is added to the system in Q21. This sensor is a movement detector. This second sensor is named M. The output of M is on if it senses movement otherwise it is off.

- If switch B is on and switch A is off then:
    o the light L turns on if the light level is low and movement is detected
    o the light L turns off after one minute if movement is not detected.

Write a Boolean expression to represent the logic of the security light system.

Universality of NAND gates

Any logic circuit can be implemented using only NAND gates.

$$NAND\ (A, B) = \overline{(A \cdot B)}$$

$$NOT(A) = NAND\ (A, A) = \overline{A \cdot A} = \overline{A}$$

$$AND\ (A, B) = NOT(NAND\ (A, B)) = \overline{\overline{(A \cdot B)}}$$

$$OR\ (A, B) = NAND\ (NOT(A), NOT(B)) = \overline{(\overline{A} \cdot \overline{B})}$$

$$NOR\ (A, B) = NOT\ (OR\ (A, B)) = NOT\ (NAND\ (NOT(A), NOT(B)))$$
$$= \overline{\overline{(\overline{A} \cdot \overline{B})}}$$

Information

Dual-in-line package (DIP) Digital Integrated Circuits(ICs or chips):

Logic gates are available as integrated circuits. An integrated circuit (IC) containing four NAND logic gates each with two inputs is shown below in both schematic form and as an actual IC.

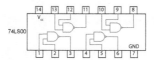

Information

NAND logic gate:

Information

NAND logic gate wired as a NOT gate:

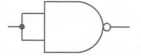

Universality of NOR gates

Any logic circuit can be implemented using only NOR gates.

$$\text{NOR (A, B)} = \overline{(A + B)}$$

$$\text{NOT(A)} = \text{NOR(A, A)} = \overline{A + A} = \overline{A}$$

$$\text{OR (A, B)} = \text{NOT(NOR (A, B))} = \overline{\overline{(A + B)}}$$

$$\text{AND (A, B)} = \text{NOR (NOT(A), NOT(B))} = \overline{(\overline{A} + \overline{B})}$$

$$\text{NAND (A, B)} = \text{NOT (NOR (NOT(A), NOT(B)))} = \overline{\overline{(\overline{A} + \overline{B})}}$$

In this chapter you have covered:

- Boolean expressions, e.g. $\overline{(A \cdot B)}$

- De Morgan's laws in a form for designing logic gate circuits

  $$A + B = \overline{(\overline{A} \cdot \overline{B})}$$

  $$A \cdot B = \overline{(\overline{A} + \overline{B})}$$

- Boolean identities

$A + 0 = A$	$A + 1 = 1$	$A + \overline{A} = 1$	$A + A = A$
$\overline{A} + 0 = \overline{A}$	$\overline{A} + 1 = 1$		$\overline{A} + \overline{A} = \overline{A}$
$0 \cdot A = 0$	$1 \cdot A = A$	$A \cdot \overline{A} = 0$	$A \cdot A = A$
$0 \cdot \overline{A} = 0$	$1 \cdot \overline{A} = \overline{A}$		$\overline{A} \cdot \overline{A} = \overline{A}$

  $$\overline{\overline{A}} = A$$

- Distribution laws

  $$A \cdot (B + C) = A \cdot B + A \cdot C \qquad A + (B \cdot C) = (A + B) \cdot (A + C)$$

- Using De Morgan's laws and Boolean identities to manipulate and simplify Boolean expressions

Did you know

Gate universality of NAND and NOR.

NAND and NOR gates possess the property of universality. This means, that a circuit consisting only of NAND gates or a circuit consisting only of NOR gates is able to perform the operation of any other gate type. The ability of a single gate type to be able to replicate the operation of any other gate type is one enjoyed only by NAND and NOR. NAND gates are preferred to NOR because
- NAND cheaper to fabricate than NOR
- NAND has a lower propagation delay than NOR.

7.1 Internal hardware components of a computer

7.1.1 Internal hardware components of a computer

Information

Processor (CPU):

The name processor was commonly used for the name of the central or general-purpose processor. Nowadays, CPU or Central Processing Unit refers to the general processor to distinguish it from other processors, e.g. Graphics Processing Unit (GPU). Originally, CPU meant processor + main memory.

Structure of a simple computer

The architecture of a simple (traditional) computer system consists of a set of independent components or subsystems which may be classified as either internal or external. The internal subsystems are:

- processor or Central Processing Unit (CPU)

- main memory (RAM)

- I/O controllers - input only, output only, both input and output

- buses

The external subsystems are on the periphery of the computer system and are known, therefore, as peripherals or peripheral devices - for example, the keyboard, visual display unit, printer, magnetic disk drive. The main processor or CPU exchanges data with a peripheral device through a part of an I/O controller called an I/O port. Peripheral devices are not connected directly to the CPU because the former often operate with signal levels, protocols and power requirements which are different from those used by a CPU. Therefore, peripherals are not under the direct control of the CPU. Figure 7.1.1 illustrates the structure of a simple (traditional) computer.

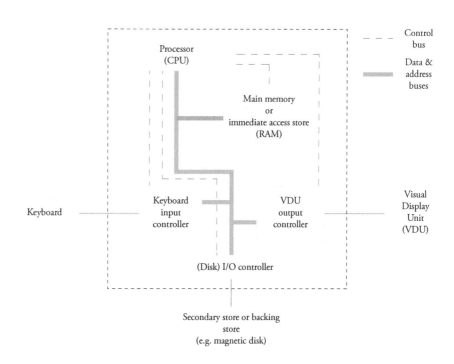

Figure 7.1.1 Block diagram of the simplified structure of a traditional (von Neumann) computer

Key concept

Peripheral:

A peripheral is a device that is connected to the computer system but which is not under the direct control of the processor. Instead the processor interacts with the peripheral indirectly via the peripheral's I/O controller which sits electrically between the peripheral and the system bus.

Key concept

System bus:

A bus that connects together processor, main memory and I/O controllers is called a system bus.

It consists of three dedicated buses:

1.   data bus
2.   address bus
3.   control bus.

Information

Bus line:

The wires of a bus are often referred to as lines or bus lines because they resemble tram lines used by trams.

Key fact

Bus width:

The number of wires in a bus is referred to as the width of the bus.

Information

Bus masters:

In the traditional shared bus system, one device takes charge of the system bus at a time, e.g. the processor or the main memory. A device that is granted access to the system bus so that it can communicate with another device is called the master during the communication and the device receiving the communication the slave.

Questions

1 The components or subsystems of a traditional von Neumann computer system are classified as either internal or external.
(a) Name the four internal components
(b) Give **three** examples of an external component

The bus subsystem

Buses can be parallel buses, which carry data words in parallel on multiple wires, or serial buses, which carry data in bit-serial form (one bit after another) in one or more communication pathways or channels (channel = pair of wires or equivalent). A parallel bus is a set of parallel wires connecting two or more independent components of a computer; for example in *Figure 7.1.2* control, data and address buses are shown connecting the processor (CPU), memory and I/O controllers. A key characteristic of the parallel bus in this example is that it is a shared transmission medium, so that only one component can successfully transmit at any one time.

A bus that connects together processor (CPU), main memory and I/O controllers has traditionally been called a system bus. Typically such a bus consists of from **50** to **100** separate wires (conducting pathways). Each wire (line) conveys a single bit at a time. The number of wires is referred to as the width of the bus. Although there are different bus designs, on a traditional system bus the lines can be classified into three functional groups: data, address and control lines. The subsets of lines are known as the data, address and control buses, respectively.

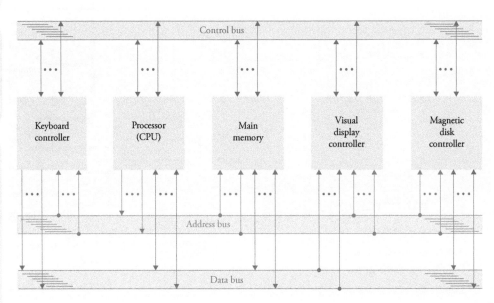

Figure 7.1.2 Internal components of a traditional shared bus computer system (von Neumann)

Questions

2 Distinguish between a parallel bus and a serial bus.

3 What is a parallel bus used for in the traditional von Neumann computer system and what name is given to this bus?

4 The system bus is subdivided into three functional groups of wires in the traditional von Neumann computer system. Name these groups.

5 What is meant by saying that this von Neumann system bus is a shared transmission medium?

Modern bus systems

The traditional computer system of von Neumann's design required that both processor (CPU) and main memory operate together at the same speed.

Modern general purpose processors operate at speeds much faster than main memory can operate. Thus the main processor or CPU in such a system will be held up waiting for a requested data word to be fetched from memory unless the CPU is decoupled from main memory in a way that allows it to do other tasks. Figure 7.1.3 shows how the bus architecture is evolving to take account of this and differences in speed of operation of other devices that are connected to the computer system. Figure 7.1.4 shows a printed circuit board (motherboard) for a relatively modern general purpose computer. In the latest processors and mother boards, the memory controller has been moved into the CPU and two separate buses are used, a memory bus and a packet-based (up to 32 bits) serial bus for peripherals.

Traditional (von Neumann) computer system data bus

The data bus, typically consisting of 8,16, 32, 64 separate lines, provides a bidirectional path for moving data and instructions between system components. The width of the data bus is a key factor in determining overall system performance. For example, if the data bus is 16 bits wide, and each instruction is 32 bits long, then the processor must access the main memory twice during each instruction cycle.

Questions

6 What is the purpose of the data bus and why is its width a factor in determining overall system performance?

Information

Serial bus:
Parallel buses suffer timing skew which limits their operating speed. and they only operate one-way at a time (half-duplex).
A serial bus does not suffer from timing skew and therefore can operate at a much higher rate than is possible with parallel buses. They can also operate in both directions simultaneously just by adding another serial channel. PCI Express, Serial ATA (SATA) and USB are all examples that support serial bus operation.

Address, data and control lines are replaced by address, data and control phases of the serial communication. which takes place in packets of bits.

The serial bus is now considered to be a point-to-point connection with one or more channels (pair of wires).

This has become an important mechanism for communicating between multiple cores and slices of main memory. One such system resembles the switching circuits of a telephone exchange which connects multiple pathways simultaneously to enable many independent calls to be made.

Key concept

Data bus:
The data bus provides a bidirectional path for moving data and instructions between system components.

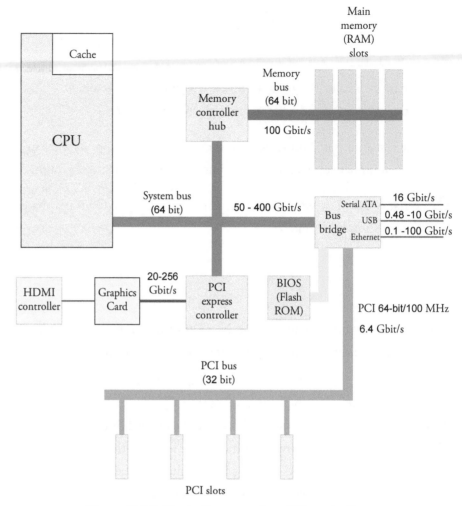

Figure 7.1.3 Block diagram of an I/O controller

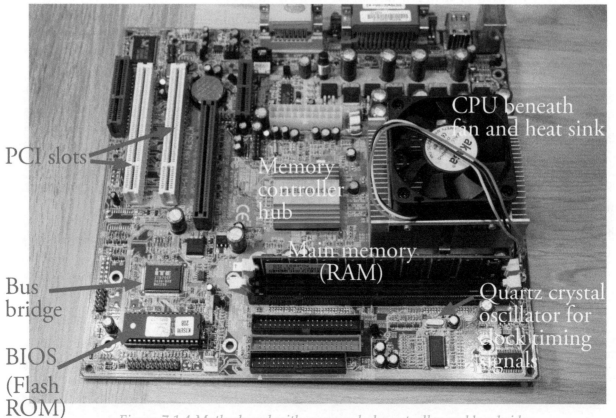

Figure 7.1.4 Motherboard with memory hub controller and bus bridge

Traditional (von Neumann) computer system control bus

The control bus is a bidirectional bus meaning that signals can be carried in both directions. The data and address buses are shared by all components of the system. Control lines must therefore be provided to ensure that access to and use of the data and address buses by the different components of the system does not lead to conflict. The purpose of the control bus is to transmit command, timing and specific status information between system components. Timing signals synchronise operations by indicating when information on the data, control and address buses is ready for consumption. Command signals specify operations to be performed. Specific status signals indicate the state of a data transfer request, or the status of a request by a system component to gain control of the system bus.

Typical control lines include:

- Memory Write: causes data on the data bus to be written into the addressed location.

- Memory Read: causes data from the addressed location to be placed on the data bus.

- I/O Write: causes data on the data bus to be output to the addressed I/O port.

- I/O Read: causes data from the addressed I/O port to be placed on the data bus.

- Transfer ACK: indicates that data have been accepted from or placed on the data bus.

- Bus Request: indicates that a component needs to gain control of the system bus.

- Bus Grant: indicates that a requesting component has been granted control of the system bus

- Interrupt request: indicates that an interrupt is pending.

- Interrupt ACK: acknowledges that the pending interrupt has been recognised.

- Clock: used to synchronise operations.

- Reset: initialises all components.

Key concept

Control bus:
The control bus is a bidirectional bus i.e. it carries signals between the processor and other system components and vice versa. The purpose of the control bus is to transmit command, timing and specific status information between system components.

Questions

 Using examples, explain the purpose of the control bus in the traditional von Neumann computer system.

Traditional (von Neumann) computer system address bus

When the processor wishes to read a word (say 8, 16, 32 or 64 bits) of data or an instruction from memory, it first puts the address of the desired word on the address bus. The width of the address bus determines the maximum possible memory capacity of the system - its address space. For example, if the address bus consisted of only 8 lines, then the maximum address it could transmit would be (in binary) 11111111 or 255 - giving a maximum memory capacity of 256 (including address 0). A more realistic minimum bus width would be 20 lines, giving a memory capacity of 2^{20}, i.e. an address space of 1048576 addressable memory locations (words). The address bus is also used to address I/O ports during input/output operations.

No of address lines, m	Maximum no of addressable locations	Maximum no of addressable locations expressed as a power of two, 2^m
1	2	2^1
2	4	2^2
3	8	2^3
4	16	2^4
8	256	2^8
16	65536	2^{16}
20	1048576	2^{20}
24	16777216	2^{24}

Table 7.1.1: Relationship between number of address lines m and maximum number of addressable memory locations

Questions

8 The address space of a particular computer system is 2^{20}. What does this mean?

9 The address bus of a traditional computer system consists of 16 lines. What is the total number of memory locations that theoretically can be addressed by this address bus?

Main memory

Main memory consists of a contiguous block of read/write, randomly accessible storage locations constructed from semiconductor technology - *Figure 7.1.5*. It is a store for addressable words, one word per location, with each word composed of the same number of binary digits - *Figure 7.1.6*

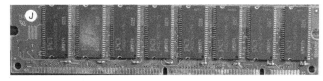

Figure 7.1.5 Main memory RAM chips

Each location is

- capable of "remembering" what was written to it

- able to change its contents to another bit pattern when a write request is received if the memory is read/write

- assigned a unique integer address by which it may be located

- capable of providing a copy of its contents when a read request is received.

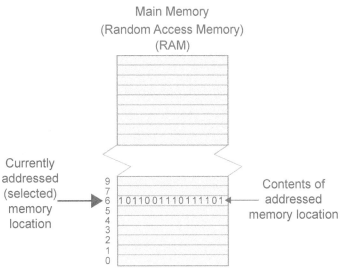

Figure 7.1.6 Main memory

The semiconductor technology used in read/write main memory means

- that the main memory is volatile, i.e. the contents of each storage location is lost when the power is removed.

- the contents of main memory are not restored when powered up again but instead each location consists of a random pattern of bits.

Storage locations may be visited (selected) one after another in any order noncontiguously, starting from anywhere in the memory. The time taken to access any particular storage location is the same.

These two facts have led to main memory being labelled Random Access Memory or RAM.

Information

von Neumann architecture:
Memory contains addressable words each composed of the same number of binary digits; addresses consist of integers running consecutively through the memory, 0, 1, 2, ...

Questions

10 How is main memory organised?

11 What is meant by volatile memory?

12 What is meant by random access in the context of main memory?

I/O Controllers

Peripheral devices cannot be connected directly to the processor. Each peripheral operates in a different way and it would not be sensible to design processors to directly control every possible peripheral. Otherwise, the invention of a new type of peripheral would require the processor to be redesigned. Instead, the processor controls and communicates with a peripheral device through an I/O or device controller.

Key concept

I/O controller:
An I/O controller is a board of electronics that enables the processor to control and communicate with a peripheral device through an I/O port.

263

The controller is a board of electronics consisting of three parts:

- An interface that allows connection of the controller to the system or I/O bus.

- A set of data, command, address and status registers (for block transfer devices the data register will be replaced by a block of storage locations).

- An interface that enables connection of the controller to the cable connecting the device to the computer.

An I/O controller presents a standard interface to the system bus so that the peripheral device appears to the processor as just a set of registers mapped onto the address space of the machine and which can be referenced by machine instructions - see *Figure 7.1.7*. This set of registers (and for block transfer devices, block of storage locations) is known as an I/O port.

I/O controllers are available which can operate both input and output transfers of bits, e.g. magnetic disk controller. Other controllers operate in one direction only, either as an input controller, e.g., keyboard controller or as an output controller, e.g., VDU controller.

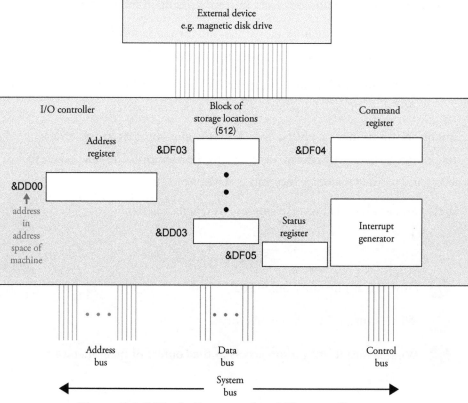

Figure 7.1.7 Block diagram of an I/O controller

Questions

13 What is an I/O controller?

14 Why is a processor not connected directly to external devices?

15 What is an I/O port?

Processor (CPU)

The processor (CPU) executes machine instructions that have been fetched along the data bus from main memory locations. The processor selects a memory location by placing the address of the location on the address bus. The data processed by machine instructions is also fetched along the data bus from main memory and the results of processing returned the same way. The control bus is used by the processor to assert actions, e.g. read from memory, write to memory, and to allow devices such as the keyboard controller to grab the attention of the processor via the interrupt mechanism when a key is pressed.

Von Neumann and Harvard architectures

General-purpose processors are designed to work well in a variety of contexts. In the von Neumann architecture, programs and data share the same memory which the processor communicates with over a shared bus called the system bus - Figure 7.1.8. As John von Neumann was working at Princeton university at the time this architecture is also known as the Princeton architecture.

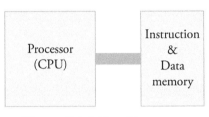

Figure 7.1.8 Von Neumann architecture

The Harvard architecture is often used in the design of processors where the context in which the processor is required to work is restricted or dedicated to a particular task, e.g. sampling and recording data from sensors. Such processors are used in embedded systems e.g., traction control systems in automobiles. In the Harvard architecture, program and data are allocated separate memories

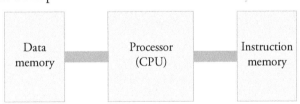

Figure 7.1.9 Harvard architecture

as shown in Figure 7.1.9. The processor is connected to both memories by separate buses so that each memory can be accessed simultaneously. The benefit of having a separate data memory is that data access is possible at a consistent bandwidth (same bit rate) which is particularly important for sampled-data systems.

The Raspberry Pi computer is based on the Harvard architecture.

The instruction sets of Harvard architecture processors can be different from that of general purpose von Neumann processors because Harvard processors need to support the context in which they will be used, e.g. graphics processing.

In graphics processing, algorithms perform identical operations on each section of the screen. For this type of processing, a processor that can multiply and

Did you know?

Sales of processors for embedded applications, e.g., mobile phones, far exceed the sale of processors for general purpose computing.

accumulate a block of data in a single instruction is very useful. Processors that perform this kind of specialised processing are called Digital Signal Processors (DSP). They are usually based on the Harvard architecture because they need to perform single instruction multiple data processing and accumulate results in an accumulator register.

Questions

16 What is the major difference between the von Neumann computer architecture and the Harvard architecture?

17 Where is each typically used?

In this chapter you have covered:

- The basic internal components of a traditional computer system
  - processor
  - main memory
  - address bus
  - data bus
  - control bus
  - I/O controllers
- The concept of a bus, parallel and serial and how address, data and control buses are used
- The difference between von Neumann and Harvard architectures and where each is typically used
- The concept of addressable memory

Information

EDSAC and SSEM:

The University of Manchester's Small-Scale Experimental Machine (SSEM) is generally recognized as the world's first electronic computer that ran a stored program—an event that occurred on 21st June 1948.

However, the EDSAC (designed and built at Cambridge university) is considered the first complete and fully operational electronic digital stored program computer. It ran its first program on 6th May 1949.

7.2.1 The meaning of the stored program concept

The stored program concept was proposed by John von Neumann and Alan Turing in separate publications in 1945. They proposed that both the program and the data on which it performed processing and calculations should be stored in memory together.

Specifically,

- The program to be executed is resident in an electronic memory directly accessible to the processor

- Instructions are fetched one at a time (serially) from this memory and executed in a processor

- Data is resident in an electronic memory directly accessible to the processor which can change it if instructed to by the executing program.

Figure 7.2.1.1 Plaque located at University of Manchester commemorating the creators of the first stored program computer

The stored program model in which program and data reside together in main memory when the program is being executed became known as a von Neumann computer. The world's first stored program electronic computer was designed and built at the university of Manchester.

The stored program concept enables computers to perform any type of computation, without requiring the user to physically alter or reconfigure the hardware.

Figure 7.2.1.2 ENIAC computer being reprogrammed by changing the wiring (*U.S. Army photo, http://ftp.arl.army.mil/~mike/comphist/*)

In contrast, to program the forerunners of the von Neumann computer and to change the data, the programmer had to manually plug in cables and set switches. This was quite tedious and time consuming. Figure 7.2.1.2 shows two programmers changing the program and data by literally rewiring the ENIAC computer, a non-stored program computer. This simple but fundamental idea of the stored program computer has been incorporated into all modern digital computers.

Program code and data are the same

The stored program concept, as embodied in the von Neumann computer, of having the program and data share the same memory means that the computer can modify its data or the program itself while it is executing.

Figure 7.2.1.3 shows the basic architecture of a von Neumann computer.

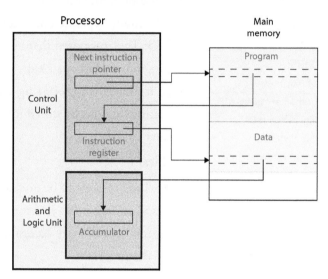

Figure 7.2.1.3 Stored program von Neumann computer basic architecture

Program code and data can be treated as if they are the same when they occupy the same memory. The memory is interpreted as an instruction when the next instruction pointer references it, and as data when an instruction references it.

Treating program code as data is useful when, for example, a program needs to be downloaded from a remote location because it can be treated as data and downloaded in the same way that an email can be.

Programs such as compilers also treat other programs as data when they read them. However, treating programs as data also has a downside. Computer viruses are programs too which get treated as data when being downloaded but as programs when the host computer is tricked into executing them.

Questions

1. What is meant by the *stored program concept*?

2. Explain what is meant by program code and data can be treated as the same thing in a von Neumann stored program computer.

3. State **one** advantage and **one** disadvantage of being able to do this.

Task

1 Explore the university of Manchester's site on the world's first stored program computer at

http://curation.cs.manchester.ac.uk/digital60/www.digital60.org/birth/index.html

In this chapter you have covered:

- the stored program concept
- why program code and data can be treated as the same thing in a von Neumann stored program computer.

Learning objectives:

■ *Explain the role and operation of a processor and its major components:*

- *arithmetic and logic unit*
- *control unit*
- *clock*
- *general purpose registers*
- *dedicated registers, including:*
  - *program counter*
  - *current instruction register*
  - *memory address register*
  - *memory buffer register*
  - *status register*

Processor

A simplified block diagram of a traditional processor is shown in *Figure 7.3.1.1*.

A typical processor or Central Processing Unit (CPU) consists of the following components:

- Control Unit, which fetches instructions from memory, decodes and executes them one at a time

- Arithmetic and Logic Unit (ALU) which performs arithmetic and logical operations on data supplied in registers, storing the result in a register. It can perform, for example, addition and subtraction, fixed and floating point arithmetic, Boolean logic operations such as AND, OR, XOR and a range of shift operations.

- Registers: general purpose, e.g. $Register_A$, and special purpose or dedicated registers, e.g. **Current Instruction Register (CIR)**, **Program Counter (PC)**, **Memory Buffer Register (MBR)**, **Memory Address Register (MAR)**, **Status Register**.

- System clock, which generates a continuous sequence of clock pulses to step the control unit through its operation.

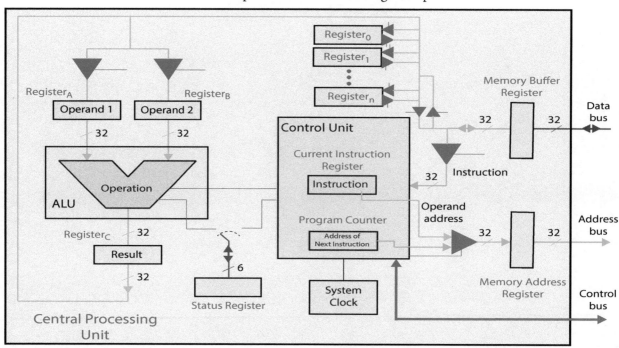

Figure 7.3.1.1 Simplified internal structure of a processor/central processing unit

The processor or central processing unit is connected to main memory by the system bus.

Questions

 General purpose registers are one major component of a traditional processor. Name and describe the **four other** major components.

Processor operation with main memory

A memory is a set of words, each with an address and a content:

- The addresses are values of a fixed size, the address length
- The contents are values of another fixed size, the word length
- A load operation is used to obtain the content of a memory word
- A store operation changes the content of a memory word.

In a von Neuman computer both program and data reside in the same memory. This memory is called main memory.

A processor interacts with this memory in 3 ways:

- by fetching instructions
- by loading a memory word into a processor register
- by changing the content of a memory word by a store operation.

The size of the registers in the processor defines the size of the processor, e.g. a 32-bit processor has registers that are 32 bits long. The length of a register is known as the word length of the processor. This word length is also usually the size of the memory word transferred in a load operation.

In Figure 7.3.1.1 the registers have a word length of 32 bits. Each is connected to a bus inside the processor which is also 32 bits wide shown as /32 in the figure.

Questions

 State **three** ways that a processor interacts with memory.

Control Unit

The control unit of the processor shown in Figure 7.3.1.1 controls fetching, loading and storing operations.

It fetches an instruction into the Current Instruction Register via the Memory Buffer Register and the data bus by

- reading the contents of the Program Counter to obtain the memory address of the memory word containing the instruction

- placing this memory address in the Memory Address Register connected to the address bus so that the addressed memory word can be selected and transferred across the data bus into the Memory Buffer Register

- transferring the instruction fetched from memory from the Memory Buffer Register into the Current Instruction Register

The control unit also

- decodes the instruction to determine if it is a load, store, arithmetic operation, or logic operation

- executes the instruction by

  ◆ using the instruction's operand fields as addresses to use in load or store operations, if required, or

  ◆ loading a memory word into a register, or

  ◆ changing a word of memory in a store operation, or

  ◆ controlling an arithmetic operation, e.g., ADD, or a logical operation, e.g., AND, in the Arithmetic and Logic Unit (ALU) using as operands the instruction's operand fields.

Questions

③ State the purpose of a processor's control unit.

④ Describe in detail the operation of a processor's control unit when executing a stored program, instruction by instruction. You should state the name and describe the role of each register in this process.

System clock

The system clock or clock is a unit inside the processor that provides regular clock pulses that the control unit uses to sequence its operations.

The clock signal is a 1-bit signal that oscillates between a "1" and a "0" with a certain frequency as shown in *Figure 7.3.1.2*. The change from "0" to "1" is called the positive edge, and the change from "1" to "0" the negative edge.

The time taken to go from one positive edge to the next is known as the clock period, and represents one clock cycle. The number of clock cycles that fit one second is called the clock frequency or clock speed.

$$\text{Clock period} \quad = \quad \frac{1}{\text{Clock frequency}}$$

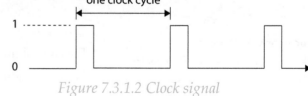

Figure 7.3.1.2 Clock signal

Table 7.3.1.1 shows some examples of clock speed/frequency for both current processors/CPUs and a very popular processor from the 1980s.

Clock frequency	Clock period/cycle	CPU
4GHz	0.25 nanoseconds	AMD 6300
900MHz	1.1 nanoseconds	ARM Cortex-A7 (Raspberry Pi 2)
1 MHz	1 microsecond	Motorola 6502 (BBC Model B computer)

Table 7.3.1.1 Clock speeds for some processors/CPUs

The number of clock cycles an instruction takes to be fetched and executed varies from processor to processor. A very simple design might use one clock cycle to fetch an instruction from memory and another clock cycle to execute the instruction as shown in *Figure 7.3.1.3*.

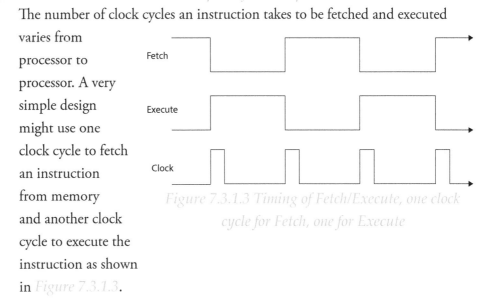

Figure 7.3.1.3 Timing of Fetch/Execute, one clock cycle for Fetch, one for Execute

A fetch phase occurs when the Fetch signal is 1 and the Execute signal is 0. An Execute phase occurs when the Execute signal is 1 and the Fetch signal is 0. Both Fetch and Execute signals are derived from the (master) clock signal and are therefore synchronised by this signal.

The number of instructions fetched and executed per second is given by

$$\text{Instructions per second} = \frac{\text{Clock frequency}}{\text{no of cycles per instruction}}$$

If the clock frequency for the 2-cycle processor design is 1 GHz then the number of instructions fetched and executed per second is

$$\text{Instructions per second} = \frac{1\text{GHz}}{2}$$

i.e. 500 million instructions per second.

Questions

5   What is the purpose of a processor's system clock?

6   What is meant clock speed?

7   With the aid of a diagram, explain how the control unit could use the system clock when an instruction in memory is executed in two clock cycles.

8   The clock frequency at which a particular processor is operated is 2GHz. The number of clock cycles per instruction is 2.
How many instructions can be executed per second in this processor?

Registers

Registers are memory locations internal to the processor that support fast access as well as rapid manipulation of their contents because they are made from the fastest memory technology.

Moving data between the ALU and registers and between registers is facilitated by dedicated pathways within the processor that the control unit can open or close relatively quickly.

However, the memory technology used and the dedicated pathways make implementing registers expensive and so the processor will have only a limited number, typically 32 but the number can range from 4 to 256. This is in contrast to memory locations in main memory which are made from much slower but cheaper technology and which are accessed over a shared pathway, the system bus. The cheap technology and shared bus make it possible to have a very large number of main memory locations, e.g. 1000 0000 0000 locations, but access is much slower than the speed the processor operates at.

> ## Questions
>
> What are processor registers?
>
> Processor registers and main memory are located in separate areas of a traditional computer system. State **four** other differences between processor registers and main memory.

General purpose registers

General purpose registers are registers that can be used by the programmer to store data, as needed. Each register will be capable of storing a memory word of a fixed size and will have a unique address known to the control unit. For example, if there are 16 general purpose registers then their addresses will be 0, 1, 2, 3, ..., 14, 15 (0, 1, 2, ..., E, F in hexadecimal).

Dedicated or special-purpose registers

Some registers are designed to be used by the control unit in a specific way, e.g. the Program Counter (PC) stores a memory address which is the address of the next instruction to be fetched and executed. The control unit sets this address to ensure it points to the next instruction. The control unit increments this address during a Fetch. It also changes this address if the current instruction is a branch instruction or a subroutine call instruction or an interrupt service routing call.

The following special-purpose registers are dedicated as follows:

- **Memory Buffer Register (MBR):** Connected to the data bus and contains a word to be stored in memory, or a word copied from memory. This is also called the Memory Data Register (MDR)

Key concept

Registers:
Registers are memory locations internal to the processor that support fast access to and manipulation of their contents because they are made from the fastest memory technology.

Key concept

General purpose registers:
General purpose registers are registers that can be used by the programmer to store data, as needed.

Key concept

Special purpose or dedicated registers:
These are registers that are used by the control unit in a specific or dedicated way, e.g. Program Counter.

Key concept

Program Counter (PC):
Points to the next instruction to be fetched and executed.

Key concept

Memory Buffer Register (MBR):
Connected to the data bus and contains a word to be stored in memory, or a word copied from memory.
This is also called the Memory Data Register (MDR).

Key concept

Memory Address Register (MAR):
Connected to the address bus so that the memory address it contains can appear on this bus and be used at the memory end of this bus to select a particular memory word.

Key concept

Current Instruction Register (CIR):
When an instruction is fetched from memory it is stored in this register while the control unit decodes and executes it.

Key concept

Status Register:
This register stores single bit condition codes each of which indicates the outcome of arithmetic and logical operations carried out in the ALU, e.g. Zero bit or flag is set to 1 if the result of the last arithmetic operation is zero otherwise it is set to 0.
The status register also has single bits to control the operation of the control unit, e.g. Interrupt Enable/Disable bit.

- **Memory Address Register (MAR):** Connected to the address bus so that the memory address it contains can appear on this bus and be used at the memory end of this bus to select a particular memory word

- **Instruction Register (IR) or Current Instruction Register (CIR):** When an instruction is fetched from memory it is stored in this register while the control unit decodes and executes it.

- **Status register:** This register stores single bit condition codes each of which indicates the outcome of arithmetic and logical operations carried out in the ALU - for example, an arithmetic operation may produce any of the following a positive, negative, zero result, a carry, overflow and the corresponding condition codes are set (made 1). Sometimes the name flag is used for a single bit condition code, i.e. a flag is set. These condition codes may subsequently be tested by the control unit when it is executing a conditional branch operation. The possible condition codes are

  - Sign: Contains the sign bit of the result of the last arithmetic operation

  - Zero: Set when the result is zero

  - Carry: Set if an operation resulted in a carry (addition) into or borrow (subtraction) out of a high-order bit. Used for multi-word arithmetic operations

  - Equal: Set if a logical compare result is equality. (Alternatively the zero flag may be used)

  - Overflow: Used to indicate arithmetic overflow.

The status register will also have single bits to control the operation of the control unit:

- Interrupt Enable/Disable: Used to enable or disable interrupts

- Supervisor: Indicates whether the processor is executing in supervisor or user mode. Certain privileged instructions can be executed only in supervisor mode, e.g. disabling interrupts, and certain areas of memory can be accessed only in supervisor mode.

Questions

11 What is meant by general purpose register?

12 What is meant by a dedicated or special purpose register?

13 State the role of each of the following:

    (a) Program Counter   (b) Memory Buffer Register   (c) Memory Address Register
    (d) Current Instruction Register   (e) Status Register.

Questions

14 Name **four** condition code flags and **two** control flags present in a typical status register.

Arithmetic and Logic Unit (ALU)

Figure 7.3.1.4 shows the ALU performing the arithmetic operation 3 + (- 5) producing the result -2.

The Negative flag condition code (N) in the status register is set to 1 because the result is negative. The Zero flag (Z), Carry flag (C), Overflow flag (O) are set to 0. The Interrupt Enable flag is 1 therefore enabling interrupts. The Supervisor mode flag (S) is 0, therefore the processor is in User mode. The Supervisor flag is set to 1 when the operating system needs to use the processor, otherwise it is 0 when a user is executing a program in the processor.

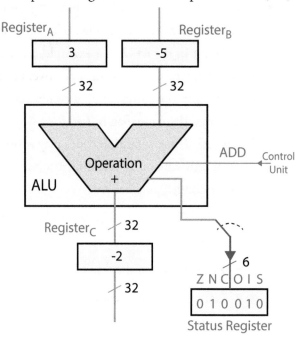

Figure 7.3.1.4 ALU performing an ADD operation

The Arithmetic and Logic Unit (ALU) performs arithmetic and logical operations on data supplied in registers, storing the result in a register as shown in *Figure 7.3.1.4*. It can perform, for example, addition and subtraction, fixed and floating point arithmetic, Boolean logic operations such as AND, OR, XOR and a range of shift operations.

Questions

15 What is the purpose of the Arithmetic and Logic Unit?

16 Describe, with the aid of a diagram, the role of registers in the execution of arithmetic operation 4 + (-4) in the Arithmetic and Logic Unit.

Tasks

1 Explore the operation of a processor using a simulator such as ASMTutor or Visual X-Toy.

Key concept

Arithmetic and Logic Unit (ALU):
The Arithmetic and Logic Unit (ALU) performs arithmetic and logical operations on the data.

Key concept

Negative flag:
The Negative flag condition code is the Sign condition code.

Information

ASM Tutor:
Available from Educational Computing Services Ltd -
www.educational-computing.co.uk
Visual X - Toy:
Available for Princeton university.
http://introcs.cs.princeton.edu/xtoy/

In this chapter you have covered:

■ The role and operation of a processor and its major components:

- arithmetic and logic unit
- control unit
- clock
- general purpose registers
- dedicated registers,
  including:
  - ◆ program counter
  - ◆ current instruction register
  - ◆ memory address register
  - ◆ memory buffer register
  - ◆ status register

■ The role and operation of a processor and its major components:

7.3 Structure and role of the processor and its components

■ 7.3.2 The Fetch-Execute cycle and the role of the registers within it

Learning objectives:

■ *Explain how the Fetch-Execute cycle is used to execute machine code programs including the stages in the cycle (fetch, decode, execute) and details of the registers used.*

Fetch-Execute cycle

A machine code program is made up of machine code instructions which are fetched from main memory, one at a time, and executed in the processor/CPU.

In *Chapter 7.3.1*, we learned that a processor executes each machine code instruction by breaking its execution into a three-step sequence with the execution synchronised by the system clock and controlled by the control unit.

This sequence of three steps is called the Fetch-Execute cycle or instruction cycle.

The first step is a fetch operation, the second a decode operation and the third step is execution.

These steps may be further broken down as follows:

(Fetch phase)

1. The address of the next instruction to be executed (held in the PC) is copied to the MAR which is connected to the address bus.

2. The instruction held at that address is fetched from memory along the data bus and placed in the MBR.

3. Simultaneously with step 2, the contents of the PC are incremented by 1 to point to the next instruction to be fetched.

4. The contents of the MBR are copied to the CIR. This frees up the MBR for the execute phase.

(Decode phase)

5. The instruction held in the CIR is decoded.

(Execute phase)

6. The instruction is executed. The sequence of micro-operations in the execute phase depends on the particular instruction being executed.

In register transfer notation, the Fetch-Execute cycle is described as follows:

$$\text{MAR} \longleftarrow [\text{PC}]$$

$$\text{MBR} \longleftarrow [\text{Memory}]_{\text{addressed}} \; ; \qquad \text{PC} \longleftarrow [\text{PC}] + 1$$

$$\text{CIR} \longleftarrow [\text{MBR}]$$

[CIR] opcode part decoded and executed

where [ ] means contents of and $\longleftarrow$ means assign.

Key concept

Machine code program:
A program consisting of machine code instructions.

Key principle

Fetch-Execute cycle:
A processor executes each machine code instruction by breaking its execution into a three-step sequence:
1.   Fetch
2.   Decode
3.   Execute

Key fact

Registers always involved in the Fetch-Execute cycle:
• Program Counter (PC)
• Memory Address Register(MAR)
• Memory Buffer Register (MBR)
• Current Instruction Register (CIR)

The PC is shown as being incremented by 1 in step 3 on the previous page.

Information

The PC is shown as being incremented by 1 in step 3 on the previous page. This assumes that every instruction is one memory word in length and therefore occupies one memory address. If this is not the case then the PC is incremented by the amount necessary for the PC to point to the next instruction to be fetched and executed.

Information

Branch instructions and effect on PC:

Branch instructions can change the contents of the PC when executed, e.g. Branch on zero <memory address> checks to see if the Zero flag in the status register is set. If it is, the contents of the PC will be replaced by the value of <memory address>. This value is the address of an instruction which the PC will now point to.

Information

Role of ALU:

The execution of an arithmetic or logical instruction will involve the ALU. The status register is updated during the execution to reflect the outcome of the arithmetic or logical operation.

Information

Role of other registers:

The execution of an instruction may involve one or more general purpose registers as well as the status register.

This cycle repeats until the execution of the machine code program terminates. Machine interrupts to the processor, if enabled, are ignored until the current Fetch-Execute cycle is completed.

Chapter 7.3.3 covers the meaning of the term opcode. Essentially it is the part of an instruction which specifies the type of operation to be carried out, e.g., ADD, SUBTRACT, AND, etc.

The operation specified by the opcode is applied to the operands part of the instruction, i.e. the part which isn't the opcode.

The word field is used to mean a part of an instruction, e.g. an operand field. In the case of multiple operands, there is more than one operand field.

The execution step of the Fetch-Execute cycle will know from the opcode if an operand field is a datum for immediate use or an address of a memory word containing a datum. If the operand is an address, the execution step will fetch this datum.

Questions

1. Name the **four** registers that are always used in the Fetch-Execute cycle.

2. Using both register transfer notation and prose, explain how the Fetch-Execute cycle is used to execute machine code programs.

In this chapter you have covered:

- *How the Fetch-Execute cycle executes machine code programs, instruction by instruction, in a repeating cycle consisting of three steps:*
  - *Fetch*
  - *Decode*
  - *Execute*
- *The registers that are always involved are*
  - *Program Counter (PC)*
  - *Memory Address Register (MAR)*
  - *Memory Buffer Register (MBR)*
  - *Current Instruction Register (CIR)*
- *These registers are used together with main memory in the Fetch-Execute cycle as shown here:*

$$\text{MAR} \leftarrow [\text{PC}]$$
$$\text{MBR} \leftarrow [\text{Memory}]_{addressed} ; \text{PC} \leftarrow [\text{PC}] + 1$$
$$\text{CIR} \leftarrow [\text{MBR}]$$
$$[\text{CIR}] \text{ opcode part decoded and executed}$$
$$\text{where } [\ ] \text{ means contents of and} \leftarrow \text{ means assign}$$

Information

Risc simulator:

A Risc simulator designed by Peter Higginson is available from

www.peterhigginson.co.uk/RISC/

■ 7.3.3 The processor instruction set

Processor instruction set

Format of instructions

The language of instruction for a digital computer is machine code; instructions consisting of sequences of binary digits which a machine can recognise and interpret. Machine code instructions are interpreted (executed) in a digital computer's processor (CPU) which must be designed so that it can understand and execute valid instructions. To understand why, consider instead a processor designed to understand certain three letter instruction words.

Table 7.3.3.1 shows examples of possible valid and invalid instructions formed from letters of the alphabet.

Valid instruction	Invalid instruction
ADD	DAD
SUB	BUS
MUL	ULM
DIV	VID

Table 7.3.3.1 3-letter valid and invalid English instruction words

Note that the instructions are of the same fixed length and only some particular combinations of letters are valid.

If these examples of valid combinations of letters correspond to the arithmetic operations, ADD, SUBTRACT, MULTIPLY, and DIVIDE then we need to include operand fields, R, B and C in each instruction so that an instruction such as ADD has something to add and somewhere to store the result. The instruction ADD R 3 4 adds together the values 3 and 4 and stores the result in R. We call ADD the operation and, R, B and C the operands. *Table 7.3.3.2* shows the new structure of two valid instructions

Valid instruction	Action
ADD R B C	Add C to B store result in R
SUB R B C	Subtract C from B store result in R

Table 7.3.3.2 Operation and two operands

Questions

1 What will be stored in R if the instruction is
(a) ADD R 3 4 (b) SUB R 4 3 (c) MUL R 4 3

Similar design constraints apply when designing the set of instructions (instruction set) that a processor (CPU) is capable of recognising as valid and then executing, i.e. instructions belonging to its instruction set. The processor or CPU will have access to registers, to memory, to an Arithmetic and Logic Unit and will also be able to make transfers of data to I/O devices such as magnetic disks.

The basic machine operations that a processor executes can be categorised as follows:

- Data processing: Arithmetic, logic and shift instructions
- Data transfers: Register and memory instructions
- I/O transfers: I/O instructions
- Control: Test, branch and halt instructions

Data processing instructions

The processor might support the instructions shown in column 1, *Table 7.3.3.3*, which also shows their abbreviated form in brackets, e.g. SUB.

Data transfer instructions

The processor might support the instructions shown in column 2, *Table 7.3.3.3*.

Control instructions

The processor might support the instructions shown in column 3, *Table 7.3.3.3*.

I/O transfer instructions

Instructions for this are not shown

Data processing	Data transfers	Control
ADD	LOAD (LDR)	COMPARE (CMP)
SUBTRACT (SUB)		
Bitwise logical AND	STORE (STR)	Unconditional branch (B)
Bitwise logical OR (ORR)		
Bitwise logical EOR (EOR)		Conditional branch (B)
Bitwise logical NOT(MVN)	MOVE (MOV)	
Logical Shift Left (LSL)		HALT (HALT)
Logical Shift Right (LSR)		

Table 7.3.3.3 Some examples of basic machine operations

but I/O transfers could be done using the given data transfer instructions if the registers and data locations in the I/O controllers for each peripheral are mapped into the addressable memory space by allocating main memory addresses to these in the same way as locations in RAM are mapped into the addressable memory space.

Operands

The next choice is how many operands? ARM processors are very popular and successful processors. ARM is the market leader (2015) for processors in smartphones and tablets and an ARM processor is the main processor in the Raspberry Pi and in the Parallela platform. ARM is a three-register architecture, meaning that a single machine code instruction can reference up to three registers. For example, the ADD instruction can specify two registers from which to read the values to be added and a third register, the destination register to store the calculated sum.

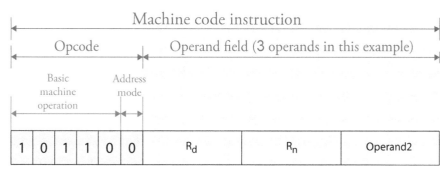

Figure 7.3.3.1 Structure of a machine code instruction with an example

Figure 7.3.3.1 shows that the structure of a machine code instruction is divided into an opcode field and an operand field. Register R_d is the destination register, register R_n contains the first input to the operation and Operand2, the second. Operand2 could be an actual value, 6, or it could be another register, R_m, containing the value to be used. The Address mode bit is used to select which is the case, e.g. 0 for value, 1 for value contained in specified register. The combined code for the basic machine operation and this address mode bit is known as the opcode or operation code field of the machine code instruction. The ARM processor has 16 programmer-accessible registers, R_0 through R_{15}. R_{15} is the Program Counter and R_{14} the link register (used to store the PC contents when a subroutine is called). Usually, another register is used for the Stack Pointer. Therefore, R_d, R_n and R_m can be any of the remaining thirteen registers, R_0 through R_{12}, e.g. R_1, R_2 and R_3, respectively.

With six bits allocated to the opcode field of the machine code instruction shown in *Figure 7.3.3.1* and every other instruction, there are a possible 2^6 different opcodes, one for each 6-bit pattern. *Table 7.3.3.4* shows how the number of possible opcodes varies with the number of bits reserved for the opcode field of a machine code instruction (remember: opcode field size is fixed at the design stage of a processor).

No of bits, n in opcode field	No of possible opcodes 2^n	No of possible opcodes
4	2^4	16
5	2^5	32
6	2^6	64

Table 7.3.3.4 No of possible opcodes for a given no of opcode field bits

Opcode	Machine code instruction format	Description
000000	LDR R_d, <memory ref>	Load the value stored in the memory location specified by <memory ref> into register R_d.
000010	STR R_d, <memory ref>	Store the value that is in register R_d into the memory location specified by <memory ref>.
000100 000101	ADD R_d, R_n, <operand2>	Add the value specified in <operand2> to the value in register R_n and store the result in register R_d. 000100 for when operand2 is a value, 000101 for when operand2 is another register, R_m. The same interpretation applies to the other two opcode instructions.
000110 000111	SUB R_d, R_n, <operand2>	Subtract the value specified by <operand2> from the value in register R_n and store the result in register R_d. For interpretation of why two opcodes, see ADD for why two opcodes.
001000 001001	MOV R_d, <operand2>	Copy the value specified by <operand2> into register R_d. For interpretation see ADD.
001010 001011	CMP R_n, <operand2>	Compare the value stored in register R_n with the value specified by <operand2>. See ADD
001100	B <label>	Always branch to the instruction at position <label> in the program.
011101 011111 011101 011111	B <condition> <label>	Conditionally branch to the instruction at position <label> in the program if the last comparison met the criteria specified by the <condition>. Possible values for <condition> and their meaning are: EQ: Equal to NE: Not equal to GT: Greater than LT: Less than.
010010 010011	AND R_d, R_n, <operand2>	Perform a bitwise logical AND operation between the value in register R_n and the value specified by <operand2> and store the result in register R_d. See ADD for why two opcodes.
010100 010101	ORR R_d, R_n, <operand2>	Perform a bitwise logical OR operation between the value in register R_n and the value specified by <operand2> and store the result in register R_d. See ADD for why two opcodes.
010110 010111	EOR R_d, R_n, <operand2>	Perform a bitwise logical eXclusive OR (XOR) operation between the value in register R_n and the value specified by <operand2> and store the result in register R_d. See ADD for why two opcodes.
011000 011001	MVN R_d, <operand2>	Perform a bitwise logical NOT operation on the value specified by <operand2> and store the result in register R_d. See ADD for why there are two opcodes.
011010 011011	LSL R_d, R_n, <operand2>	Logically shift left the value stored in register R_n by the number of bits specified by <operand2> and store the result in register R_d. See ADD for why there are two opcodes.
111100 111101	LSR R_d, R_n, <operand2>	Logically shift right the value stored in register R_n by the number of bits specified by <operand2> and store the result in register R_d. See ADD for why there are two opcodes.
111110	HALT	Stops the execution of the program.

Table 7.3.3.5 6-bit opcodes mapped to machine operations. Reproduced with permission of AQA. Currently only in specimen papers and has therefore not been through the complete rigorous question paper process and is liable to change. Please consult AQA's website for the most recent version of the specification.

Table 7.3.3.5 shows a possible mapping of some 6-bit opcodes (5 bits for basic machine operation, 1 bit for address mode) to machine operations for an imaginary processor.

Instruction set

The simple operations referenced in Table 7.3.3.5 may be combined together in sequences to perform quite complicated tasks.

The set of 28 bit patterns (strings of bits) shown in the opcode column of Table 7.3.3.5 represent these operations for a given processor and are known as the processor instruction set. Note that if Table 7.3.3.5 shows all the operations that a processor has been designed to understand and interpret then four bit patterns do not correspond to any defined machine operations because for a 6-bit opcode field, there are 32 possible bit patterns but only 28 are used to define opcodes. We therefore use the following definition of instruction set:

The set of bit patterns for which machine operations have been defined.

An instruction set is processor specific

An instruction set is specific to a particular processor for the following reasons:

- The machine operations that a processor is designed to perform varies in number and type from processor to processor, e.g. from the ARM® Cortex®-A7 CPU used in the Raspberry Pi 2 to the Intel® Core™ i7 CPU used in laptops and PCs.
- The number of bits allocated to the opcode field can also vary from processor to processor as well as how they are mapped to the operations that the processor supports. Therefore, machine code programs written for the ARM Cortex-A7 CPU will not run on an Intel Core i7 CPU.
- The number of possible operands, their type and the number of bits reserved for each may also vary from processor to processor.
- The design of a processor's control unit instruction decoder circuits reflects the structure of the machine code instructions and will not therefore be able to decode instructions designed for a different processor.

Structure of machine code instructions

We have learned that a machine code instruction is divided into an opcode part and an operand part as shown again in Figure 7.3.3.2.

Opcode	Operand(s)

Figure 7.3.3.2 Format of a machine code instruction

The machine code instruction with format MOV R_d, <operand2> has two possible opcodes which in binary are 001000 and 001001.

- opcode 001000 moves the value that is <operand2> into the register R_d, e.g., 001000 0000 0100 1111. This instruction is broken down as shown in Figure 7.3.3.3. The destination register is R_0 (binary code 0000) and <operand2> is replaced by the value 0100 1111$_2$ (79$_{10}$).

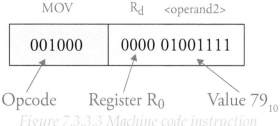

Figure 7.3.3.3 Machine code instruction

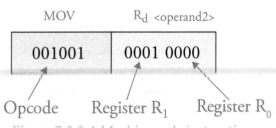

MOV R_d <operand2>

| 001001 | 0001 0000 |

Opcode   Register R_1 Register R_0

Figure 7.3.3.4 Machine code instruction

• opcode 001001 moves the value stored in the register specified by <operand2> into the register R_d, e.g., 001001 0001 0000.

This instruction is broken down as shown in *Figure 7.3.3.4*. The destination register is R_1 (binary code 0001) and <operand2> is replaced by register R_0 (binary code 0000). If when the processor executes this instruction the value 45_{10} is stored in register R_0 then at the end of the execution register R_1 will also contain 45_{10}.

The structure that has been used to illustrate machine code is a simplified one. It is not a good idea to design an instruction set that doesn't map to the word length of a memory word which is typically a multiple of eight. The word length of registers is usually a multiple of eight too, e.g. 32 bits. The unit of transfer between processor and main memory for load and store operations is usually the same as the word length of registers, e.g., 32 bits if registers are 32 bits. Bits of a memory word that are not needed for a particular machine code instruction are ignored by the instruction decoder.

The machine code instruction with format LOAD R_d, <memory ref> has a single opcode which is 000000 in binary. R_d is the destination register and <memory ref> is replaced by the memory address of a memory word stored in main memory. This instruction is broken down as shown in *Figure 7.3.3.5*. For example, 000000 0011 0100 1111 copies the memory word whose memory address is 0100 1111 into register R_3 (binary code 0011).

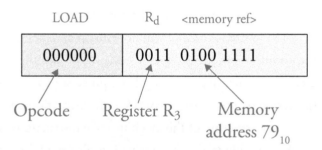

LOAD R_d <memory ref>

| 000000 | 0011 0100 1111 |

Opcode   Register R_3 Memory address 79_{10}

Figure 7.3.3.5 Machine code instruction

Questions

2   Eight bits are reserved for the opcode field of a particular processor's instruction set.
  (a) What is the total number of codes that could be used as opcodes for this processor?
  (b) Why might only some of these 8-bit codes be valid?
  (c) The 8-bit opcode is subdivided into two parts. What are the two parts?

Questions

3 What is meant by *processor instruction set*?

4 Explain using LOAD, STORE, ADD that machine code instructions consist of an opcode and one or more operands which may be value, memory address or register.

5 What is meant by saying that an instruction set is processor specific?

Task

1 You are required to design an instruction set for a processor based on a two register architecture in which the destination register is always the register called the accumulator. The processor must be able to add and subtract. The only instructions allowed to interact directly with main memory are load and store. The first input to an arithmetic operation is always read from the accumulator. The second input is read from one of fifteen other registers. Values may be set up in all sixteen registers either by a load instruction or by a move instruction. The second operand of a move instruction is always a value. The processor's instruction set must support four control instructions:

1.   branch on zero
2.   branch on negative
3.   branch unconditionally
4.   Halt

Branch instruction 1 tests the zero flag and branch instruction 2, the negative flag of the status register. All three branches use a single operand which is a value (positive or negative) to add to the current value of the program counter. The status register and program counter are separate from the sixteen registers also used by the instruction set. Registers have a word length of 16 bits as does main memory. Main memory consists of 256 memory words. Some instructions may not use all 16 bits. The processor will use those bits which define the instruction.

In this chapter you have covered:

■   The meaning of 'processor instruction set' and that an instruction set is processor specific

■   The structure of machine code instructions which is an opcode and one or more operands (value, memory address or register)

7.3 Structure and role of the processor and its components

■ *Learning objectives:*

- *Understand and apply immediate and direct addressing modes*

Information

0x:

0x indicates a hexadecimal number, e.g. 0x3F.

R0

before

| ? |

after

| 0xFF |

Figure 7.3.4.1 register R0 before and after execution of instruction MOV R0,#0xFF

Key concept

Immediate addressing:
The operand is the datum.

Key concept

Direct addressing:
The operand is the address of the datum.

■ 7.3.4 Addressing modes

Immediate addressing

When the addressing mode is immediate addressing the operand is the datum.

For example, the MOV operation copies the value specified by <operand2> into register R_d.

$$MOV\ R_d,<operand2>$$

If R_d is register R0 and <operand2> is **0xFF** in hexadecimal (**255** in decimal) then the assembly language instruction is as follows

$$MOV\ R0,\#0xFF$$

The # in front of **0xFF** indicates that the mode of addressing is immediate addressing. The contents of register R0 will be the binary equivalent of hexadecimal value **FF** after this instruction is executed - *Figure 7.3.4.1*.

Questions

1. Register R0 contains the datum 43_{10}, register R1 the datum 56_{10}. What will register R0 contain after each of the following assembly language instructions have been executed?
Express your answer in decimal.
   (a) MOV R0,#0x5E
   (b) ADD R0,R1,#0x5E

Direct addressing

When the addressing mode is direct addressing the operand is the address in memory where the datum can be found.

For example, the LDR operation loads the value stored in the memory location specified by <memory ref> into register R_d.

$$LDR\ R_d,<memory\ ref>$$

If R_d is register R0 and <memory ref> is in hexadecimal **0xFCC0** (**64704** in decimal) then the assembly language instruction is as follows

$$LDR\ R0,0xFCC0$$

Note that in this instruction there is no #. The absence of the # symbol indicates that this is direct addressing.

The operand 0xFCC0 is the main memory address of a memory location containing the datum to be used when this instruction is executed. The contents of register R0 will therefore be 0x4D (we can omit the leading 00) after this instruction is executed because memory location with address 0xFCC0 contains the datum 0x4D - *Figure 7.3.4.2*.

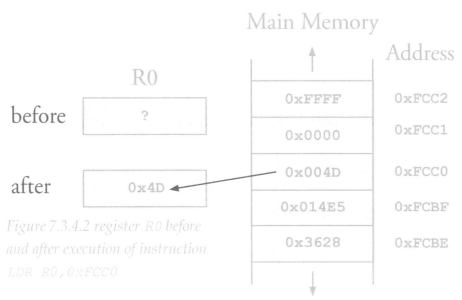

Figure 7.3.4.2 register R0 before and after execution of instruction LDR R0,0xFCC0

Questions

2 Register R0 contains the datum 43_{10}, main memory contents are as shown in *Figure 7.3.4.2*. What will register R0 contain after the following assembly language instruction has been executed? Express your answer in decimal.

        LDR R0,0xFCC0

3 In the assembly language instruction STR R$_d$,<memory ref>, the STR operation stores the value that is in register R$_d$ in a memory location specified by <memory ref>. Register R0 contains the datum 43_{10}, register R1 the datum 56_{10}, main memory contents are as shown in *Figure 7.3.4.2*. What will the memory locations 0xFCC1 and 0xFCC2 contain after the following two instructions have been executed? Express your answers in decimal.

        STR R0,0xFCC1

        STR R1,0xFCC2

4 Main memory contents are as shown in *Figure 7.3.4.2* What will be stored in register R1 after the following instructions are executed? Express your answer in decimal.

        LDR R0,0xFCC0

        ADD R1,R0,#0xFCC0

In this chapter you have covered:

■ Immediate addressing: the operand is the datum

■ Direct addressing: the operand is the address of the datum

Learning objectives:

■ *Understand and apply the basic machine-code operations of*

- *load*

- *add*

- *subtract*

- *store*

- *branching (conditional and unconditional)*

- *compare*

- *logical bitwise operators (AND, OR, NOT, XOR)*

- *logical*

  ▪ *shift right*

  ▪ *shift left*

- *halt*

■ *Use the basic machine-code operations above when machine-code instructions are expressed in mnemonic form- assembly language, using immediate and direct addressing*

Key concept

Load-store architecture:
No direct manipulation of memory contents. A value in memory that needs to be processed must be loaded into the processor (core) first, processed and then stored back in memory.

Information

See Table 7.3.3.5 in Chapter 7.3.3 for AQA instruction set.

■ 7.3.5 Machine-code and assembly language operations

Load-Store architecture

In a load-store architecture the only instructions that work directly with memory are load and store instructions or their equivalent. A value in memory that needs to be processed must be loaded into the processor (core) first, processed and then stored back in memory.

Load

A load register operation is used to transfer a copy of a datum from a specified location, e.g. main memory location 102, to a symbolically named register, e.g. R0.

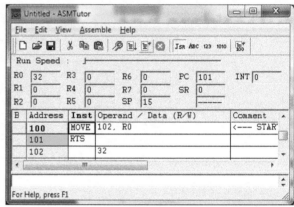

Figure 7.3.5.1 ASMTutor after executing the machine code equivalent of MOVE 102, R0

For example using direct addressing, LDR R0, 102 transfers the contents of memory location with address 102 into register R0. In some instruction sets, the mnemonic MOV or MOVE is used instead of the mnemonic LDR, and the order of the operands can be reversed. The simulator ASMTutor shown in *Figure 7.3.5.1* is one that uses MOVE instead of LDR for a load operation. It also reverses the order of the operands.

Figure 7.3.5.1 shows an example of an assembly language program which transfers a copy of the datum 32 from memory location 102 to register R0. The assembly language program ends with RTS (ReTurn from Subroutine) because ASMTutor expects the last instruction to be RTS in order to work correctly. Note that memory location with address 102 in this example contains 32.

Figure 7.3.5.2 shows the register state just before the machine code equivalent of MOVE 102, R0 is executed.

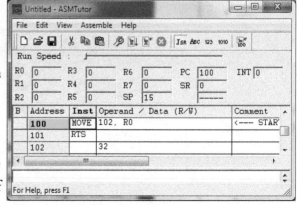

Figure 7.3.5.2 ASMTutor just before executing the machine code equivalent of MOVE 102, R0

Memory address (in decimal)	Main memory contents (in decimal)
102	21
103	42
104	84

Figure 7.3.5.4

Figure 7.3.5.3 shows the result when memory location 102 contains 64.

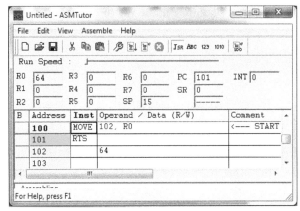

Figure 7.3.5.3 Just after with 102 containing 64

Questions

1   The assembly language instruction LDR R0, 102 transfers a copy of the contents of memory location 102 to register R0. *Figure 7.3.5.4* shows the contents of memory locations 102, 103 and 104.

What does register R0 contain after the following instructions, expressed in assembly language, are executed in machine code?

(a) LDR R0, 102   (b) LDR R0, 103   (c) LDR R0, 104

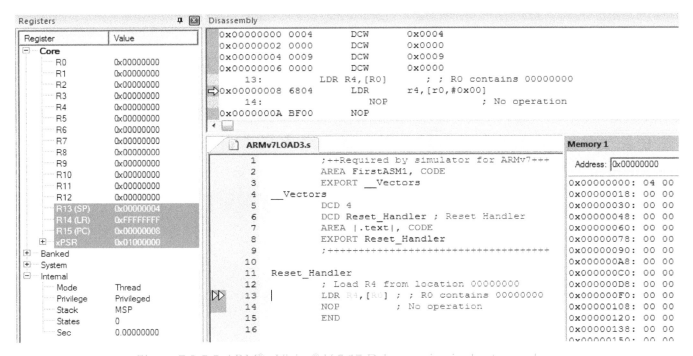

Figure 7.3.5.5 ARM® μVision® V 5.17 Debugger in single-step mode

Information

Figure 7.3.5.5 shows a screenshot of the ARM μVision simulator in debugger mode single-stepping through an assembly language program written for an ARM Cortex processor. ARM instruction sets use LDR but the reference to a memory location is not direct. Instead, the memory reference must be obtained from a register. This example uses register R0.

[R0] means contents of register R0. LDR R4, [R0] loads register R4 with the contents of memory location 0x00000000 as this is the memory address stored in register R0. The notation 0x indicates a hexadecimal number.

Figure 7.3.5.6 shows the result of executing the instruction **LDR R4, [R0]**.

The ARM μVision simulator simulates the execution of instructions for the Cortex™-M family of ARM microcontrollers. These microcontrollers implement the **ARMv7** instruction set. In order for this simulator to function, every assembly language program must start with the preamble shown in *Figures 7.3.5.5, 7.3.5.6*. The user chooses the identifier in **AREA FirstASM1, CODE**, i.e. **FirstASM1**, but the rest of the preamble must conform to that given.

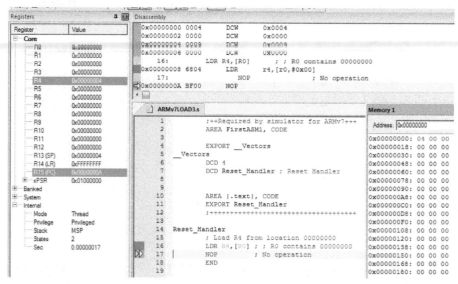

Figure 7.3.5.6 ARM® µVision® V 5.17 Debugger in single-step more

STORE

A store operation, STR, transfers a copy of the contents of a register to a specified memory location,

e.g. **STR R4, 0x20000000**

If **R4** contains **0x00000065** then execution of the machine code equivalent of this instruction will change the contents of memory location, address **0x20000000**, to the value **0x65**.

Figure 7.3.5.6 shows register **R4** preset with value **0x00000065**, register **R0** preset with value **0x20000000**, and memory location **0x2000000** initialised to **0x00000000**. The next instruction to be executed is **STR R4, [R0]** which is equivalent to

STR R4, #0x20000000

Figure 7.3.5.8 shows memory location 0x20000000's contents with value **0x65**, the result of executing **STR R4, [R0]**.

The ARM μVision simulator is configured so that 0x20000000 is the first available location that a program may write to.

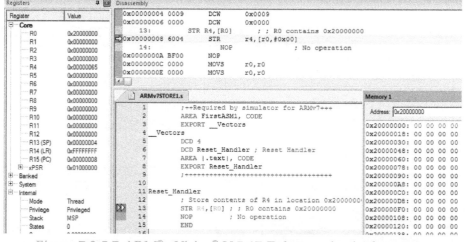

Figure 7.3.5.7 ARM® µVision® V 5.17 Debugger in single-step more

Figure 7.3.5.8 ARM® µVision® V 5.17 Debugger in single-step more

Questions

2 The assembly language instruction STR R0, 102 transfers a copy of the contents of register R0 to memory location with decimal address 102. What are the contents of memory location 102 after this instruction is executed in machine code when the value in R0 is decimal 67?

MOVE

A MOVE operation copies a value from source to destination. The source could be a register, an immediate value (or a memory location but not in the case of ARM processors). The destination could be another register (or a memory location but not in the case of ARM processors).

For example, the ARM processor instruction set has a MOV instruction (MOVS in ARMv7 to update status register as well). MOV R$_d$, <operand2> copies the value specified by <operand2> into register R$_d$. For example, MOV R2, #36 copies the value 36 into the register R2. # indicates immediate addressing.

MOV R1, R2 copies the value in register R2 into register R1. Figure 7.3.5.9 shows an assembly language program, MOV.s, prepared in Notepad++ and then loaded into ArmSim# version 1.9.1 for assembling and executing one instruction at a time. Register contents are shown in the window on the left. Note how registers R2 and R3 are changed by the two different MOV operations. The hash symbol # before the decimal value 36 indicates immediate addressing, i.e. the operand is the value to be used. As with ASMTutor, the last instruction must be an instruction that enables ArmSim# to function correctly. This instruction is SWI 0x11.

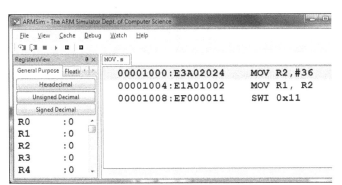

Figure 7.3.5.9 Single stepping through execution of machine code equivalent of assembly language program containing MOV R$_d$, <operand2> for an immediate operand and a register operand

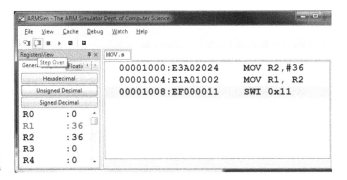

ArmSim simulates ARMv5 instruction set architecture.

It can be downloaded from

http://armsim.cs.uvic.ca/DownloadARMSimSharp.html

Questions

3 The assembly language instruction MOV R0, R1 transfers a copy of the contents of register R1 to register R0. What does register R0 contain after the following instructions, expressed in assembly language, are executed in machine code?

(a) MOV R0, #78   (b) MOV R1, #25 followed by MOV R0, R1

ADD

An add operation ADD R$_d$, R$_n$, <operand2> is used to add the value specified in <operand2> and the value in register R$_n$, storing the result in register R$_d$. <operand2> may be an immediate value or a register.

For example, ADD R2, R3, #1 when executed in machine code adds 1 to the contents of register R3 before storing the result in register R2.

Figure 7.3.5.10 shows ArmSim# stepping through program ADD1.s one instruction at a time. This program assigns 24 to R3 and 36 to R2. It adds 1 to a copy of the 24 stored in R3 then stores the result 25 in R2.

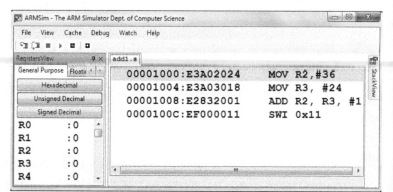

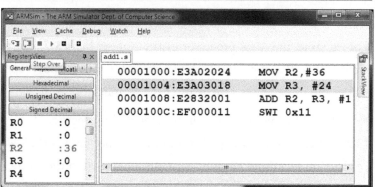

Task

① Using a text editor such as Notepad++, create the file ADD32.s with the following contents:

```
MOV R4, #25
MOV R5, #43
ADD R5, R4, #32
SWI 0x11
```

Load ADD32.s into ArmSim# and single step through the instructions. Observe how registers R4 and R5 change.

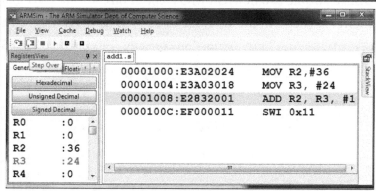

Task

② Using a text editor such as Notepad++, create the file ADD.s with the following contents:

```
MOV R4, #25
MOV R5, #43
MOV R3, #1
ADD R5, R4, R3
SWI 0x11
```

Load ADD.s into ArmSim# and single step through the instructions. Observe how registers R3, R4 and R5 change.

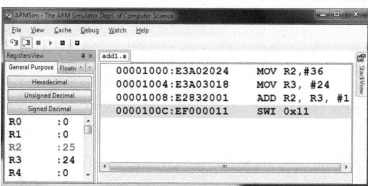

Figure 7.3.5.10 Before and after state of registers R2, R3 for execution of ADD R2, R3, #1

Questions

④ Write an assembly language program that stores the result of adding the contents of registers R1, R2, R3 in R0. The program will need to initialise R1 with decimal 5, R2 with decimal 3 and R3 with decimal 6.

SUBTRACT

A subtract operation SUB R_d, R_n, <operand2> is used to subtract the value specified in <operand2> from the value in register R_n before storing the result in register R_d. <operand2> may be an immediate value or a register.

For example, SUB R2, R3, #1 when executed in machine code subtracts 1 from the contents of register R3 before storing the result in register R2.

Figure 7.3.5.11 shows the before and after contents of the registers R2 and R3.

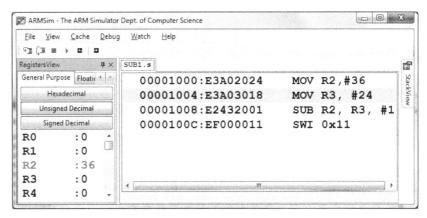

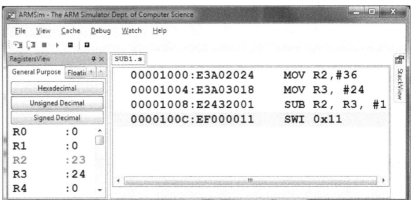

Figure 7.3.5.11 Before and after state of registers R2, R3 for execution of SUB R2, R3, #1

Task

3 Using a text editor such as Notepad++, create the file SUB5.s with the following contents:

```
MOV R4, #25
MOV R5, #43
SUB R5, R4, #5
SWI 0x11
```

Load SUB5.s into ArmSim# and single step through the instructions. Observe how registers R4 and R5 change.

Questions

5 Write an assembly language program that stores the result of subtracting the contents of register R1 from R2 in R0. The program will need to initialise R1 with decimal 5 and R2 with decimal 13.

Status register

The status register contains flags called condition codes which are set or reset to reflect the outcome of the last machine operation, e.g. if the result of an arithmetic operation was zero then the zero flag is set. A flag is a single bit code that can be set (binary 1) or reset (binary 0). A status register consists of at least four condition codes:

- Zero flag - set if the result of the last machine operation stores zero in the results register
- Negative flag - set if the result of the last machine operation stores a negative value in the results register
- Carry flag - set if the result of an *unsigned operation* overflows the result register or as a result sometimes of performing two's complement signed arithmetic.
- Overflow flag - set if the result of a *signed operation* overflows the result register.

Moving zero into a register can set the Z(ero) flag as will an arithmetic operation if the result is zero.

Moving a negative value into a register can set the N(egative) flag as will an arithmetic operation if the result is negative. A carry can be produced when a machine performs two's complement arithmetic or when it performs unsigned addition.

Figure 7.3.5.12 shows an assembly language program created in ASMTutor. It has been assembled so it can be executed. The first screenshot shows that the next instruction to be executed is MOVE #0, R0. The second screenshot shows the effect on the status register of executing this instruction. The zero flag has been set in the status register (indicated by a Z).

The third screenshot shows that the negative flag has been set in the status register as a result of the machine executing the instruction MOVE #-1, R1. Note the value stored in R1 is 65535_{10} or 1111111111111111_2, which is the two's complement representation for -1_{10}.

The fourth screenshot shows the effect on the status register of subtracting decimal 5 (register R2) from 0 (register R0). The negative flag is set because the result is negative.

Figure 7.3.5.13 shows that when the largest positive number 0111111111111111_2 ($7FFF_{16}$) is added to itself, overflow results and the overflow flag is set. The negative flag is also set because the result, 65534_{10}, that is stored in register R0 is interpreted as -2_{10} by the machine.

Questions

6 The format of the MOVE operation in an instruction set is MOV R_d, \<operand2\> which is interpreted as copy the value specified by \<operand2\> into register R_d. Assuming that MOV can set the condition codes.
Which, if any, status register condition codes are set when the machine code equivalents of the following are executed

(a) MOV R0, #-1   (b) MOV R1, #0

(c) MOV R2, #23?

7 The format of the SUBTRACT operation in an instruction set is SUB, R_d, R_n, \<operand2\> which is interpreted as subtract the value specified in \<operand2\> from the value in register R_n and store the result in register R_d. Register R0 stores decimal 7. Which status register condition codes are set, if any, when the machine code equivalents of the following are executed

(a) SUB R1, R0, #9   (b) SUB R1, R0, #7

(c) SUB R1, R0, #5?

R0 0	R3 0	R6 0	PC 100
R1 0	R4 0	R7 0	SR 0
R2 0	R5 0	SP 15	-----

B	Address	Inst	Operand / Data (R/W)
	100	MOVE	#0, R0
	101	MOVE	#-1, R1
	102	MOVE	#5, R2
	103	SUB	R2, R0
	104	MOVE	#-1, R0

R0 0	R3 0	R6 0	PC 101
R1 0	R4 0	R7 0	SR 2
R2 0	R5 0	SP 15	--Z--

B	Address	Inst	Operand / Data (R/W)
	100	MOVE	#0, R0
	101	MOVE	#-1, R1
	102	MOVE	#5, R2
	103	SUB	R2, R0
	104	MOVE	#-1, R0

R0 0	R3 0	R6 0	PC 102
R1 65535	R4 0	R7 0	SR 1
R2 0	R5 0	SP 15	-N---

B	Address	Inst	Operand / Data (R/W)
	100	MOVE	#0, R0
	101	MOVE	#-1, R1
	102	MOVE	#5, R2
	103	SUB	R2, R0
	104	MOVE	#-1, R0

R0 65531	R3 0	R6 0	PC 104
R1 65535	R4 0	R7 0	SR 1
R2 5	R5 0	SP 15	-N---

B	Address	Inst	Operand / Data (R/W)
	100	MOVE	#0, R0
	101	MOVE	#-1, R1
	102	MOVE	#5, R2
	103	SUB	R2, R0
	104	MOVE	#-1, R0

Figure 7.3.5.12 Single-stepping an assembly language program in ASMTutor to show the effect on the status register

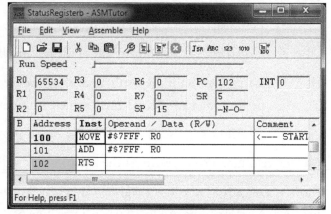

Figure 7.3.5.13 Shows the result of adding the most positive value $7FFF or $7FFF_{16}$ to itself

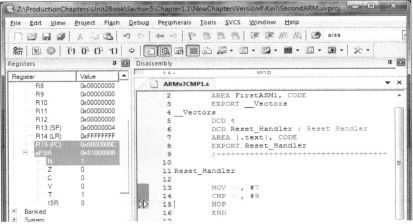

Figure 7.3.5.14 ARM µVision simulating the execution of CMP R0, #9

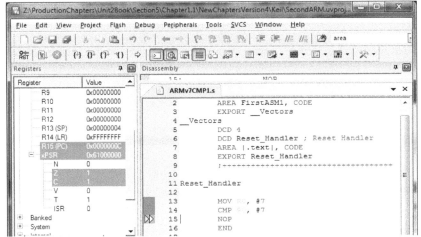

Figure 7.3.5.15 ARM µVision simulating the execution of CMP R0, #7

COMPARE

Compare instructions may be used to compare the contents of two registers or the contents of a register and an immediate value. For example, CMP R0, R1 compares the contents of registers R0 and R1. If the contents of these registers are equal, the zero flag in the status register is set. A compare operation performs a subtraction and uses the result to determine whether the two operand's values are equal or not. If unequal then the negative flag will be set if the subtraction result was negative. Figure 7.3.5.14 shows ARM µVision simulating the execution of CMP R0, #9 with decimal 7 stored in R0. The negative flag is set indicating that the operation [R0] - 9 has been performed by CMP. The notation [] means 'contents of'.

Figure 7.3.5.15 shows the result of CMP R0, #7 with decimal 7 stored in R0. Note that the zero flag is set. The carry flag is also set because two's complement arithmetic sometimes sets this flag.

Questions

8   What is the state of each condition code after the following comparison operations are executed in machine code? R0 contains the value decimal 9. Assume that CMP behaves as shown above.
(a) CMP R0, #15   (b) CMP R0, #7   (c) CMP R0, #9

Branching (conditional and unconditional)

Normally, a processor executes one instruction after another in a linear fashion. This means the next instruction to execute is found immediately following the current instruction. Branch instructions allow for a different order of execution. For example, the B loop instruction in Table 7.3.5.1 causes the previous instruction to be repeated indefinitely. The previous instruction is labelled loop so that the branch instruction can refer to it. The assembler will convert this symbolic label into a memory address when it translates the assembly language program into its machine code equivalent - object code column in Table 7.3.5.2.

Assembly language instructions or statements are divided into four fields separated by spaces or tabs as shown in Table 7.3.5.1.

Label field	Opcode field	Operand field(s)	Comment field
	MOV	R0, #1	; initialise counter to 1, R0 will hold a running count, R0 = 1
loop	ADD	R0, R0, #1	; increment counter by 1, R0 = R0 + 1
	B	loop	; repeat previous instruction
	END		; this is a pseudo-op that marks the end of the program to the assembler

Table 7.3.5.1 ARM assembly language program showing how instructions are divided into four fields

AQA uses HALT

The label field is optional and starts in the first column. It is used to identify the position in memory of the current instruction. It must be unique within the program. The opcode field expresses the processor command to execute. The operand field specifies where to find the data the command uses when it executes. ARM processor instructions have 0, 1, 2, 3 or 4 operands separated by commas. We will consider instructions that use only 0, 1, 2 or 3 operands.

The comment field is optional and is ignored by the assembler. It allows a programmer to write a few words describing the purpose of the instruction, e.g. 'increment counter by 1', to make it easier to understand. A semicolon (;) is used to separate the operand and comment fields.

The assembler translates assembly language source code into object code. Object code consists of the machine instructions executed by the processor. *Table 7.3.5.2* shows ARM processor (Thumb-2 instruction set) object code alongside its equivalent assembly language source code. The first column shows the address in RAM of each machine code instruction, e.g. 0x00000008. The second column the opcode + operands, e.g. 1C40. The third, fourth and fifth columns show the corresponding assembly language source code. The comment field has been omitted. *Figure 7.3.5.16* shows ARM µVision simulating this program. The loop label has been replaced in the instruction B loop by the memory address 0x000000A corresponding to label loop. In object code this is translated into the value to 'add' to the current address because ARM uses

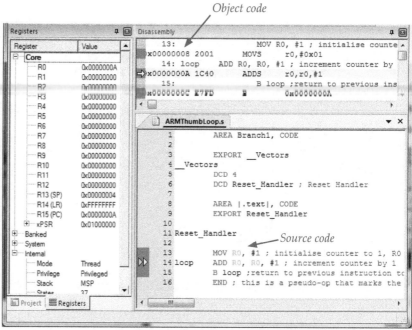

Object code

Source code

Figure 7.3.5.16 ARM µVision simulating the execution of a program that uses an unconditional branch instruction, B

Address	Object code	Label	Opcode	Operand
0x0000008	2001		MOV	R0, #1
0x000000A	1C40	loop	ADD	R0, R0, #1
0x000000C	E7FD		B	0x000000A

Table 7.3.5.2 ARM assembly language program showing both source and object code

Decimal	Hexadecimal	Object code byte
8	8	20
9	9	01
10	A	1C
11	B	40
12	C	E7
13	D	FD

Table 7.3.5.3 Memory map for ARM machine code program

relative addressing[1]. The new address becomes the address of the next instruction to be fetched and executed. In this case FD in hexadecimal or -3 in decimal because two's complement coding is used for numbers.

Table 7.3.5.3 shows the memory map for the program's machine code. Note that 13_{10} is the address of byte value FD or -3_{10}. $13_{10} - 3_{10} = 10_{10} = A_{16}$. A_{16} is the address of instruction opcode 1C which is ADD in assembly language mnemonics.

Unconditional branch

The unconditional branch instruction B label always causes execution to branch (jump) to the instruction at the address indicated by label. Using direct addressing this would be for the example program

B 0x000000A

---

1   relative addressing not covered in AQA specification

Conditional branch

There is another kind of branch called a conditional branch. In this type of branch a condition must be true for branching of program execution to occur.

The instruction immediately before a conditional branch must be a COMPARE instruction. Execution of this instruction affects the condition code flags which conditional branch instructions examine before deciding whether or not to branch (SUBTRACT can be used instead of COMPARE, e.g. is an alternative to CMP R0, R1).

CMP R0, R1	Condition	Condition codes
R0 = R1	Equal	Zero flag set, Z = 1
R0 <> R1	Not Equal	Zero flag not set, Z = 0
R0 > R1	R0 Greater Than R1	Z = 0, N = 0
R0 < R1	R0 Less Than R1	Z= 0, N = 1

Table 7.3.5.4 Condition and condition codes for SUB and CMP

Table 7.3.5.5 shows the four conditional branch instructions, BEQ, BNE, BGT and BLT.

Instruction	Description	Condition codes
BEQ <label>	Branch if operands being compared are equal	Z = 1
BNE <label>	Branch if operands being compared are not equal	Z = 0
BGT<label>	Branch if first signed operand is greater than second signed operand	Z = 0, N = 0
BLT <label>	Branch if first signed operand is less than second signed operand	Z = 0, N = 1

Table 7.3.5.5 Conditional branch instructions

Figure 7.3.5.17 shows the simulation of conditional branch BEQ loop.

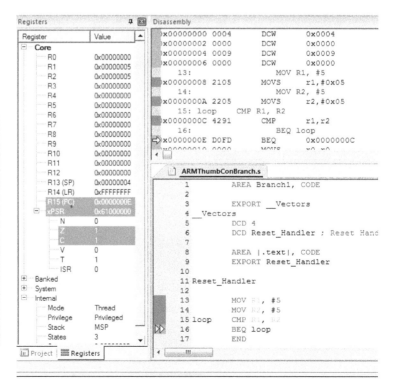

Questions

9 Explain what the following snippet of assembly language code does when its machine code equivalent is executed

```
        MOV R0, #12
        MOV R1, #6
loop    ADD R1, R1, #1
        CMP R1, R0
        BNE loop
        HALT   ; Stops the execution
```

Figure 7.3.5.17 ARM µVision simulating the execution of a program that uses conditional branch instruction, BEQ

Questions

10 Explain what the following snippets of assembly language code do when their machine code equivalent is executed

(a)
```
        MOV R0, #12
        MOV R1, #6
loop    SUB R0, R0, #1
        CMP R0, R1
        BGT loop
        HALT   ; Stops the execution
```

(b)
```
        MOV R0, #12
        MOV R1, #6
loop    ADD R1, R1, #1
        CMP R0, R1
        BLT loop
        HALT
```

11 What other conditional branch instruction would result in the code behaving in a similar way if used in place of BGT and BLT in (a) and (b)?

Logical bitwise operators

When designing digital logic gate circuits gates are used, such as AND, OR, NOT, which convert single bit input signals into single bit output signals.

For example, with the AND gate, if the inputs are 1 and 0 then the output is 0 because 1 AND 0 = 0.

Using AND, OR, NOT and XOR as operators in assembly language programs is slightly different. The inputs are typically 32-bit numbers and the output is a single 32-bit number. The inputs are transformed into the output by applying 32 logic operations, e.g. AND, at the same time in a bitwise fashion.

The format for ARM processors for the logical operations AND, OR and XOR is

$$\text{Logical operation } R_d, R_n, \text{<operand2>}$$

This means perform a bitwise logical operation between the value in register R_n and the value specified by <operand2> and store the result in register R_d. The symbolic opcode for the AND operation is AND; for the OR operation it is ORR and for XOR it is EOR.

The format for ARM processors for the logical operation NOT is

$$\text{MVN } R_d, \text{<operand2>}$$

This means perform a bitwise logical NOT operation on the value specified by <operand2> and store the result in register R_d.

AND

Figure 7.3.5.18 shows ARM μVision simulating 1111_2 AND 0001_2. The result is 0001_2 when AND R0, R0, R1 is executed in machine code. This instruction ANDs the contents of registers R0 and R1 and stores the result in R0, the register specified as the first operand.

A mask operation is one that isolates bits to be tested. The logical AND can be used in this role. Suppose that we need to test the three least significant bits of a 32-bit word

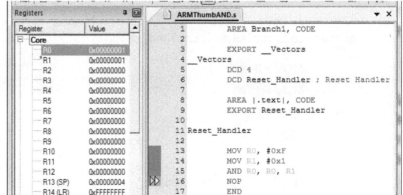

Figure 7.3.5.18 ARM μVision simulating the execution of a program that applies a bitwise AND operation to operands 0xF and 0x1 i.e. 1111_2 AND 0001_2

then we would choose the mask 0x00000007 because the last three bits are 111_2 (7_{16}) and the other bits are 0. If the bit pattern to be tested is stored in R0 then R1 will contain the state of the three least significant bits and zeroes everywhere else after executing

AND R1, R0, #0x7

To know if all three least significant bits are 1 then compare R1 with 0x7 as follows

CMP R1, #0x7

The zero flag will be set by CMP if they are.

OR

Figure 7.3.5.19 shows ARM μVision simulating 1000_2 OR 0111_2. The result is 1111_2 when ORR R0, R0, R1 is executed in machine code. This instruction ORs the contents of registers R0 and R1 and stores the result in R0, the register specified as the first operand.

XOR

XOR is the eXclusive-OR operation.

ARM names the operator for this operation EOR (Exclusive-OR)

Figure 7.3.5.20 shows ARM μVision simulating 1000_2 XOR 0111_2. The result is 1111_2 when EOR R0, R0, R1 is executed in machine code. This instruction Exclusive-ORs the contents of registers R0 and R1 and stores the result in R0, the register specified as the first operand.

NOT

To perform a bitwise logical NOT operation the instruction

MVN R$_d$, <operand2>

This instruction NOTs the value specified by <operand2> and stores the result in register R$_d$.

Figure 7.3.5.21 shows ARM μVision simulating NOT 0x00000000.

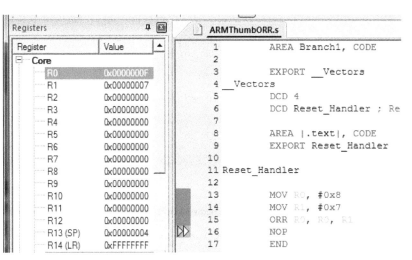

Figure 7.3.5.19 ARM μVision simulating the execution of a program that applies a bitwise OR operation to operands 0x8 and 0x7 i.e. 1000_2 OR 0111_2

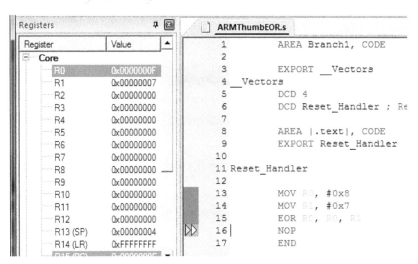

Figure 7.3.5.20 ARM μVision simulating the execution of a program that applies a bitwise XOR operation to operands 0x8 and 0x7 i.e. 1000_2 XOR 0111_2

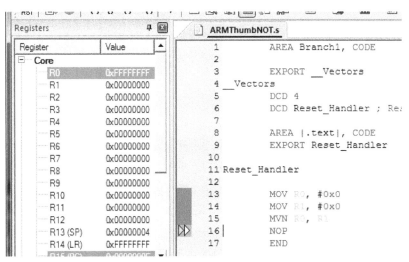

Figure 7.3.5.21 ARM μVision simulating the execution of a program that applies a bitwise NOT operation to operand 0x00000000, i.e. NOT 00000000000000000000000000000000$_2$

The result is $11111111111111111111111111111111_2$ when MVN R0, R1 is executed in machine code. The result expressed in hexadecimal is FFFFFFFF. Note that R1 was assigned 0x0 in a MOV operation first.

Questions

12   What will the contents of register R0 be after the machine code equivalent of the following snippets of assembly language code are executed

(a)   MOV R0, #0xFF   (b)   MOV R0, #0xFF   (c)   MOV R0, #0x0

         EOR R0, R0, R0   MOV R1, #0x7   MOV R1, #0x7

         HALT   AND R0, R0, R1   ORR R0, R0, R1

                                             HALT   HALT

13   A certain process may begin if bits 1, 3 and 5 of an 8-bit word are set. The state of the other bits may be ignored. Write the assembly language instructions to determine if the process may begin. You should assume that bit 1 is the least significant bit and that register R0 contains the 8-bit word.

14   Write an assembly language instruction using ORR to set bit 4 of register R0. Assume bits are numbered from the right 1...8 with bit 1 the least significant bit.

15   Write an assembly language instruction to isolate bits 1 and 3 of register R0 so that the state of each may be tested by other instructions. Assume bit numbering as in Q14.

16   "We use the logical OR to make bits become one, and we use the logical AND to make bits become zero." Explain using examples the meaning of this statement.

17   Register R0 contains a 32-bit word that represents the state of 32 pixels of a black and white image with colour depth one bit per pixel. Write a single assembly language instruction to invert the state of each pixel stored in R0. Write another instruction to restore the stored state.

Logical shift operations

A logical shift treats the bit pattern as being an unsigned pattern of bits. A shift operation takes two inputs, one the number of shifts to apply, *n*, and the other the bit pattern to be shifted by n bits. For example, the bit pattern in *Figure 7.3.5.22 (a)* when shifted by one bit to the left becomes the bit pattern shown in *Figure 7.3.5.22(b)*.

1	0	1	1	0	1	1	0

Figure 7.3.5.22(a) 8-bit bit pattern before it is shifted left one bit

0	1	1	0	1	1	0	0

Figure 7.3.5.22(b) 8-bit bit pattern after it has been shifted left one bit

Logical shift left operation

With a logical shift left the bit pattern is moved to the left with the least significant bit position replaced by a zero. The carry bit will contain the last bit shifted out. For the example in *Figure 7.3.5.22* the carry bit will contain 1 after shifting left one bit. The bit pattern in *Figure 7.3.5.22(a)* is unsigned decimal 178 or B2 in hexadecimal. In ARM assembly language, the 32-bit register R0 contains $B2_{16}$ after MOV R0, #0xB2 is executed. The ARM instruction LSL R1, R0, #1 shifts the bit pattern in R0 left one bit and stores the result 164_{16} or 356_{10} in R1. Notice that the value stored in R1 is double the value in R0. This is equivalent to multiplying by 2^1. If the shift operation is LSL R0, #2 and R0 contains 178_{10} or $B2_{16}$ then $2C8_{16}$ or 712_{10} will be stored in R1. This is equivalent to multiplying by 2^2.

Figure 7.3.5.23 shows the result of applying logical shift left to 0x1 eight times. The loop was stepped through eight times to change the pattern in R0 from 0x00000001 to 0x00000100. (Note these are hex numbers)

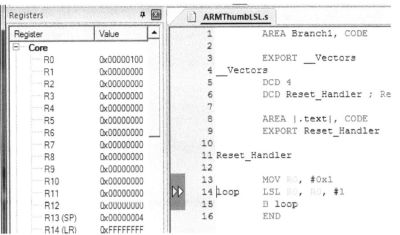

Questions

18 Rewrite

```
loop    LSL R0, R0, #1
        B loop
        END
```

to obtain the bit pattern 0x00000100 from the bit pattern 0x00000001 stored in R0 without a loop.

Figure 7.3.5.23 Logical Shift Left by one bit applied 8 times by single-stepping through loop eight times

Questions

19 The decimal number 4 is stored in register R0. Write an assembly language instruction that multiples this number by 2^4.

20 Using *Figure 7.3.5.22* as a template, record the state of R0 after the following assembly language program is executed in machine code. Assume R0 is an 8-bit wide register. Include the carry bit in your answer.

> MOV R0, #3
>
> LSL R0, R0, #7
>
> HALT

Logical shift right

With a logical shift right the bit pattern is moved to the right with the most significant bit position replaced by a zero. The carry bit will contain the last bit shifted out.

For the example in *Figure 7.3.5.24* the carry bit will contain 0 after right shifting one bit. The bit pattern in *Figure 7.3.5.24(a)* is unsigned decimal 178 or B2 in hexadecimal. In ARM assembly language, the 32-bit register R0 contains $B2_{16}$ after MOV R0, #0xB2 is executed. The ARM instruction LSR R1, R0, #1 shifts the bit pattern in R0 right one bit and stores the result 59_{16} or 89_{10} in R1. Notice that the value stored in R1 is half that in R0. This is equivalent to dividing an unsigned number by 2^1. If the shift operation is LSR R1, R0, #2 and R0 contains 178_{10} or $B2_{16}$ then $2C_{16}$ or 44_{10} will be stored in R1. This is equivalent to unsigned integer division by 2^2, with the remainder 1 stored in the carry bit.

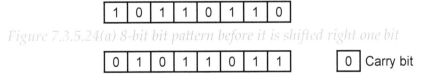

Figure 7.3.5.24(a) 8-bit bit pattern before it is shifted right one bit

| 0 | 1 | 0 | 1 | 1 | 0 | 1 | 1 | | 0 | Carry bit |

Figure 7.3.5.24(b) 8-bit bit pattern after it is shifted right one bit

Questions

21 R0 contains 0x00000100. What does it contain after LSR R0, R0, #8 in machine code is executed?

22 The decimal number 64 is stored in register R0. Write an assembly language instruction that divides this number by 2^4. The result should be stored in register R1.

23 Using *Figure 7.3.5.24* as a template, record the state of R0 after the following assembly language program is executed in machine code. Assume R0 is an 8-bit wide register. Include the carry bit in your answer.

MOV R0, #195

LSR R0, R0, #7

HALT

HALT

When a **HALT** instruction is encountered in an executing machine code program the execution of the program is stopped.

Questions

Use AQA's instruction set from *Table 7.3.3.5* in *Chapter 7.3.3* to answer these questions.

24 The high level language program statement "Sum := Sum + 100;" assigns to variable Sum the result of adding decimal number 100 to Sum. The symbol ":=" is the assignment operator. Write the equivalent assembly language instructions for this statement. Assume that memory location with address 0x1000 is used to store the current value of variable Sum.

25 Write the equivalent assembly language instructions for high level language statement

If Sum > 5 Then Sum := Sum + 1 Else Sum := Sum - 1;

Assume that memory location with address 0x1000 is used to store the current value of variable Sum.

26 Write the equivalent assembly language instructions for high level language statement

While Sum < 10 Do Sum := Sum + 1;

Assume that memory location with address 0x1000 is used to store the current value of variable Sum.

27 Write the equivalent assembly language instructions for high level language statement

Repeat Sum := Sum - 1 Until Sum = 0;

Assume that memory location with address 0x1000 is used to store the current value of variable Sum which is decimal 10.

28 Write the equivalent assembly language instructions for high level language statement

Sum := Sum * 8;

Assume that memory location with address 0x1000 is used to store the current value of variable Sum, an unsigned number.

29 Write the equivalent assembly language instructions for high level language statement

If (SwitchSettings BitWiseAND 4) = 1 Then Sum := 0 ;

Assume that memory location with address 0x1000 is used to store the current value of variable SwitchSettings, an unsigned number and memory location 0x1004 the current value of variable Sum.

30 Use an assembly language simulator to check your answers.

In this chapter you have covered:

- The basic machine-code operations of
  - load - LDR R_d, <memory ref>
  - add - ADD R_d, R_n, <operand2>
  - subtract - SUB R_d, R_n, <operand2>
  - store - STR R_d, <memory ref>
  - branching (conditional and unconditional)
    - B <label>
    - BEQ <label>
    - BNE <label>
    - BGT <label>
    - BLT <label>
  - compare - CMP R_n, <operand2>
  - logical bitwise operators
    - AND - AND R_d, R_n, <operand2>
    - OR - ORR R_d, R_n, <operand2>
    - NOT - MVN R_d, <operand2>
    - XOR - EOR R_d, R_n, <operand2>
  - logical
    - shift left - LSL R_d, R_n, <operand2>
    - shift right - LSR R_d, R_n, <operand2>
  - halt - HALT
- The use of the basic machine-code operations above when machine-code instructions are expressed in mnemonic form - assembly language, using immediate and direct addressing
- The instructions set of assembly language mnemonics identified by AQA to be used in questions - see *Table* 7.3.3.5 in *Chapter* 7.3.3. Question papers will supply the list of mnemonics and their description so that they do not need to be memorised.

7.3 Structure and role of processor and its components

■ 7.3.6 Interrupts

The role of interrupts

Virtually all computers provide a mechanism by which a program currently executing on the processor may be interrupted by a module such as an I/O controller, seeking the attention of the processor. The module generates a signal called an interrupt signal which is sent along a control line to the processor. Thus an interrupt may be defined as follows:

> *An interrupt is a signal from some device/source seeking the attention of the processor.*

If interrupts are enabled then, on receipt of an interrupt, the currently executing program is suspended in an orderly fashion and control is passed to an interrupt service routine. The currently executing program is suspended in such a way that its execution can be resumed without error after the servicing of the interrupting device has been carried out.

> ### Key concept
>
> **Interrupt:**
> An interrupt is a signal from some device/source seeking the attention of the processor.

Sources of interrupt

There are many sources of interrupt. *Table 7.3.6.1* shows the main ones and their priority with **1** being the highest and **4** the lowest.

Class of interrupt	Source of interrupt	Priority
Hardware failure	Power failure Memory parity	1
Program	Arithmetic overflow Division by zero Attempt to execute an illegal machine instruction Reference outside a user's allowed memory space Supervisor call to cause mode to switch from user to privileged	2
Timer	Real time clock This allows the operating system to perform certain functions at regular intervals of time	3
I/O	Generated by an I/O controller to signal normal completion of an operation or to signal a variety of error conditions, e.g. disk block of data transfer into main memory completed, keyboard key pressed, printer ready to accept next block/line of characters	4

Table 7.3.6.1 Classes of interrupt

The role of interrupt service routines (ISRs)

What happens when, for example, a key on the keyboard is pressed, thus generating an interrupt? A small program called an interrupt service routine (ISR) or interrupt handler is executed to transfer the character code value of the key pressed into main memory. **A different ISR is provided for each different source of interrupt**.

The effect on the fetch-execute cycle

A typical sequence of actions when an interrupt occurs would be:

1. The processor must complete the current fetch-execute cycle for the current program if begun;

2. The contents of the program counter, which points to the next instruction of the current program to be executed, must be stored away safely so it can be restored after servicing the interrupt;

3. The contents of other registers used by the current program are stored away safely for later restoration;

4. The source of the interrupt is identified;

5. Interrupts of a lower priority are disabled;

6. The program counter is loaded with the start address of the relevant interrupt service routine;

7. The interrupt service routine is executed.

After the interrupt service routine has completed its execution:

1. The saved values belonging to the current program for registers other than the program counter are restored to the processor's registers;

2. Interrupts are re-enabled;

3. The program counter is restored to point to the next instruction to be fetched and executed in current program.

The need to save the volatile environment

The volatile environment of the processor refers to the contents of processor registers, e.g. the program counter, the general purpose registers, the status register. Running the interrupt service routine causes the contents of processor registers to change. Unless the volatile environment is saved before these changes occur, restoring the contents of the affected registers will be impossible as will returning the processor to the exact state it was in just before executing the interrupt service routine.

Key concept

Interrupt service routine:
An interrupt service routine is a small piece of program code written to process an event such as a key on a keyboard being pressed.

Key concept

Volatile environment:
The volatile environment of the processor refers to the contents of processor registers.

To service an interrupt, the program counter contents must be changed from the memory address of the next instruction to be executed of the program that is being interrupted to the memory address of the first instruction of the interrupt service routine responsible for servicing the interrupt. The interrupt enable/disable flag of the status register must be changed to disable interrupts of a lower priority. The interrupt service routine may well make use of one or more of the general processor registers. Hence the need to save the volatile environment before switching execution to the interrupt service routine.

Questions

1. What is an interrupt?

2. Give **three** examples of sources of interrupt.

3. Describe the role of interrupts.

4. Describe the role of an interrupt service routine.

5. Describe the typical sequence of actions when an interrupt occurs and its effect on the fetch-execute cycle.

6. What is meant by the volatile environment?

7. Why is it necessary to save the volatile environment while an interrupt is being serviced?

In this chapter you have covered:

- The role of interrupts
- The role of interrupt service routines (ISRs) and
  - their effect on the fetch-execute cycle
  - the need to save the volatile environment while the interrupt is being serviced

7.3 Structure and role of the processor and its components

7.3.7 Factors affecting processor performance

Learning objectives:

■ *Explain the effect on processor performance of:*

- *multiple cores*
- *cache memory*
- *clock speed*
- *word length*
- *address bus width*
- *data bus width*

7.3.7 Factors affecting processor performance

How many instructions can be executed per second?

We have learned already about the basic computational model of CPU and memory from earlier chapters in *Section 7*. In this model, the program is fetched instruction by instruction from main memory and executed in the CPU. The executing program accesses data in main memory while it is executing. *Figure 7.3.7.1* shows this basic model. The fetching, decoding and execution of an instruction is synchronised with the CPU's clock.

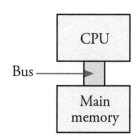

Figure 7.3.7.1 Basic computational model

Information

No of clock cycles per instruction:

The number of clock cycles that an instruction takes to execute is determined by its complexity and the design of the control unit in the CPU. For a given Instruction Set Architecture (ISA), the same instruction may take longer to execute on one processor than another operating at the same clock frequency. The difference is in the design of the control unit.

The number of clock cycles ("ticks") of the CPU's clock it takes the CPU to execute an instruction varies from instruction to instruction with load instructions which load data from memory taking the most.

Suppose, *the average number of clock cycles per instruction = 2*

then *the average number of instructions executed per clock cycle = $\frac{1}{2}$ = 0.5*

If the CPU operates at a clock frequency of 800 MHz then there are 800 million clock cycles per second.

Using this, we calculate that

the average number of instructions executed per second is 0.5 x 800

$$= 400 \text{ million per second}$$

Cycles per instruction (CPI)

Cycles per instruction (clock cycles per instruction) is one aspect of a processor's performance. When evaluating processor performance the average number of clock cycles per instruction is often used.

Information

Average no of clock cycles per instruction:

The percentage of instructions that are load, store, integer arithmetic, branches varies from program to program so the average no of clock cycles per instruction will vary from program to program.

Questions

 The performance of two processors with the same instruction set architecture but operating at different clock frequencies is assessed by measuring the average number of cycles per instruction (CPI) for various programs compiled by the same compiler and executed on each processor. Which processor do you think was the faster at executing these programs? Justify your answer.

Processor 1: Clock frequency 5 GHz   CPI = 3

Processor 2: Clock frequency 3 GHz   CPI = 1.5

Information

Listed below in order of popularity, as of 2015, are some of the most common ISAs (most popular first) :

• ARM
• IA-32 (Intel® x86)
• Intel® 64 (Intel® x86-64)
• IA-64 (Intel® Itanium®)

Information

Clock speed or rate:

Clock speed can be adjusted in the BIOS.

Information

Tools for exploring the hardware of a computer system:

Speccy®: www.piriform.com/speccy

CPUID: www.cpuid.com / softwares/cpu-z.html

Key concept

Core:

A processing unit consisting of ALU + Control unit + Registers within a CPU.
A CPU or processor with just one core is called a single-core CPU.
A CPU with more than one core is called a multi-core CPU, e.g. a quad-core processor has four cores.

CPU time

CPU Time is the amount of time it takes the CPU to execute a particular program. CPU time is a function of the number of instructions in the program, the clock cycle time and average CPI:

$$\text{CPU time} = \text{instruction count} \times \text{CPI} \times \text{clock cycle time}$$

CPU time can be reduced by reducing any or all of the quantities on the right-hand side of the above equation.

Instruction count can be reduced by

- inspecting the compiled code and replacing sections of it with code that uses fewer instructions, written directly in assembly language by hand
- redesigning the compiler to produce fewer machine code instructions for a given program, i.e. better optimisation.

To reduce CPI and clock cycle time we must focus on the processor (CPU) itself.

Questions

 What affects the amount of time it takes a CPU to execute a particular program?

How can we improve processor performance?

CPI and clock cycle time are related to how the processor operates. To improve its performance we need to reduce the

- average CPI by redesigning the processor, using multiple cores, increasing memory bandwidth (number of bits transferred per second), or pre-fetching data and instructions and storing these in fast access memory (cache) located on processor chip.

- clock cycle time by clocking the processor at a higher rate.

Multiple cores

Arithmetic instructions are executed using the Arithmetic and Logic Unit (ALU). If the number of ALUs is increased from one to four then a single arithmetic instruction can use all four ALUs at the same time. For this to be possible,

1. The data must lend itself to being divided into four streams, one per ALU.

2. Four cores (ALU + Control Unit + Registers [+ Cache]) are required

This means that all the arithmetic instructions to which this applies for a given program can be executed in a quarter of the time. Single Instruction Multiple Data (SIMD) stream processing, as it is known, requires special control units to decode and execute instructions that are to be executed in parallel.

Data can also be pre-fetched at the same time the processors are busy decoding and executing arithmetic instructions. The pre-fetched data is stored in fast to access memory on the processor chip so as not to hold up the processor.

Figure 7.3.7.2 shows a schematic for an ARM® Cortex®-A7 quad-core 32-bit processor based on ARM's licensed v7-A instruction set architecture (ISA). It has four CPUs or cores labelled 1, 2, 3 and 4. Each core has its own data cache as well as an instruction cache enabling instructions to be pre-fetched as well. SIMD operations for handling audio and video processing as well as graphics and gaming processing rely on a special control unit called the NEON Data Engine. Floating point operations take considerably longer than fixed point and integer operations (fixed point data can be treated and processed as integers). The A9 processor also includes a dedicated Floating Point Unit specially designed to allow the CPU to offload floating point operations to this unit.

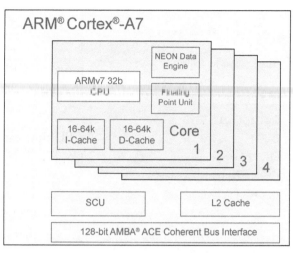

Figure 7.3.7.2 ARM® Cortex®-A7 quad-core processor

Figure 7.3.7.3 shows the Parallella computer platform which is an energy efficient, high performance, credit card sized computer based on the Epiphany multicore chips from Adapteva®. This desktop version cost £150 and is used for developing and implementing high performance, parallel processing. It uses a Zynq dual-core ARM A9 processor to launch and run programs which use the 16-core Epiphany coprocessor for parts of the program that can be executed in parallel. The Epiphany coprocessor is also available with 64 cores. The Parallela's Ethernet connection allows multiple units to be interconnected to make a cluster.

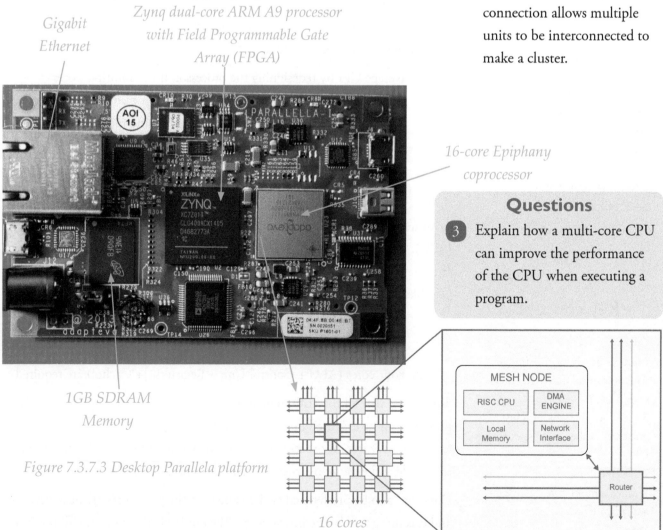

Gigabit Ethernet

Zynq dual-core ARM A9 processor with Field Programmable Gate Array (FPGA)

16-core Epiphany coprocessor

1GB SDRAM Memory

Figure 7.3.7.3 Desktop Parallela platform

16 cores

Questions

3 Explain how a multi-core CPU can improve the performance of the CPU when executing a program.

Bus width effect on processor performance

Main memory or RAM is controlled by a circuit called a memory controller which is a part of the CPU. The memory controller is connected to main memory by a memory bus as shown in *Figure 7.3.7.4*.

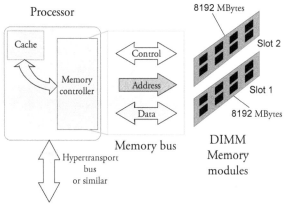

Figure 7.3.7.4 Memory bus

In modern computer systems every byte in memory has its own address. The data bus part of the memory bus is typically **64, 128, 192 or 256** bits wide on a modern general purpose Intel or AMD CPU. **64** bits means that when **64** bits are transferred along the data bus, these **64** bits have come from 8 memory addresses.

Modern computer systems use *synchronous dynamic random access memory* (SDRAM) that is dynamic random access memory (DRAM) synchronized with the system/memory bus.

DDR3-1600 memory used in the computer on which this book was written stands for double data rate type three synchronous dynamic random-access memory. It is operated at a clock rate or clock speed of approximately 800MHz but because data is transferred on both the rising edge of the clock signal and the falling edge, twice as much data is transferred per clock cycle - *Figure 7.3.7.5*.

Each transfer consists of **64** bits, the width of the data bus (single channel). The *memory data bus must also operate at the same frequency as memory* because it has to be synchronised with the DDR memory.

A processor should take less time executing a program if more data can be transferred each time memory is accessed. *A wider data bus allows more data to be transferred in one go.* However, the speed at which the transfer takes place is also a factor. This is why both data bus width and memory bus clock rate must be taken into account.

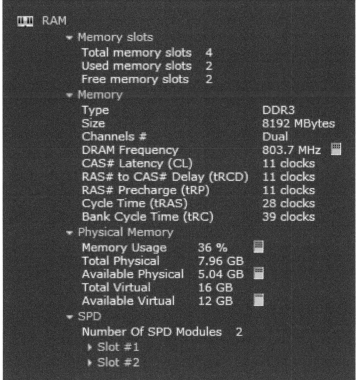

Figure 7.3.7.5 Details of RAM in author's computer

Extension material: *Memory bandwidth and effect on processor performance*

Memory bandwidth is the rate at which data can be read from or stored in main memory by a processor. Memory bandwidth is usually expressed in units of bytes per second.

Memory bandwidth = memory clock rate x bits transferred per clock cycle / 8

For example, bits transferred per clock cycle = **64** bits x **2** x no of channels

(Multiple by 2 when Double Rate Dynamic RAM (DDR3) is used)

No of channels = 2, clock rate = 800MHz (8×10^6),

Memory bandwidth = $800 \times 10^6 \times 64 \times 2 \times 2/8 = 256 \times 10^8$ bytes per second = 25.6 Gigabytes per second

$$= 25.6 \text{ GB/s}$$

This is a theoretical maximum because memory doesn't respond immediately to a read or write request. This is called latency, in particular, Column Access Strobe (CAS) latency - *Figure 7.3.7.5*. It is the delay time between the moment a memory controller tells the memory module to access a particular memory column on a RAM module, and the moment the data from the given location is available on the module's output pins. To overcome this latency, which can be as much as 11 clock cycles or more (see *Figure 7.3.7.5*), cache memory is employed.

Cache memory is faster to access than main memory because

(a) its technology is different from main memory technology

(b) the bus speed of the bus that accesses cache memory is much higher than the memory bus speed connecting main memory to the CPU.

Questions

4　Describe the effect on memory bandwidth of increasing
(a) the width of the data bus from **64** bits to **128** bits
(b) the clock rate that memory uses from **666.6MHz** to **800MHz**.

5　Explain why the transfer speed of bits along the data bus is not the only factor that determines the time taken to transfer data between processor and main memory.

The effect of cache on processor performance

CPU cache is memory on the CPU chip used by the central processing unit (CPU) of a computer to reduce the average time to access data from main memory.

The cache is a small amount of fast but expensive memory which stores copies of the data from frequently used main memory locations, data to be written to main memory and pre-fetched instructions.

When the processor attempts to read a word of main memory, a check is made first to determine if the word is in the cache. If it is, a copy of the word is transferred to the processor. This is a much faster operation than accessing main memory. If not, a block of main memory, consisting of a fixed number of words, is transferred into the cache and then a copy of the referenced word is transferred to the processor.

Similarly, when the processor needs to write to main memory it will write to the cache instead which is a much faster operation than writing directly to main memory.

Figure 7.3.7.6 shows the cache hierarchy and its role in the Fetch-Execute cycle. L1 cache has near zero latency but only a limited amount is provided because it is expensive. The L2 memory cache is cheaper to make than

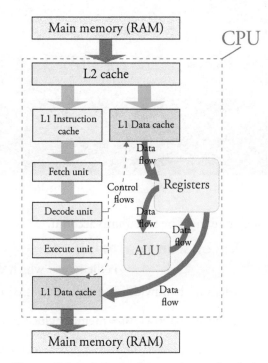

Figure 7.3.7.6 Cache hierarchy and role in Fetch-Execute cycle

Cores	6
Threads	6
Name	AMD FX-6300
Code Name	Vishera
Package	Socket AM3+ (942)
Technology	32nm
Specification	AMD FX-6300 Six-Core Processor
Family	F
Extended Family	15
Model	2
Extended Model	2
Stepping	0
Revision	OR-C0
Instructions	MMX (+), SSE, SSE2, SSE3, SSSE3,
Virtualization	Supported, Disabled
Hyperthreading	Not supported
Fan Speed	2129 RPM
Bus Speed	200.9 MHz
Rated Bus Speed	2411.0 MHz
Stock Core Speed	3500 MHz
Stock Bus Speed	200 MHz
Average Temperature	15 °C

    ▾ Caches

L1 Data Cache Size	6 x 16 KBytes
L1 Instructions Cache Size	3 x 64 KBytes
L2 Unified Cache Size	3 x 2048 KBytes
L3 Unified Cache Size	8192 KBytes

Figure 7.3.7.7 Cache present in AMD® FX-6300 CPU

L1 cache but is slower to respond than the L1 cache, and therefore it has some latency but still much less than main memory. Some systems use an additional layer of cache between main memory and L2 cache called L3 cache with latency greater than L2 cache but still less than main memory. More L3 cache is provided than L1 and L2 cache because it is cheaper than these.

Figure 7.3.7.7 shows the L1, L2 and L3 caches incorporated into AMD's FX-6300 CPU and their memory sizes. Note that there are two L1 caches, one for data and one for instructions.

Key concept

Cache memory:

A small amount of faster memory than main memory, that stores copies of the data from frequently used main memory locations, data to be written to main memory and pre-fetched instructions. L1 and L2 cache are usually located on the CPU chip. Slower L3 cache is often located on the motherboard.

The cache memory approach relies for its effectiveness on the fact that when a block of data is fetched into the cache to satisfy a single memory reference, it is likely that future references will be to other words in the block.

Questions

6 Explain how cache memory may be used to improve the performance of a processor.

The effect of word length on processor performance

The instruction set architecture of a processor is designed to work with registers of a given word length (number of bits). In a 32-bit processor, the registers are 32 bits in length, in a 64-bit processor, 64 bits. A machine code instruction will manipulate 32 bits at a time in a 32-bit processor and the unit of transfer between processor and main memory will also be 32 bits. In each case, 32 bits are presented for manipulation or transfer in 32-bit long registers.

If we need to work with 64 bits but are restricted to using a 32-bit processor then we have to use more 32-bit machine code instructions to accomplish the same task than would be the case if we could use 64-bit machine code instructions. A program compiled for a 32-bit machine is thus likely to have more instructions to execute than the same program compiled for a 64-bit processor other things being equal. More instructions to execute means more CPU time.

Questions

7 Explain the effect on processor performance of processor word length.

The effect of address bus width on processor performance

The language of digital computers is binary. Addresses of memory words are no different and are also expressed at the machine level in binary. Addresses can and are treated as data to be manipulated. The address bus width tends therefore to mirror the word length of the processor and therefore its registers. Although 8-bit processors have tended to be different by using an address bus width of 16 lines. More address lines means more bytes can be addressed.

Processor	No of bytes that can be addressed
8-bit	256
16-bit	65,536
32-bit	4,294,967,296
64-bit	18,446,744,073,709,551,616

Table 7.3.7.1 Effect on no of bytes that can be addressed when address bus width is increased

Table 7.3.7.1 shows how the number of bytes that a processor can address increases with word length of processor. At present 64-bit processors are designed with a lower figure for the width of the address bus of 48 bits as 18,446,744,073,709,551,616 bytes is of the order of petabytes for 64-bit wide address bus. Memory of this capacity would cost a lot of money!

Questions

 Explain the effect on processor performance of address bus width.

Summary

To improve the performance of a processor timewise, CPU time needs to be reduced so that programs take less time to execute. CPU time is defined as follows: CPU time = instruction count x CPI x clock cycle time

To reduce CPU time the following need to be reduced

1. Instruction count

   • influenced by the design of the compiler or whether sections of code have been rewritten in assembly language to use fewer instructions.

2. CPI (cycles per instruction) and clock cycle time

   • influenced by the design of the processor and its operation.

CPI can be reduced by

• increasing the word length of the processor

• redesigning its control unit to take less time decoding and executing instructions

• using multiple cores

• increasing memory bandwidth (number of bits transferred per second)

   ◆ by increasing the width of the data bus for a given clock rate

   ◆ by clocking the memory bus at a higher rate for a given width of data bus

• pre-fetching data and instructions and storing these in fast access memory (cache) located on processor chip.

Clock cycle time can be reduced by increasing the clock speed and clocking the processor at a higher rate.

To improve the performance of a processor regarding the number of memory words it can address, the width of the address bus needs to be increased.

In this chapter you have covered:

■   Explanations of the effect on processor performance of:

- multiple cores

- cache memory

- clock speed

- word length

- address bus width

- data bus width

7.4 External hardware devices

Information

Barcode symbols:
A combination of several bars that make up an individual character or digit is often called a symbol. The set of symbols available for a specific barcode standard is referred to as its symbology. All these different symbologies can be read with a laser beam.

Key concept

One-dimensional barcode:
Barcodes are said to have one dimension if there's a single line (such as a line traced by a scanner's laser) that can cross all lines of the symbol.

Did you know?

Universal Product Code (UPC):
The first-ever product carrying a UPC code in its packaging was scanned June 26th 1974. It was a 10-pack of chewing gum, now on display at Smithsonian Institution's National Museum of American History in Washington, D.C.

■ 7.4.1 Input and output devices

Barcode reader

A barcode reader, or barcode scanner, is an electronic device for reading barcodes printed on items such as cans, packaging, and the covers of books or magazines. A barcode is a sequence of white and black bars (*Figure 7.4.1.1*) that encodes information such as a product identifier. The product identifier is usually printed in human-readable form beneath the barcode.

978-0-9927536-2-7

Figure 7.4.1.1 Barcode encoding the characters 978-0-9927536-2-7

A barcode reader consists of a light source (low-powered laser diode), a lens, photoelectric detectors (photodiodes) and decoder circuitry to analyse the barcode's image data and generate character codes. The scanner uses the light source to illuminate the black and white bands. More light is reflected from a white band than from a dark band. The pattern of reflection is converted from optical form to electrical form by photoelectric detectors in the barcode reader.

The electrical form of the reflection data is analysed and the barcode is decoded into character form. The path of a red laser beam as it moves over the barcode is shown in *Figure 7.4.1.2*. The relative time the beam spends scanning dark bars and light spaces which encode a character is measured and a lookup table is then used to translate this time into the corresponding character.

1234

Figure 7.4.1.2 Laser beam scan of barcode

The scanner outputs the character codes, e.g. ASCII codes, as a sequence of binary digits for processing by a computer.

The line of the laser beam shown in *Figure 7.4.1.2* is the reason why barcodes that are scanned in this way are known as one-dimensional barcodes.

A major advantage of one-dimensional barcodes is that they can be decoded very reliably even when the items tagged with such barcodes are moving at high speed. They are also relatively cheap to use because the technology has been

Learning objectives:

■ *Understand that:*

• *the issue of scale, for software the whole world over, creates potential for individual computer scientists and software engineers to produce great good, but with it comes the ability to cause great harm*

■ *Be able to discuss the challenges facing legislators in the digital age*

Case study continued

After their rescue on July 29th and arrest after returning to England Dudley and Stephens went to trial and Brooks turned state's witness. Defending killing Parker before his natural death they argued that his blood would be better preserved for them to drink. They freely confessed to killing and consuming Parker but claimed they had done so out of necessity. Parker was an orphan without dependents whilst Dudley and Stephens had families that depended upon them.

At the time maritime law was not clear cut on such cases and in such circumstances the custom of the sea applied as practised by the officers and crew of ships and boats in the open sea.

Questions for discussion

1 Suppose you were the judge at their trial. Putting aside the question of maritime law and assuming that you were making a moral judgement, how would you rule and what argument would you use to justify your ruling?

(The actual ruling is available from https://en.wikipedia.org/wiki/R_v_Dudley_and_Stephens)

The case of the Crown versus Dudley and Stephens in 1884 was important for two reasons. Firstly, it established a precedent, throughout the common law world, that necessity is not a defence to a charge of murder. Secondly and more importantly, it highlighted that morality is more than a matter of cost-benefit analysis and calculating consequences but has more to do with the proper way for human beings to treat one another. Morality implies certain moral duties and human rights so fundamental that they rise above a matter of simply calculating consequences.

Questions for discussion

2 Suppose you were asked to draw up a list of fundamental moral duties and human rights. What would be on your list? You could use a search engine to research the general consensus on these but try yourself or discuss the question with others first. Bear in mind that your generation, the digital native one, may disagree with what you find on the World Wide Web which could reflect what has been framed by an older generation labelled digital immigrants.

The Global Information Society and a new Digital Ethics

Society is shaped by the technology at its disposal:

"The handmill gives you society with the feudal lord; the steam-mill the society with the industrial capitalist." Karl Marx

The information society that we live in today has been shaped by the information and communication technologies of the global networking of the digital computer.

"The digital computer and networking give you the Global Information Society"

Whilst previous societies have evolved relatively slowly, the Global Information Society has burst into existence in a relatively short period of time by comparison. Berkeley's School of Information Management and Systems estimated that humanity had accumulated approximately 12 exabytes of data in the course of its entire history before the advent of the desktop digital computer. Since then there has been an explosion in data. For example, in just one year, 2002, more than 5 exabytes of data were produced and recorded. According to IDC, in 2013 the digital universe contained some 4.4 zettabytes, a thousand-fold increase on 2002, roughly. Whilst bringing enormous benefits and opportunities, the information revolution's enormous growth rate has posed a conceptual, ethical and cultural challenge of how to put in place a viable philosophy and ethics of information.

The European Data Protection Supervisor (EDPS), an independent institution of the EU, published a report in 2015 entitled

"Towards a New Digital Ethics"

(https://secure.edps.europa.eu/EDPSWEB/webdav/site/mySite/shared/Documents/Consultation/Opinions/2015/15-09-11_Data_Ethics_EN.pdf)

At its core is the protection of human dignity:

"An ethical framework needs to underpin the building blocks of this digital ecosystem. The EDPS considers that better respect for, and the safeguarding of, human dignity could be the counterweight to the pervasive surveillance and asymmetry of power which now confronts the individual. It should be at the heart of a new digital ethics."

Asymmetry of power and pervasive surveillance

Asymmetry of power

Coded algorithms automate operations or actions according to a logic that differs little from that which humans have applied for centuries. Replacing the human brain by a digital computer enables more consistency, greater speed of calculation and more control. However, it adds an additional dimension that is not possible with a human agent: computers do not only carry out actions using information in the form of programmed instructions but they can also produce information that coded algorithms can capture and report.

Key principles

Protection of personal data: EU Charter of Fundamental Rights Article 1 defines the right of an individual to protection of their personal data via data protection principles the following principles -necessity, proportionality, fairness, data minimisation, purpose limitation, consent and transparency. These apply to data processing in its entirety, to collection as well as to use.

Key concept

Personal data: Data about any living person.

Task

Data Protection Act
1. Look at the eight principles of the Data Protection Act 1998 at https://ico.org.uk/for-organisations/guide-to-data-protection/ and see if you can match these to the EU Charter principles.
2. Look at Regulation (EU) 2016/679 which applies to all 28 EU countries from 25 May 2018 and Directive (EU) 2016/680 which requires member states to enact legislation by 6 May 2018.

Key concept

Asymmetry of power: Computers do not only carry out actions using information in the form of programmed instructions but they can also produce information that coded algorithms can capture and report. However, whilst you have some control over the former in that you have initiated the action, e.g. a search, you seemingly have much less control over the latter.

Key concept

Machine learning:
Machine learning is the science of getting computers to act without being explicitly programmed. This approach enables patterns in and links between data to be discovered autonomously once the machine has been "trained" on a large enough dataset. Examples are speech recognition and language translation software, and self-driving cars.

Key concept

Information:
Data is how information is represented.

Key concept

Knowledge:
Knowledge is usable information.

Key concept

Pervasive surveillance:
Capturing of small data from individuals' online actions and utterances as they go about their daily lives. These data flows have been labelled 'data exhaust'.

"Information Technology alone has this capacity to both automate and reflect information (informate)" - Professor Shoshana Zuboff. However, whilst you have some control over the former in that you have initiated the action, e.g. a search, you seemingly have much less control over the latter (e.g. collecting, storing and associating with you information about what you are searching for) and certainly many people do not perceive that the latter is happening behind the scenes. This is what is meant by asymmetry of power.

Visiting a particular website results in your visit being logged, tracked with cookies and then combined with information already held about you to send you personalised advertisements. You can see what is happening behind the scenes using packet capture software such as Wireshark. For example, visiting the New York Times' website results in the communication of information to the following other sites (as of October 2015):

https://www.doubleclickbygoogle.com/

http://www.conversantmedia.com/

http://www.facebook.com

Pervasive surveillance

The logic in automation is the logic of action, i.e. do this followed by do that, whereas the logic of information reflection is the logic of accumulation. The latter has given rise to huge datasets labelled Big Data (see Chapter 11.1) and the impetus to analyse large datasets using machine learning techniques. Contributing to this Big Data phenomena in a major way is the capturing of small data from individuals' online actions and utterances as they go about their daily lives. Nothing is too trivial or unimportant for this data harvesting, from Facebook 'likes' and clicks on links, to smartphone location data. Such data (representation of information) is aggregated, analysed, packaged and sold.

These data flows have been labelled 'data exhaust' because they are the byproduct of users' actions as they go about their daily business interacting with computer systems. Google and Facebook are among the largest and most successful Big Data companies because they sweep up this data exhaust. In 2015, Google's search engine was the most visited engine and Facebook the most visited social media site.

Although Google started out with no intention of offering advertisers space on their search results' Web pages, they eventually gave in to the need to generate revenue via an advertising model rather than a fees-for-service one because the latter might have impacted on the expansion of their user base. This advertising approach depended upon the acquisition of personal data as the raw material that after analysis and application of machine learning would sell and target advertising through a unique auction model reliant upon the accumulation of huge quantities of personal data to make it work with increasing precision and success.

Google's business is thus the auction business and its customers are advertisers. AdWords, Google's algorithmic auction method for selling online advertising, analyses massive amounts of data to determine which advertisers get which one of eleven sponsored links on each search results page (http://archive.wired.com/culture/culturereviews/magazine/17-06/nep_googlenomics?currentPage=all).

Case study

In 2009 Google published a research paper in the prestigious scientific journal Nature that described a method to track influenza-like illness in a population by analyzing large numbers of Google search queries. The researchers reported that they could accurately estimate the current level of weekly influenza activity in each region of the United States, with a reporting lag of about one day.
(http://static.googleusercontent.com/media/research.google.com/en//archive/papers/detecting-influenza-epidemics.pdf)
"This seems like a really clever way of using data that is created unintentionally by the users of Google to see patterns in the world that would otherwise be invisible," said Thomas W. Malone, a professor at the Sloan School of Management at MIT.
Shortly after its publication, H1N1, a new strain of a particularly virulent strain of flu hit the United States. In order to track and contain the outbreak before it became pandemic, the Centers for Disease Control and Prevention (CDC) requested that doctors inform them of new flu cases. Unfortunately, this reporting at best involved a two-week lag, too long to enable effective control of the outbreak.

Questions for discussion

3. "What companies know about me from my behavior online cannot hurt me. In fact, it is more likely to benefit me."

4. "What information I give out about myself is a fair tradeoff for benefits that I receive."

5. "Surrendering personal data for perceived benefits is not a square deal because I cannot control all the ways that my personal data will be used."

6. "I am powerless to stop my personal data being used for purposes that I am unaware of because the services that I use for free in exchange for surrendering my data are an integral part of my life."

7. "I am just amazed at all the innovative services, e.g. Google translate, DropBox, GoogleDocs, Apps or education, YouTube, etc, that I can get for free by interacting online. It doesn't bother me that my personal data and activities online can be used by the data scientists and data mining experts to create the weird and wonderful algorithms behind all these services."

8. Google's use of user-generated data to support public health efforts in significant ways is a benefit to society and therefore outweighs the concerns raised by two privacy organisations that Google could be compelled by court order to release sensitive user-specific information - the Electronic Privacy Information Center (https://www.epic.org) and the US Patient Privacy Rights organisation (https://patientprivacyrights.org).

Key principle

Linking of information:
Two pieces of information about a person might individually be harmless but less so if linked.

For example:

1. Tony Blair is a former British Prime Minister
2. Tony Blair has a home in London
Google's street view map of Tony Blair's London home is now blurred. Google are required now to offer to blur properties visible in Street View after a European court ruling in favour of people's 'right to be forgotten'.

1. Dick Cheney was US Secretary of Defense during Operation Desert Storm, the 1991 invasion of Iraq
2. Dick Cheney has been fitted with a heart pacemaker, recently.

The pacemaker was specially adapted for Dick Cheney so that it would be resistant to hacking and disruption. This must be very reassuring to the rest of the population which has to make do with pacemakers that are vulnerable to hacking.

Case study - adapted with permission from Forbes.com

The chief data scientist, Andrew Pole, of a US retail chain, Target, successfully figured out how to answer the question, "If we wanted to know if a customer is pregnant, even if she didn't want us to know, is it possible? ", by analysing data that the company collected on customers' spending habits.

As Pole's computers crawled through the collected personal data, he was able to identify about 25 products that, when analyzed together, allowed him to assign each shopper a "pregnancy prediction" score. More importantly, he could also estimate her due date to within a small window, so Target could send coupons timed to very specific stages of her pregnancy. The sending of such coupons did result in an unexpected outcome when a Target store was visited by an angry man to complain that Target was sending his teenage daughter coupons for baby clothes and cribs even though she was certainly not pregnant and was still at high school.

The manager was bemused and could only apologise profusely and then again a few days later by phone.

On the phone, though, the father was somewhat apologetic. "I had a talk with my daughter," he said. "It turns out there's been some activities in my house I haven't been completely aware of. She's due in August. I owe you an apology."

Target changed their mailing policy to mask the fact that they knew a lot more about their customers than their customers realised. So they started mixing coupons for other things with the baby item coupons so that the pregnant woman did not think that she had been spied on.

Questions for discussion

Revisit questions 3 to 6 shown again below, to see if you would respond in the same way after reading the case study above.

3 "What companies know about me from my behaviour online cannot hurt me. In fact, it is more likely to benefit me."

4 "What information I give out about myself is a fair tradeoff for benefits that I receive."

5 "Surrendering personal data for perceived benefits is not a square deal because I cannot control all the ways that my personal data will be used."

6 "I am powerless to stop my personal data being used for purposes that I am unaware of because the services that I use for free in exchange for surrendering my data are an integral part of my life."

The issue of scale

Google is the pioneer of hyperscale, the ability at relatively low cost to scale processing quickly across thousands of commodity computers housed in data centres. Other hyperscale businesses such as Facebook, Twitter, Alibaba, Baidu, Amazon, and Yahoo also possess this ability. Smaller firms without hyperscale revenues can leverage some of these capabilities by using a cloud facility such as Amazon's Elastic Cloud facility.

Having this hyperscale ability enables many results to be extracted from individuals' personal data that would have remained unknown but for the scaling of the processing it makes possible, as well as the support for massive datasets of personal information it grants. The extracted information can be of benefit to society but it also has the potential for misuse if the processing is used for social or economic discrimination, unsolicited advertising, or reputational damage.

This hyperscale ability also provides the capacity for sharing information amongst individuals on a global scale through social media sites, tweets, online blogs, etc., from which individuals derive much benefit of a social nature. All of this has been made possible by coded algorithms devised and deployed by computer scientists and software engineers. However, the free access and facilities provided by Internet companies to enable this sharing comes at a cost which may be difficult for the individual to assess or for that matter for anyone to know how the information surrendered freely will be used in the future.

"The Web means the end of forgetting" Jeffrey Rosen

YouTube demonstrates that people's eccentric behaviour can be distributed around the world without their knowledge or control as they may not know their behaviour was captured in a video or that the video has been uploaded to YouTube. Whilst access to lots of information is made possible by the hyperscale reach provided through the Internet, it also provides access to aspects of people's lives that were formally private. Sometimes people do knowingly give away or surrender their privacy, but it is also the case that sometimes they are innocent victims because of circumstances beyond their control. It is very difficult to protect privacy in such cases.

Information

Hyperscale computing:
In computing, hyperscale is the ability of an architecture to scale appropriately and quickly in a cost-effective manner as increased demand is added to the system. Hyperscale computing is necessary in order to build a robust and scalable cloud, big data, map reduce, or distributed storage system and is often associated with the infrastructure required to run large distributed sites such as Facebook, Google, Microsoft Azure or Amazon AWS.

Key fact

Memories for life:
The ability to record memories, and store them indefinitely in digital form in virtually unlimited quantities has been dubbed the phenomenon of memories for life. Photographs and documents featuring you may turn up in other people's memory banks. "The Spy in the Coffee Machine" © Kieron O'Hara and Nigel Shadbolt 2008, reproduced with permission of the publishers Oneworld Publications.

Questions for discussion

Topic: Practical obscurity

Practical obscurity is an important factor in the preservation of privacy. If the representation of information does not permit it to be easily queried, e.g. the information is on paper in a filing cabinet, then the extraction of important knowledge (usable information) is made more difficult.

9   Why does the ability to collect and process data on a mammoth scale in the way achieved by Google and other hyperscale companies reduce practical obscurity?

Information

The Web means the end of forgetting:
New York Times article by Jeffrey Rosen
http://www.nytimes.com/2010/07/25/magazine/25privacy-t2.html?pagewanted=all&_r=0

Key concept

Cookie:

A cookie is the standard way that a website uses to track its visitors to the site. They are little pieces of data harmless in themselves that are used to inform a website that a particular visitor to the website has returned. This is generally seen as a positive thing.

A benefit is that cookies allow e-commerce sites to maintain a virtual shopping basket for the visitor between visits. However, some cookies collect data across many websites, creating 'behavioural profiles' of people. These profiles can then be used to decide what content or adverts to show you. This use of cookies for targeting in particular is what recent changes in UK law were designed to address by requiring websites to inform and obtain consent from visitors for the use of cookies. The law's aim is to give web users more control over their online privacy.

Task

Cookie Law:

Find out about Cookie law which was adopted by all EU countries in May 2011 and required an update in the UK to the Privacy and Electronic Communications Regulations.

The challenges facing legislators in the digital age

There is a general feeling that a person's privacy has shrunk in the global information society. There are something like five hundred companies that are able to track every move you make on the Internet, mining the raw material of the Web and selling it to marketers.

"Personal data are purchased, aggregated, analyzed, packaged, and sold by data brokers who operate, in the US at least, in secrecy – outside of statutory consumer protections and without consumers' knowledge, consent, or rights of privacy and due process" (*U.S. Committee on Commerce, Science, and Transportation, 2013*).

The law often places constraints on what computer scientists and software engineers are allowed to do, but equally the nature of software, data, and information, and the degree and scale of control over software available to this group constrain what the lawyers and legislators can achieve when local laws run up against the global Internet.

"In today's digital environment, adherence to the law is not enough; we have to consider the ethical dimension of data processing."

(*Towards a New Digital Ethics*)

This is the case whether the right under scrutiny is any one of copyright, trademark, privacy, or freedom of expression. Can a law made in one country be successfully applied to the global Internet whose content, algorithms and access embed value judgments from different cultures, societies and legal systems?

Case study

Guardian article: Right to be forgotten: Swiss cheese Internet, or database of ruin?

Read this Guardian article by Julia Powles at
http://www.theguardian.com/technology/2015/aug/01/right-to-be-forgotten-google-swiss-cheese-internet-database-of-ruin

Questions for discussion

10   Do you think that one country should have the authority to control what content someone in another country can access on the Internet? Justify your opinion.

11   In respect of the Internet, should the reach of the law for each of the following apply (i) globally or (ii) locally with each country deciding what law to apply

(a) copyright (b) trademark (c) privacy (d) freedom of expression

Software and their algorithms embed moral and cultural values

Any artifact that interacts with human beings and that is able to change the dynamics of social processes is not value free.

Social processes are the ways in which individuals and groups interact, adjust and re-adjust and establish relationships and patterns of behaviour.

To be value free means to be without bias or to use criteria that do not reflect prejudice or cultural attitudes.

Cultural attitudes reflect the culture of a society and are expressed through the ideas, customs, and social behaviour that are held to define the society. British culture, for example, means to act fairly and justly; respect for the right of free expression; respect for the rule of law and the democratic process; respect for a free press (free from Government control); the right to protest in an orderly manner; and much more. Other cultures place a different emphasis on free speech, etc.

Email was the first killer application built on top of the Internet. It changed a major social process dramatically, i.e. the way that we communicate, but if you were not digitally connected then you could not use it. Although this is less true today there are sectors of the world's population who are unable to communicate via email because they do not have access to the necessary resources.

Case study

The architecture of a place functions as a form of regulation; it constrains the behaviour of those who interact with it, often without them even realizing it. Build a bridge so low that buses cannot pass under it then it is possible to exclude people from travelling to what lies beyond the bridge, if economic circumstances mean that buses are their only means of travel. If these circumstances are associated with lack of education and therefore employment opportunities then it becomes a form of segregation, all the more worse if the lack of education opportunities and employment are linked to ethnicity.

The architecture of a place is the way it is because of how the built-environment was designed. The design is not value free if it has been based on criteria which are subjective, i.e. not objective. If the design was objective then the object of connecting one side of the bridge to the other would have applied equally to both buses and cars.

Questions for discussion

12 Think of **two** other ways in which the design of the architecture of the built-environment constrains access to certain social groups?

13 Generally speaking, securing privacy by controlling access is an inalienable right. After all privacy is a human right. What is morally wrong then with applying design to public places in a way that affects some peoples' access but protects other peoples' right to privacy?

14 Can you imagine a situation where the designers set out with the intention of creating fair access but are prevented from doing so by circumstances beyond their control?

Background

The algorithms of the Internet allow data about people to be collected in the following ways:

• Volunteered data – created and explicitly shared by individuals, e.g. social network profiles.
• Observed data – captured by recording the actions of individuals, e.g. location data when using cell phones.
• Inferred data – data about individuals based on analysis of volunteered or observed information, e.g., credit scores.

From your discussions you may have concluded that the architecture of the built-environment can be said to embed moral and cultural values, i.e. it is not value free.

This is also true of the Internet, the World Wide Web and other applications built on top of the Internet such as social media because each of these has been designed. Each has a particular architecture shaped by its designers in its hardware, software, and its algorithms, none of which can be value free because design decisions are always taken which inevitably embed moral and cultural values. Thus the design and operation of the Internet, the World Wide Web and other applications that rely on the Internet must also raise questions of justice, fairness and democracy.

This matters even more because there are major differences between the built environment and the architecture of the Internet, World Wide Web and these other applications.

- The first is one of scale, the Internet's reach is global whereas that of public space is local.

- Secondly, the Internet, World Wide Web and other Internet-based applications embody not only the logic of action, i.e. automation, but also the logic of information reflection or accumulation which facilitates a form of control.

- Thirdly, the distinction between hardware and software is blurred because cloud computing effectively delivers physical hardware packaged as software i.e. a virtual machine running the operating system of your choice and virtual storage such as DropBox. Users can gain access in minutes to virtualised, scalable hardware resources (e.g., Amazon's Elastic Cloud) which obviates the need to purchase the equivalent physical hardware. As there is no physical hardware to dismantle, terminating or halting such a provision also takes only minutes.

Cloud computing also decouples the physical possession of data from their ownership. It means dealing now with the issues of ownership of virtual assets and access to those virtual assets, i.e. the right to ownership and the right to usage. For example, if your personal data is aggregated and subjected to machine learning algorithms that derive new information about you, who owns this new information and who has the right to access this information?

Information

Cloud service providers:

Amazon Web Services -
https://aws.amazon.com
Google Cloud -
https://cloud.google.com
Microsoft Azure:
https://azure.microsoft.com

Case study

There are a number of large gateways into China through which Internet access for Chinese citizens is controlled. The Chinese telecom companies that control these gateways are required by the Chinese government to configure their routers to use DNS servers that screen and filter out content that the Chinese government objects to because, according to Western opinion, of a fear of losing control to forces other than the Chinese government. While the primary purpose of routers is to direct or route Internet traffic to its correct destination, they can also be configured in this way to block content and thereby prevent information from getting to its destination. Routers can also be configured to block access to websites by their URL, e.g. Twitter.com and forbidden web page content by inspecting the packets of information, any content that mentions Tiananmen Square. The router, DNS server, and the software they use become a censor in these circumstances.

Questions for discussion

15 (a) Do you think that the world at large has an inalienable right to influence public opinion in China?

(b) What would be your motives if you do believe this?

16 What should be the limits of freedom of expression on social media sites?

17 Is it wrong for a search engine to return a list of web pages according to a profile that they have built up about you? Why?

18 Should governments make policies to govern access to certain web sites?

Information

Example:
URL to use to explore how China controls its citizens access to the Internet:
http://www.howtogeek.com/162092/htg-explains-how-the-great-firewall-of-china-works/

Task

Read
(1)
http://www.wired.com/2015/07/hackers-remotely-kill-jeep-highway/
(2)
http://www.theguardian.com/technology/2014/jun/29/facebook-users-emotions-news-feeds

Background

How Tor works:
https://www.torproject.org/about/overview

Software can produce great good but with it comes the ability to cause great harm

It is not always enough to encrypt communications over the Internet because the packets that carry the encrypted communication also carry tracking data in plaintext form, i.e. the source and destination IP addresses, e.g. your computer's IP address and the IP address of the website that you are visiting. These IP addresses must be machine readable for the Internet to function and route packets successfully. Internet Service Providers can sell this tracking data to marketers and in some countries are required to keep and reveal this information to the authorities on demand. The packets can also be examined in transit by packet sniffing software snooping in on the communication.

Preserving privacy means not only hiding the content of messages, but also hiding who is talking to whom. The Tor project and the Tor software that it developed has made this tracking much more difficult as well as providing encryption of the content of messages. As a software tool for anonymous and confidential communication, it has been used successfully by journalists to

Background

Deep Web DVD:

Now available to purchase from www.amazon.com.

URL: http://www.amazon.com/ Deep-Web-Directors-Keanu-Reeves/dp/B017WUEJ52

Information

Banning use of free or shared WiFi and Tor:

In December 2015 in the wake of the Paris attacks, it was reported that France's law enforcement authorities were proposing new legislation to forbid the use of free or shared WiFi during a state of emergency. They were also proposing that anonymous browsers like Tor should be blocked in general.

Background

Bitcoin:

Bitcoin is a decentralized digital currency or virtual currency. It uses peer-to-peer technology to operate with no central authority or banks.

communicate more safely with whistleblowers and dissidents. It has proved to be an effective tool to circumvent censorship of the Internet in countries such as China and Iran and as a building block for other software designed to protect privacy.

However, the Tor software has also been used to hide criminal activity and other undesirable activities. A question mark also hangs over whether Tor is secure against monitoring by governments as it was originally developed, built and financed by the US military which released it for general use in 2004, ostensibly to improve the cover of its spies overseas by masking their Internet activities amongst the activities of a diverse group of people to whom the Tor software was now available. If it is not secure against government monitoring, it might be difficult to know because the authorities would be careful about revealing their hand.

Case study

The Dark Web is the World Wide Web content that exists on underground networks which use the public Internet but which require specific software such as Tor for access. The Dark Web forms part of the Deep Web, the part of the Web not indexed by search engines. In the Deep Web there are several online shopping sites that specialise in connecting sellers of illicit goods with willing buyers.

The online black market Silk Road launched in February 2011 used the anonymising tool Tor to protect the identities of buyers, sellers and the site's administrators. Payment was made in Bitcoin, allowing buyers a relatively high amount of protection. Ross William Ulbricht, its creator, was arrested in October 2013. On May 29, 2015, Ulbricht was handed five sentences to be served concurrently, including two for life imprisonment, without the possibility of parole. He was also ordered to forfeit $183 million obtained from his criminal activities that he held in Bitcoins, beyond the reach of the authorities until he was forced to hand over the encryption keys. In a letter to Judge Forrest before his sentencing, Ulbricht stated that his actions through Silk Road were committed through libertarian idealism and that "Silk Road was supposed to be about giving people the freedom to make their own choices" and admitted that he made a "terrible mistake" that "ruined his life".

Watch the film Deep Web by Alex Winter, if you can, which explores how the designers of the Deep Web and Bitcoin are at the centre of a battle for control of how the Internet may be used and its effect on our digital rights.

Questions for discussion

19) In 2014 Google launched a service in response to a European Court ruling to allow Europeans to ask for personal data to be removed from online search results.

(a) Why might removal of personal data from search engine results not be sufficient to comply with the right to be forgotten?

(b) If on the grounds of freedom of speech it is a human right to be able to access information, why might forcing people to conduct searches with engines that are able to access the Deep Web be undesirable?

20) "Software such as Tor should be banned because although it can be used for morally sound purposes it can also be used for criminal and immoral acts." Do you agree or disagree with this statement and why?

Questions

1) What is meant by personalised search results?

2) What is meant by personalised advertisements?

3) Some search engines return search results to fit the profile of the person making the query. State **two** dangers to individuals and society of providing such personalised search.

4) Social media and search engine companies collect personal data from users to make their services more useful to users. Explain why it can be beneficial for the user to give up personal data in this way and why it might not.

5) Software can produce great good but with it comes the ability to cause great harm. Using at least one example, explain the meaning of this statement.

6) Software and their algorithms embed moral and cultural values. Using at least one example, explain the meaning of this statement.

7) Why do legislators face difficulty enacting legislation where the Internet is concerned?

8) Developments in computer science and digital technology have dramatically altered the shape of information flows in society. The labels *asymmetry of power* and *pervasive surveillance* have been applied to these flows. What is the meaning of each of these labels?

9) Processes involving humans communicating with machines have been replaced by machine processes, i.e. machine to machine communication with machines making decisions and taking actions according to the code (automated algorithms) that they are programmed with. Machines in these cases could be embedded computers or nodes in a network such as the Internet, for example. Describe **two** examples of applications where machine to machine communication is relied on substantially. Software engineers and computer scientists have responsibilities in the algorithms that they devise and the code that they deploy. What precautions should be observed by computer scientists and software engineers in the development of the two applications that you have described?

In this chapter you have covered:

- What it means for a person to act morally

- How ethics, a set of principles that applies to a society, can inform a person's reasoning when making moral judgements

- How the nature of software, data, and information and its global scale make it difficult to legislate for on the scale of the Internet especially when it crosses cultural divides, i.e. encounters a different culture

- Equally how the nature of software, data, and information and its global scale creates opportunities through social media, email, blogging, etc. for people to express themselves freely, to share information and ideas freely, and to associate freely

- The manner in which
  - developments in computer science and the digital technologies have dramatically altered the shape of communications and information flows in societies, giving rise to an asymmetry of power and pervasive surveillance
  - software is designed so cannot be value free and therefore will inevitably embed moral and cultural values. This places responsibilities on computer scientists and software engineers to act morally and ethically

- That the ability of computer scientists and software engineers to scale software and processing quickly for marginal cost offered creates the potential for great good through access to information whilst software can also be misused to cause great harm

- The difficulty of applying law made in one country to the global Internet whose content, algorithms and access embed value judgments from different cultures, societies and legal systems, e.g. online privacy versus freedom of speech

9.1 Communication

■ 9.1.1 Communication methods

Serial data transmission

In serial data transmission, single bits (binary digits) are sent one after another along a single wire by varying the voltage on the wire. *Figure 9.1.1.1* shows a simple electrical circuit for sending single bits coded as 0 volts and 5 volts. When the switch is in position A the lamp bulb is connected to 5 volts. When the switch is in position B the lamp bulb is connected to 0 volts. We need to decide what the signal lamp on and the signal lamp off represent.

Figure 9.1.1.1 Simple circuit for sending binary digits serially

Key principle

Serial data transmission:
In serial data transmission, single bits (binary digits) are sent one after another along a single wire.

If single bits are being sent along the wire, then we have one of two possible binary digit values to represent at any moment, 0 or 1. We may choose to let the state *lamp on* represent binary digit 1 and the state *lamp off* represent binary digit 0. In which case, the equivalent signals travelling along the signal wire represent binary digit 1 by 5 volts and binary digit 0 by 0 volts. The binary digits represent data and the voltages 0 volts and 5 volts their signal equivalent. *Figure 9.1.1.2* shows the transmission of a sequence of data bits using signals of 0 volts and 5 volts.

Information

In Figure 9.1.1.1 the current travels along a single wire loop. The moving electric charge picks up electrical energy in the battery and delivers this energy to the lamp bulb.

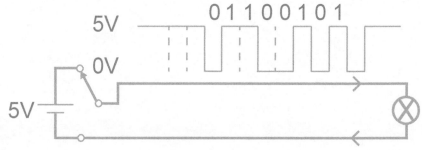

Figure 9.1.1.2 Serial data transmission of a sequence of data bits sent as electrical signals

Questions

1 What is serial data transmission?

Key principle

Parallel data transmission

In parallel data transmission, bits are sent down several wires simultaneously. The connecting cable consists of many wires.

Figure 9.1.1.3 shows two parallel interfaces connected by a parallel connection that uses eight data wires labelled 0 to 7, one ground (GND) wire, one clock signal (CLK) wire. The clock signal wire is set to 5 volts or 0 volts. The data wires are set to 5 volts or 0 volts.

The receiver reads the data bits in one go by sampling the voltage on each data wire when it receives the clock signal pulse ⌐ on the clock wire.

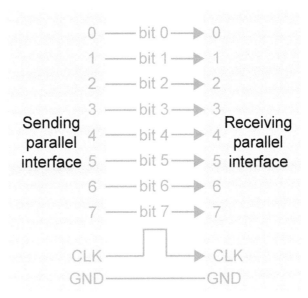

Figure 9.1.1.3 Parallel data transmission along an 8-bit data bus, controlled by a clock pulse to signal the arrival of 8 data bits

Questions

2   What is parallel data transmission?

Advantages of serial over parallel

Parallel data transmission has a limited data rate and distance at which it can be reliably operated compared with serial. The limited data rate and distance of parallel data transmission are caused by skew and crosstalk.

Skew is the phenomenon where the bits travel at slightly different speeds down each wire in a parallel bus. This includes the clock signal as well. The reading of the data on the data lines is synchronised with the clock signal. If data and clock signal get out of step to such a degree that the data lines are sampled before the clock signal has appeared or after it has disappeared then data will not be read correctly. A higher clock rate means narrower clock pulses and shorter time intervals between pulses. The consequence is a narrower sampling time window which means less tolerance of skew. The longer the parallel bus the more data bits on each wire can get out of step with each other and the clock signal.

Crosstalk is induced signals in adjacent wires of a parallel bus caused when a signal on one or more wires varies rapidly. The longer a wire and the more rapid the variation in voltage in adjacent wires the greater the effect.

Serial data transmission doesn't suffer from skew because it doesn't use a separate clock signal and crosstalk is minimised because there are fewer wires in close proximity and techniques can be applied relatively cheaply to guard against crosstalk. It is also considerably cheaper over long distances than parallel would be, simply because fewer wires are used.

A parallel interface is simpler to design than a serial one. The parallel interface just requires a buffer of the same width as the data to be transmitted or received. A serial interface must perform a parallel to serial conversion and vice versa and so is a little more complicated to design than a parallel interface. However, a parallel interface requires more pins than a serial one.

Questions

3 State **two** disadvantages of parallel data transmission when compared with serial data transmission.

Synchronous and asynchronous data transmission

Serial interfaces are divided into two groups: synchronous or asynchronous.

Synchronous serial data transmission is a form of serial communication in which the communicating endpoints' interfaces are continuously synchronized by a common clock. Synchronisation may take the form of special synchronising bit patterns that are sent periodically or which are attached to a block of data. It may also take the form of a special clock line as shown in *Figure 9.1.1.4* which is an I2C interface.

In the Inter-Integrated Circuit (I2C, pronounced I-two-C) synchronous serial interface, used by microcontroller-based systems such as the Raspberry Pi, the clock signal requires its own wire and so adds to the total number of wires that connect the communicating devices.

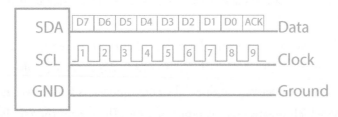

Figure 9.1.1.4 Synchronous serial data transmission for an I2C interface

Figure 9.1.1.4 shows the three pin and three wire interface for I2C. The data bits **D7** to **D0** are individually clocked into the receiving interface by **8** clock pulses. The receiving I2C interface places an acknowledgement bit onto the data wire on receipt of the **9**th clock pulse.

Whatever the type of synchronous serial interface, a clock signal is associated with its data line(s) and this clock signal is used by all the devices connected to the serial bus to synchronise all data transfers.

Information

Serial ports:

Desktop PCs used to have at least one serial port called the COM port but the advent of USB meant manufacturers stopped supplying PCs with serial ports. They are absent from tablets and smart phones where the space for ports is limited. However, the demise of serial ports is greatly exaggerated. Serial ports are everywhere, in everything from industrial automation systems to scientific instrumentation and in Internet of Things (IoT) devices. The Arduino has at least one TTL serial port for transmitting and receiving serial data.

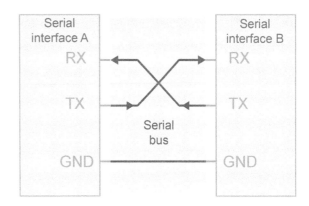

Figure 9.1.1.5 Asynchronous serial data transmission between two interfaces supporting transmit (TX) and receive (RX) in both directions simultaneously

Another example of a synchronous interface used by embedded microcontroller systems is the Serial Peripheral Interface bus (SPI).

Synchronous serial communication is used in telecommunication systems which the Internet relies upon. These are time-division systems which continuously send frames of bits between nodes. The nodes are kept in sync by synchronisation frames which are sent periodically and which distribute the common clock signal derived from an atomic clock. This enables very high data transfer rates not achievable with asynchronous data transfer.

Asynchronous means that data is transferred without support from an external clock signal. No clock wire is required so reducing the number of wires by one and the number of connecting pins in each interface by one as well.

Figure 9.1.1.5 shows a serial interface A connected to another serial interface B by a serial bus consisting of three wires, one to transmit from interface A to interface B and one to transmit from interface B to interface A. Both interfaces share a common ground wire.

Key concept

Asynchronous data transmission:

Asynchronous means that data is transferred without support from an external clock signal. No clock wire is required.

Asynchronous serial data transmission sends **7** or **8** data bits at a time and an optional parity bit framed by start and stop bits in the **RS232/RS422** protocol as shown in *Figure 9.1.1.6*. These **7** or **8** bits often represent character data from the ASCII character data set.

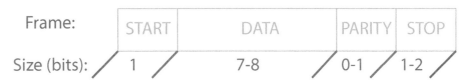

Figure 9.1.1.6 Asynchronous serial data transmission frame

The serial interface is usually a part of an integrated circuit called a UART (Universal Asynchronous Receiver Transmitter) that buffers a serially received data byte before placing it on an internal 8-bit bus as shown in Figure 9.1.1.7.

The UART buffers a byte from the 8-bit data bus before clocking it out onto the serial TX wire framed in start and stop bits. The UART performs serial to parallel conversion and vice versa. If the parity bit system is being used, it also generates a parity bit as well as checking the received data for parity errors.

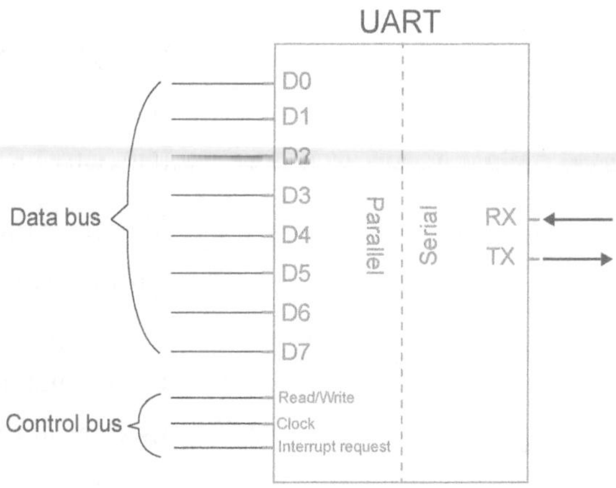

Figure 9.1.1.7 UART

Questions

4 Define the following modes of data transmission
(a) synchronous
(b) asynchronous

Information

Ethernet and USB:
These are serial data transmission protocols that both encode timing information in the communication symbols, i.e. the bit patterns or codes that they use. This coding therefore delivers both a clock signal and data, so both can be classified as synchronous.

Comparison of synchronous and asynchronous data transmission

RS232/RS422 asynchronous serial data transmission is relatively cheap because it requires less hardware than synchronous serial data transmission and is appropriate in situations where messages are generated at irregular intervals, for example from embedded systems used in scientific instruments as initiation of a transfer is relatively quick. However, two in nine or ten bits are control bits thus a significant proportion of the data transmission conveys no information.

Synchronous data transmissions requires the distribution of a stable clock signal. In parallel synchronous data transmission this limits the distance and clock speed. This can also limit serial synchronous data transmission if a separate clock wire is used. However, in time-division multiplexed synchronous serial data transmission, this is less of a problem because all clocks are kept in synchronisation with a master clock by periodically sending synchronising frames and thus doing away with the need for a separate clock wire. High speed data transmission is achievable with this method.

Questions

5 Compare synchronous and asynchronous data transmission.

The purpose of start and stop bits

In asynchronous serial data communication such as RS232 the data are words of a certain word length, for example, a byte, each word is delimited by start and stop bits as shown in Figure 9.1.1.6. In asynchronous serial data transmission the transmitter and receiver are not kept synchronised between transmissions. Instead, the receiver is synchronised with the transmitter only at

Key concept

Start and stop bits:

The start bit signals the arrival of data at the receiver. This enables the receiver to sample the data correctly by generating clock pulses synchronised to the bits in the received data. Effectively, transmitter and receiver clocks are synchronised by the arrival of a start bit.

Both transmitter clock and receiver clock must have been set up previously to "tick" at the same rate when running. Other parameters must agree in both transmitter and receiver interface such as the number of data bits that will be sent, the number of stop bits and whether parity is used or not and if so, what parity, even or odd. These parameters are set up once before either interface is used.

the time of transmission. This allows data to be transmitted intermittently such as when typing characters on a keyboard.

Start bit

The arrival of data at the receiver is signalled by a special bit called a start bit. As the arrival of data cannot be predicted by the receiver, the transmission is called asynchronous.

The start bit is used to wake up the receiver. The receiver's clock is set ticking by the start bit. The clock is just a circuit that is designed to generate a preset number of pulses at fixed intervals which are used to sample the data bits as they arrive one after another. The signal changes in the serial data transmission take place at regular time intervals so the receiver must operate a timing device set at the same rate as the transmitter, so the received bits can be read at the same regular time intervals.

The transmitter also operates a timing device, a clock, that is set at a rate determined by the baud rate (see Chapter 9.1.2). Again this can be as simple a circuit to generate a preset number of pulses at fixed intervals of time.

It is important that the receiver reads each bit during the time that it is not changing, i.e. in the time interval between when changes can take place. This is why the receiver's timing device needs to be brought in step or synchronism with the transmission's timing.

Figure 9.1.1.8 shows two computers, A and B, with a TTL serial connection between their serial ports. TTL is Transistor-Transistor Logic and is a logic that operates between 0 volts and 5 or 3.3 volts. TTL relies on circuits built from bipolar transistors to achieve switching and maintain logic states.

For the link from computer A to computer B, the data wire is kept at the voltage level corresponding to a binary digit 1 when not sending – the idle state. A data transmission is started by changing the voltage level to the level for binary digit 0. This is the start bit. The transmitter (TX) then follows the start bit with 7 or 8 data bits depending on how the serial port has been configured. The least significant data bit (LSB) is sent first and

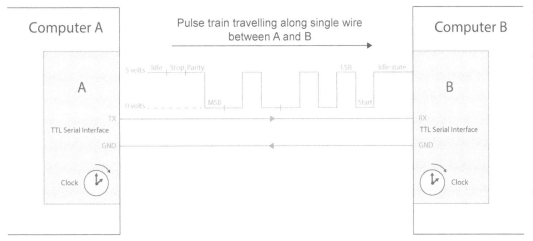

Figure 9.1.1.8 Asynchronous serial data transmission between the TTL serial interface of two computers, A and B

the most significant data bit (MSB) last. If parity is enabled, the last data bit is followed by a parity bit.

Stop bit

Finally, the transmitter attaches a stop bit. The voltage level chosen for the stop bit is the level for binary digit 1. The time interval for the stop bit allows the receiver (RX) to deal with the received bits, i.e. transfer them into the RAM of the computer, before receiving and processing the next serial frame as shown in *Figure 9.1.1.9*. Two stop bits are used if the receiver needs more time to deal with the received bits.

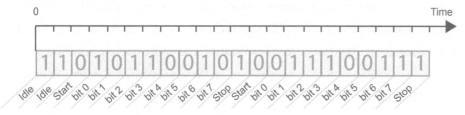

Figure 9.1.1.9 Asynchronous serial data transmission frame showing transmission of two bytes without parity

Questions

6 Describe the purpose of start and stop bits in asynchronous data transmission.

In this chapter you have covered:

- Serial and parallel transmission methods and the advantages of serial over parallel transmission
- Synchronous and asynchronous data transmission and how they compare with each other
- The purpose of start and stop bits in asynchronous data transmission

9.1 Communication

Key concept

Baud rate: The maximum rate at which signals on a wire or line may change.

1 baud: One signal change per second.

9.1.2 Communication basics

Baud rate

The baud rate sets the maximum frequency at which signals may change. To understand the meaning of baud rate consider the following simplified switching system shown in Figure 9.1.2.1. Switch A operates at the baud rate. For example if the baud rate is 1 baud then the switch remains connected to one of the four electrical voltages for one second. At the end of each second, the switch can switch the connection to any one of the four possible voltages. The changeover happens in a time period very much smaller than one second (theoretically, it happens instantaneously). Thus, the output signal that appears on the signal wire may change every one second but no quicker. If the baud rate is 10 baud then the switch can change position every tenth of a second.

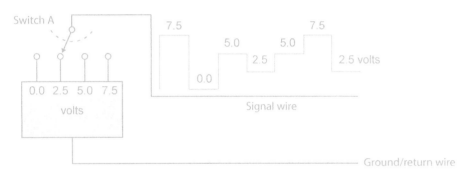

Figure 9.1.2.1 Simplified switching system illustrating baud rate

For example, a computer's serial port may be set to send at 1 baud, the signal sent out by the computer can change only at the end of each elapsed second.

Table 9.1.2.1 shows the rates of signal change for some baud rates.

Baud rate	Time between signal changes (s)	Rate of signal changes (changes per second)
1	1	1
2	0.5	2
4	0.25	4
1000	0.001	1000
10000	0.0001	10000

Table 9.1.2.1 Relationship between baud rate and rate of signal changes

Questions

1. How often may switch A change if the baud rate is 100 baud?

2. How many times a second can the switch change if the baud rate is 1000 baud?

Bit rate

Bit rate is measured in bits per second. It is the number of bits transmitted per second. The bit rate is the same as the baud rate when one bit is sent between consecutive signal changes. However, it is possible to send more than one bit between signal changes if more than two voltage levels are used to encode bits. If the voltages 0 volts, 2.5 volts, 5 volts and 7.5 volts are used, then the decimal numbers in *Table 9.1.2.2* can be encoded.

Signal level (volts)	Decimal number	Binary number
0	0	00
2.5	1	01
5	2	10
7.5	3	11

Table 9.1.2.2 Linking signal levels and number of bits they encode

Figure 9.1.2.2 shows how two bits of data can be encoded per time slot on a **1** baud line, giving a bit rate of **2** bits per second.

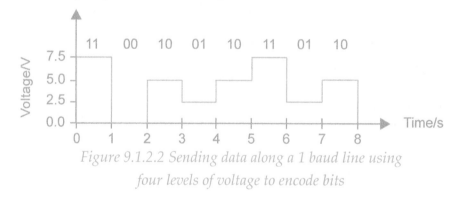

Figure 9.1.2.2 Sending data along a 1 baud line using four levels of voltage to encode bits

From this we may conclude that the relationship between but rate and baud rate is

bit rate = baud rate x the no of bits per signal (voltage)

Questions

3 What is meant by (a) baud rate (b) bit rate?

4 Explain the difference between baud rate and bit rate.

5 The following voltage levels expressed in volts are chosen to encode bits:

-6.0, -4.5, -3.0, -1.5, +1.5, +3.0, +4.5, +6.0

How many bits represent these voltages?

6 For the voltages given in question 5 write down one possible set of corresponding bit patterns (an example of a bit pattern is 01).

7 If the baud rate of the line is 900 baud what is the bit rate for the voltage levels given in question 5?

Bandwidth

Bandwidth is a measure of how fast the data may be transmitted over the transmission medium. The greater the bandwidth, the greater the rate at which data can be sent.

The bandwidth of a transmission medium, e.g. copper wire, is the range of signal frequencies that it may transmit from one end of the wire to the other without significant reduction in strength. Bandwidth is measured in hertz (Hz), e.g. 500Hz. The hertz is a unit of frequency equal to one cycle per second. Figures 9.1.2.3 and 9.1.2.4 show the effect of the transmission medium on two different frequencies.

Figure 9.1.2.3 Low-frequency signal injected onto wire at A arrives at B with its strength relatively undiminished

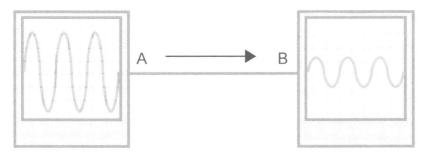

Figure 9.1.2.4 Higher-frequency signal injected onto wire at A arrives at B with its strength diminished significantly

Although a given signal may contain frequencies over a very broad range, any medium used to transmit the signal will be able to accommodate only a limited band of frequencies. This limits the bit rate that can be carried on the transmission medium. Figure 9.1.2.5 shows the effect of a 500 Hz bandwidth signal channel, e.g. a copper wire, on a transmission with bit rate of 2000 bits per second.

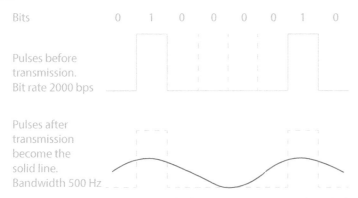

Figure 9.1.2.5 A 2000 bps transmission over a 500 Hz signal channel

Key concept

Latency:
Latency is the time delay that can occur between the moment something (an action) is initiated and the moment its first effect begins.

Latency

Latency is the time delay that can occur between the moment something (an action) is initiated and the moment its first effect begins. In a wide area network involving satellites, significant time delay occurs because of the physical distance between the ground stations and the geostationary satellite.

Requesting and receiving a web page can involve a considerable time delay, even though the bit rate of the uplink and downlink to the satellite is high, i.e. the bandwidth is large. The speed of microwaves is 3×10^8 m/s. With a round-trip distance of over 143,200 km, the propagation time delay is approximately 0.4 s.

Questions

 What is latency in the context of communications?

Key concept

Communication protocol:
A set of pre-agreed signals, codes and rules to be used for data and information exchange between computers, or a computer and a peripheral device such as a printer, that ensure that the communication is successful.

Information

Handshaking protocol:
The sending and receiving devices exchange signals to establish that the receiving device is connected and ready to receive. Then the sending device coordinates the sending of the data, informing the receiver that it is sending. Finally, the receiver indicates it has received the data and is ready to receive again.

Protocol

A communication protocol is a set of pre-agreed signals, codes and rules used to ensure successful communication between computers or a computer and a peripheral device such as a printer.

A protocol will govern such things as:

- Physical connections – e.g. RS423 serial
- Data format – packet/frame size
- Error detection and correction
- Cabling – Cat 5, Optical fibre
- Speed – baud rate, bit rate
- Flow control
- How data is to be sent

For example, serial data communication, uses a handshaking protocol to control the flow of data. In a handshaking protocol, the sending device checks first to see if the receiving device is present. If it is present, the sending device then enquires if the receiving device is ready to receive. The sending device

C	→	Are you ready?	→	P
C	←	Yes I am	←	P
C	→	Here it is (Start bit)	→	P
C	←	Busy	←	P
C	→	That's it (Stop bit)	→	P
C	←	I'm ready again	←	P

Table 9.1.2.3 Handshaking protocol: computer = C, printer = P

waits for a response which indicates that the receiving device is ready to receive. On receipt of this signal, the sending device coordinates the sending of the data and informs the receiver that it is sending the data. The sender then waits for the receiver to become ready to receive more data.

Questions

 10 What is a communications protocol?

Understand the relationship between bit rate and bandwidth

There is a direct relationship between bit rate and bandwidth. The greater the bandwidth of the transmission system, the higher the bit rate that can be transmitted over that system. If the data rate of the digital signal is W bits per second (bps) then a very good representation can be achieved with a bandwidth of 2W Hz.

For example, *Figure 9.1.2.6* shows a **4 x 5** chequered board of black and white squares. Suppose that the information contained within this board of which squares are black and which white is sent as a bit stream row by row, starting from the top left square. The bits and the corresponding stream of voltage pulses are also shown in the figure. The fundamental frequency with which the pulses alternate between **5 volts** and **0 volts** is W/$_2$ Hz where **W** is the bit rate in bits per second.

Key principle

Bit rate and bandwidth:
The greater the bandwidth of the transmission system, the higher the bit rate that can be transmitted over that system.

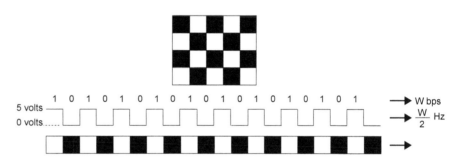

Figure 9.1.2.6 A chequered pattern being encoded in bits and sent serially as a bit stream at W bps

We know from section 5.6 that a square wave is made of harmonics of the fundamental frequency, *f*. Therefore, the bandwidth of the communication channel must allow at least the first harmonic which is 3*f* to travel without significant reduction in amplitude. A bandwidth of four times the fundamental frequency, *f*, should therefore be adequate,

i.e. 4 x W/$_2$ = 2W Hz.

Questions

11 What is the relationship between bandwidth and bit rate?

In this chapter you have covered:

- Definitions for
  - baud rate
  - bit rate
  - bandwidth
  - latency
  - protocol
- The difference between baud rate and bit rate
- The relationship between bit rate and bandwidth

9.2 Networking

Learning objectives:

■ *Understand*

- *physical star topology*

- *logical bus network topology*

■ *Differentiate between both*

■ *Explain their operation*

■ *Compare each (advantages and disadvantages)*

■ 9.2.1 Network topology

Topology

The way computers are cabled together or linked to form a network is very important. The term topology is used to describe the layout of a network. When the computers that are linked are in close proximity, e.g. in a single building, the network is called a local area network.

The topology in *Figure 9.2.1.1(a)* is a mesh and that in *Figure 9.2.1.1(b)* is a bus.

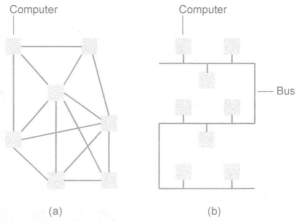

Figure 9.2.1.1 Two different network layouts

Star topology

The most common physical network topology is the star which is shown in outline in *Figure 9.2.1.2*. The centre of the star is either a network switch or a central computer.

> **Key concept**
>
> **Network topology:**
> The shape, layout, configuration or structure of the connections that connect devices to the network.

> **Key concept**
>
> **Local Area Network (LAN):**
> Linked computers in close proximity or in a small geographical area.

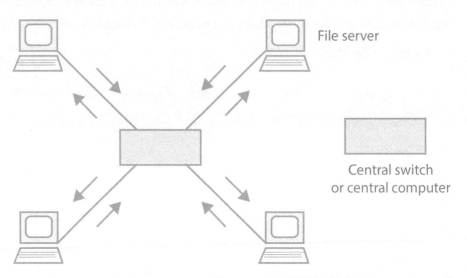

Figure 9.2.1.2 Star network topology

A computer communicates on the network through a network interface card or network adapter. A network adapter plugs into the motherboard of a computer and into a network cable. Network adapters perform all the functions required to communicate on a network. They convert data between the form stored in the computer and the form transmitted or received on the cable (Figure 9.2.1.3).

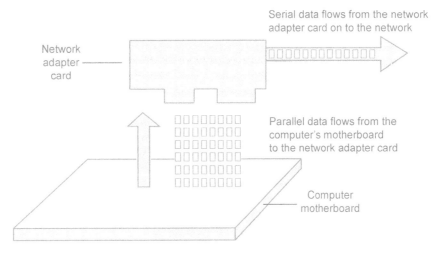

Figure 9.2.1.3 Network adapter

A network adapter receives data to be transmitted from the motherboard of a computer into an area of memory called a buffer. The data in the buffer is then passed through some electronics that calculates a checksum value for the block of data (CRC) and adds address information, which indicates the address of the destination card and its own address, which indicates where the data is from; each network adapter card is assigned a permanent unique address at the time of manufacture. The block is now known as a frame.

Ethernet bus protocol uses the frame structure shown in Figure 9.2.1.4.

Destination address	Source address	Type	Data	CRC
6 bytes	6 bytes	2 bytes	46 - 1500 bytes	4 bytes

Figure 9.2.1.4 Ethernet frame

The network adapter then transmits the frame one bit at a time onto the network cable. The address information is sent first, followed by the data and then the checksum. In the Ethernet protocol, each network card is assigned a unique address called its MAC address. MAC stands for Media Access Control. A MAC address is a **48**-bit address normally expressed in hexadecimal and separated into **6** bytes, e.g. **00-02-22-C9-54-13**. Part of the MAC address identifies the manufacturer. Each network card manufacturer has been allocated a block of MAC addresses to assign to their cards.

Figure 9.2.1.5 shows how three computers connected via T-pieces to a bus can send Ethernet frames to each other.

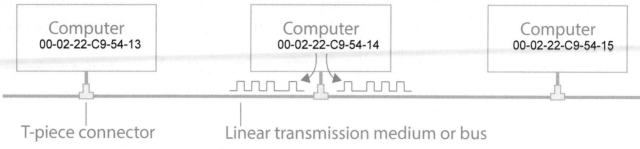

Figure 9.2.1.5 Bus network topology

Figure 9.2.1.6 shows a physical bus network that uses the transmission medium of coaxial cable to interconnect network adapters and their computers. Since the bus transmission medium is a shared medium only one computer can send at a time. However, because it is a shared medium, every network adapter is able to "see" each transmitted Ethernet frame. Each network adapter checks Ethernet frames to see if the destination address field contains the adapter's MAC address. If it does it buffers the frame and reads the data. Collisions can occur when two adapters try to send at the same time. Each will stop transmitting and delay sending again for a random time period. If collisions occur too frequently the speed of communication over the network is reduced.

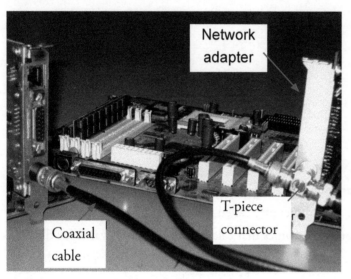

Figure 9.2.1.6 Physical bus network using coaxial cable to interconnect network adapters

Switched Ethernet

The solution to the collision problem is to restrict the communication channel to just each pair of sending and receiving computers, at a time. To cope with more than one computer sending at the same time, the transmissions are buffered and then sent in turn to the corresponding receiving computer. A fast switch is required to make the temporary bus connection between each pair of sending and receiving computers. This is what an Ethernet switch is designed to do.

In switched Ethernet the LAN is wired in star topology with the nodes (computers or workstations) connected to a central switch (*Figure 9.2.1.7*).

Even though the physical layout or topology is a star, the LAN still behaves as a bus. We say that the network physically wired in a star topology can behave logically as a bus network by using a bus protocol and appropriate

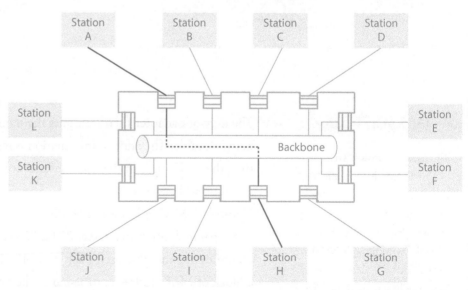

Figure 9.2.1.7 Central switch details and computers or workstations connected in a star configuration to this central switch

physical switching. The central switch queues frames until each frame can be placed onto the backbone. The switch ensures that collisions do not occur. For example, if computer A launches an Ethernet frame for computer H, the switch creates a temporary exclusive connection from computer A to computer H. If computer B simultaneously launches an Ethernet frame for computer D, the switch will buffer the frame until the backbone becomes free. Switched Ethernet eliminates collisions, so its performance is superior to Ethernet LANs based on multidrop coaxial cable.

In switched Ethernet a separate cable is run from a central switch to each workstation. If there are *n* workstations, there are *n* separate

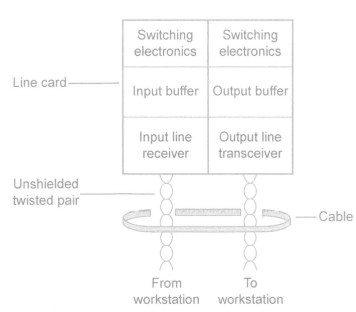

Figure 9.2.1.8 A line card connected to a cable containing two unshielded twisted pairs

cables. At the switch end, a cable is connected to a line card. Therefore, for *n* cables there are *n* line cards. Figure 9.2.1.8 shows a cable connected to a line card. Figure 9.2.1.9 shows a network cable plugged into the Ethernet switch and a cutaway of two twisted pairs emerging from CAT5 cable terminated by an RJ45 connector. To enable bidirectional data transfer, the cable consists of two independent pairs of wires. One pair of wires forms the input circuit and the other the output circuit. The wires in each pair are twisted together, hence the name twisted pair.

Figure 9.2.1.9 Cat 5 network cable showing two twisted pairs: Orange + White & Orange, Blue + White & Blue

A workstation may be a workstation computer, a server, a dumb terminal or some other device. A workstation transmits a packet of data to the line card along the input pair. The packet is stored in the input buffer of the line card. The switching electronics reads the destination address contained in the packet then routes the packet along a backbone in the switch to the line card connected to the destination. A backbone is a high-speed bus.

Figure 9.2.1.10 shows a 10/100 Mbps Ethernet network adapter that connects to the PCI bus of a computer.

Figure 9.2.1.10 10/100 Mbps Ethernet network adapter that plugs connects to the PCI bus of a computer

Questions

1. In the context of networking, what is a topology?

2. Draw a diagram that illustrates the essentials of a bus network.

3. Draw a diagram that illustrates the essentials of a star network.

4. Explain how a network wired in star topology can behave logically as a bus network.

5. What is a network adapter?

6. What is a MAC address?

7. Explain the collision problem in the context of a bus network.

8. How does switched Ethernet overcome the collision problem?

Comparing bus and star networks

Bus and star topologies appear very similar in the way that they are physically wired using the current switch-based hardware. Even thin-client systems, which can be considered to resemble a traditional star network, use an Ethernet bus switch to connect a central server to nodes.

In a traditional star network, each link from node to central computer is an independent link. Each link is therefore secure from eavesdropping by other nodes.

If a link to a node goes down, the other links and nodes are unaffected. However, if the central computer / central switch goes down, the whole network will fail.

In a true star-based network, the speed of each link to the central computer should remain high, because the links are not shared. Traffic between nodes in a switch-based bus network will not be adversely affected if a node goes down, unless the traffic involves the broken node or the node is a domain server that validates users when they attempt to log in. Unplugging a network cable in a switch-based bus network will not affect the rest of the network. In a coaxial cable bus network, a break in the cable stops the whole network from working. All connected nodes are able to read the frames travelling on the coaxial cable bus network. Therefore coaxial cable bus networks are not secure against eavesdropping. The frames in a coaxial cable Ethernet bus network can collide when multiple nodes send at the same time, causing a noticeable slowdown. Although collisions between frames in switch-based Ethernet bus networks cannot occur, performance can be affected when traffic volumes are high, because the buffers in the switches suffer overflow.

A wireless network is a broadcast network, so it is less secure than a cabled switch-based Ethernet network unless wireless encryption is enabled. In a wireless network without encryption, it is possible to eavesdrop on traffic intended for other computers. A wireless network can also suffer congestion because the channels are shared.

Questions

9 Discuss the advantages and disadvantages of operating a logical bus network topology wired as a physical star topology. You may wish to make reference in your answer to a physical bus topology and a traditional star topology.

In this chapter you have covered:

- The operation of
  - physical star topology
  - logical bus network topology
- Differences between both
- The advantages and disadvantages of each

9.2 Networking

Key concept

Peer-to-peer network:
A network in which there is minimal or no reliance on dedicated servers. All computers are equal, and are called peers. Each peer may act as both a client and server.

■ 9.2.2 Types of networking between hosts

Peer-to-peer networking

In a peer-to-peer (**P2P**) network there is minimal or no reliance on dedicated servers.

All computers are equal hence the name peer.

Each computer can communicate with any other computer on the network to which it has been granted access rights.

Each peer computer acts as a client when initiating requests to another computer(s) for resources and as a server when satisfying requests from another computer(s).

Figure 9.2.2.1 shows a wired peer-to-peer local area network and the possible communication paths between peers.

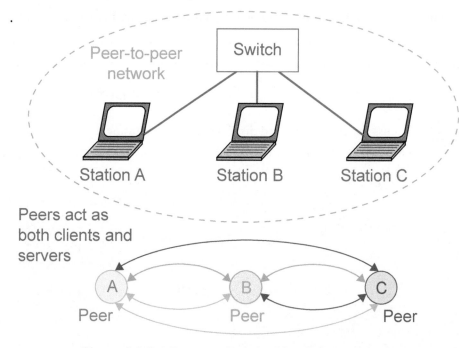

Figure 9.2.2.1 Peer-to-peer wired local area network

There is no central control and normally there is no administrator responsible for the entire network. The user at each computer acts as a user and an administrator, determining what data, disk space and peripherals on their computer get shared on the network.

Security control is limited because it has to be set on the computer to which it applies. The computer user typically sets the computer's security and they may choose to have none. It is possible to give password protection to a resource on the computer, e.g. a directory, but there is no central login process where a user's access level is protected by a single password. A user logged in at one peer computer is able to use resources on any other peer computer if the resources are unprotected by passwords or if the user knows the relevant password. Peer-to-peer networks can be as small as two computers or as large as thousands of computers.

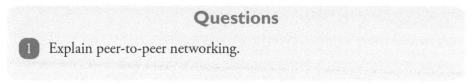

Questions

1. Explain peer-to-peer networking.

Peer-to-peer local area networks

A peer-to-peer local area network (LAN) is a good choice for environments where:

- there are fewer than 10 users
- the users are all located in the same area and the computers will be located at user desks
- security is not a major concern, so users may act as their own administrators to plan their own security
- the organisation and the network will have limited growth over the foreseeable future.

For Windows 7 desktop operating system, the maximum number of peers permitted in a peer-to-peer local area network is 20 as revealed by the command NET CONFIG SERVER as shown in Figure 9.2.2.2.

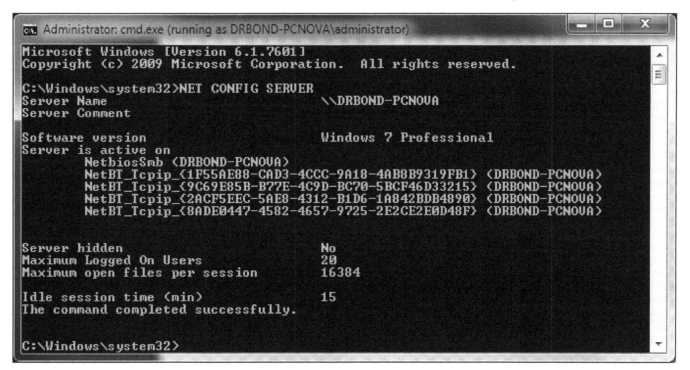

Figure 9.2.2.2 NET CONFIG SERVER command run in Windows 7 console

Questions

2. Describe the circumstances when peer-to-peer is an appropriate choice for local area networks.

Server-based network

A peer-to-peer local area network, with computers acting as both client and server, is seldom adequate for a system with more than 10 users. Therefore, most networks use dedicated servers. A server-based local area network is a client-server network in which resources, security, administration and other functions are provided by dedicated servers. Clients request services that are satisfied by dedicated servers.

A dedicated server is one that functions solely as a server and is not used as a client or workstation. Servers are usually optimised in both hardware and operating system to quickly service requests from network clients and to ensure the security of files and directories. Larger networks with a higher volume of traffic employ more than one server.

Clients use servers for services such as file storage and printing in a local area network. Client computers are usually less powerful than server computers. A server can also authenticate users attempting to log on at client workstations; it stores the client users' IDs and passwords for this purpose. Typically, school networks are server-based networks (thick-client networks): a central domain controller stores user accounts and a central file server stores users' work and some applications that users download into the client machines they work at.

Information

Hosts in networks:
A host is a computer or device that is accessible over a network.

Key concept

Server-based network:
A server-based local area network is a client-server network in which resources, security, administration and other functions are provided by dedicated servers. Clients request services that are satisfied by dedicated servers.

Questions

 3 Explain how a server-based local area network differs from a peer-to-peer local area network and why it is considered a client-server network.

Client-server and peer-to-peer networking architectures

Web browsing and sending email are client applications that rely on an underlying network architecture to interact with the corresponding server applications, a web server and an email server, respectively.

Both clients and servers are software applications. They conform to one of two particular application architectures used in modern networking:

1. the client-server architecture

2. the peer-to-peer (P2P) architecture

Web servers and email servers are examples of server-based systems.

Client-server networking architecture

In a client-server architecture, there is an always-on host, called the server, which services requests from many other hosts, called clients. A classic example is the web application for which an always-on web server services requests

Key concept

Client-server architecture:
In a client-server architecture, there is an always-on host, called the server, which services requests from many other hosts, called clients. For example, when a web server receives a request from a client host for a web page, it responds by sending the requested web page to the client host.

from browsers running on client hosts. When a web server receives a request from a client host for a web page, it responds by sending the requested web page to the client host.

In the client-server architecture, clients do not directly communicate with each other. For example, two web browsers do not directly communicate. This is very different from the peer-to-peer architecture where peers can communicate with each other because peers can act as both client and server (Figure 9.2.2.1).

Another characteristic of the client-server architecture is that a server has a fixed, well-known address in TCP/IP networks, called an IP address. A client can always contact the server by sending a packet to the server's IP address and get a response because the server is always on.

Search engines such as Google and Bing employ more than one server (hundreds of thousands, in fact) in order to meet demand. However, to the client these servers appear as a single machine, a virtual server.

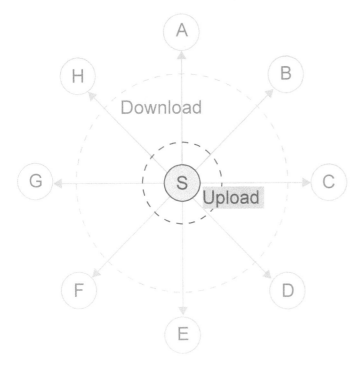

Figure 9.2.2.3 Client-server architecture

Questions

4. What is meant by client-server architecture and describe a situation where it is used?

Figure 9.2.2.3 shows a server, S, connected to eight clients, A to H. The server may be capable of uploading (transferring to clients) at a rate of, say, 5000 KiB/s whilst each client may be capable of downloading at a rate of, say, 500 KiB/s, i.e. a ratio of ten to one. If the server application running at the server is an FTP server delivering eight copies of a file to an FTP client application running at each of the eight clients then the server is more than capable of serving each client at their download rate of 500 KiB/s. Therefore, a file of size 500 KiB (500 x 1024 bytes) will take one second to download to all eight clients. Figure 9.2.2.4 shows an FTP client downloading a file from an FTP server.

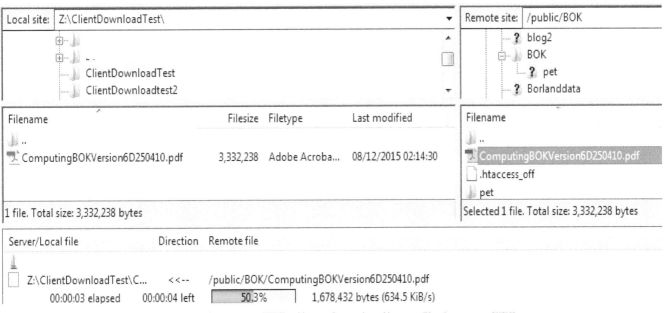

Figure 9.2.2.4 shows an FTP client downloading a file from an FTP server

Increasing the number of clients to twenty reduces the download rate because the server's upload rate of 5000 KiB/s is now shared by 20 clients. This means a maximum download rate of $5000/_{20}$ KiB/s per client = 250 KiB/s. This is less than the client's maximum of 500 KiB/s.

One solution is to add another server so that the demand from twenty clients is shared now between two servers. This should restore the download rate to 500 KiB/s assuming that each client is able to operate at a download speed of 500 KiB/s.

Peer-to-peer networking architecture

The client-server model works well for many applications. However, if many clients are downloading very large files from a server, then download speeds diminish unless more servers are added. It would be better if uploads could be shared amongst both servers and clients. This would lighten the load on servers and reduce the amount of server bandwidth that clients have to pay for. In fact, web hosting could be eliminated altogether. Client hosts not only download a file, but can upload what they have obtained to others as well. Client hosts are perfectly capable of doing both at the same time. They are then called peers rather than clients. *Figure 9.2.2.5* shows how separate parts of a file are uploaded to three peers which in turn upload what they have to their peers. Peer distribution can start whilst each peer is still downloading their part of the file from the server. The server doesn't have to be a dedicated server but can be another peer that happens to have the file that other peers want to download.

> **Key concept**
>
> **Peer-to-peer architecture:**
> In a peer-to-peer architecture, client hosts not only download a file, but can upload what they have obtained to others as well. Client hosts are capable of doing both at the same time. They are then called peers rather than clients.

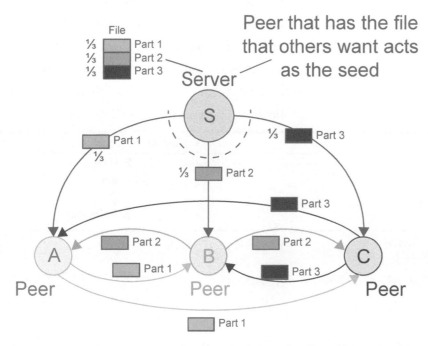

Figure 9.2.2.5 shows peers uploading and downloading files using FTP

BitTorrent came up with a protocol for distributing large files in this way. BitTorrent doesn't overload servers that provide the download since it relies on peers contributing upload capacity. The result is that large files can be received

Did you know?

Jaan Tallinn was one of the co-founders and authors of Skype. Read an interview with Jaan at http://affairstoday.co.uk/interview-jaan-tallinn-skype/

faster than would be the case in a client-server architecture where downloads rely on just a central server.

Decentralized P2P networks have several advantages over traditional client-server networks. P2P networks scale well because they don't rely on costly centralized resources. Scaling doesn't lead to a deterioration in download speed because P2P networks use the processing and networking power of the end-users' machines which grows in direct proportion to the network itself.

The costs associated with a large, centralized infrastructure are virtually eliminated because the processing power and bandwidth reside in the peers within the network.

Investigation

1. Peer-to-peer (P2P) architecture became widely used and popularized by file-sharing applications such as Napster and Kazaa. Research the history of Napster and Kazaa.

2. Skype originally relied on a form of P2P architecture. Research the history of Skype and why its P2P supernodes were replaced with Linux boxes hosted by Microsoft.

Questions

5. Explain what is meant by peer-to-peer architecture and describe a situation where it is used?

In this chapter you have covered:

- peer-to-peer networking
- client-server networking
- situations where they might be used

9.2 Networking

■ 9.2.3 Wireless networking

The purpose of WiFi

WiFi was invented to provide a wireless connection between computing devices and to enable these devices to connect to the Internet via a bridge between a wireless LAN and a wired LAN known as an access point.

WiFi or Wi-Fi® is officially called IEEE 802.11, because of the naming scheme that the IEEE (Institute of Electrical and Electronic Engineers) uses to name their standards. The 802 part means a Local Area Network (LAN) as wireless is short-range, and the .11 part is for wireless.

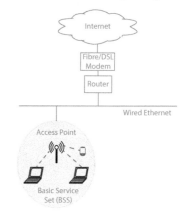

Figure 9.2.3.1 Wireless Access Point connection to Internet

Figure 9.2.3.1 shows WiFi providing wireless connections to computing devices such as laptops, tablets and smartphones that are close to an access point. The access point is also connected to a wired local area network (Ethernet) which in turn provides wired access to the Internet via a router and modem (Digital Subscriber Line (DSL) or optical fibre).

Wireless networking uses radio waves from the electromagnetic spectrum in two bands of frequencies centred around 2.4 and 5 GHz. Very importantly, these two bands of frequencies do not require licensing to use them unlike the mobile phone network spectrum which uses expensive licensed frequencies.

Table 9.2.3.1 shows the standards as they have evolved over the years from 802.11 to 802.11ac. Maximum speeds are very rarely achieved for reasons that will be given later.

> **Key concept**
>
> **WiFi LAN or WLAN:**
> A wireless local area network that is based on international standards laid down by the organisation known as the IEEE.
> It is used to enable devices to connect to a local area network wirelessly.

> **Information**
>
> **802.11 mobile and portable devices:**
> A requirement of the 802.11 standard is to handle mobile as well as portable wireless stations. A portable station is one that is moved from location to location, but that is only used while at a fixed location. Mobile stations actually access the LAN while in motion.

802.11 Standard	Year	Frequency (GHz)	Maximum speed (Mbps)
-	1997	2.4	2
b	1999	2.4	11
a	1999	5	54
g	2003	2.4	54
n	2009	2.4 & 2.5	150
ac	2013	2.4 & 5	Typical 800 (theoretical1.3 Gbps)

Table 9.2.3.1 WiFi standards

1. What is the purpose of WiFi?

2. In a wired network, data travels between wired devices by electrical means. What is the equivalent means by which data travels in a wireless network?

Key concept

Frame/packet:
A frame or packet is a unit of transfer consisting of data, addresses and control information.

Components for wireless networking

Wireless networks typically consist of the following major physical components:

- Stations: computing devices with wireless network interfaces

- Access Points (APs): provide the wireless-to-wired bridging function in which wireless frames are converted to wired frames - usually Ethernet frames (a frame is a unit of transfer consisting of data, addresses and control information; sometimes called a packet); access points are also used to control access to a wireless network by authenticating users or devices that wish to join the network

- Wireless medium: to move frames from station to station, the 802.11 standard uses a wireless medium consisting of two frequency bands, 2.5 GHz and 5 GHz, each divided into channels

- Distributing system: used to connect several access points to form a large coverage area of the same LAN, e.g. a hotel with WiFi access in rooms. The APs are often connected by a wired Ethernet backbone.

Information

Wireless propagation characteristics:
Propagation characteristics are dynamic (not static) and unpredictable.

In WiFi, devices (stations) belong to what is called a Basic Service Set (BSS) which is simply a group of stations that communicate with each other wirelessly in an area (green shading) defined by the propagation characteristics of the wireless medium and called the basic service area (Figure 9.3.2.2).

BSSs are of two types:

- Independent BSS: stations communicate with each other directly and therefore must be within direct communication range. Independent BSSs are used to create short-lived networks, e.g. for a meeting in a conference room. This type of BSS network is commonly known as an ad hoc network because of its limited duration, small size and focused purpose.

- Infrastructure BSS: infrastructure BSSs always use at least one access point and access points are used for all communications including communication between stations. Two hops are therefore used to send frames.

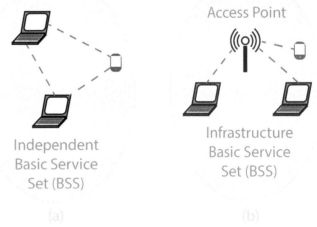

Independent Basic Service Set (BSS)

Access Point

Infrastructure Basic Service Set (BSS)

(a) (b)

Figure 9.2.3.2 (a) independent BSS (b) infrastructure BSS

Information

BSSID address:
A BSSID address is used to identify a wireless LAN. Stations in the same area may be assigned to a Basic Service Set (BSS) to form a LAN. The LAN is then identified by its BSSID.
In infrastructure networks, the BSSID is the MAC address used by the wireless interface in the access point. It is a 48-bit identifier for the BSS.

The originating station transfers the frame to the access point (first hop) which then relays it to the destination station (second hop). This lifts the restriction that stations must be in range of each other. They only have to be in range of an access point belonging to the BSS. Secondly, access points can buffer frames so that stations which are battery-powered can be powered down until they need to transmit and receive frames, e.g. wireless sensors.

The stations must have the capability to send and receive over a WiFi connection. *Figure 9.2.3.3* shows an EDIMAX® wireless network adapter that plugs into a USB port of a computer. This particular adapter has MAC address 001F1FCD5D7A.

All adapters, wireless or wired have a unique MAC address so that they can be identified.

The tall slim tubular structure is its antenna through which it radiates and receives radio waves on specific frequencies designated by the IEEE.

A wireless network adapter is also known as a wireless interface.

Desktop computers can have a wireless network adapter installed on their motherboard in a PCI slot and tablets and smartphones use a built-in wireless network adapter.

Within each BSS, stations communicate directly with an Access Point (AP), similar to a mobile phone network base station. The Access Point acts as a bridge between a wireless and a wired local area network. When a device searches for WiFi connectivity, it sends messages to discover which APs are in its transmission range.

*Figure 9.2.3.3 EDIMAX®
USB port wireless adapter
802.11b/g*

This results in a list of names such as shown in *Figure 9.3.2.4*: *educational-computing* and *Kevin Bond's Guest Network*. These are user-friendly names, commonly known as Service Set Identifiers / Identities (SSIDs), used to identify a service set to users of the wireless network.

The user-friendly name, or SSID, maps to the BSSID which is the MAC address equivalent. It is the BSSID that is sent in wireless frames to identify the access point.

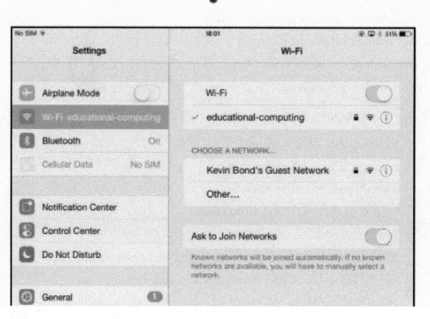

Figure 9.2.3.4 IPad WiFi settings screen showing two APs

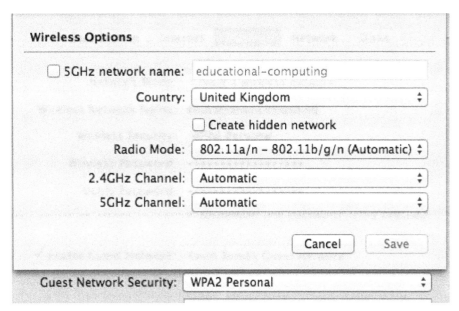

Figure 9.2.3.5 Wireless radio frequency options for wireless network with SSID educational-computing

Figure 9.2.3.5 shows the settings for an AP with SSID *educational-computing*. The AP automatically chooses either 2.4 GHz or 5 GHz depending on which currently provides the better transmission, and then within the chosen band a particular channel[1].

Questions

3 Name and describe **four** major physical components that may be found in a wireless network.

4 What is the purpose of an SSID?

Carrier Sense Multiple Access with Collision Avoidance (CSMA/CA)

Channel selection

Each access point (AP) operates on a given frequency channel, e.g. channel 36. Both the 2.4 GHz and the 5 GHz frequency bands are divided into a number of such channels, each with a predetermined width. Figure 9.2.3.6 shows that the channels for the 5 GHz band are 20 MHz wide. For example, channel 36 is centred on the frequency 5180 GHz and it covers the range 5170 to 5190 GHz.

Figure 9.2.3.6 Operating channel bands and frequencies for 5 GHz wireless transmission in Europe

In order for a station to communicate with its access point, it selects the channel that its AP is using. This means that all the stations in the same basic

---

1   Explained in the next section.

service set, e.g. *educational-computing*, use the same channel. Therein lies a problem, as more stations join a basic service, the transmission rate usually goes down which is one reason why the maximum transmission rate is rarely achieved. The AP will actually tell the stations to use a lower transmission rate if there is too much traffic from too many devices.

Questions

5 What is meant by channel selection in wireless networking?

Interference

WiFi is prone to interference from other sources as well as from stations using a particular basic service because

- the frequency bands used by WiFi are unlicensed and so WiFi is not the sole user of the spectrum. The spectrum is used by lots of other equipment over which the basic service set has no control, e.g. microwave ovens used to heat and cook food in the kitchen

- its maximum transmit power is restricted to a very low level because it is unlicensed

- it is typically used indoors where there are lots of objects to block the signal or reflect and echo a transmitted signal into the path of another

Noise

The circuits used in WiFi generate unwanted electrical noise (random electrical fluctuations) which can mask signals of too low power.

Collisions

When two stations, A and B are transmitting at similar times their frames will collide if they are within interference range of each other which is the case when they both use the same access point (*Figure 9.2.3.7*). The outcome is determined by the signal-to-interference + noise ratio (SINR) of each.

Figure 9.2.3.8 shows the overlap of two frames one from A and one from B. The greater the overlap with another frame, the higher the chance that neither frame will be properly decoded at the receiver.

Information

Signal to Interference + Noise Ratio (SINR):

Radio wave communication relies on differentiating a signal from background noise and interference. If the signal power level falls below the noise + interference power level, it becomes more difficult to extract the signal. The ratio of signal power level to noise + interference power level is a measure of how easy or difficult it is to extract a signal

$$SINR = \frac{\text{Signal power}}{\text{Interference + Noise power}}$$

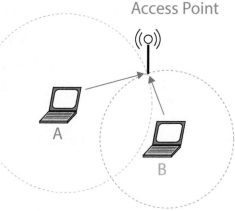

Access Point

Figure 9.2.3.7 shows the energy of two frames spreading through the air and crossing at the access point

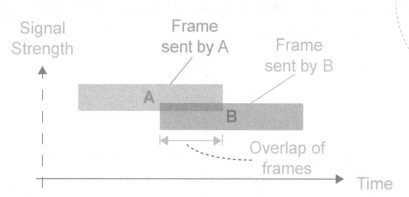

Figure 9.2.3.8 Two frames overlapping in time. A is a stronger signal than B

Questions

6 What is meant by a collision in wireless networking?

Collision avoidance

The approach in wireless networking to this problem is to try to avoid collisions in the first place by requiring WiFi-enabled devices to be aware of whether other devices are currently transmitting, i.e. sensing other device's transmissions. A device can transmit only if others are not. It is a bit like a crossroads controlled by Give Way signs. You can proceed across the crossroads as long as you can see that your intended path is clear of other traffic (Figure 9.2.3.9). If two road users arrive at the crossroads at the same time, each can sense that it is not safe for both to proceed if it will result in crossing each other's path. Instead, each delays their movement until they can interpret what the other's intentions are. The delay is a random amount of time whilst some form of mutual coordination for a safe crossing is achieved.

Multiple access

The WiFi channel through which the WiFi signals travel is a shared medium, shared between devices on this channel, e.g. channel **36**. For this reason, we say it is multi-access or a multiple access medium. Access must be coordinated and controlled.

Carrier Sense Multiple Access/Collision Avoidance (CSMA/CA) explained

The CSMA/CA protocol was designed to allow a station to send as long as no other station is sending. It is called Carrier Sense Multiple Access (CSMA) because each station tries to sense the presence of others on the shared medium. It is called Collision Avoidance (CA) because each station tries to avoid a collision by not sending when another station is sending.

Figure 9.2.3.10 shows station A transmitting a frame to station B. The dotted red circle with A at its centre shows the reach of A's transmission. Station C is within this reach and so is able to sense that A is currently transmitting. If station C was also transmitting at the same time to, say a station D, but with enough signal strength to also reach station B, then B might not be able to decode the transmission from A because both transmissions interfere with each other in the receiver B's electronics.

The CSMA/CA protocol requires that the receiving station, for whom the transmission is intended, sends back an acknowledgement (ACK) signal to the sending station on successfully receiving and decoding the transmission (Figure 9.2.3.11). This is how the sending station knows that its transmission got through. If an acknowledgement is not received then the sending station will know that a collision has occurred and its transmission did not get through.

Key concept

Collision:
A collision occurs when two transmitters are within interference range of each other, and they send at similar times. What actually collides are frames, one from each transmitter. The result is that neither frame will be properly decoded at the receiver. A frame is a unit of digital data transmission.

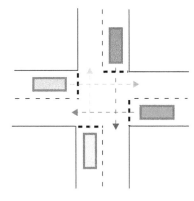

Figure 9.2.3.9 Crossroads

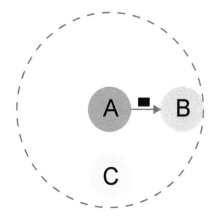

Figure 9.2.3.10 Station A transmitting to station B but with the transmission also reaching station C

The situation shown in *Figure 9.2.3.12* can arise when two stations, A and C that wish to transmit cannot detect the transmissions of each other because they are not within each other's wireless reach. Station A may start transmitting but the out-of-range C cannot sense this and so starts transmitting as well. C's transmission to D reaches B at about the same time that A's does. A collision arises at B between A's transmission and C's which results in neither transmission being decoded by B. B will therefore not send an ACK to A. The use of an acknowledgement signal enables stations to detect a collision and to take remedial action which consists of sending the frame again after a delay of an appropriate amount of time.

We have simplified the scenario to make a point. In an infrastructure BSS where everything goes through an access point, B could be an access point shared by A, C and D. A may in fact be sending to C via B and C could be sending, via B, to D.

Before sending, a station has to observe a wait and listen period. If during this period the station does not detect any transmissions, it can start transmitting at the end of the period as shown for station A in *Figure 9.2.3.13*.

If a station that wants to send senses that the channel is busy at any time during the wait and listen period, then the station does not transmit. C starts its *wait & listen* period just after A's. It senses during this period that A starts sending. It waits a frame + ACK + a little bit more before starting another *wait & listen* period.

It is still possible that a collision can occur even though a sending station

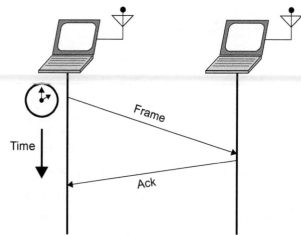

Figure 9.2.3.11 Timing for the sending of a frame, its processing at the receiver, and the sending of an acknowledgement signal to the sender

Figure 9.2.3.12 Station A transmitting to station B and station C transmitting to D at a similar time with neither A nor C able to sense the other

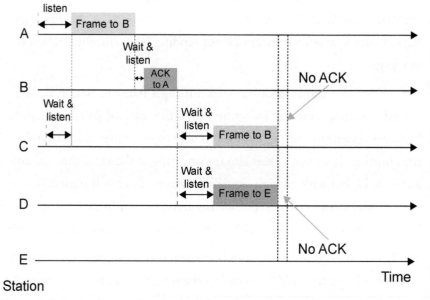

Figure 9.2.3.13 Shows the timing for the sending of frames by A C, D and an ACK from B to A, a collision occurs between frames from C and D which is detected by both not receiving the corresponding ACK

waited and found the channel idle before sending. Another station might have begun sending at the same time because it began its waiting period at the same time and also concluded that the channel was idle. This is shown in Figure 9.2.3.14 where both C and D start sending at the same time and cause a collision. However, neither receives an acknowledgement signal within the expected window of time and so both conclude that an error has occurred.

If both resend at the same time the same result ensues.

The solution in this circumstance is for stations C and D to employ a contention window of say size 15. Such a window is divided into 15 equal-sized time slots. Stations C and D then each choose one of the time slots at random, e.g. C might choose slot 3 and D slot 7 (there remains a small chance that they could choose the same slot). C will now listen for the wait & listen period + 3 time slots; D will now listen for the wait & listen period + 7 time slots. If one or the other finds the channel idle after its wait then each can send.

To prevent collisions 802.11 allows a station to use Request To Send (RTS) and Clear To Send(CTS) signals to obtain exclusive use of the channel for sending. This is necessary if many collisions are occurring such as when there are many hidden stations. Too many collisions reduces transmission speed. The sending station sends an RTS frame to the target station. The target station responds by transmitting a CTS frame. The sending station now sends the data frame to the target. The target responds by returning an ACK frame.

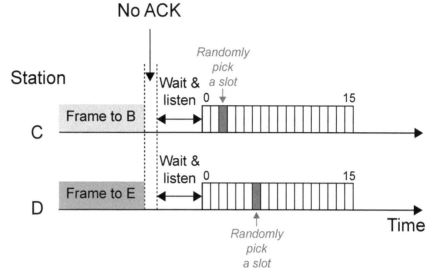

Figure 9.2.3.14 Shows stations C and D in addition to a wait & listen period backing off a randomly determined number of time slots between 0 and 15 after concluding by receiving no ACK that that a collision has occurred

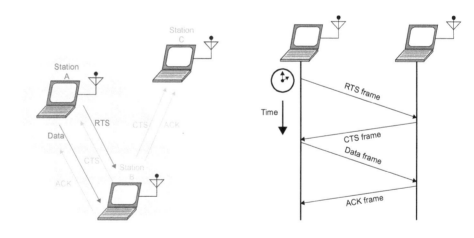

Figure 9.2.3.15 Using RTS and CTS to reserve channel for one station to send to another collision-free

Information

Wireless communication symbol for an antenna:

Figure 9.2.3.15 shows the RTS frame, CTS frame, data frame and ACK frame forming a single atomic transaction between sending and receiving stations.

If the target station receives an RTS it responds with a CTS.

The RTS silences stations within its range and the CTS silences stations within its range. In this way collisions that result from the hidden station problem shown in *Figure 9.2.3.12* are avoided.

In *Figure 9.2.3.15* station A is able to reach station B but not station C whilst station B is able to reach both. Station A sends an RTS to station B, B responds with a CTS which reaches both A and C. C now avoids sending until it receives an indication that the transaction between A and B is over. This is the ACK signal. Meanwhile A receives the CTS signal and proceeds to send the data frame. A finishes sending and then waits for the ACK signal from B.

Questions

7 What is meant by multiple access in wireless networking?

8 Explain the CSMA/CA protocol used in wireless networking.

9 What is the hidden node problem in wireless networking?

10 What is the purpose of RTS and CTS in CSMA/CA wireless networking?

11 RTS and CTS add extra time to a data transmission between two stations. Under what circumstance would they be used?

Securing wireless networks
WPA/WPA2

Wi-Fi Protected Access (WPA) and Wi-Fi Protected Access II (WPA2) are two security protocols developed by the Wi-Fi Alliance to secure wireless computer networks. WPA was a backwards-compatible temporary measure adopted before WPA2's development was complete. WPA/WPA2 replaced WEP which is easily broken because it is a stream cipher which exclusive-ORs the data stream with a fixed key stream (see **RC4** *Chapter 5.6.10*).

User's data sent between two devices, e.g. a wireless station and an access point needs to be private to those two devices, i.e. kept confidential by securing against unauthorised access. Unfortunately, radio transmissions over a wireless network are easily intercepted and read by third parties unless encrypted.

They are also open to spoofing, i.e. purporting to originate from a genuine user when they don't. Message authentication lets communicating partners who share a secret key verify that a received message originates with the party who claims to have sent it.

Messages can also be easily intercepted and altered in transit by a third party. Message integrity checks allow such alterations to be detected.

Key concept

Security:
Security means protecting against unauthorised access, alteration or deletion.

Key concept

Authentication:
Proving that the user is who they say they are.

Key principle

Access control WPA/WPA2:
To join a WPA/WPA2-secured personal wireless network, a user (client) has to successfully negotiate an authentication stage which checks that the client knows a pre-shared secret key (PSK).

Key principle

Pre-shared secret key (PSK):
In WPA/WPA2 personal, the access point and stations that are allowed to join the wireless network share a secret key called the Pairwise Master Key (PMK). This is a 256-bit key (32 bytes).

Key principle

Generating the PMK:
In WPA/WPA2 personal, the 256-bit Pairwise Master Key (PMK) is generated from a passphrase/password known to the user and the SSID. The passphrase is a plaintext string.

Access control and authentication

To join a WPA/WPA2-secured personal wireless network, a user (client) has to successfully negotiate an authentication stage which checks that the client knows a pre-shared secret key (PSK). This checking is based on a message authentication code (Message Integrity and Authentication Code or MIAC, abbreviated further to MIC) generated from the pre-shared secret key. The checking is done at the access point. The access point is responsible for controlling access to the wireless network.

Pre-shared secret key

In WPA/WPA2 personal, the access point and stations that are allowed to join the wireless network share a secret key called the Pairwise Master Key (PMK). This is a 256-bit key (32 bytes). Fortunately, users/clients don't have to remember this key. Instead, clients share a passphrase/password consisting of up to 133 ASCII characters which is set up on the access point for a specific SSID. The PMK is generated by combining the SSID and this passphrase. To join a known SSID network, a user enters the passphrase for this specific SSID at their wireless station. The wireless station now has everything it needs to calculate its own copy of the PMK for this SSID network. For example, if the passphrase/password is LetMeIn and the SSID is MyWirelessNetwork then the generated PMK could be c4f9 400d 1cc7 cc3c 6b68 5b12 13a8 20dc

Pairwise Transient Key (PTK)

The PMK is never transmitted to avoid an unauthorised third party obtaining a copy.

How is it possible then for both access point and station to demonstrate that they possess the same pairwise master key (PMK) without sending each their copy of the PMK?

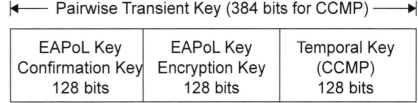

Figure 9.2.3.16 Pairwise Transient Key for Counter Mode with CBC-MAC Protocol (CCMP)

The solution is for both wireless station and access point to use a Pairwise Transient Key (PTK) derived from the PMK and to demonstrate to each other knowledge of this PTK.

Extension material beyond A-level

Knowledge is demonstrated using the Key Confirmation Key to produce a message authentication code which the station sends to the access point. If more than one wireless station has joined the network then each station-access point pairing will have its own PTK.

The Pairwise Transient Key is a collection of other keys as shown in Figure 9.2.3.16:
- Key Confirmation Key (KCK) – used to prove possession of the PMK
- Key Encryption Key (KEK) – used to encrypt the Group Transient Key (GTK)
- Temporal Key (TK) – used to secure data traffic once connection is established
- The PTK temporal key is used to secure unicast (communication between a single sender and a single receiver over a network) data transmissions.

The Group Transient Key is used to secure multicast/broadcast transmissions.

The pairwise transient key CCMP uses CCM, a provably secure cipher based on an AES block encryption algorithm.

The particular algorithm used by the transmissions shown in Figures 9.2.3.17-21 is the 128-bit AES block cipher one, a very secure cipher.

Questions

12 What are WPA and WPA2?

13 State and explain **three** reasons why wireless networks need to be secured.

Information (This material is not required for A-level

Four-way handshake

Communications begin with an unauthenticated supplicant (client device, e.g. station 1) attempting to connect with an authenticator (802.11 access point). The client sends an Extensible Authentication Protocol (EAP)-start message. This begins a series of message exchanges called a **four-way handshake** to authenticate the client. *Figure 9.2.3.17* shows a simplified version of this exchange.

Message 1:

The authenticator sends an unencrypted message to the supplicant which contains the authenticator-generated random number ANonce (*Figure 9.2.3.18*).

Nonces are random numbers which are used once (**N**umber **ONCE**).

Message 2:

The supplicant knows its own PMK, the value of ANonce sent to it, its own MAC address, the supplicant's MAC address and its own nonce, SNonce which it generates.

It now has all it needs to generate its copy of the pairwise transient key (PTK) - see *Figure 9.2.3.21*. It responds to the authenticator by sending its SNonce in unencrypted form across the channel (*Figure 9.2.3.19*). The authenticator now has all it needs to calculate its copy of the PTK.

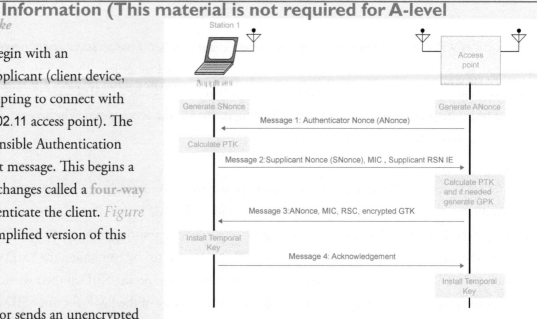

Figure 9.2.3.17 The Pairwise Transient Key (PTK) is computed at the station and the access point it is connecting to so that each has a copy

```
○ ○ ○                              ⊠ 418 18.444511000 72:73:cb:b7
▷ Frame 418: 160 bytes on wire (1280 bits), 160 bytes captured (1280 bi
▷ Radiotap Header v0, Length 25
▷ IEEE 802.11 Data, Flags: ......F.C
▷ Logical-Link Control
▽ 802.1X Authentication
    Version: 802.1X-2004 (2)
    Type: Key (3)
    Length: 95
    Key Descriptor Type: EAPOL RSN Key (2)
  ▷ Key Information: 0x008a
    Key Length: 16
    Replay Counter: 0
    WPA Key Nonce: b46af319764776c3a6e031251920dae3810204d098b151dd...
    Key IV: 00000000000000000000000000000000
    WPA Key RSC: 0000000000000000
    WPA Key ID: 0000000000000000
    WPA Key MIC: 00000000000000000000000000000000
    WPA Key Data Length: 0
```

ANonce

Figure 9.2.3.18 Message 1 frame captured with Wireshark®

Screenshot reproduced by permission of the Wireshark Foundation

```
○ ○ ○                              ⊠ 424 18.449397000 Apple_e8:e3:09 72:7:
▷ Frame 424: 180 bytes on wire (1440 bits), 180 bytes captured (1440 bits) on
▷ Radiotap Header v0, Length 25
▷ IEEE 802.11 QoS Data, Flags: ......T
▷ Logical-Link Control
▽ 802.1X Authentication
    Version: 802.1X-2001 (1)
    Type: Key (3)
    Length: 117
    Key Descriptor Type: EAPOL RSN Key (2)
  ▷ Key Information: 0x010a
    Key Length: 0
    Replay Counter: 0
    WPA Key Nonce: ff41683c4814e9322014da33e5fc60b04c9d1858e803bbe7...
    Key IV: 00000000000000000000000000000000
    WPA Key RSC: 0000000000000000
    WPA Key ID: 0000000000000000
    WPA Key MIC: 57673428683c62ad358d58dc0095c133
    WPA Key Data Length: 22
  ▷ WPA Key Data: 30140100000fac040100000fac040100000fac020000
```

SNonce

Message Authentication & Integrity Code (MIC) generated using the KCK key from PTK

Supplicant RSN Information Elements (IE)

Figure 9.2.3.19 Message 2 frame captured with Wireshark

Information

Message 2 includes a MIC. This is a message digest that has used the EAPoL Key Confirmation Key (KCK) from the supplicant's copy of the PTK. The authenticator now uses its copy of KCK and the received message to calculate the corresponding MIC. The two MICs, one received and the other calculated, are compared.

Message 3:

If the MICs agree, the authenticator sends an acknowledgment message to the supplicant confirming that it has been authenticated and is now allowed to join the network and to install the PTK data encryption key (Figure 9.2.3.20). The authenticator awaits confirmation from the supplicant that it has installed the data encryption key (temporal key) before it installs its copy. The same GTK is used for all stations.

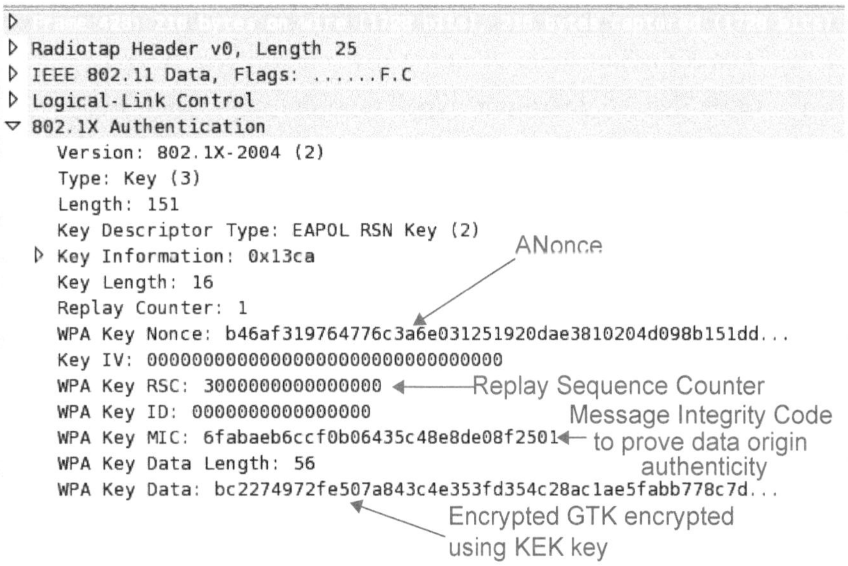

Message 4:

The supplicant responds with an acknowledgement message (Figure 9.2.3.21) confirming to the authenticator that it has installed the temporal key (data encryption key) that should be used from now on to encrypt data transmissions as well as to generate the MIC to protect the integrity of the data as well as authenticate its origin. The authenticator now installs its copy of the temporal key.

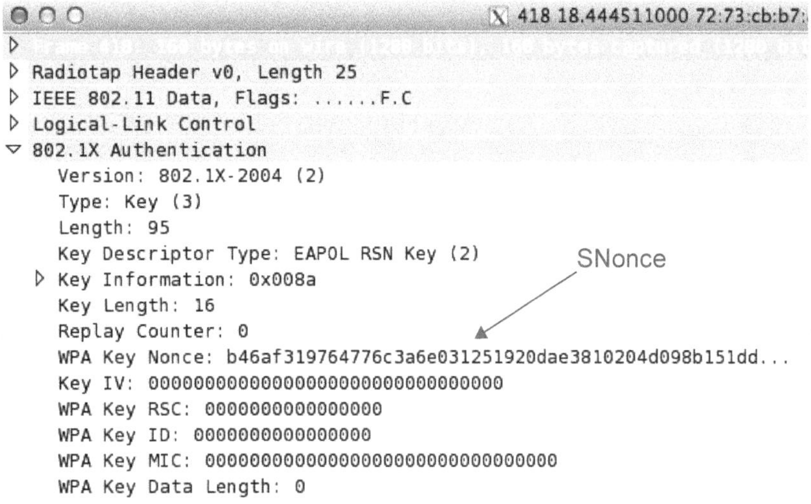

```
▷
▷ Radiotap Header v0, Length 25
▷ IEEE 802.11 Data, Flags: ......F.C
▷ Logical-Link Control
▽ 802.1X Authentication
    Version: 802.1X-2004 (2)
    Type: Key (3)
    Length: 151
    Key Descriptor Type: EAPOL RSN Key (2)
  ▷ Key Information: 0x13ca                    ANonce
    Key Length: 16
    Replay Counter: 1
    WPA Key Nonce: b46af319764776c3a6e031251920dae3810204d098b151dd...
    Key IV: 00000000000000000000000000000000
    WPA Key RSC: 3000000000000000 ←——— Replay Sequence Counter
    WPA Key ID: 0000000000000000              Message Integrity Code
    WPA Key MIC: 6fabaeb6ccf0b06435c48e8de08f2501◄— to prove data origin
    WPA Key Data Length: 56                             authenticity
    WPA Key Data: bc2274972fe507a843c4e353fd354c28ac1ae5fabb778c7d...
                                             Encrypted GTK encrypted
                                             using KEK key
```

Figure 9.2.3.20 *Message 3 frame captured with Wireshark*

```
● ● ○                              ⊠ 418 18.444511000 72:73:cb:b7:
▷
▷ Radiotap Header v0, Length 25
▷ IEEE 802.11 Data, Flags: ......F.C
▷ Logical-Link Control
▽ 802.1X Authentication
    Version: 802.1X-2004 (2)
    Type: Key (3)
    Length: 95
    Key Descriptor Type: EAPOL RSN Key (2)      SNonce
  ▷ Key Information: 0x008a
    Key Length: 16
    Replay Counter: 0
    WPA Key Nonce: b46af319764776c3a6e031251920dae3810204d098b151dd...
    Key IV: 00000000000000000000000000000000
    WPA Key RSC: 0000000000000000
    WPA Key ID: 0000000000000000
    WPA Key MIC: 00000000000000000000000000000000
    WPA Key Data Length: 0
```

Figure 9.2.3.21 *Message 4 frame captured with Wireshark*

Task

1. Download and install Wireshark from www.wireshark.org on a computer with a wireless interface. In Wireshark, select the wireless interface and enable monitor mode. Start capturing wireless frames whilst at the same time connecting to a wireless network access point. Stop the capture once you are connected. Set the filter in the main window filter to EAPoL so that you can see four messages similar to those above. Expand the Authentication part of the frame and examine messages 1 to 4 in turn as above. What you will see will depend on the wireless protocol that you have chosen and the cipher suite supported by your wireless interface. Clear the EAPoL filter and search for Beacon, Probe Request and Probe Response frames.

Extension material (Beyond A-level)

Figure 9.2.3.22 shows a block diagram of the computation of the PTK.

A random number generator at the access point generates the first nonce (ANonce) and another random number generator at the station generates the second Nonce (SNonce). ANonce is short for Authenticator Nonce and SNonce is short for Supplicant Nonce. A new and different ANonce and a new and different SNonce are generated when a station that has disassociated itself from the access point reconnects. This means that a new and different PTK is generated.

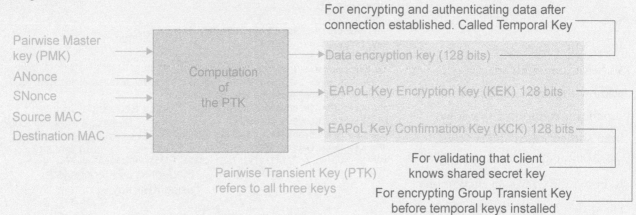

Figure 9.2.3.22 Computing the Pairwise Transient Key (PTK) takes place at the station and the access point it is connecting to so they both have a copy. EAPoL is Extensible Authentication Protocol over LAN

Figure 9.2.3.23 shows two networked connected stations each with a different paired temporal key (data encryption and MIC key).

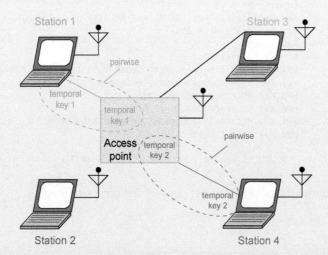

A temporal key is used to encrypt data transmissions and to create MICs to protect and authenticate the data

Figure 9.2.3.23 Station 1 and the access point are connected with a pair of keys, temporal key 1; station 4 and the access point are connected with a different pair of keys, temporal key 2.

Information

Man-in-the middle attack:
In cryptography and computer security, a man-in-the-middle attack is an attack where the attacker secretly relays and possibly alters the communication between two parties who believe they are directly communicating with each other.

Information

Replay attack:
In network security, a replay attack is a form of network attack in which a valid data transmission is maliciously or fraudulently repeated or delayed.
One way that replay attacks are defeated is to use the sequence number of packets. If stations and access points record the highest received sequence number then they can reject packets with lower sequence numbers which occur with replayed packets.

Questions

14. Why is relying on PMK, source and destination addresses alone as input to the PTK computation not as secure as the method which includes two nonces?

Key principle

Media Access Control (MAC) address white list filtering:
In MAC address white list filtering, the access point has an internal table of MAC addresses which it consults to decide whether to permit access to the network or not.

Key principle

SSID broadcast disabled protection:
Wireless stations require a knowledge of the SSID in order to join the network. If broadcast, the SSID appears in the network settings window of stations within range.
In this form of protection, an access point disables broadcasting its SSID to wireless stations. Thus, only clients who already know the pre-configured SSID can establish a connection, others will not be able to (without a bit of extra effort).

Media Access Control (MAC) address white list filtering

A wireless network could not use any form of encryption for its packets but instead rely on filtering of packets. MAC address white list filtering is one such form of filtering. MAC addresses are 48-bit addresses uniquely assigned to each wireless network interface card. In MAC address white list filtering, the access point has an internal table of MAC addresses which it consults to decide whether to permit access to the network or not. If the supplicant's MAC address is on this list then it may join the wireless network controlled by this access point. If its MAC address is not on the list then the access point will reject any attempt that the supplicant makes to join the network. Whilst MAC address white list filtering gives a wireless network some additional protection, MAC filtering can be defeated by a spoofer who learns the MAC address of a valid wireless network interface card, i.e. one on the white list, by scanning wireless traffic and then replacing a validated one with their own MAC. Task 1 with Wireshark should have revealed that MAC addresses do not get encrypted when travelling over the air between computer and wireless access point. A MAC address is "glued" into a network card, but it is possible to command the operating system to change information about the MAC address in every data packet it sends out to the network. In this way a spoofer could gain access to the white list protected network.

SSID broadcast disabled protection

Access points have the option to disable broadcasting their SSID. This means that the SSID will not appear in the client's network settings window (see *Figure 9.2.3.4*). Clients who already know the pre-configured SSID can establish a connection, others will not be able to (without a bit of extra effort). Unfortunately, clients who already know the SSID cause the SSID to be revealed to snoopers when establishing a connection with the access point. Before the authentication stage begins, the client sends a Probe Request message and receives a Probe Response from the access point in return as shown in *Figure 9.2.3.24*. The (unencrypted) SSID is present in these packets, therefore reducing the effectiveness of disabling broadcasting of the SSID.

To discover the SSID, a snooper might first send a deauthentication message to the stations that are connected to force them to disconnect and reconnect. Reconnecting should cause Probe and Response Request messages to be broadcast which reveal the SSID.

```
259 Probe Response, SN=1192, FN=0, Flags=.......C, BI=100, SSID=Kevin Bond's Guest Network
```

Figure 9.2.3.24 Probe and Response Request frame/packets captured with Wireshark to reveal the SSID

Questions

15 What is (a) MAC address white list filtering? (b) SSID broadcast disabled protection?

16 Explain why both MAC address white list filtering and SSID broadcast disabled protection are insufficient alone to protect a wireless network.

In this chapter you have covered:

- The purpose of WiFi
- The components required for wireless networking
- How wireless networks are secured
- The wireless protocol Carrier Sensing Multiple Access with Collision Avoidance (CSMA/CA) with and without Request to Send/Clear to Send (RTS/CTS)
- The purpose of Service Set Identifier (SSID)

9.3 The Internet

9.3.1 The Internet and how it works

The structure of the Internet

The term 'internet' is a combination of 'inter' and 'net'. The 'net' refers to a computer network and 'inter' refers to interconnections between two or more computer networks and computers or devices with computing capability on these networks. This is how the Internet began back in the 1970s. The problem was how to connect packet-switched networks located in North America and Europe. It was solved by Robert Kahn, Vint Cerf and others, and the Internet was born. Any network of computer networks is an internet or internetwork. NHS workers use a secure private internet to access patient records. The network used by the general public for e-mail and web page access is a special internet called the Internet. It consists of a network of interconnected computer networks and computers using a globally unique address space (IP addresses) based on Internet Protocol (IP), and Transmission Control Protocol (TCP) to support public access to e-mail and web pages, among other things. Figure 9.3.1.1 shows how computer networks and computers are connected by the Internet.

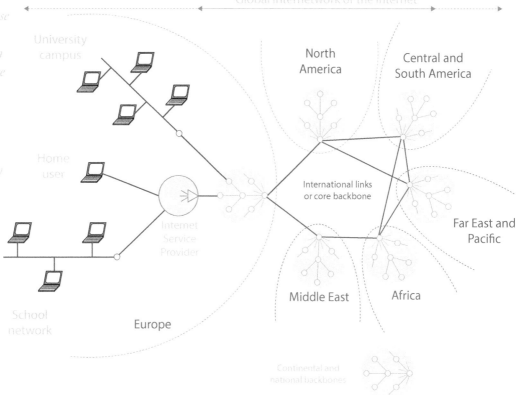

Figure 9.3.1.1 General architecture of part of the Internet

Europe, Africa, the Middle East, North America, Central and South America, the Far East and the Pacific are linked by very high-speed connections which form the core backbone of the Internet. Each continent has a backbone of very high-speed links which interconnect routers located in each country. Routers are special packet switches that receive incoming packets of data along one link and send them as outgoing packets on another link.

Open architecture networking

The Internet uses open architecture networking. Designers are free to design networks however they want, but all these different networks can be connected to and communicate over the Internet because of the way that the Internet has been designed. Each network is connected to the Internet through a router (a special router called a gateway router).

Until recently, the end-system devices in these networks that connected to the Internet were desktop computers and powerful servers but now a wider range of devices are being connected to the Internet. These end-systems are referred to as hosts because they host (i.e. run) application programs such as a Web browser program, a Web server program, an email client program, etc. Each host has a user-friendly memorable hostname, e.g. www.aqa.org.uk.

Questions

1. Explain the term internet.

2. What is the Internet?

The role of packet switching and routers

The role of packet switching is to support end-to-end communication of a message between two hosts located in different parts of an internet. Messages split into smaller segments called packets travel along independent paths through a network of packet switches called routers. Each packet sent by a host contains the IP (Internet Protocol) address of the destination host. Each router uses the destination IP address to choose from among its outgoing links one along which the packet can reach its destination.

Within national boundaries, networks belonging to large businesses and organisations such as universities are connected directly to the national backbone. Smaller organisations and home users of the Internet connect to an Internet Service Provider (ISP), which connects to the national backbone. Figure 9.3.1.2 shows three networks connected by routers.

The design of the Internet is based on the Catenet (internet) concept of a network of networks. This concept describes data packets flowing essentially unaltered throughout an internet with their source and destination addresses (IP addresses) that of the endpoint systems (now referred to as end-systems) sending and receiving the packets, respectively.

The key idea of a packet switched network is built-in redundancy supporting multiple pathways between endpoints. The concept of a packet switched network occurred quite independently to two researchers, Paul Baran (USA) and Donald Davies (UK) around the same time in the early 1960s. Both advocated building a distributed network that looked rather like a fishnet - Figure 9.3.1.3 - consisting of switching nodes connected by links in such a way that allowed multiple pathways through the network between endpoints, e.g. endpoint X and endpoint Y.

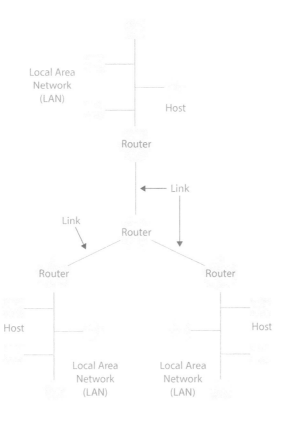

Figure 9.3.1.2 Connecting three LANs by routers

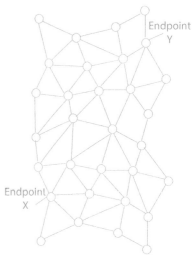

Figure 9.3.1.3 Distributed network of switching nodes (routers) resembling a 'fishnet'

Baran's and Davies' second proposal was to introduce redundancy when sending messages. The messages were to be split into a number of fixed-length "message blocks" which Davies christened packets.

The radical idea was to allow the packets of a message to travel along independent paths through the network of routers.

Any packet that did not get through was sent again. The sending station would wait a certain period of time for an acknowledgement packet to be sent by the receiving station. If one was not received within this wait-time then the sending station would send a copy of the packet again but in a different direction through the network.

In 1961 Leonard Kleinrock showed that packet switching was a better switching method than circuit switching[1]. Figure 9.3.1.4 shows Leonard Kleinrock photographed standing before an early packet switch called an Interface Message Processor (IMP).

Figure 9.3.1.4 An early packet switch (reproduced with kind permission of Professor Leonard Kleinrock)

1   Not in AQA A-level specification

Circuit switching connects two endpoints with a complete end-to-end electrical circuit for communication by exclusively allocating all the switches and their links along a single pathway for the duration of the communication. No other endpoints can use the same pathway if it is already in use.

By contrast, packet switching allows packets from different messages to use the same nodes and links at the same time. This makes better use of the network's bandwidth, defined as its maximum capacity for sending information.

The built-in redundancy of packet switching means better congestion handling, e.g. if a particular route is busy then packets may be rerouted along a different, less busy route. It also means that the network can withstand switching nodes going down. This means that cheaper, less reliable nodes may be used.

The Internet uses packet switching.

Question

3 Explain the role of packet switching and routers in a packet switched network.

Packet transmission

The packet is the unit of communication in the Internet.

In its simplest form, a packet consists of three parts:

Source address	Destination address	Application data

When computer X, connected to the Internet, wishes to send a message or a document to computer Y, also connected to the Internet, computer X splits the message or document into chunks; *Figure 9.3.1.5* shows five chunks: A, B, C, D and E. Computer X then generates as many packets as there are chunks, placing each chunk in the application data part of the next available packet. The unique address of the sending computer is placed in the source address part of each packet and the unique address of the receiving computer is placed in the destination address part of each packet.

Each packet is then dispatched to the Internet through a router. The packets are sent independently through a series of interconnected routers until they reach their destination. Each router examines the destination address of a packet it receives to determine what to do with it. Computer Y could reply to computer X by a similar process.

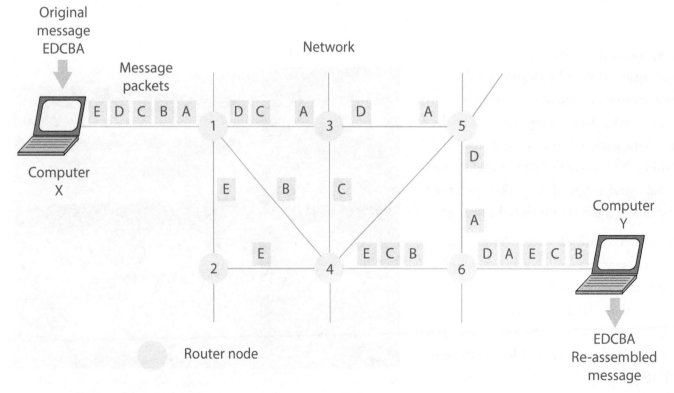

Figure 9.3.1.5 Routing of packets A, B, C, D and E through a packet-switched network

The end-to-end principle

Cerf and Kahn proposed that the two communicating computers, X and Y in our example, should be the endpoints of the communication. The end-to-end principle states that the two endpoint hosts should be in control of the communication. The role of the Internet is to move packets between these two endpoints.

This has several advantages:

- The sending application in Computer X and the receiving application in Computer Y are able to survive a partial network failure. The failure is detected and the packets that did not get through are resent.
- Packets can be rerouted around failures very quickly and sent along alternative paths.
- The Internet can grow easily because control resides in the endpoints (end-systems, e.g. Computer X) not in the Internet.
- There is no requirement for Internet routers to notify each other as endpoint connections are formed or dropped; this simplifies the design of routers.
- The integrity and security of each packet sent is handled by the endpoints (end-systems), which simplifies the role of the Internet.
- Each endpoint need only be aware of the router to which it is directly connected and, optionally, a name resolution service that converts user-friendly hostnames (Computer X) into their corresponding IP addresses.

Single logical address space

The end-to-end principle requires that each computer using the Internet should be uniquely identified. Cerf and Kahn proposed that each computer be labelled with a globally unique address known as an IP address. Their numbering system, called IPv4, is used today and allows 2^{32} different addresses. All these unique addresses make up a single logical address space. At the binary level, an IPv4 address consists of 32 bits (4 bytes).

Cerf and Kahn split an IP address into two parts (*Figure 9.3.1.6*):

- bits that identify the network connected to the Internet (NetID) and
- bits that identify a host (strictly speaking a network interface) connected to the network (HostID).

The thinking behind this was that since the Internet is made up of networks, being able to identify each network would help routers enormously in the task of routing packets to the correct destination network.

An Internet address can be expressed in dotted decimal notation, where each byte of the 32-bit IP address is written in decimal, separated by a dot:

196.100.11.4

The network ID might be 196.100.11 and the host ID, 4.

Questions

4 Explain the end-to-end principle.
5 State **five** advantages of an internet designed using the end-to-end principle.

31	0
NetID	HostID

Figure 9.3.1.6 IPv4 address structure

Router

Routers are used because it is not practical to connect every host directly to every other host. Instead a few hosts connect to a router, which connects to other routers, and so on, to form a network (*Figure 9.3.1.2*).

A router receives packets from one host or router and uses the destination IP address that they contain to pass on the packets, correctly formatted, to another host or router.

Figure 9.3.1.7 shows the hierarchy of routers for a single country. Each router in this hierarchy maintains a table of other routers, computers and networks it is directly connected to and enough information about the hierarchical structure of the Internet to route a packet to the desired destination.

For example, the IP address range 202.0.0.0 to 203.255.255.255 has been allocated to the Asia-Pacific region. A host on a school network in England wishing to communicate with a host on a network in Malaysia will send packets to the router on the school network. This router will pass the packets onto the local router it is connected to. The local router will pass these packets on to the regional router it is connected to. The regional router will pass packets on to the national router it is connected to, and so on, until the router of the destination network is reached. Each router in the path uses a part of the IP address to make the routing decision. In this example the decision is to route packets up the national hierarchy because 202/203 addresses are outside England.

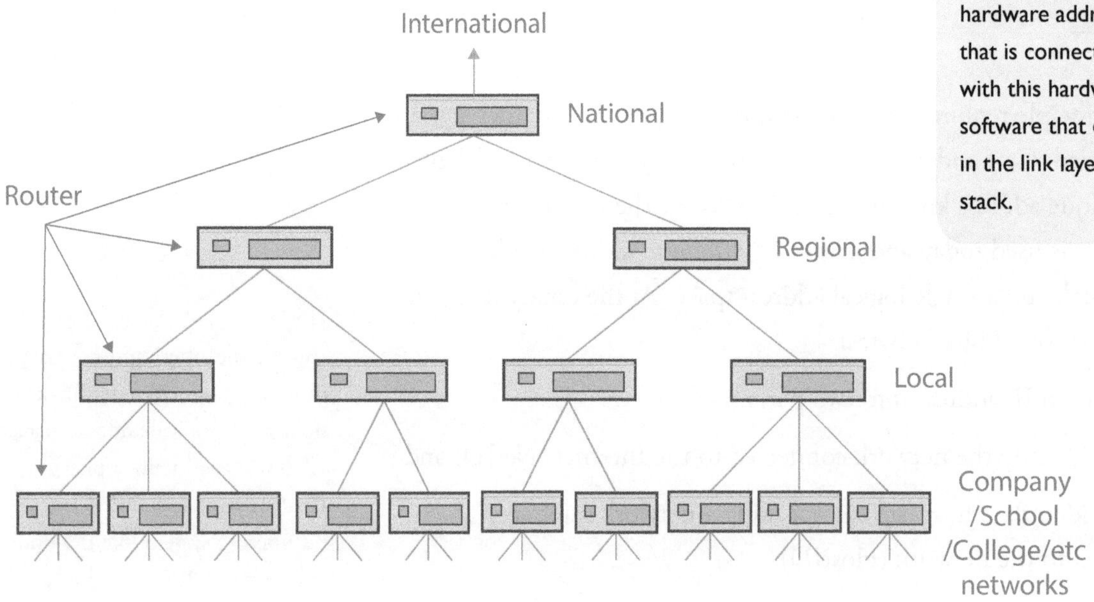

Figure 9.3.1.7 Routing hierarchy for one country

> ### Key point
>
> **Difference between a router and a switch**
> A router receives packets from a host or router on an incoming link and uses the destination IP address that they contain to pass on the packets, correctly formatted, to another host or router connected to an outgoing link. The software that does this is located in the network layer of the protocol stack. The router acts as a kind of packet switch with the ability to determine, on the basis of IP address, which outgoing link of several to use.
>
> A data link switch such as an Ethernet switch has several ports but each switch port connects to one device at most. The switch learns the hardware address of each connected device and the port it is connected to. It is then able to map a packet's destination hardware address to a port to use that is connected to the device with this hardware address. The software that does this is located in the link layer of the protocol stack.

Questions

6 Explain why routers are used.

7 What is a router?

8 How are routers organised in the Internet?

Gateway

Gateways are special routers that provide an interface between two or more dissimilar networks. Gateways translate one network layer protocol into another, translate link layer protocols, and open sessions between application programs.

Gateways allow two or more networks that use different link or network protocols to be connected so that information can be passed from one system to another.

For example, in *Figure 9.3.1.8* a Local Area Network (LAN) is connected to the Internet through a gateway, *Gateway 1*, and another LAN is connected through another gateway, *Gateway 2*. The LANs use a protocol that differs in certain respects from the Wide Area Network (WAN) protocols used

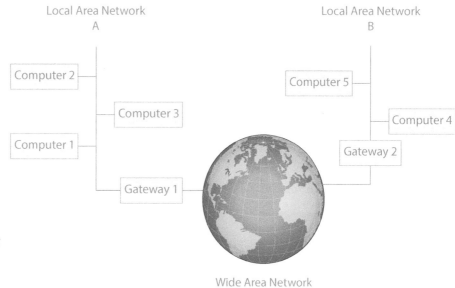

Figure 9.3.1.8 Gateway connections to the Internet

on the Internet. The gateway does the job of translating the LAN frame into its equivalent WAN frame and vice versa. Sometimes gateways are called gateway routers.

Another common use of gateways is to enable LANs that use TCP/IP and Ethernet to communicate with mainframes that use other protocols.

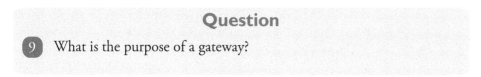

Question

9 What is the purpose of a gateway?

The main components of a packet

Messages or application data are split into chunks and the chunks together with headers are sent in packets through the Internet's packet-switched network from an instance of an application, e.g. Web browser, running on a host one endpoint, to an instance of an application, e.g. Web server, running on a host at another endpoint.

The two hosts on which the applications are sending and receiving must be identified by numbers called source and destination IP addresses. Routers will use these IP addresses to route the packets through the packet switched network.

Two applications sending to and receiving from each other, are identified by numbers called port numbers.

Hosts use the port numbers to allocate the received packets to the corresponding destination application and to send the required reply to the corresponding sending application.

The packets may be received out of sequence. Therefore, to re-assemble them in the correct order, they each need a sequence number with the first message packet numbered 1, the second, 2 and so on.

Received packets are acknowledged if the endpoint-to-endpoint connection requires it. For this, each packet belonging to a message is assigned an acknowledgement number before it is sent. The receiver replies with a packet to the sender constructed with the received acknowledgement number to indicate that the packet with this number was received successfully.

Packet transmission errors can occur for a variety of reasons but it must be possible for the receiver to detect when errors have occurred. A checksum (e.g. CRC) attached to each packet is used for error detection.

Packets travel along transmission media consisting of wires, fibre-optic cable and radio frequency links. To launch a packet onto or to receive a packet from any of these requires a layer of hardware called a network interface. Each sending/receiving host's network interface hardware needs to be assigned a "fixed" unique hardware address called a link layer address. Similarly, each router will need link layer hardware, uniquely identified by a link layer hardware address, because routers are also connected to transmission media.

A packet is structured into a series of headers which contain all of the above information and the message chunk or data - Figure 9.3.1.9. The data D and the headers H_T, H_N, H_L make up each packet (and a checksum appended to the end of the packet).

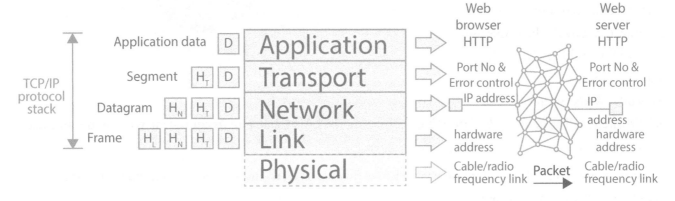

Figure 9.3.1.9 The protocol stack for TCP/IP showing how different headers are added to the payload data - see Chapter 9.4.1

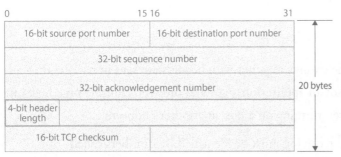

Figure 9.3.1.10 TCP header, H_T

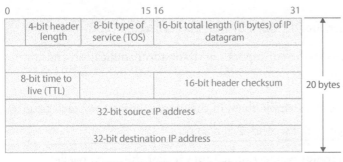

Figure 9.3.1.11 IP header, H_N

TCP header

Figure 9.3.1.10 shows some of the detail in the header labelled H_T in Figure 9.3.1.9. H_T is called the TCP header. The key fields to note are the port numbers and the sequence number fields.

IP header

Figure 9.3.1.11 shows some of the detail in the header labelled H_N in Figure 9.3.1.9. H_N is called the IP header. The time-to-live field is used in order to stop a lost packet wandering the Internet forever. The key fields to note are the source and destination IP addresses and the time to live fields.

Frame header

Figure 9.3.1.12 shows an example of a link layer header for Ethernet. In Ethernet, a CRC checksum, which is not shown in the figure, is added after the application data. The length field value is for the entire frame including application data but excluding the CRC checksum.

48-bit destination address	48-bit source address	16-bit length field	16-bit type field

Figure 9.3.1.12 Link layer header, H₁

The type field identifies the type of data, e.g. ARP request which maps an IP address to a hardware address. The destination and source addresses are hardware addresses usually assigned to the network interface card by its manufacturer. In the Ethernet protocol, the hardware addresses are known as MAC addresses or Media Access Control addresses. The key fields to remember are the hardware destination and source address fields.

Figure 9.3.1.13 shows the main components of a packet.

Hardware destination address	Hardware source address	Source IP address	Destination IP address	Source port no	Dest. port no	Sequence no	Data

Figure 9.3.1.13 Main components of a packet

Questions

10 What are the main components of a packet?

How routing is achieved across the Internet

Figure 9.3.1.14 shows, for a simplified network scenario, the routing of a packet from end-system host X to end-system host Y.

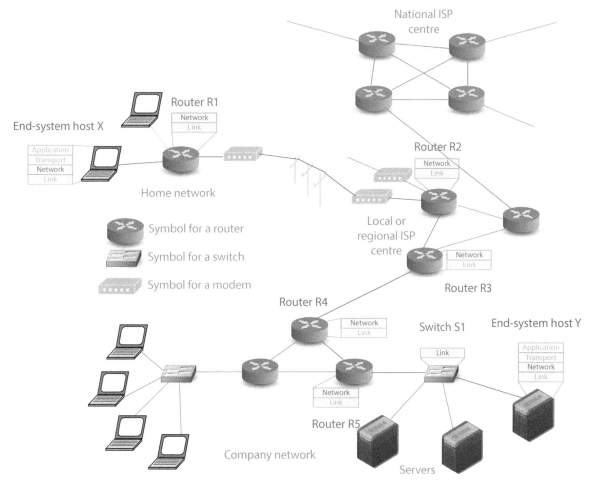

Figure 9.3.1.14 Routing of a packet from end-system X to end-system Y through the Internet by network IP address

Routing refers to the network-wide process that determines the end-to-end paths that packets take from source to destination. Routing is necessary when the destination is not directly reachable.

A router receives a packet on an input link and transfers the packet to the appropriate output link. This is known as forwarding. Every router has a forwarding table. A router forwards a packet by using the destination IP address in the arriving packet's header as an index to an entry in the router's forwarding table. This entry indicates the router's outgoing link to use to forward the packet.

Using a driving analogy, routing would be equivalent to an ordered list of roads that need to be travelled to get from place X to place Y. Forwarding would be equivalent to choosing the exit to take at the junctions/roundabouts connecting each road segment to the next.

Routers play a crucial role in both the process of forwarding and the process of determining the paths to follow. A router uses algorithms known as routing algorithms to calculate these paths and perform packet switching when forwarding a packet. The routing algorithm determines the values that are inserted into the forwarding table of each router. In the decentralised model, each router executes a part of a distributed routing algorithm relevant to its location in the hierarchy of routers (see Figure 9.3.1.7).

In Figure 9.3.1.14, host X is sending a message to host Y. The message might be an HTTP GET message to an HTTP server Y (see Chapter 9.3.2). The transport layer of the TCP/IP protocol stack in host X adds a transport header to the message packet generated by the application layer to produce a transport layer segment. This segment then passes to the network layer which adds its own header to it to create an IP datagram which then passes to the link layer. This layer adds its own header and a checksum trailer to create a link frame. This frame is delivered to the physical medium where it travels to router R1.

R1 strips away the link layer header and trailer to extract the IP datagram which then passes to the network layer. The network layer consults its forwarding table to determine that the datagram should be sent onto the outgoing link that connects R1 to router R2. The datagram is passed to the link layer that adds the correct link layer header and trailer to create a new frame. The link layer then passes the frame to the physical medium which transfers it to router R2.

The process that occurred at R1 now repeats at router R2. R2 consults its forwarding table to find which outgoing link to use, i.e. the one joined to router R3. This process continues until the frame arrives at the end-system host Y.

At host Y, the headers are stripped away progressively as the packet is passed up the protocol stack until only the message remains. The last header, the transport header, is removed by the transport layer before the message is delivered to an application layer process, e.g. an HTTP server.

Routers require just two layers for this task: the network and link layers of the protocol stack.

Note that the source and destination IP addresses set by host X remain the packet's source and destination IP addresses throughout the journey through the routers from host X to host Y. However, the link layer hardware source and destination hardware addresses are changed for each hop.

Table 9.3.1.1 shows a simplified example of a forwarding table for a router with four links, numbered 0 to 3. The router has IP address 146.97.33.2. It connects to hosts with dotted-decimal IP addresses beginning with 142, 144, 152, 155 via other routers.

Destination address prefix	Link interface
10001110	0
10010000	1
10011000	2
10011011	3

Table 9.3.1.1 Simplified forwarding table

For example, www.southamption.ac.uk has IP address 152.78.118.52. The router with the forwarding table shown in *Table 9.3.1.1* routes packets it receives with destination IP address 152.78.118.52 to the link interface numbered 2.

Questions

11 Explain how routing is achieved across the Internet.

12 Which addresses remain unaltered throughout routing and which change?

13 Explain why some addresses must change and some must not.

Uniform Resource Locator

A uniform resource locator (URL) is a short string that represents the target of a hyperlink; it was introduced in early 1990 in Tim Berners-Lee's proposals for hypertext. A URL specifies which server to access, the access method and the location in the server. *Figure 9.3.1.15* shows that a URL consists of several parts. The simplest version contains three parts:

- How: defines which protocol is to be used

- Where: defines the host

- What: specifies the name of the requested object and the complete path to it.

Figure 9.3.1.15 Structure of a URL

Questions

14 What is a URL and what does it specify?

15 Give an example of a URL, different from the one above. Identify its how, where and what parts.

Domain name and IP address

In the early days of the Internet, users of Internet applications such as e-mail were required to enter IP addresses when they wanted to set the destination and source addresses of an e-mail they were sending.

An IP or Internet Protocol address in the context of the Internet is a globally unique, 32-bit (IPv4) or 128-bit (IPv6), logical address which identifies a host connected to and directly reachable from the Internet. This wasn't a problem while the number of IP addresses in use was very small. However, as the number of networks began to grow, it became a lot harder to use IP addressing directly.

The Domain Name System (DNS) was invented so that users could use a memorable name called a domain name to refer to a network and a Fully Qualified Domain Name (FQDN) to refer to a host on that network. For example, the IP address 144.173.6.226 has the memorable fully qualified domain name emps.exeter.ac.uk. (FQDN end with a full stop but this is often omitted). For convenience, people often use 'domain name' when they mean fully qualified domain name.

How domain names are organised

The Domain Name System (DNS), part of which is shown in *Figure 9.3.1.16*, is a hierarchical system of names and abbreviations. The root is abbreviated to a full stop. Using this domain name hierarchy, an example of a domain name is ags.bucks.sch.uk. This domain name was used to identify a network of computers with network ID 195.112.56 located at a school in Buckinghamshire in the UK when the school hosted its own servers.

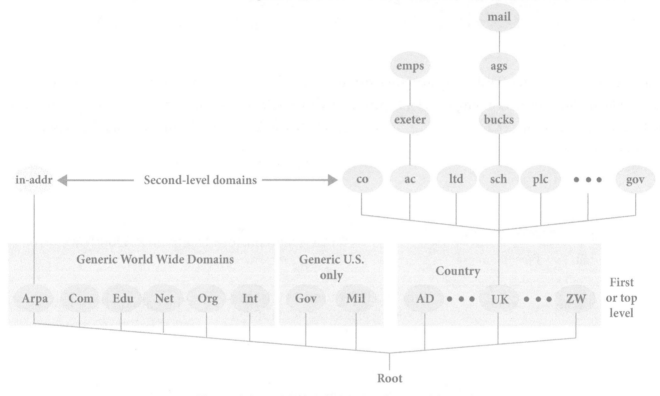

Figure 9.3.1.16 Domain Name System hierarchy

A particular host on this network was <u>mail.ags.bucks.sch.uk</u>. This name (hostname) is an example of a fully qualified domain name (FQDN). An FQDN uniquely identifies a host. When the host ID of this computer, 124, is added to the network ID, the IP address becomes 195.112.56.124.

In <u>mail.ags.bucks.sch.uk.</u> the domain *uk* includes all hosts that use the top-level domain name suffix 'uk'.

The second-level domain *sch* includes all the hosts that use 'sch', the third-level domain *bucks* includes all the hosts in Buckinghamshire, and the fourth-level domain *ags* includes all the hosts in the organisation AGS with globally unique IP addresses. Finally, *mail* is the public name of the host. *Table 9.3.1.2* shows the interpretation of some top-level domain names. *Table 9.3.1.3* shows the interpretation of some second-level domain names.

Domain Name	Type of organisation
com	Commercial
edu	Educational
org	Non-commercial
uk	Located in UK

Table 9.3.1.2 Some top level domain names

Domain Name	Type of organisation
co	Commercial
ac	Academic, higher education or further education
sch	School
uk	Located in UK

Table 9.3.1.3 Some second level domain names

Questions

17 How is the domain name system organised?

18 Give **two** examples of top level domain names and **two** examples of second level domain names.

19 Give the meaning associated with each domain name given in Q18.

Purpose and function of the Domain Name System (DNS) and DNS Servers

People prefer to use the user-friendly memorable form of hostname, i.e. its fully qualified domain name, e.g. university-of-exeter.ja.net.

However, routers prefer fixed-length IP addresses. In order for the needs of each to be met a directory service is used that translates hostnames to IP addresses e.g. university-of-exeter.ja.net → 146.97.144.42.

This is the main purpose of the Internet's Domain Name System (DNS).

Domain Name System servers translate FQDNs into IP addresses.

The DNS is a distributed database implemented in a hierarchy of DNS servers, and an application-layer protocol that allows hosts to query the distributed database to resolve domain names into IP addresses before connecting to other hosts on the Internet.

No single DNS server has all the mappings for all the hosts in the Internet. Instead the mappings are distributed across the DNS servers.

DNS also provides a few other services in addition to translating hostnames into IP addresses:

- Host aliasing - A host with a complicated hostname can have one or more alias names. For example, www.exeter.ac.uk and admin.ex.ac.uk are alias hostnames for a server with hostname webdata02.ex.ac.uk and IP address 144.173.6.226 that hosts University of Exeter's website as well as other sites. The hostname webdata02.ex.ac.uk is said to be the canonical hostname (CNAME).

- Mail server aliasing - user-friendly memorable email addresses such as fred@hotmail.com are aliases. The hostname of the mail server hotmail.com that is used for Fred's email will almost certainly be more elaborate than this, e.g. the canonical hostname of the alias hotmail.com is actually origin.sn145w.snt145.mail.live.com with server IP address 155.55.152.112. DNS can be used by a mail application, e.g. Microsoft Outlook, to obtain the canonical hostname for a supplied hostname as well as the IP address of the host. Aliasing also allows a Web server and a mail server to have identical aliased hostnames: e.g. company.co.uk.

- Load distribution - servers such as Web servers may be replicated if they host busy sites. Each server runs on a different end system with each having a different IP address. The set of IP addresses for these server end-systems is associated with just one canonical hostname. The DNS database contains this set of addresses. A DNS server responds with the entire set of IP addresses when hit with a client request to translate a hostname into an IP address. Clients normally pick the first IP address in the set they come across. The DNS server rotates the order of IP addresses in each reply so that the traffic is distributed amongst the replicated Web servers (the same is true of mail servers).

Questions

20 What is the main purpose of the Domain Name Service?

21 What services are performed by DNS servers?

A very useful tool to use when exploring the DNS system is the Unix DNS tool dig. It is also available to use in Linux and Mac OS X operating systems. The Raspberry Pi[2] computer connected to the Internet may be used to explore the use of *dig* but *dnsutils* will need to be installed first as follows:

sudo aptget install dnsutils

Another useful tool available in both Microsoft Windows and Unix/Linux/Mac OS X systems is nslookup. This tool maps domain name to IP address.

For example, *nslookup* www.aqa.org.uk returns the answer 194.34.8.20.

The tool *dig* may be used to query DNS name servers as shown in *Table 9.3.1.4*.

Command	Description	Result
dig NS .	Returns the hostnames of the name servers located at the root of the domain name system. The root is represented by a full stop. Note that there are thirteen root servers. NS means name server.	d.root-servers.net. e.root-servers.net. f.root-servers.net. g.root-servers.net. h.root-servers.net. i.root-servers.net. j.root-servers.net. k.root-servers.net. l.root-servers.net. m.root-servers.net. a.root-servers.net. c.root-servers.net.
dig NS uk.	Returns the hostnames of name servers for the domain name uk. located in the top level of the domain name system. Nominet UK is responsible for nic.uk.	dns1.nic.uk. nsd.nic.uk. and several others.
dig NS ac.uk.	Returns the hostnames of name servers in the domain with domain name ac.uk. and located in the second level of the domain name system.	auth03.ns.uu.net. ns4.ja.net. and several others.
dig NS bris.ac.uk.	Returns the hostnames of name servers for the domain name bris.ac.uk. located in the third level of the domain name system.	irix.bris.ac.uk. ncs.bris.ac.uk. ns3.ja.net.
dig A irix.bris.ac.uk.	Returns the IP address of the DNS server irix.bris.ac.uk. A means address.	137.222.8.143
dig A snowy.cs.bris.ac.uk.	Returns the IP address of the host with hostname snowy. cs.bris.ac.uk.	137.222.103.3
dig +trace www.aqa.org. uk @a.root-servers.net.	This will report all the DNS servers that are consulted in resolving www.aqa.org.uk. NOTE a.root-servers.net must end with a full stop.	194.34.8.20 (AQA Education 194.34.8.0/24)

Table 9.3.1.4 Using the dig command to query the DNS system

For more examples of the use of the *dig* command see

www.cyberciti.biz/faq/linux-unix-dig-command-examples-usage-syntax

2   Raspberry Pi is a trademark of the Raspberry Pi Foundation

Tasks

1. Use the URL http://simpledns.com/lookup-dg.aspx to access a DNS delegation trace utility. Use this utility to trace the DNS server queries for a host snowy.cs.bris.ac.uk. Note that the trace begins with a DNS root server chosen from the list of possible root servers, and proceeds down the hierarchy of name servers until the IP address of snowy.cs.bris.ac.uk is obtained.

2. Use the nslookup command to look up the IP address of the following www.exeter.ac.uk, www.manchester.ac.uk, www.bristol.ac.uk.

3. Use the dig command to find the hostnames of third level DNS servers for the University of Exeter (hint: use the information in Table 9.3.1.3 to target exeter.ac.uk.). Repeat the exercise for the Computer Science department, University of Washington in the USA (hint: target cs.washington.edu.). If you do not have access to the dig command you can use the site referenced in Question 1.

4. Install PingPlotter - https://www.pingplotter.com. Choose the following targets: www.exeter.ac.uk, www.manchester.ac.uk, www.bristol.ac.uk. In each case observe the route. Does each route have anything in common? Also make a note of each destination IP address then use each recorded destination IP address in the url window of a browser in turn. Why might some IP addresses return a web page and others a *Request rejected* message?

5. Use ipconfig/all in Windows command line to discover your computer's IP address, the default gateway and the physical/hardware address (MAC address) of its network card.

6. Install Wireshark - https://www.wireshark.org. Familiarise yourself with Wireshark by capturing a few packets and examining their contents.

Internet registries

Private companies and organisations called Internet registrars are responsible for registering Internet domains and therefore domain names to people, businesses and organisations, domain names such as educational-computing.co.uk. A registrar is an online retailer where domains (domain names) can be bought.

The world is divided into five geographical regions for the purposes of Internet registries: Canada, USA, and some Caribbean Islands (ARIN), Africa (AFRINIC), Asia/Pacific Region (APNIC), Europe, the Middle East and Central Asia (RIPE), Latin America and some Caribbean Islands (LACNIC).

Regional Internet Registrars delegate responsibility for registering domain names to their customers, which include Internet Service Providers and other organisations. The Regional Internet Registry for Europe is RIPE (Réseaux IP Européens).

RIPE has delegated to Nominet to hold the official registry for all .UK domain names. Nominet is therefore an Internet registrar. Nominet provides a WHOIS tool that can be used to find out if a .UK domain name is registered and if it is, provide details of the registration including the registrant. Nominet sets the policies and rules that relate to the management of .UK. It does delegate

Task

7. Use the WHOIS service of Nominet (www.nominet.uk/whois) to look up the registration of the following: (i) co.uk. (ii) ac.uk, (iii) org.uk. (iv) plc.org. (v) me.uk. (vi) ags.bucks.sch.uk. (vii) commonweal.co.uk. (viii) lordwilliams.oxon.sch.uk.

registration to third parties, e.g. RM Education PLC, but third party registrars are required to follow Nominet's policies and rules in respect of .UK domains.

Internet registries store registered domain names and the details of the registrants, e.g. domain name educational-computing.co.uk has been registered by Educational Computing Services Ltd, the registrant.

The registrant or their ISP will supply the IP address of a DNS server(s) (the registrant's or the ISP's) for this domain name to their Internet registrar. This registrar will then place an entry for this domain name and supplied IP address at the corresponding level in the Domain Name Server System.

Registering a domain name and associating it with a range of IP addresses

Suppose that you wanted a domain name for a group of servers, including a Web server, that you intend managing yourself.

You have chosen myowndomain.co.uk as your domain name.

You have obtained Internet connectivity, by contracting with and connecting to, a local ISP (Internet Service Provider). You have purchased a gateway router which will be connected via DSL (Digital Subscriber Line) to a router in your local ISP.

Your local ISP has granted you a block of IP addresses, one of which you will assign to the Web server (www.myowndomain.co.uk), one to the gateway router (gateway.myowndomain.co.uk) and another to the DNS server (dns.myowndomain.co.uk).

You will need to check with an Internet registrar that your domain name, myowndomain.co.uk, has not been registered already. If it hasn't, it may now be registered with your Internet registrar.

You will also need to provide the IP address of your DNS server to your Internet registrar. Your registrar will then place an entry for your DNS server (domain name and corresponding IP address) in the .co.uk second level domain servers. After this is done, the IP address for your domain name and therefore your DNS server can be obtained via the DNS system on request.

You must provide entries in your DNS server that map the hostname of your Web server, e.g. www.myowndomain.co.uk to its IP address. You will need entries also for all your other publicly available servers.

Suppose that your ISP provided you with a block of 8 IP addresses expressed as 144.173.6.176/29 (a prefix). This is interpreted as 29 bits for the network ID and 3 bits for the host ID (0..7) starting with host ID 144.173.6.176. Therefore, the range of the block of IP addresses is 144.173.6.176 to 144.173.6.183.

Routers need to become aware directly or indirectly of your network ID and range of IP addresses so that packets can be routed to your network. This is achieved by your ISP which will inform the ISPs it is connected to by sending them 144.173.6.176/29 and they in turn will propagate your network ID and range of IP addresses to others. Eventually all Internet routers will know a subset of your network ID and therefore will be able to forward packets destined for your Web server, etc. *Figure 9.3.1.17* shows a hierarchy of routers and their simplified routing tables. Router 1 routes using the most significant byte of an IP address, Router 2 the next most significant and so on. Router **5** is the gateway router for domain myowndomain.co.uk. It has the fully qualified domain name gateway.myowndomain.co.uk.

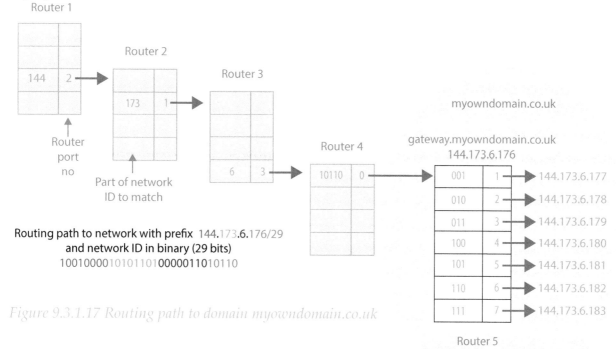

Figure 9.3.1.17 Routing path to domain myowndomain.co.uk

Tasks

8 Visit the web page https://ipinfo.io/AS786 and discover how many IP addresses with the prefix **129.12.0.0/16** i.e. 16-bit NET ID **129.12** are allocated to the University of of Kent.

9 Visit the web page https://ipinfo.io/AS786 and locate the prefix **192.150.184.0/24** assigned to the University of Manchester. Explain why for this prefix only **256** IP addresses can be allocated to this University. What is the network ID for this block of IP addresses?

10 The web page https://ipinfo.io/AS786 shows that **512** IP addresses are allocated to the University of Northumbria at Newcastle at prefix **192.173.2.0/23**. How many bits are allocated for the host ID and how many for the network ID? What is the network ID?

In this chapter you have covered:

- The structure of the Internet
- The role of packet switching and routers
- The main components of a packet
- The definition of a
  - router
  - gateway
- How routing is achieved across the Internet
- The term 'uniform resource locator' (URL) in the context of internetworking
- The terms 'domain name' and 'IP address'
- How domain names are organised
- The purpose and function of the Domain Name System (DNS) and its reliance on the DNS server system
- The service provided by Internet registries and why they are needed.

9.3 The Internet

Learning objectives:

- *Understand how a firewall works (packet filtering, proxy server, stateful inspection)*

- *Explain symmetric and asymmetric (private/public key) encryption and key exchange*

- *Explain how digital certificates and digital signatures are obtained and used*

- *Discuss worms, Trojans and viruses, and the vulnerabilites that they exploit*

- *Discuss how improved code quality, monitoring and protection can be used to address worms, trojans and viruses.*

9.3.2 Internet security

Firewalls

A firewall is a combination of hardware and software that isolates an organisation's internal network from the Internet at large, allowing some packets to pass and blocking others. *Figure 9.3.2.1* shows a firewall located between an organisation's local area network and the router that connects, via an ISP, the organisation's network to the Internet. With all network traffic entering and leaving the organisation's network passing through the firewall, the firewall is able to allow authorised traffic through whilst blocking unauthorised traffic. Two ways by which a firewall can control traffic are

- traditional packet filtering

- stateful inspection of packets

> **Key term**
>
> **Firewall:**
> A firewall is a combination of hardware and software that isolates an organisation's internal network from the Internet at large, allowing some packets to pass and blocking others.

Packet filtering

Packet filtering is done by a packet filter acting on a network-layer datagram (see *Figure 9.3.1.9* in *Chapter 9.3.1*). Network-layer datagrams contain source and destination IP addresses, source and destination port numbers, protocol type: TCP, UDP, ICMP (Internet Control Message Protocol) and so on; ICMP message type; some flags, SYN, and ACK related to theTCP connection three-way handshake (*Figure 9.3.2.2*). The packet filter is set up to make decisions according to

> **Key term**
>
> **Packet filtering:**
> Packet filtering is done by a packet filter acting on a network-layer datagram.

- IP source or destination address

- Protocol type

- Source and destination port numbers

- ICMP message type (see *Table 9.3.2.1*)

- TCP flag bits: SYN, ACK, etc, (see *Figure 9.3.2.2*)

- Different rules for datagrams entering and leaving the network

- Different rules for different firewall interfaces.

ISP & DNS servers

Web server

Firewall

Interface 1

Interface 2

Internet gateway

E

A   B   C   D

Private Local Area Network

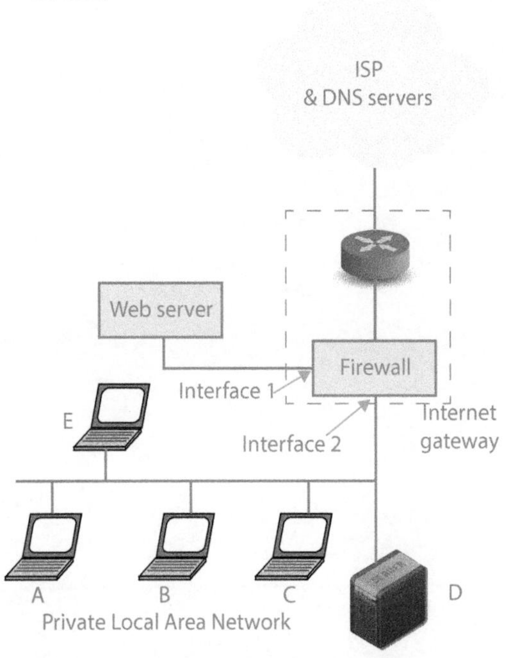

Figure 9.3.2.1 Local Area Network behind a firewall

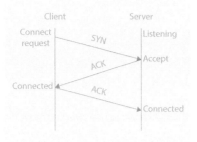
Information

ICMP message types:

ICMP type	Code	Description
0	0	echo reply
3	1	destination host unreachable
3	3	destination port unreachable
8	0	echo request
11	0	TTL expired

Table 9.3.2.1 Some ICMP message types

Key term

Stateless packet filtering:
Information about packets is not remembered by the firewall. This type of firewall can be tricked very easily by hackers because allow/deny decisions are taken on a packet by packet basis and these are not related to the previous allowed/denied packets.

For example, a datagram arriving at the firewall from the Internet with IP destination address of the Web server shown in Figure 9.3.2.1 and destination port number 80 will be allowed through the firewall interface connected to the Web server. However, if the destination IP address was that of server D connected to the firewall's second interface then the datagram could be blocked for all ports except those related to an FTP connection.

A datagram arriving at the firewall from the Internet with IP destination address of the Web server shown in Figure 9.3.2.1 and destination port number 23 might be blocked by the firewall from passing through the firewall interface connected to the Web server.

Information

ICMP message datagrams have a type and a code field, and contain the header and the first 8 bytes of the IP datagram that caused the ICMP message to be generated.

Ping is a software utility used to test the reachability of a host on an Internet Protocol (IP) network and to measure the round-trip time for messages sent from the originating host to a destination computer and back. Suppose *ping* sends an ICMP type 8 code 0 message (see Table 9.3.2.1 - echo request) to the Web server in Figure 9.3.2.1. The ping ICMP type 8 code 0 message is a request to the Web server to reply to the sender with ICMP type 0 code 0 - echo reply. The reply will contain the originator's IP address, i.e. the Web server's IP address. That's fine because the ping echo request was addressed in the first place to this Web server. However an attacker could do more by guessing the IP address range of the organisation hosting the Web server and proceeding to carry out a ping sweep across this IP address range in the hope that other hosts will be discovered. To prevent this, the firewall can be configured to block all ICMP echo request packets.

Task

 Use ping to test if ICMP echo requests are blocked by a firewall:
(a) www.ucl.ac.uk   (b) www.bristol.ac.uk
(c) www.educational-computing.co.uk

Stateless packet filtering

Stateless packet filters do not match return packets with outgoing packet flow, and therefore ignore whether a connection has been established. Instead they focus on source and destination IP address, source and destination port numbers and protocol type. A set of rules are constructed called a ruleset and then expressed in the syntax of a particular firewall scripting language.

Suppose we want to allow inbound mail (SMTP, port 25) but only to the Internet gateway shown in Figure 9.3.2.1.

Figure 9.3.2.3 shows how the rule for this could be expressed. Figure 9.3.2.3(a) shows the table starting out in the default state which is to block everything (*). Figure 9.3.2.3(b) shows the rule that allows an inbound connection to port 25 on the Internet gateway. Port 25 is the Simple Mail

Transfer Protocol service for both sending and receiving electronic mail.

If the policy is to allow any host on the local area network to also send email from any one of its ports to the outside world via the Internet then hosts must be allowed to connect to port 25 on an external host. The rule to do this is shown labelled '(a) Outgoing' in *Figure 9.3.2.4*.

The second rule labelled (b) 'Incoming', *Figure 9.3.2.4* is necessary to allow ACK packets to enter the local area network which is necessary part if a TCP connection is to be established with an external host - see *Figure 9.3.2.2*.

Action	Source	Port	Destination	Port	Comment
Block	*	*	*	*	Default

(a) Incoming

Action	Source	Port	Destination	Port	Comment
Allow	*	*	Gateway	25	Connection to Gateway SMTP port

(b) Incoming

Figure 9.3.2.3 Firewall ruleset tables

	Action	Source	Port	Destination	Port	Flags	Comment
(a) Outgoing	Allow	192.168.1/24	*	*	25	*	LAN host packets to external host SMTP port
(b) Incoming	Allow	*	25	192.168.1/24	*	ACK	External host response

192.168.1/24 means all hosts on network with NetworkID 192.168.1

Figure 9.3.2.4 Firewall ruleset for SMTP

Stateful inspection packet filtering

In **stateful inspection packet filtering**, TCP (and UDP) connections are tracked and connection information is used to make filtering decisions. A connection table of current outbound TCP connections is maintained. Suppose an attacker attempts to send a bogus packet into the local area network behind the firewall by sending a datagram with the ACK flag set from TCP source port 80, source address 137.248.8.9 to destination port 49923 and destination IP address 95.144.156.56. This masquerades as a genuine HTTP response from an external Web server at 137.248.8.9 to a Web page request from internal host with IP address 95.144.156.56. When this packet reaches the firewall, the firewall checks its access control list in *Table 9.3.2.2* which indicates the connection table, *Table 9.3.2.3*, must also be checked before permitting this packet to enter the local area network. On checking, the firewall sees that this packet is not part of an ongoing TCP connection, and rejects the packet.

> **Key term**
>
> **Stateful inspection packet filtering:**
> If the firewall remembers connection information for previously passed packets, then the firewall is performing stateful inspection packet filtering.

Action	Source address	Destination address	Protocol	Source port	Destination port	Flag bit	Check connection table
Allow	95.144.156/24	External to 95.144.156/24	TCP	>49152	80	Any	
Allow	External to 95.144.156/24	95.144.156/24	TCP	80	>49152	ACK	X
Deny	All	All	All	All	All	All	All

Table 9.3.2.2 Access control list for stateful filter - this is scanned for a match from row 1 downwards

Information

Client-server TCP connections:

Server ports are assigned to numbers < 1023 permanently, e.g. 20, 21 for FTP, 23 for Telnet 25 for server SMTP, 80 for HTTP. Client ports are numbers > 49152 allocated dynamically and valid only for the duration of the communication.

The boundary values of the port number ranges, e.g. 1023, are reserved and therefore not available.

Key term

Firewall proxy server:
A firewall proxy server works at the application level of the TCP protocol stack and therefore is able to filter by application protocol type, e.g. HTTP, and provide authorisation by user (stateless and stateful operate at the level of hosts via IP addresses) and what content users may access.

Source address	Destination address	Source port	Destination port
95.144.156.56	130.88.98.244	49917	80
95.144.156.44	144.173.6.226	49918	80
95.144.156.21	129.11.26.33	49919	80

Table 9.3.2.3 Connection table for stateful filter

Proxy server

Figure 9.3.2.5 shows communication between two computers connected through a third computer acting as a proxy. The proxy acts on behalf of both Alice and Bob to allow dialogue to take place indirectly between the two. The proxy is able to mediate the communication because it is aware from whom the request comes, to whom the request is directed, and the type of request. It might be the case that Alice is not allowed to contact Bob because he is on a banned list called a blacklist. It might be the case that Alice is not authorised to communicate with Bob in a particular way.

Translating this analogy into proxies in computer networks, a proxy server is a server (an application-specific server running on a host) that acts as an intermediary for requests from clients seeking resources from other servers. The proxy server would form part of the firewall protection shown in *Figure 9.3.2.1*. A client, say host A in the private local area network, connects to the proxy server, requesting some service, such as a Web page, or other resource available from a different server. The proxy server evaluates the request and decides whether to allow it. If it does the proxy server allows an indirect network connection between the client, host A, and the requested network service, e.g. a Web page from a remote Web server located somewhere in the Internet. The Web server that serves up the Web page will only be aware of the proxy server not the real source of the request, host A. As far as the Web server is concerned the client that made the request was the proxy server acting as a client.

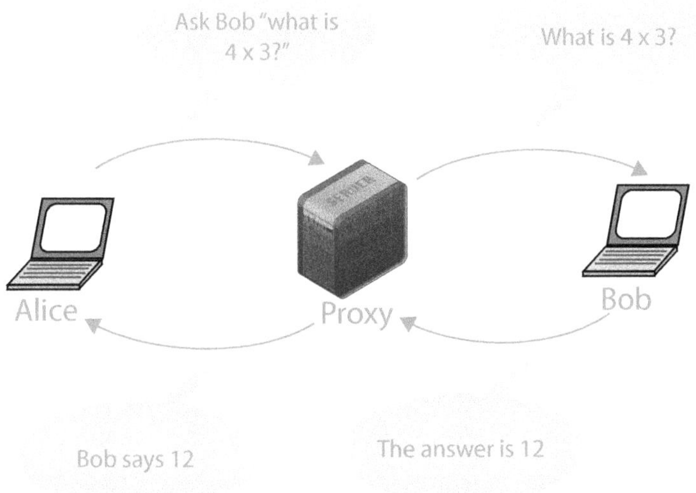

Similarly, host A gets the Web page from the proxy server. If the proxy server has cached this Web page from a previous occasion then it could, if necessary, serve up the cached copy. Host A will be unaware of the origin of Web page it is served, proxy server or remote server.

Proxy servers work at the application level of the TCP protocol stack and so are aware of the type

Figure 9.3.2.5 Communication between two computers connected through a third computer acting as a proxy. Bob engages in a dialogue with the proxy server but doesn't know that the dialogue is driven by Alice with whom he is communicating without knowing it.

of request they receive from clients behind the firewall by the application protocol that is used, e.g. SSH, HTTP request.

A content-filtering web proxy server provides control over the content that may be relayed in one or both directions by filtering by URL (and DNS) or by keywords in the content.

The proxy server may also scan incoming content in real time for viruses and other malware and block such content from entering the network.

Question

 Stateless packet filtering, stateful inspection packet filtering and proxy servers are three kinds of firewall techniques. Explain by examples how they differ from each other.

Encryption

Encryption is the process of obtaining ciphertext from plaintext. Plaintext is understandable (English) text. The intention of encryption is to render plaintext incomprehensible to all but those granted the means to reverse the process, i.e. decrypt the ciphertext.

The encryption process requires two inputs: the plaintext and the encryption key. The decryption process also requires two inputs: the ciphertext and the decryption key.

Encryption is covered in *Chapter 5.6.10*.

Symmetric encryption

Shared private key

In symmetric encryption the communicating parties use the same key for encryption and decryption. Symmetric key encryption is also known as private key or secret key encryption because the key used must be private and known only to the communicating parties. If not, then anyone intercepting encrypted messages can use a knowledge of the key and the encryption algorithm to decrypt the messages.

For example, if Alice wanted to use symmetric encryption to send an encrypted message to Bob then Alice would use the private key *k*, agreed with Bob, to encrypt the plaintext form of the message. Bob would use the same private key *k* to decrypt the received encrypted message. Bob could reply with his own encrypted message which he has also encrypted with private key *k* (*Figure 9.3.2.6*).

Using symmetric encryption, Alice and Bob are able to communicate securely through a communication channel.

However, there is a potential problem with use of a single private key. Let's suppose that Alice gets to choose the key. She now has to communicate the key to Bob. They could agree to meet so that Alice could, by whispering into Bob's ear, communicate the key securely. However, in a networked world, Alice and Bob may never meet and may never communicate except over a network, e.g. the Internet. However, to communicate the key securely to Bob via a network connection, Alice needs to secure the channel through the network.

How can she do this if she hasn't yet distributed the private key? She needs the secure channel

> **Key term**
>
> **Symmetric encryption:**
> Symmetric encryption uses the same secret key to perform both the encryption and decryption processes.

Message M — Private key, k — Private key, k — Message M

Encrypted with key k → Encrypted message M → Decrypted with key k

Communication channel

Figure 9.3.2.6 Secure communication channel using symmetric encryption

to distribute the key. This "chicken and egg" situation is known as the key distribution problem of symmetric encryption.

Asymmetric encryption (public key/private key encryption)

Secure communication in the world of online transactions

The key distribution problem of symmetric encryption becomes an even more challenging one in the world of online transactions which the World Wide Web has made possible. Many transactions take place online through online stores where goods may be bought with a credit or debit card. All these transactions need to take place through secure channels of communication to protect a purchaser's payment details. Securing each channel with a separate symmetric encryption private key shared in advance between seller and customer would be a nightmare:

- The seller would have to store a large number of private keys, one for each customer buying goods.
- Each key would have to be distributed to the corresponding customer who would have to remember the key and for which seller.

A mechanism for secure communication is needed which

- reduces the number of keys that need to be remembered
- allows two parties to exchange information secretly, but with no pre-arranged symmetric encryption private key

One solution is public key/private key encryption to secure a communication channel. This secure channel can then be used to distribute a temporary symmetric encryption key to be used for securing credit/debit card details. This temporary shared key is called a session key because it is only used for the duration of the transaction.

Public key encryption

In public key encryption two mathematically related keys are used:

- a public key p_k
- a private or secret key s_k

Public key encryption has two clear advantages over private key encryption:

- The online seller has only to store a single private key s_k rather than sharing, storing and managing N different secret symmetric encryption keys (i.e. one for each buyer).
- The number and identities of potential buyers need not be known at the time of key generation.

Public key encryption is an asymmetric encryption scheme, asymmetric because only one of the paired keys, the private key s_k is secret. The public key p_k can be freely shared with any party. Thus an online seller makes their public key p_k available to any buyer. A buyer can then use the seller's public key to establish a secure channel over which they can send their credit card information securely to complete a purchase. The seller uses their private key s_k, which only they know, to decrypt the buyer's credit card information to process the transaction or, if symmetric encryption is used for the latter, to set up a secure means of communicating a shared private session key.

If the key pair is chosen well:

- The private key cannot be derived from the public key
- The public key encrypted messages can only be decrypted by the corresponding private key.

In practice, encrypting and decrypting with public key encryption is far slower than with symmetric encryption. For this reason, public key encryption is often used to solve the problem of sharing a secret key for use in a symmetric encryption scheme.

One public key encryption scheme that is employed in online transactions to provide one-way secure communication and authentication is the RSA cryptosystem which is named after its inventors Rivest, Shamir and Adleman.

The following RSA section (included as enrichment material) is beyond A Level.

The RSA public key/private key cryptosystem

Let us to suppose that Alice wishes to receive secure messages from other people. She proceeds as follows:

- Alice selects two distinct prime numbers p and q and then forms her public modulus $N = pq$.

  N must be sufficiently large to ensure that no adversary could factor N = pq except by luck. This means that p and q each need to be more than 150 digits long, and not be too close to each other.

- Alice then chooses her public exponent e to be relatively prime to $(p-1)(q-1)$, with $1 < e < (p-1)(q-1)$.

- Alice chooses the pair (N, e) as her public key and she publishes this.

- Her private key is the unique integer, d such that
  ed mod (p − 1)(q − 1) = 1 and 1 < d < (p − 1)(q − 1)
  or in congruence notation as ed = 1 (mod b) where b = (p - 1)(q - 1)
  d is the mod (p - 1)(q - 1) multiplicative inverse of e

Bob has a message which he wishes to send to Alice (*Figure 9.3.2.7*).

He proceeds as follows:

- Bob encodes the characters of his message as a string of integer codes M, e.g. 1521112325981720......
- Bob looks up Alice's public key (N, e)
- Bob splits the integer encoded form of the message M into a sequence of blocks $M_1, M_2, M_3, ..., M_i$ where each M_i is an integer that satisfies $1 \leq M_i < N$.

Information

Prime number:

A prime number is a natural number greater than 1 that cannot be expressed as the product of two smaller natural numbers. Note that this means 1 is not a prime number.

In other words: a number that has only two factors: 1 and itself, e.g. 2, 3, 5, 7, 43.

Relatively prime:

Two natural numbers are relatively prime if they have no common divisor apart from 1.

E.g. 4 and 7 are relatively prime but 7 and 14 are not.

One-way function:

Exponentiation to the power e modulo N is one-way function: relatively easy to compute but hard to invert. The private key d is known as a trapdoor because it makes inversion possible.

It is easy to multiply two numbers, p and q but apparently hard to factor a number pq into a product of two others when it is large. Try factoring 7859112349338149.

Exponentiation:

Exponentiation means raising a number x to the power y; it is written x^y.

A useful property of exponentiation is that raising a number x to the power y and then raising the result to the power z yields the same result as raising x to the power z and raising that result to the power y,
  i.e. $(x^y)^z = x^{yz} = (x^z)^y$

This is true even if the exponentiation uses modular arithmetic.

Figure 9.3.2.7 RSA Public key/Private key encryption

- Bob then encrypts these blocks as $C_i = M_i{}^e \bmod N$ and sends the encrypted blocks to Bob.

Alice decrypts the encrypted message blocks as follows:

- Alice decrypts each C_i to recover M_i using her private key d by calculating $M_i = C_i{}^d \bmod N$
- Alice then converts the string of integer codes, M_i, back into their equivalent characters to recover the plaintext form of the message Bob has sent her.

Example

Suppose Alice chooses primes p = 7 and q = 11. So N = 77, (p − 1)(q − 1) = 60 and she chooses e = 7, since 7 and 60 are relatively prime.

Alice then calculates her private key using ed = 1 (mod (p -1)(q - 1) to be d = 43, since 43 x 7 = 301 = 1 mod 60

Hence Alice's public key is the pair (N, e) = (77, 7) and her private key is d = 43.

If Bob wants to send the plaintext message M = 4 to Alice he encrypts it as ciphertext C = M^e mod 77 = 4^7 mod 77 = 16384 mod 77= 60 (mod 77).

(Use Windows calculator in Scientific mode for the mod operation)

Alice then decrypts C using her private key to recover the message

$$M = C^d \bmod 77 = 60^{43} \bmod 77 = 4 \;(\bmod\; 77)$$

Background

Public key/private key encryption schemes rely on the discrete logarithm problem to make it difficult to discover the private key. A very simple example that illustrates this problem is as follows:

To encrypt integer 19 raise it to the power 43 and then find the remainder after dividing by 77, the result is the encrypted value 61

$$19^{43} \bmod 77 = 61$$

To recover the unencrypted value 19, an exponent must be found for which

$$61^d \bmod 77 = 19$$

If we try d = 1, 2, 3, 4, 5, 6, 7 we find that 7 does.

Thus, $\qquad 61^7 \bmod 77 = (19^{43})^7 \bmod 77 = 19^{43 \times 7} \bmod 77 = 19$

by replacing 61 by (19^{43}).

Now suppose, we encrypt 2137 by raising it to the power of 17 and finding the remainder after division by 3233, the result is the encrypted value of 2137

$$2137^{17} \bmod 3233 = 166$$

To recover the unencrypted value 2137, an exponent d must be found for which

$$166^d \bmod 3233 = 2137$$

If we try d = 1, 2, 3, ..., 2753 we find that 2753 does.

Now suppose we use exponent 65537 and a 2048-bit modulus such as the one shown in the information panel on next page labelled Public modulus. We would find that d would be the 2048-bit value labelled Private exponent in the information panel. Using the public exponent 65537 and the public modulus in the margin we could encrypt integers up to 256 digits long. To decrypt we would use the private exponent shown in the margin and the same public modulus. The public key is (public exponent, public modulus) and the private key is (private exponent).

The discrete logarithm problem is the difficulty with which the private exponent can be discovered given only the public exponent, the public modulus and the result from encryption. The last example illustrates that this becomes an exceedingly difficult task when the number of bits used for the public key and the private key is a large number.

Tasks

The discrete logarithm problem:

This is the problem of finding x where

$$a^x \equiv b \pmod{n}$$

Watch the Khan Academy video "The discrete logarithm problem"

https://www.khanacademy.org/computing/computer-science/cryptography/modern-crypt/v/discrete-logarithm-problem

RSA encryption:

Watch the Khan Academy video "RSA encryption part 1"

https://www.khanacademy.org/computing/computer-science/cryptography/modern-crypt/v/intro-to-rsa-encryption

Questions

 Two computers, X and Y, communicate securely using public/private key encryption. X and Y each has a public key and a private key. X encrypts a message that it sends to Y using Y's public key. Explain why the message should not be encrypted with:

(a)   X's private key

(b)   X's public key

Task

Explore the Wolfram programming lab:

The Wolfram programming language is a useful language with which to explore encryption, factoring, modular arithmetic and a lot of other concepts.

https://lab.wolframcloud.com/app/

Key exchange

Diffie-Hellman key exchange

Diffie-Hellman exponential key agreement or key exchange provides a way for Alice and Bob to agree on a key *k* while communicating over an insecure network channel. The key *k* is used only for one communication session. It is then discarded. Hence the name session key.

A modulus N is made available publicly for network users to use to secure their communications.

Alice privately selects a large random number s_A, and calculates

$$p_A = 2^{s_A} \pmod{N}.$$

Alice's private key is s_A. Alice sends p_A to Bob.

An eavesdropper, Eve, who intercepts p_A will find it extremely difficult to discover Alice's private key s_A from a knowledge of $2^{s_A} \pmod{N}$.

Bob also privately chooses a large random number s_B and calculates
$p_B = 2^{s_B} \pmod{N}$. Bob sends p_B to Alice.

Information

Public exponent:

65537

Public modulus:

2945766458199006354518714370
7899373134590389698365517414
7436531255410052428401668999
1569699787388856353829206878
9960515720869761675361593675
0142684142154547677777091183
0025184723218753394504845305
8775378412564817224035219475
4009164712998755052650119170
0526487333570141735966271760
9983903002107163226848818840
0158224961738996272694978348
3911617160808460658137438912
5352226641602068091100881754
2406869405300299433220109635
6829801571379647912703834109
7645087806299949060364755202
6457247820594217256398577789
2068763898076972147981555129
2545752837433987680744224926
6349409655365479329715297233
8693514772681326828715360798
3,

Private Exponent:

1867954933393873782460117671
2588036509564176191840855893
9517636845023894270709928136
2736371572765095935920688763
2530923178172720077279660496
3035074348530733667898444472
3319447437745471314964559885
5861378703165672432312367837
3851608513401624463708037482
1711090843470222168596156702
9856585454957802300706215013
4902084633057718998128856073
0634048021082866988921193324
8345789361959152473636354183
1163718788584849254198077263
3601888977561074349848200284
5117747384513278257497790608
7498040258768855234664650244
7343908134657726546395530654
5636669349253657671182525663
8729925941579363805926939935
4303032695385463103575787950
5

Alice has her private key s_A and Bob's public key p_B.

Bob has his private key s_A and Alice's public key p_A.

Bob and Alice can now calculate their shared secret key, k.

Alice uses her private key s_A to calculate $k_A = p_B{}^{s_A} = (2^{s_B} \pmod N)^{s_A} \bmod N$

Bob uses his private key s_B to calculate $k_B = p_A{}^{s_B} = (2^{s_A} \pmod N)^{s_B} \bmod N$

But $(2^{s_B} \pmod N)^{s_A} = (2^{s_A} \pmod N)^{s_B}$, therefore $k_A = k_B = k$, the shared secret key.

The shared secret key k may now be used for symmetric encryption of messages between Alice and Bob.

SSH

SSH, or secure shell, is a secure protocol and the most common way of safely administering remote servers. Symmetric keys or shared secret keys are used by SSH in order to encrypt the entire connection between client and server.

The secret key is created through a process known as key exchange. This exchange results in the server and client both arriving at the same key independently by a process similar to that described in the previous section.

The symmetric encryption key created by this procedure is session-based and is the key used to encrypt the data sent between server and client, e.g. credit card details.

SSH utilizes asymmetric encryption during the initial key exchange process used to set up the symmetrical encryption key used to encrypt the session between two parties. The two parties exchange public keys (see p_A and p_B in previous section) in order to produce the shared secret key k used for symmetrical encryption.

Task

Diffie-Hellman key exchange:
Watch the Khan Academy video "Public key encryption: What is it?"

https://www.khanacademy.org/computing/computer-science/cryptography/modern-crypt/v/diffie-hellman-key-exchange-part-1

Question

3 Describe **two** different methods for communicating a shared secret symmetric encryption key k via an insecure network channel.

Digital certificate

When a website is visited that supports the Secure HyperText Transfer Protocol HTTPS, e.g. https://www.google.co.uk, the identity of the website is "proved" with public key encryption. It is important that the authenticity of the website is checked, i.e. that it really is the genuine site and not a man-in-the-middle attacker placed between a visitor and a website, impersonating both.

With a man-in-the-middle attack, the browser thinks it is talking to the web site on an encrypted channel, and the website thinks it is talking to the browser, but they are both talking to the attacker who is sitting in the middle. All traffic passes through this man-in-the-middle, who is able to read and modify any of the data.

Operating systems and browsers typically have a list of certificate authorities that they implicitly trust. If a website

Figure 9.3.2.8 Digital certificate warning that web site authenticity cannot be guaranteed

presents a certificate that is signed by an untrusted certificate authority, the browser warns the visitor that something could be amiss - *Figure 9.3.2.8*. Certificates are files containing information about the owner of a website, and the public half of an asymmetric key pair (e.g. RSA). A certificate authority (CA) digitally signs the certificate to verify that the information in the certificate is correct. By trusting the certificate, you are trusting that the certificate authority has done its due diligence.

A website that supports HTTPS should have a certificate and a corresponding public key. This will enable a connection to be made between a web browser and the website using the Transport Layer Security (TLS) protocol. The browser must also support the TLS protocol.

When a web browser uses HTTPS to visit a website such as https://www.google.co.uk, a TLS connection is established between the web browser and the website. TLS is used to encrypt data sent between both and to prove the identity of the server.

Question

 (a) What is a digital certificate?

(b) Explain how it is used to authenticate a website that supports HTTPS.

Authentication

The web browser starts the TLS connection by telling the website which ciphersuites it supports i.e. it tells the website which types of encryption it is able to use. The website https://cc.dcsec.uni-hannover.de/ will report what ciphersuites your browser supports, e.g. **ECDHE-RSA-AES256-SHA** which means Elliptic Curve Diffie-Hellman Exchange which is used to share a symmetric key, RSA for authentication, **AES256** is the symmetric encryption algorithm to use and SHA is the hash function used to create a message digest.

The web browser generates a 128-bit random number called a nonce which it sends to the website. The website encrypts this nonce using its RSA private key and sends the encrypted nonce to the web browser. The web browser decrypts this encrypted nonce using the trusted-certificate-authority-validated public key belonging to the website. A match confirms that the website knew the private key half of the public key/private key pair and therefore is authentic. The same nonce is never used twice to prevent a bogus site replaying the encrypted nonce which it had intercepted and recorded on a previous occasion.

Digital signature

A digital signature is a cryptographic technique that can be used in a digital world when you want

- to indicate that you are the owner or creator of a document, or
- to affirm that you agree with a document's content.

For Bob to know that a document genuinely came from Alice, he needs some way to authenticate the document. This is what Alice does to make this possible:

- Alice digitally signs the document with her private key s_A using a public key/private key encryption algorithm as shown in *Figure 9.3.2.9* to produce Enc(M), the digital signature

- Alice then sends Enc(M), the encrypted form of M to Bob

- Bob decrypts Enc(M) using Alice's public key p_A as shown in *Figure 9.3.2.10* and recovers the document M from Alice.

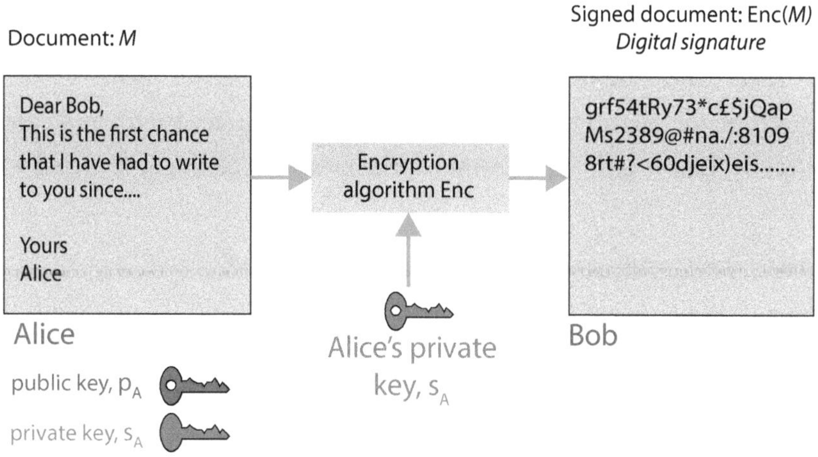

Does the digital signature Enc(M) meet the requirements of being verifiable and unforgeable?

Yes, because applying Alice's public key to the digital signature, Enc(M) recovers the original document, M. Alice's public key and private key are associated mathematically. If document M had been signed with a private key different from Alice's then applying Alice's public key to Enc(M) would not have recovered M.

The only person who could have signed M is therefore Alice because she is the person who generated the pair of keys (p_A, s_A). This assumes that Alice has not given away her private key or had it stolen.

Also, if Alice or anyone else should alter the original document from M to M_1, the signature that Alice created for M will not be valid for M_1 because Dec(Enc(M)) does not equal M_1. Thus digital signatures also provide message/document integrity, allowing the receiver

- to verify that the message/document was not tampered with in transit

- to verify that the original document has not been tampered with at source.

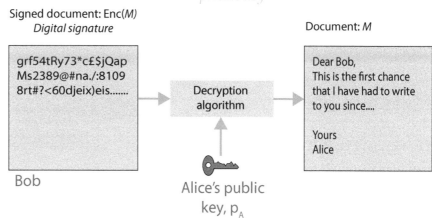

Document: *M*

Dear Bob,
This is the first chance that I have had to write to you since....

Yours
Alice

Alice

public key, p_A
private key, s_A

Encryption algorithm Enc

Alice's private key, s_A

Signed document: Enc(*M*)
Digital signature

grf54tRy73*c£$jQap
Ms2389@#na./:8109
8rt#?<60djeix)eis.......

Bob

Figure 9.3.2.9 Digital signing of Alice's document with Alice's private key

Signed document: Enc(*M*)
Digital signature

grf54tRy73*c£$jQap
Ms2389@#na./:8109
8rt#?<60djeix)eis.......

Bob

Decryption algorithm

Alice's public key, p_A

Document: *M*

Dear Bob,
This is the first chance that I have had to write to you since....

Yours
Alice

Figure 9.3.2.10 Bob verifies that the document came from Alice by decrypting the encrypted document using Alice's public key

Key term

Digital signature:

A digital signature is a cryptographic technique that can be used in a digital world when you want

- to indicate that you are the owner or creator of a document, or
- to affirm that you agree with a document's content or
- to verify that the message/document was not tampered with in transit or
- to verify that the original document has not been tampered with at source.

Message digest

Encryption and decryption are computationally intensive. Digitally signing a document by encrypting the whole document is therefore expensive computationally.

To reduce the computation overhead a hash function H is used.

This function takes a message/document M, of arbitrary length and computes H(M), a fixed-length "fingerprint" of the message/document M called a message digest.

Alice now digitally signs the message digest rather than the message/document itself to create a digital signature.

As H(M) is generally of much shorter length than the original message/document M, creating the digital signature consumes much less computational effort.

Alice now sends the document M followed by the digital signature to Bob as shown in Figure 9.3.2.11.

On receipt of M, Bob uses the hashing function H to produce a hash of document M as shown in Figure 9.3.2.12.

On receipt of the digital signature, Bob decrypts it using Alice's public key p_A to obtain the message digest or hash produced by Alice if she genuinely signed the document. If the two hashes match then Bob can conclude that Alice was the signer of the document and that the document has not been tampered with whilst in transit.

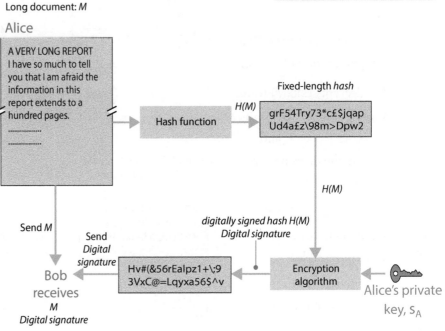

Figure 9.3.2.11 Using Alice's private key to create a digital signature from the hash of document M

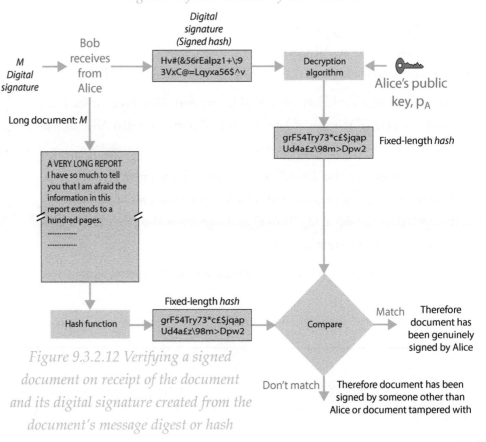

Figure 9.3.2.12 Verifying a signed document on receipt of the document and its digital signature created from the document's message digest or hash

Question

5 (a) What is a digital signature?

(b) Explain how it is used to authenticate the author of an electronic document.

(c) Explain how a digital signature can be used

(i) to discover that a digitally signed electronic document has been tampered with

(ii) to challenge the author when they say that they did not sign to say that they agree with its contents.

6 Explain how signing a long electronic document or message with a digital signature might differ from signing a short document or message.

7 Two computers, X and Y, communicate securely using public/private key encryption. X and Y each have a public key, a private key, and a hash function H that generates a message digest of a plaintext message of arbitrary length. Computer X sends a plaintext message and a digital signature in encrypted form to Computer Y as shown in *Figure 9.3.2.13*. Computer Y processes the received transmission as shown in *Figure 9.3.2.13*.

State what processing takes place at each of the stages indicated by a ringed numeral. Where a key is used, specify which key.

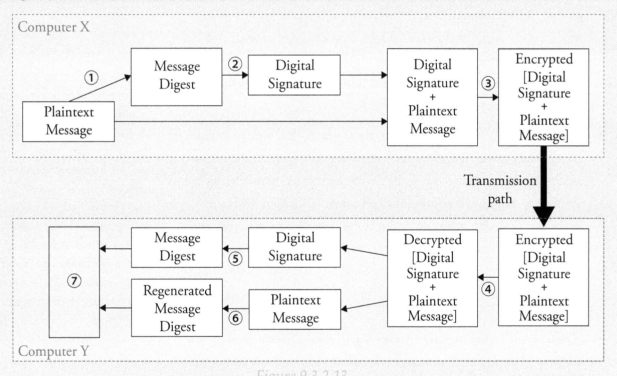

Figure 9.3.2.13

Worms, Trojans and viruses

The devices that we connect to the Internet enable us to do useful things such as exchange email messages, obtain search engine results, view Web pages and so on. However, our devices may be subject to infection by malicious software (malware) which can do all sorts of harmful things such as delete files, take control of our devices, install spyware that can steal private information such as passwords, debit and credit card details. Examples of types of malware are worms, Trojans and viruses. Worms and viruses are self-replicating and are thus able to spread from one computer to another.

Worms

Worms are malicious software that can enter a computer from the Internet without any explicit user interaction by exploiting a vulnerability in a running network application program, e.g. the Conficker computer worm that targeted flaws in Windows OS software to propagate. The worm in the newly infected computer scans the Internet, searching for other hosts running the same vulnerable network application. On discovering other vulnerable hosts, it sends a copy of itself to those hosts.

Unlike a computer virus, a worm does not need to attach itself to an existing program or file because they are self-contained programs. Worms are one way of installing a backdoor in the infected computer to allow the creation of a "zombie" computer under control of the worm author. Networks of such machines are often referred to as botnets and are very common use is the sending of junk email called spam.

Trojans

A Trojan horse or Trojan is a type of malicious software that is often disguised as legitimate software. Users are typically tricked into loading and executing Trojans on their systems. Once activated, Trojans can enable cybercriminals to spy on you, steal your sensitive data, and gain backdoor access to your system. Unlike computer viruses and worms, Trojans are not able to self-replicate.

Trojans are classified according to the type of actions that they can perform on the infected computer. A selection is shown below.

- A Backdoor Trojan enables remote control over the infected computer by a cybercriminal or hacker to do anything they wish on the infected computer – including sending, receiving, launching, and deleting files, displaying data, and rebooting the computer. Backdoor Trojans are often used to link a group of victim computers to form a botnet or zombie network that can be used for criminal purposes

- Trojan-Banker programs are designed to steal account data for online banking systems, e-payment systems, and credit or debit cards from infected computers

- Trojan DDoS are programs that conduct DDoS (Distributed Denial of Service) attacks against a targeted web address. They send multiple requests from your computer and several other infected computers that attack and overwhelm the target address leading to a denial of service at the target address computer, typically a server

- Trojan-Downloaders can download and install new versions of malicious programs onto your computer – including Trojans and adware

- Trojan-Ransom can modify data on your computer – so that your computer doesn't run correctly or you can no longer use specific data. The criminal will only restore your computer's performance or unblock your data, after you have paid them the ransom money that they demand

- Trojan-Mailfinder is a program that can harvest email addresses from your computer.

Key term

Worm:

A computer worm is a self-contained program that attacks a system and tries to exploit a specific vulnerability in the target. It replicates itself in order to spread to other computers. Unlike a computer virus, it does not need to attach itself to an existing program or file but instead it exploits vulnerabilities in network application software running on the infected host. The aim of a worm is often to take over a computer for the purposes of creating a botnet for sending spam and Distributed Denial of Service (DDoS) attacks.

Key term

Trojan:

A Trojan horse or Trojan is a type of malicious software that is often disguised as legitimate software. Unlike computer viruses and worms, Trojans are not able to self-replicate.

Users are typically tricked into loading and executing Trojans on their systems. Once activated, Trojans can enable cyber-criminals to spy on you, steal your sensitive data, and gain backdoor access to your system.

Viruses

A virus is malicious software attached to another file which infects and harms a user's computer when the user is tricked into opening the file, e.g. an email attachment containing the virus' executable code. Opening such an attachment inadvertently runs the malware on their computer. Once executed, the virus is able to replicate and then spread by sending an identical email with the same malicious attachment to, for example, every recipient in the user's address book.

Viruses piggy-back on seemingly legitimate files but they require some form of user interaction to infect the user's computer.

Key term

Virus:
A computer virus is malicious software that requires some form of user interaction to infect a user's computer because the user needs to be tricked into opening the file to which the virus is attached. Viruses are not stand-alone programs but are always embedded in another program or file. Once the virus is executed it can replicate and infect other computers.

Question

 8 Explain the differences between worm, virus and Trojan malware.

Code quality

One way of securing computers against malicious attacks is to improve the quality of the code, from operating systems to application programs, which executes on computers. Attackers exploit vulnerabilities in code in order to get a computer to execute their malicious software.

For example, the command shell in the Windows operating system is a separate software program, CMD. exe, that executes programs and displays their output as individual characters on the screen. It is known to have vulnerabilities.

For instance, one of the commands it can execute is the echo command which is shown in *Figure 9.3.2.14* being used once to output the string "Hello World" and once to output the name of the current directory stored in the environment variable %CD%. On the second occasion, a new directory has been created beforehand using

```
C:\Windows\system32\cmd.exe

C:\>cd test

C:\test>echo "Hello World"
"Hello World"

C:\test>echo %CD%
C:\test

C:\test>md "NewTest&ping 8.8.8.8"

C:\test>dir
 Volume in drive C is WINDOWS
 Volume Serial Number is 20F0-B3D7

 Directory of C:\test

24/01/2016  15:54    <DIR>          .
24/01/2016  15:54    <DIR>          ..
24/01/2016  15:54    <DIR>          NewTest&ping 8.8.8.8
               0 File(s)              0 bytes
               3 Dir(s)  1,756,534,038,528 bytes free

C:\test>cd "Newtest&ping 8.8.8.8"

C:\test\NewTest&ping 8.8.8.8>echo %CD%
C:\test\NewTest

Pinging 8.8.8.8 with 32 bytes of data:
Reply from 8.8.8.8: bytes=32 time=27ms TTL=54
Reply from 8.8.8.8: bytes=32 time=27ms TTL=54
Reply from 8.8.8.8: bytes=32 time=27ms TTL=54
Reply from 8.8.8.8: bytes=32 time=27ms TTL=54

Ping statistics for 8.8.8.8:
    Packets: Sent = 4, Received = 4, Lost = 0 (0% loss),
Approximate round trip times in milli-seconds:
    Minimum = 27ms, Maximum = 27ms, Average = 27ms

C:\test\NewTest&ping 8.8.8.8>
```

Figure 9.3.2.14 Exploiting a vulnerability in cmd.exe, the command line interpreter in the Windows operating system to run the ping program

the command md "NewTest&ping 8.8.8.8" and made the current directory. The command shell program CMD. exe is tricked into executing ping 8.8.8.8 because & is interpreted by the command shell as the separator of multiple commands on one command line. CMD.exe runs the first command echo c:\test\NewTest1, and then the second command, ping 8.8.8.8 because NewTest is separated by & from ping 8.8.8.8 in %CD%.

Figure 9.3.2.15 shows the same exploit causing calc.exe to execute. A third example could replace calc.exe with malware.exe.

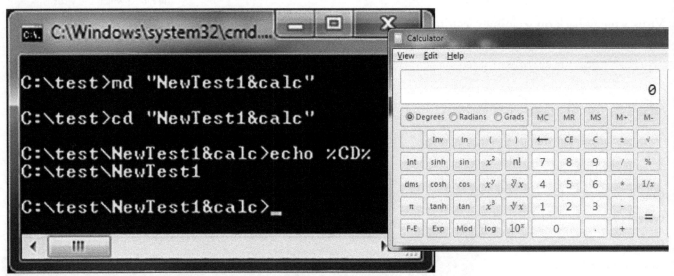

Figure 9.3.2.15 Exploiting a vunerability in cmd.exe, the command line interpreter in the Windows operating system to run Windows calculator calc.exe

CMD.exe can also execute batch files. There are batch files in systems that have been running for years which contain echo %CD% commands probably with a pipe, e.g. echo %CD% > logfile.txt.

If Microsoft's recommended fix to change echo %CD% to echo "%CD%" has not been done then running any batch file that has not been fixed could allow malware to execute.

The contents of environment variable %CD% can be changed with the SET command outside of the batch file containing echo %CD%,

e.g. SET CD=c:\test\NewTest&malware. If this is the value of %CD% when the batch file is executed the malware program will be executed.

Buffer overflow

A common vulnerability exploited by worms and viruses is buffer overflow. The Stuxnet worm used buffer overflow and some other techniques. It was widely suspected of targeting Iran's nuclear enrichment programme and may have destroyed 1,000 centrifuges, reduced output and sowed chaos.

Another way that malicious code can be executed is to place this code in the buffer that is being caused to overflow and to overwrite the return address so it points back into the buffer.

Patching or updating software is usually an effective way to remove vulnerabilities to worms and viruses. Coding to standards that avoid creating code vulnerabilities in the first place is a better way.

Background

Figure 9.3.2.16 shows a simplified case of how buffer overflow can occur when a call is made to a library routine **input(Password)** that reads keyboard input from a user one character at a time. The routine copies each character's byte-value, in turn, into the memory reserved in the stack frame for the call to **IsPasswordValid()** labelled **Password** (the stack frames for the calls to **input** and **stringCompare** are not shown). Seven bytes have been allocated in this current stack frame to **Password** according to the declaration **"chararray[7] Password;"** in the program source code. These seven bytes constitute a buffer. *Figure 9.3.2.16* shows the result of the user typing password **"1234567"** and then on another attempt to login, password **"123456789ABCDEF"**.

Notice that the library routine **input** stores the first character of the password in the byte pointed to by **Top of Stack Pointer**, the next in the byte above and so on. Notice also that the longer password overwrites the **Previous Stack Frame Pointer** and the **Return Address** areas of the stack frame. This is because the library routine **input (Password)** does not apply array bounds checking when the 8th byte and subsequent bytes are written to **Password**. Buffer overflow occurs and the return address is corrupted. This return address is used to return to the routine **main** but this will not happen because the return address now points to somewhere else in the memory of the computer. It is likely that this will cause an exception (*Figure 9.3.2.17*). Now suppose the **15** character password is chosen so that the return address on the stack is overwritten with the address of the **else output ("Access allowed");** line of code. The result will be that the user will be granted access to the system.

In a different scenario, buffer overflow could replace the return address on the stack with the address of the malicious code of a worm or a virus.

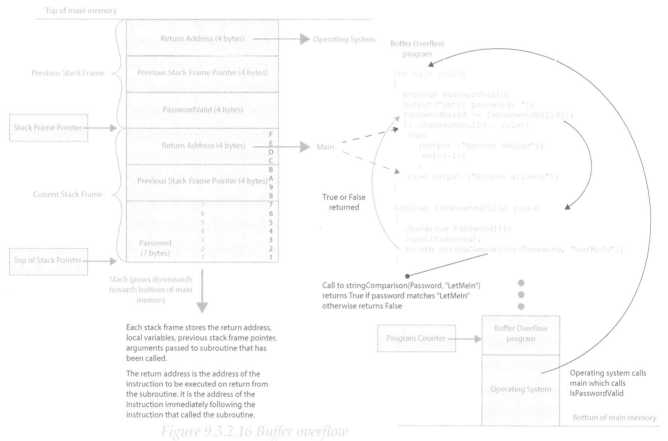

Figure 9.3.2.16 Buffer overflow

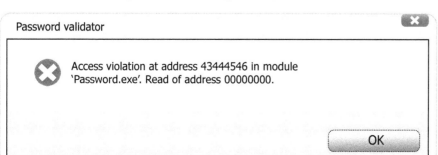

Figure 9.3.2.17 Exception caused by Buffer overflow

Monitoring and protection

Firewalls are designed to monitor packets and offer protection against attempts to exploit weaknesses in the TCP/IP protocol suite which worms and Trojans can exploit.

Digital certificates enable HTTP and FTP to be reliably secured against attacks. Digital certificates also offer protection against downloading and installing malicious software by validating that the software is from a trusted source. Downloading from untrusted sources has the potential to install a Trojan.

Anti-virus and anti-malware software are designed to monitor and protect against attempts to exploit weaknesses in operating systems by hooking deep into the operating system's core or kernel and function.

Any time the operating system accesses a file, the protection software scans the file to check it is a 'legitimate' file or not. If the file is identified as malware by the virus/malware scanner, the access operation will be stopped, the file will be dealt with by the scanner in a predefined way and the issue reported to the user. The goal of the anti-virus and anti-malware software is to stop any malicious operations on the system before they can occur. Anti-virus and anti-malware software should be kept up-to-date as new threats emerge on a regular basis.

Some viruses infect files such as MS-Word documents and MS-Excel spreadsheets because the applications allow strings of program commands called "macros" to be stored in document and spreadsheet files. Clicking on the document or spreadsheet file launches the corresponding application which will run the malicious commands/code/script unless users have disabled execution of macros in these applications.

Information

CERT:

CERT was founded in November 1988 in response to the Morris worm incident, which brought 10 percent of Internet systems to a halt in November 1988. Since 1988, CERT has handled more than 300, 000 computer security incidents.

CERT conducts secure coding research and eliminate vulnerabilities in software caused by quality of coding.

Analysis indicates that the majority of incidents are caused by Trojans, social engineering, and the exploitation of software vulnerabilities, including software defects, design decisions, configuration decisions, and unexpected interactions among systems, e.g. print spooler exploit in Windows - https://www.youtube.com/watch?v=Fy0S9KMNjnY which was also implicated in the Stuxnet worm.

Information

Social Engineering:

This is when attackers set out to gain the trust of a user so that they can steal user information or dupe them into downloading malicious software.

Attackers exploit the lack of knowledge of many users about how technology functions in order to launch their attacks, e.g. a Trojan attack.

Non-technical users can avoid social engineering attacks by following some simple guidelines which are intended to offer some protection against such attacks, for example:

- Never open email attachments unless they are from a trusted source.
- Pay heed to warnings that state that the website or software you are about to download does not have a valid certificate.
- Disable macros in applications that allow them.

General guidelines:

- Always make sure updates are installed for both operating system and application code.
- Keep anti-virus and anti-malware software up-to-date.
- Use a firewall.
- Run a security check on your system using Microsoft Baseline Security Analyser.

Questions

9　Worms, viruses and trojans exploit vulnerabilities in computer systems. Describe **one** vulnerability that is exploited by a

(a) worm　　　　　　　　(b) virus　　　　　　　　(c) Trojan.

10　How might the quality of operating system and application code affect whether a system is vulnerable to worms, viruses and Trojans?

11　How can monitoring and protection be used to prevent worms, viruses and Trojans from infecting systems?

In this chapter you have covered:

■　How a firewall works by packet filtering, proxy server, and stateful inspection

■　Symmetric and asymmetric (private/public key) encryption and key exchange

■　How digital certificates and digital signatures are obtained and used

■　Worms, Trojans and viruses, and the vulnerabilities that they exploit

■　How improved code quality, monitoring and protection can be used to address worms, trojans and viruses.

9.4 The Transmission Control Protocol/ Internet Protocol (TCP/IP) protocol

■ 9.4.1 TCP/IP

The role of the four layers of TCP/IP protocol stack

Networking protocols were designed to make possible communication between application programs executing on different hosts whilst hiding the complexities of the underlying network from these application programs.

A host, or host computer, is any computer system that connects to an internet and runs applications.

The term process is used for an instance of a program in execution, so it is actually processes in different hosts connected by a network that are communicating.

Layered organisation

Networking protocols are usually developed in layers.

Each layer is responsible for a different part of the communication process. The software that implements a protocol is called protocol software and the software that implements a suite of protocols such as TCP/IP, a protocol stack. The TCP/IP protocol suite consists of four conceptual layers: application, transport, network or IP (Internet layer), and link layers (*Figure 9.4.1.1*). It is implemented in software as the TCP/IP protocol stack in separate software modules corresponding to the individual layers of the protocol suite.

Each layer and therefore each software module has a different responsibility. The protocol stack is installed on each computer either as a part of the operating system or as a software library.

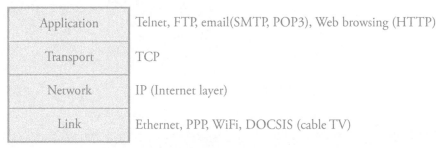

Application	Telnet, FTP, email(SMTP, POP3), Web browsing (HTTP)
Transport	TCP
Network	IP (Internet layer)
Link	Ethernet, PPP, WiFi, DOCSIS (cable TV)

Figure 9.4.1.1 The four layers of the TCP/IP protocol suite and stack

Application programs interact with the software stack via an Application Programming Interface (API). The de facto standard is the socket API.

The following Python code snippet shows a client application using the socket API to set up a socket to send a message to a server:

```
clientSocket = socket(socket.AF_INET, socket.SOCK_STREAM)
message = "Hello Server"
clientSocket.sendTo(message, (serverName, serverPort))
```

420

Key term

Application layer:

Application layer protocols are used to exchange data between programs running on the source and destination hosts. It is the application layer that provides the interface between these programs and the underlying network over which the programs' messages are transmitted, e.g. HTTP message GET / which fetches the default Web page from a Web server.

Key term

Transmission Control Protocol (TCP):

TCP enables applications executing on two hosts to establish a connection and exchange application-layer messages through a reliable byte-stream channel (pipe) for data flows between the two end systems.

Key term

Function of Transport layer:

The basic function of the transport layer is

- to accept messages/data from the layer above it
- split these into smaller units called segments if necessary
- pass these segments to the network or IP layer
- ensure that all the segments arrive correctly at the other end
- reassemble the received segments, which it gets from the network layer, in the correct order to form the message/data to pass to the layer above.

The transport layer is a true end-to-end layer which carries messages/data all the way from the source to the destination.

Figure 9.4.1.2 shows a client process and a server process that use the socket API from the TCP/IP protocol stack to send and receive messages via a TCP/IP connection pipe established between client and server.

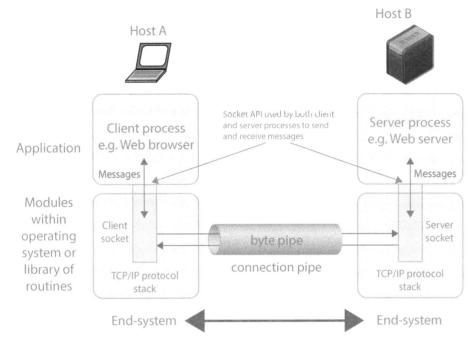

Figure 9.4.1.2 Sending and receiving messages using the socket API

Application layer

A process in one end-system (host) uses the application layer of TCP/IP to exchange packets of information with a process in another end-system. The packets of information at the application layer are called messages.

The application layer uses different application-layer protocols for different applications. For example, if the application is designed to enable Web pages to be fetched from a Web server then the application will use either the HTTP application-layer protocol or the HTTPS application-layer protocol. An application-layer protocol defines the kind of messages to send. In the case of HTTP or HTTPS, one such message could be a GET message.

Transport layer

The transport layer of the protocol stack is a piece of software in each host. This software implements the transport protocol known by the name Transmission Control Protocol (TCP). TCP enables applications executing on two hosts to establish a two-way connection and exchange application-layer messages through a reliable byte-stream channel (pipe) for data flows in either direction between the two end-systems as shown in *Figure 9.4.1.2*. It also allows the connection to be terminated.

TCP breaks long messages into shorter segments which it sends as separate transport-layer packets known as TCP segments.

The application at the sending side (e.g. a Web browser using the application-layer protocol HTTP) pushes messages (e.g. GET) through a TCP/IP socket.

The transport-layer protocol TCP has the responsibility of getting the messages to the socket of the receiving application process, e.g. a Web server listening on port 80. Port numbers such as port 80 are 16-bit numbers used for application and service identification on the Internet.

TCP does everything in its control to guarantee delivery of the application-layer message and also guarantee that the received TCP segments will be reassembled in the correct order to form the message to be passed to the application-layer and then the corresponding application process.

Once the TCP has established a connection:

- it monitors the connection for transmission errors and responds when an error is detected by retransmitting the segment that suffered the error

- it detects when a connection is broken

- it performs flow control by speed matching sender and receiver

- it provides congestion control when the network is congested.

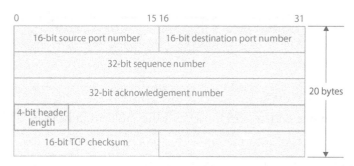

Figure 9.4.1.3 TCP header

The format of a TCP segment is covered in *Chapter 9.3.1 (Figure 9.3.1.10)*. The header part of a TCP segment contains the source and destination port numbers as shown in *Figure 9.4.1.3*. Port numbers bind to sockets so that the TCP layer can identify the application that data is destined for.

Network or IP layer

The TCP layer uses the IP layer to carry its segments. Each TCP segment is encapsulated in an IP packet before it is sent across the internet. The network or IP layer in hosts and routers move these packets known as IP or Internet Protocol packets from one host to another without regard to whether these hosts belong to the same network or different networks. The Internet Protocol is a connectionless protocol which just provides a best effort but not guaranteed way of delivering packets called datagrams. The reliability of the transmission is left to the layer above, the transport layer.

Getting to the destination host may require many hops via intermediate routers along the way.

Both routers and hosts are assigned IP addresses by which they may be identified. An IP address (Internet Protocol address) is a logical 32-bit (IPv4) or 128-bit quantity (IPv6). The IP layer in the sending host attaches the source (sending host) and destination (receiving host) IP addresses to the packets handed to it from the transport layer. The IP layer then passes these packets to the layer below, the link layer. The IP layer also receives packets from the link layer, removes the source and destination IP addresses then passes them to the transport layer.

The format of an IP packet is universal so that all routers recognise it (see Chapter 9.3.1). This makes it possible for IP packets to pass through almost every network of networks, e.g. the Internet.

Both hosts and routers need to use the network or IP layer of the TCP/IP protocol stack but since the job of a router is dedicated to routing packets, a router only requires use of the network and link layers of the TCP/IP stack. The IP layer in a router must have sufficient knowledge of other routers and links in its internet to be able to make routing decisions for packets that pass through it.

Together TCP and IP hide the differences between the underlying networks through which packets pass when going from source to destination host.

Link layer

The link layer handles all the physical details of interfacing with the network cable or wireless connection. It includes the network interface card (network adapter) and a device driver. TCP/IP protocol supports many different types of link layer, depending on the type of networking hardware being used. One example is Ethernet.

The link layer adds source and destination hardware addresses (e.g. MAC addresses) to packets that it receives from the IP layer then dispatches the packets onto the local cable or wireless connection.

If the packet is destined for a host on another network, the link layer destination address is the hardware address of the gateway (router) to the internet which the other network is connected to.

Key term

Link layer:
The link layer handles all the physical details of interfacing with the network cable or wireless connection.
The link layer adds source and destination hardware addresses (e.g. MAC addresses) to packets that it receives from the IP layer then despatches the packets onto the local cable or wireless connection.

In an Ethernet local area network (LAN) these hardware addresses are Ethernet card addresses, or MAC addresses - see the following section on MAC addresses. Figure 9.4.1.4 shows a packet despatched by the link layer of a host with IP address 174.89.0.54 to a remote host with IP address 210.5.0.67. Figure 9.4.1.4 shows the first, second and last hop of many hops.

Note that the link layer hardware address changes from hop to hop whilst the source and destination IP addresses remain constant. This is because the link layer's role is to stream bytes between directly connected machines, hosts and routers. It is the link layer that puts bits onto the network cable or wireless connection. Sending to a remote machine is done in hops where each hop is a direct connection (link) between a host and a router, a router and a host, a router and another router, or two directly connected hosts.

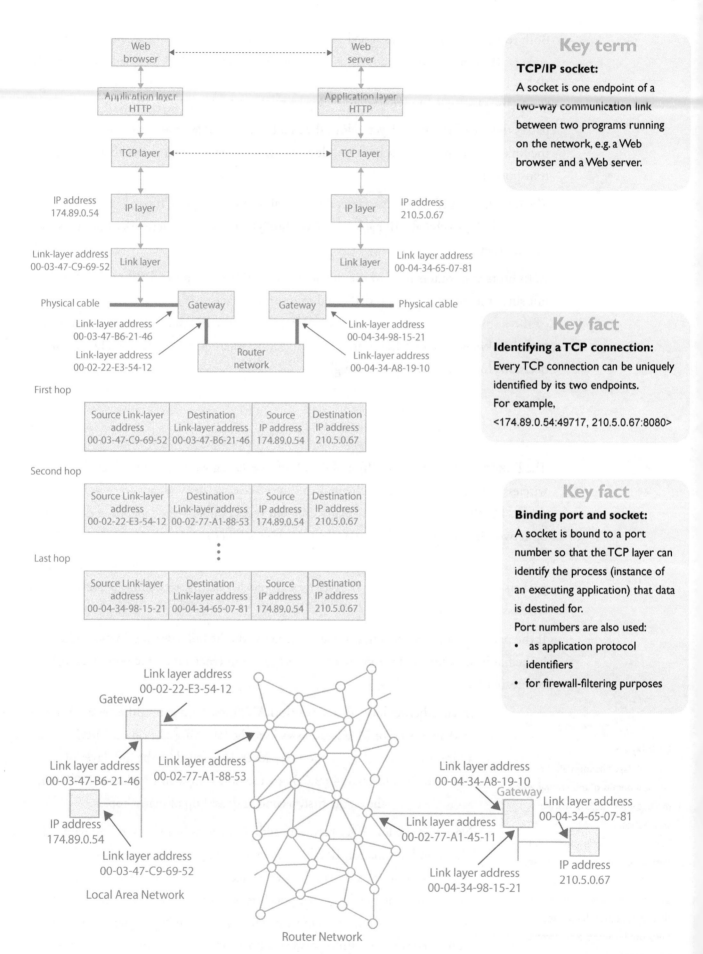

Figure 9.4.1.4 TCP/IP protocol stack and the role of the link layer in the communicating hosts and intermediate routers

Questions

1. Describe three tasks performed by the transport layer of the TCP/IP protocol stack.

2. Name one application-layer protocol.

3. Explain why the source and destination IP addresses of a packet remain the same whilst link layer addresses need to change when a packet is sent from a host to a server on a different network.

4. Describe the role of the different layers of the TCP/IP stack in each of the host, the server, and intervening routers when a Web browser running on a host uses the TCP/IP protocol stack to send an HTTP GET message to a Web server running on a different network.

The role of sockets in TCP/IP

A socket is one endpoint of a two-way communication link between two programs running on the network, e.g. a Web browser and a Web server. A socket is bound to a port number so that the TCP layer can identify the executing application that data is destined for.

> An endpoint is a combination of an IP address and a port number.

Every TCP connection can be uniquely identified by its two endpoints. This fact allows multiple connections to exist between a host and a server as shown in Figure 9.4.1.5.

A socket is created as a two-way resource (capable of both sending and receiving), even if it is only used in one direction by program code.

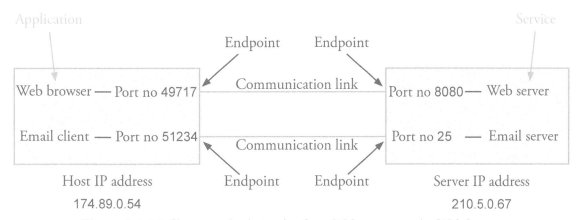

Figure 9.4.1.5 Shows endpoint pairs for a Web server and a Web browser, an email client and an email server

A procedure called *bind*, performed on the client side and the server side, tells the operating system which local IP address/port no pair to associate with the socket before a connection is established (on the client side the bind procedure may be called as part of the connect operation). On the server side, the bind procedure establishes the IP address/port no pair that the server listens on to accept client connections.

Figure 9.4.1.6 shows an HTTP server listening on port 8080 for connection requests from client hosts. The client shown is called *localhost*. It has IP address 127.0.0.1 (known as the *loopback IP address*). A TCP socket has been created and the bind operation applied to assign the socket to the IP address/port no pair 127.0.0.1:49717 (client port numbers are in the range 49152-65535) . The colon symbol (:) is used to separate the IP address 127.0.0.1 from the port number 49717. The client host sends a TCP connect request through this socket to the listening socket of the HTTP server. This server has been set up on the same machine so also has *localhost* as its computer name and the same IP address 127.0.0.1. The name *loopback IP address* derives from the fact that TCP/IP stack packets sent to the network adapter of the machine are looped back to another TCP/IP stack within the same machine. The server has created a listening socket that is bound to the IP address/port no pair 127.0.0.1:8080.

On receipt of a connection request from the client on the listening socket, the server decides whether it will accept this request or not. If it accepts, it creates a new TCP socket (*connection socket* in *Figure 9.4.1.6*) which it then binds to 127.0.0.1:8080. *Figure 9.4.1.7* shows a three-way handshake which takes place to establish this TCP connection between server and client.

The established TCP connection between HTTP client and HTTP server (*connection socket* to *connection socket*) is uniquely identified by its two endpoints: <127.0.0.1:49717, 127.0.0.1:8080>. Having established this TCP connection, the HTTP server now returns to listening on its *listening socket* for connection requests.

Figure 9.4.1.6 shows Python 3.4 code for both the HTTP client and the HTTP server. The HTTP server runs (`httpd.serve_forever()`) until it is shutdown.

Information

Normally, the two IP addresses in an end-to-end connection will be different, but in this example the loopback address is being used so that students can try the code out using just their machine (with their machine acting as both client and server).

Key term

TCP/IP socket:
A socket is one endpoint of a two-way communication link between two programs running on the network, e.g. a Web browser and a Web server.

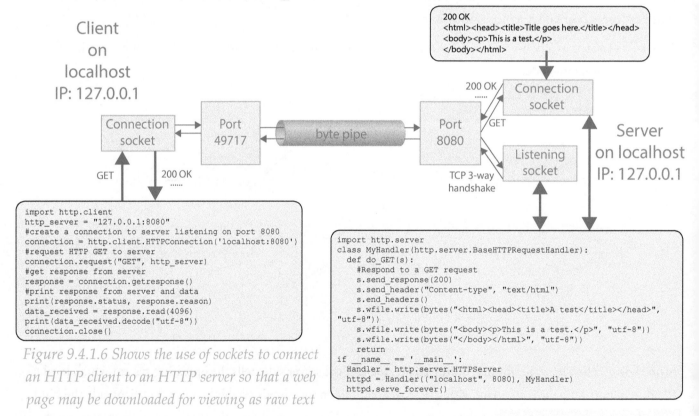

Figure 9.4.1.6 Shows the use of sockets to connect an HTTP client to an HTTP server so that a web page may be downloaded for viewing as raw text

The HTTP client requests a web page from the HTTP server by using the HTTP GET command. In Python 3.4 code this is `connection.request("GET", http_server)` where `http_server` is an identifier for "127.0.0.1:8080". This request is directed at port 8080 on the server. On receiving this packet, the server identifies the TCP connection as <127.0.0.1:49717, 127.0.0.1:8080> and routes the packet to the corresponding connection socket (*Figure 9.4.1.6*). The HTTP server responds by sending 200 OK followed by a page of HTML through this

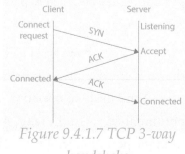

Figure 9.4.1.7 TCP 3-way handshake

426

TCP connection to the HTTP client. The client-side Python 3.4 code `print` statements output the response to the client's console.

Figure 9.4.1.8 shows a web browser using URL localhost:8080 rendering the HTML received from localhost:8080 in the browser's window as "This is a test". To do this, the web browser has connected to the HTTP server, sent a GET request using the established TCP connection, received back 200 OK and the HTML with content "This is a test".

Figure 9.4.1.8 Shows the same HTML rendered in a browser window

Questions

5. What is a TCP/IP socket?

6. Why is a socket bound to a port number?

7. How is each TCP connection uniquely identified?

8. Describe the role of sockets in the TCP/IP stack when a web browser on a host with IP address 195.61 3.4.7 connects with a web server listening on port 80 on a machine with IP address 210.56.78.3 to download a web page.

Well-known ports and client ports

Port numbers are 16-bit numbers which are also known by their associated service names such as "telnet" for port number 23 and "http" (as well as "www") for port number 80. Hosts running services, hosts accessing services on other hosts, and intermediate devices such as firewalls and NATs all need to agree on which service corresponds to a particular destination port. Many services have a default port which servers usually listen on. These ports are recorded by the Internet Assigned Numbers Authority (IANA) through the service name and port number registry.

Port numbers are subdivided into three ranges of numbers:

- the System Ports or Well-known Ports use the range 0-1023

- the User Ports or Registered Ports use the range 1024-49151

- the Dynamic Ports or Private or Ephemeral Ports use the range 49152-65535

The first two ranges are assigned by IANA. The third range is used by clients. A port number from the dynamic ports range (or private port or ephemeral port range) is allocated temporarily to a connection socket requested by a client application. Hence, these are also called client ports. Client port numbers are never allocated permanently.

Table 9.4.1.1 shows some examples of well-known port numbers and their corresponding service names.

Service name	Port number	Description
FTP	21	File Transfer Protocol (control)
FTP-data	20	File Transfer Protocol (data)
SSH	22	Secure Shell Protocol
SMTP	25	Simple Mail Transfer Protocol
HTTP	80	World Wide Web HTTP
POP3	110	Post Office Protocol Version 3
HTTPS	443	HTTP protocol over TLS/SSL

Table 9.4.1.1 Some examples of well-known port numbers and their corresponding service name

Questions

9 Explain what the well-known ports and client ports are used for and the differences between them.

10 The following information was captured by packet capture software monitoring the network adapter of a host when a Web browser sent an HTTP message to a Web server:

```
50268 192.168.2.22 64.29.1.45.9 80 HTTP GET /books.html
```

For this captured transmission state

(a) the source IP address   (b) the port no associated with the sending application's connection socket

(c) the destination IP address   (d) the port no associated with the connection socket in the destination

(e) the application-layer message.

11 In the same capture session, the following information was captured immediately after books.html was transferred to the client:

```
50272 192.168.2.22 64.29.1.45.9 80 HTTP GET /img/AQAUnit2.jpg
50268 192.168.2.22 64.29.1.45.9 80 HTTP GET /img/AQAUnit2.jpg
```

(a) What is the meaning of each line of this capture?

(b) The first number in the second line is the same as the first number in Q10. What explanation can you give for the two numbers being the same?

The role of MAC addresses

A MAC (Media Access Control) address is a 48-bit address expressed in hexadecimal and separated into 6 bytes, e.g. 00-02-22-C9-54-13 - see Chapter 9.2.1. It is the physical or hardware address of the network adapter and is designed to be unique. Hosts and routers communicate with the network through a network adapter attached to the host or router. Network adapters perform all the functions required to communicate on a network. They convert data from the form stored in the host/router to the form transmitted or received on the cable or wireless link and vice versa. The MAC address of a network packet on the network cable (or received via a wireless link) is read and compared by a network adapter

Key term

MAC address:

A MAC (Media Access Control) address is a 48-bit address expressed in hexadecimal and separated into 6 bytes, e.g. 00-02-22-C9-54-13.

The MAC address identifies the network adapter connected to the network so that a packet's destination hardware address can be matched to a particular host with this adapter as its address.

with its own unique assigned MAC address. If it matches then the network adapter passes the packet to the link layer software of the TCP/IP stack.

Questions

12 What is the role of Media Access Control (MAC) addresses?

13 The following information was captured by packet capture software monitoring the network adapter of a host when a Web browser sent an HTTP message to a Web server:

```
50268 192.168.2.22 64.29.1.45.9 80 74:d4:35:94:ad:53 70:73:cb:b2:f7:d0 HTTP GET /books.html
```

What do the numbers 74:d4:35:94:ad:53 and 70:73:cb:b2:f7:d0 represent?

In this chapter you have covered:

■ The role of the four layers of the TCP/IP stack (application, transport, network, link)

■ The role of sockets in the TCP/IP stack

■ The role of MAC (Media Access Control) addresses

■ What the well-known ports and client ports are used for and their differences

9.4 The Transmission Control Protocol/ Internet Protocol (TCP/IP) protocol

■ 9.4.2 Standard application layer protocols

FTP (File Transfer Protocol)

File Transfer Protocol (FTP) is an application layer protocol that enables files on one host, computer B, to be copied to another host, computer A. One host runs an FTP client and the other an FTP server.

FTP servers use two ports: port **21** for commands and port **20** for data.

Figure 9.4.2.1 shows an FTP client connected to an FTP server via TCP so that it can send a command request for a file Test.txt located on the FTP server. The FTP response is to send file Test.txt through the TCP connection to the FTP client.

Port **57359** is bound to the TCP socket on the client side, whilst on the server side, port **21** is bound to the command socket and port **20** to the data socket.

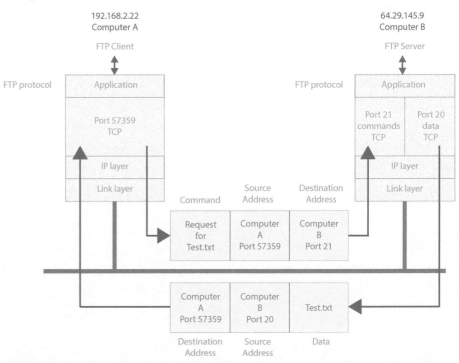

Figure 9.4.2.1 FTP transfer of file Test.txt from Computer B to Computer A

The client may need to navigate the directory structure of the server, create new directories, rename files and directories, delete files and directories. These are sent to the server as command requests.

FTP client software and FTP server

Figure 9.4.2.2 shows FTP client software (FileZilla) running on a computer with IP address 192.168.2.22 connected to an FTP server running on a computer with IP address 64.29.145.9. This server is located in the USA whilst the client computer is in the UK.

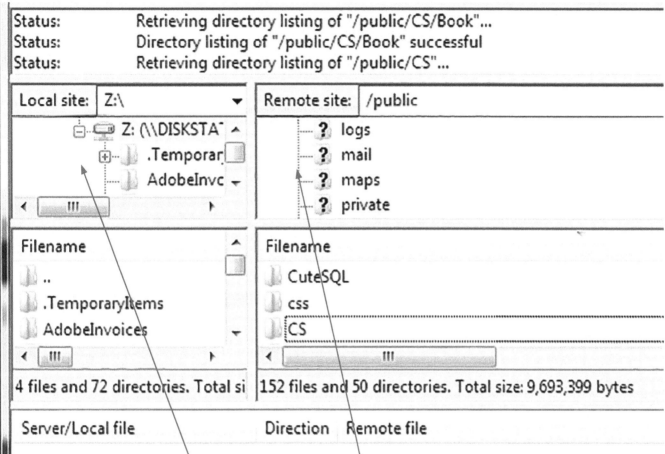

Figure 9.4.2.2 FTP client using FileZilla FTP client software connected to an FTP server

Anonymous and non-anonymous access

Some FTP servers restrict access to their service and require users to use a registered user name and password (non-anonymous access). Other FTP servers do not restrict access but may prompt users for a user name; then the user name is normally 'anonymous'. The user may be prompted for a password too. If the user name is 'anonymous', it is sufficient to supply an e-mail address as the password. *Figure 9.4.2.3* shows the user name *Anonymous* being set up on a Cerberus FTP server. *Figure 9.4.2.4* shows an FTP client connected to this FTP server (Cerberus FTP server obtainable from www.cerberusftp.com).

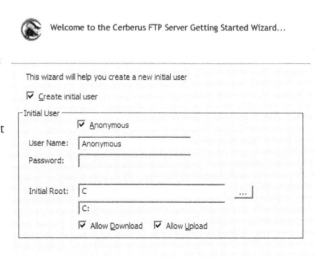

Figure 9.4.2.3 Setting up Cerberus FTP server

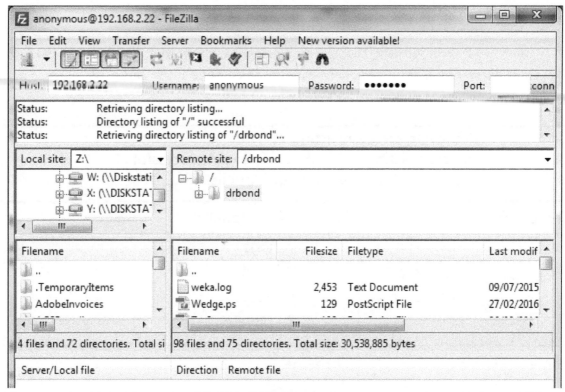

Figure 9.4.2.4 FTP client using FileZilla FTP client software connected to a Cerberus FTP server

Questions

1 A file Test.txt stored on a computer on one network is to be copied to another machine on a different network which is reachable from the first computer.

(a) What type of software running on the first computer could enable this to be done?

(b) What type of software running on the second computer could enable this to be done?

(c) Why might it be necessary to send commands as well as file data across the connection between the two computers? Give an example of one command.

HTTP (Hypertext Transfer Protocol)

Hypertext Transfer Protocol (HTTP) is a very simple application-level protocol. In this protocol, a client computer sends a request message to the server and the server responds with a response message (*Figure 9.4.2.5*). In the example in *Figure 9.4.2.5* the file index.html has been requested. The response message may contain many forms of data. The most popular form of data is text formatted using Hypertext Markup Language (HTML).

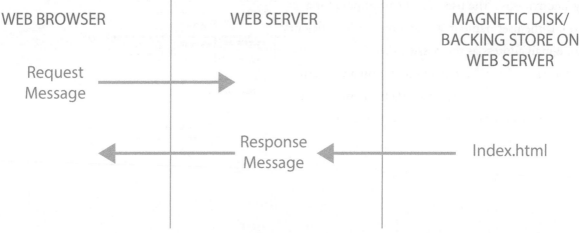

Figure 9.4.2.5 HTTP request-response messages

Other data, such as images or audio files, may also be transmitted. TCP establishes a connection between the client computer and the server computer so that HTTP has a pathway for its request and response messages.

The simplest request message is

```
GET / <Return key pressed>

<Return key pressed>
```

This gets the default web page, index.html, for the given site. HTTP finishes with the connection after the response message is sent; the TCP connection is broken unless specifically requested to stay connected. A web page returned by an HTTP GET request is a text file containing content to be displayed together with instructions on how to style and structure this content when displayed.

Here is what a web browser does:

1. It accepts a URL from a user, e.g. www.educational-computing.co.uk/books.html.

2. It extracts the FQDN (Fully Qualified Domain Name - host name + domain name - e.g. www.educational-computing.co.uk) and uses a DNS server to translate it into an IP address. DNS is another application layer protocol.

3. It sends a GET request for the web resource specified in the URL; the request is sent to a web server at this IP address – port 80 unless another port number is specified.

4. It receives the file returned by the web server.

5. It renders this file's contents in a web browser window; that means it uses the style and structure instructions to display the content appropriately.

6. If this file contains other URLs, e.g. a reference to a graphic, then the browser should issue a GET to obtain this resource from the web server, e.g. GET /images/flower.jpg, and, when received, display it according to the instructions on style and structure.

To obtain a web page other than the default web page, the web browser sends an HTTP GET request message with the structure

```
GET <path to resource> <Return key pressed>

<Return key pressed>
```

For example,

```
GET /books/books.html <Return key pressed>

<Return key pressed>
```

Questions

2 Explain how a web browser and a web server interact via the HTTP protocol when the web browser is used with URL www.educational-computing.co.uk/books.html.

HTTPS (Hypertext Transfer Protocol Secure)

Hypertext Transfer Protocol over Secure Sockets (HTTPS) is a web protocol that encrypts and decrypts user page requests as well as the pages that are returned by the web server. HTTPS uses the Secure Sockets Layer (SSL) beneath the HTTP application layer. HTTPS uses port 443 instead of port 80 in its interactions with TCP/IP. *Figure 9.4.2.6* shows the SSL sublayer which encrypts the HTTP GET / request before sending it through the TCP connection to the Web server www.site.co.uk. Both the request and the response are encrypted.

HTTPS has been used for a long time for securing payment transactions on the Web but it is now being more widely used for general Web access.

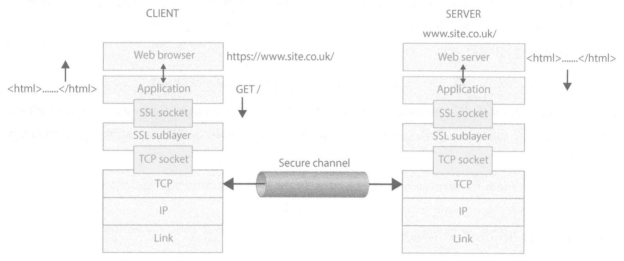

Figure 9.4.2.6 Fetching a Web page using HTTPS

SSL provides a simple Application Programmer Interface (API) with sockets similar to TCP's API. When an application wishes to use SSL, the application includes SSL classes/libraries.

SSL provides encrypted communication but it also embodies support for data integrity, server authentication, and client authentication. SSL secures TCP. As such it can be used by any application that runs over TCP, e.g. SMTP and POP3.

Questions

3 Give **two** reasons why Web browsers have been redesigned to use HTTPS rather than HTTP when interacting with Web servers.

4 In what way does the use of the TCP/IP stack differ when HTTPS is used instead of HTTP?

SMTP (Simple Mail Transfer Protocol) and POP3 (Post Office Protocol (v3))

Simple Mail Transfer Protocol (SMTP) is used by e-mail clients to send e-mail. It is a relatively simple text-based protocol. One or more recipients of a message are specified then SMTP is used by the email client to transfer the message text to a mail server listening on port 25. The mail server takes care of delivering the mail to the ultimate destination using SMTP. The user who retrieves the message from the destination mail server uses the application-layer protocol POP3 to retrieve the stored mail. POP3 uses well known port 110. POP3 is Post Office Protocol version 3. E-mail is stored in a mailbox and a user does not need to be connected for mail to be sent to them. The server holds incoming mail until the user connects and requests the mail.

There are other email protocols that may be used instead of SMTP and POP3.

The POP3 protocol defines commands that can be used to retrieve a mail message, e.g. the command `RETR no`, where `no` is the position number of the message in the mailbox. The command `LIST` returns a list of these numbers. `DELE no` marks an email for deletion.

For creating and sending email the SMTP protocol supports commands such as

- `MAIL FROM:` - defines the e-mail address of the sender of the message.
- `RCPT TO:` - defines the e-mail address of a recipient of the message. Repeating this command once for each recipient means you can send one piece of mail to many users without having to repeat the entire process over and over again.
- `DATA` marks the start of the data portion of the message, essentially everything that you would consider "content", this includes the "To:", "From:", "CC:" etc. as these are not commands but simple informational components making up a header which the e-mail client picks out of the content and displays in a far nicer format. Just as a reminder - anything which is in the content can be faked as it is content and so consequently cannot be validated.

Questions

5. A TCP connection to port 110 of a POP3 mail server `pop3.apm-internet.net` was established by an email client to a user's mailbox stored on the mail server. Give **two** examples of POP3 commands that might be sent by the email client over this TCP connection when the user is browsing their emails.

SSH (Secure Shell)

SSH is used for encrypted communication between two computers over a TCP/IP network. It uses port **22**.

SSH provides a secure channel over an unsecured network in a client-server architecture, connecting an SSH client application with an SSH server. Common applications include remote command-line login and remote command execution, but any network service can be secured with SSH. SSH was developed independently of SSL and doesn't therefore use SSL but it is similar in that it supports encryption of the communication, both client and server authentication, and data integrity.

Using SSH for remote management

Managing computers and networks remotely can be done and was done previously using clear-text protocols and unsecured channels. For this an administrator (or another user) uses Telnet software and the TCP/IP protocol to establish an unsecured TCP connection through which operating system commands could be sent to the remote computer. To log in to the remote computer, a Telnet client sends the account name and password in clear-text form through a TCP connection to a Telnet server running on the remote machine. Any eavesdropper could easily obtain the transmitted login details by tapping into the TCP connection. Once obtained the eavesdropper could use these details to log in to the remote computer.

SSH is a secure replacement for Telnet. Both SSH client and SSH server software encrypt messages before they are sent through a TCP connection.

Figure 9.4.2.7 shows a screenshot of a Windows computer connected to a remote computer, an Apple MacBook Pro. The account accessed on the Mac belongs to user *drbond*. The Windows computer is shown logged into the Apple computer having passed authentication by password. The Windows computer has navigated, using the command `cd`, the directory structure on the Mac to a directory named `myIOSProjects`. A directory listing is then obtained using the Unix command `ls`.

The Windows computer's IP address is 192.168.2.22 and the Apple Macbook Pro computer's IP address is 192.168.2.21.

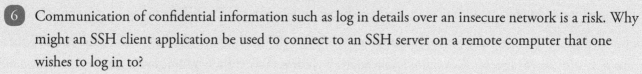

```
██ Command Prompt - plink drbond@192.168.2.21

Microsoft Windows [Version 6.1.7601]
Copyright (c) 2009 Microsoft Corporation.  All rights reserved.

C:\Users\drbond>plink drbond@192.168.2.21
Using username "drbond".
Using keyboard-interactive authentication.
Password:
Last login: Thu Mar  3 15:29:47 2016 from 192.168.2.22
←[?1034hKevin-Bonds-MacBook-Pro:~ drbond$ cd myIOSProjects
Kevin-Bonds-MacBook-Pro:myIOSProjects drbond$ ls
Project1                  setup_paserver.zip
Project2                  untitled folder
Kevin-Bonds-MacBook-Pro:myIOSProjects drbond$
```

Figure 9.4.2.7 Using an SSH client on a Windows computer to connect to an SSH server running on a remote computer so that the remote computer, an Apple Macbook Pro, can be managed

Background

Plink (PuTTY Link) is a command-line connection tool written for Microsoft's Windows operating system and similar to UNIX's SSH application. Openssh is a fork(version) of SSH which has been released under an open source licence. It is now supported in Microsoft's Windows PowerShell.

Questions

6 Communication of confidential information such as log in details over an insecure network is a risk. Why might an SSH client application be used to connect to an SSH server on a remote computer that one wishes to log in to?

In this chapter you have covered:

■ The following application layer protocols:
  - FTP (File Transfer Protocol)
  - HTTP (Hypertext Transfer Protocol)
  - HTTPS (Hypertext Transfer Protocol Secure)
  - POP3 (Post Office Protocol (v3))
  - SMTP (Simple Mail Transfer Protocol)
  - SSH (Secure Shell)

■ The use of FTP client software and an FTP server

■ Using SSH for remote management of a computer

■ The use of an SSH client to make a TCP connection to a remote port for the purpose of sending commands to this port using application level protocols

■ Using SSH to log in securely to a remote computer and execute commands

■ The role of an email server in retrieving and sending email

■ The role of a web server in serving up web pages in text form

■ The role of a web browser in retrieving web pages and web page resources and rendering these accordingly.

9.4 The Transmission Control Protocol/ Internet Protocol (TCP/IP) protocol

9.4.3 IP address structure

> **Key concept**
>
> **Host or host computer:**
> TCP/IP defines the term host or host computer as any computer system that connects to an internet and runs applications.

> **Key concept**
>
> **Uniform addressing scheme:**
> A uniform addressing scheme is a logical addressing scheme, independent of the underlying physical network. Each address conforms to a common format defined by a standard, e.g. IPv4.

> **Key concept**
>
> **Interface:**
> The boundary between a host/ router and the physical link that connects the host to an internet is called an interface.

> **Key fact**
>
> **Routers have multiple interfaces:**
> Routers have multiple interfaces because routers are connected to two or more links.

A single uniform system

The physical architecture of an internet in which router(s) interconnect physical networks (LANs) as shown in *Figure 9.4.3.1* was covered in *Chapter 9.3.1*. TCP/IP systems use a software protocol stack in each host and router to hide the physical architecture from hosts and routers. This software turns an internet into a single uniform system or virtual network which enables users, application programs and higher layers of the protocol software stack to communicate seamlessly using a uniform addressing scheme called the IP address scheme.

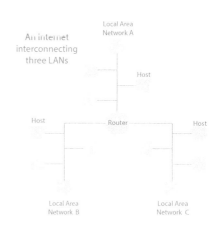

Figure 9.4.3.1 An internet consisting of three local area networks interconnected by a single router

Uniform addressing scheme

If an internet is viewed as a single, uniform system then all its host computers must use a uniform addressing scheme in which each address is unique. Physical network addresses are not good candidates for this uniform addressing scheme because physical networks can differ in their technologies and because each technology defines its own address format.

To guarantee uniform addressing for all hosts, the TCP/IP protocol software defines an addressing scheme that is independent of the underlying physical network. This scheme is administered by the Internet Protocol (IP) part of TCP/IP.

Hosts are connected into a network via a single physical link, e.g. an Ethernet cable. When the IP layer of the TCP/IP stack in a host sends an IP datagram it does so over this link. The boundary between the host and the physical link is called an interface. Routers are connected to two or more links because a router's job is to forward a datagram it receives on one link to another one of its connected links. The boundary between a link and the router is also called an interface. A router thus has multiple interfaces, one for each of its links. The IP protocol requires that each host and router interface has its own IP address. The IP version 4 (IPv4) standard specifies that each host interface is assigned a unique 32-bit number known as the host interface's Internet Protocol address or IP address or Internet address. The IP version 6 (IPv6) standard specifies that each host interface is assigned a unique 128-bit number. Users, application programs and higher layers of the protocol software stack use these logical addresses, i.e. IP addresses, to communicate through the Internet with each other without regard to whether the sending and receiving hosts are on the same physical network or a different one and without needing to know physical addresses.

Figure 9.4.3.2 shows IPv4 addresses assigned to host and router interfaces.

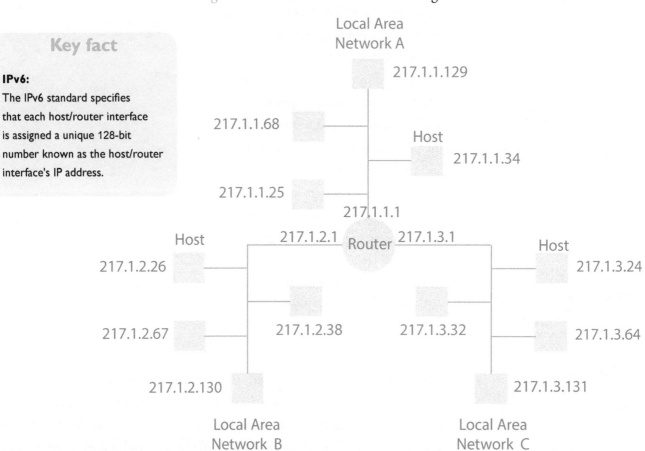

Figure 9.4.3.2 IP addresses, expressed in dotted decimal notation, assigned to host and router interfaces for an internet interconnecting three local area networks, A, B and C via a single router

Dotted decimal notation

The binary form of IP addresses was designed for reading/processing by machine. Although IPv4 addresses are 32-bit numbers, users rarely enter or read IP addresses in binary. Therefore, the software that interacts with users employs a notation called dotted decimal notation which is more convenient for humans to understand. In this notation, each 8-bit section of a 32-bit number is expressed as a decimal value separated from its neighbour by a full stop. Table 9.4.3.1 shows some examples of 32-bit binary numbers and their equivalent dotted decimal forms.

32-bit binary number	Equivalent dotted decimal
01011100 00010111 00011101 10100010	92.23.29.162
01001110 10010111 11101100 00000001	78.151.236.1
11011001 00000001 00000001 10000001	217.1.1.129

Table 9.4.3.1 Examples of 32-bit binary numbers and their equivalent in dotted decimal notation. The first row is colour-coded to show the correspondence between the 8-bit sections and their decimal equivalent.

Questions

 Convert the following IPv4 32-bit addresses from binary to their equivalent dotted decimal form

(a) 11001100 00111111 01010101 00111111   (b) 11011001 10000111 00011001 00010011

Subnet

In *Figure 9.4.3.2* one router with three interfaces is used to interconnect twelve hosts.

The four hosts in local area network A and the router interface to which they are connected all have an IP address of the form 217.1.1.x with x chosen from the range 1 to 254. This means IP addresses in this range are guaranteed to have the same most significant 24 bits in their IP address, i.e. 11011001000000010000001 (see last row of *Table 9.4.3.1*).

In IP terms, local area network A connecting four host interfaces and one router interface forms a subnet.

IP addressing assigns an address to this subnet in the form a.b.c.d/x which is expressed as 217.1.1.0/24, where the /24 notation indicates that the most significant 24 bits of the IPv4 32-bit IP address define the subnet address.

Additional hosts added to local area network A will be required to have interfaces with an address of the form 217.1.1.x. This means that network A can use 256 different IP addresses, i.e. 217.1.1.0 to 217.1.1.255.

However, 217.1.1.0 and 217.1.1.255 are both reserved IP addresses not to be used for host/router interface identification, this leaves 254 IP address for identifying host/router interfaces.

Figure 9.4.3.2 contains two other subnets:

- 217.1.2.0/24

- 217.1.3.0/24

Key concept

Subnet:
A network of directly connected interfaces.

Subnet address:
IP addressing assigns an address to a subnet in a format a.b.c.d/x which enables the network to be identified, e.g. 217.1.1.0/24 where the value 24 indicates that the most significant 24 bits identify the network.

Questions

 How many bits identify the network in each of the following subnet addresses:

(a) 129.12.0.0/16   (b) 192.173.2.0/23?

The division of IP address into network ID and host ID

We have learned that an IP address is assigned to a host interface. Conceptually, each 32-bit IP address (IPv4) (and each 128-bit IP address (IPv6)) is divided into two parts:

- a prefix or network identifier part (Net ID)

- a suffix or host identifier part (Host ID)

The prefix (most significant bits) identifies the physical network to which the host computer is connected. This physical network is called a subnet. The prefix is more commonly known as the network ID or Net ID.

In *Figure 9.4.3.2*, the network ID is given by the most significant 24 bits of the IP address, e.g. 217.1.2 in IP address 217.1.2.3.

Key concept

Division of an IP address:

Conceptually, each 32-bit IP address (IPv4) (and each 128-bit IP address (IPv6)) is divided into two parts:

1. a prefix or network identifier part (Net ID)
2. a suffix or host identifier part (Host ID)

The prefix (most significant bits) identifies the physical network to which the host computer is connected. This physical network is called a subnet. The prefix is more commonly known as the network ID or Net ID.

The suffix identifies a particular host interface connected to the subnet. The suffix is more commonly known as the Host ID.

The suffix identifies a particular host interface connected to the subnet. The suffix is more commonly known as the Host ID. In *Figure 9.4.3.2*, the Host ID is given by the least significant 8 bits of the IP address, e.g. 3 in 217.1.2.3.

This division is used as the basis of traffic routing between the physical networks making up the Internet.

For example, suppose a host with host interface IP address 217.1.1.25 in local area network A wishes to send an IP datagram to a host with host interface IP address 217.1.3.64 in local area network C.

The LAN A host's IP software is able to determine by examining the destination's IP address that the destination host is on a different subnet (217.1.3.0/24) with network ID 217.1.3 and therefore cannot be reached directly.

The LAN A host therefore sends the IP datagram to the router interface 217.1.1.1.

This router examines the network ID of the destination's IP address contained in the IP datagram and forwards this datagram to its interface with IP address 217.1.3.1 since this interface is connected to subnet 213.1.3.0/24. This interface places the IP datagram onto the link it is connected to and which host interface 217.1.3.64 is also connected.

The IP datagram is is then read by host interface 217.1.3.64.

The Global Internet

Every interface on every host and router in the global Internet must have an IP address that is globally unique (except for interfaces behind NATs - see *Chapter 9.4.8*). IP addresses are assigned in a coordinated manner so that routing is facilitated. The strategy is called Classless InterDomain Routing (CIDR). It generalises subnet addressing to the global Internet. As with subnet addressing, the 32-bit IP address in IPv4 is divided into two parts using the same dotted decimal form a.b.c.d/x, where x indicates the number of bits for the prefix. The prefix constitutes the network part of the IP address.

Every organisation that wishes to send and receive e-mail, or gain access to the Internet, needs at least one globally unique IP address.

An organisation is typically assigned more than one unique IP address as a block of contiguous addresses with a common prefix. The IP addresses of all devices within the organisation will share this common prefix.

For example, the organisation Jisc Services Limited, more commonly known as Janet, is a private, UK government-funded organisation, which provides computer network and related collaborative services to UK research and education (Further and Higher). To see how blocks of contiguous IP addresses are assigned for the Janet network visit https://ipinfo.io/AS786. *Table 9.4.3.2* shows a sample of these blocks.

Netblock	Description	No of IP addresses
129.12.0.0/16	University of Kent	65536
192.195.42.0/23	University of Ulster	512

Table 9.4.3.2 Sample of IP address contiguous block allocation within the Janet organisation.

The University of Kent has subdivided its block of IP addresses into 128 subnets. *Table 9.4.3.3* shows a sample of these addresses of these subnets.

129.12.0.0/23	129.12.2.0/23	129.12.4.0/23 1	29.12.6.0/23
●	●	●	●
●	●	●	●
129.12.248.0/23	129.12.250.0/23	129.12.252.0/23	129.12.254.0/23

Table 9.4.3.3 Sample of subnet addresses for University of Kent.

Table 9.4.3.4 shows binary equivalent of the subnet addresses shown in *Table 9.4.3.3* and the corresponding Network ID expressed in binary. Note that the most significant 16 bits of each subnet Network ID is the same. This corresponds to the prefix for the University of Kent given by 129.12.0.0/16.

Subnet Block	Equivalent binary value	Network ID (prefix)
129.12.0.0/23	10000001 00001100 00000000 00000000	10000001 00001100 0000000
129.12.2.0/23	10000001 00001100 00000010 00000000	10000001 00001100 0000001
129.12.4.0/23	10000001 00001100 00000100 00000000	10000001 00001100 0000010
129.12.6.0/23	10000001 00001100 00000110 00000000	10000001 00001100 0000011
●	●	●
●	●	●
129.12.248.0/23	10000001 00001100 11111000 00000000	10000001 00001100 1111100
129.12.250.0/23	10000001 00001100 11111010 00000000	10000001 00001100 1111101
129.12.252.0/23	10000001 00001100 11111100 00000000	10000001 00001100 1111110
129.12.254.0/23	10000001 00001100 11111110 00000000	10000001 00001100 1111111

Table 9.4.3.4 Network IDs for the subnets for University of Kent. The university's Network ID is shown in red

Using IP address prefix to route an IP datagram

Suppose that an IP datagram is addressed to a remote destination whose IP address is 129.12.3.237. When an organisation is allocated a block of IP addresses these are registered and Internet routers are supplied with the organisation's Network ID expressed in a.b.c.d/x form. For example, Internet routers store the following for the University of Kent Network ID: 129.12.0.0/16. The most significant 16 bits of 129.12.0.0, the prefix, are used by Internet routers to relay the IP datagram to the gateway router to the University of Kent's network. Once this IP datagram has reached this gateway router, this routing table is searched to determine how to route the IP datagram within the University of Kent. If this gateway router is connected to 128 links (subnets) then the routing table will contain an entry for each link which corresponds to its subnet address or Network ID (see *Table 9.4.3.4*), e.g. the first entry will be 129.12.0.0/23, the second entry 129.12.2.0/23, etc. The binary equivalent of the IP datagram's destination address 129.12.3.237 is (the most significant 23 bits are shown in red)

10000001 00001100 00000011 11101101

The gateway router's routing table entries indicate that the most significant 23 bits of the IP datagram should be examined to determine which subnet to forward it to. The 23-bit prefix of 129.12.3.237 in binary is

10000001 00001100 0000001

Writing this in 32 bits by adding nine trailing zeroes we get

10000001 00001100 00000010 00000000

In dotted decimal notation, this 32-bit binary value is **129.12.2.0** which is the Network ID of the second subnet. The gateway router will use this result to forward the IP datagram to the second link. The host with host interface **129.12.3.237** is connected to this link as shown in *Figure 9.4.3.3.* so the IP datagram has reached its destination.

In practice it is more likely that the gateway router will be connected to a hierarchy of routers internal to the university with the links to the subnets connected to the routers in the last stage of this hierarchy. In this way, each final stage router will require fewer interfaces, perhaps just eight and likewise, the gateway router could require only eight interfaces.

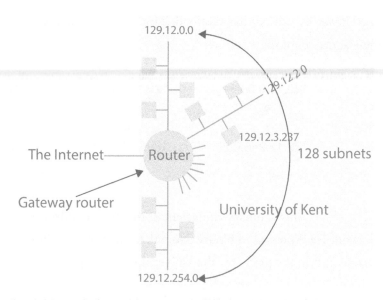

Figure 9.4.3.3 Gateway router at University of Kent connected to 128 subnets within university.

Table 9.4.3.5 shows a section of the University of Kent's gateway router subnet Network IDs stored as 32-bit values assuming that the university's network is organised as shown in *Figure 9.4.3.3*. Note that nine trailing zeroes have been added to each 23-bit prefix to create 32-bit values. These nine least significant bits are reserved for the Host IDs of host interfaces connected to a subnet. Note that the same Host IDs can be used in each subnet because when combined with the 23-bit subnet address a unique IP address always results.

Network ID	Link no
10000001 00001100 00000000 00000000	1
10000001 00001100 00000010 00000000	2
10000001 00001100 00000100 00000000	3
10000001 00001100 00000110 00000000	4
• •	• •
10000001 00001100 11111000 00000000	125
10000001 00001100 11111010 00000000	126
10000001 00001100 11111100 00000000	127
10000001 00001100 11111110 00000000	128

Table 9.4.3.5 Network IDs for the subnets for University of Kent expressed as 32-bit values and the corresponding Link no expressed in decimal.

Questions

3 The following 32-bit value is an entry in the University of Kent's gateway router routing table (see *Table 9.4.3.5*) **10000001 00001100 00000110 00000000**

Which of the following destination IP addresses expressed in dotted decimal notation match this entry

(a) **129.12.7.38** (b) **129.12.6.123** (c) **129.12.5.223** (d) **129.13.6.45?**

Questions

4 An IP datagram is addressed to a remote destination whose IP address is 129.12.33.114. Internet routers forward this datagram to the gateway router at the University of Kent. Explain how this datagram is forwarded to the host interface with IP address 129.12.33.114 within the University of Kent's network. You may assume that Figure 9.4.3.3 describes this university's network setup.

In this chapter you have covered:

- How an IP address is split into a network identifier part and a host identifier part
- The background knowledge needed to understand this splitting of the IP address:
  - Uniform addressing scheme
  - Dotted decimal notation
  - The meaning of the term subnet and subnet address expressed in the form a.b.c.d/x
  - The division of an IP address into a prefix and a suffix
  - The prefix is the network identifier part and the suffix the host identifier
  - Generalisation of subnet addressing to the global Internet
  - Using an IP address prefix to route an IP datagram

9.4 The Transmission Control Protocol/ Internet Protocol (TCP/IP) protocol

9.4.4 Subnet masking

Learning objectives:

■ *Know how a subnet mask is used to identify the network part of the IP address*

Subnet mask

We learned in *Chapter 9.4.3* that a 32-bit IP address in IPv4 is divided into two parts using the dotted decimal notation a.b.c.d/x, where x indicates the number of bits for the prefix. The prefix constitutes the network part of the IP address. For example, we can divide 129.12.7.38/23 into a prefix and suffix expressed in binary as follows

```
                           ◄──────  23 bits  ──────►
129.12.7.38     = 10000001 00001100 0000011|1 00100110

129.12.7.38/23 = 10000001 00001100 0000011| (prefix)

129.12.7.38     =                          |1 00100110 (suffix)
                                           ◄── 9 bits ──►
```

The suffix is the Host ID. In this example nine bits are allocated to the suffix.

The prefix is the Network ID or subnet address. In IPv4 it is expressed as a 32-bit value by replacing the suffix or Host ID part with zeroes. For example, the Network ID of the host interface with IP address 129.12.7.38 is in binary

```
        10000001 00001100 00000110 00000000
```

which in dotted decimal form is 129.12.6.0/23.

Therefore to obtain the Network ID for a given IP address we need to know how many bits are assigned to the prefix part. This is known as the subnet mask. The Network ID is also known as the subnet address.

Given a 32-bit IP address such as 129.12.7.38 it is possible to obtain its Network ID expressed as a 32-bit value by a bitwise AND operation applied to the 32-bit mask derived from the subnet mask and the IP address. If the subnet mask is 23 then the 32-bit mask for the bitwise AND operation will consist of twenty three ones for the most significant bits followed by nine zeroes.

```
        32-bit mask = 11111111 11111111 11111110 00000000

        129.12.7.38 = 10000001 00001100 00000111 00100110
AND     ───────────────────────────────────────────────────
        129.12.6.0  = 10000001 00001100 00000110 00000000
```

The result of the AND operation is the Network ID or subnet address expressed in 32 bits.

> ## Key concept
>
> **Subnet mask:**
> The subnet mask is the number of bits assigned to the prefix part of an IP address. The prefix identifies the Network ID or subnet address.

> ## Key concept
>
> **Using a subnet mask:**
> The subnet mask is used by a computer/router to obtain the Network ID or subnet address of the subnet to which its network interface is connected. This may be done with an AND operation applied to the computer interface's IP address and a mask of the same number of bits constructed from the subnet mask.

Figure 9.4.4.1 shows the Internet Protocol version 4 (TCP/IPv4) Properties window of a Microsoft Windows 7 computer. The field labelled subnet mask shows the AND mask that is used by this computer when it needs to know to which subnet it is connected.

Why does a computer need to be able to "calculate" the subnet address of the subnet it is connected to?

When a computer wishes to send an IP datagram to another computer it needs to know whether or not it is directly connected to this computer, i.e. connected to the same subnet as the destination. If linked directly by wire or wireless, then the hardware address of the destination computer is obtained and attached to the IP datagram. The wire or wireless frame encapsulating the datagram is then sent over the direct link to the destination computer.

A computer determines to which IPv4 subnet it is connected by applying a bitwise AND operation to its IP address and the 32-bit mask derived from the subnet mask. The destination's subnet is determined in a similar way.

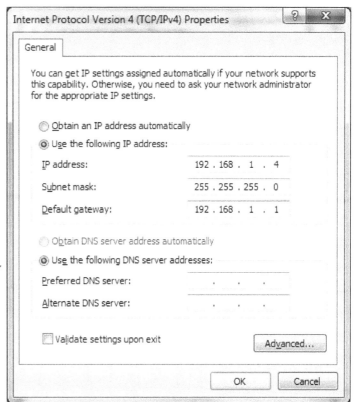

Figure 9.4.4.1 IPv4 properties window of a Microsoft Windows computer showing the subnet mask that is ANDed with the IP address to obtain the subnet address.

If the destination computer is not on the same subnet then the sending computer obtains the hardware address of the gateway router to which it is directly connected. It then uses this hardware address to send the IP datagram to this router. The gateway router will use its routing tables to forward the IP datagram to the subnet of the destination computer so the datagram is able to reach its destination.

Figure 9.4.4.1 shows that the TCP/IP software on the Windows 7 computer has recorded 192.168.1.1 as the IP address of the default gateway. The subnet address of the Windows 7 computer and the default gateway can be calculated as follows

```
       255.255.255.0 = 11111111 11111111 11111111 00000000 (mask)
       192.168.1.4   = 11000000 10101000 00000001 00000100 (sending computer's IP address)
AND    ─────────────────────────────────────────────────────
       192.168.1.0   = 11000000 10101000 00000001 00000000 (subnet address /Network ID)


       255.255.255.0 = 11111111 11111111 11111111 00000000 (mask)
       192.168.1.1   = 11000000 10101000 00000001 00000001 (default gateway IP address)
AND    ─────────────────────────────────────────────────────
       192.168.1.0   = 11000000 10101000 00000001 00000000 (subnet address /Network ID)
```

This shows that the Windows 7 computer and the default gateway are on the same subnet (192.168.1.0) and therefore directly connected.

Questions

1. *Table 9.4.4.1* shows subnet masks and IP addresses expressed using IPv4 dotted decimal notation

Subnet mask	IP address	Network ID or subnet address
255.255.255.0	192.168.2.15	
255.255.0.0	192.168.253.234	
255.255.252.0	192.168.253.234	

Table 9.4.4.1 Subnet masks and IP address expressed using IPv4 dotted decimal notation

Complete the Network ID column for the given subnet masks and IP addresses.

2. A computer with a host interface IP address 192.168.1.5 sends an IP datagram to a computer with IP address 192.168.2.3. In each case the subnet mask expressed in IPv4 dotted decimal notation is 255.255.255.0. The default gateway for the computer 192.168.1.5 is 192.168.1.1. Explain why the IP datagram is sent to the default gateway for forwarding to 192.168.2.3.

In this chapter you have covered:

■   How a subnet mask is used to identify the network part of the IP address

9.4 The Transmission Control Protocol/ Internet Protocol (TCP/IP) protocol

9.4.5 IP standards

Internet addressing 1969

ARPANET, the forerunner to the Internet, consisted initially of four nodes. Each node was an Interface Message Processor (IMP) - see *Chapter 9.3.1* for an image of an IMP.

In 1969, several months before the first of the four original ARPANET nodes became operational, Stephen Crocker at UCLA authored the first Request For Comment, RFC 1, "Host Software" - https://tools.ietf.org/html/rfc1.

RFC 1 proposed specifications for the Interface Message Processor software and host-to-host connections in which **5** bits were allocated to a message's destination address. The allocation of **5** bits would theoretically provide 2^5 or 32 destination addresses as follows:

```
00000 00001 00010 00011 00100 00101 00110 00111

01000 01001 01010 01011 01100 01101 01110 01111

10000 10001 10010 10011 10100 10101 10110 10111

11000 11001 11010 11011 11100 11101 11110 11111
```

An increase in the total number of addresses could be achieved by adding more bits to these binary codes. Each additional bit doubles the total number of addresses. *Table 9.4.5.1* shows the total number of addresses for 6, 7 and 8 bits respectively.

Number of address bits	Total number of addresses
6	64
7	128
8	256

Table 9.4.5.1 Total number of addresses for a given number of bits

The emergence of electronic mail

ARPANET was envisaged by its designers to be a network for facilitating resource and file transfer. They did not forsee the emergence of electronic mail and the unexpected growth in the ARPANET network that followed as a result.

A radical change took place in 1974 with the design of TCP. TCP makes the hosts responsible for the reliability of transmission instead of the network as was the case with ARPANET. RFC 675 "Specification of Internet Transmission Control Program", December 1974, contains the first attested use of the term internet, as a shorthand for internetworking. TCP/IP followed later in the decade and the Internet was born along with IP addressing.

Internet addressing 1981 and IPv4

RFC 791 (1981) - https://tools.ietf.org/html/rfc791 - introduced the Internet Protocol standard, later known as IPv4, expanding the size of each IP address to a 32-bit code divided into a network prefix and a host prefix. The address length of 32 bits provides a theoretical pool of 2^{32} or approximately 4.3 billion unique Internet addresses.

However, as far back as the early 1990s it was forecast that the Internet would run out of IPv4 addresses and that a transition to a new version of the protocol offering a larger address space would be required if the problem was to be avoided. In February 2011, IANA allocated the last remaining pool of unassigned IPv4 addresses to a regional registry (the regional registries are ARIN, RIPE NCC, APNIC, LACNIC, and AfriNIC). Organizations acquire IPv4 addresses from their Regional Internet Registry (RIR) or their service providers. Service providers acquire their IPv4 addresses from their Regional Internet Registry. ARIN (American Registry for Internet Numbers) ran out of IPv4 addresses on 24th September 2015.

IPv6

In response to the projected problem of running out of IPv4 addresses, the technical community came up with a specification for IP version 6 (IPv6) in the mid-1990s.

IPv6 allocates 128 bits for IP addresses. This gives a theoretical total number of addresses of 2^{128} or roughly 3.4 x 10^{38} addresses. This is more than enough for the foreseeable future. By way of comparison, the number of addresses required to uniquely label all the grains of sand on planet earth would be 7.5 x 10^{18}. However, adoption of IPv6 is not a straightforward matter because the public Internet is an IPv4 router network designed to work with 32-bit addresses not 128-bit addresses. Whilst new IPv6-capable systems can be made backwards compatible, i.e. send route and receive IPv4 datagrams, already deployed IPv4-capable systems are not capable of handling IPv6 datagrams.

Questions

1 What is the theoretical total number of IP addresses for
   (a) IPv4?   (b) IPv6?

2 Why was IPv6 introduced?

In this chapter you have covered:

■ *Two standards of IP address, v4 and v6*

■ *Why v6 was introduced.*

9.4 The Transmission Control Protocol/ Internet Protocol (TCP/IP) protocol

9.4.6 Public and private IP addresses

Key fact

Private IPv4 address spaces:
The address spaces 10.0.0.0/8, 172.16.0.0/12 and 192.168.0.0/16 are reserved for private IPv4 TCP/IP networks.

Private IPv4 address ranges:
192.168.0.0 - 192.168.255.255
172.16.0.0 - 172.31.255.255
10.0.0.0 - 10.255.255.255

Private address spaces

The address spaces 10.0.0.0/8, 172.16.0.0/12 and 192.168.0.0/16 are the three regions of the IPv4 address space that are reserved (RFC 1918 - https://tools.ietf.org/html/rfc1918) for private TCP/IP networks. Addresses in these address spaces are known as private addresses. The use of private IP addresses requires no coordination by IANA (Internet Assigned Numbers Authority) or an Internet registry because they are only unique within a private TCP/IP network. Private addresses can be reused in any private TCP/IP network which means that they are not unique across the public, global Internet.

Table 9.4.6.1 shows the range of private IP addresses for each reserved address space.

Address space	Range	Total no of addresses
192.168.0.0/16	192.168.0.0 - 192.168.255.255	65,536
172.16.0.0/12	172.16.0.0 - 172.31.255.255	1,048,576
10.0.0.0/8	10.0.0.0 - 10.255.255.255	16,777,216

Table 9.4.6.1 The three private IP address spaces, their range and total number

Key concept

Non-routable IP address:
Private IP addresses are non-routable.
Routers in the public, global Internet will reject IP datagrams with source and/or destination IP addresses which fall within a private address range and will therefore not route them.

Routable IP addresses:
Public IP addresses are routable IP addresses because their assignment is coordinated by IANA and the Regional Internet registries to ensure that hosts/routers are uniquely identified globally. Routing tables in routers contain globally unique address information to enable successful and unambiguous routing of IP datagrams.

Non-routable IP addresses

Hosts within a given private TCP/IP network can send IP datagrams to each other using addresses assigned to each which are chosen from a private address space, e.g. 192.168.0.0/24. However, IP datagrams forwarded from the private network into the larger public, global Internet cannot use these addresses as source or destination address because there will be many other connected networks which use addresses from the same private address space. Routers in the public, global Internet will reject such IP datagrams and will not route them. Private IP addresses are therefore said to be non-routable.

Routable IP addresses

The assignment to hosts of IP addresses is coordinated by IANA and the Regional Internet Registries to ensure that each host's IP address is globally unique. This enables routers of the global, public Internet to use the source and destination public IP addresses of two communicating hosts to route IP datagrams through the Internet from one host to the other. Public IP addresses are routable IP addresses because the coordination provided by IANA and the Regional Internet registries ensures that routing tables in routers contain globally unique address information to enable successful and unambiguous routing of IP datagrams.

Questions

1. Read sections 1 to 4 of RFC 1918 (https://tools.ietf.org/html/rfc1918) then answer the following questions

   (a) Give **three** examples where external connectivity of hosts and routers in an organisation's TCP/IP network might be unnecessary.

   (b) Give **one** reason why it is good practice to use private IP addresses where possible in IPv4 TCP/IP local area networks that are connected to the Internet.

2. State the **three** regions of the IPv4 address space that are reserved for private TCP/IP networks.

3. Distinguish between routable and non-routable IP addresses.

In this chapter you have covered:

- *The three IPv4 address spaces that are reserved for private TCP/IP networks*

- *How to distinguish routable from non-routable IP addresses*

9.4 The Transmission Control Protocol/ Internet Protocol (TCP/IP) protocol

9.4.7 Dynamic Host Configuration Protocol (DHCP)

Obtaining a host address

How does a host get an IP address for its network interface when it joins a subnet?

One way of doing this is for the host's user to assign an IP address to the host interface that connects to the subnet.

This approach assumes

- some expertise on the part of the user

- that the user is able to choose an IP address which is not already in use

- that the user is able to choose an IP address whose network identification part matches the subnet address

Assigning an IP address is not all that will need to be done.

A subnet mask will also need to be assigned so that the host interface can determine the subnet address of the subnet to which it is connected.

The IP address of at least one DNS server will also need to be assigned to the host interface so that the host can consult this server to convert domain names into their IP addresses.

The network's administrator will know how to set up hosts and could be called to the host to configure it. However, this is not always convenient.

For example, the host in question could be a laptop attempting to connect wirelessly to a wireless subnet belonging to a cafe offering free WiFi access to its customers.

Functions of the DHCP system

The Internet Engineering Task Force specified a solution to the above problem in RFC 2131 (https://www.ietf.org/rfc/rfc2131.txt) .

The Dynamic Host Configuration Protocol (DHCP) provides configuration parameters to Internet hosts. DHCP consists of two components:

- a protocol for delivering host-specific configuration parameters from a DHCP server to a host, e.g. subnet mask

- a mechanism for allocation of IP addresses to hosts.

DHCP supports three mechanisms for IP address allocation.

- In "automatic allocation", DHCP assigns a permanent IP address to a client

Key point

Functions of the DHCP system:

1. To allocate IP addresses to hosts via three mechanisms:
   - automatic allocation of a permanent IP address
   - dynamic allocation of a temporary IP address (limited period of time)
   - conveying a manually assigned IP address to a host

2. To deliver host-specific configuration parameters such as subnet mask to a host.

- In "dynamic allocation", DHCP assigns an IP address to a client for a limited period of time (or until the client explicitly relinquishes the address)

- In "manual allocation", a client's IP address is assigned by the network administrator, and DHCP is used simply to convey the assigned address to the client.

A particular network will use one or more of these mechanisms, depending on the policies of the network administrator.

In addition to host IP address assignment, DCHP also allows a host to learn additional information, such as the subnet mask for the subnet it is connected to, the address of its first hop-router (often called the default gateway) to which it sends IP datagrams for hosts on different subnets, and the address of a DNS server.

Figure 9.4.7.1 shows the TCP/IPv4 Properties window for a Microsoft Windows 7 host. It shows the manually configured properties for the host interface's IP address, subnet mask and default gateway. The DNS servers have not been configured. If the radio buttons "Obtain an IP address automatically" and "Obtain DNS server address automatically" were selected then these property fields would be completed automatically by preconfigured information obtained from a DHCP server in a client-server operation.

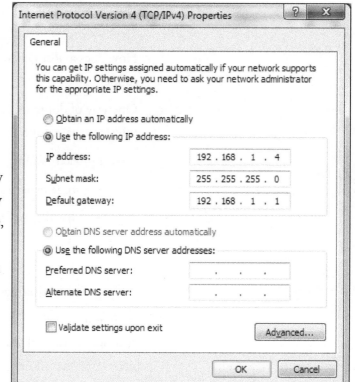

Figure 9.4.7.1 TCP/IPv4 properties window for a Microsoft Windows 7 host

The four-step DCHP process

Step 1

The first task of a new host (client) that wishes to join an existing TCP/IP network is to find a DHCP server. It does this by broadcasting a DHCP discover message over the network. The host at this point does not know the subnet address of the network or the IP address of any DHCP server. So it uses a special broadcast destination address of 255.255.255.255 and a "this host" source IP address of 0.0.0.0. This broadcast will reach all nodes attached to the subnet.

Step 2

A DHCP server receiving a DHCP discover message responds to the client with a DHCP offer message that is broadcast to all nodes on the subnet, again using the IP broadcast address of 255.255.255.255. The DHCP offer message contains the proposed IP address for the client, the network mask, an IP address lease time (the amount of time for which the IP address will be valid), and a transaction ID extracted from the DHCP discover message which links this message with the new client.

Step 3

The new client responds to the offer with a DHCP request message which echoes back the configuration parameters.

Step 4

The server responds to the DHCP request message with a DHCP ACK message, confirming the requested parameters.

Purpose of DHCP system

The primary purpose of DHCP is to automate the setting up of hosts that are connecting to a TCP/IP network. This is particularly important where hosts come and go frequently and IP addresses are needed only for a limited period of time, e.g., in a wireless LAN. Another example would be an ISP that has 16000 residential customers but no more than 4000 are ever online at the same time. In this case, rather than needing a block of 16384 addresses, a DHCP server that assigns addresses dynamically needs only a block of 4096 addresses (e.g. a block of the form a.b.c.d/22).

Each time a host joins the network, the DHCP server allocates an arbitrarily chosen IP address from its current pool of available IP addresses. Each time a host leaves, its address is returned to the pool.

Key point

Purpose of the DHCP system:
The primary purpose of DHCP is to automate the setting up of hosts that are connecting to a TCP/IP network.

Questions

1. What is the primary purpose of the DHCP system?

2. Give **two** examples where using DHCP to configure new client hosts is preferable to manual configuration by other means.

3. Explain the function of the DHCP system.

4. Why is a DHCP server required in a network that uses DHCP?

In this chapter you have covered:

■ The purpose and function of the DHCP system

9.4 The Transmission Control Protocol/ Internet Protocol (TCP/IP) protocol

■ 9.4.8 Network Address Translation (NAT)

Learning objectives:

■ *Explain the basic concepts of NAT and why it is used*

> **Key Concept**
>
> **Network Address Translation (NAT) protocol:**
> The NAT protocol is specified in RFC 2663 and RFC 3022. Network Address Translation is a method by which a device, e.g. a router, is used to connect an isolated address realm assigned private unregistered addresses, e.g. a LAN, to an external realm assigned globally unique registered addresses, e.g. the Internet.

Using non-routable IPv4 addresses with a NAT-enabled router
Obtaining blocks of routable IPv4 addresses to cover every computing device in a home, small office or school LAN is problematic because of the shortage of such addresses. However, if such computing devices wish to connect to the public Internet and communicate with other Internet-connected TCP/IP-enabled devices then a solution is required which allows devices to use IP addresses drawn from the non-routable IP address spaces 10.0.0.0/8, 172.16.0.0/12, 192.168.0.0/16.

The current approach to the problem is to use a NAT-enabled router. The NAT-enabled router has an interface that is part of the LAN as shown in *Figure 9.4.8.1*. The subnet address of this LAN is 192.168.1.0/24 and the IP addresses of the interfaces in this subnet are the private, non-routable addresses. 192.168.1.1, 192.168.1.2, 192.168.1.3 and 192.168.1.4, respectively. Devices within the home LAN can send IP datagrams to each other using 192.168.0/24 addressing. However, IP datagrams forwarded beyond the home LAN into the global Internet cannot use these addresses because 192.168.1.0/24 addresses will be rejected by Internet routers.

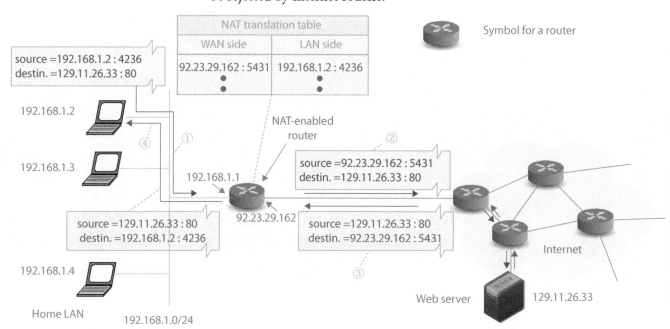

Figure 9.4.8.1 NAT-enabled router connecting a Home LAN to the Internet

The NAT-enabled router deals with this issue by presenting itself to the outside world not as a router but as a single device with a single IP address. In *Figure 9.4.8.1* all traffic leaving this NAT-enabled router for the global Internet has a source IP address of 92.23.29.162. All traffic entering this router must have a destination address of 92.23.29.162. The role performed by this NAT-enabled router is to hide the details of the home LAN from the outside world.

NAT translation table

If all IP datagrams arriving from the Internet have the same destination IP address, 92.23.29.162, i.e. the NAT router's Wide Area Network(WAN) interface address, how does the router know to which LAN host it should forward the IP datagram? The answer is the NAT Translation table in the NAT-enabled router together with the use of port numbers. *Figure 9.4.8.2* shows the rear of a NAT-enabled router.

Figure 9.4.8.2 NAT-enabled router showing four LAN sockets labelled Ethernet 1, 2, 3 and 4, a WAN socket, and a broadband socket (an alternative way of connecting to the Internet)

The use of port numbers

To understand how port numbers are used to enable LAN hosts to use the WAN, consider the example shown in *Figure 9.4.8.1*. In this figure, LAN host with IP address 192.168.1.2 requests a Web page from a Web server with IP address 129.11.26.33 listening on port 80. The LAN host assigns an arbitrarily chosen source port number 4236 to the request and sends the IP datagram into the LAN as a link-layer packet addressed to the NAT-enabled router - see *Figure 9.4.8.1* ①. Note that the destination IP address is 129.11.26.33 and the destination port number is 80.

The NAT-enabled router receives the IP datagram and makes two changes to this datagram:

- It generates a new source port number 5431 for the datagram and replaces the original source port number 4236 with this new source port number
- It replaces the source IP address 192.168.1.2 with its WAN-side IP address 92.23.29.162.

The NAT-enabled router adds the entry 92.23.29.162 : 5431   192.168.1.2 : 4236 to its NAT translation table as shown in *Figure 9.4.8.1.* and sends the IP datagram ② into the public Internet.

When generating a replacement source port number, the NAT router chooses a source port number which is not currently present in the NAT translation table. Port numbers are 16-bit numbers so the NAT router with a single WAN-side IP address is able to support 2^{16} simultaneous connections.

The Web server responds with an IP datagram whose destination address is the WAN-side IP address of the router, and whose destination port number is 5431 - see *Figure 9.4.8.1* ③. Note that the Web server is not aware that the Web page request has come from the LAN host with interface IP address 192.168.1.2.

On arrival at the NAT-enabled router, the received datagram's destination IP address 92.23.29.162 together with the destination port number 5431 is matched to the corresponding entry in the NAT translation table to obtain the LAN host IP address and port number. The router then constructs an IP datagram using these as destination IP address and destination port number, respectively, before dispatching this datagram into the home LAN where it is read by host 192.168.1.2 and passed to the application (identified by port number 4236) that initiated the Web page request - see *Figure 9.4.8.1* ④.

Questions

1 Why does an IPv4 TCP/IP LAN need a NAT-enabled router if hosts with private IP addresses are to connect to the Internet?

2 Explain how port numbers are used to enable LAN hosts using private IPv4 addresses to exchange IP datagrams with the global Internet.

3 Port numbers are associated in the TCP/IP specifications with layer 4, the Application layer, of the TCP/IP protocol stack (*Chapter 9.4.1*). How does the use of port numbers by the NAT protocol differ from their use by the Application layer protocol?

4 The end-to-end principle is one of the underlying system principles of the Internet (*Chapter 9.4.1*).
(a) Why is the NAT protocol a violation of this principle?
(b) Why might using IPv6 addressing obviate the need for the NAT protocol?

In this chapter you have covered:

■ The basic concepts of NAT:

- A method used to connect an isolated address realm assigned private unregistered addresses, e.g. a LAN, to an external realm assigned globally unique registered addresses, e.g. the Internet.

- A NAT-enabled router enables this connection to the outside world by presenting itself not as a router to the the world but as a single device with a single IP address.

- The internal hosts are identified by port no and their interaction with the outside world is recorded in a NAT-enabled router in its NAT translation table which maps the host port no to a router port no.

■ NAT is necessary because of the scarcity of sufficient blocks of IPV4 addresses

9.4 The Transmission Control Protocol/ Internet Protocol (TCP/IP) protocol

9.4.9 Port forwarding

Key Concept

Port forwarding:
In port forwarding, specific
router ports (TCP and UDP)
are opened up so that the
router is able to direct all traffic
arriving at these ports to a
specific internal IP address.

Port forwarding is one method by which clients in other LANs connected to
the Internet may reach servers assigned private unregistered IP addresses and
located behind a NAT router in another LAN. For example, in Figure 9.4.9.1
two servers, a Web server listening on port 80 and a multiplayer Minecraft
server listening on port 25565, are located in Home LAN 1 behind a NAT-
enabled router. Both have private, unregistered and therefore non-routable
IPv4 addresses. Clients in other LANs such as Home LAN 2 and Home LAN
3 can request Web pages from the Web server in Home LAN 1 by sending
their HTTP requests in IP datagrams, marked for the attention of TCP port
80, to the router interface with routable IP address 92.23.29.162. This router
will consult its port mapping table and find that 92.23.29.162 : 80 maps to
192.168.1.4 : 80 on the internal network. The HTTP request IP datagram will
then be forwarded to the Web server in Home LAN 1 at 192.168.1.4.

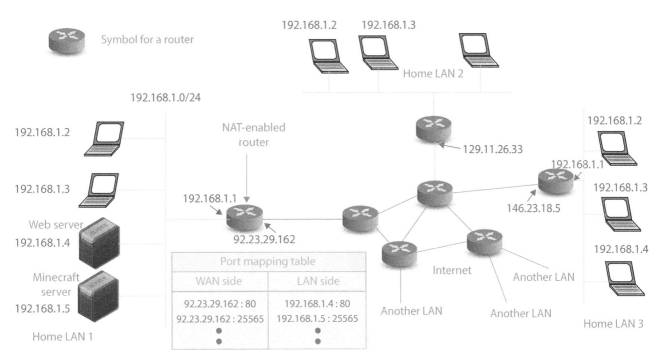

Figure 9.4.9.1 Port forwarding to enable access from the Internet to a Web server and a Minecraft server
assigned unregistered private addresses in home LAN 1

In a similar manner, clients in other LANs may connect to the Minecraft server
in Home LAN 1 via port forwarding set up in the NAT-enabled router with
public IP address 92.23.29.162.

Figure 9.4.9.2 shows the setup window for port forwarding for a NAT-enabled
router.

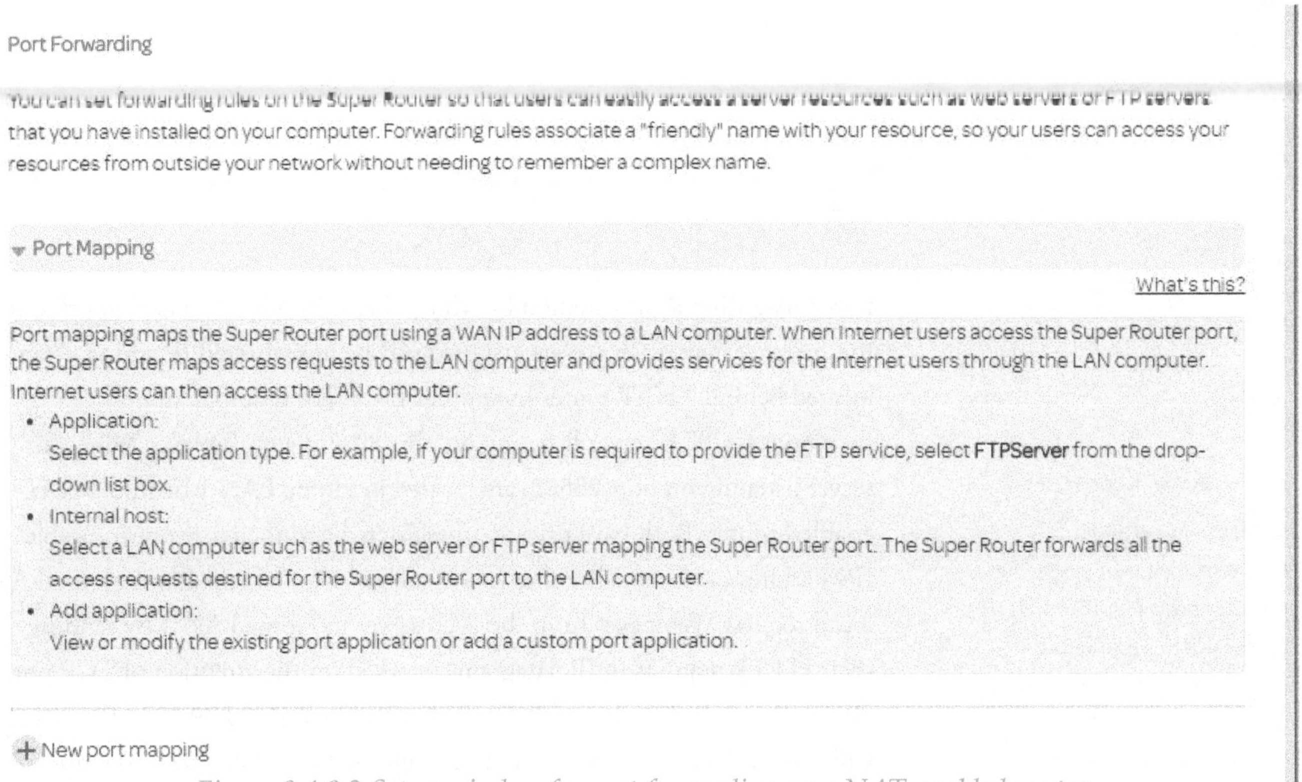

Port Forwarding

You can set forwarding rules on the Super Router so that users can easily access a server resource such as web servers or FTP servers that you have installed on your computer. Forwarding rules associate a "friendly" name with your resource, so your users can access your resources from outside your network without needing to remember a complex name.

▼ Port Mapping

What's this?

Port mapping maps the Super Router port using a WAN IP address to a LAN computer. When Internet users access the Super Router port, the Super Router maps access requests to the LAN computer and provides services for the Internet users through the LAN computer. Internet users can then access the LAN computer.

- Application:
  Select the application type. For example, if your computer is required to provide the FTP service, select **FTPServer** from the drop-down list box.
- Internal host:
  Select a LAN computer such as the web server or FTP server mapping the Super Router port. The Super Router forwards all the access requests destined for the Super Router port to the LAN computer.
- Add application:
  View or modify the existing port application or add a custom port application.

➕ New port mapping

Figure 9.4.9.2 Setup window for port forwarding on a NAT-enabled router

The port mapping table that enables port forwarding uses private IPv4 address for the internal servers. It is therefore important that the IP addresses of these servers do not change because if they do the mapping will no longer work. These private IP addresses must be assigned to the servers as static IP addresses. This may be done in one of two ways:

- The network administrator sets up these addresses in DHCP so that they are assigned permanently by DHCP

- DHCP is not used and these addresses are assigned at the servers by using network configuration software running on the servers.

Questions

1 In what circumstance would port forwarding be used?

2 A Web server connected to a LAN uses the private IP address 172.31.78.4. The Web server listens for HTTP requests on port 80. A NAT-enabled router with two interfaces, 172.31.78.1 and 146.31.18.97 is also connected to this LAN. Its 146.31.18.97 interface is connected to the Internet. Explain how the port mapping table in this router would be set up to allow port forwarding of HTTP requests arriving from the Internet.

3 The Web server in Question 2 is switched off for maintenance for two days. When it is brought back online, port forwarding no longer works. State **one** likely reason why port forwarding no longer works and suggest a solution.

In this chapter you have covered:

■ The basic concept of port forwarding and why it is used.

9.4 The Transmission Control Protocol/Internet Protocol (TCP/IP)

9.4.10 Client-server model

What is it?

When you order a pizza from a pizza delivery service, called Pizza House, you are accessing the service offered by Pizza House, the server, as one client amongst many. Your REQUEST is processed by Pizza House which generates a RESPONSE by creating the pizza you ordered before arranging for it to be delivered to you. This is an example of a client-server model. In this model, we expect a server to be available continuously, i.e. Pizza House will continue to service orders from clients **24** hours a day, seven days a week – *Figure 9.4.10.1.*

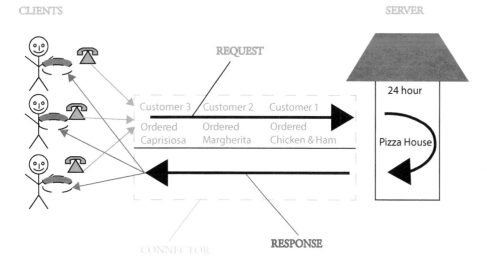

Figure 9.4.10.1 The client server model for Pizza House service

There is a protocol that client and server use in this scenario that is common to many similar scenarios in which a customer (client) orders something over the telephone or online from a supplier (server):

1. there is a menu to choose from that defines the identifier for the resource, e.g. Margherita;

2. a request which begins "I would like to order…" and ends with "for delivery to **42** Acacia Avenue, Dingley Dell, NeverNeverLand";

3. the server issues a response to the request addressing it to the client.

The protocol is the "glue" or connector that enables the client-server interaction to perform as expected.

The client-server model is the most commonly employed of the architectural styles for when one application interacts with another. A server is one application, a client is another. A server application listens for requests, from client applications, for services which it offers and the client applications consume these services.

A client application, needing a service to be performed, sends a request to the server application via a standard interface protocol e.g. HTTP.

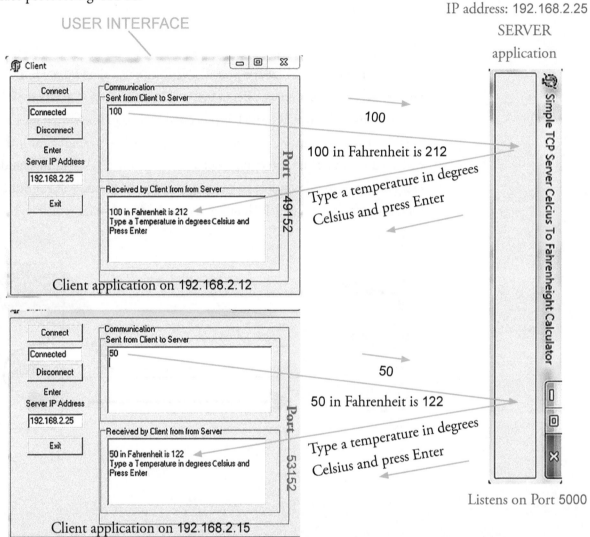

Figure 9.4.10.2 Client-server operation, server application offers a temperature conversion service, client applications request this service

Background

Callback:

A callback function is typically a Javascript function. A reference to the callback function is passed to the server along with the request. The server invokes this function on the client whenever a response to the request is ready at the server.

The server application either rejects or performs the request and sends a response back to the client application (possibly invoking a callback function in the client application).

A server application, on the other hand, waits for requests to be made and then reacts to them. A server application is usually a non-terminating process (i.e. on or running all the time). It is usually designed to provide a service to more than one client application.

The server application shown running in Figure 9.4.10.2 performs a temperature conversion service, e.g. 100°C → 212°F, when it receives a client application request for this service (server port 5000). Included in the request is the temperature to be converted, the IP address of the client application, e.g. 192.168.2.15, and the port number on the client, e.g. **53152**, that is connected to the requesting client application. The response of the server application is to return the temperature in Fahrenheit to the requesting client application, using as return address the client application's IP address and port number. The client application connects to the server application for this service. In this example, the connection uses the Telnet (a less secure alternative to SSH) protocol.

Figure 9.10.4.2 illustrates a very important principle: Separation of Concerns. The client application is developed quite separately from the server application. The client application focuses on the user interface design and the server application focuses on the design for the processing and formatting of data. Both designs can be changed without regard to each other whilst preserving a uniform interface between the two, e.g. the Telnet protocol.

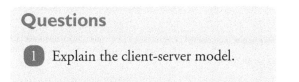

Questions

1 Explain the client-server model.

Background

API:

An API is an application programming interface. An application programming interface separates the data from the operations that may be performed on the data. Applications that use a particular API do not know how the data is stored only how to access it via API calls.

REST

The idea of REST is that application data can be queried and changed using verbs and nouns, represented by HTTP methods and URLs, respectively. A REST request will typically return data in a machine-readable form, such as JSON or XML.

Suppose that you wanted to order a book from Amazon, the online bookseller. Do you have to download a special app to do this or can you use software that you have on your computer

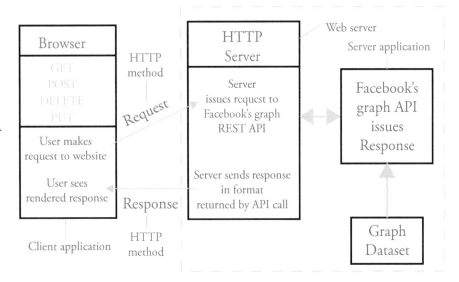

Figure 9.4.10.3 Interaction via an HTTP server between a browser and a server application accessing Facebook's social network graph

already? Of course, the answer is that you can use browser software you have on your computer already. Typing the following URL (uniform resource locator) into the address bar of your browser returns a web page that contains information about a resource that Amazon uniquely identifies with the ID **0241003008**, i.e. the book *Very Hungry Caterpillar Board Book*: http://www.amazon.co.uk/Very-Hungry-Caterpillar-Board-Book/dp/0241003008/

Amazon's web site is a web service based on a design pattern called REST which stands for REpresentational State Transfer. Central to the concept of REST is the notion of resources. Resources are represented by URIs or Uniform Resource Identifiers, the Amazon example is one such URI. There are two types of URI: URLs and URNs. We will focus on URLs (Uniform Resource Locators). Another key aspect of the design of REST web services is that resources should be linked together and representations of these resources should enable a user to move from one resource to another by following these links.

Figure 9.4.10.3 show an interaction via an HTTP server between a client application, a browser, and a server application, that provides a Facebook RESTful web service that accesses Facebook's social network graph dataset of Facebook users. Facebook's graph API is an application programming interface (API) that is run on Facebook servers. If the following URL is typed into the browser's address bar for the scenario in Figure 9.4.10.3 then what is returned is a representation that the browser renders as shown in Figure 9.4.10.4:

https://graph.facebook.com/4?oauth_token= CAACE......

See Task 1 below for how to get an access token (CAACE....) to use with oauth_token.

```
{
    "id": "4",
    "first_name": "Mark",
    "gender": "male",
    "last_name": "Zuckerberg",
    "link": "https://www.facebook.com/zuck",
    "locale": "en_US",
    "name": "Mark Zuckerberg",
    "username": "zuck"
}
```

Figure 9.4.10.4 Mark Zuckerberg's User node in Facebook's social network graph, node id is 4. Mark's home page is www.facebook.com/Zuck

In the Facebook social network graph, Mark Zuckerberg's user node has the identifier "4", not surprisingly his identifier was one of the very first to be allocated. The representation returned is expressed in JSON (JavaScript Object Notation)

By following the link in the representation shown in *Figure 9.4.10.4*, a client application, i.e. a browser, can obtain the next resource representation, Mark Zuckerberg's Facebook home page, from the server application. Facebook's social network graph is, in 2015, the largest social network dataset in the world.

Figure 9.4.10.5 shows how the client application's state changes as it interacts with the server application which in turn accesses Facebook's social network graph dataset. Thus, the client application changes (Transfers) to a new State when it obtains a new resource REpresentation from the server application, this is why REST stands for REpresentational State Transfer!

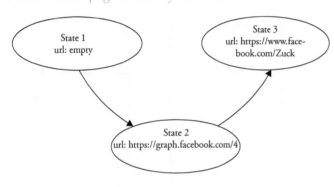

Figure 9.4.10.5 The client application's changes of state, each transition to a new state causes the server application to transfer a representation to the client application

Questions

2 Explain with an example what is meant by REST.

The REST architecture is characterised by

- Client-server: separation between server application that offers a service, and the client application that consumes it

- Stateless: each request from a client application must contain all the information required by the server application to carry out the request. Session state is kept entirely on the client not at the server

- Uniform interface: the method of communication between a client application and a server application must be uniform, e.g. via HTTP requests and responses

- Code-on-demand: server applications can provide executable code or scripts for client applications to execute in their context

- Cacheable: the server application must indicate to the client application requests that can be cached.

- Every resource has a unique ID, e.g. https://graph.facebook.com/4

- Multiple representations of resources provided for different needs, e.g. html, JSON, XML, jpeg, png, gif, csv

- Resources are linked together, e.g. Facebook's social network graph.

Uniform interface

Communication between the client application and the server application typically uses HTTP as the uniform interface. HTTP provides four principle methods for Creating, Retrieving, Updating and Deleting a resource. The methods are sometimes referred to as CRUD operations:

- C – Create
- R – Retrieve
- U – Update
- D - Delete

The HTTP methods that map onto these operations are shown in Table 9.4.10.1.

The REST API created and run at the server may be connected to a relational database such as MySQL. In which case the HTTP verbs will be converted into SQL equivalent database commands as follows :

- GET → SELECT
- POST → INSERT
- DELETE → DELETE
- PUT → UPDATE

HTTP method	Action	Examples

GET	**Retrieve** a resource or a collection of resources	Retrieve Mark Zuckerberg's social network graph entry –
		`GET /4 HTTP/1.1`
		`Host: graph.facebook.com`
		Retrieve AQA CS Unit 2 main sections
		`GET /v1/csunit2s/ HTTP/1.1`
		`Host: cs.apispark.net`

POST	**Create** a new resource	Creates a new resource –
		`POST /v1/csunit2s/ HTTP/1.1`
		`Host: cs.apispark.net`
		`{ "id": "7", "title": "Fundamentals of compter organisation and architecture", "link":["a test"] }`

PUT	**Update** or replace an existing resource	Updates a resource, "computer" misspelt–
		`PUT /v1/csunit2s/7 HTTP/1.1`
		`Host: cs.apispark.net`
		`{ "id": "7", "title": "Fundamentals of computer organisation and architecture", "link":["a test"] }`

DELETE	**Delete** a resource	Deletes a resource, 8 –
		`DELETE /v1/csunit2s/8 HTTP/1.1`
		`Host: cs.apispark.net`

Table 9.4.10.1 The four HTTP methods for CRUD

in order to carry out operations on the database (see Chapter 10.4 for SQL commands).

The REST API may also be connected to a NOSQL database such as MongoDB.

Multiple representations of resources

What is returned to the client application is not the resource but a representation of the resource. The REST service provided by the server application is usually designed to provide at least JSON and XML representations. Figure 9.4.10.6 shows the JSON response and Figure 9.4.10.7 shows the equivalent XML response. The URL in each case is

https://cs.apispark.net/v1/csunit2/6

```
var http = require('http');
var work = require('./mydatabase');
var mysql = require('mysql');
var db = mysql.createConnection({
        host: '127.0.0.1',
        user: 'myuser',
        password: 'mypassword',
        database: 'mydatabase'
});
```

Table 9.4.10.2 Server-side Javascript to set up a MySQL database connection to database, mydatabase. This is part of a larger script that runs under node.js.

The client application has no knowledge of how the resource is actually stored on the server. The resource sits behind an interface which hides this information. This means that the resource can be restructured without affecting any client application which simply continues to use the uniform interface of HTTP CRUD operations.

```
GET /v1/csunit2s/6 HTTP/1.1
Host: cs.apispark.net
Content-Type: application/json
Authorization: Basic
NjY1ZjkyNDUtZTUzNy00MjViLWJhZGI·····
Accept: application/json
Cache-Control: no-cache
```

To access these urls login credentials are required.

Information

APISpark:
(http://restlet.com/products/
apispark/). It's an online
platform that allows you to
design your APIs following
REST principles and then
host them. The data are
also managed by the
platform. Users need to
have authorisation to use a
resource which is obtained
by just registering to use
APISpark.

```
{
   "id": "6",
   "link": [
        "https://cs.apispark.net/v1/csunit2s/subsections/6.1",
        "https://cs.apispark.net/v1/csunit2s/subsections/6.2",
        "https://cs.apispark.net/v1/csunit2s/subsections/6.3"
   ],
   "title": "Fundamentals of computer systems"
}
```

Figure 9.4.10.6 JSON representation returned to client application

```
GET /v1/csunit2s/6 HTTP/1.1
Host: cs.apispark.net
Content-Type: application/xml
Authorization: Basic
NjY1ZjkyNDUtZTUzNy00MjViLWJhZGI·····
Accept: application/xml

Cache-Control: no-cache
```

```
<Csunit2>
   <id>6</id>
   <link>
        <link>https://cs.apispark.net/v1/csunit2s/subsections/6.1</link>
        <link>https://cs.apispark.net/v1/csunit2s/subsections/6.2</link>
        <link>https://cs.apispark.net/v1/csunit2s/subsections/6.3</link>
   </link>
   <title>Fundamentals of computer systems</title>
</Csunit2>
```

Figure 9.4.10.7 XML representation returned to client application

Every resource has an ID

Resources may be individual resources or collections of resources.

For example, the URL https://cs.apispark.net/v1/csunit2s/subsections/

returns links to all the subsections whereas the URL

https://cs.apispark.net/v1/csunit2s/subsection/6.1

returns just subsection 6.1.

Resource linking

Facebook's social network graph consists of ————

- nodes (e.g. a User, a Photo, a Page, a Comment)

- edges (e.g. connections between Users, Pages, etc)

- fields (info about Users, such as the birthday of a User, or the name of a Page).

So it should be possible to navigate from node to node by following edges, e.g. "likes". If we start with a user with Userid **784889091561000** (this is a fictional example), we need our client application, e.g. POSTMAN, to send the following request to Facebook's server application to access the open graph(og) part of the social network graph:

https://graph.facebook.com/784889091561000/og.likes?oauth_token= CAACE......

Figure 9.4.10.8 shows a section of the response from the application server.

> See Task 1 below for how to get an access token (CAACE....) to use with oauth_token.

Questions

3 In the context of REST explain, with examples, what is meant by
(a) uniform interface
(b) multiple representations
(c) every resource has an id
(d) resources are linked.

4 What is meant by CRUD?

5 A REST API is connected to a server-side relational database. What SQL commands will the HTTP verbs, GET, POST, DELETE and UPDATE map to?

```
{
  "data": [
    {
      "id": "670741596309143",
      "from": {
        "id": "784889091561000",
        "name": "Fred Bloggs"
      },
      "start_time": "2014-06-17T15:48:54+0000",
      "publish_time": "2014-06-17T15:48:54+0000",
      "application": {
        "name": "Og_likes",
        "namespace": "likes",
        "id": "193042140809145"
      },
      "data": {
        "object": {
          "id": "222386191275871",
          "url": "http://www.needateacher.co.uk/",
          "type": "website",
          "title": "http://www.needateacher.co.uk/"
        }
      },
```

Figure 9.4.10.8 Section of the response from application server. The id's have been altered for privacy reasons

Tasks

1 For this exercise you will need to be on Facebook. Launch Facebook's social network graph explorer tool, https://developers.facebook.com/tools/explorer and select the GET method. Enter /me into the field next to GET. Click on Get Access Token and in the pop-up screen select the items that you wish to view. Click on submit.

2 Using Facebook's social network graph explorer tool, enter the following in the GET field:
`search?q=secondary school&type=place&center=51.8168, -0.8124&distance=10000`
The response should be information about schools in the Aylesbury area –
`latitude 51.8168, longitude -0.8124, radius distance 10000 metres.`

3 Continuing on from Task 1. Select version v2.2 (Facebook reduced information returned in later versions). Enter /4 into the address bar next to GET. Click on submit. Copy the link to Mark Zuckerberg's home page and visit it in a browser.

4 Google supports several REST web services, one is finding directions. Try the following URL:
https://maps.googleapis.com/maps/api/directions/json?origin=Aylesbury Grammar School&destination=Tesco Tring Road

5 Experiment with changing the origin and destination parameter values for the URL in Task **4**.

Tasks

6　Another Google REST service in staticmap. Try the following URL in a browser.

https://maps.googleapis.com/maps/api/staticmap?center=Aylesbury Bucks&zoom=13&size=600x300&maptype=roadmap&format=png

7　Experiment with the center parameter value for the URL in Task 6 and the maptype (roadmap, satellite, terrain, hybrid).

Information

Google Maps Javascript reference:
https://developers.google.com/maps/documentation/javascript/reference#Map

8　Install POSTMAN REST client from Google Chrome store. Once installed run it from outside Chrome web browser. Select the normal page and the GET method.
Enter http://www.youtypeitwepostit.com/api/ onto the GET line. Click Send. You should get a response which is a collection of posts to a message board.

9　Use url http://www.youtypeitwepostit.com/api/. Select POST and raw then enter the following below the raw bar:

```
{
"template": {
            "data": [
                 {
                      "prompt":
"Text of message",
                      "name":
"text",
                      "value":
"Arfur"
                 }
            ]
        }
}
```

Click Send.

10　Using POSTMAN, check that the new message has been posted to the message board using GET. Click on the hyperlink URL, e.g. http://www.youtypeitwepostit.com/api/25134141254238784, so that it appears in the GET line. (Id 25134141254238784 must exist for this to work). Change GET to DELETE and Send. Check that this message has been deleted by doing a GET on http://www.youtypeitwepostit.com/api/.

11　Explore http://petstore.swagger.io/. Read the instructions very carefully and try
(a) GET (b) POST (c) PUT (d) DELETE

12　Obtain an API key from flickr (Yahoo). Enter the following URL into a browser URL address bar to use the REST web service of Flickr inserting your API key where indicated:
https://api.flickr.com/services/rest/?method=flickr.photos.search&api_key=this is where you put your key&format=json&nojsoncallback=1&text=cats&extras=url_o

Find a jpg image in the JSON response and copy its URL into a browser address bar.

13　Create a REST web service with APISpark.

Table 9.4.10.3 shows Javascript code embedded in an HTML web page, `GoogleMap.html`. This HTML file uses a Google map api Javascript library at http://maps.googleapis.com/maps/api/js. The script calls a REST API provided by Google to pull down a road map. After loading this web page the browser executes the Javascript function `initialize()`. This function loads the map data into the web page using a call to an API constructor `google.maps.Map`. This creates a new map inside the given HTML container, the Div element, identified by the identifier "`googleMap`". The script section is placed at the end of the web page to ensure that it is executed after the web page is loaded. The function `initialize` also places a marker on the map, using the latitude and longitude coordinates.

Tasks

14 Experiment with the values assigned in `mapOptions`:

(a) Change `zoom` from 1 to 20. Note that the map object can be dragged to move location.

(b) Change ROADMAP to SATELLITE.

(c) Change the latitude and longitude to match your location.

(d) Change the marker text that appears when the mouse is over the marker on the map.

```html
<!DOCTYPE html>
<html>
  <head>
    <script
      src="http://maps.googleapis.com/maps/api/js">
    </script>
  </head>
  <body>
    <div id="googleMap" style="width:600px;height:400px;"></div>
    <script>
      function initialize()
        {
          var LatitudeLongitude = new google.maps.LatLng(51.8168, -0.8124);
          var mapOptions = {
                            zoom: 15,
                            center: LatitudeLongitude,
                            mapTypeId:google.maps.MapTypeId.ROADMAP
                          }
          var map = new google.maps.Map(document.getElementById('googleMap'),
                        mapOptions);
          var marker = new google.maps.Marker({
                                      position: LatitudeLongitude,
                                      map: map,
                                      title: 'Marker test!'
                                    });
        }
      initialize();
    </script>
  </body>
</html>
```

Table 9.4.10.3 Web page GoogleMap.html that contains a Javascript script to load a Google roadmap centred on latitude 51.8168 and longitude -0.8124 at zoom level 15.

Table 9.4.10.4 shows a Javascript client side script that accesses a REST web service at

https://cs.apispark.net/v1/csunit2s/subsections/subsubsections/5.1.1

> To access this url login credentials are required.

The response is then rendered by adding it to the paragraphs according to their class ids, greeting id, greeting title, greeting-link. The script uses jQuery, $ is short for jQuery, e.g. $.ajax is equivalent to jQuery.ajax.

Figure 9.4.10.9 shows the response rendered in a browser window.

```
<!DOCTYPE html>
<html>
  <head>
    <title>Hello jQuery</title>
    <script src="https://ajax.googleapis.com/ajax/libs/jquery/1.10.2/jquery.min.js">
    </script>
  </head>
  <body>
    <div>
      <p class="greeting-id">The ID is </p>
      <p class="greeting-title">The title is </p>
      <p class="greeting-link">The link is </p>
    </div>
  </body>
  <script>
    $.ajax({
      headers: {"Authorization": "Basic replace with access token here"},
      dataType: "json",
      url: "https://cs.apispark.net/v1/csunit2s/subsections/subsubsections/5.1.1"
    }).then(function(data) {
        $('.greeting-id').append(data.id);
        $('.greeting-title').append(data.title);
        $('.greeting-link').append(data.link);
    });
  </script>
</html>
```

> Save this script with extension .html. Launch in Google Chrome. If an access token is not supplied then the Javascript console window will show the error message:
> Failed to load resource: the server responded with a status of 401 (Unauthorized)

> You will need to register with **cs.apispark.net** and set up your own REST service. The urls used here are the author's own setup.

Table 9.4.10.4 HTML web page containing a jQuery Javascript script to access a REST web service

The ID is 5.1.1

The title is Natural numbers

The link is https://cs.apispark.net/v1/csunit2s/subsections/subsubsections/contents/5.1.1

Figure 9.4.10.9 Response to jQuery Javascript rendered in a browser window

Comparing JSON and XML

JSON is more compact than XML and therefore quicker to parse but this comes at the price of security compared with XML. XML is text/parsing, not code execution, whereas JSON is a subset of Javascript and is parsed by Eval() which is also used to execute Javascript and therefore could execute malicious code inserted into the JSON unless precautions are taken to prevent this. XML has namespaces whereas JSON does not - so it cannot support multiple instances of the same field name in a data-interchange. However, JSON does have advantages over XML which the JSON.org site summarises as:

- JSON (JavaScript Object Notation) is a lightweight data-interchange format. It is easy for humans to read and write. It is easy for machines to parse and and generate.

- XML is less easy for humans to read and write and less easy for machines to parse and generate.

Questions

6 Give **three** advantages that JSON has over XML. **7** Give **two** advantages that XML has over JSON.

Websocket protocol

The use of HTTP is well suited to the applications described so far. However, in applications which require the server to send data to the client the very moment when it knows that new data is available, HTTP is inadequate because it is client-driven.

The HTML5 WebSocket specification defines an API that establishes a full-duplex communication channel operating through a single socket over the Web between a web browser and a server. HTML5 Websocket has been designed for real-time, event-driven web applications. The Websocket protocol creates a persistent connection between the client and the server in which both parties can start sending data at any time.

As soon as a connection to the server is established, the client application can start sending data to the server using the `send('a message')` method on the connection object.

Equally the server application can send messages to the client application at any time.

The http:// is replaced by ws:// in a url, e.g. ws://echo.websocket.org,

https:// is replaced by wss://, e.g. wss://echo.websocket.org.

The Websocket protocol is used where multiple users need to interact in real time such as in multiplayer games.

Tasks

15 Visit http://demo.kaazing.com/livefeed/ to see a live demo that uses the WebSocket protocol.

16 Try the echo test at https://www.websocket.org/echo.html

Questions

8 Explain why the Websocket protocol has replaced the HTTP protocol for a certain type of client-server interaction.

In this chapter you have covered:

- The client-server model
- The Websocket protocol
- The principles of Web CRUD Applications and REST:
  - CRUD is an acronym for
    - C – Create
    - R – Replace
    - U – Update
    - D – Delete

- REST enables CRUD to be mapped to database functions (SQL) as follows:
  - GET → SELECT
  - POST → INSERT
  - DELETE → DELETE
  - PUT → UPDATE
- Comparing JSON (Javascript Object Notation) with XML

9.4 The Transmission Control Protocol/ Internet Protocol (TCP/IP) protocol

■ 9.4.11 Thin- versus thick-client computing

Key Concept

Thick-client:

A thick-client is a computer workstation with non-volatile local storage, e.g. magnetic hard disk or solid state disk. The magnetic disk or solid state disk stores an operating system, application programs and local files.

Thick-client network:

The thick-client is connected in a client-server network to a file server and a domain controller. The domain controller validates users when they initiate a login session. The central file server stores users' files.

Thick-client computing:

The operating system that runs in the thick-client is loaded from the thick-client's local store. Applications are loaded from the thick-client's local store and run in the thick-client workstation.

Key Concept

Thin-client:

A thin-client is a diskless workstation with a little RAM, a low specification CPU, a network interface adapter with a boot ROM, interfaces for keyboard, mouse, VDU, and possibly interfaces for other peripherals.

Thick-client

A thick-client is a computer workstation (*Figure 9.4.11.1*) with non-volatile local storage, e.g. magnetic hard disk or solid state disk. The magnetic disk or solid state disk stores an operating system, application programs and local files.

Thick-client network

The thick-client is connected in a client-server network to a file server and a domain controller. The domain controller validates users when they initiate a login session. The central file server stores users' files.

Thick-client computing

The operating system that runs in the thick-client is loaded from the thick-client's local store, i.e. its magnetic hard disk or solid state disk. Applications that are used by the thick-client are loaded from its local store. It may also load some applications from the file server or an application server. However, what distinguishes thick-client computing from thin-client computing is that applications run in the thick-client workstation whereas for the thin-client workstation applications run, by default, in a central server.

Figure 9.4.11.1 Thick-client workstation with 1 TB magnetic disk

Thin-client

In a thin-client network, the client is a diskless workstation with a little RAM, a low specification CPU, a network interface adapter with a boot ROM, interfaces for keyboard, mouse, VDU, and possibly interfaces for other peripherals. The boot ROM on the network card is used to load a stripped-down operating system from a central server as well as to obtain an IP address and other networking configuration information, e.g. a subnet mask and a gateway IP address.

Key Concept

Thin-client networking:

The boot ROM on the network card is used to load an operating system from a central server as well as to obtain an IP address and other networking configuration information, e.g. a subnet mask and a gateway IP address. Users sit at a thin-client workstation and log into the server.

Thin-client computing:

The central server is an application server, a file server and a domain controller all rolled into one. The central file server stores users' files. The central application server stores applications. The central domain controller stores user accounts and validates users when they initiate a login session.

By default all applications run at the server.

Information entered by the user operating at the thin-client workstation gets sent to the central server which processes it before returning an updated image to the thin-client's screen.

Information

PiNet:

A thin-client network for Raspberry Pi thin-clients derived from LTSP - see http://pinet.org.uk/.

Terminal server:

Thin-clients behave in a similar manner to dumb terminals used in a previous era of computing for providing input and receiving results from application programs running in mainframes.

The central server in a thin-client network serves clients which act like these dumb terminals, hence the label terminal server.

Thin-client networking

The central server is an application server, a file server and a domain controller all rolled into one. The domain controller validates users when they initiate a login session. The central file server stores users' files. Users sit at a thin-client workstation and log into the server. Figure 9.4.11.2 shows a diskless thin-client workstation.

Thin-client computing

By default all applications run at the server. If the server has sufficient RAM, a sufficiently powerful multicore CPU and the speed of the network is adequate then a user unacquainted with thin client architecture will think that the applications they are using are running in their client workstation. Information entered by the user at the thin-client workstation gets sent to the central server which processes it before returning an updated image to the thin-client's screen.

Figure 9.4.11.2 Jammin LTSP diskless thin-client workstation with its own VDU, USB keyboard, mouse, and connected to a client-server network.

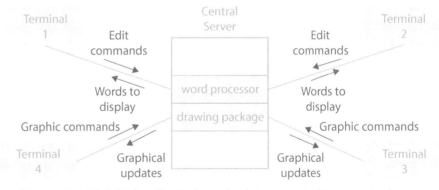

Figure 9.4.11.3 Thin-clients (terminals) connected to a central server

LTSP

Figure 9.4.11.2 shows a diskless workstation called a Jammin that is supported by the Linux Terminal Server Project (LTSP[1]) - http://www.ltsp.org. Linux is very good at disk caching and code sharing. The Linux server requires about 250 MiB before any clients are added and then 50 MiB for each client.

---

1   LTSP is a registered trademark of DisklessWorkstations.com, LLC

Key point

Thin- versus thick-client:
Software maintenance:
- Single point of control in thin-client for patches/updates and installations of new applications
- Updates/patches and installations of new applications at each thick-client

Hardware maintenance:
- Life expectancy or mean-time-between-failure of thin-client workstations longer than thick-client workstations by about two years

Security:
- Unauthorised software cannot be installed, virus and spyware infections are not possible because of absence of local storage in a thin-client

Cost:
- Lower specifications for CPU, less RAM, no magnetic hard drive/SSD for thin-client compared with thick-client means lower cost to produce

Power consumption:
- Lower specifications and less hardware means thin-client workstations can consume about one-seventh the power that PC thick-client does

Reduced licensing costs:
- Only as many licences as will be used, need to be purchased in a thin-client system but as many licences as thick-clients are needed in a thick-client system

Apps best run in a thick-client:
- Applications that result in considerable latency such as graphic intensive and video editing ones. These require a lot of processing power, large amount of RAM, large file sizes and higher network bandwidth

Questions

1. Estimate the amount of RAM in MiB required in a Linux Server supporting 100 thin-clients. Compare this with the amount of RAM installed in a thick-client workstation that you have access to (or go online to a computer retailer and obtain a figure for a typical thick-client).

Comparison of thin- and thick-client computing

In a thin-client network there is a single-point of control for patches/updates and for installation of new applications, the terminal server. In contrast workstations in a thick-client network require new applications to be installed and patches/updates to be applied at each workstation.

Software maintenance

In the thick-client scenario, there is a software maintenance overhead on each client. Patches/updates will need to be applied from time to time to the operating system installed on the hard disk drive/SSD of each client. Similarly, patches need to be applied to applications installed on the hard disk drive/SSD of each client. If the number of thick clients is significant, e.g. **50+**, this is a time-consuming activity.

In a thin-client network, patches/updates are applied to the software stored on the terminal server. This is much less time consuming because the maintenance occurs on just one machine.

Hardware maintenance

Fanless thin-clients have no mechanical moving parts which is the principle cause of failure in thick-clients with magnetic hard disk drives and fans to cool the CPU. The life expectancy of thin-clients is about two years longer than thick clients with magnetic storage.

Security

One of the primary benefits of using thin-client hardware is security. The absence of local storage means that users are unable to install unauthorised software onto the system. There is also no local storage to infect with viruses or spyware. Virus protection is applied at the terminal server where it is centrally managed.

Cost

Thin client hardware has a very low price tag compared with thick-client workstations. The cost of a thin-client station in a Raspberry Pi LTSP thin-client network is £20 to £30. The Jammin series are about £200 but have **2-4** GiB memory and a fast Gigabit network adapter.

Power consumption

Thin client devices tend to consume much less power than thick-client workstations. Power consumption varies among makes and models, but some estimates indicate that thin-client devices only consume about one-seventh the power of PC thick-clients.

Reduced licensing costs

In a thick-client environment application software is installed on each client. If the software requires a licence then the total number of licences that need to be purchased equals the total number of thick-clients, assuming that users can work at any thick-client. In a thin-client environment only as many licences as will be used, need to be purchased as the licensed application software runs in the terminal server whilst being accessible from any thin-client.

Applications that are best run in a thick-client workstation

Thin-client computing works well for typical applications such as email, web browsing, office applications such as word processing but it doesn't work quite so well for high-level graphics processing and video editing because there will be considerable latency because of the higher processing power, larger RAM, larger file sizes and network bandwidth required for these applications. These applications are best suited to running in a thick-client.

Questions

2   Facing tighter budgets and the need to be more responsive to public requirements, local and city councils are finding it increasingly difficult to meet targets with their existing PC-centric computer infrastructures of 4500+ machines.
    (a) Give **four** reasons why a solution to this problem could be to replace the thick-client systems (PC-centric) with a thin-client system.
    (b) Suggest **one** reason why a thin-client system might not be the best option for the following
        (i) the architects department   (ii) computer science students in local council schools

3   In Business Studies lessons at one school, students need to use stand-alone machines. Before each lesson the teacher has found it is necessary to reset all twenty machines to their base configuration, spending 15 or 20 minutes each time on this task. Explain why replacing the stand-alone machines by a thin-client network could improve this situation.

4   Explain why clients in a thin-client network have been called dumb terminals.

In this chapter you have covered:

■   The meaning of

  • thin-client

  • thick client

■   and compared and contrasted thin-client computing with thick-client computing.

10.1 Conceptual data models and entity relationship modelling

Data modelling

What is a data model?

Just as a designer of a new type of aircraft or building will build models to help his or her understanding of the task so a database designer will build models to help his or her understanding of the task of creating a database. The models that the database designer builds are called data models.

> Formally,
> *A data model is a method of describing the data, its structure, the way it is inter-related and the constraints that apply to it for the given system or organisation.*

Requirements analysis

Before building a database system a systems analyst or systems analysts will establish:

- the applications the database must support – the processing and user requirements;

- the data that must be stored in order to satisfy the needs of the variety of users in an organisation – the data requirements;

- the constraints or rules that apply to that data – the data constraints.

From the analysis, a data model is constructed that will provide a conceptual model of the real-world system from which a database can be logically designed and then physically built using a particular Database Management System.

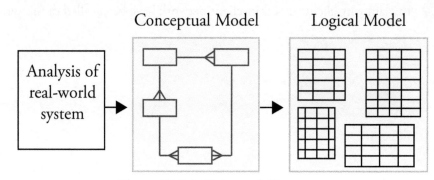

Conceptual Model   Logical Model

Analysis of real-world system

Figure 10.1.1 Data modelling stages

Data Requirements

Data requirements are usually expressed in English statements, e.g.

> 'Each module of study offered by a college has a module code, a module title and a credit value.'

Data constraints are also usually expressed in English statements, e.g.

'Students may not study more than three modules per term.'

Conceptual data model

The conceptual data model is created during the analysis phase of a project from the data requirements. It summarises these requirements in a formal way that makes it easier for the analyst to check with the customer that the data requirements of their organisation have been covered completely and accurately.

The model should contain no references to physical details of database construction because that would make it difficult for a customer who is not technically minded to understand.

Formally,
A conceptual model is a representation of the data requirements of an organisation constructed in a way that is independent of any software that is used to construct a database.

A conceptual model consists of

- a diagram showing the entities and relationships

- a formal description of each entity in terms of its attributes

- descriptions of the meaning of relationships

- descriptions of any constraints on the system and of any assumptions made

The terms entity, attribute and relationship are defined and explained below.

Entity

An example of an entity is a **Student**. Students are of interest to an organisation such as a school or college. The college will need to record the name of each student currently enrolled, his/her date of birth, home address, and other data about the student.

Formally,
An entity is an object, person, place, concept, activity, event or thing of interest to an organisation and about which data are recorded.

Key concept

Conceptual data model:
A conceptual model is a representation of the data requirements of an organisation constructed in a way that is independent of any software used to construct a database.

Key concept

Entity:
An entity is an object, person, place, concept, activity, event or thing of interest to an organisation and about which data are recorded.

Questions

1 List **three** entities for each of the following organisations:

(a) Hospital

(b) Lending library

(c) Athletics club

Attribute

The particular items of data such as name, date of birth, home address, etcetera belonging to an entity such as Student are called attributes.

Formally,
An attribute is a property or characteristic of an entity.

Key concept

Attribute:
An attribute is a property or characteristic of an entity.

Questions

2 List **two** attributes of each of the following entities that belong to a hospital in-patient system:

(a) Patient

(b) Ward

(c) Nurse

Entity occurrence or instance

A college will record the details of all its students.

The details of a particular student are referred to as an instance or occurrence of the entity **Student**.

Figure 10.1.2 shows four examples of instances / occurrences of the entity **Student**.

Attributes

Entity Occurrence or Instance →

Student Enrolment Number	Surname	Forename	Date of birth	Address	Tel. No
1	Briggs	Sarah	19/1/80	42 Benn Av.	433991
2	Carter	David	22/2/80	10 Acacia Av.	484132
3	Teng	Lee	13/4/80	23 Queens Road	472611
4	Khan	Imran	29/5/80	3 Stannier St	447334

Figure 10.1.2 Instances of the entity Student

Key concept

Entity identifier:
The entity identifier is an attribute or combination of attributes which uniquely identifies an instance or occurrence of the entity. Sometimes referred to loosely but incorrectly as the primary key.

Entity identifier

An organisation will need to select or identify a particular occurrence of an entity from among others. It does this with the entity identifier. This is sometimes referred to loosely but incorrectly as the primary key.

Formally,
The entity identifier is an attribute or combination of attributes which uniquely identifies an instance or occurrence of the entity.

Suppose that each student is assigned a number called the **student enrolment number**, such that no two students have the same number. This number is then unique to each student. Therefore, by making this number an attribute of the entity **Student** it can be used as this entity's identifier. An entity identifier must have a value, it can never be null, i.e. without a value.

If no single attribute possesses the property of uniqueness, then two or more attributes must be selected to achieve this goal. Such a combination of attributes is known as a composite entity identifier.

For example, the entity **ClassRoomTimeTable** has the following attributes:

Class Room Number, Period Of Day, Day Of Week, Class Code, Subject Code

Some example occurrences are shown in Figure 10.1.3.

Entity **ClassRoomTimeTable**

Class Room Number	Period Of Day	Day Of Week	Class Code	Subject Code
1	1	Monday	12C1	CS
2	2	Monday	12C1	CS
1	1	Tuesday	13D2	Phy
1	2	Tuesday	12C1	CS

Entity Occurrence or Instance

Figure 10.1.3 Sample occurrences of the entity ClassRoomTimeTable

Attribute **Class Room Number** alone is not sufficient to uniquely identify a single occurrence of this entity, but when it is combined with **Period Of Day** and **Day Of Week** then it becomes possible to identify a single occurrence. The entity identifier is thus the composite identifier **Class Room Number, Period Of Day** and **Day Of Week**.

A composite identifier must be **minimal**, i.e. it should contain the minimum number of attributes possible. For example, if attribute **Class Code** was added to the composite identifier it would be longer than necessary. Whereas, if attribute **Day Of Week** was removed it would no longer be unique so would not be an entity identifier.

Questions

3 How many occurrences of an entity must a value of an entity identifier identify?

    A. None   B. One or more

    C. Zero or more   D. Exactly one

4 A **CarForSale** entity has the following attributes:

Manufacturer Name, Model Name, Registration Number, Engine Size, Body Colour, Trim Colour, Mileage, Year Of Registration, MOT Date, Price

Which of the following would be suitable as an entity identifier?

      (a) Year Of Registration and Model Name

      (b) Manufacturer Name and Model Name

      (c) Year Of Registration, MOT Date and Model Name

      (d) Registration Number

      (e) Registration Number, Year Of Registration

5 A Reservation entity in a hotel room booking system has the following attributes:

    Surname Of Guest, Forename of Guest, Home Address, Contact Telephone Number, Room Number, Date Room Booked For, Number Of Nights, Date Reservation Made

Which of the following would not be suitable as an entity identifier and why?

      (a) Surname Of Guest

      (b) Surname Of Guest, Forename Of Guest and Home Address

      (c) Room Number and Date Room Booked For

      (d) Surname Of Guest, Room Number and Date Room Booked For

Questions

6   Which attributes of the following entities would make suitable entity identifiers?

       a) Patient

       b) Ward

       c) Nurse

Entity relationship modelling

Entity description

Consider a school scenario consisting of students and staff. An analyst has recorded two entities **Student** and **Staff** and noted the following in *Table 10.1.1*.

Key concept

Entity description:
A formal description of an entity consisting of its name and attributes with the entity identifier indicated by being underlined, e.g.
GP(GPId, GpName).

Entity	Example
Student	A person who is a enrolled at the school to study one or more courses
Staff	A person who is employed by the school, e.g. teacher, technician, secretary, caretaker

Table 10.1.1

The analyst has also recorded the attributes of each entity as follows

> **Student**: StudentEnrolmentNo, Surname, Forenames, DateOfBirth, Address, TelNo

> **Staff**:   StaffNo, Surname, Forenames, DateOfBirth, Address, TelNo, Qualifications, Salary, TypeOfStaff, Grade, SubjectsTaught, ContractHours, Permanent

The entities can now be formally described in the following succinct fashion called an *entity description*:

> Student (<u>StudentEnrolmentNo</u>, Surname, Forenames, DateOfBirth, Address, TelNo)

> Staff (<u>StaffNo</u>, Surname, Forenames, DateOfBirth, Address, TelNo, Qualifications, Salary, TypeOfStaff, Grade, SubjectsTaught, ContractHours, Permanent)

The convention is to underline the entity identifier.

Formally,
An entity description is a formal description of an entity consisting of its name and attributes with the entity identifier indicated by being underlined, e.g.
GP(*GPId*, *GPName*)

Questions

7 A hospital is organised into a number of wards staffed by nurses. The attributes of the entities Ward and Nurse are listed below
Ward: WardName, NumberOfBeds
Nurse: StaffNumber, Surname, Forename

Write the entity descriptions for these two entities.

8 An airline owns a number of aeroplanes. Each aeroplane has an aeroplane identification number and type recorded, along with the number of seats in that aeroplane. Flight staff employed by the airline have their staff number, name and specialism recorded.

The attributes of the entities Aeroplane and FlightStaff are listed below

Aeroplane: AeroplaneIdNo, Type, NumberOfSeats
FlightStaff: StaffNumber, Name, Specialism

Write the entity descriptions for these two entities.

Key concept

Relationship:
A relationship is a two-way association or link between two entities.

Relationships

Within an organisation or within a system in an organisation, entities do not exist in isolation but have links with other entities.

Formally,
A relationship is a two-way association or link between two entities.

For example,

- A patient is *nursed by* nurses   the *nursed by* relationship associates a patient with nurses who nurse that patient
- A nurse *nurses* patients   the *nurses* relationship associates a nurse with the patients who the nurse nurses

In the school example, a link exists between the entities **Student** and **Staff**. Students are taught by staff whose role is teaching, and staff whose role is teaching teach students. In the direction from student to staff, the relationship has the name **Is Taught By**. In the direction from staff to students the relationship has the name **Teaches**.

Degree of a relationship

When the data requirements are described more precisely as follows:

> *A member of staff may teach zero or more students (zero because not all staff teach, e.g. caretaker) and a student is taught by one or more members of staff*

It becomes clear that a member of staff who teaches may teach many students and a student may be taught by many members of staff.

Formally,
The degree of a relationship between two entities refers to the number of entity occurrences of one entity which are associated with just one entity occurrence of the other and vice versa.

A relationship therefore has a degree as well as a name.

The degree of a relationship may be one of the following:

- one-to-one

- one-to-many

- many-to-one

- many-to-many

The relationships between entities are best represented diagrammatically in an entity-relationship or E-R diagram.

Entities in an E-R diagram are represented by rectangles containing the name of the entity.

Rectangle containing the name of the entity → **Student** ← Entity name should be singular

Figure 10.1.4 Entity symbol on an E-R diagram

A relationship is represented by a line drawn between two associated entities with a shape resembling a crow's foot drawn at the many end of the relationship if this exists.

The four types of relationship are represented diagrammatically in *Figure 10.1.5*.

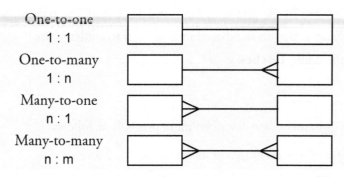

Figure 10.1.5 Diagrammatic representations of relationship degrees

It is good practice to label each relationship that appears on an E-R diagram with its name (two-way relationship, so two names).

Relationship names should be chosen so sentences that are meaningful can be constructed describing the relationship using the entity names and the relationship names.

Figure 10.1.6 shows an E-R diagram for the two entities **Student** and **Staff** drawn with two separate one-to-many relationships showing that **Staff** *Teaches* **Student** and **Student** *Is Taught By* **Staff**.

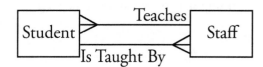

Figure 10.1.6 Student-Staff E-R Diagram with separate one-to-many relationships

Figure 10.1.7 shows an E-R diagram in which the two one-to-many relationships have been replaced by a single many-to-many one.

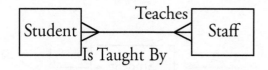

Figure 10.1.7 Many to many E-R diagram

However, it is not always necessary to label both ends of a relationship. Often, common sense dictates that a single label describes a relationship adequately. This label is placed in the middle of the relationship line connecting the two entities.

Questions

9 For each of the following relationship definitions choose the correct degree classification:

(a) Each hospital ward has zero or more patients whilst a patient is assigned to a single ward.

	Ward		Patient
(i)	m	:	n
(ii)	1	:	n
(iii)	n	:	1
(iv)	1	:	1

(b) Each patient is assigned a single hospital consultant, whilst each hospital consultant is responsible for one or more patients.

	Patient		Consultant
(i)	m	:	n
(ii)	1	:	n
(iii)	n	:	1
(iv)	1	:	1

(c) Each lorry driver is assigned their own lorry and each lorry is driven by one driver.

	Driver		Lorry
(i)	m	:	n
(ii)	1	:	n
(iii)	n	:	1
(iv)	1	:	1

(d) A computer may contain zero or more application programs and each may be installed on zero or more computers.

	Computer		Program
(i)	m	:	n
(ii)	1	:	n
(iii)	n	:	1
(iv)	1	:	1

Resolving many-to-many relationships

The entities in many-to-many relationships would record data as multiple facts not single facts unless this situation is resolved by creating a link entity and one-to-many relationships as shown below. For example, a firm that sells computer parts receives orders for parts from other businesses. A typical official order appearing on a form as shown opposite consists of several lines, labelled 1, 2, 3, etc. called order lines. Each order line lists a specific part and quantity ordered. If we record these multiple lines in an **Order** entity we will make it difficult

> Order No: 12345
>
> 1.   6 x CPU
>
> 2.   10 x RAM
>
> 3.   5 x Video Card

to query the entity for specific data, e.g. how many CPUs were ordered on the order with OrderNo 12345? Or, how many CPUs have been ordered in total this year? Much better to separate out the lines and store them separately but linked to the order on which they appear.

Two entities for this ordering system are **Order** and **Part**, but a third entity exists that is not so obvious, **OrderLine**, corresponding to the separate lines of the order.

Figure 10.1.8 shows that each order is for many parts and that a part can appear on many orders, a many-to-many relationship but each order is made up of many order lines each containing an order for a particular part, a one-to-many relationship.

Each part may appear in an order line in different orders. If all the order lines over all the orders are grouped together in an entity called **OrderLine** (the link entity) then we have another one-to-many relationship, this time between **Part** and **OrderLine**.

Order(<u>OrderNo</u>, ...)
Part(PartNo, Description, ...)

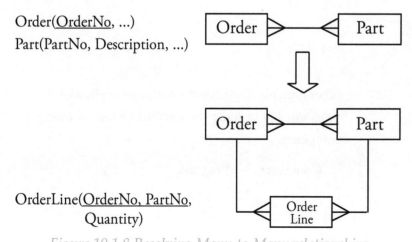

OrderLine(<u>OrderNo, PartNo,</u>
     Quantity)

Figure 10.1.8 Resolving Many-to-Many relationships

It may be necessary, to re-draft an Entity-Relationship diagram several times before completing the modelling satisfactorily. The goal is to resolve each many-to-many relationship into two one-to-many relationships and a link entity. The process of drafting raises the analyst's level of understanding of the data requirements each time it is attempted.

Questions

10 The data requirements for a hospital in-patient system are defined as follows:

A hospital is organised into a number of wards. Each ward has a ward number and a name recorded, along with a number of beds in that ward. Each ward is staffed by nurses. Nurses have their staff number and name recorded and are assigned to a single ward.

Each patient in the hospital has a patient identification number, and their name, address and date of birth are recorded. Each patient is under the care of a single consultant and is assigned to a single ward. Each consultant is responsible for a number of patients. Consultants have their staff number, name and specialism recorded.

(a)   In data modelling, what is

   (i) an attribute

   (ii) a relationship?

(b)   State **four** entities for the hospital in-patient system and suggest an identifier for each of these entities.

(c)   Draw an entity-relationship diagram that shows **three** relationships that can be inferred from these data requirements.

In this chapter you have covered:

- The meaning of data model
- How to produce a data model from given data requirements for a simple scenario involving multiple entities.
- How to produce entity relationship diagrams representing a data model and entity descriptions in the form:
              Entity1 (Attribute1, Attribute2, ...)
- What is meant by entity description
- The meaning of entity identifier
- Using underlining to identify the attribute(s) which form the entity identifier
- Identifying the degree of a relationship
- How to resolve many-to-many relationships

Relational database model

Logical database model

Over the years several different ways of modelling data logically have been tried.

Modelling data logically emphasises that we are still engaged in a stage of modelling which is independent of a particular database system, e.g. Microsoft Access or MySQL. No details of how the data is to be physically stored and accessed will be considered.

The focus of interest in this chapter is the relational model and relational database. In this model:

> *A relational database is a set of relations or a collection of tables.*

A later chapter covers an alternative model, the fact-based model.

The conceptual model in the previous chapter concentrated on the structure and meaning of the data for a specific organisation, without answering the question: "how should the data be structured and interpreted in a software system?"

A logical database model concentrates on the structure and meaning of the data in a particular database approach or system, e.g. the relational database model approach in which relationships between entities are modelled by shared or common attributes alone.

The goal of the logical model is to create schemas from which a database can be physically built. A schema is another name for a plan describing what is to be built.

Relational Data Model
Mathematical relation

We focus first on the approach to logical data modelling known as relational modelling.

This type of modelling is based upon a mathematical concept called a relation. For example, if we have two sets named *SetOfStudents* and *SetOfSubjects*, respectively, and populated as follows

$$SetOfStudents = \{Sarah, Jim, Kevin\}$$

$$SetOfSubjects = \{CS, Physics, Maths\}$$

Background

Mathematical relation:

Relation *Studies* is a subset of the Cartesian product

SetOfStudents x *SetOfSubjects*

or an element of the power set

℘ (*SetOfStudents* x
          SetOfSubjects).

See Unit 1 4.2.2.

and a relationship between these two sets, called **Studies**, then we might model this relationship as a set of ordered pairs as follows

Studies = {(Sarah, Physics), (Jim, Physics),(Jim, Maths) }

The ordered pair, (Sarah, Physics), records that Sarah studies Physics.

The set **Studies** is a subset drawn from the set of all possible ordered pairs formed from the two sets *SetOfStudents* and *SetOfSubjects*.

Questions

 Write down the set of all possible ordered pairs formed by the Cartesian product of *SetOfStudents* and *SetOfSubjects* of which (Sarah, Physics) is one example.

This way of organising these facts and their relationship uses the concept of a relation – a relation corresponds to a relationship such as **Studies** used in the above example.

We can use the relation to obtain information. For example, we can conclude that Kevin does not study any of the subjects in *SetOfSubjects*, Sarah and Jim study Physics and Jim also studies Maths.

Key concept

Relation:
A relation in the relational data model can be regarded loosely as a form of table, with attributes being named columns of the table.

Relational data model relation

A relation in the relational data model can be regarded loosely as a form of table, with attributes being named columns of the table. More precisely, the table is a depiction of the relation presenting actual values for the relation in tabular form.

Rows of values of the table are called tuples. They correspond to instances of records in a programming language.

Key concept

Attribute:
An attribute is a named column of a table.

Relation **ClassRoomTimeTable**

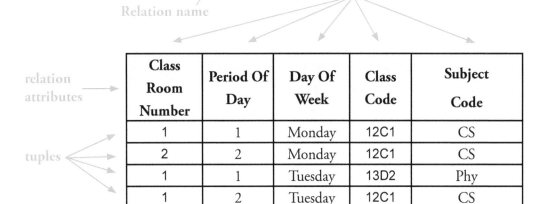

Class Room Number	Period Of Day	Day Of Week	Class Code	Subject Code
1	1	Monday	12C1	CS
2	2	Monday	12C1	CS
1	1	Tuesday	13D2	Phy
1	2	Tuesday	12C1	CS

Figure 10.2.1 Table depiction of relation ClassRoomTimeTable

Primary key

Relations are written in the following format:

Relation name (Attribute1, Attribute2, Attribute3, etc)

With the primary key, Attribute1, underlined.

> *The attribute, or combination of attributes, which uniquely identifies a single occurrence (tuple) of the relation is underlined. This attribute, or combination of attributes, is called the **primary key** of the relation.*

If a combination of attributes is required to ensure uniqueness then all the attributes in the combination are underlined. In this instance, the primary key is called a composite primary key.

For example, the relation **ClassRoomTimeTable** is written as follows:

ClassRoomTimeTable(ClassRoomNumber, PeriodOfDay, DayOfWeek, ClassCode, SubjectCode)

With the attribute combination *ClassRoomNumber, PeriodOfDay* and *DayOfWeek* chosen as the primary key.

A value of this primary key, such as "2, 2, Monday" selects just one row or tuple of the table because the combination is unique in the table. It is also minimal, i.e. has no more attributes than necessary. If we removed one of *ClassRoomNumber, PeriodOfDay, DayOfWeek* we forfeit uniqueness.

ClassRoomNumber, PeriodOfDay, DayOfWeek, ClassCode although unique is not minimal because it has one more attribute than is necessary to ensure uniqueness, i.e. *ClassCode* is unnecessary.

Key concept

Primary key:
The attribute or combination of attributes which uniquely identifies a single occurrence or tuple of the relation. It is indicated by being underlined.

Key concept

Composite primary key:
Minimal combination of attributes that uniquely identifies a single occurrence or tuple of the relation.

Questions

 A **SwimmingGalaRaceResult** relation has the following attributes:

GalaNo, RaceNo, StrokeNo, Distance, SwimmerNoOfWinner, WinningTime

Which of the following would be suitable as a primary key and why?
- (a) SwimmerNoOfWinner
- (b) RaceNo
- (c) GalaNo, RaceNo, StrokeNo
- (d) GalaNo, RaceNo
- (e) GalaNo, SwimmerNoOfWinner

Questions

3   A **CDTrack** relation in a CD music collection system has the following attributes:

CompactDiscId, TrackNo, TrackDuration, SongId

(a) Which of the following would not be suitable as a primary key and why?

   (i) CompactDiscId, SongId
   (ii) TrackNo, SongId

   (iii) SongId
   (iv) CompactDiscId, TrackNo

(b) What is the name given to a primary key that consists of more than one attribute?

Key concept

Foreign key:
A foreign key is an attribute in one relation/table which is also the primary key of another relation/table. It forms a link between two relations/tables via this attribute.

Foreign Key

In a relational database, relationships are modelled by the foreign key mechanism.

For example, in a hospital system the relationship between the two entities **Ward** and **Patient** has degree one-to-many as shown in Figure 10.2.2. Each ward is occupied by zero or more patients.

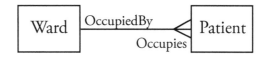

Figure 10.2.2 E-R diagram for the entities Ward and Patient

The entity definitions from the conceptual modelling stage are

   Ward (<u>WardName</u>, NoOfBeds)

   Patient (<u>PatientNo</u>, Name, HomeAddress, DateOfBirth, Gender)

The equivalent relations are defined as follows:

   Ward (<u>WardName</u>, NoOfBeds)

   Patient (<u>PatientNo</u>, Name, HomeAddress, DateOfBirth, Gender, *WardName*)

The relationship between the two entities is represented in the relation **Patient** by the additional attribute *WardName*. Foreign keys are usually indicated by italicising them or placing a line over them.

WardName is the primary key of the relation **Ward** as well as the entity identifier of the entity **Ward** and is known as a foreign key in the relation **Patient**.

WardName is therefore common to both **Patient** and **Ward**.

> *A foreign key is an attribute in one relation/table that is also the primary key of another relation/table. It forms a link between two relations/tables via this attribute.*

Link between mathematical relation and relational model relation

If we have sets *SetOfStudentForenames* and *SetOfStudentIds* as follows

SetOfStudentForenames = {Sarah, Jim, Kevin}

SetOfStudentIds = {1, 2, 3}

and a relation **Student** as follows

Student (<u>StudentId</u>, Forename)

where possible values of *StudentId* are chosen from the *SetOfStudentIds* and possible values of *Forename* are chosen from *SetOfStudentForenames*.

Then we have the relationship of *StudentId* value 1 to *Forename* value "Jim" modelled by the relation **Student** as follows

StudentId 1 is **Student** with *Forename* Jim

This appears as one tuple in the table depiction (two-dimensional array) of the relation as shown in *Table 10.2.1*.

StudentId	Forename
1	Jim
2	Kevin
3	Sarah

Table 10.2.1 Relation Student as a table of values

Similarly, if we have sets *SetOfSubjectIds* and *SetOfSubjectNames* as follows

SetOfSubjectNames = {CS, Physics, Maths}

SetOfSubjectIds = {1, 2, 3}

and a relation **Subject** as follows

Subject (<u>SubjectId</u>, SubjectName)

then we can say for example that

SubjectId 1 is a **Subject** with SubjectName "CS"

as shown in *Table 10.2.2*.

SubjectId	SubjectName
1	CS
2	Physics
3	Maths

Table 10.2.2 Relation Subject as a table of values

Figure 10.2.3 shows the entity-relationship (E-R) diagram from the conceptual modelling stage, the stage before the relational database modelling stage. The diagram conveys that a student studies zero or more subjects and a subject is studied by zero or more students (actually the E-R diagram needs an additional symbol on each crow foot to indicate "zero or more").

Figure 10.2.3 E-R diagram from conceptual modelling stage

In the relational model we use only relations.

Mathematically these are sets of ordered pairs.

Therefore, we need another relation **Studies**. This is shown below for the relational database model and as a mathematical relation.

Relational database model

Studies(<u>StudentId, SubjectId</u>)

Primary key is composite, consisting of the combination

StudentId, SubjectId

Mathematical relation model

Studies = {(1,2),(1,3),(2,1),(2,3),(3,2)}

Table 10.2.3 shows a depiction of relation **Studies** with values corresponding to the ordered pairs.

StudentId	SubjectId
1	2
1	3
2	1
2	3
3	2

Table 10.2.3 Relation Studies as a table of values

Figure 10.2.4 shows the E-R diagram after the relational modelling stage. The entity **Studies** has now been included (on an E-R diagram we use the term entity).

A student is associated with zero of more subjects and a subject is associated with zero or more students. The relation **Studies** provides the link that we need between the relations **Student** and **Subject**. That is why we call the entity on the E-R diagram corresponding to this relation, a **link** entity.

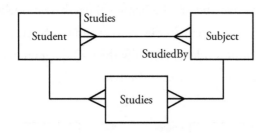

Figure 10.2.4 E-R diagram after relational modelling stage

The relational database model thus consists of the three relations

> **Subject** (<u>SubjectId</u>, SubjectName)
>
> **Student** (<u>StudentId</u>, Forename)
>
> **Studies**(<u>StudentId, SubjectId</u>)

Many-to-many relationships in the conceptual model must be modelled in the relational model by relations that support one-to-many relationships otherwise problems arise. If the one-to-many relationships don't exist then they must be created. The previous example illustrates how this can be achieved.

Key concept

Modelling many-to-many relationships:
Many-to-many relationships in the conceptual model must be modelled in the relational model by relations that support one-to-many relationships otherwise problems arise, e.g. querying can be problematic.

Questions

4. The entities **Ward** and **Nurse** are defined below

   Ward(<u>WardName</u>, NoOfBeds)

   Nurse(<u>StaffNo</u>, Name)

   Using the entity-relationship diagram shown below, define the relations which correspond to these two entities, i.e. add a foreign key to one of the entities to model the relationship.

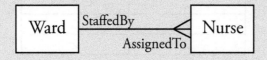

Questions

5   Each patient is registered with one GP whereas a GP has many patients. The entity definitions for these data requirements are

> **GP**(<u>GPId</u>, GPName)
>
> **Patient**(<u>PatientNo</u>, Name, HomeAddress, DateOfBirth, Gender, NHSNo)

and E-R diagram is

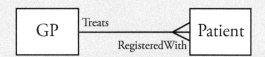

Define relations for these data requirements.

6   A competition is made up of many events. Each event involves many teams and a team participates in many events. The entity-relationship diagram for this competition is shown below

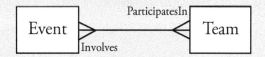

The entities **Event** and **Team** are described as follows

> **Event**(<u>EventId</u>, EventDescription, Date, Time)
>
> **Team**(<u>TeamId</u>, TeamName, ContactTelNo)

(a)   Modify this entity-relationship diagram so that its entities may be modelled in a relational database.

(b)   Using the new E-R diagram from (a) write down the relations.

Questions

7 The entity-relationship diagram for a hospital system is shown below.

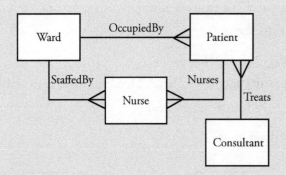

The entities and their attributes for this E-R diagram are:

Ward(<u>WardName</u>, NoOfBeds)

Patient(<u>PatientNo</u>, Name, Address, DateOfBirth, Gender)

Nurse (<u>StaffNo</u>, Name, Rank)

Consultant (<u>StaffNo</u>, Name, Specialism)

A patient is nursed by one or more nurses and a nurse nurses one or more patients but not every patient on a ward.

(a)   Modify the entity-relationship (E-R) diagram so that its entities may be modelled in a relational database.

(b)   Using the new E-R diagram from (a) write down the relations.

Foreign key already present

Sometimes the foreign key attribute is already present in the entity at the many end of a one-to-many relationship. For example, the entity definitions for the entities **Customer**, **AuctionItem** are

Customer (<u>CustomerId</u>, Name, Address)

AuctionItem (<u>ItemId</u>, AuctionPrice, PaidYN, CustomerId)

A data tuple is never created for **AuctionItem** without the *CustomerId* of the customer who has bought the item at auction. If no items are sold **AuctionItem** will be empty.

Foreign Keys in One-To-One Relationships

As an example of a one-to-one relationship consider the E-R diagram of *Figure 10.2.5*, in which the **Drives** relationship represents the fact that each taxi driver drives one car at a time and that each car is driven by only one taxi driver at a time. It might make sense to model with separate entities if drivers are assigned and re-assigned to different cars, frequently.

Figure 10.2.5 One-to-one relationship

The entities and their attributes are:

Driver(<u>DriverId</u>, DriverName, Gender, ….)

Car(<u>CarId</u>, CarModel, ………)

To convert these entities into relations, first write down the relations ignoring the relationship **Drives**.

Then represent the relationship Drives by adding foreign keys. However, unlike previous examples we now have a choice. We can add the foreign key CarId to Driver or we can add the foreign key DriverId to Car or we can do both.

If we do both then we get relations as follows

Driver(<u>DriverId</u>, DriverName, Gender, *CarId*, …..)

Questions

8 **Driver** and **Car** could have been combined into one entity.

    (a) Why might doing this not always be sensible?
    (b) In what circumstances would using just one foreign key
        be sensible?

Foreign Keys in Recursive Relationships

Some nurses are in charge of other nurses. *Figure 10.2.6* shows how this is represented in an entity-relationship diagram. The relationship in this case is said to be recursive.

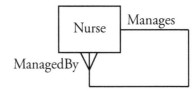

Figure 10.2.6 Recursive relationship

The entity **Nurse** has the attributes:

Nurse(<u>StaffNo</u>, Name, Rank)

The relation **Nurse** has the attributes:

Nurse(<u>StaffNo</u>, Name, Rank, *ManagerStaffNo*)

The attribute *ManagerStaffNo* is a foreign key whose values are taken from the range of values of the attribute *StaffNo*.

Some example occurrences of the relation Nurse are listed in *Table 10.2.4*

Table **Nurse**

StaffNo	Name	Rank	Manager StaffNo
1	Sarah Briggs	Staff Nurse	3
2	John Doe	Staff Nurse	3
3	Sue Cripps	Ward Sister	4
4	Mary Downs	Senior Nurse	Null

Table 10.2.4 Example occurrences of the relation Nurse

Note that it is possible to have no value at all in a foreign key column, i.e. a null value, in any relationship, recursive or not. If a value is present then there must be a matching value present in the primary key column, e.g. 3.

Questions

9 Some teachers manage other teachers.

The entity description for the **Teacher** entity is as follows

Teacher `Manages`
ManagedBy

   Teacher (TeacherId, Name, *SubjectId*)

   Write the relation **Teacher** to model the relationship.

10 A blood donor service uses a relational database to keep track of donors and their donations of blood. Each donor, on registering to give blood for the first time, is assigned a unique donor identification number and has their surname, forename, address, telephone number, date of birth and blood type recorded. Each time a donor gives blood the quantity of blood given and the date of giving are recorded together with the identification number attached to the vessel in which the blood is stored. Each vessel is assigned a unique identification number and is used once only. Two entities for this system are **BloodDonor** and **BloodGiven**.

(a) List the attributes of the following entities underlining the entity identifier attribute(s) in each case

   (i) **BloodDonor**

   (ii) **BloodGiven**

(b) Draw an entity-relationship diagram showing the degree of the relationship for the two entities **BloodDonor** and **BloodGiven**.

(c)

   (i) What is a relational database?

   (ii) What is a foreign key in the context of a relational database?

   (iii) State how the relationship between **BloodDonor** and **BloodGiven** is represented in a relational database.

   (iv) State the relations and their attributes for this blood donor service scenario. Underline the primary keys.

In this chapter you have covered:

- Modelling data logically
- Relational modelling and the relational database model
- Modelling relationships by foreign key mechanism
- The link between mathematical relation and relational model relation
- Use of link relation to model many-to-many relationship

10.3 Database design and normalisation techniques

Learning objectives:
- *Normalise relations to third normal form*
- *Understand why databases are normalised*

■ Normalisation techniques

Repeating groups

Table 10.3.1 shows a fictitious sample of general practitioners (GPs) and their patients' names and identification numbers.

In the British National Health Service,

- Each patient is registered at any one time with just one GP

- A GP has zero or more registered patients.

Expressing this table as a relation

GP (<u>GPId</u>, GPName, Patient)

GPId values are drawn from a simple domain or set of values, the natural numbers. *GPName* values are also drawn from a simple domain of alphabetic strings. However, patient values are not drawn from a simple domain of values but one with structure of array of *PatientId, PatientName*. If relations are to be usable, e.g. queried, then their attributes must all be drawn from simple domains of values. No column or combination of columns must contain multiple values per row.

Key concept

Repeating group:
Domain for attribute(s) is a structured type so an instance is a group of values, known as a repeating group because its group-like structure repeats from row to row.

| | | Repeating group / PatientId / PatientName |
GPId	GPName	Patient
1	Smith	718 Bloggs 345 Khan 234 Teng 456 Nunn
2	Smith	1118 Archer 1305 Ali 2214 Singh 6541 Nunn
3011	Minns	8600 Bloggs 4341 Sorensen 1678 Ng 2999 Zog

Table 10.3.1 GPs and their patients

The **GP** relation is said to be unnormalised because of the multiple values in the *Patient* column in each row. This state is caused by the *Patient's* domain of values being a group of values, known as a repeating group - so named because its group-like structure repeats from row to row.

Problems occur if a relation is unnormalised

One of the problems with the unnormalised **GP** relation is that there is no space available in row 1 of its table for a new patient that registers with Dr Smith. Row 1 would have to be deleted, the new patient details added to the repeating group and the new record appended to the end of the table.

> **Repeating group**
> *Domain for attribute(s) is a structured type so an instance is a group of values, known as a repeating group because its group-like structure repeats from row to row.*

To indicate that a relation contains a repeating group a line is placed above the attribute(s) that contain groups of values

GP (<u>GPId</u>, GPName, $\overline{\text{Patient}}$)

The solution to the repeating group problem in this example is to remove the *Patient* values to their own relation called **Patient** as shown below, and to add the primary key of the **GP** relation to this new relation to model the link between **GP** and Patient relations as follows

GP (<u>GPId</u>, GPName)

Patient (<u>PatientId</u>, PatientName, *GPId*)

There is now no repeating group in either relation – see *Table 10.3.2* – and what's more

Every non-key attribute is a fact about the key,
the whole key and nothing but the key.

where key means primary key.

Because this is the case we then can say that relations **GP** and Patient are fully normalised.

Key concept

Single-Valued Fact (SVF):

When a relation is fully normalised, instances of a single-valued fact (SVF) will be recorded just once, in just one place.

Single-valued facts assert that one thing is associated with just one other thing.

Some examples of a single-valued fact are:

1. A teacher has a name. Given a value of ***TeacherId***, it is a fact that there is just one value of ***TeacherName*** associated with this value.

2. A student has a name. Given a value of ***StudentId***, it is a fact that there is just one value of ***StudentName*** associated with this value.

The instances of single-valued facts for the fully normalised **GP** and **Patient** relations are recorded just once, in just one place:

- *GPId determines GPName* because, given a specific value of *GPId*, say 2, there is just one and only one value of *GPName*, Smith, associated with this value of *GPId*.

- *PatientId* determines *PatientName* because, given a specific value of *PatientId*, say 1305, there is just one and only one value of *PatientName*, Ali, associated with it.

Information

Determinant

Another way of expressing a single-valued fact is to draw a determinancy diagram.

$$PatientId \rightarrow PatientName$$

The diagram asserts that attribute *PatientId* determines attribute *PatientName* and therefore *PatientId* is a determinant. There is a single value of *PatientName* for each value of *PatientId*, i.e. given a value of *PatientId* such as 345 the name Khan is returned from a search of the **Patient** table – Table 10.3.2. However, it is not true that there is only one value of *PatientId* associated with each value of *PatientName*. Two patients can have the same name but must have different values of *PatientId*, e.g. given the name Bloggs a search of the **Patient** table returns the values of *PatientId* 718 and 8600.

We say that *PatientId* determines *PatientName* or *PatientName* depends upon or is functionally dependent upon *PatientId* or is a fact about *PatientId*.

Determinants are useful because from a list of determinants drawn up from the data requirements, it is possible to immediately write down a set of fully normalised relations.

Values in cells must be atomic

Table 10.3.2 shows the **Patient** relation in table form with each cell occupied by a single atomic value. Atomic means that the value is as simple as it can be, i.e. it cannot be broken down any further without losing meaning. The patient values that have come from *Table 10.3.1* have been separately recorded in attributes *PatientId* and *PatientName* to achieve atomicity.

Not all rows in *Table 10.3.2* show actual data. This fact is indicated by ellipses, •••, in cells. Ellipses can also be shorthand for multiple rows.

Key principle

Atomicity:
Values in cells must be atomic.

PatientId	PatientName	GPId
718	Bloggs	1
345	Khan	1
234	Teng	1
456	Nunn	1
1118	Archer	2

PatientId	PatientName	GPId
1305	Ali	2
2214	Singh	2
6541	Nunn	2
•••	•••	•••
•••	•••	•••
8600	Bloggs	3011
4341	Sorensen	3011
1678	Ng	3011
2999	Zog	3011

Table 10.3.2 Patient relation table form

Questions

1. Write down the determinants from the data in Table 10.3.1. Using these determinants can you see how to write down the normalised relations?

2. The relation **Ward** is unnormalised

   Ward (<u>WardName</u>, WardType, Patient)

   Table 10.3.3 shows the Ward relation in table form.

WardName	WardType	Patient
Nightingale	Orthopaedic	1456 Smith 1497 Smart
Barnard	Cardiac	1461 Berry 1468 Singh 1478 Alton
Seacole	Medical	1472 Harley 1421 Sven
Guttman	Geriatric	1483 Noggs 1305 Ali 1678 Ng

Table 10.3.3 Ward relation in table form

(a) What makes the **Ward** relation unnormalised?

(b) Derive the fully normalised relations corresponding to the **Ward** relation.

Normalisation where relationship is many-to-many

Figure 10.3.1 is an E-R diagram for a school scenario in which

- a teacher teaches one subject to one or more students

- a student is taught by one or more teachers

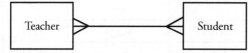

Figure 10.3.1 E-R diagram for **Teacher**, **Student** *entities*

Table 10.3.4 shows that teacher *Mead,* for example, teaches students *Bond, Afridi, Smith, Ng* and *Ali* English.

TeacherId	TeacherName	Student
1234	Mead	15898 Bond English 24298 Afridi English 32145 Smith English 11023 Ng English 18769 Ali English
5678	Davies	24298 Afridi Physics 32145 Smith Physics 11023 Ng Physics
9123	Younis	15898 Bond Maths 32145 Smith Maths 11023 Ng Maths
4532	Ferris	15898 Bond Maths 45910 Singh Maths 19462 Gurung Maths

Table 10.3.4 shows the **Teacher Teaches** *table for a sample of teachers and the students that they teach*

The table contains a repeating group and so its relation is unnormalised.

We indicate the repeating group with an overline as follows

TeacherTeaches (TeacherId, TeacherName, $\overline{\text{Student}}$)

where the *Student* repeating group is an array of *StudentId, StudentName, SubjectName.*

A first step to resolving the issue is to eliminate the repeating group, *Student,* in the **TeacherTeaches** relation. The simplest way of doing this is to make a new row in **TeacherTeaches** for each row of the repeating group and to replace the *Student* column by three columns *StudentId, StudentName, SubjectName,* respectively. This step is called putting the relation in First Normal Form or 1NF.

We have now achieved atomicity.

The **TeacherTeaches** relation is now

> **TeacherTeaches** (<u>TeacherId</u>, TeacherName, <u>StudentId</u>, StudentName, SubjectName)

Task

 Draw up the table for this new form of the relation using the data in Table 10.3.4.

Clearly it is not true for this new form of the relation **TeacherTeaches** that

> *Every non-key attribute is a fact about the key, the whole key and nothing but the key.*

For example, *TeacherName* is a fact about *TeacherId* which is only part of the key.

Questions

 What is
    (a) *StudentName* a fact about?
    (b) *SubjectName* a fact about?

If we remove these facts from **TeacherTeaches** to new relations we get

> **Teacher** (<u>TeacherId</u>, TeacherName, SubjectName)

> **Student** (<u>StudentId</u>, StudentName)

leaving

> **TeacherTeaches** (<u>TeacherId, StudentId</u>)

These three relations are fully normalised.

Renaming **TeacherTeaches**, **Teaches** we have

> **Teaches** (<u>TeacherId, StudentId</u>)

We can safely delete all tuples in relation **Teaches** that reference a particular teacher who leaves the school. At the same, the references in **Teaches** to students taught by this teacher are removed but we don't in the process delete the corresponding student tuples in the relation **Student**. The integrity of the database is preserved.

If we acted instead on the 1NF relation (at top of page) then we would lose some student names and potentially all references to a student still at the school. This would be an inconsistency in the database.

E-R modelling approach to normalisation

Can we arrive at a fully normalised set of relations by any other route? The answer is yes. Often conceptual modelling, i.e. entity-relationship modelling, leads to relations in the relational model that are already fully normalised.

Figure 10.3.2 arrived at by entity-relationship modelling, has produced a set of fully normalised entities from which fully normalised relations follow which correspond to the fully normalised relations in the previous section. The entity **Teaches** already has the necessary foreign keys, *TeacherId* and *StudentId*.

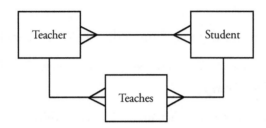

*Figure 10.3.2 E-R diagram for **Teacher**, **Student** and **Teachers** entities*

Questions

④

SalesmanId	CustomerId	Salesman
1	1 2	Archer
2	3 4	Dent
3	5 6	Rogers

(a) Explain why this table is unnormalised.

(b) Normalise the relation for this table into a set of fully normalised relations.

 ⑤

PatientId	GPId	GPName
1	1	Biggs
2	1	Biggs
3	2	Smith
4	2	Smith
5	3	Timms
6	3	Timms

The table contains redundant data (unnecessary duplication). The values of GPName, highlighted in red, may be deleted without loss of information. We say that the table therefore contains redundant data. For example, PatientId value 2 in row 2 is associated with GPId value 1. Therefore, GPName of GPId 1 can be looked up in row 1.

Normalise the data in the table into a set of fully normalised relations.

Questions

 A student is taught by one or more tutors and a tutor teaches one or more students as shown in the table below.

TutorNo	StudentNo	TutorName	StudentName
1	1	Ainsley	Khan
1	2	Ainsley	Carter
1	3	Ainsley	Chandai
2	4	Svensen	Smith
2	2	Svensen	Carter
2	1	Svensen	Khan

(a) Does this table contain any redundant data?

(b) Is this table fully normalised? Justify your answer.

7

PatientNo	PatientName	WardName	WardType
1456	Smith	Nightingale	Orthopaedic
1461	Berry	Barnard	Cardiac
1468	Thomas	Barnard	Cardiac
1472	Harley	Guttman	Orthopaedic
1478	Smith	Barnard	Cardiac
1483	Noggs	Spens	Geriatric
1497	Smith	Nightingale	Orthopaedic

(a) In what ways does this table contain redundant data?

(b) Split the relation corresponding to this table into two separate relations, ensuring that each table for the new relations contains no redundant data.

(c) Select and indicate a primary key for each new relation.

(d) Are each of the new relations fully normalised? Justify your answer.

Why normalise databases?

It should be clear now why a set of fully normalised relations are desirable. For fully normalised relations

- All possible relationships between the data are allowed for

- Unnecessary duplication of data is avoided and storage space saved

- Altering data is not unnecessarily time-consuming

- Altering data does not lead to inconsistencies

A fully normalised set of relations contains no redundant data.

There may be duplication of data in a fully normalised set of relations but it is non-redundant and necessary duplication.

Normalising relations to third normal form

Why don't we just use E-R modelling to arrive at a set of fully normalised relations?

If we have an alternative then we have a means of checking the completeness, accuracy and consistency of the E-R model.

In this section, we describe a formal technique for arriving at a set of fully normalised relations which is an alternative to E-R modelling.

This formal normalisation technique consists of stages known as Normal Form (NF).

Starting with the unnormalised relations

- Remove repeating groups to place relation in First Normal Form (1NF)

- Remove partial dependencies to place relation in Second Normal Form (2NF)

- Remove transitive dependencies to place relation in Third Normal Form (3NF)

A relation which is in 3NF is automatically in 2NF. A relation which is in 2NF is automatically in 1NF.

Information

There are several higher forms of normalisation than 3NF. These forms are used in highly specialised cases. In normal cases, a relation that is in 3NF is also in these higher forms.

One in particular is worth mentioning because it has its own name, Boyce-Codd Normal Form (BCNF).

We have already used the informal test for BCNF in earlier sections

Every non-key attribute is a fact about the key, the whole key and nothing but the key.

It contains within it the tests for 2NF and 3NF

Consider the following simple example.

Un-normalised Relation **StudentClass**

StudentClass (ClassId, ClassDescription,StudentId, StudentName)

ClassId	ClassDescription	StudentId	StudentName
A1	Art 1	1 2 3	Bloggs Garcia Begum
A2	Art 2	4 5 6	Mertems Becker Zhu
B1	Biology 1	1 3 5	Bloggs Begum Becker
B2	Biology 2	2 4 6	Garcia Mertems Zhu

*Table 10.3.5 shows the **StudentClass** table in unnormalised form because of a repeating group*

1NF

First Normal Form – remove repeating group to produce a relation in which all the data values in its table are atomic values.

The easiest way to do this is create a table for each row in the repeating group as shown in Table 10.3.6.

Note that 1NF is formally defined as

> **A relation is in 1NF if and only if every non-primary key attribute is functionally dependent on the primary key** – see page 497.

Information

Functional dependency:
Given a relation R, attribute R.B, e.g. *PatientName*, is functionally dependent on attribute R.A, e.g. *PatientId*, if and only if each value of R.A is associated with precisely one value of R.B, at any one time.

Full Functional dependency:
Given a relation R, attribute R.B, e.g. *ProductId* , is fully functionally dependent on attribute R.A, e.g. *OrderNo, OrderLineNo* if it is functionally dependent on R.A and not functionally dependent on any subset of R.A (where A and B may be composite, i.e. consist of more than one attribute).

ClassId	ClassDescription	StudentId	StudentName
A1	Art 1	1	Bloggs
A1	Art 1	2	Garcia
A1	Art 1	3	Begum
A2	Art 2	4	Mertems
A2	Art 2	5	Becker
A2	Art 2	6	Zhu
B1	Biology 1	1	Bloggs
B1	Biology 1	3	Begum
B1	Biology 1	5	Becker
B2	Biology 2	2	Garcia
B2	Biology 2	4	Mertems
B2	Biology 2	6	Zhu

Table 10.3.6 shows the StudentClass table in 1NF

StudentClass (<u>ClassId, StudentId</u>, ClassDescription, StudentName)

2NF

Second Normal Form – Remove any non-primary key attributes that are not a fact about the whole of the primary key to separate relations to get here.

ClassDescription is a fact about *ClassId* and not *StudentId*. *StudentName* is a fact about *StudentId* and not *ClassId*.

> **StudentClass** (<u>ClassId</u>, StudentId)
>
> **Class** (<u>ClassId</u>, ClassDescription)
>
> **Student**(<u>StudentId</u>, StudentName)

3NF

Third Normal Form - The next stage is to remove any non-primary key attributes that are both a fact about the key and other non-key attributes to separate relations to get here.

There aren't any so the 2NF relations are already in 3NF. Note that this is not always the case.

> **StudentClass** (<u>ClassID</u>, StudentID)
>
> **Class** (<u>ClassID</u>, ClassDescription)
>
> **Student**(<u>StudentId</u>, StudentName)

Check:

> ***Every non-key attribute is a fact about the key, the whole key and nothing but the key.***

Key point

A relation which is in 3NF is automatically in 2NF. A relation which is in 2NF is automatically in 1NF.

In normal cases, a relation that is in 3NF is also in the higher forms such as BCNF.

Background

Fourth stage:
Boyce-Codd Normal Form (BCNF) reached by removing remaining anomalies arising from functional dependencies.

Background

BCNF informally:
Every non-key attribute is a fact about the key, the whole key and nothing but the key.

Questions

8 The relation **GP** is unnormalised

GP (<u>GPId</u>, GPName, P̄atient)

The table opposite shows some data for this relation.
the patient data is a combination of *PatientId* and
PatientName.

GPId	GPName	Patient
1	Smith	718 Bloggs 345 Khan 234 Teng 456 Nunn
2	Brown	1118 Archer 1305 Ali 2214 Singh 6541 Nunn

(a) Place this relation in 1NF (hint: result is a single
relation). Justify your answer.
(b) Place this 1NF relation in 2NF (hint: result is two relations). Justify your answer.
(c) Place the 2NF relations in 3NF. Justify your answer.

Normalising relations to third normal form for a given scenario

We start by considering a simple scenario for which the data requirements are
as follows:

> *A school offers a number of different courses. Students enrol to study one
> or more courses up to a maximum of three. A particular course is taught
> by one teacher only but a teacher may teach more than one course.
> When students enrol they are each allocated a unique student identifier
> and have their name, gender and courses they enrol for recorded. Each
> course has a course title and a unique course code. Teachers are assigned
> a unique teacher identifier and have their name recorded.*

Instead of identifying the entities and their relationships, we will immediately
write down a single relation called **StudentCourse** consisting of every single
attribute identified in the data requirements. To give flesh to this task we
also construct the table equivalent of this relation and populate it with some
example data. The primary key is *StudentId*.

The **StudentCourse** relation is unnormalised because it contains a repeating
group consisting of *CourseCode*, *CourseTitle*, *TeacherId*, *TeacherName*.

StudentCourse (<u>StudentId</u>, StudentName, Gender,

CourseCode, CourseTitle, TeacherId, TeacherName)

Table **StudentCourse**

StudentId	StudentName	Gender	CourseCode	CourseTitle	TeacherId	TeacherName
15898	Bond	M	AQA0643	A Level CS	1234	Mead
			UCL0675	A Level Maths	5678	Davies
			EDE0187	A Level Art	9123	Milsom
24298	Smith	F	UCL0675	A Level Maths	5678	Davies
			AQA0643	A Level CS	1234	Mead
			AQA0432	A Level ICT	1234	Mead
10598	Robert	M	EDE0187	A Level Art	9123	Milsom
			UOC0987	A Level French	4567	Crapper
			AQA0432	A Level ICT	1234	Mead
13497	Nixon	F	UOC0987	A Level French	4567	Crapper

Table 10.3.7 Table StudentCourse unnormalised

Repeating group shown in red.

Stages of normalisation

1NF: **Remove repeating groups to place relation in First Normal Form.**

The First Normal Form of the table, Table 10.3.8 is shown below.

StudentId	StudentName	Gender	CourseCode	CourseTitle	TeacherId	TeacherName
15898	Bond	M	AQA0643	A Level CS	1234	Mead
15898	Bond	M	UCL0675	A Level Maths	5678	Davies
15898	Bond	M	EDE0187	A Level Art	9123	Milsom
24298	Smith	F	UCL0675	A Level Maths	5678	Davies
24298	Smith	F	AQA0643	A Level CS	1234	Mead
24298	Smith	F	AQA0432	A Level ICT	1234	Mead
10598	Robert	M	EDE0187	A Level Art	9123	Milsom
10598	Robert	M	UOC0987	A Level French	4567	Crapper
10598	Robert	M	AQA0432	A Level ICT	1234	Mead
13497	Nixon	F	UOC0987	A Level French	4567	Crapper

Table 10.3.8 Table StudentCourse in First Normal Form

StudentId on its own no longer satisfies the criterion of uniqueness and so a new primary key must be found. *StudentId* together with *CourseCode* becomes the new primary key.

The relation in first normal form is

   StudentCourse(<u>StudentId</u>, <u>CourseCode</u>, StudentName,
            Gender, CourseTitle,TeacherId, TeacherName)

2NF:

Second Normal Form - Every non-primary key attribute is functionally dependent on the whole of the primary key.

The next stage is to remove any non-primary key attributes that depend only upon part of the primary key to separate relations to achieve Second Normal Form.

This step will transform a relation that is in 1NF to two or more relations that are in 2NF form. Note that a relation that is in 1NF may already be in 2NF if the condition for 2NF is also satisfied.

Attributes *StudentName*, *Gender* depend upon (are facts about) *StudentId* not *StudentId*, *CourseCode*, the new primary key. Attributes *CourseTitle*, *TeacherId* and *TeacherName* depend upon (are facts about) *CourseCode* not *StudentId*, *CourseCode*.

Therefore, we create two new relations called **Course** and **Student** leaving a reduced **StudentCourse** relation as shown below:

> **Course**(<u>CourseCode</u>, CourseTitle, TeacherId, TeacherName)
>
> **Student**(<u>StudentId</u>, StudentName, Gender)
>
> **StudentCourse**(<u>StudentId, CourseCode</u>)

3NF:

> Third Normal Form - The next stage is to remove any non-primary key attributes that are not solely directly dependent on the key to separate relations.

This step will transform a relation that is in 2NF to two or more relations that are in 3NF. Note that a relation that is in 2NF may already be in 3NF if the condition for 3NF is also satisfied.

TeacherName is dependent on the primary key *CourseCode* of relation **Course** but it is also dependent upon *TeacherId*. So relation **Course** is not in 3NF. Relation **Student** and relation **StudentCourse** are already in 3NF.

> **Task**
>
> Discuss why *TeacherName* is dependent on the primary key *CourseCode* of relation **Course.** Look at the data requirements.

Therefore, we create a new relation called **Teacher.** *TeacherName* is removed from relation **Course** together with a copy of attribute *TeacherId* as shown below. A copy of *TeacherId* must be left behind in relation **Course** otherwise it will not be possible to determine the teacher assigned to teach a particular course.

> **Course**(<u>CourseCode</u>, CourseTitle, TeacherId)
>
> **Teacher**(<u>TeacherId</u>, TeacherName)
>
> **StudentCourse**(<u>StudentId, CourseCode</u>)
>
> **Student**(<u>StudentId</u>, StudentName, Gender)

We have arrived at a set of relations in which there is no unnecessary duplication, i.e. no redundancy. Updating the database is straightforward and avoids potentially inconsistent results. For example, if a teacher marries and changes their surname, the change is made in one place only. In the unnormalised table, if the teacher name to be changed is Mead, this requires changing in three places. If, let's say, the changes are carried out in only two of the three places accidentally, then the database will inconsistently reflect the new status of teacher Mead. The changes will also take longer to make in the case of the unnormalised database.

Questions

 Table 10.3.9 shows some data for a TeacherTeaches relation

TeacherTeaches (TeacherId, TeacherName, Student)

The data requirements are summarised as follows
- a teacher teaches one or more students
- a student is taught by one or more teachers
- a teacher may teach more than one subject

The student data is composed of *StudentId, StudentName, SubjectName*.

TeacherId	TeacherName	Student
1234	Mead	15898 Bond English 24298 Afridi English 32145 Smith English 15898 Bond French 24298 Afridi French
5678	Davies	24298 Afridi Physics 32145 Smith Physics 11023 Ng Physics
9123	Younis	15898 Bond Maths 32145 Smith Maths 32145 Smith RS
4532	Ferris	15898 Bond Maths 45910 Singh Maths 45910 Singh GS

Table 10.3.9 **TeacherTeaches** table

(a) Place this relation in 1NF.

(b) Place this relation in 2NF.

(c) Place this relation in 3NF.

Questions

10 Swimming galas take place at different venues during the course of the swimming season. Each gala consists of several races. Each gala race consists of several swimmers and is for one particular swimming stroke, e.g. breast stroke and one particular distance, e.g. 50m. Races are numbered starting from 1 for each gala. All galas code the strokes in the same way: strokes are numbered from 1 and each has a stroke name, e.g. 1 is always breast stroke. Each venue has a unique name, e.g. Leeds. Each swimmer is assigned a country-wide unique swimmer number so that no two swimmers will use the same swimmer number at any gala. The swimmer's time for a race is recorded.

The unnormalised relation corresponding to Table 10.3.10 showing swimming gala data (note for space reasons, distance is not included) is

Gala (<u>SwimmerNo</u>, Name, GalaNo, Venue, RaceNo
StrokeNo, StrokeName, Time)

Normalise this relation to produce a set of relations in 3NF.

SwimmerNo	Name	GalaNo	Venue	RaceNo	StrokeNo	StrokeName	Time
1	Bond	1	Leeds	1	1	Breast	1.30
				3	3	Crawl	0.30
		2	Derby	1	3	Crawl	0.32
				6	1	Breast	1.33
		3	Oxford	1	5	Medley	2.14
				3	4	Back	0.59
		10	Hove	10	2	Fly	1.15
123	Teng	10	Hove	1	2	Fly	1.16
				13	4	Back	0.58
		21	Bristol	1	4	Back	0.57
				26	2	Fly	1.17
		45	Swindon	1	1	Breast	1.34
				31	5	Medley	2.16

Table 10.3.10 shows a sample of swimming gala data

Questions

11 An agency arranges bookings of live bands for a number of venues. The data requirements are defined as follows.

- Each band is registered with the agency and is assigned a unique BandId

- Each band is managed by a manager

- A manager may manage several bands

- Each manager is registered with the agency and is assigned a unique ManagerId by the agency

- Each venue is registered with the agency and is assigned a unique VenueId

- The agency records the following details

  - o Manager name

  - o Band name

  - o Venue name

  - o Date of a booking, band booked and venue for booking

The constraints are

A band will never have more than one booking on any particular date.

Agency (<u>ManagerId</u>, ManagerName, <u>BandId,BandName,BookingDate,VenueId,VenueName</u>)

Normalise this relation to produce a set of relations in 3NF.

Table 10.3.11 shows a sample of agency data.

ManagerId	ManagerName	BandId	BandName	BookingDate	VenueId	VenueName
1	Bloggs	1	Nice	3/10/2015	1	Arch
				10/10/2015	2	Ten
				17/10/2015	3	Macs
				24/10/2015	4	Friars
		2	Loud	3/10/2015	5	Oak
				10/10/2015	6	Elm
				17/10/2015	7	Caesars
				24/10/2015	8	Locarno
2	Ramases	3	Riff	3/10/2015	9	Mill
				10/10/2015	10	Floss
				17/10/2015	11	Riverside
				24/10/2015	12	Cult
		4	Moss	3/10/2015	13	Goth
				10/10/2015	14	Cairns
				17/10/2015	15	Boot
				24/10/2015	16	Mod

Table 10.3.11 shows a sample of the agency's data

Problems occur if a relation is not fully normalised

Now we have a little more experience working with relations/tables that are not fully normalised we can revisit the issues that arise with such relations and describe these using the examples that we have considered. The issues are:

1. Redundant data:

   Clearly, the table **StudentClass**, *Table 10.3.6*, contains unnecessary repetition of data, e.g. *ClassDescription* data such as Art 1 corresponds to *ClassId* A1 but the same information is repeated unnecessarily on rows 2 and 3. We don't need Art 1 to be repeated on rows 2 and 3. We say that the table contains redundant data.

2. Data anomaly on deletion:

   Clearly the table **StudentCourse**, *Table 10.3.8*, contains unnecessary repetition of data. Let's suppose, student 13497 Nixon leaves the school. We delete Nixon's tuple from table **StudentCourse**. We lose value 4567 Crapper but it still exists in the table in tuple with *StudentId* 10598. But let's suppose that this student now leaves the school. We delete this student's tuple but in the process we also lose the information that teacher with *TeacherId* 4567 has name Crapper and that they can teach course UOC0987.

3. Data inconsistency on update:

   Also, if Smith in *Table 10.3.8* were to change her surname, it will need to be changed in three places which again could lead to an inconsistency if this is done incompletely. Also, the changes in each case will consume more time than would be necessary if the data to be changed were recorded just once.

4. Data anomaly on insert:

   Suppose a new student, Bunter, joins the school and is assigned *StudentId* value 7. If this student is inserted into *Table 10.3.6* before being allocated to any classes then the primary key, *ClassId*, *StudentId* will be null, 7 respectively. This is not allowed because no part of a primary key may be null, i.e. without a value.

Extension Material

Boyce-Codd Normal Form

We have already stated that Boyce-Codd Normal Form is the next stage after 3NF.

Informally, when a relation is in BCNF, every attribute which is not part of the primary key, is a fact about the key, the whole key and nothing but the key ("so help me Codd").

Formally,

BCNF	**a relation is in Boyce-Codd Normal Form (BCNF) if and only if every determinant is a candidate key.**

We have already seen that determinants are useful. From a list of determinants drawn up from the data requirements, it is possible to immediately write down a set of fully normalised relations in BCNF.

We have also seen that

The BCNF test will immediately reveal if there are any redundant data in a relation or table.

BCNF & 3NF	**3NF and BCNF are equivalent for a relation with only one candidate key.**

Candidate key	**A candidate key is an attribute or combination of attributes that has the property of uniqueness and minimality. Such a key distinguishes one row of a table (one tuple of a relation) from another.**

Minimality	**The minimum number of attributes which guarantee uniqueness are used.**

A relation may have more than one candidate key. One is chosen as the **primary key** and the others are **alternate keys**.

For example, if each student is allocated a locker to store their things and pays a refundable deposit, the **Student** relation becomes

Student(StudentId, StudentName, LockerNo, Deposit)

Both *StudentId* and *LockerNo* each determine *StudentName*

and both *StudentId* and *LockerNo* are unique and candidate keys for the **Student** relation but only one can be chosen as primary key.

Extension Questions

12 The table below shows some sample data for relation **Patient**.
Patient is not fully normalised

PatientId	GPId	GPName	PatientName
1	1	Biggs	Singh
2	1	Biggs	Brown
3	2	Smith	Mian
4	2	Smith	Fadhil
5	3	Biggs	Fadhil
6	3	Biggs	Brown

(a) State which of the following are candidate keys for relation **Patient**.

      (i) PatientId

      (ii) GPId

      (iii) GPName

      (iv) PatientName

(b) Draw a determinancy diagram – see page 500 - for the
    Patient table.

(c) Normalise the relation **Patient** for the data in the table into
    a set of relations in BCNF.

(d) Why is the set of BCNF relations identical to the 3NF set?

13 For the scenario in Q10

(a) Draw a determinancy diagram.

(b) List the determinants in this scenario.

(c) List the candidate keys.

(d) Produce a set of normalised relations in BCNF directly from
    the list of determinants.

In this chapter you have covered:

■ Normalising database relations to third normal form (3NF)

- remove repeating groups → First Normal Form (1NF)

- remove partial dependencies → Second Normal Form (2NF)

- remove transitive dependencies → Third Normal Form (3NF)

■ A database is normalised so that

- all possible relationships between the data are allowed for

- unnecessary duplication of data is avoided and storage space saved

- altering data is not unnecessarily time-consuming

- altering data does not lead to inconsistencies.

Learning objectives:

■ Be able to use SQL to

• retrieve data from multiple tables of a relational database

• update data in tables of a relational database

• insert data into tables of a relational database

• delete data in tables of a relational database

■ Be able to use SQL to define a database table.

Using SQL to retrieve, update, insert and delete data

Querying a database

The main purpose of storing data in a database is to enable applications to interrogate the database for information. This interrogation is called querying the database.

Structured Query Language (SQL)

Structured Query Language (SQL) can be used to query a database. It is a simplified programming language.

Although SQL is an ANSI (American National Standards Institute) and ISO/IEC JTC1 (Joint Technical Committee 1) standard, there are different versions of the SQL language. However, to be compliant with the ANSI/ISO standard, they all support at least the major commands (such as SELECT, UPDATE, DELETE, INSERT, WHERE) in a similar manner.

Retrieving data from a single table

Table 10.4.1 shows data for the **Student** relation

Student (StudentId, StudentName, Gender)

The following query, expressed in SQL, will retrieve all of the data in the **Student** relation

```
SELECT *
  FROM Student;
```

The wildcard character * matches the attribute list

StudentId, StudentName, Gender

StudentId	Student Name	Gender
1	Ames	M
2	Baloch	F
3	Cheng	F
4	Dodds	M
5	Groos	M
6	Smith	F

Table 10.4.1 Relation Student in table form

The ANSI/ISO SQL standard requires that a semicolon is used at the end of the SQL statement but some systems relax this requirement. When writing SQL the convention is to use upper case for the SQL commands.

If we wanted just the data for *StudentName* we would refine the query as follows

```
SELECT StudentName
FROM Student;
```

We could refine the search even further by adding a WHERE clause that applies a search condition as follows

```
SELECT StudentName
FROM Student
WHERE Gender = 'F';
```

The result set that would be returned when this query is applied to relation **Student** would be as follows

Baloch

Cheng

Smith

because only these rows of the table/tuples of the relation match the search condition Gender = 'F'.

Gender = 'F' is actually called a predicate because it evaluates to either TRUE or FALSE.

If we also wanted the values of *StudentId* returned then the query would be

```
SELECT StudentId, StudentName
FROM Student
WHERE Gender = 'F';
```

Questions

 Write an SQL query that returns the names of all students in *Table 10.4.1* who are male.

Retrieving data from multiple tables

Table 10.4.2 shows data in table form for the **Ward** relation

Ward (<u>WardName</u>, NurseInCharge, NoOfBeds)

Table 10.4.3 shows data in table form for the **Patient** relation

Patient (<u>PatientId</u>, Surname, WardName)

The two relations are linked via a shared or common attribute *WardName*. The existence of an attribute common to both relations is not enough to join data from the corresponding tables correctly, as the following SQL query demonstrates

```
SELECT Ward.WardName, Ward.NurseInCharge,
       Patient.PatientId
FROM Ward, Patient;
```

The part of the query `Ward.WardName` references the *WardName* attribute in relation **Ward** and the part `Patient.PatientId` references *PatientId* attribute in relation **Patient**.

The `FROM Ward, Patient` part joins both relations without regard for the way that the data is actually linked via matching values of the shared attribute, *WardName*. The result set returned by the query is shown in *Table 10.4.4*.

WardName	NurseInCharge	NoOfBeds
Victoria	Sister Bunn	30
Aylesbury	Sister Moon	40

Table 10.4.2 Relation Ward in table form

PatientId	Surname	WardName
1	Bond	Aylesbury
2	Smith	Victoria
3	Jones	Aylesbury
4	Biggs	Victoria

Table 10.4.3 Relation Patient in table form

Victoria	Sister Bunn	1
Victoria	Sister Bunn	2
Victoria	Sister Bunn	3
Victoria	Sister Bunn	4
Aylesbury	Sister Moon	1
Aylesbury	Sister Moon	2
Aylesbury	Sister Moon	3
Aylesbury	Sister Moon	4

Table 10.4.4 Result set ignoring relationship between Ward and Patient

The problem is caused by the fact that our query does not make use of the common attribute that models the real world relationship between ward and patient, *WardName*.

When the search condition

WHERE Ward.WardName = Patient.WardName

is added to the SQL query we are able to exclude values that are not linked by the attribute *WardName* and to include only those that are. This SQL query will return the result set that corresponds to the real world situation shown in *Table 10.4.5*.

Aylesbury	Sister Moon	1
Victoria	Sister Bunn	2
Aylesbury	Sister Moon	3
Victoria	Sister Bunn	4

```
SELECT Ward.WardName, Ward.NurseInCharge, Patient.PatientId
    FROM Ward, Patient
        WHERE Ward.WardName = Patient.WardName;
```

The two relations have been joined on their common attribute, *WardName*, i.e. where the value of *WardName* is the same in both relations.

Table 10.4.5 Result set taking account of relationship between Ward and Patient

Writing the query as follows would return the same result set because dropping the relation name prefix before *NurseInCharge* and *PatientId* in the SELECT part of the SQL query is allowed where there is no ambiguity as to what is intended.

```
SELECT Ward.WardName , NurseInCharge, PatientId
    FROM Ward, Patient
        WHERE Ward.WardName = Patient.WardName;
```

Background

Integrity:
Means maintaining the accuracy and consistency of the data and relationships between data.

Questions

2 Write the SQL query that returns from *Tables 10.4.2* and *10.4.3* the name of the nurse in charge of the ward, surnames of all patients in their ward and the ward name.

Referential integrity:
Each foreign key value must have a matching primary key value in a related table, or be Null.

Role of a foreign key

What purpose does a foreign key serve if it doesn't automatically join the corresponding two relations?

The answer is so that the relational database system can perform a referential integrity check, i.e. check that the referenced primary key value exists before it is used as a foreign key in another relation. For example, if an attempt is made to add a new patient to the **Patient** table, either 'Victoria' or 'Aylesbury' must be chosen for *WardName* because these are the only two values present in the linked-to table **Ward**. The database system would use a referential integrity check to trap any other entered value for *WardName* and report an error.

Null:
Special value that is used to indicate the absence of any data value.

Similarly, if an attempt was made to delete the row in the **Ward** table for 'Victoria' ward, an error would occur because this value is used in the **Patient** table. In both of the cases described, preventing these changes occurring maintains the integrity of the data in the database of those attributes which make references to other attributes.

Ordering the result set returned by a query

We can order a result set returned by a query in ascending or descending order with the keyword ORDER BY qualified by one of the keywords ASC or DESC. If the qualifier is omitted then ASC is assumed. For example, we can place the result set returned in ascending order on *WardName* by the query opposite.

Table 10.4.6 shows the outcome of applying this query to the **Ward** and **Patient** relations.

```
SELECT Ward.WardName, NurseInCharge, PatientId
FROM Ward, Patient
  WHERE Ward.WardName = Patient.WardName
    ORDER BY Ward.WardName ASC;
```

Aylesbury	Sister Moon	1
Aylesbury	Sister Moon	3
Victoria	Sister Bunn	2
Victoria	Sister Bunn	4

Table 10.4.6 Result set ordered on WardName in ascending alphabetic order

Questions

 3   Write the SQL query that returns the names of both nurses and their patients, from *Tables 10.4.2* and *10.4.3*, ordered in descending patient name order.

Using more than one search condition

We may refine the query to return only those matches for which the number of beds is more than **30**. We can do this by adding the search condition `Ward.NoOfBeds > 30`

and connecting it logically to the search condition `Ward.WardName = Patient.WardName`

with the logical connective AND as follows

```
SELECT Ward.WardName, NurseInCharge, Patient.PatientId
  FROM Ward, Patient
    WHERE Ward.WardName = Patient.WardName
      AND Ward.NoOfBeds > 30
    ORDER BY WardName ASC;
```

Aylesbury	Sister Moon	1
Aylesbury	Sister Moon	3

The result set returned when this query is applied is as shown above right. Ward Aylesbury has **40** beds. Ward Victoria does not appear because this ward has only **30** beds and so is ruled out by the search condition

`Ward.NoOfBeds > 30.`

Questions

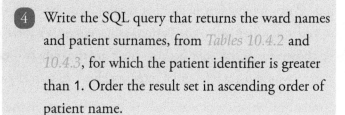 4   Write the SQL query that returns the ward names and patient surnames, from *Tables 10.4.2* and *10.4.3*, for which the patient identifier is greater than 1. Order the result set in ascending order of patient name.

Relational or comparison operators for search condition

Table 10.4.7 shows comparison operators that may be used in SQL queries.

Comparison Operator	Description
=	Equal to
<	Less than
>	Greater than
<=	Less than or equal to
>=	Greater than or equal to
<>	Not equal to
IN	The IN operator is used to compare a value to a list of literal values that have been specified or returned from another SQL query, e.g. `IN (SELECT PatientId FROM Patient).`

Table 10.4.7 Comparison operators for SQL queries

Questions

5 Write the SQL query that returns the ward names and patient surnames , from *Tables 10.4.2* and *10.4.3*, for which the patient identifier is less than or equal to **3**. Order the result set in descending order of patient identifier.

Ordering on more than one attribute

Table 10.4.8 shows two database tables, **Customer** and **Order**, respectively.

The effect of applying the following SQL query to this database

```
SELECT Customer.CustomerName , Order.OrderNo
   FROM Customer, Order
      WHERE Customer.CustNo = Order.CustNo
         ORDER BY Customer.CustomerName, Order.OrderNo;
```

is to return the following result set with columns *CustomerName*, *OrderNo*.

Note that, the result set is ordered on the first column, *CustomerName* and then the second *OrderNo*.

Blue Jack Aqua Center	1001
Blue Jack Aqua Center	1009
Sight Diver	1005
Sight Diver	1007
Tom Sawyer Diving Centre	1003
Tom Sawyer Diving Centre	1004

CustNo	Customer Name	Location
1221	Kauai Dive Shoppe	Kapaa Kauai
1351	Sight Diver	Kato Paphos
1356	Tom Sawyer Diving Centre	Christiansted
1380	Blue Jack Aqua Center	Waipahu
2156	Davy Jones' Locker	Vancouver

OrderNo	CustNo	SaleDate
1007	1351	20140412
1009	1380	20140417
1004	1356	20140420
1005	1351	20141106
1003	1356	20141113
1001	1380	20141202

Table 10.4.8 Tables Customer and Order

1007	
1009	
1004	
1005	
1003	
1001	

In the **Order** table, the order of the values of *OrderNo* for the orders placed by these customers is shown on the left. The data is extracted in this order. It is next sorted on the first column, *CustomerName* to produce the order of values shown on the right abbreviated. The rows with the same *CustNo* values are then sorted on *OrderNo* to produce the result set that is returned by the SQL query.

Blue...	1009
Blue...	1001
Sight...	1007
Sight...	1005
Tom...	1004
Tom...	1003

Logical operators for search condition

Table 10.4.9 shows some of the logical operators that can be used in SQL queries.

Logical Operator	Description
AND	The AND operator connects multiple search conditions in an SQL statement's WHERE clause that must all be true for a successful match.
OR	The OR operator allows multiple conditions to be combined in an SQL statement's WHERE clause any of which can be true for a successful match.
NOT	The NOT operator reverses the meaning of the logical operation with which it is used e.g. NOT (age > 14 AND age < 19).

Table 10.4.9 Logical operators for SQL queries

When more than one logical operator is used in a statement, NOT is evaluated first, then AND, and finally OR.

To impose a different order of evaluation parentheses can be added to the query. The logical conditions inside parentheses are evaluated independently before logical operators outside of the parentheses are applied.

Table 10.4.10 and *Table 10.4.11* show data for relations **Borrower** and **BooksOnLoan**.

BorrowerId	Surname	Initial
1	Smith	K
2	Barnes	W
3	Minns	M

ISBN	CopyNo	BorrowerId	DateDueBack
9781907982514	1	2	10/9/2014
9781907982514	2	1	4/9/2014

Table 10.4.10 Table showing some values for the relation Borrower

Table 10.4.11 Table showing some values for the relation BooksOnLoan

The result set returned when the following SQL query is applied to these tables is

Barnes, W
Smith, K

```
SELECT Borrower.Surname, Borrower.Initial
    FROM Borrower
        WHERE BorrowerId IN BooksOnLoan;
```

The search condition `WHERE BorrowerId IN BooksOnLoan`

matches *BorrowerId* 2 and 1 because these *BorrowerId*s are present in the **BooksOnLoan** table.

The result set returned when the following SQL query is applied to these tables is

Minns, M

```
SELECT Borrower.Surname, Borrower.Initial
    FROM Borrower
        WHERE BorrowerId NOT IN BooksOnLoan;
```

The search condition `"WHERE BorrowerId NOT IN BooksOnLoan"` matches *BorrowerId* 3 because this *BorrowerId* is not present in the **BooksOnLoan** table.

The result set returned when the following SQL query

is applied to these tables is shown below

Smith, K

```
SELECT Borrower.Surname, Borrower.Initial
FROM Borrower
WHERE BorrowerId IN (SELECT BorrowerId
            FROM BooksOnLoan
WHERE BooksOnLoan.DateDueBack < '5/9/2014');
```

The search condition

```
WHERE BorrowerId IN (SELECT BorrowerId
    FROM BooksOnLoan
        WHERE BooksOnLoan.DateDueBack < '5/9/2014')
```

matches *BorrowerId* 1 because this *BorrowerId* has a *DateDueBack* value of '4/9/2014' in the **BooksOnLoan** table and this value is less than '5/9/2014'.

The result set returned when the following SQL query is applied to these tables is shown below

Barnes W

```
SELECT Borrower.Surname, Borrower.Initials
FROM Borrower
    WHERE BorrowerId =
        (SELECT BorrowerId
            FROM BooksOnLoan
                WHERE BooksOnLoan.ISBN = 9781907982514
                    AND BooksOnLoan.CopyNo = 1);
```

Relation **Country** is

Country (<u>Name</u>, Capital, Population, Area)

Table 10.4.12 shows some data in table form for relation **Country**.

The result set returned when the following SQL query

```
SELECT Name, Capital, Population
 FROM Country
 WHERE (Population < 7000000)
   OR  (Population > 30000000);
```

is applied to this **Country** relation with attributes *Name, Capital, Population, Area* is shown below

Argentina	Buenos Aires	32300003
Brazil	Brasilia	150400000
Colombia	Bagota	33000000
El Salvador	San Salvador	5300000
Guyana	Georgetown	800000

Name	Capital	Population	Area
Argentina	Buenos Aires	32 300 003	2777815
Bolivia	La Paz	7 300 000	1098575
Brazil	Brasilia	150 400 000	8511196
Canada	Ottawa	26 500 000	9976147
Chile	Santiago	13 200 000	756943
Colombia	Bagota	33 000 000	1138907
Cuba	Havana	10 600 000	114524
Ecuador	Quito	10 600 000	455502
El Salvador	San Salvador	5 300 000	20865
Guyana	Georgetown	800 000	214969

Table 10.4.12 Table for relation Country showing some values

Questions

6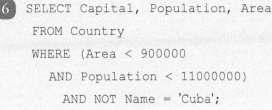
```
SELECT Capital, Population, Area
 FROM Country
 WHERE (Area < 900000
   AND Population < 11000000)
   AND NOT Name = 'Cuba';
```

What result set is returned when this SQL query is applied to the data in *Table 10.4.12*?

Questions

7
```
SELECT Capital, Population
 FROM Country
   WHERE Name IN ('Chile',
'Cuba', 'Guyana');
```

What result set is returned when this SQL query is applied to the data in *Table 10.4.12*?

Questions

8 Rewrite the query in Q7 so that it uses OR instead of IN.

Deleting data in a single table

The DELETE statement is used to delete rows of a table.

```
DELETE FROM table_name
        WHERE some_column = some_value;
```

The WHERE clause specifies which row or rows should be deleted. If the WHERE clause is omitted, all rows will be deleted!

For example referencing *Table 4.10.12*,

```
DELETE FROM Country
        WHERE Capital = 'Brasilia';
```

deletes the row Brazil, Brasilia, 150400000, 8511196.

Questions

9 Write the SQL statement to delete the row with BorrowerId 3 in the Borrower table shown in *Table 10.4.10*.

10 Write the SQL statement to delete the row(s) with Population > 15000000 in the Country table shown in *Table 10.4.12*.

Inserting data in a single table

The **INSERT INTO** statement inserts a new row into a table. It is possible to write this statement in two forms.

The first form does not specify the column names where the data will be inserted, only their values:

```
INSERT INTO table_name
        VALUES (value1, value2, value3, ...);
```

The second form specifies both the column names and the values to be inserted:

```
INSERT INTO table_name (column1, column2, column3, ...)
        VALUES (value1, value2, value3, ...);
```

In the first form, a value of the correct data type must be supplied for every attribute of the relation and the order of the supplied values must be the same as the corresponding columns.

In the second form, a value for every specified column must be supplied and each value must match in data type the corresponding specified column, i.e. value1 corresponds to column1, value2 to column2, etc. The value Null will be inserted for any columns not referenced.

For example, for relation **Ward**, *Table 10.4.2*, reproduced here

First form:

```
INSERT INTO Ward VALUES ('Gresham', 'Mr Oonga', 20);
```

WardName	NurseInCharge	NoOfBeds
Victoria	Sister Bunn	30
Aylesbury	Sister Moon	40

Table 10.4.2 Relation Ward in table form

Second form:

```
INSERT INTO Ward (WardName, NurseInCharge) VALUES ('Savernake', 'Sister Teng');
```

This second form creates a new row in *Table 10.4.2* with values 'Savernake', 'Sister Teng', Null

Questions

11　Write the SQL statement to add a new row to the Ward table (*Table 10.4.2*) for ward 'Amersham', containing **25** beds. The nurse in charge is 'Sister Brody'.

12　Write the SQL statement to add a new row to the Country table (*Table 10.4.12*) for 'UK', 'London'.

Updating data in a single table

The UPDATE statement is used to update an existing row of a table.

```
UPDATE table_name
  SET column1 = value1, column2 = value2, ...
    WHERE some_column=some_value;
```

For example,

```
UPDATE Ward
        SET NurseInCharge = 'Mr Ali',
                        NoOfBeds = 25
                WHERE WardName = 'Victoria';
```

Questions

13　Write the SQL statement to update the row of the Country table (*Table 10.4.12*) for 'UK' to add population **64100000**, area **243610**. Assume that an insert statement has inserted 'UK', 'London' already as in Q12.

Data Manipulation Language (DML)

SQL qualifies as a data manipulation language because it can be used to retrieve, insert, delete and update the data content of databases. It is possible to practise using and writing SQL to manipulate data in a database online at

http://www.w3schools.com/sql/default.asp.

The tutorials on this site use the Northwind sample database (included in MS Access and MS SQL Server).

This site also contains a handy SQL quick reference that can be consulted at

http://www.w3schools.com/sql/sql_quickref.asp. Online SQL tests are also available at this site.

Using SQL to create a database

Data Definition Language (DDL)

Data Definition Language is a standard for commands that define the different structures in a database. DDL statements create, modify and remove database objects such as tables, indexes, and users.

CREATE TABLE command

The CREATE TABLE command is used to create a table in a database.

Tables are organized into rows and columns. Each table must have a name. The structure and name of a table is created with a statement of the form

```
CREATE TABLE table_name
  (
    column_name1 data_type(size),
    column_name2 data_type(size),
    column_name3 data_type(size),
      ....
  );
```

The column_name parameters specify the names of the columns of the table.

The data_type parameter specifies what type of data the column can hold (e.g. VARCHAR, INTEGER, DECIMAL, DATE, etc...).

The size parameter sets a limit on the length of values of the data type, e.g. VARCHAR(10) sets a limit of 10 characters. The size parameter may be omitted.

For example,

```
CREATE TABLE Person
  (
    PersonId SMALLINT,
    Surname VARCHAR(25),
    FirstName VARCHAR(25),
    Address VARCHAR(25),
    City VARCHAR(25)
  );
```

The *PersonId* column is of type SMALLINT and will hold an integer containing up to 5 decimal digits (SQL : 1999 standard).

The *Surname, FirstName, Address,* and *City* columns are of type VARCHAR and will hold characters up to a maximum length of 25 characters.

This DDL statement when executed will create an empty **Person** table with structure as follows

PersonId	Surname	FirstName	Address	City

The empty table can be filled with data using the INSERT INTO statement.

SQL Constraints

SQL constraints are used to specify rules for the data in a table and are applied either at the level of column or at the level of the table.

Column level:

```
        CREATE TABLE table_name

          (

          column_name1 data_type(size) constraint_name,

          column_name2 data_type(size) constraint_name,

          column_name3 data_type(size) constraint_name,

          ....

          );
```

In SQL, we have the following constraints:

- NOT NULL - Indicates that a column cannot store NULL value

- UNIQUE - Ensures that each row for a column must have a unique value

- PRIMARY KEY - A combination of a NOT NULL and UNIQUE. Ensures that a column (or combination of two or more columns) has a unique identity which helps to find a particular record in a table more easily and quickly

- FOREIGN KEY - Ensure the referential integrity of the data in one table to match values in another table

- CHECK - Ensures that the value in a column meets a specific condition

- DEFAULT - Specifies a default value when none specified for this column

To see an application of these we will use the **Ward**, **Patient** scenario from *Table 10.4.2* and *Table 10.4.3* suitably modified and with a *Gender* attribute to illustrate use of the CHECK constraint.

Table level: Column level

```
    CREATE TABLE Patient

      (

        PatientId SMALLINT PRIMARY KEY,

        Surname VARCHAR(25) NOT NULL,

        FirstName VARCHAR(25),

        Gender CHAR(1) CHECK (Gender = 'M' OR Gender='F'),

        WardName VARCHAR(25) FOREIGN KEY

            REFERENCES Ward(WardName)

      );


    CREATE TABLE Ward

      (

        WardName VARCHAR(25) PRIMARY KEY,

        NurseInCharge VARCHAR(25) NOT NULL,

        NoOfBeds SMALLINT

      );
```

There is a variation on syntax for specifying primary key. It can also be defined at table level as shown below. You will need to check which syntax is accepted by the database system that you use. A foreign key is expressed at table level as shown below.

Table level:

```
         CREATE TABLE Patient
           (
              PatientId SMALLINT,
              Surname VARCHAR(25) NOT NULL,
              FirstName VARCHAR(25),
              Gender CHAR(1) CHECK (Gender = 'M' OR Gender='F'),
              WardName VARCHAR(25),
              PRIMARY KEY(PatientId),
              FOREIGN KEY(WardName)
              REFERENCES Ward(WardName)
           );
```

Composite primary key

A composite primary key can only be defined by a named constraint at the table level as follows. The example below also shows how foreign keys can be defined by a named constraint as well, necessarily so if the foreign key is composite. In the example below, *EnrolClassNoPK* is the name of a named constraint that defines a composite primary key, *YearNo, ClassNo, StudentId* for the **EnrolForClass** relation. *EnrolClassFK* is the name of a named constraint that defines the foreign key *YearNo, ClassNo* that references the primary key *YearNo, ClassNo* in the **Class** relation (not shown).

```
CREATE TABLE EnrolForClass
  (
     StudentId CHAR(6),
     YearNo CHAR(4)
     ClassNo CHAR(8),
     Grade CHAR(2),
     CONSTRAINT EnrolClassPK PRIMARY KEY (YearNo, ClassNo, StudentId),
     CONSTRAINT EnrolClassFK FOREIGN KEY (YearNo, ClassNo)
        REFERENCES Class (YearNo, ClassNo),
     CONSTRAINT EnrolStudentFK FOREIGN KEY (StudentId)
        REFERENCES Student (StudentId)
  );
```

Data types

Table 10.4.13 shows some general data types used in SQL (SQL:1999 standard) when defining tables using CREATE TABLE.

CHARACTER(n) or CHAR(n)	Character string. Fixed-length n. Default length is 1 when n is omitted. Use CHAR when the sizes of the column data entries don't vary much.
VARCHAR(n) or CHARACTER VARYING(n) or CHAR VARYING(n)	Character string. Variable length. Maximum length n. Default length is 1 when n is omitted. Use VARCHAR when the sizes of the column data entries vary considerably.
NCHAR(n)	National character string type that uses fixed width Unicode string. Width specified by n.
NCHAR VARYING(n)	National character string type that uses variable width Unicode string. Maximum width specified by n.
BOOLEAN	Stores TRUE or FALSE values.
SMALLINT	Integer numerical (no decimal). Signed unless keyword UNSIGNED present. Precision 5. Exact numeric type.
INTEGER	Integer numerical (no decimal). Signed unless keyword UNSIGNED present. Precision 10. Exact numeric type.
DECIMAL(p, s) or DECIMAL	Exact numerical, precision p, scale s. Example: decimal (5, 2) is a number that has 3 digits before the decimal point and 2 digits after the decimal point. Exact numeric type so can be used to represent money. Can omit (p, s) to obtain default precision and scale.
FLOAT(p) or FLOAT	Approximate numerical, mantissa precision p. A floating number in base 10 exponential notation. The size argument for this type consists of a single number specifying the minimum precision. Approximate numeric type. Can omit (p) to obtain default precision.
REAL	Approximate numerical, mantissa precision 7.
DATE	Stores year, month, and day values.
TIME	Stores hour, minute, and second values.

Table 10.4.13 Table for some general data types used in SQL:1999 (ISO/IEC 9075-2:1999 (E))

Database Engine to practise with

SQLite is a self-contained, server-less, zero-configuration, transactional SQL database engine. The code for SQLite is in the public domain and is thus free for use for any purpose, commercial or private. It is obtainable from http://www.sqlite.org/. There are several other database engines that can be used instead of SQLite, some come with a graphical user interface manager.

Command line operation

To use SQLite requires the `sqlite3` program, "sqlite3.exe". Typing `sqlite3` at the command prompt of a console or terminal window, optionally followed by the name of the file that holds the SQLite database, starts the SQLite database engine. If the file holding the database does not exist, a new database file with the given name will be created automatically. If no database file is specified, a temporary database is created, then deleted when the `sqlite3` program exits unless saved with the `.save` filename command. The engine can also be started by clicking on `sqlite3.exe` in the usual manner. That was how the window shown in *Figure 10.4.1* was opened.

When started, the `sqlite3` program shows a brief banner message as shown in *Figure 10.4.1*, before prompting to receive SQL. SQL statements (terminated by a semicolon) can be entered at the command prompt followed by pressing the "Enter" key to execute the SQL.

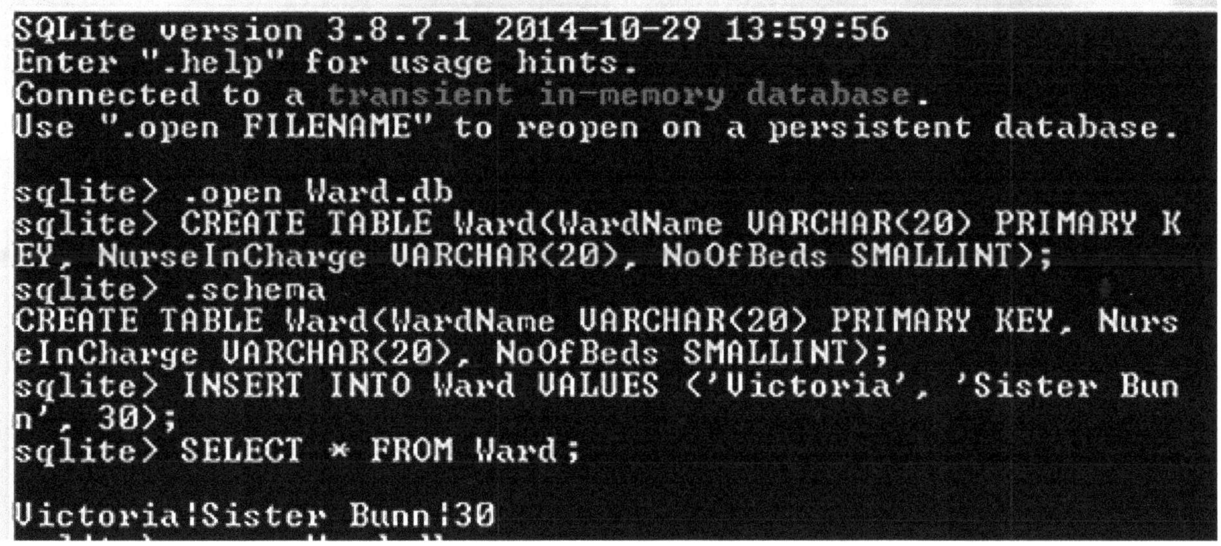

```
SQLite version 3.8.7.1 2014-10-29 13:59:56
Enter ".help" for usage hints.
Connected to a transient in-memory database.
Use ".open FILENAME" to reopen on a persistent database.

sqlite> .open Ward.db
sqlite> CREATE TABLE Ward(WardName VARCHAR(20) PRIMARY K
EY, NurseInCharge VARCHAR(20), NoOfBeds SMALLINT);
sqlite> .schema
CREATE TABLE Ward(WardName VARCHAR(20) PRIMARY KEY, Nurs
eInCharge VARCHAR(20), NoOfBeds SMALLINT);
sqlite> INSERT INTO Ward VALUES ('Victoria', 'Sister Bun
n', 30);
sqlite> SELECT * FROM Ward;

Victoria|Sister Bunn|30
```

Figure 10.4.1 SQLite running in a console window

Figure 10.4.1 also shows a database, `Ward.db` being created (it didn't previously exist) with the command `.open` and command line argument `Ward.db`.

`.open Ward.db`

If it does exist then it will be opened by the same command and command line argument.

Next, the database's first table is created with the Data Definition Language (DDL) command

```
CREATE TABLE Ward (WardName VARCHAR(20) PRIMARY KEY, NurseInCharge VARCHAR(20),
                   NoOfBeds SMALLINT);
```

The data types applied to the attributes are VARCHAR(**20**) and SMALLINT.

The command `.schema` when executed at the command prompt returns the DDL script that was used to create tables and any other structures such as indices, triggers, etc.

The DML command to add to table **Ward** the tuple `('Victoria', 'Sister Bunn', 30)`

is as follows   `INSERT INTO Ward VALUES ('Victoria', 'Sister Bunn', 30);`

Confirmation of the success of this insert is shown in *Figure 10.4.1* using the Data Manipulation Language (DML) query   `SELECT * FROM Ward;`

Next, the database's second table, **Patient**, is created with the Data Definition Language (DDL) command below, also shown in *Figure 10.4.2*.

```
CREATE TABLE Patient
    (PatientId SMALLINT PRIMARY KEY, Surname VARCHAR(20), WardName VARCHAR(20),
     FOREIGN KEY(WardName) REFERENCES Ward(WardName));
```

This table is linked to the Ward table by a foreign key which is created in table Patient by

```
FOREIGN KEY(WardName) REFERENCES Ward(WardName)
```

Figure 10.4.2 Creating table Patient with one row of values

The DML command to add to table **Patient** the tuple `(2, 'Smith', 'Victoria')`

is as follows   `INSERT INTO Patient VALUES (2, 'Smith', 'Victoria');`

The value 'Victoria' used for the attribute *WardName* of **Patient** satisfies the referential integrity condition of existence of this value in the **Ward** table. If it didn't the INSERT action would be aborted and the reason for the failure to carry out the command reported in an explanatory error message.

Confirmation of the success of this insert is shown in *Figure 10.4.2* using the Data Manipulation Language (DML) query   `SELECT * FROM Patient;`

> ## Questions
>
> **14** Write the DDL statements to create tables in database **Library** for the relations
>
> > **Borrower** (<u>BorrowerId</u>, Surname, Initial)
> > **BooksOnLoan** (<u>ISBN, CopyNo</u>, BorrowerId, DateDueBack)
>
> as shown in *Tables 10.4.10* and *10.4.11*.

In this chapter you have covered:

- How to use SQL to
  - retrieve data from multiple tables of a relational database using SELECT FROM WHERE
  - update data in tables of a relational database using UPDATE SET WHERE
  - insert data into tables of a relational database using INSERT INTO VALUES
  - delete data in tables of a relational database DELETE FROM WHERE
- How to use SQL to define a database table using CREATE TABLE.

▨ 10.5 Client server databases

Learning objectives:

▪ *Know that a client server database system provides simultaneous access to the database for multiple clients*

▪ *Know how concurrent access can be controlled to preserve the integrity of the database*

Client server database system

Simultaneous access

In a multi-user client server database system, stored data items in a database on a server may be accessed simultaneously by programs running on client workstations as shown in Figure 10.5.1.

The database server allows users at client workstations to retrieve information (read operation) stored in the database and modify this information (update/insert/delete operations).

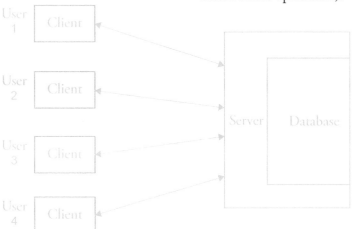

Typically, a user reads data items from one or more database tables before modifying one or more of these data items. A database transaction is a group of these operations. Each operation must succeed before the entire database transaction is considered successful. If an operation fails, a database transaction allows the program to back out from all previous operations and leave the database in its original state.

Figure 10.5.1 Client server database system with users 1 to 4

Key term

Client server database:
In a multi-user client server database system, stored data items in a database on a server may be accessed simultaneously by programs running on client workstations.

Key term

Concurrent access:
Means access occurs at the same time or over the same time interval.

Concurrent access

Transactions submitted by users at client workstations can sometimes target the same data items in the database. Access to the same data items by different users can occur over the same time interval, i.e. concurrently. This can result in an inconsistent database if not carefully controlled.

An inconsistent database is one in which the state of the database does not truly reflect reality, e.g. the number of airline seats sold should be 120 but the database has recorded only 118 seats sold. The integrity of the data in the database will be affected. Data integrity refers to the accuracy and consistency of the data in the database.

Lost update

To illustrate this potential problem consider an airline flight reservation database system which stores information about each flight such as:

- flight number
- date of flight
- number of seats sold
- the number of seats left to sell

Suppose that a computer terminal located in a travel agent's office in Birmingham attempts to book three seats about the same time as a terminal located in a travel agent's in Swindon attempts to book five seats on the same flight. They each request copies of data for this flight from the server located in London. *Figure 10.5.2* illustrates what could happen. The problem that ensues is known as the **lost update problem**. This occurs when two transactions that access the same database items have their operations interleaved in such a way that makes the value of some database item incorrect.

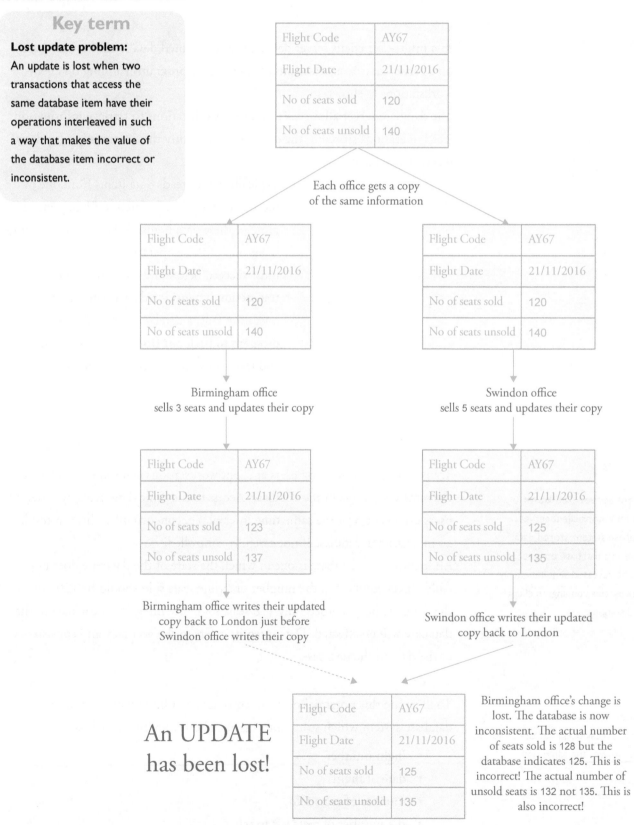

Key term

Lost update problem:
An update is lost when two transactions that access the same database item have their operations interleaved in such a way that makes the value of the database item incorrect or inconsistent.

Flight Code	AY67
Flight Date	21/11/2016
No of seats sold	120
No of seats unsold	140

Each office gets a copy of the same information

Flight Code	AY67
Flight Date	21/11/2016
No of seats sold	120
No of seats unsold	140

Flight Code	AY67
Flight Date	21/11/2016
No of seats sold	120
No of seats unsold	140

Birmingham office
sells 3 seats and updates their copy

Swindon office
sells 5 seats and updates their copy

Flight Code	AY67
Flight Date	21/11/2016
No of seats sold	123
No of seats unsold	137

Flight Code	AY67
Flight Date	21/11/2016
No of seats sold	125
No of seats unsold	135

Birmingham office writes their updated
copy back to London just before
Swindon office writes their copy

Swindon office writes their updated
copy back to London

An UPDATE has been lost!

Flight Code	AY67
Flight Date	21/11/2016
No of seats sold	125
No of seats unsold	135

Birmingham office's change is lost. The database is now inconsistent. The actual number of seats sold is 128 but the database indicates 125. This is incorrect! The actual number of unsold seats is 132 not 135. This is also incorrect!

Figure 10.5.2 Lost update problem

If we consider the detail of how individual seats are booked then we see that it is a two-stage process as shown in *Figure 10.5.3*:

1. The database is first queried to obtain the seating plan for a specific flight, e.g. flight **AY67** on 21/11/2016, using an SQL Select statement sent from the client to the database server

2. The SQL query results returned are used to select a seat which is not already reserved (SeatBooked = FALSE) and then an SQL update operation is sent to the database server to set the chosen seat to reserved (SeatBooked = TRUE) for the given flight and date.

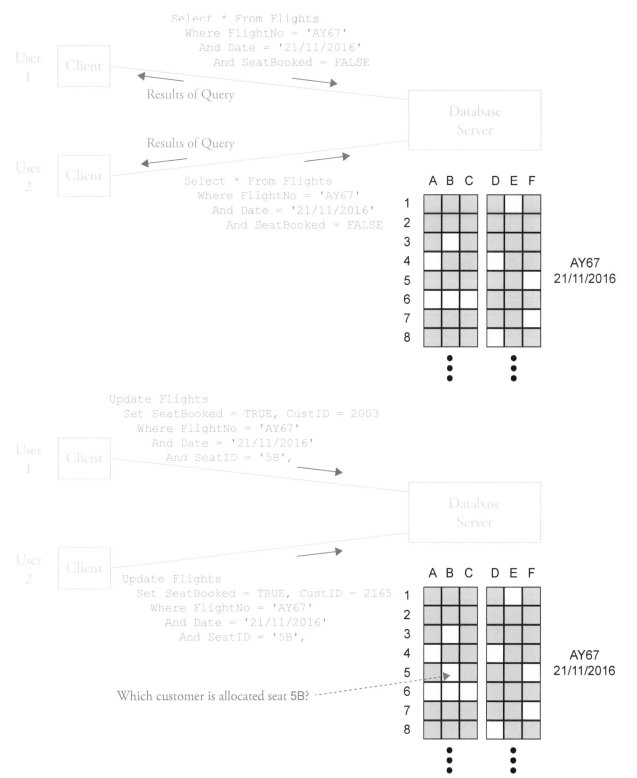

Figure 10.5.3 Two users, User 1 and User 2, attempting to reserve the same seat at the same time and in the process allowing one user to overwrite the other's reservation

A problem arises if the SQL Update operations proceed as shown in *Figure 10.5.3*. Both User 1 and User 2 believe that seat **5B** is available at the time when they each send an SQL Update operation to the database server to reserve seat **5B**. The database can only record this seat as being booked by one customer, either the customer with CustID **2003** or the customer with CustID **2165**. If a database server allows uncontrolled access to a specific record in the manner described then it will become inconsistent, i.e. its record of the bookings will not agree with its users' record. To avoid this problem the database server must control concurrent access to its database.

Key concept

Record lock:

A record lock is a concurrency control method which can prevent a lost update. The lock ensures exclusive-access to a record when it is being updated. Other transactions are blocked from accessing the record until after it has been updated and the change permanently recorded. The blocked transactions then see the updated record.

Record locking

One approach relies upon a locking mechanism. Consider a simplified version of the scenario shown in *Figure 10.5.3* in which relation Flight consists of attributes, FlightNo and NoOfSeatsSold. Its table depiction consisting of two columns is shown in *Table 10.5.1*.

FlightNo	NoOfSeatsSold
1	50
2	120
3	87
4	156

Table 10.5.1 Relation Flight consisting of two columns in table form

Now suppose that two clients, User 1 and User 2, attempt to access the same row of the Flight table, e.g. row 1.

Let User 1 retrieve row 1 first. After that, assume that User 2 retrieves the same row.

Time	User 1	User 2
	postgres=# BEGIN; USER 1 starts transaction BEGIN	postgres=# BEGIN; USER 2 starts transaction BEGIN
	postgres=# SELECT * FROM Flight WHERE FlightNo = 1 FOR UPDATE; FlightNo | NoOfSeatsSold -------------------------- 1 | 50	
		postgres=# SELECT * FROM Flight WHERE FlightNo = 1;
	postgres=# UPDATE Flight SET NoOfSeatsSold = 52 WHERE FlightNo = 1; USER 1 sells 2 seats UPDATE 1	BLOCKED
	postgres=# COMMIT; USER 1 ends transaction COMMIT ————————————————▶ postgres=#	UNBLOCKED - Select query now executes
		FlightNo | NoOfSeatsSold -------------------------- 1 | 52
		postgres=# COMMIT; USER 2 ends transaction COMMIT postgres=#

Table 10.5.2 User 1 and User 2 interacting concurrently with the Flight table

Table 10.5.2 shows User 1 using the BEGIN command to start a transaction on the PostgreSQL database containing the table Flight. User 1 wishes to update the NoOfSeatsSold field of the record in the first row.

It locks this record with the SQL command

```
SELECT * FROM Flight WHERE FlightNo = 1 FOR UPDATE;
```

The "`SELECT * FROM Flight WHERE FlightNo = 1`" part queries the database. The database server returns the query result

```
FlightNo | NoOfSeatsSold
--------------------------------
   1     |      50
```

The "`FOR UPDATE`" part locks the record to prevent other users from accessing this record until the lock is released. This lock is known as an exclusive-lock for this reason.

User 2 sends the following SELECT query to the database server just after User 1 gets the query result shown above

```
SELECT * FROM Flight WHERE FlightNo = 1
```

User 2's query is blocked because the record with FlightNo = 1 is locked.

User 1 then sends the following UPDATE command to the database server

```
UPDATE Flight SET NoOfSeatsSold = 52 WHERE FlightNo = 1;
```

To commit this update to the database and end the transaction, User 1 sends the COMMIT command.

This update is applied and the lock is removed. Whereupon, the pending SELECT query from User 2 is executed by the database server and the following query results are returned to User 2

```
FlightNo | NoOfSeatsSold
--------------------------------
   1     |      52
```

Note that the `NoOfSeatsSold` reflects the update applied by User 1.

If User 2 had attempted a "`SELECT * FROM Flight WHERE FlightNo = 1 FOR UPDATE;`" just after User 1 had set an exclusive-lock then it would have been blocked. Only when User 1's transaction was finished would User 2 been granted an exclusive-lock. User 2 could then have applied an update to the `NoOfSeatsSold` field of record 1. This is how locking can be used to prevent the Lost Update problem occurring.

In the example, the lock applied to the `Flight` record/row of the table where `FlightNo = 1`. If User 2 had chosen to query a different row then User 2 would not have been blocked. For a similar reason, User 2 would not have been blocked from updating a different row of the `Flight` table.

Serialisation

The isolation level of a transaction determines what data the transaction can see and whether it can modify a data item or not when other transactions are executing concurrently. The highest level of isolation is SERIALIZABLE. The default level is often READ COMMITTED. This is a lower level of isolation. READ COMMITTED does not prevent the LOST UPDATE problem whereas SERIALIZABLE does.

The isolation provided by each is as follows:

READ COMMITTED (Not in AQA specification but included because it is relevant to understanding serialisation)
An SQL operation can only see rows committed before the transaction began. It does not prevent the situation when a modification by one transaction is overwritten by another executing concurrently.

SERIALIZABLE
1. A transaction cannot read data written by a concurrent uncommitted transaction.

2. A transaction can only see data that was committed before it began even when this data has been modified and committed by another transaction.

3. A transaction cannot modify a data item that has been modified by a concurrent transaction.

If the isolation mode is set to SERIALIZABLE then the database server can detect and prevent the LOST UPDATE problem occurring. A characteristic of the LOST UPDATE problem is that the transactions that cause this conflict are not serialisable, i.e. do not behave as if they were executed one right after another in a serial fashion.

The isolation level can be set using the SET TRANSACTION CHARACTERISTICS command or the SET SESSION CHARACTERISTICS. These set the default transaction characteristics for a transaction and for subsequent transactions of a session, respectively.

Time	User 1	User 2

	`SET SESSION CHARACTERISTICS AS TRANSACTION ISOLATION LEVEL READ COMMITTED;`
	`SET`
	`postgres=# BEGIN;` USER 1 starts transaction
	`BEGIN`	

		`SET SESSION CHARACTERISTICS AS TRANSACTION ISOLATION LEVEL READ COMMITTED;`
		`SET`
		`postgres=# BEGIN;` USER 2 starts
		`BEGIN` transaction

	`postgres=# SELECT * FROM Flight WHERE` `FlightNo = 1;` FlightNo | NoOfSeatsSold ---------------------- 1 | 50	
		`postgres=# SELECT * FROM Flight WHERE` `FlightNo = 1;` FlightNo | NoOfSeatsSold ---------------------- 1 | 50

	`postgres=# UPDATE Flight SET NoOfSeatsSold`
	`= 52 WHERE FlightNo = 1;`
	`UPDATE 1` USER 1 sells 2 seats	

		`postgres=# UPDATE Flight SET`
		`NoOfSeatsSold = 51 WHERE FlightNo = 1;`
		BLOCKED TEMPORARILY

	`postgres=# COMMIT;`
	`COMMIT` ⟶
	`postgres=#`
		UNBLOCKED

		`UPDATE 1` USER 2 sells 1 seat
		`postgres=# COMMIT;`
		`COMMIT`
		`postgres=#`

	`postgres=# SELECT * FROM Flight WHERE` `FlightNo = 1;` FlightNo | NoOfSeatsSold ---------------------- LOST UPDATE 1 | 51	SHOULD BE 53, 2 SOLD BY USER 1 and 1 SOLD BY USER 2

Table 10.5.3 User 1 and User 2 interacting concurrently with the `Flight` table when isolation level is READ COMMITTED

Table 10.5.3 shows User 1 and User 2 interacting concurrently with the `Flight` table when the isolation level is READ COMMITTED. This setting fails to prevent the Lost Update problem. What is needed is a way of detecting and preventing concurrent transactions that would not execute serially, if attempted. Figure 10.5.4 shows User 2's attempt to update the same record as User 1 but later in time than User 1. The database server forces User 2 to abort its update because the server has concluded that it would not be possible to serialise these updates. When

User 2 restarts the transaction it finds that the `NoOfSeatsSold` field has been updated. User 2 uses the new value 52 recorded in the database, adding one to calculate the value **53** which it uses to update the database.

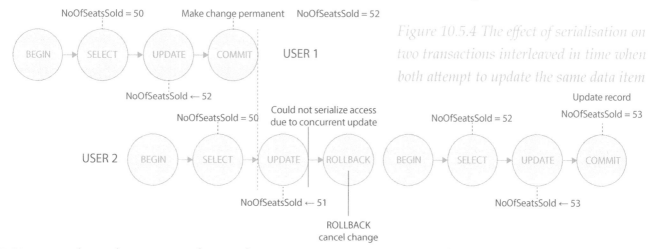

Figure 10.5.4 The effect of serialisation on two transactions interleaved in time when both attempt to update the same data item

Table 10.5.4 shows the sequence of events for two users interacting concurrently with a postgreSQL database when the transaction isolation is set to SERIALIZABLE.

Time	User 1	User 2

	`SET SESSION CHARACTERISTICS AS TRANSACTION ISOLATION LEVEL SERIALIZABLE;`
	`SET`
	`postgres=# BEGIN;` USER 1 starts transaction
	`BEGIN`	

		`SET SESSION CHARACTERISTICS AS TRANSACTION ISOLATION LEVEL SERIALIZABLE;`
		`SET`
		`postgres=# BEGIN;` USER 2 starts transaction
		`BEGIN`

	`postgres=# SELECT * FROM Flight` `WHERE FlightNo = 1;` FlightNo | NoOfSeatsSold ------------------------- 1 | 50	
		`postgres=# SELECT * FROM Flight` `WHERE FlightNo = 1;` FlightNo | NoOfSeatsSold ------------------------- 1 | 50

	`postgres=# UPDATE Flight`
	`SET NoOfSeatsSold = 52 WHERE FlightNo = 1;`
	`UPDATE 1` USER 1 sells 2 seats	

	`postgres=# COMMIT;` USER 1 ends transaction `COMMIT` Change made permanent `Postgres=#`	
	USER 2 cannot see the change even though it is now permanent	`postgres=# SELECT * FROM Flight` `WHERE FlightNo = 1;` FlightNo | NoOfSeatsSold ------------------------- 1 | 50
	USER 2 is stopped from updating the database because its data is out of date. If allowed it would overwrite the change that USER 1 made and lead to a LOST UPDATE.	`postgres=# UPDATE Flight SET NoOfSeatsSold = 51 WHERE FlightNo = 1;` Could not serialize access due to concurrent update

	`postgres=# SELECT * FROM Flight WHERE`
	`FlightNo = 1;`
	Database is consistent FlightNo | NoOfSeatsSold
	------------------------- 	
	    1 | 52
		`postgres=# ROLLBACK;` USER 2 ends transaction
		`ROLLBACK` Update aborted
		`postgres=#`

	USER 2 must try again to update the database adding 1 to 52 not 1 to 50: `UPDATE Flight SET NoOfSeatsSold = 53`
	`WHERE FlightNo = 1;`
		`postgres=# SELECT * FROM Flight WHERE`
		`FlightNo = 1;`
		Database is consistent FlightNo | NoOfSeatsSold
		------------------------- 	
		    1 | 52

Table 10.5.4 Effect of serialisation on two transactions interleaved in time when both update the same data item and the isolation level is SERIALIZABLE

Key concept

Serialisation:
Serialisation attempts to serialise access to a data item in order to detect and prevent the lost update problem occurring. Transactions attempting to alter a data item that is currently the subject of another transaction are detected and aborted. Any temporary changes cancelled.

Key concept

Timestamp ordering:
A timestamp is a unique identifier created by a database server that indicates the relative starting time of a transaction. The database records the transaction timestamp of the last transaction to read data item X and the transaction timestamp of the last transaction to write data item X.
The database server applies rules using these to determine if a transaction's actions will result in the integrity of the database being compromised. If it will the server aborts the transaction.

Timestamp ordering

A transaction is a unit of work. When a transaction is committed its work is done and any change (update, insert, delete) is made permanent. Until a transaction is committed changes are registered with the database server but are not actually applied to the database. They are considered temporary changes which means that they can be undone or rolled back (ROLLBACK).

Temporary changes are made first to allow the database system to check for concurrency violations. If none have occurred then the changes are applied permanently to the database. However, if the database system detects a concurrency violation then the transaction is aborted and no permanent change is made to the database. Any temporary change must be undone. This is called ROLLBACK.

Typically, timestamp values are assigned in the order in which transactions are submitted to the system, so a transaction timestamp can be thought of as the *transaction start time*. We refer to the timestamp of transaction T as TS(T). A simple counter which starts at zero can be used as the source of transaction number. Each new transaction causes the counter to be incremented and the resulting new counter value is assigned to the transaction.

The database server records the largest timestamp for a data item, X, when a read transaction is performed on the data item, X - ReadTS(X). It records separately, the largest timestamp for a data item, X, when a write transaction is performed on the data item, X - WriteTS(X). The counter starts initially at zero.

Let's suppose User 1 begins a transaction, T_1, that contains a Read request followed by a Write request. The timestamp counter is incremented and its new value 1 (it started at 0) assigned to transaction T_1.

User 2 begins a transaction T_2 and is assigned transaction time stamp value 2. T_2 also contains a Read request and a Write request. Now suppose the time ordering of these Read and Write requests is as shown in *Table 10.5.5*. User 2 completes before User 1. Therefore, User 1's Read data is potentially out of date. Therefore, User 1's transaction, T_1 must be aborted.

User 1	TS(T)	User 2	Counter	ReadTS(X)	WriteTS(X)
			0	0	0
Starts a transaction	1		1	0	0
Read request	1		1	1	0
	2	Starts a transaction	2	1	0
	2	Read request	2	2	0
	2	Write request	2	2	2
Write request	1				

Table 10.5.5 Timestamp ordering protocol ensures serializability among transactions in their conflicting read and write operations

The following rules are used with timestamps to determine whether a transaction operation is allowed or not.

Rules:

1. Transaction T_1 issues a WriteItem(X) operation:

```
If ReadTS(X) > TS(T1) Or WriteTS(X) > TS(T1)
   Then abort and rollback T1 and reject the operation.
   Else
      If WriteTS(X) <= TS(T1)
         Then execute the WriteItem(X) operation of T1
             and set WriteTS(X) to TS(T1)
```

> Another transaction has read X since T_1 started or another transaction has modified X since T_1 started

> Another transaction modified X but before T_1 started

2. Transaction T_1 issues a ReadItem(X) operation:

```
If WriteTS(x) > TS(T1)

   Then abort and rollback T1 and reject the operation.

   Else
      If WriteTS(x) <= TS(T1)

         Then execute the ReadItem(x) operation of T1

                 and set ReadTS(x) to the larger of TS(T1)

                 and the current ReadTS(x)
```

> Another transaction modified X after T_1 started

> Another transaction modified X but before T_1 started

If we revisit the User 1 and User 2 lost update problem, then an attempt by User 1 to update the Flight record for which FlightNo = 1 will result in User 1's transaction being rescheduled because User 2's transaction timestamp has a larger counter value than User 1's.

Commitment ordering

Commitment ordering is used in client server database systems such as mobile banking, and e-commerce.

A transaction is an "all or nothing" unit of work. A transaction is either committed, i.e. its effects on all the resources (data items) involved become permanent, or it is aborted (rolled back), i.e. its effects on all the resources are undone. The term that summarises this is atomicity:

> *In database systems, an atomic transaction is an indivisible and irreducible series of database operations such that either all occur, or nothing occurs.*

When a transaction is in conflict with another transaction, i.e. committing both would lead to database inconsistency such as the lost update problem, one of the transactions is aborted and started again. This is a form of concurrency control.

Concurrency control applied to a client server database system where clients are mobile devices presents its own special problems. Mobile devices move from base station to base station and the connection with the database server can be intermittent. What happens if a transaction is started on a mobile device which fails to complete in a reasonable time because the connection is lost? There is a danger, if locking is used, of a data item being locked in exclusive-access mode for a lengthy period of time thus preventing other transactions from completing.

Key concept

Commitment ordering:
Used in a distributed database system such as mobile device client server systems where transactions are created locally on the mobile device before being sent to the server for execution. The transactions are scheduled at the server so that they are committed in an order that avoids concurrency conflict.

One solution is for transactions to be done locally on the mobile device before they are sent to the server for the final stage. In a non-distributed system, the transactions are created centrally at the server. However, mobile device database systems uses a distributed model in which the transactions are generated locally. Relative timestamps are assigned locally to operations (Read, Update, Insert, Delete). The list of operations with timestamps is then transferred to the server. The absolute time of the execution of the operations is calculated in the server using the relative timestamps. The server uses a scheduling algorithm to produce a commit order which avoids conflict between transactions. This is what is meant by commitment ordering.

Questions

1. What is a client server database system?

2. What is meant by concurrent access?

3. What is the Lost Update problem?

4. Describe three methods that are used in non-distributed client server database systems to prevent the Lost Update problem occurring.

5. Describe a method used in distributed client server database systems such as mobile banking to prevent the Lost Update problem occurring.

In this chapter you have covered:

- Client server database systems which provide simultaneous access to a database for multiple clients
- How concurrent access can be controlled to preserve the integrity of the database
  - Record locks
  - Timestamp ordering
  - Serialisation
  - Commitment ordering

11.1 Big Data
Section 1

■ 11.1 Big Data

Did you know?

On Saturday, August 3, 2013 in Japan, people watched an airing of "Castle in the Sky", and at one moment they took to Twitter so much that a one-second peak of 143,199 tweets per second was recorded. This was a world record.

Key concept

Big Data:
Big Data is the term applied to datasets whose size is beyond the ability of traditional software tools to capture, manage and process; or whose production rate exceeds the ability of this software to respond in a timely manner; or the dataset lacks the necessary structure to be stored and processed in the relational model.
A dataset is a collection of data.

What is Big Data

The term Big Data is described as data that can't be processed or analysed using traditional processes or tools because it falls into one or more of the following categories:

■ too big to fit into a single server

■ too heterogeneous (diverse in character or content) - structured, semi-structured or totally unstructured

■ its production can occur at very high rates.

To give you an example of the challenges of Big Data, on a typical day in 2015, 500 million tweets were sent with an average of 5,700 tweets per second (TPS). During the 2010 World Cup, the influx of tweets - from every shot on goal, penalty kick and yellow or red card - repeatedly took its toll and made Twitter unavailable for short periods of time. Twitter had reached the limit of throughput on their storage systems. The MySQL storage system Twitter employed was having trouble processing tweets at the rate that they were showing up, and the solution of throwing more machines at the problem, each with a new MySQL database, was deemed a sticking plaster solution whilst a complete redesign of their system was undertaken. The bottlenecks in the system were the system's inability to handle concurrency effectively - multiple tweets arriving simultaneously - and the system's inability to handle the storage requirements.

Twitter's solution was to create a sharded and fault-tolerant distributed database system. A database shard is a horizontal partition of data in a database, e.g. the first 10,000 rows. Each shard is then held on a separate database server instance, to spread load.

Volume, Velocity and Variety

The three defining characteristics of Big Data are

1. Volume - data to be analysed is too big to fit into a single server

2. Velocity - speed at which data must be processed to keep up, if the *data is at rest* it can be batch processed but if it is *data in motio*n, i.e. streamed data, then processing needs to take place in real time.

3. Variety - data can appear in many forms from structured through semi-structured to unstructured.

This is summarised pictorially in *Figure 11.1.1*.

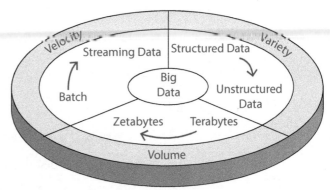

Figure 11.1.1 Schematic of the three V's, Volume, Velocity and Variety

Questions

1. What is meant by ***Big Data*?**

2. Name the **three** defining characteristics of Big Data.

Volume

Volume in Big Data refers to the size of the data to be processed. Data-analysis scenarios that process hundreds of terabytes or petabytes fall into the Big Data category if that data must be analysed as a single dataset.

A physical data centre that hosts an exabyte of data is not necessarily dealing with Big Data. This data might be nightly backups stretching back over ten years. However, if, say, a petabyte of data needs to be analysed to answer a given question, then this is definitely a Big Data problem. Thus the "Big" in Big Data is more than an assessment of the size of the data to be stored, it really relates to the processing of this size of data.

When the data volumes that needed to be processed outgrew the storage and processing capabilities of a single host an alternative to the traditional data processing approach was required.

In a traditional data processing system,

- file blocks belonging to a file of data would be stored on a single server

- The program written to execute this traditional data processing activity would also execute in a single server.

In the Big Data era, the blocks of a file have to be distributed across more than one server simply because there are too many of them to fit one server. In traditional data processing systems the block size is typically 512 bytes whereas in a Big Data processing system, the block size is typically 64 or 128 megabytes.

Secondly, the program that does the processing must now be written so that it can execute on more than one machine at the same time.

Summarising, the Big Data approach to processing a dataset that has already been collected and stored (data at rest) relies on

- a distributed file system
- a way to parallelise and execute programs

Questions

3. Explain the meaning of the Big Data characteristic known as **volume**.

4. Explain how Big Data processing system differs from a traditional data processing system.

Distributed File System

A distributed file system is one in which the blocks of individual files are spread across more than one server. Google's distributed file system is GFS. Yahoo, Facebook, and Twitter use HDFS, the Hadoop Distributed File System. Both systems use racks of servers with network switches interconnecting servers in a rack and servers in other racks. *Figure 11.1.2* shows a schematic consisting of several servers connected via a network switch within a rack, Rack 1 and to another rack, Rack 2.

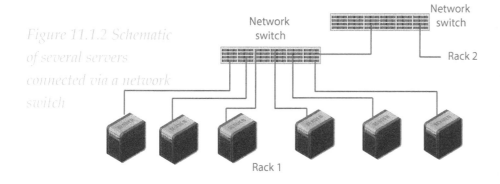

Figure 11.1.2 Schematic of several servers connected via a network switch

Network switch
Network switch
Rack 2
Rack 1

Figure 11.1.3 shows racks of commodity servers at one of Google's data centres. The data centre houses some 100,000 commodity servers consuming a total power of 40 Megawatts. This is roughly the total power output of Coolkeeragh power station in Northern Ireland.

Both GFS and HDFS are fault-tolerant. They need to be because of their reliance on commodity magnetic disk hard drives and servers. Commodity magnetic disk hard drives have a Mean-Time-To-Failure of about 300,000 hours or a probability of failing within an hour of 1 in 300,000. With one hundred thousand servers in a data centre this means a probability that a disk drive will fail in the next hour of about 33%.

Figure 11.1.4 shows Google's first server rack. Their first search engine ran on this system

Figure 11.1.3 Racks of commodity servers at one of Google's data centres (image Google/Connie Zhou)

Figure 11.1.5 shows in HDFS that each block belonging to a particular file is written three times with at least one block written to a different server rack, e.g. Block 2, Block 2' and Block 2".

Information

Figure 11.1.4 shows Google's first server rack circa 1999. Their first search engine ran on this. It was retired from service after five years to the Computer History museum, Mountain View, California, USA.

Information

HDFS stores files across a cluster. A Hadoop cluster is a special type of computational unit designed specifically for storing and analysing large datasets across a distributed computing environment. One machine in the cluster is designated as the NameNode and another machine as JobTracker - these are the masters. The rest of the machines in the cluster act as both DataNode and TaskTracker; - these are the slaves. Hadoop clusters are often referred to as "shared nothing" systems because the only thing that is shared between nodes is the network that connects them.

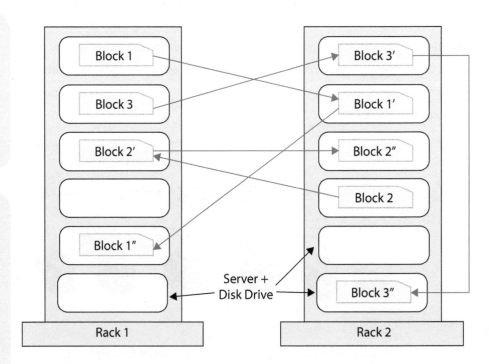

Figure 11.1.5 In HDFS each block is written three times and at least one of the three is written to a different server rack

Both GFS and HDFS are scalable. More servers (known as nodes) can be added if the file grows in size because all the racks of servers are interconnected and the file system is able to keep track of which blocks belong to which file wherever the blocks are stored whether Rack 1 or Rack 10,000.

Questions

5 What is meant by a *distributed file system*?

6 What is meant by *fault-tolerant*?

7 Explain how fault-tolerance is achieved in HDFS.

8 What is meant by the term *scalable* in the context of HDFS and GFS?

Tasks

1 Watch a YouTube video about a Facebook data centre

https://www.youtube.com/watch?v=0pB9falsA9k

Information

Vertical scaling:

Takes place in a single server when more CPUs, memory, hard drives are added.

Horizontal scaling:

Takes place when more servers are added. It is like adding another lane to a two-line highway to make a three-lane highway in order to accommodate the increase in traffic.

Function-to-data model

The second aspect of the Big Data approach is parallelising the execution of programs. This is done with the function-to-data model. In the function-to-data model because there is so much data, the analysis program is sent to the data, i.e. a copy is sent to each server. This model is used in Hadoop which is an open source highly scalable, distributed batch processing system for large datasets. At the heart of of the function-to-data model is a technique borrowed from functional programming called MapReduce.

All MapReduce programs that run natively under Hadoop are written in Java, and it is the Java Archive file (jar) that's distributed by the JobTracker to the various Hadoop cluster nodes to execute map and reduce tasks.

Information

MapReduce

MapReduce is a programming model which uses a parallel, distributed algorithm to process large datasets "at rest" in a cluster. MapReduce takes an input, splits it into smaller parts, executes the code of the mapper on every part, then gives all the results to one or more reducers that merge all the results into one.

For example, suppose that we wanted to demonstrate determining the number of times each word appears throughout a collection of texts, e.g. the novels *War and Peace*, *Les Miserables*, *Three Men in a Boat* and *Fireside Stories*.

First, the files containing the text of these novels would be copied from where they are stored to Hadoop's distributed file system HDFS as shown in Figure 11.1.6.

Next a copy of a Map function would be distributed to each HDFS server. In this example, the Map function would be something along the lines

```
function wordcountMap (lineoftext)
  {for (word in lineoftext.split(" ")) {emit (word, 1)}}
```

Information

Traditional database systems use special database servers of high reliability. Such systems attempt to solve the scaling problem by vertical scaling. This is an expensive option because highly-reliable components are expensive.

Google's solution was to scale horizontally using much cheaper commodity hardware. Commodity hardware is cheaper but less reliable. Google's solution was to build in fault-tolerance so that the failure of a component would not bring down the system.

The collection of key-value pairs emitted by each copy of map would be stored temporarily before being grouped and sorted by shuffle and sort operations, e.g. all <A, 1> key-value pairs would be grouped together and placed before all <About, 1> key-value pairs. Finally, copies of a Reduce function count all <A, 1>s, all <About, 1>s and so on to produce a total count for each word.

```
function wordcountReduce (word, value)
  {sum = 0
  for (nextvalue in value) {sum += nextvalue}
  emit(word, sum)
  }
```

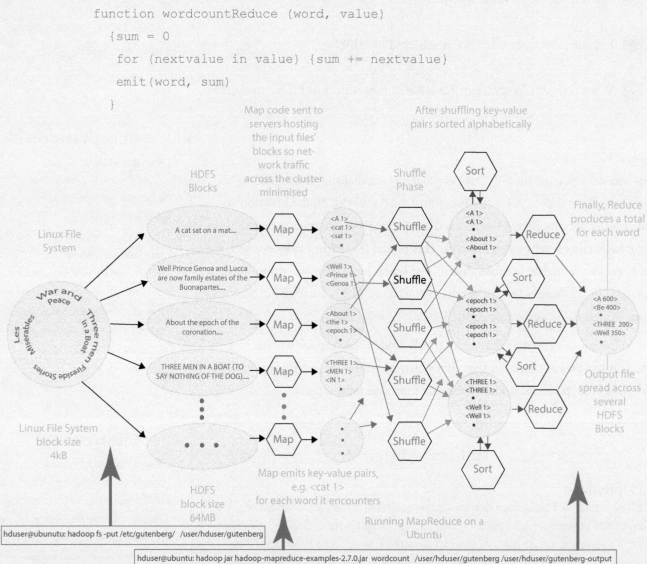

Figure 11.1.6 MapReduce applied to text of several novels. The text is copied from the host operating system to Hadoop's HDFS file block system which sits on top of the host file system

Extension Question

9 Describe MapReduce in the context of counting word occurrences in a large dataset consisting of text.

Variety

Data can appear in many forms from structured through semi-structured to unstructured.

Structured data

Structured data is data that can be represented in tabular form. Such data is modelled in the relational model as described in Chapter 10.2. Structured data lends itself to formal modelling of the data before building a database because the data has a clear and identifiable structure. In the relational model, the data is structured into tuples that record values for a fixed number of predefined attributes, e.g. attributes StudentId, StudentSurname, etc.

Semi-structured data

This is data such as XML- or JSON-formatted files that do not have a formal structure but nevertheless have some structure, albeit of a variable kind. Figure 11.1.7 shows two related examples that are XML-formatted. The structure of each memo is clearly identified by tags that could be predefined but the actual structure of each memo cannot be formally modelled because it is not consistent. No schema is enforced to ensure consistency.

```
<memo>
  <to>Sarah</to>
  <from>Fred</from>
  <about>Milk for tea and coffee </about>
  <status>Urgent</status>
  <message>
     Don't forget to buy a pint of milk!
  </message>
</memo>

<memo>
  <to>Fred</to>
  <from>Sarah</from>
  <about>Milk for tea and coffee </about>
  <moan>I am always buying the milk</moan>
  <reply>Bought one pint!</reply>
</memo>
```

Figure 11.1.7 Two related examples of XML data showing the semi-structured nature of this type of data

Unstructured data

This is data such as text whose content is so variable that

- it cannot be modelled in advance or
- it cannot be fitted to a column-row structure required by relational database modelling or
- its (key) elements are not identified with tags.

Information

The simple, structured data managed by legacy Relational database management systems (RDBMS) invented in the 70s continue to be used for simple, structured data. They are not suitable for complex data because such data does not easily fit the row and column format required by relational databases. Data that fits the latter is highly structured and can be pre-modelled prior to collection and storing.
However, a different kind of data classified as semi-structured or unstructured now predominates.
Unstructured data can be difficult to pre-model because of its lack of structure. It is also characterised by sheer volume and frequency of generation. Examples are Web logs of events such as mouse clicks on Web pages; text, images, video, audio, sensor readings, output from scientific modeling, and other complex data types streaming into data centres today.
New data processing techniques must be applied to extract the value contained within this data.
Algorithms tailored to both the data and the questions that can be answered are applied to each of the data types such as images, video, or audio.
The Big Data approach is then able, by linking the results, to deliver insights that would not be possible otherwise.

Examples include, the body of e-mail messages, web pages, text files, video, images, data from sensors. Even though each of these examples does have structure it is not of the semantic kind, e.g. a Web page contains HTML mark-up such as paragraph tags, but this is solely for the purpose of rendering the Web page and not for specifying its meaning (semantics) and therefore what information it conveys.

Questions

10 Explain the meaning of the Big Data characteristic known as *variety*.

Velocity

Velocity refers to whether the data is in motion and with what frequency or at rest.

Data at rest is data that has been stored on some permanent data storage device. The data may be processed at any time because it is permanently stored and speed of processing is not critical as the rate of arrival and processing of this data can be controlled. Big Data at rest is usually batch processed. In batch processing, processing, once started, is carried out to completion without user interaction.

Data in motion is data that is streamed at some frequency continuously, e.g. 1000 events per second. There is an expectation that it will be collected at the rate it arrives. In stream processing, data is processed as it arrives and before it is stored permanently.

In the Big Data scenario, this data is likely to arrive at a high rate, and from multiple sources simultaneously - e.g. log data, Twitter streams, and RSS feeds. The site http://developer.usa.gov/1usagov sends event notifications at the rate of less than 10 per second. The stream is composed of JSON events, each of which is generated every time someone clicks on any US .gov or .mil URL that has been shortened. When this site is launched in a browser a simple long-lived HTTP connection is established and data is subsequently streamed back to the browser until the HTTP connection is ended. 10 events or less per second is manageable by one machine but what if the velocity was increased to about 46,000 events per second - see www.internetlivestats.com. This equates to the rate at which Google receives search hits.

Imagine that Google streamed these search request events to the world. Any system receiving these would have to cope with collecting the events at a velocity of 46,000 per second. This would require scaling the collection part of the system so that it would cope, i.e. the equivalent of adding some more lanes to a highway.

Information

Figure 11.1.8 shows a basic stream of event-driven data passing from source to sink in Spring XD, a stream processing system applied to Big Data. The source converts data arriving at unpredictable times into an internal message format. The messages travel along channels between any number of processors. One kind, a "wire tap", is shown in the figure. The data travelling in the stream is tapped into and some processing carried out. In this example it is a simple count of tweets arriving from Twitter. The main stream is set up and deployed with the shell command

stream create tweetcount --definition "tap:stream:tweets>aggregate-counter" --deploy true

The wire tap is set up with

stream create tweets --definition "twitterstream | file" --deploy true

Using Spring XD a unified, distributed, and extensible system for data ingestion, real time analytics, batch processing, and data export

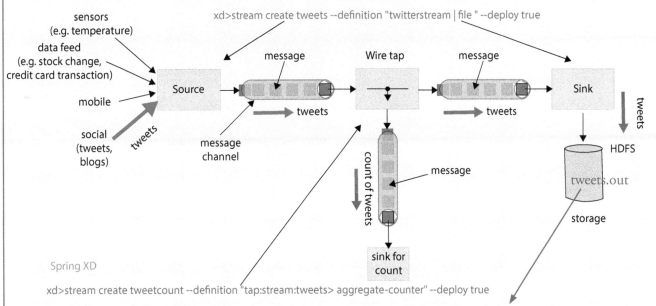

{"created_at":"Wed Jul 08 12:26:35 +0000 2015","id":618758072752832512,"text":"RJ is going to use \"big data..
{"created_at":"Wed Jul 08 12:26:36 +0000 2015","id":618758078813573120,"text":"@ukieandyt @uk_ie @doct...
{"created_at":"Wed Jul 08 12:26:39 +0000 2015","id":618758090146607104,"text":"Big Data: Genomical ....
{"created_at":"Wed Jul 08 12:26:44 +0000 2015","id":618758110690308096,"text":"RT @BigDataBlogs: ....

Figure 11.1.8 Streaming using Spring XD tool to pull tweets from Twitter, perform some processing on the stream as it is in motion with a tap into the stream and storing all tweets received in tweets.out for later batch processing

The role of the sink is to store the stream data permanently. This could be as a file using the file system of the operating system or it could be HDFS, for example, a distributed file system built on top of the native file system of the operating system. In addition to the stream data being "tapped into". It could be processed in transit before being stored, e.g. case converted from lower case to upper case. Figure 11.1.9 shows the visualisation of tweets filtered by the "lang" field in tweets at a wire tap. The visualisation updates in real time. To see this in action download the video from www.educational-computing.co.uk/CS/Book/Videos/TweetLang.avi.

A stream can be thought of as a series of connected operators. The initial set of operators (or single operator) are typically referred to as source operators. These operators read the input stream and in turn send the data downstream. The intermediate steps comprise various operators that perform specific actions. Finally, for every way into the in-motion analytics platform, there are multiple ways out, and in streams these are outputs called sink operators - see Figure 11.1.8. In a more technical sense, a stream is a graph of nodes connected by edges. Each node is an operator.

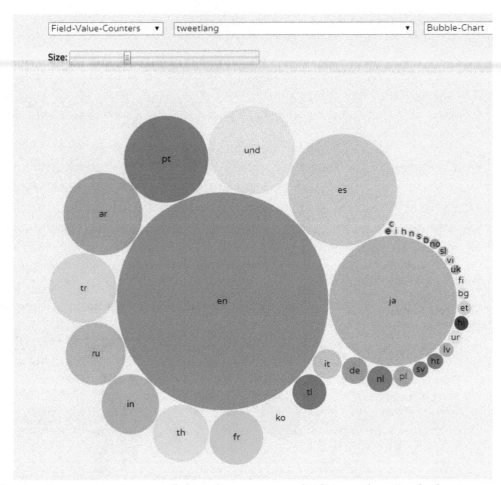

Figure 11.1.9 Spring XD analytics showing visualisation in real time of tweets broken down by the "lang" field and piped via the following tap:

stream create tweetlang --definition "tap:stream:tweets > field-value-counter --fieldName=lang" --deploy true

Questions

11 Explain the meaning of the Big Data characteristic known as ***velocity***.

Machine learning

Machine learning techniques are needed to discern patterns in data and to extract useful information. Big Data datasets are analysed with machine learning techniques which enable the value in the datasets to be extracted. This can take the form of a predictive model that can then be used in the algorithm that processes streaming data to extract the value from the data in the stream.

The value of data in large datasets was revealed in 2009 when a new flu virus, H1N1 hit the streets. Public Health authorities feared a pandemic on the scale of the 1918 Spanish flu that killed millions.

Doctors were requested to inform health authorities of new flu cases. However, people might feel ill for days but wait before seeing a doctor. With other delays in the reporting system and a rapidly spreading disease the authorities were unable to get a clear picture.

About the same time, Google engineers had reported in the science publication Nature how Google could "predict" the spread of the winter flu in the United States, not just nationally, but down to specific areas of the States by what people searched for on the Internet using the three billion search queries a day that they were receiving and saving. This led to Google identifying the areas infected by the flu virus.

Google processed some 450 million different mathematical models in order to test search terms, comparing their predictions against actual flu cases from 2007 and 2008. The result was their software found a combination of 45 search terms that, when used together in a mathematical model, strongly correlated their predictions with the official historical figures. The result: Google could tell where the flu had spread in near real time, not a week or two after the fact. Google's result was built on Big Data. It is Big Data and machine learning applied to Big Data that enables the value in data to be extracted and used to provide useful insights of significant value.

To understand how machine learning applied to a dataset or datasets can produce a predictive model, consider a much simpler case of trying to find the relationship between growth rate of something of interest and temperature. *Figure 11.1.10* shows some data plotted on an x-y graph together with a best-fit straight line generated using linear regression, a common machine learning technique. The programming language used was R, a strongly functional programming language for statistical computing. The code to produce this graph and to generate the model and plot the best-fit straight line is shown below.

```
R programming language
> temperature <- c(10,20,30,40,50,60,70,80,90,100,110,120,130,140
,150)
> growthrate <- c(20,26,38,49,45,55,55,55,67,74,74,77,83,95,108)
> plot(temperature, growthrate)
> model <- lm(growthrate~temperature)
> abline(model)
```

Information

R programming language:
R is a free software environment for statistical computing and graphics.
R can be downloaded from https://cran.rstudio.com/.
It can also be run online at www.getdatajoy.com

The model generated by the program was

```
growthrate = 0.5371 x temperature + 21
```

This model could be used as shown in *Figure 11.1.11* in a coded algorithm applied to the data stream of temperature data to predict growth rate and take action if it was too slow.

Figure 11.1.10
Plot of growth rate against temperature generated in the programming language R

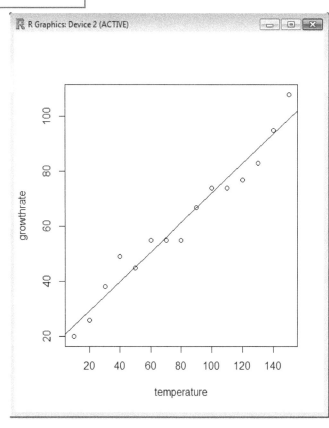

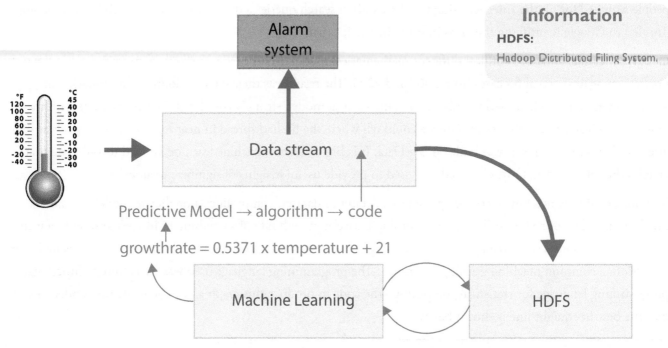

Information

HDFS:

Hadoop Distributed Filing System.

Figure 11.1.11 Predictive model algorithm applied to stream data from a temperature sensor

Generating a predictive model is done with the data at rest. The model is then applied to streaming data. A classic example is fraud detection on credit card transactions - see http://www.fico.com/en/wp-content/secure_upload/FICO_Real_Time_Fraud_3095IN.pdf.

Recommendation systems also fall into this category - see http://techblog.netflix.com/2012/04/netflix-recommendations-beyond-5-stars.html.

Questions

12 Explain how machine learning is used in Big Data systems to leverage value in stored datasets. Give real examples of **two** different types of machine learning Big Data systems.

Programming tasks

1 Gain access to the R programming system and launch the GUI. Create your own example dataset of temperature and growth rate.

2 Plot these with growth rate on the y-axis and temperature on the x-axis.
```
> plot(temperature, growthrate)
```

3 Create a linear regression model to fit a best-fit straight line to your data, e.g. `model <- lm(growthrate~temperature)`

4 Plot the best-fit line from the given model using
```
> abline(model)
```

5 View this model with command `model`.

Section 2

Functional programming is a solution to the Big Data processing problem

The functional programming paradigm (see Chapters 12.1.1 to 12.3.1) makes it easier to write correct and efficient distributed code because functional programming languages support

- immutable data structures
- statelessness
- higher-order functions

Using functional programming, a developer composes a program by assembling a series of functions.

An immutable data structure is a data structure whose state cannot be modified after it is created.

There are no assignment statements in functional programming, so once something is given a value of 5, let's say, it continues to have that value.

This is quite important because when we call a function, say one that squares its input, we always expect *square (3)* to be 9, for example. If, however, we called a different function, say, one that returned the state of the balance of a bank account, we wouldn't expect to get the same result everytime because bank account balances fluctuate. Whereas the square function operates in a stateless manner, the function to discover a bank balance operates on a system which is not stateless. The result returned depends on both the input and the current state of the system in a system with state. If there is state to be affected then it is possible to write functions that in addition to returning a result also alter state. This is called a side-effect of calling the function. If a function is labelled pure, it has no side-effect. Functions in a pure functional programming languages are pure.

Therefore programs written in a pure functional programming language consist only of pure functions. This means the programs can be reasoned about mathematically to check that they do what they are expected to do even when run in parallel, i.e. that they are correct. There is no state to consider as well.

Higher order functions compose, which means that a function can be passed as an argument to another function, e.g.

reduce (map (list of things))

It follows that it is very easy to see which parts of code are independent and arrange for these to run in parallel. The independence is a consequence of immutability and statelessness.

If it is possible to execute code in parallel on a different part of a dataset then we can scale the hardware horizontally, i.e add more servers if more data needs to be processed. The code can be just copied, distributed and run on the additional servers.

Learning objectives:
- Know that when data size are so big as not to fit on a single server:
  - the processing must be distributed across more than one machine
  - functional programming is a solution, because it makes it easier to write correct and efficient distributed code.
- Know what features of functional programming makes it easier to write:
  - correct code
  - code that can be distributed across more than one server

Principle

Functional programming (FP) is based on a simple premise: Programs are constructed using only pure functions—in other words, functions that have no side effects. A function has a side effect if it does something other than simply return a result, e.g. update a counter that the function relies on when calculating the result to return.

Questions

13 Explain what is meant by
(a) immutability (b) statelessness
(c) higher-order functions.

14 What features of functional programming make it easier to
(a) write correct code
(b) distribute code to run across more than one machine?

Section 3

Learning objectives:

■ *Be familiar with the:*

- *fact-based model for representing data*

- *graph schema for capturing the structure of the dataset*

- *nodes, edges and properties in graph schema*

Principle

Fact-based model:

- Raw data stored as atomic facts

- Each fact captures a single piece of information (i.e. atomic)

- Facts are kept immutable and eternally true by using timestamps

- Each fact is made identifiable so that query processing can identify duplicates (facts with same identity)

- A nonce is used to make identical facts identifiable (a nonce is a randomly generated 64-bit number)

Information

Immutability in the fact-based model:

The immutability concept applied to datasets in the fact-based model was borrowed from functional programming.

Fact-based model

The fact-based model is a conceptual model for modelling data. Physical models based on the fact-based model are Bigtable used by Google, Cassandra used by Apple, Facebook, EBay, Twitter, Instagram. It models data in a completely different way from the relational model and it fits the Big Data approach better than the relational model does. Each fact within a fact-based model captures a single piece of information.

Data is immutable

In the fact-based model data is immutable, i.e. it cannot be altered except to delete data which has been entered erroneously as a result of human error. This is completely different from the relational model in which data is mutable, i.e. can be overwritten with new values in an update operation. In the relational model, an erroneous entry caused by human error cannot be undone once committed, i.e. it is not possible to go back to a previous value. *Table 11.1.1* shows a section of student data from a fact-based model system. As students move from year to year they move classes. This information is recorded as a historical record, e.g. student 1 was assigned to class Year 11 D on 03/06/2014 and then roughly a year later to class Year 12 B on 27/08/2015. The historical record for 03/06/2104 is not removed because in the fact-based model, data is immutable.

StudentId	YearClass	TimeStamp
1	Year 11 D	03/06/2014 10:35:16
2	Year 11 A	03/06/2014 10:38:05
3	Year 11 D	03/06/2014 10:44:45
1	Year 12 B	27/08/2015 12:45:51
2	Year 12 E	26/08/2015 11:15:31

Table 11.1.1 Student data for a fact-based model

If data had been modelled using the relational model then student 1's data would have been updated, and in the process the value Year 11 D would have been overwritten with the value Year 12 B.

The ability of a Big Data system to store vast quantities of data in a single dataset lends itself well to the fact-based model which requires a change to be recorded as a new fact and not applied as an update - the master dataset continually grows with the addition of immutable, timestamped data.

Human fault tolerance

People will make mistakes. The impact of such mistakes is minimised in the fact-based model because it is an immutable data model, no data can be lost. If bad data is written, earlier (good) data units still exist.

In comparison, in the relational model, a mistake can cause data to be lost because values are overwritten in the database.

Data is true forever

The key consequence from immutability is that each piece of data is true in perpetuity, i.e. forever: a piece of data, once true, must always be true.

Simplicity

Databases based on the relational model rely on indexes to retrieve and update data. These must be built and subsequently modified as data is updated/altered/deleted.

In the fact-based model, data is immutable so all that is required is the ability to append new data units to the master dataset. This does not require an index for the data. This is a significant simplification.

Atomic facts

In the fact-based model, data is broken down into fundamental units that are called facts. A fact, for example, is student 1 is in class Year 10 D. Another fact is, student 1 is in class Year 12 B. What differentiates these two facts in time are their timestamps, 03/06/2014 10:35:16 and 27/08/2015 12:45:51.

A fact possesses two core properties:

- it is atomic

- it is timestamped.

Facts are atomic because they can't be subdivided further into anything meaningful.

Collective data such as the classes for a student and their subjects studied are represented as multiple, independent facts as shown in Figure 11.1.12.

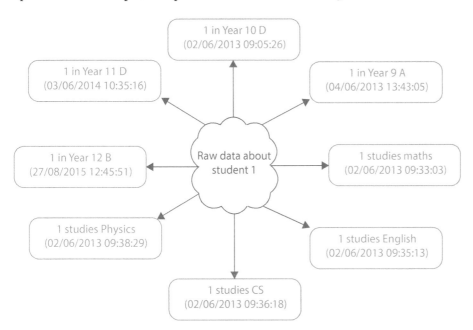

Figure 11.1.12 Collection of independent facts for student 1

As a consequence of being atomic, there is no redundancy of information across distinct facts. The timestamps make each fact immutable and eternally true. Also, storing atomic facts makes it easy to handle partial information about an entity without introducing NULL values by simply leaving out the missing information.

Principle

Facts in graph schema:

Each fact modelled in the graph schema represents either a piece of information about an entity, e.g. entity student has surname Alex, or a relationship between entities, e.g. student **1** visits intranet page

http://192.168.0.32/physics

student Alex is friends with student Kevin.

Graph schemas

Let's suppose that in addition to storing facts about students our dataset also stores facts about which intranet web pages students visit and for each page the total visits from all students. Each fact for this dataset represents either a piece of information about a student or a relationship between a student and an intranet web page. A graph schema can be used to describe this scenario.

A graph schema captures the structure of a dataset stored using the fact-based model. Structure means a description of the types of facts contained in the dataset, e.g. student has surname of data type string, and a description of the relationships between the entities. In *Figure 11.1.13* student and intranet page are entities because students visit intranet pages.

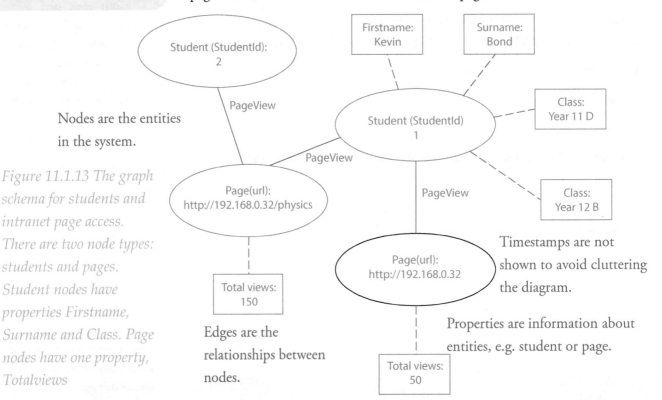

Nodes are the entities in the system.

Figure 11.1.13 The graph schema for students and intranet page access. There are two node types: students and pages. Student nodes have properties Firstname, Surname and Class. Page nodes have one property, Totalviews

Edges are the relationships between nodes.

Timestamps are not shown to avoid cluttering the diagram.

Properties are information about entities, e.g. student or page.

Concept

Graph schema:

A graph schema captures the structure of a dataset stored using the fact-based model. Structure means a description of the types of facts contained in the dataset, e.g. student has surname of data type string, and a description of the relationships between entities, e.g. student visits intranet page, student and intranet page are entities

The graph in *Figure 11.1.13* represents the facts for the student and intranet page access dataset. The graph highlights the three core components of a graph schema—nodes, edges, and properties:

- Nodes are the entities in the system. In this example, the nodes are students and pages.

- Edges are relationships between nodes. In this example an edge between a student and a page represents the relationship between a page and a user who has visited this page.

- Properties are information about entities. In this example, *surname, firstname, class, total views.*

Edges are strictly between nodes and are shown visually connected by a solid line. Dashed lines are used for connecting properties to the corresponding node.

In the example an intranet page is able to identify a student by *StudentId*, e.g. student 1. A relationship labelled "PageView" exists between a student and a page.

Another way that an intranet page could identify students is by using a cookie. The intranet site places a cookie on the student's computer and when a student returns to this intranet site, the student is identified by the stored cookie, e.g. cookie *abs123*. At some point, the intranet site might be able to associate student 1 with this cookie if it is stored on student 1's computer. A node labelled *Student(CookieId) abs123* could then be connected to node labelled *Student (StudentId) 1* by the relationship labelled "Equivalent".

One of the attractive features of the fact-based model is that it is very easy to add new types of information to the schema just by defining new node, edge, and property types. Existing fact types are unaffected because facts are atomic.

Information

Graph schema:

The graph schema provides a complete description of all the data contained within a dataset.

Principle

Nodes, edges, properties:

The three core components of a graph schema are nodes, edges, and properties.

Tasks

2 Research Google's data storage system, Bigtable (http://static.googleusercontent.com/media/research.google.com/en//archive/bigtable-osdi06.pdf) and Google's Cloud Bigtable (https://cloud.google.com/bigtable/).

3 Research Amazon's Cloud Search system (http://aws.amazon.com/cloudsearch/).

Questions

15 Describe the fact-based model.

16 What are the **two** core properties that a fact possesses?

17 What is meant by *atomic fact*?

18 What does each fact modelled in a graph schema represent?

19 In the fact-based model, what is (a) a node   (b) an edge   (c) a property?

20 Complete the graph schema in *Figure 11.1.14* to represent the following facts:
   (a) Alex, Kevin, and Sue are friends
   (b) Alex's age is 23, Kevin's is 24 and Sue's is 22
   (c) Alex lives in Reading, Kevin lives in Aylesbury, Sue lives in Bristol

21 Alex and Sue each post a message on an electronic message board. Extend your graph schema to include these facts.
   What use would be made of timestamps in this graph schema?

22 Why does the fact-based model require Big Data techniques?

23 Give **three** advantages of the fact-based model over the relational model.

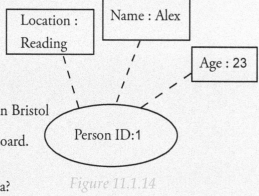

Figure 11.1.14

In this chapter you have covered:

■   'Big Data' is a catch-all term for data that can't be processed or analysed using traditional processes or tools because it is

- too big to fit into a single server
- too heterogeneous
- its production can occur at high rates.

■   Big Data is described in terms of

- volume - data to be analysed is too big to fit into a single server
- velocity - refers to whether the data is in motion and with what frequency or at rest. Data in motion is data that is streamed at some frequency continuously, e.g. 1000 events per second. Data at rest is data that has been stored on some permanent data storage device.
- variety - data in many forms such as structured, unstructured, text, multimedia. The data is said to be heterogeneous.

■   When dataset size is so big as not to fit on a single server:

- the processing must be distributed across more than one machine
- functional programming is a solution, because it makes it easier to write correct and efficient distributed code.

■   The features of functional programming that make it easier to write:

- correct code - immutable data structures, statelessness: pure functions
- code that can be distributed across more than one server - immutable data structures, statelessness, higher-order functions.

■   The fact-based model for representing data is a conceptual model for modelling data - data is broken down into fundamental units that are called facts. Each fact captures a single piece of information. Data is immutable, human fault-tolerant and true forever. Data is modelled in a completely different way from the relational model. Better fit with Big Data approach than relational model.

■   Graph schema - captures the structure of a dataset stored using the fact-based model. Structure:

- the types of facts contained in the dataset
- the relationships between the entities.

■   Graph schema drawn in a graph-like structure with

- Nodes - the entities in the system
- Edges - the relationships between nodes
- Properties - information about entities.

12.1 Functional programming paradigm

12.1.1 Function type

What is a function?

Loosely speaking, a function is a rule that, for each element in some set A of inputs, assigns an output chosen from set B but without necessarily using every member of B.

For example, the function f

$$f : \{0,1,2,3\} \rightarrow \{0,1,2,3,4,5,6,7,8,9\}$$

maps 0 to 0, 1 to 1, 2 to 4 and 3 to 9 when the rule is: output the square of the input.

Function as process

In function as process, a function is a rule that tells us how to transform some information into some other information, e.g. the integer 2 into its square 4.

Function as object

In function as object, the function is a thing in its own right.

For example, a pencil sharpener is an object. If the focus of attention is a pencil then the pencil sharpener just represents a process - sharpening pencils, input: unsharpened pencil; output: sharpened pencil.

In the function as process view, we are applying the function *sharpen* to pencils; it's the pencil that counts. But we can also think about the pencil sharpener as a thing in its own right, when we empty it of pencil shavings, or worry about whether its blade is sharp enough. This is the function as object view.

Key principle

Function as process:
A function is a rule that tells us how to transform some information into some other information.

Function as object:
The function is a thing in its own right.

Questions

A function f
$$f : \{0,1,2,3\} \rightarrow \{0,1,2,3, ..., 25, 26, 27\}$$
maps 0 to 0, 1 to 1, 2 to 8, 3 to 27.

1. What is the rule?

A function f
$$f : \{0,1,2,3\} \rightarrow \{0,1,2,3, 4, 5, 6\}$$
maps 0 to 0, 1 to 2, 2 to 4, 3 to 6.

2. What is the rule?

Key principle

Function type:

A function f which takes an argument of type A and returns a result of type B has a function type which is written

$A \rightarrow B$

What is a function type?

Just as data values (e.g. 6, 9.1, True) have types (integer, real, Boolean respectively) so do functions. Function types are important because they state what type of argument a function requires and what type of result it will return.

A function f which takes an argument of type A and returns a result of type B has a function type which is written

$$A \rightarrow B$$

To state that f has this type, we write

$$f : A \rightarrow B$$

For example,

1) $squareroot : real \rightarrow real$

2) $square : integer \rightarrow integer$

The function named *squareroot* applied to an argument of data type *real* produces a result of data type *real*, e.g.

$$squareroot\ (4.0) \rightarrow 2.0$$

The function named *square* applied to an argument of data type *integer* produces a result of data type *integer*, e.g.

$$square\ (2) \rightarrow 4$$

Domain and co-domain

If $f : A \rightarrow B$ is a function from A to B we call the set A, the domain of f, and the set B the co-domain of f. The domain and co-domain are always subsets of objects in some data type. For example, if A is a subset of domain data type *integer* then its values might be 0, 1, 2, 3, ..., 149, 150. Often it is just convenient to use the data type directly,

$$square : integer \rightarrow integer$$

The function *square* then has an argument type, *integer* and a result type, *integer* even though in practice a subset of integers only will be used.

Practical Activity

Use a text editor such as NotePad++ to write Haskell programs. Save these Haskell programs using extension .hs.

Figure 12.1.1.1 shows NotePad++ being used to create a function named *square* with one parameter *x* of data type *Integer* and a body *x*x*. This file has been saved with filename `square.hs` in folder `c:\book\haskell`.

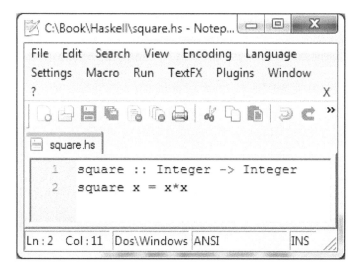

Figure 12.1.1.1 NotePad++ editor showing square.hs

The :: operator (read as *has type*) is used in Haskell to express what type an expression has.

Integer is the type of mathematical integers (*int* could have been used and is the type of integers that fit into a word on the computer - this will vary from computer to computer).

Launch WinGHci if you are using a machine running the Windows operating system (ghci on Linux-based machines). The WinGHci window is shown in *Figure 12.1.1.2*.

Key concept

Domain and co-domain:
If $f : A \rightarrow B$ is a function from A to B, we call the set A, the domain of f, and the set B the co-domain of f.

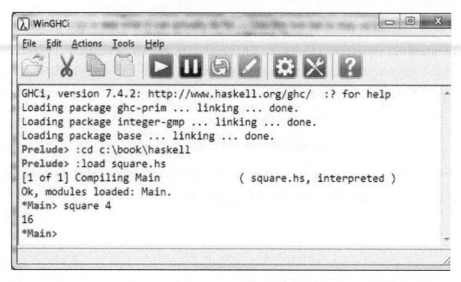

Figure 12.1.1.2 WinGHCi showing square.hs loaded, compiled and run

At the Prelude prompt (Prelude>) type the command to change to a specified folder.

`:cd c:\book\haskell` followed by <return>.

Commands begin with a colon, i.e. :

Now load the file containing the program defining the function *square*.

At the Prelude prompt type

`:load square.hs` followed by <return>.

WinGHCi will perform a compilation of a module called `Main` in order to run `square.hs` interactively.

If there are no errors loading and compiling the Prelude prompt will be replaced by the prompt `*Main`.

At the `*Main` prompt, type

`square 4` followed by <return>.

The correct answer, 16, is displayed.

To return to the Prelude prompt, type :module or :m

In this chapter you have covered:

- Function as process

- Function as object

- Function, f, has a function type, $f: A \rightarrow B$ where the type is $A \rightarrow B$.

- A is the argument type, and B is the result type.

- A is called the domain and B is called the co-domain.

- The domain and co-domain are always subsets of objects in some data type.

12.1 Functional programming paradigm

12.1.2 First-class object

First-class objects (or values)

First-class objects (or values) are objects which may

- appear in expressions (expressions such as $5 + 3 \times y^3$)

- be assigned to a variable

- be assigned as arguments to functions

- be returned by function calls

Typical first-class objects in many programming languages are integers, floating-point values, characters and strings.

For example,

$x := 5$ is an assignment statement in which the first-class value 5 is assigned to the variable x.

```
MyStringVar := Uppercase('Hello World!')
```

is an assignment statement containing a function call `Uppercase` with argument

'Hello World!'

which is a first-class value of type string. This function returns a first-class value of type string

'HELLO WORLD!'

Functions as first-class objects

In functional programming languages and in some imperative programming languages a function is a first-class object. This means that it can

- appear in expressions

- be assigned to a variable

- be passed as an argument to another function

- be returned as the result of a function call.

For example, in Python a function may be created and assigned to a variable v using the keyword `lambda` as follows

$x**2$ means x^2

$$v = lambda\ x:\ x**2$$

It may be called in a print procedure to square the value 5 as follows

```
print (v(5))
```

Figure 12.1.2.1 shows the above coded and executed in IPython using Python **3.4.1.**

Key principle

First-class object:

First-class objects (or values) are objects which may:
- appear in expressions
- be assigned to a variable
- be assigned as arguments in function calls
- be returned as a function call result.

```
In [1]: v = lambda x: x**2

In [2]: print(v(5))
25
```

Figure 12.1.2.1 function as argument

Information

Alternatively,

```
def square(x):
    return x*x

v = square
print(v(5))
```

The value **25** is returned by the call `v(5)` and the procedure `print` then outputs this value to the screen.

The function is defined with

$$\text{lambda x: x**2}$$

This is an anonymous function with one argument `x` and a body `x**2`. It is a first-class object because it can be assigned to a variable and passed as an argument to another function/procedure.

The following Python code defines a function `exp` with one argument `n` that returns a function also with one argument `x` and a body `x**n`.

$$\text{def exp (n): return lambda x: x**n}$$

```
In [8]: def exp (n): return lambda x: x**n

In [9]: f = exp(3)

In [10]: print (f(4))
64
```

Figure 12.1.2.2 Another function as argument

`exp(3)` returns a function with body `x**3`

`exp(10)` returns a function with body `x**10`

$$\text{f = exp(3)}$$

$$\text{print (f(4))}$$

If `exp(3)` is assigned to `f` then `f` references a function with body `x**3`, i.e if `f` is called, it will return a function with body `x**3`.

For example, if `f` is called with argument **4** then the function with body `x**3` is returned with `x` replaced by **4**. The function call `f(4)` will therefore return 4^3 which is **64**. We can then display this value on a screen with the `print` procedure.

Questions

1 What requirements must be satisfied for an object or value to be classified as first class?

2 A function f takes one argument n and returns a function with body x^n. f is a first-class object. It is assigned to variable g as follows

$$g = f(10)$$

What is returned by the call

(a) $g(2)$ (b) $g(3)$ (c) $g(5)$

Functions as arguments

Functions as arguments is particularly useful when a common underlying pattern can be identified. For example, suppose we need to double the result of squaring, cubing, etc. Although trivial, it does illustrate how this generalisation could be used for more complicated cases.

We first define a function `double` which takes a single argument `afunction`. The argument `afunction` is a function type. The function `double` returns `2*afunction`.

In Python 3.4, `double` would be defined as follows

```
def double (afunction)
        return 2*afunction
```

We can now define maths functions `square`, `cube` and so on in Python 3 as follows

```
def square(x):
        return x*x

def cube(x)
        return x*x*x
```

Now we can use `double`, `square` and `cube` as follows

```
double(square(4))
```

The function call `double(square(4))` returns **32**.

```
double(cube(4))
```

The function call `double(cube(4))` returns **128**.

In Haskell, for the same problem, we have an argument to `function double`:

```
afunction x  of type (Integer -> Integer)
```

When `function double` is called it returns

a function of type

```
(Integer -> Integer)
```

with body

```
(2*afunction) x
```

> **Key principle**
>
> **Functions as arguments:**
> Functions as arguments is particularly useful when a common underlying pattern can be identified. The common programming patterns that recur in code, but which are used with a number of different functions can be abstracted and then given a general name, e.g. **sum** where summing might be a sequence of natural numbers, numbers squared, numbers cubed, terms in an infinite series, etc.

afunction x   (2*afunction) x

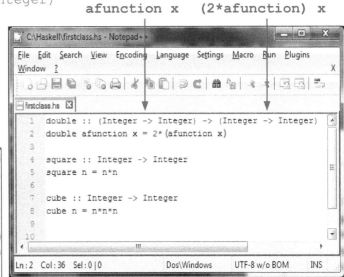

Figure 12.1.2.3 Haskell version of Python code

`double(square)` is applied to argument 5 to produce 50.

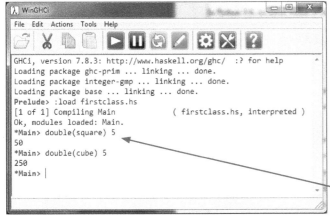

Figure 12.1.2.4 Execution in WinGHCi

Programming task

1 Using a text editor such as NotePad++ enter the following Haskell program and save as summy.hs.

```
summy :: (Integer -> Integer) -> (Integer -> Integer)
summy afunction 0 = 0
summy afunction x = (afunction x) + summy afunction (x - 1)

square :: Integer -> Integer
square n = n*n

cube :: Integer -> Integer
cube n = n*n*n

identity :: Integer -> Integer
identity n = n
```

Launch WinGHCi and at the **Prelude** prompt type

`:load summy.hs` (your working directory must contain summy.hs).

At the `*Main` prompt try the following

(a) `summy(square) 5`

(b) `summy(cube) 5`

(c) `summy(identity) 5`

Now

(d) Explain how `summy` in each case arrives at the observed output.

In this chapter you have covered:

- What is meant by first-class object or value

- Functions as first-class objects in functional programming languages and in imperative programming languages that support such objects

- A function as an argument to another function

- Returning a function as a function call result

12.1 Functional programming paradigm

12.1.3 Function application

Computations

The arithmetic expression 3 × 4 + 2 represents a computation which can be described with reductions as follows

$$3 \times 4 + 2 \rightarrow 12 + 2 \rightarrow 14$$

The given expression describes a single computation.

Formula

A formula is an expression containing variables. It represents a whole class of computations, since the variable(s) can assume different values.

For example, the formula corresponding to the computation above

$$a \ x \ b \ + \ c$$

uses the variables a, b, c.

Substituting integers for the variables, a, b, c, produces an expression whose value can be computed. For example, $a = 3$, $b = 4$, $c = 2$

$$3 \times 4 + 2 \rightarrow 12 + 2 \rightarrow 14$$

The formula a x b + c describes one computation for each possible combination of values for a, b, c.

Since there are an infinite number of integers, the formula represents an infinite number of computations.

Procedural and Functional Abstraction

The formula a x b + c is an abstraction because it omits the actual numbers to be used in the computation. The formula a x b + c represents a computation method, a procedure. Such an abstraction is called a procedural abstraction, since the result of the abstraction is a procedure, a method.

In general, there are many methods for obtaining a desired result.

The result of a procedural abstraction is a procedure, not a function. To get a function another abstraction, which disregards the particular computation method, must be performed.

The result of this abstraction is a function and the abstraction is called functional abstraction. The focus is then on the input(s) and the output.

For example, suppose we wished to calculate the sum of the first n natural numbers. We have two choices of method or formula for calculating this sum:

$$\frac{n \times (n + 1)}{2}$$

and

$$1 + 2 + 3 + 4 + \dots + (n - 1) + n$$

The above two methods are examples of procedural abstraction.

The black box in *Figure 12.1.3.1* hides the particular method used to calculate the sum for a particular n and so is an example of functional abstraction.

Figure 12.1.3.1 Calculation of sum of first n natural numbers

All that a user needs to know are the number and order of the inputs and the name of the function in order to be able to apply the function to these inputs.

Parameters

The formula used to define a function is sometimes called the body of the function. The name used for the quantity that can vary is called the parameter of the function. Therefore in the example above n is the parameter.

The function associated with the formula $\frac{n \times (n + 1)}{2}$ is given a name, e.g. sum.

To use the sum function, we apply it to an argument.

For instance, to find the sum of the first 6 natural numbers, the function sum is applied to the argument 6.

Thus the parameter, n, is the name used in the function body to refer to the argument, 6.

To compute the value of the function for some argument, replace the parameter in the body of the function by the argument and compute the expression.

For example,

$$n = 6 \longrightarrow \frac{n \times (n + 1)}{2}$$

$$= \frac{6 \times (6 + 1)}{2}$$

$$= \quad 21$$

Function Application

Note that the name given to a function does not involve the parameter. The name of the function above is sum not sum(n) or sum n which is the notation for sum applied to n. We call a function applied to its argument(s) a *function application*. A function application is when the function is applied to a particular argument, e.g. 6 in sum(6) or sum 6.

A function add takes two integer arguments and returns their sum. In Haskell this function could be written as follows:

```
add :: Integer -> Integer -> Integer
add x y = x + y
```

Application of this function to arguments 3 and 4 would be written as follows

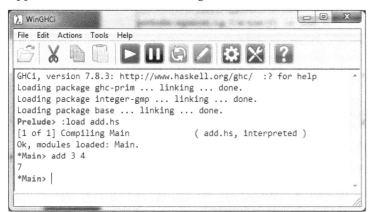

Key principle

Function application:
Function application is the process of giving particular inputs to a function, e.g. add (3, 4) represents the application of the function add to integer arguments 3 and 4.

Information

Function type:
Function add has function type
add: integer x integer → integer
which is expressed in Haskell as

```
add :: Integer -> Integer
                 -> Integer
```
See Unit 1 Chapter 4.2.2 for an explanation of the Cartesian product integer x integer.

Questions

1. In Haskell a function square is defined as follows
```
square :: Integer -> Integer
square n = n*n
```
What is the result of the function application
(a) square 3   (b) square 5?

2. What is the parameter in the function square defined in question 1?

3. What are the values of the arguments used in question 1?

4. What is meant by function application?

In this chapter you have covered:

■ What is meant by

  • a computation

  • a formula

  • procedural and functional abstraction

  • parameter of a function

  • argument of a function

■ Function application is when a function is applied to a particular argument, e.g. 6 in Sum(6) or Sum 6.

12 Fundamentals of functional programming

12.1 Functional programming paradigm

Learning objectives:

■ *Know what is meant by partial function application for two and three argument functions.*

■ *Be able to use the notations*
function: data type → (data type → data type)
which is equivalent to
function: data type → data type → data type
for example,
  add: integer → (integer → integer)
which is equivalent to
  add: integer → integer → integer

■ *Know that for an example such as function add*
  add: integer → (integer → integer)
means add can take a single argument of type integer and return a more specialised function (integer → integer) which takes a single integer argument and returns an integer.

Information

Remember:
Functions are not partial, it is their application which is partial.

■ 12.1.4 Partial function application

Some "partially applicable" devices

A radio can be viewed as a partially applicable function. Its main function is to transform electromagnetic(radio) waves into sound waves, but before listening to a radio broadcast a radio station is selected by frequency, e.g. 101 MHz.

Hence, the radio first takes a radio station frequency as argument and then the radio waves to be transformed.

In itself, the radio is quite a general function with many different broadcast frequencies to choose from. By selecting a specific broadcast frequency, the radio's function is specialised into one dedicated to transforming electromagnetic waves for this particular frequency. This is still a function.

General function:

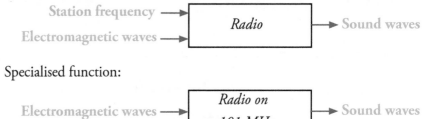

Specialised function:

In conclusion, for this example, a partially applicable function is a function that given its first argument returns a new, more specialised, function. If you supply this new function with an argument, you get the final result.

This is what is meant by partial function application.

In this example, a function moves from being a two-argument function to being a one-argument, more-specialised function. The function application of the original function is applied to just one of its arguments but not both.

In general, in partial function application, the function application of the original function is applied to just some of its arguments but not all.

The example shown in *Figure 12.1.4.1* illustrates how a more -specialised function `add2` with one argument is created in Haskell from an addition function, `add`, with two arguments.

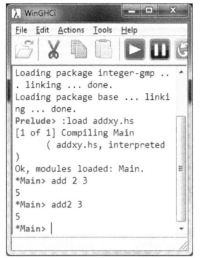

Figure 12.1.4.1 Example of partial function application for a two-argument function add x y

Figure 12.1.4.2 Shows bracket notation
Integer -> (Integer -> Integer)

Three input device

If the radio has more than one band (e.g. FM and AM), then it will have three inputs:

General function:

First, a band is selected, e.g. FM, creating a two argument function.

Specialised function:

Then, a station frequency is selected to produce an even more specialised function:

Partial application for two-argument functions

Consider the function add which adds together two integer arguments and returns an integer result.

$$add\ x\ y = x + y$$

This function can be viewed as a box, with two input arrows and an output arrow.

This function takes a pair of integers and returns an integer, i.e.

$$\underbrace{Integer \rightarrow Integer}_{Input} \rightarrow \underbrace{Integer}_{Output}$$

If we apply the function to two arguments, the result is a number; so that, for instance, add 2 3 equals 5.

What happens if add is applied to one argument 2? Pictorially we have

What is the output of this function application to one argument?

It is actually another function of a more specialised nature, this time a function add2 with one argument y.

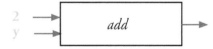

This new function will return 2 + y.

So for function application add2 3 the value 5 is returned.

Function add2 maps an integer to an integer, i.e. in Haskell

$$\underbrace{Integer \rightarrow Integer}_{Input \quad Output}$$

The function `add2` is a function. It is function `add` partially applied to one argument, the argument that substitutes for input x, i.e. in Haskell

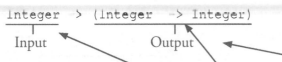

We feed in the particular value, 2, for input x and get as output a function `add2` which takes an integer and returns an integer.

The function `add2` is denoted by output

as shown in *Figure 12.1.4.2*.

This is an example of a general principle: any function taking two or more arguments can be partially applied to one or more arguments.
It also means that

$$\text{Integer -> Integer -> Integer}$$

is equivalent to

$$\text{Integer -> (Integer -> Integer)}$$

as shown in Figure 12.1.4.1 and Figure 12.1.4.2.

Questions

1. A computer can be considered a "partially applicable" device.
   A computer is used to calculate some output from a given input, but before performing the calculation, it is provided with a program – its first argument.

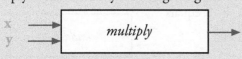

   Redraw the figure to show the computer as a "partially applicable" device executing a program with the name prog1.

2. A function multiply calculates x * y for integer arguments.

   Redraw the figure to show this function partially applied to the argument 10.

3. In Haskell the partially applied multiply function in question 2 has the function type
   $$\text{Integer -> (Integer -> Integer)}$$
   Give the meaning of this notation.

4. Explain why a radio can be viewed as supporting partial function application.

5. Explain why function type
   $$\text{Integer -> Integer -> Integer}$$
   can be interpreted as function type
   $$\text{Integer -> (Integer -> Integer)}$$

Partial application for three-argument functions

Now consider the function `addxyz` which adds together three integer arguments and returns an integer result.

```
add x y z = x + y + z
```

This function can be viewed as a box, with three inputs and an output.

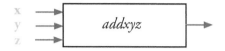

This takes three integers and returns an integer, i.e. in Haskell

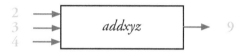

If we apply the function to three arguments, the result is a number; so that, for instance, `addxyz 2 3 4` equals 9.

What happens if `addxyz` is partially applied to one argument 2? Pictorially we have

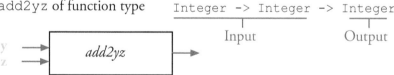

This function application computes `2 + y + z.`

If we treat `2 + y + z` as a new function it represents a function `add2yz`, with two inputs, `y, z`.

The function `addxyz` partially applied to argument x = 2 returns a function `add2yz` of function type

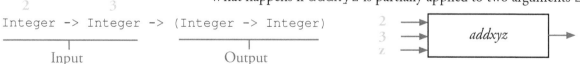

Function `add2yz` is thus a two argument function.

What happens if `addxyz` is partially applied to two arguments 2 and 3?

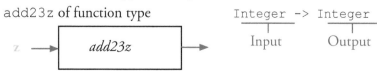

This function application computes `2 + 3 + z.` If we treat `2 + 3 + z` as a new function it represents a function `add23z`, with one input z. The function `addxyz` applied to arguments x = 2, y = 3 returns a function `add23z` of function type

For example, if argument z = 4,
function application `add23z 4 = 2 + 3 + 4 = 9`

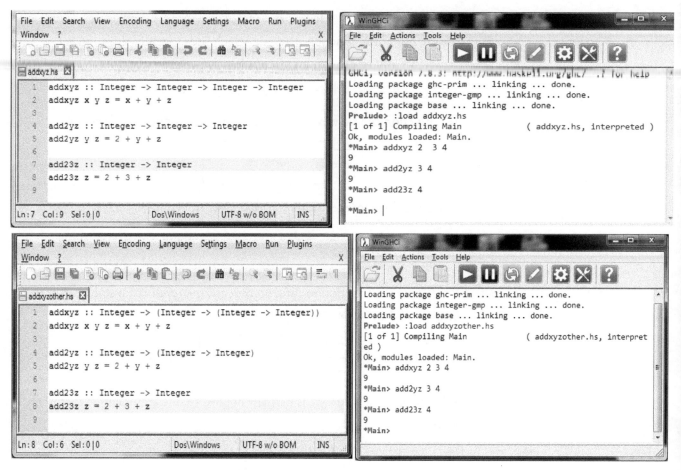

Figure 12.1.4.3 Shows partial function application for three-argument function addxyz

Programming task

1 Using a text editor such as NotePad++ write a Haskell program for functions `multiplyxy` which takes two integer arguments and returns x times y. Function `multiplyxy` has function type

```
Integer -> Integer -> Integer
```

Using the existing definition of `multiplyxy`, add the function `multiply2y` which takes one integer argument y and returns 2 times y.

Function `multiply2y` has function type

```
Integer -> Integer
```

Save as multiplyxy.hs.

Launch WinGHCi and at the **Prelude** prompt type

`:load multiplyxy.hs` (your working directory must contain multiplyxy.hs).

Test function `multiplyxy` with x = 2 and y = 3

Test function `multiply2y` with y = 3

Questions

6 A function `multiplyxyz` takes three integer arguments `x`, `y`, `z` and returns `x * y * z`. The function is applied to arguments 2 and 3 as shown below.

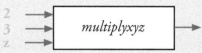

Which of the following represent(s) the type of `multiplyxyz` with `x = 2` and `y = 3`?

    1.   `Integer -> Integer -> (Integer -> Integer)`

    2.   `Integer -> (Integer -> Integer -> Integer)`

    3.   `Integer -> Integer -> Integer -> Integer`

    4.   `Integer -> (Integer -> Integer)`

7 The function `multiplyxyz` is applied to argument 2 as shown below.

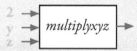

Which of the following represent(s) the type of `multiplyxyz` with `x = 2`?

    1.   `Integer -> (Integer -> Integer -> Integer)`

    2.   `Integer -> (Integer -> (Integer -> Integer))`

    3.   `Integer -> Integer -> Integer -> Integer`

    4.   `Integer -> (Integer -> Integer)`

    5.   `Integer -> Integer -> Integer`

In this chapter you have covered:

- Partial function application means any function taking two or more arguments can be partially applied to one or more arguments.

- The use of notations

  function: data type → (data type → data type)

  which is equivalent to

  function: data type → data type → data type

  for example,

  add: integer → (integer → integer)

  which is equivalent to

  add: integer → integer → integer

- add: integer → (integer → integer) means add can take a single argument of type integer and return a more specialised function (integer → integer) which takes a single integer argument and returns an integer.

Learning objectives:

■ *Know what is meant by composition of functions*

Key principle

Function composition:
Function composition or functional composition combines two functions to get a new function.

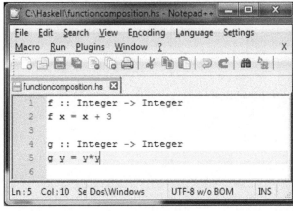

Figure 12.1.5.2 Defining functions f and g

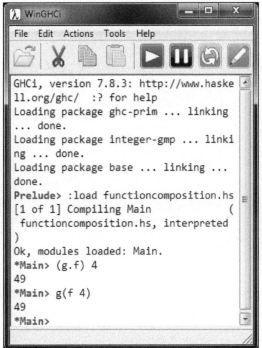

Figure 12.1.5.3 Application of the function composition (g.f) to argument 4

12.1.5 Composition of functions

Function composition

The operation function composition combines two functions to get a new function.

Given two functions $f: A \rightarrow B$

$g: B \rightarrow C$

function $g \circ f$, called function composition of g and f, is a function whose domain is A and co-domain is C.

$$g \circ f: A \rightarrow C$$

domain of f is A
co-domain of f is B
domain of g is B
co-domain of g is C
(See Chapter 12.1.1)

Note that the co-domain of f must be the same as the domain of g.

For example,

suppose $f(x) = x + 3$
and $g(y) = y^2$
then $g \circ f = g(f(x)) = g(x + 3) = (x + 3)^2$

Function g is applied to the result of applying function f, i.e. g is applied to $x + 3$. Since function g squares its argument, g applied to $x + 3$ is $(x + 3)^2$.

Applying the composition $g \circ f$ to argument **4**, we get f applied to **4** first then g applied to the result as follows

$$g \circ f\, 4 = (4 + 3)^2 = 7^2 = 49$$

Function composition is one of the simplest ways of structuring a program. In function composition a number of things are done one after another. This allows a separation of concerns so that each part can be designed and implemented independently.

In Haskell the function composition operator is '.' In function composition the operator is placed between the two functions of the composition. The operator has the effect of passing the output of one function as input to the other function as shown in *Figure 12.1.5.1*.

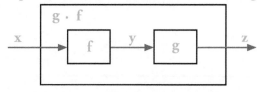

Figure 12.1.5.1 Function composition for functions f and g, g.f

Figure 12.1.5.3 shows (*g.f*) applied to argument **4** two ways. *Figure 12.1.5.2* shows *g* and *f* being defined.

Sometimes it is not possible to use Haskell's function composition operator. For example, if we wanted to find the sum of the squares of two integers, say 4 and 5 then we would use the expression

```
sum (square 4) (square 5)
```

This is still function composition.

Programming tasks

1. Using a text editor such as Notepad++, enter the following Haskell code and save as doublesquare.hs

```
square :: Integer -> Integer
square x = x*x
double :: Integer -> Integer
double w = 2*w
```

Launch WinGHCi then at the Prelude prompt type

`:load doublesquare.hs`

At the *Main prompt write function compositions using the function composition operator '.' to

(a) double the square of 6

(b) square the result of doubling 6

(c) repeat (a) and (b) without using the function composition operator.

2. Define a function add which takes two integer arguments and returns their sum. Incorporate this definition into doublesquare.hs and save as addsquare.hs.

Launch WinGHCi then at the Prelude prompt type

`:load addsquare.hs`

At the *Main prompt write a function composition which adds the squares of 2 and 3. Note you will not be able to use the function composition operator for this.

3. Change the argument type from Integer to Float in both functions add and square. Save as addsquarefloat.hs.

Launch WinGHCi then at the Prelude prompt type

`:load addsquarefloat.hs`

Haskell has a built-in function sqrt which takes one argument of type Float and returns a Float.

At the *Main prompt write a function composition which calculates the square root of the sum of the squares of 3 and 4. Note you will not be able to use the function composition operator for this.

Questions

1. What is function composition?

2. Function f applied to x and function g applied to y are defined as follows
$$f(x) = x - 3$$
$$g(y) = y^3$$
The domains and co-domains of f and g are $\mathbb{N}$
What is $g \circ f$ applied to x?

3. Two functions f and g have the following function types
$$f\!: A \to B$$
$$g\!: C \to D$$
Explain why it is not possible to have the function composition $g \circ f$.

4. In Haskell, a function *add* has the following function type
```
add :: Integer -> Integer -> Integer
```
A function *square* has the following function type
```
cube :: Integer -> Integer
```
Function *add* is defined as follows
```
add x y = x + y
```
Function *cube* is defined as follows
```
cube z = z*z*z
```
What is the result of the function composition
```
add (cube 3) (cube 4)?
```

In this chapter you have covered:

■ The meaning of function composition:

- function composition combines two functions to get a new function
- function $g \circ f$ is called function composition of g and f
- $g \circ f$ is a function whose domain is A and co-domain is C if $f\!: A \to B$
  $g\!: B \to C$
- f is applied first and then g is applied to the result

12 Fundamentals of functional programming

12.2 Writing functional programs

Learning objectives:

- *Have experience of constructing simple programs in a functional programming language.*
- *Use higher-order functions.*
- *Have experience of using the following in a functional programming language.*
  - *map*
  - *filter*
  - *reduce or fold*

12.2.1 Functional language programs

Haskell

WinGHCi and GHCi

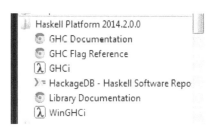

Figure 12.2.1.1 Start menu

After installing Haskell (www.haskell.org), launch WinGHCi (assuming the installation is for Microsoft® Windows®) - see *Figure 12.2.1.1*. A prompt with `Prelude>` at the beginning should appear in the window - see *Figure 12.2.1.2*. This tells you that the interpreter is ready to accept commands, and that the only loaded module at this moment is **Prelude**, which contains the most basic functions and data types in Haskell. The application is running an instance of a **Read Eval Print Loop** (**REPL**), or in other words an interpreter.

Figure 12.2.1.2 Initial screen

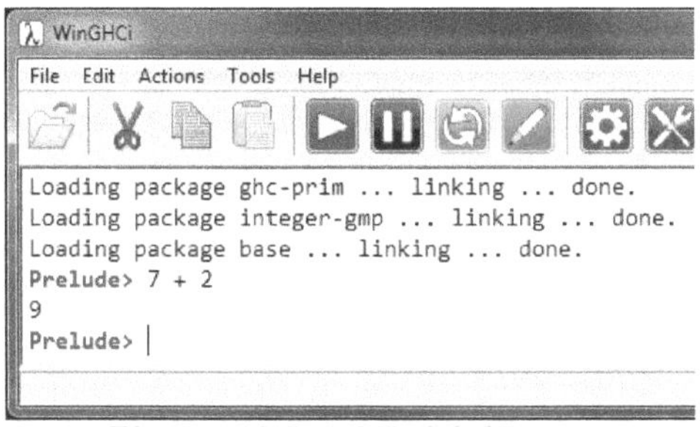

In WinGHCi, you input an expression and press the Enter key. The expression gets evaluated, and the result is shown in the screen.

For example, `7 + 2` as shown in *Figure 12.2.1.3*.

Haskell can also evaluate expressions that contain rational numbers,

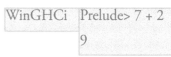

WinGHCi	Prelude> 7 + 2
	9

Figure 12.2.1.3 REPL in action

e.g. Prelude> 1/2 + 1/3
     0.8333333333333333

Haskell also has a command line application called **GHCi**. If you launch this you may look up the standard functions built in to the language. For example, typing **s** into GHCi at the **Prelude** prompt and pressing the Tab key, causes a list of all possible functions beginning with the letter **s** to appear as shown in *Figure 12.2.1.4*.

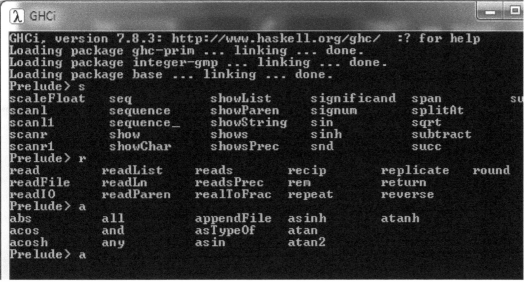

Figure 12.2.1.4 GHCi command line interpreter

In WinGHCi , to see all the definitions in a module: **Prelude>** `:browse Prelude`

If you then type **q** and press Tab again, only one possibility is left, **sqrt**, which is automatically displayed ready to be used. To find the square root of 2, just write at the **Prelude** prompt:

GHCi	Prelude> sqrt 2
	1.4142135623730951

```
Prelude> sqrt 2
```

Programming tasks

1 Try (a) `sqrt 3`   (b) `div 5 2`   (c) `mod 5 2`   (d) `cos 0`

(e) `(^) 2 4`   (f) `(^) 2 8`   (g) `gcd 128 32`   (h) `lcm 4 5`

(i) `take 5 "Hello World!"`   (j) `drop 6 "Hello World!"`

(k) `splitAt 6 "Hello World!"`   (l) `words "The black cat sat on the mat"`

Working with characters, numbers, strings and Booleans

Character values can be created in two different ways:

- Writing the character itself between single quotes, like `'a'`

- Writing in decimal between `'\` *and* `'`, or in hexadecimal between `'\x` *and* `'` using the Unicode standard, e.g. the character `'a'` can be written as `'\97'` or `'\x61'`.

Using WinGHCi, the actual type of an expression can be checked by using the

WinGHCi	Prelude> :t 'a'
	'a' :: Char

`:t` command, followed by the expression itself. For example, typing `:t 'a'`.

The :: symbol means "is of type". **Char** is a pre-defined type in Haskell.

WinGHCi	Prelude> import Data.Char
	Prelude Data.Char> :t toUpper
	toUpper :: Char -> Char

Only a few functions are loaded by default. The **import** command is used to add more functions, e.g. to import the **Data.Char** module use `import Data.Char`. The prompt of the interpreter changes to reflect the fact that now two different modules are loaded, **Prelude** and **Data.Char**.

Click on Help and select Libraries documentation to see other modules that are available.

In Haskell, everything has its own type including functions. We see that the type of the function `toUpper` is `Char -> Char`.

The arrow -> syntax is used to specify the type of a function. In this case,

WinGHCi	Prelude Data.Char> chr 98
	'b'
	Prelude Data.Char> :t chr
	chr :: Int -> Char

`toUpper` is a function taking a character (the `Char` on the left side) and returning another one (because of the `Char` on the right side).

Function types may be specified with a different data type before and after the arrow as shown in *Figure 12.2.1.5*.

Figure 12.2.1.5 Function type with different argument and result data types

For functions with more than one argument, each argument type is separated from the next with a single arrow. For example, the `max` function takes two ordinal arguments, e.g. of type `Integer`, and returns the smallest one.

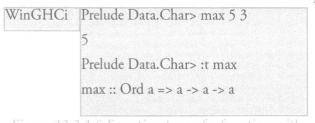

WinGHCi	Prelude Data.Char> max 5 3
	5
	Prelude Data.Char> :t max
	max :: Ord a => a -> a -> a

Figure 12.2.1.6 Function type of a function with two arguments

Information

`=>`:

Everything before `=>` is a class constraint. `Ord a =>` means that the type of the arguments and return value must be members of the Ord class.

Ord contains all data types that allow data values to be put into an order e.g. numerical order or alphabetical order.

Its function type is expressed as `a -> a -> a` because this function is polymorphic, i.e. it will work with any ordinal type - *Figure 12.2.1.6*.

`Ord` is the language-defined name for an ordinal type.

Programming tasks

2 At the **Prelude** prompt in WinGHCi type `import Data.Char`.
   Try (a) `chr 48`   (b) `chr 49`   (c) `chr 50`   (d) `chr 57` (e) `chr 65`
   (f) `chr 127`   (g) `ord '0'`   (h) `ord '1'` (i) `ord '2'`   (j) `ord '9'`
   (k) `ord 'A'`   (l) `min 45 32`

Numbers

Haskell supports a great variety of number types.

- `Int` is a fixed-precision integer type with at least range $[-2^{29} .. 2^{29-1}]$. These are bounded, machine integers, represented by 29-bit signed binary at least. The exact range for a given implementation can be determined by using `minBound` and `maxBound`.

- `Integer` is an unbounded integer type (mathematical integers, also known as "bignums"): it can represent any value without a fractional part without underflow or overflow. This is very useful for writing code without caring about the range.

- Exact rational numbers using the `Ratio` type. Rational values are created using `n % m`.

- `Float` and `Double` are floating-point types of single and double precision, respectively.

Haskell provides functions to convert between types. *Table 12.2.1.1* shows a sample of these.

Function	Module
`truncate`	
`round`	In module `Prelude`
`floor`	
`ceiling`	
`toRational`	In module `Data.Ratio`
`fromRational`	
`%`	

Table 12.2.1.1 Some functions that convert between number types

Programming tasks

3 Try (a) `truncate 45.34` (b) `round 45.6`
   (c) `ceiling 5.3` (d) `floor 5.3`

4 Type `import Data.Ratio` to add this library to Prelude. Try
   (a) `toRational 0.5`
   (b) `toRational 0.25`
   (c) `toRational 0.125`

```
WinGHCi   Prelude> truncate 6.7
6
Prelude> round 6.7
7
Prelude> ceiling 6.2
7
Prelude> floor 6.7
6
Prelude Data.Ratio> import Data.Ratio
Prelude Data.Ratio> 1%2 + 1%4
3 % 4
Prelude Data.Ratio> toRational 6.7
7543529375845581 % 1125899906842624
Prelude Data.Ratio> fromRational (6 % 3)
2.0
Prelude> import Data.Ratio
Prelude Data.Ratio> :m - Data.Ratio
Prelude>
```

Key point

Infix operators as functions:
Functions whose name is built entirely by symbols, like +, must be called using infix syntax: writing them between the arguments, instead of in front of them. So you write x + y, not + x y. To use a symbol function in the normal fashion, you must use parenthesis as follows
`(+) x y`.

Key point

^:

^ is the exponentiation operator, e.g. 4^2 = 16 because it is 4 raised to the power of 2.
We can also write this in Haskell as (^) 4 2.

Infix operators

The infix operators +, −, *, /, ^ are used as follows

> **Prelude**> 4 + 5
> 9

They may also be used in a similar way that a function is applied by placing the operator in brackets as follows

> **Prelude**> (+) 4 5
> 9

Care must be taken with negative numbers, e.g. −4 in the vicinity of an infix operator or any of the functions (+), (−), (*), (/), (^). We must wrap in parentheses the expression it applies to, e.g. 4 * (−3) = −12 where the parentheses have been used to surround (−3).

Programming tasks

5 Try (a) `(+) 9 7` (b) `(*) 3 4` (c) `(/) 4 3` (d) `(−) 4 3`
   (e) `(−) 4 (−3)`

Relational operators

Op	Description	Op	Description	Op	Description
==	Equal to	>	Greater than	<	Less than
>=	Greater than or equal to	<=	Less than or equal to	/=	Not equal to

Strings

If characters are grouped together then we have what is called a string. In Haskell a string is enclosed in double quotes, e.g. `"Hello World!"`.

If the WinHGCi interpreter is asked what type is a string, it responds with `[Char]`. The square brackets, `[ ]` surrounding `Char` indicate that `"Hello World!"` is not `Char` but a list of characters, each of type `Char`. Lists are the most commonly used data structure in functional programming. We study lists in greater detail in the next chapter.

WinGHCi	Prelude> :t "Hello World!"
	"Hello World!" :: [Char]

Information

++ operator:

++ can also be used to concatenate two lists, e.g.

```
[1,2,3,4] ++ [5,6,7,8]
= [1,2,3,4,5,6,7,8]
```

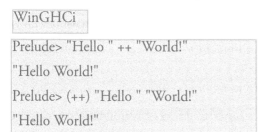

WinGHCi
Prelude> "Hello " ++ "World!"
"Hello World!"
Prelude> (++) "Hello " "World!"
"Hello World!"

Joining two strings together is called concatenation.

The ++ function is used for this, e.g.`"Hello " ++ "World!"`

or `(++) "Hello " "World!"`

WinGHCi
Prelude> True && True
True
Prelude> True && False
False
Prelude> True || True
True
Prelude> False || False
False
Prelude> not True
False
Prelude> not False
True

Booleans

The truth values, true and false, are represented in Haskell by the literal constants `True` and `False` respectively.

Boolean operators

Op	Description	Op	Desccription	Op	Description
&&	and	||	or	not	not

Anonymous function

An anonymous function is one that is not given a name but instead is defined as follows

$$(\backslash x\ ->\ x\ +\ 2)$$

This means given a value for x add 2 to it. The argument to this anonymous function is x and the result returned is the value of the expression `x + 2`. To apply this anonymous function we supply an actual argument e.g. 4 as follows

$$(\backslash x\ ->\ x\ +\ 2)\ 4$$

A shorthand form of this is possible if the function is an operator:

$$(+2)\ 4$$

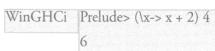

WinGHCi	Prelude> (\x-> x + 2) 4
	6

Information

Anonymous functions:

Anonymous functions are useful where there is no requirement to make the function visible to other parts of the program code or to reuse the function. They are often used for callback functions in event-driven programming.

Programming tasks

6. Write anonymous functions and apply these to the integer 5
   (a) double a given integer (b) double a given integer and add 3

Conditional expressions

We can write general conditional expressions by means of the if ... then ... else construct, e.g. the value of the following expression

$$\text{if condition then x else y}$$

is x if the condition is `True` and is y if the condition is `False`.

Programming tasks

 7 Write an anonymous function that outputs `True` if x = 2*y otherwise `False`

Using the two-argument anonymous function, arguments x and y

$$(\text{\textbackslash}x\ y\ \text{->}\ \text{if}\ x\ \text{>=}\ y\ \text{then}\ x\ \text{else}\ y)$$

We can apply this function to x = 4 and y = 5 as follows

WinGHCi	(\x y -> if x >= y then x else y) 4 5
(\x y -> if x >= y then x else y) 4 5	
5	

Key point

let:

It is possible to make temporary definitions in WinGHCi or GHCi using let as follows:
`let x = 5`

Using let to make temporary definitions

It is possible to make temporary definitions in WinGHCi or GHCi using `let` as follows:

$$\text{let}\ x\ =\ 5$$

We can use `let` to name and define a function `square` as follows

WinGHCi	Prelude> let square x = x*x	
	Prelude> square 4	`let square x = x * x`
	16	

Pattern matching

Pattern matching is an important aspect of Haskell and functional programming languages in general.

The left-hand side of equations such as `fac 0 = 1` and

`fac n = n * fac (n - 1)` contain the patterns 0 and n, respectively.

When a function is applied these *patterns* are matched against argument values. If the match succeeds, the right-hand side of the equation is evaluated and returned as the result of the application. If it fails, the next equation is tried. If all equations fail, an error results. All the equations that define a particular function must appear together, one after another. The definition of the `fac` function is a recursive one because `fac` refers to itself on the right-hand side of the second equation.

Using a text editor to create Haskell functions

It is often more convenient to use a text editor such as NotePad++ or WordPad to write Haskell programs. These Haskell programs should be saved with extension `.hs`.

Switch WinGHCi to the directory in which the Haskell program file was saved, e.g. `c:\book\haskell`, by typing at the Prelude prompt the following command,

`:cd c:\book\haskell` followed by the Enter key

Programming tasks

 8 Write a named function using `let` to
(a) double a given integer
(b) cube a given integer

The Haskell program, e.g. `factorial.hs` may then be loaded into WinGHCi at the **Prelude** prompt as follows

> `:load factorial.hs` followed by the Enter key

WinGHCi will perform a compilation of a module called `Main` in order to run `factorial.hs` interactively.

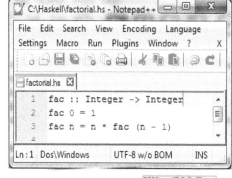

If there are no errors loading and compiling, the **Prelude** prompt will be replaced by the prompt `*Main`.

To return to **Prelude** at any time, type `:m`.

We are now ready to run the factorial program.

At the `*Main` prompt type

> `fac 6` followed by the Enter key

The correct answer, **720**, is displayed.

WinGHCi

```
Prelude> :load factorial.hs
[1 of 1] Compiling Main        ( factorial.hs, interpreted )
Ok, modules loaded: Main.
*Main> fac 6
720
```

Programming tasks

9 Use a text editor to create the following two functions, one after another in the same file, `cubedouble.hs`: `cube x` and `double x` where `x` is an Integer.

Try:

(a) `cube 3` (b) `double 6` (c) `double (cube 4)`

Higher-order functions

Much of the power of a functional language comes from advanced use of functions. In particular, a function that takes a function as an argument or returns a function as a result (or does both) is a higher-order function. Higher-order functions make it possible to define very general functions that are useful in a variety of applications.

Map

Our first example of a higher-order function is the map function. This function applies a given function to each element of a list, returning a list of results. For example, to apply the `abs` function to every element of the integer list

`[-1,-2,-3,-4]` we do the following

> `map abs [-1,-2,-3,-4]`

The `abs` function returns the absolute value of its argument, e.g. `abs −3` is +3. The map function applies the `abs` function to each value in the list, i.e.

> `abs −1`   `abs −2`   `abs −3`   `abs −4`

Key concept

Higher-order function
A function that takes a function as an argument or returns a function as a result (or does both) is said to be a higher-order function.

Key principle

Map:
Map is a higher-order function that applies a given function to each element of a list, the results in a new list.

WinGHCi
```
Prelude> map abs [-1,-2,-3,-4]
[1,2,3,4]
```

$$\text{map } f\ [x_1, x_2, ..., x_n] == [f\ x_1, f\ x_2, ..., f\ x_n]$$

```
Prelude> map (+3) [1,2,3,4]
[4,5,6,7]
```

To add 3 to every element of the integer list [1,2,3,4] do the following

```
map (+3) [1,2,3,4]
```

To multiply every element of the integer list [1,2,3,4] by 3 do the following

```
map (*3) [1,2,3,4]
```

```
Prelude> map (*3) [1,2,3,4]
[3,6,9,12]
```

Programming tasks

10 Try the following in WinGHCi or GHCi

(a) `map (/2) [2,4,6,8]`

(b) `map (\x -> x*x) [1,2,3]`

(c) `map (\x -> x*x) [1..100]`

(d) `map (\x -> x^2) [1..100]`

(e) `map (\x -> x^2) [1..1000]`

(f) `map sqrt [1..16]`

(g) `:m Data.Char`

   `map toUpper ['a'..'z']`

(h) `map words ["hello world", "the sun has got`
                          `its hat on"]`

(i) `map ($ 4) [(10*),(5+), sqrt, (^2)]`

Information

Function application operator $:

Can be used with map to map a function application over a list of functions, i.e. $ is replaced in turn by each function. In Q10(i) ($ 4) gets mapped over the list. The list happens to be a list of functions. So every function in the list gets applied to 4.

Key principle

Filter:
The filter function is a higher-order function that processes a data structure, e.g. a list, in some order to produce a new data structure containing exactly those elements of the original data structure that match a given condition.

Filter

The filter function is a higher-order function that processes a data structure, e.g. a list, in some order to produce a new data structure containing exactly those elements of the original data structure that match a given condition. For example, filter can apply the even function to every element of the integer list [1,2,3,4,5,6,7,8] and return a list containing integers that possess the property of evenness

```
filter even [1,2,3,4,5,6,7,8]
```

Similarly, filter can also apply the odd function to every element of the integer list [1,2,3,4,5,6,7,8] and return a list containing integers that possess the property of oddness

```
filter odd [1,2,3,4,5,6,7,8]
```

```
Prelude> filter even [1,2,3,4,5,6,7,8]
[2,4,6,8]
```

```
Prelude> filter odd [1,2,3,4,5,6,7,8]
[1,3,5,7]
```

Programming tasks

11 Try the following in WinGHCi or GHCi

(a) `filter (\x -> x > 3) [0..10]`

(b) `filter (\x -> (mod x 3)== 0) [1..100]`

(c) `:m Data.Char`

   `filter isUpper ['!'..'z']`

(d) `map (*2) $ filter odd [1..100]`

Information

Function application operator $:
When a $ is encountered, the expression on its right is applied as the argument to the function on its left, e.g. in 11(d) filter odd [1..100] is evaluated first, the result then becomes the argument to map (*2).

Reduce or fold

Reduce or fold is the name of a higher-order function which reduces a list of values to a single value by repeatedly applying a combining function to the list of values.

In the folding or reduction process, a function, e.g. `sum`, is applied to the list element by element, returning something such as the total `sum` of all elements. A fold takes a binary function, a starting value (often called an `accumulator`), and a list to fold up. The fold reduces the entire list down to a single accumulator value. In Haskell folding from the left is done with `foldl`. For example to sum a list of integers `[1,2,3,4]` using `foldl` do the following

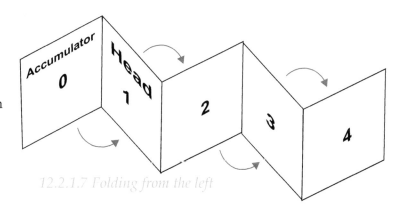

12.2.1.7 Folding from the left

```
foldl (+) 0 [1,2,3,4]
```

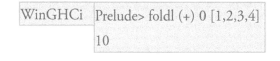

WinGHCi   Prelude> foldl (+) 0 [1,2,3,4]
10

`foldl` takes three arguments: the binary function `(+)`, the `accumulator` which has value `0`, and the list `[1,2,3,4]`. Binary means the function `(+)` takes two operands. The first of these is the `accumulator`. The second operand starts with the first element of the list (the head). `(+)` returns their sum and this becomes the new `accumulator`. `foldl` then applies `(+)` to the new `accumulator` value and the second element in the list to produce a new value of the `accumulator` and so on until all the integers in the list are summed.

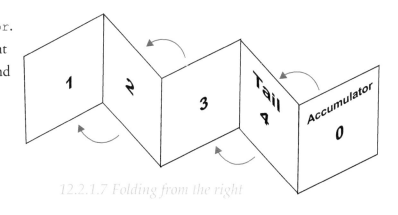

12.2.1.7 Folding from the right

To start the traversal from the opposite end of the list, the tail, we use `foldr` as follows

```
foldr (+) 0 [1,2,3,4]
```

WinGHCi   Prelude> foldr (+) 0 [1,2,3,4]
10

`foldr` differs from `foldl` in the order of the arguments which the function is applied to.

For example, if the function applied is `(^)`, exponentiation, then

the new value of accumulator = current list value ^ old value of accumulator.

With `foldr (^) 2 [1,2,3]` in WinGHCi, the accumulator is 2.

The list is folded from the right as follows

WinGHCi

Prelude> foldr (^) 2 [1, 2, 3]
1

```
list value^ accumulator

   3^2  =  9

   2^9  =  512

   1^512  =  1
```

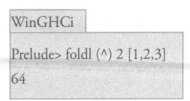

With `foldl (^) 2 [1,2,3]` in WinGHCi, the accumulator is 2. The list is folded from the left as follows

```
accumulator ^ list value

        2^3 = 8

        8^2 = 64

        64^1 = 64
```

Programming tasks

12 Try the following in WinGHCi or GHCi

(a) `foldl (+) 0 [1..1000]`

(b) `foldl (*)1 [1..3]`

(c) `map(^2)[1..3]`

(d) `foldl (+)0 $ map (^2) [1..3]`

(e) `foldr (++) "!" ["Hello ", "World"]`

(f) `foldl (++) "!" ["Hello ", "World"]`

Questions

1 In a functional programming language, a higher-order function `map` takes two arguments, a function `f`, and a list and applies the function `f` to each element of the list returning the results in a new list.

(a) A function named `square` is defined below

```
square x = x * x
```

The result of making the function call `square 2` is 4.

Calculate the result of making the function call

Function call	Result
`map square [1,2,3,4]`	

(b) Another function defined as `(++ "!")` takes a single string argument and returns a string which is the concatenation of the string argument with !

`++` is the concatenation operator. For example,

```
(++ "!") "Wow" returns "Wow!"
```

Calculate the result of making the function call

Function call	Result
`map (++ "!") ["SLAP", "BAM",` `"WALLOP"]`	

Questions

2 In a functional programming language, a higher-order function `filter` takes two arguments, a function `f` that returns a Boolean value, and a list and applies the function `f` to each element of the list returning the results in a new list.

A function defined as `(>4)` takes a single integer argument and returns true or false depending upon whether the integer is greater than 4 or not.

Calculate the result of making the function call

Function call	Result
`filter (>4) [5,3,6,2,-1]`	

3 In a functional programming language, a higher-order function `foldl` takes as arguments a binary function, `f`, e.g. `(+)`, a starting value called the accumulator, and a list, and returns a single value. A new accumulator value is calculated as follows if function `f` is `(+)`

      new accumulator = old accumulator + a list value

Calculate the result of making the function call where f is `(*)` and `*` is the multiplication operator.

Function call	Result
`foldl (*) 1 [5,3,6,2]`	

4 Using the higher-order functions `map`, `filter` and `foldl`.

Calculate the result of making the function call

Function call	Result
`foldl (+) 0 $ filter (>14) $ map (*3) [3..8]`	

`$` means evaluate the rightmost expression first.

In this chapter you have covered:

- Constructing simple programs in a functional programming language.
- Using higher-order functions.
- Using the following functional programming language higher-order functions:
  - map
  - filter
  - reduce or fold.

12 Fundamentals of functional programming

12.3 Lists in functional programming languages

12.3.1 List processing

Learning objectives:

- Be familiar with representing a list as a concatenation of a head and a tail

- Know that the head is an element of the list and the tail is a list

- Know that a list can be empty

- Describe and apply the following operations:
  - return head of list
  - return tail of list
  - test for empty list
  - return length of list
  - construct an empty list
  - prepend an item to a list
  - append an item to a list

Key concept

List:

A list is a collection of data items stored in no particular order, having the following properties:
- data items may be inserted or deleted at any point in the list
- data items may be repeated in the list
- lists may contain any type of object
- a particular list may contain different object types

A list is represented by square brackets enclosing list values separated by commas. For example:

[Emma, John, Fred, Janet]

What is a list?

A list is a collection of data items stored in no particular order, having the following properties:

- data items may be inserted or deleted at any point in the list

- data items may be repeated in the list

- lists may contain any type of object

- a particular list may contain different object types

A list is represented by square brackets enclosing list values separated by commas. For example:

[Emma, John, Fred, Janet]

is a list consisting of the items Emma, John, Fred, Janet.

A more complex example of a list containing different types of item (including another list) is:

[Mick, 46, 5.15, London, [Spurs, Chelsea]]

This type of list of mixed-type items is not supported by all programming languages that support list processing.

Element of a list

We refer to a data item in a list as an element or item of a list, e.g. Emma is an element or item of the first example list above.

Empty list

If all the elements of a list are removed we still have a list but it is now an empty list. The empty list is denoted by square brackets as follows [ ].

Thus every list is either **empty** or **non-empty**.

Representing a list as a concatenation of a head and a tail

A non-empty list may also be written in the form h:t where h is the first item in the list and t the remainder of the list. t is itself a list.

For example,

the list [1,2,3] = 1 : [2,3]

We call the element 1 the head of the list and [2,3] the tail of the list. : is called the list constructor operator.

Return head of list

In an imperative programming language, the function call

head(list)

returns the element at the head of list if list is non-empty, otherwise an error is reported.

e.g. for list [Emma, John, Fred, Janet]

head([Emma, John, Fred, Janet]) will return Emma.

In the functional programming language Haskell, a function that returns the item at the head of a list, h : t is defined as follows

```
head          :: [a] -> a
head (h : _)   = h
```

where h is the head. The underscore represents an anonymous variable which is the mechanism used by Haskell to ignore a value.

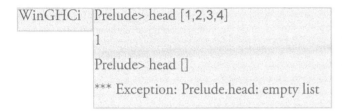

Using WinGHCi, the pre-defined function head applied to [1,2,3,4] returns 1. Applying head to the empty list [] causes an exception.

Return tail of list

In an imperative programming language, the function call

tail(list)

returns a new list containing all but the first element of the original list, list.

e.g. for list [Emma, John, Fred, Janet]

tail([Emma, John, Fred, Janet]) returns [John, Fred, Janet]

In Haskell, a function that returns the tail of a list, h : t is defined as follows

```
tail :: [a] -> [a]        WinGHCi  prelude> tail [1,2,3,4]
tail(_:t) = t                      [2,3,4]
```

where t is the tail.

Test for empty list

In an imperative programming language, a function call

empty(list)

returns True if list is an empty list or False otherwise.

In Haskell, a function null that returns True if list is an empty list or False otherwise is defined as follows

```
null :: [a] -> Bool        WinGHCi  prelude> null []
null[] = True                       True
null (_ : _) = False                prelude> null [1,2,3,4]
                                    False
```

where [] is the empty list.

593

Questions

1   What result is returned by the following functions applied to the list
    Towns where
    Towns = [Swindon, Aylesbury, Banbury, Stevenage, Slough]
    (a) empty(Towns)   (b) head(Towns)   (c) tail(Towns)
    (d) head(tail(Towns))
    (e) tail(tail(tail(tail(Towns))))

Information

Convention for representing lists:

In Haskell it is an informal convention to write variables over lists in the form xs, ys (pronounced 'exes', 'whyes') and so on, with variables x, y, ... for list elements. For example, x : xs is a list with head element x and tail xs.

Return length of list

In Haskell, a function `length` that returns the length of a list `h:t` is defined as follows

```
length :: [a] -> Integer
length [] = 0
length (h:t) = 1 + length t
```

WinGHCi prelude> length [1,2,3,4]
4

The length function uses recursion to calculate the length of list `h:t`.

`h` has a length of `1` to which we add length of the list `t`. The list `t` is the original list minus its head.

Key principle

length(list):
The operation `length(list)` returns the number of elements in the lists, i.e. its length.

Construct a list from the empty list

Every list can be built from the empty list by repeatedly applying the list constructor operator `':'`. For example, the list `[1,2,3,4]` can be created as follows

```
[]   4:[] = [4]   3:[4] = [3,4]   2:[3,4] = [2,3,4]
1:[2,3,4] = [1,2,3,4]
```

OR

```
      1:2:3:4:[]
```

WinGHCi Prelude> 4:[]
[4]

Prelude> 1:2:3:4:[]
[1,2,3,4]

The operator `:` serves a special role: it is a constructor of lists, since every list can be built up in a unique way from `[]` and `':'`. The form `1:2:3:4:[]` is called the list constructor form of the list `[1,2,3,4]`.

Key principle

The : list constructor operator:
Every list can be built from the empty list by repeatedly applying the list constructor operator ':', e.g.
`1:2:3:4:[] = [1,2,3,4]`

Questions

2   Write the list constructor form of a list for the following lists
    (a) [6,3,8,1]   (b) [2]

594

Prepend an item to a list

Prepend is when an item is added to the beginning of a list. For example, in Haskell the following code prepends 0 to the list [1,2,3,4]

```
0 : [1,2,3,4]
```

```
WinGHCi Prelude> 0:[1,2,3,4]
[0,1,2,3,4]
```

Key principle

Prepend:
To prepend an item to a list we add the item to the beginning of the list using the ':' operator.
E.g. `0 : [1,2,3,4] =`
`[0,1,2,3,4]`

Questions

3 What lists result from the following prepend operations
(a) 6 : [5,4]   (b) 4 : []   (c) 4 : [1, 2, 3]?

Append an item to a list

Append is when an item is added to the end of a list. For example, item 5 is appended to list [1,2,3,4] to produce the new list [1,2,3,4,5].

A user can define a function `append` in Haskell that appends an item y to a list x : xs as follows using the function `reverse` which is built-in to Haskell

```
append :: a ->[a] -> [a]
append y (x : xs) = reverse(y : reverse(x : xs))
```

For example, `append 5` [1,2,3,4] returns [1,2,3,4,5]

```
WinGHCi *Main> append 5 [1,2,3,4]
[1,2,3,4,5]
```

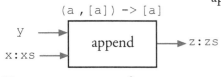

Two argument input function is first treated as a function with a single argument y which returns as result a new function x:xs -> z:zs.

Therefore if for y, the value 5 is input and then for x:xs the value [1,2,3,4] is input, the final result is [1,2,3,4,5]. This step by step process is expressed in Haskell as

`a -> [a] -> [a]`

Append is an example of the principle that any function taking two or more arguments can be partially applied to one or more arguments.

```
(a ,[a]) -> [a] => a ->([a] -> [a]) => a -> [a] -> [a]
```

The function first reverses the list x : xs. It then prepends the item y to the reversed list and then finally reverses the result. For example, if we wish to append 5 to [1,2,3,4]

Reverse: [4,3,2,1]

Prepend: 5 : [4,3,2,1] = [5,4,3,2,1]

Reverse: [1,2,3,4,5]

Key principle

Append:
To append an item to a list we add the item to the end of the list.
E.g. `append 5 [1,2,3,4]` returns [1,2,3,4,5]

Questions

4 What is returned when the function append y (x:xs) is called as follows
(a) append 6 [1]   (b) append 5 [3,2]?

5 Define the function
```
listproduct :: [Integer] -> Integer
```
which returns the product of a list of integers or 1 if the list is empty.

Programming tasks

1 The function `max` is built-in to Haskell. It takes two arguments of an ordinal type and returns the larger of the two. Use WinGHCi and enter the following at the **Prelude** prompt:

```
Prelude> max 9 3
```

Now try (a) `max 46 57` (b) `max 46 43`

```
WinGHCi Prelude> max 9 3
9
```

2 Create the following Haskell program in a text editor such as Notepad++ and save as `maxy.hs`.

```
maxy :: (Ord a) => [a] -> a
maxy [] = error "no maximum of empty list!"
maxy [x] = x
maxy (x:xs) = max x (maxy xs)
```

`Ord` is Haskell's ordinal data type, `(Ord a) =>` specifies that the values of `a` must belong to an ordinal type.

Load this program into WinGHCi using the command

`:load maxy.hs`

Try (a) `maxy []`   (b) `maxy [4]`

  (c) `maxy [34,23,7,67,31]`

In this chapter you have covered:

■ Representing a list as a concatenation of a head and a tail, e.g. the list `[1,2,3]` = `1 : [2,3]` where `:` is the list constructor operator, `1` is the head element and `[2,3]` is the tail

■ The empty list `[]`

■ The following operations on lists:

- The operation *head of list* returns the element at the head of the list

- The operation *tail of list* returns a list which is the original list minus the first element, the head

- The operation *empty list* tests for an empty list returning either `True` or `False`

- The operation *length of list* returns the length of the given list

- Every list can be built starting from the empty list by repeatedly applying the construction operator `':'`,

   e.g. `[]`   `4:[]` = `[4]`   `3:[4]` = `[3,4]`

- Prepend operation which is when an item is added to the beginning of a list

- Append operation which is when an item is added to the end of a list.

Index

Symbols

R

Radio frequencies (RF) 320

Radio frequency Identification (RFID) 320

RAM 257, 260, 263, 311, 323

Random Access Memory 263

Randomness 202

Range for a given number of bits 57

Range of numbers in unsigned binary in n bits 46

Rational number approximation to a real number 22

Rational numbers 6

Rational numbers as recurring decimals 9

Rationals as terminating decimals 8

Raw data 556

RAW image file 318

RC4 207

Read Eval Print Loop (REPL) 581

Reading file contents byte by byte 114

Read-write head 323

Real number line 14

Real numbers 14

Receiver 349

Record lock 536

Reduce 589

Reduced Instruction Set Computer 283

Reduced licensing costs 473

Reduce function 548

Redundancy 100, 178

Redundancy theorem 251

Redundant data 506, 515

REFERENCES 532

Referential integrity 521

Regional Internet Registry 448

Regional registries 448

Registers 270, 274

Registers always involved in the Fetch-Execute cycle 278

Relation 487, 502, 519

Relational database 486

Relational database model 486

Relational model 486

Relational modelling 486

Relational operators 522, 584

Relationship 480, 558, 559

Relationship between bit rate and bandwidth 355

Relationship name 481

Relative error 75

Relatively prime 406

Remainder 193

Repeating group 498, 499, 502

REPL 581

Replay attack 380

Representational State Transfer 461

Representation of two's complement floating point binary 61

Representation problem 70

Request message 432

Request To Send (RTS) 375

Requirements analysis 474

Reset 261, 293

Resolution of a bitmap 144

Resolution of an ADC 132

Resolution of computer displays 145

Resolving many-to-many relationships 484

Response message 432

REST 461, 462

REST request 461

REST web services 461

Retina displays 145

Retrieving data from a single table 519

Retrieving data from multiple tables 520

RFC 447

RFID 320

RFID device 320

RFID price smart tag 321

RFID reader 320

RFID system 320

RFID tag 320

RFID tag characteristics 321

RFID transponder 320

RISC 283

RJ45 connector 359

RJ45 socket 360

RLE 179

RLE packet 179

Role of a compiler 225

Role of a foreign key 521

Role of an assembler 225

Lightning Source UK Ltd.
Milton Keynes UK
UKHW050648060720
366093UK00001B/1

9 780992 753627